Contemporary Strategy Analysis

Concepts, Techniques, Applications

Third Edition

Robert M. Grant

First published 1991
Second edition published 1995
Reprinted 1995, 1996 (twice), 1997 (twice)
Third edition published 1998
Reprinted 1998, 1999(twice)

Blackwell Publishers Inc.
350 Main Street
Malden, Massachusetts 02148
USA

Blackwell Publishers Ltd
108 Cowley Road
Oxford OX4 1JF
UK

Library of Congress Cataloging-in-Publication Data
Grant, Robert M.
    Contemporary strategy analysis : concepts, techniques,
  applications / Robert M. Grant. —3rd ed.
      p.   cm.
    Includes index.
    ISBN 0–631–20780–5
    1. Strategic planning. I. Title.
HD30.28.G72   1998
  658.4'012—dc21

                                                         97–47751
                                                         CIP

British Library Cataloguing-in-Publication Data
A CIP catalogue record for this book is available from the British Library

Typeset by AM Marketing
Printed and bound in Great Britain
by MPG Books Ltd, Bodmin, Cornwall

This book is printed on acid-free paper

Contents

Preface

This third edition of *Contemporary Strategy Analysis* combines continuity and change. My objectives remain the same. As I wrote in the preface to the first edition, "The objective of this book is to provide a guide to business strategy analysis that combines rigor with relevance and applicability. The origins of the book lay in my dissatisfaction with the available strategic management texts. These thousand-page monsters were analytically flabby, provided inadequate coverage of the latest thinking by academics and practitioners, lacked penetrating insight into the fundamental issues of business success, and failed to communicate the excitement of the subject matter."

The distinguishing features of the book also remain the same. The guiding principle of the book is a focus on the underlying determinants of business success. This emphasis on fundamentals is the basis of the book's practicality. Rather than provide the compendium of checklists and buzzwords so prevalent among many practitioner-oriented strategy guides, I have tried to develop a more profound knowledge of the critical characteristics of companies, markets, and the competitive process. This focus on the drivers of superior performance means that *competitive advantage* forms the central theme of the book.

So what is new about the third edition? I have been influenced by two sets of forces: feedback from customers and recent developments in the field of strategy. Fortunately, both sets of forces have been complementary. Customers, both students and professors, pointed to the need for more on strategy implementation. At the same time, most of the key developments in the theory and practice of strategic management have been within the firm. Interest in organizational capability, flexibility, innovation, and the pursuit of shareholder value have important implications for how companies are structured and the systems through which they are managed. In response, I have added two entirely new chapters: one on company goals and performance management (Chapter 2), another on organization structure and management systems (Chapter 6). At the same time, I continue to reject the conventional (and mistaken) dichotomy between strategy formulation and strategy implementation. A strategy that cannot be implemented is worthless: strategy must be formulated with a view to its implementation. Hence, organization structure and management systems are introduced as fundamental tools for strategy analysis. Subsequent chapters that apply these fundamental tools to particular types of strategy and particular types of business provide an integrated analysis of strategy formulation and implementation. Nevertheless, I have had to draw limits as to how far down the implementation path that it is sensible to travel. Strategy implementation ultimately takes us into functions such as finance, marketing, operations, human resource management, and management information systems, areas that have their own bodies of knowledge—and textbooks.

My commitment to keep the book at the forefront of new developments in strategic management has resulted in the additions of new topics and techniques. The field continues to advance at a blistering pace. In many cases, we are seeing the influx of ideas whose implications are not yet clear, and strategic innovations whose lessons have yet to be learned. For this reason, I have added a final chapter that looks at emerging trends in strategy as we enter a new millennium.

I have relied heavily on the ideas and insights of other people. I should like to thank all those who have taken the time and trouble to share their wisdom, thoughts, and opinions with me. Among the many comrades-in-arms who have been sources of ideas and suggestions, I should like to thank Paul Almeida, Charles Baden Fuller, Tony Boardman, Andrew Campbell, Bill Finnie, Peter Grinyer, Sebastian Green, Gary Hamel, Ann Huff, Dan McAllister, John McGee, John Kay, Shiv Mathur, Peter McKiernan, Elaine Romanelli, Dick Rumelt, Rami Shani, J.-C. Spender, John Stopford, Howard Thomas, Margarethe Wiersema, and George Yip. Thanks, too, to my students at Georgetown School of Business—they continue to be my major source of learning.

Robert M. Grant
Washington, D.C.
October 1997

To Sue

Robert M. Grant was born in Bristol, England and lives in Washington D.C., where he is Professor of Management at Georgetown University School of Business. He has also taught at California Polytechnic, UCLA, University of British Columbia, London Business School, City University, and St. Andrews University. He was a student at the London School of Economics. His business experiences range from producing pork pies (Kraft Foods) and retreading tires (Firestone), to strategy consulting with American Express, ENI, and other companies. His research interests are in corporate diversification, organizational capabilities and knowledge management, and strategic and organizational change within the oil and gas industry.

I.

The Concept of Strategy

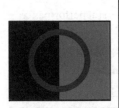

1

The Concept of Strategy

> Strategy is the great work of the organization. In situations of life or death, it is the Tao of survival or extinction. Its study cannot be neglected.
> —Sun Tzu, *The Art of War*

◆ INTRODUCTION AND OBJECTIVES

Strategy is about winning. This chapter investigates the role of strategy in organizational and personal success—not only in its business context, but also in relation to other fields of human endeavor including warfare, entertainment, politics, and sport. We examine the nature of strategy, and we distinguish strategy from planning. Strategy is not a detailed plan or program of instructions; it is a unifying theme that gives coherence and direction to the actions and decisions of an individual or organization.

We go on to examine the role of analysis in strategy formulation. If strategy is purely a matter of intuition and experience, then there is little point in studying this book—the only way to learn is to go and do. The key premise that underlies this book is that there are concepts, frameworks, and techniques that are immensely useful in formulating and implementing effective strategies.

By the time you have completed this chapter, you will be able to:

♦ Identify the contribution that strategy can make to successful performance—both for individuals and for organizations.

♦ Describe the origins and development of business strategy.

♦ Recognize the multiple roles of strategy within an organization.

Though its primary purpose is to guide management decisions toward superior performance through establishing competitive advantage, strategy also acts as a vehicle for communication and coordination within an organization. Finally, you will be equipped not only with insight into the fundamentals of business success, but with a specific framework that shows how strategy is a link between the firm and its business environment. This link provides the foundations for further learning about how to formulate winning strategies.

Since the purpose of strategy is to help us to win, we start by looking at the role of strategy in success.

THE ROLE OF STRATEGY IN SUCCESS

Exhibits 1.1, 1.2, and 1.3 outline examples of success in three very different fields of endeavor: Madonna in popular entertainment, General Giap and the North Vietnamese armed forces in warfare, and Bill Clinton and Tony Blair in politics. Can the success of these diverse individuals and the organizations they led be attributed to any common factors?

For none of these four people can success be attributed to overwhelmingly superior resources:

♦ Madonna possesses vitality, intelligence, and a tremendous capacity for work, but lacks outstanding talents as a vocalist, musician, actress, or any other of the principal vocations within popular entertainment.

♦ The military, human, and economic resources of the Vietnamese communists were dwarfed by those of the United States and South Vietnam. Yet, with the evacuation of U.S. military and diplomatic personnel from Saigon in 1975, the world's most powerful nation was humiliated by one of the world's poorest.

♦ The election triumphs of Bill Clinton in 1996 and Tony Blair in 1997 were against an ideological tide of conservatism. Clinton had to overcome the Republican landslide of 1994 and record disapproval ratings, while Blair was handicapped by the supposed unelectability of the British Labor Party.

Nor can success be attributed either exclusively or primarily to luck. Among all four, lucky breaks provided opportunities at critical junctures. None, however, was the beneficiary of a consistent run of good fortune. More important than luck was the ability to recognize opportunities when they appeared and to have the clarity of direction and the flexibility necessary to exploit these opportunities.

It is my contention that the key common ingredient in all four success stories is the presence of a soundly formulated and effectively implemented *strategy*. These strategies did not exist as a plan; in several cases the strategy was not made explicit. Yet in all four, we can observe a consistency of direction based upon a

EXHIBIT 1.1

Madonna

In 1978 at the age of 20, Madonna Louise Ciccone traveled to New York to find work as a dancer. A succession of small-time dancing and singing jobs eventually led to a recording contract, and her first album, *Madonna*, released in 1984, eventually sold close to 10 million copies worldwide. Her second album, *Like a Virgin*, released in 1985, sold over 12 million copies. During the next ten years Madonna achieved a remarkable feat. She succeeded in a building an image for herself that transcended any single field of entertainment. She became not only a pop singer, but also an actor and an author. She became the world's highest paid female entertainer earning $80 million between 1985 and 1991—with $20 million in 1991 alone.

It is difficult to attribute Madonna's success to outstanding talent. Although she has evoked comparison with stars of the past—Monroe, Garbo and Mae West—her capabilities are modest even by the standards of modern popular music. She lacks the voice of Whitney Houston, the dancing ability of Michael Jackson, and the songwriting talent of Sinead O'Connor. Under any conventional criteria it is difficult to regard her as outstandingly beautiful.

To diagnose her success, it is first worth noting that she is not the product of any media organization or protégé of any entertainment entrepreneur. Madonna's success is the result of her own efforts. She fought her way into the pop music business and since her initial success has directed her own career. On her own initiative, she flew to Los Angeles in 1982 to persuade Freddie De Mann, Michael Jackson's manager, to take her on and eventually to drop Jackson. The relationship has continued. Madonna is chairman of her group of companies, De Mann is president. By 1992, her staff had grown to 150, all of whom were personally picked by Madonna.

Madonna's drive and purposefulness has powered her career. Her chameleon-like transformations in appearance and image, and her movement between live performances, music videos, recorded music, movies, and publishing belie a remarkable dedication to a single goal: the quest for superstar status. For over ten years, Madonna has worked relentlessly to market herself and to maintain and renew her popular appeal. She is widely regarded as a workaholic who survives on little sleep and rarely takes vacations. "I am a very disciplined person. I sleep a certain number of hours each night, then I like to get up and get on with it. All that means that I am in charge of everything that comes out." Her career has been largely undeflected by other goals. Most of her personal relationships have acted as stepping stones to career transitions. Her transition from dancing into music was assisted by relationships first with a rock musician, and later with disc jockey John Benitex. Her move into Hollywood followed her brief marriage to actor Sean Penn and an affair with Warren Beatty. As Jeff Katzenberg, former head of Disney studios observed: "She has always had a vision of exactly who she is, whether performer or businesswoman, and she has been strong enough to balance it all. Every time she comes up with a new look it is successful. When it happens once, OK, maybe it's luck; but twice is a coincidence, and three times it's got to be a remarkable talent. And Madonna's on her fifth or sixth time." There are striking parallels between the careers of Madonna and Evita Peron, whom Madonna portrayed in the screen version of the Lloyd Webber musical. The two shared humble origins, astuteness in making the right connections, mastery of the strategic use of sex, and an unfailing knack for being in the right place at the right time.

Madonna has demonstrated an acute awareness of the keys to success in the world of "show biz." In terms of generating publicity and popular interest she is masterful, walking a fine line between the shocking and unacceptable. There is nothing novel in the use of sex as a marketing tool: her innovation has been in the subtle and not-so-subtle suggestions of sexual deviance, the portrayal of pornographic imagery (often under the banner of "art"), and the juxtaposition of sexual and religious themes. While developing her customer appeal, she has also recognized the importance of the "gatekeepers" to the channels of distribution by carefully nurturing relationships with key producers and promoters.

In product development and marketing, she has followed a "product life cycle" approach. This can be seen in her different images from street kid, to glamorous femininity, to soft-porn goddess with a hint of sado-masochism sexuality, to mother. It is also clear in her shifting emphasis between different media. As her recorded music

EXHIBIT 1.1

(Continued)

sales waned (her sales peak occurred with her *True Blue* album), she focused more on live performances, the nine shows of her "Blond Ambition" tour grossing $40 million in 1991. Throughout the 1990s, she has concentrated increasingly on movies, with limited success until *Evita* in 1996. As a result, every time her career appears to be in decline, she has shown a remarkable ability to stage publicity coups and renew her image and appeal.

Her approach involves very careful exploitation of her own talents and endowments. Her foremost ability is designing and projecting images that combine music, dance, theater, physical presence, and her sense of style. Her weaknesses as an entertainer are compensated for by her heavy reliance on technology, sexual suggestion, and an array of support personnel including musicians, dancers, and designers. These are effectively integrated through her own creative vision and design capability.

Above all, like all other successful purveyors of fantasy (Walt Disney Company for example), Madonna's success depends upon her obsessive attention to detail. Her insistence on control is reflected in the organization of her business interests. Most of her entertainment ventures have been owned and operated by her own companies, including Boy Toy Inc. (publishing), Siren films, and Slutco Inc. (video). In 1992 she formed Maverick Inc., a joint venture with Time Warner. In addition to her share in Maverick's profits she

is paid $8 million a year in salary until 1997. Her desire for commercial and artistic control has resulted in her refusal to endorse or advertise products. The one exception was with Pepsi which, in exchange for making three advertisements, paid her $3 million and sponsored her concert tour.

The Maverick venture represents yet another stage in Madonna's strategic evolution. Now that her own career approaches maturity, Maverick provides a vehicle for using her creative and promotional intuition and experience and the wealth of talented specialists that she has gathered around her to develop new entertainers and enterprises. As Madonna noted: "I've met these people along the way in my career and I want to take them everywhere I go. I want to incorporate them into my little factory of ideas. I also come into contact with a lot of young talent that I feel entrepreneurial about." Although several of Madonna's projects have lost significant sums of money (notably the *Erotica* book), the overall financial returns to Madonna's business empire have been impressive. Her personal net worth exceeds $100 million. As Harry Scolinos, a Los Angeles attorney observes: "I would take her street-smart business sense over someone with a Harvard MBA any day."

Source: "Madonna Is America's Smartest Business Woman," *Business Age,* June 1992, pp. 66–69.

---

clear understanding of the "game" being played and an acute awareness of how to maneuver into a position of advantage.

♦ Madonna's preeminence as a "superstar" and her earnings over the ten-year period 1984–1993 have been built upon a multimedia, multimarket strategy spanning recorded music, concert tours, music videos, films, and books with an appeal based upon successive renewals of her image and brilliant marketing through exploiting sexuality and sexual imagery and challenging conventional standards of decency.

♦ The victory of the Vietnamese communist forces over the French and then the Americans is a classic example of how a sound strategy pursued with total commitment over a long period can succeed against vastly superior resources. The key was Giap's strategy of a protracted war of limited engagement. With American forces constrained by domestic and international opinion from using their full military might, the strategy was unbeatable

EXHIBIT 1.2

General Giap and the Vietnam Wars, 1948–1975

"As far as logistics and tactics were concerned, we succeeded in everything we set out to do. At the height of the war the army was able to move almost a million soldiers a year in and out of Vietnam, feed them, clothe them, house them, supply them with arms and ammunition and generally sustain them better than any army had ever been sustained in the field . . . On the battlefield itself, the army was unbeatable. In engagement after engagement the forces of the Vietcong and the North Vietnamese Army were thrown back with terrible losses. Yet, in the end, it was North Vietnam, not the United States that emerged victorious. How could we have succeeded so well yet failed so miserably?"[1]

Despite having the largest army in Southeast Asia, North Vietnam was no match for South Vietnam so long as it was backed by the world's most powerful military and industrial nation. South Vietnam and its United States ally were defeated not by superior resources but by a superior strategy. North Vietnam achieved what Sun Tzu claimed was the highest form of victory: the enemy gave up.

The prime mover in the formulation of North Vietnam's military strategy was General Vo Nguyen Giap. In 1944, Giap became head of the Vietminh guerrilla forces. He was commander-in-chief of the North Vietnamese Army until 1974 and Minister of Defense until 1980. Giap's strategy was based upon Mao Tse Tung's three-phase theory of revolutionary war: first, passive resistance during which political support is mobilized, second, guerrilla warfare aimed at weakening the enemy and building military strength, finally, general counteroffensive.[2] In 1954, Giap began the final phase of the war against the French and the brilliant victory at Dien Bien Phu fully vindicated the strategy. Against South Vietnam and its U.S. ally, the approach was similar. Giap explained his strategy as follows:

> Our strategy was . . . to wage a long-lasting battle . . . Only a long-term war could enable us to utilize to the maximum our political trump cards, to over-

come our material handicap, and to transform our weakness into strength. To maintain and increase our forces was the principle to which we adhered, contenting ourselves with attacking when success was certain, refusing to give battle likely to incur losses . . .[3]

The strategy built on the one resource where the Communists had overwhelming superiority: their will to fight. As Clausewitz, the nineteenth century military theorist, observed: war requires unity of purpose between the government, the military, and the people. Such unity was never achieved in the United States The North Vietnamese, on the other hand, were united in a "people's war." Capitalizing upon this strength necessitated "The Long War." As Prime Minister Pham Van Dong explained: "The United States is the most powerful nation on earth. But Americans do not like long, inconclusive wars . . . We can outlast them and we can win in the end."[4] Limited military engagement and the charade of the Paris peace talks helped the North Vietnamese prolong the conflict, while diplomatic efforts to isolate the United States from its Western allies and to sustain the U.S. peace movement accelerated the crumbling of American will to win.

The effectiveness of the U.S. military response was limited by two key uncertainties: what were the objectives and who was the enemy? Was the U.S. role one of supporting the South Vietnamese regime, fighting Vietcong terrorism, inflicting a military defeat on North Vietnam, or combating world communism? Lack of unanimity over goals translated into confusion as to whether America was fighting the Vietcong, the North Vietnamese, the communists of Southeast Asia, or whether the war was military or political in scope. Diversity of opinion and a shifting balance of political and public opinion was fatal for establishing a consistent long-term strategy.

The consistency and strength of North Vietnam's strategy allowed it to survive errors in implementation. In particular, Giap was undoubtedly premature in launching his general offensive.

1. Col Harry G. Summers Jr., *On Strategy,* (Novato, CA: Presidio Press, 1982): 1

2. G.K. Tanham, *Communist Revolutionary Warfare* (New York: Praeger, 1961): 9–32

3. Vo Nguyen Giap, *Selected Writings* (Hanoi: Foreign Language Publishing House, 1977).

4. J. Cameron, *Here Is Your Enemy* (New York: Holt, Rinehart, Winston, 1966).

EXHIBIT 1.2

(Continued)

Both the 1968 Tet Offensive and 1972 Easter Offensive were beaten back, inflicting heavy losses on North Vietnamese regulars and Vietcong. Giap was replaced as Commander-in-Chief by General Van Tien Dung, who recognized that the Watergate scandal had so weakened the U.S. presidency that an effective American response to a new communist offensive was unlikely. On April 29, 1975, Operation Frequent Wind began evacuating all remaining Americans from South Vietnam, and the next morning North Vietnamese troops entered the Presidential Palace in Saigon.

EXHIBIT 1.3

Bill Clinton and Tony Blair

Political commentators have noted numerous similarities between the president of the United States and the British prime minister: both are baby-boomers who were educated at Oxford, both are lawyers who married lawyers, both are skilled debaters and highly effective oral communicators, both see themselves as revitalizing and modernizing their parties around a vision of a society based on a dynamic market economy, a limited role of government, a strong social conscience, and a well-understood set of moral commitments. The two have even shared some of the same political advisers. Our interest is in the strategic similarities between Clinton's victory in the November 1996 presidential election and Blair's victory in the May 1997 parliamentary election.

In both instances, electoral victory was in the face of some daunting opposition. In both countries, the ideological swing of the 1990s was strongly to the right. Left-wing policies, and socialism in particular, had become viewed as impediments to a dynamic market economy driven by technology and entrepreneurship and to individual liberty. Both the U.S. Democratic Party and the British Labor Party were viewed as having their ideological and emotional roots in a bygone era of big government, labor unions, and macroeconomic management. Bill Clinton's prospects for reelection were especially dim in view of the landslide victory of the Republicans in the 1992 congressional elections and the declining reputation of the president as a result of policy setbacks and personal scandal. For Tony Blair, the greatest obstacle was the Conservative Party's status as the natural party of government and the widespread skepticism over the electability of Labor.

The essence of the Clinton strategy of 1995–1996 and Blair strategy of 1996–1997 was a rightward repositioning of policies and electoral perceptions that would permit their respective parties to follow the rightward shift in popular political opinion and to capture the middle ground from their opponents. In pursuing this approach, both leaders were adopting a fundamental strategic principle arising from elementary game theory: where two players compete and customer preferences are distributed around a modal point, then maximizing market share implies positioning one's offering to appeal to median customer preferences.

Both sought to establish themselves in positions of moral leadership. At the White House, while Dick Morris was busily appropriating the most popular elements of the Republicans' "Contract with America" for the Clinton electoral platform, Clinton's advisors and counselors were formulating a message of moral and cultural leadership that transcended specific economic and policy issues and established Clinton as a proponent of family values, supporter of law and order, protector of children and the social fabric of the community, and a world leader. In a

EXHIBIT 1.3

(Continued)

similar vein, Blair had little difficulty in establishing moral superiority above the sleaze-tainted Tories.

Both Clinton and Blair were committed to moderation in taxation, smaller government, a "tough on welfare, tough on crime" stance, and abandonment of pro-labor union traditions in favor of a strong pro-business orientation.

Their election strategies capitalized on key party and personal strengths. Both emphasized their appeal to traditional supporters: women, immigrants, and ethnic minorities. Both sought to exploit their campaign advantages of communication ability, social skills, and telegenic image to the maximum.

Both showed effective leadership of their campaigns. Despite an undistinguished first presidency in terms of melding an effective executive, the appointment of Leon Panetta as White House Chief of Staff inaugurated a new era of consistency, purpose, and attention to detail. The Clinton campaign made particular use of the advantages of incumbency, not least in fundrais-

ing. Most of all, Clinton showed the same energy, persistence, and perseverance that earned him the title of "Comeback Kid" during the 1992 presidential campaign. Blair's leadership of the British Labor Party was even more impressive. During 1995–1997 he systematically remodeled the party, expelling the motley fringe of radicals characterized as the "Loony Left" and dismantled many of his party's ties to socialist principles and to the trade union movement.

Both were favored by the propensity of their opponents to self-destruct. Though both Clinton and Blair showed a determination to keep their eyes on the prize, the electoral efforts of both Republicans and Conservatives were weakened by internal division over fundamental policy issues. Moreover, the rightward shifts by the American Democrats and the British Labor Party to capture the political middle ground were made all the easier by their opponents vacating this territory: the Republicans were consumed by their post-1994 radical zeal, the British Conservatives labored under their Thatcherite legacy.

once it began to sap the willingness of the U.S. government to persevere with a costly, unpopular foreign war.

♦ The electoral victories of Clinton and Blair vindicate a classic strategy principle: in a two-firm market with distributed customer preferences, market share is maximized by targeting median-customer preferences. Thus, in a two-party political system, vote maximization requires targeting the "swing voter" in the same way that the quest for market share in news weeklies and soft drinks results in *Time* and *Newsweek* and Coca-Cola and Pepsi competing for the middle ground with similar offerings.

We can go further. What do these examples tell us about the characteristics of a strategy that are conducive to success? Four common factors stand out. These are illustrated in Figure 1.1.

1. **Goals that are simple, consistent, and long term.** All four endeavors feature notable single-mindedness of goals.
   ♦ Madonna's career features a relentless drive for stardom. Male attachments have provided stepping stones to new phases of her career and most other dimensions of her life have been subordinated to her career as an entertainer.

FIGURE 1.1
The Common Ele-
ments of Successful
Strategies

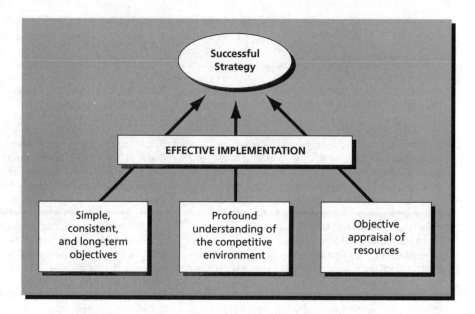

- North Vietnamese efforts were unified and focused on the ultimate goal of reuniting Vietnam under communist rule and expelling a foreign army from Vietnamese soil. By contrast, U.S efforts in Vietnam were bedeviled by confused objectives. Was the United States supporting an ally, stabilizing Southeast Asia, engaging in a proxy-war against the Soviet Union, or pursuing an ideological struggle against world communism?
- Though their opposition was deflected by issues of ideology and party doctrine, both Bill Clinton and Tony Blair uniquely focused their campaigns upon the goal of being elected to government.

2. **Profound understanding of the competitive environment.** All four individuals designed their strategies around a deep and insightful appreciation of the arena in which they were competing.
   - Fundamental to Madonna's continuing success has been a shrewd understanding of the ingredients of stardom and the basis of popular appeal. This extends from the fundamental marketing principle that "sex sells" to recognition of the need to manage the critical channels of distribution and appease their gatekeepers.
   - Giap understood his enemy and the battlefield conditions where he would engage them. Supporting the military effort was an acute awareness of the political predicament of U.S. presidents in their efforts to conduct a foreign war. This was key to the core element of North Vietnamese strategy: undermining the will of the American people to support the war effort.
   - Clinton and Blair each showed an acute awareness of the mood and preferences of their respective electorates and the weaknesses of their opponents. Both were willing to abandon long-standing policy principles and party dogma in order to maximize electoral appeal.

3. **Objective appraisal of resources.** All four strategies were effective in exploiting internal strengths, while protecting areas of weakness.

   ♦ By positioning herself as a "star," Madonna exploited her abilities to develop and project image, to self-promote, and to exploit emerging trends, while avoiding being judged simply as a rock singer or an actress. Her live performances rely heavily on a large team of highly qualified dancers, musicians, vocalists, choreographers, and technicians, thus compensating for any weaknesses in her own performing capabilities.

   ♦ Giap's strategy was carefully designed to protect against his army's deficiencies in arms and equipment, while exploiting the commitment and loyalty of his troops.

   ♦ Clinton's and Blair's election strategies exploited the candidates' youth, sociability, and superb debating skills while limiting their vulnerability to weaknesses associated with their privileged backgrounds and limited political experience.

4. **Effective implementation.** Without effective implementation, the best laid strategies are of little use. Critical to the success of Madonna, Giap, and Blair are their effectiveness as leaders in terms of eagerness to make decisions, energy in implementing them, and effectiveness in demanding loyalty and commitment from subordinates. All four individuals established organizations that were structured for effective strategy implementation. Critical to such organizations were a highly effective marshaling of resources and capabilities, as well as appropriate responses to the requirements of the competitive environment. In Clinton's case, the effectiveness of his organization compensated for many of his personal weaknesses in leadership and suspect moral fiber.

These observations about the role of strategy in success can be made in relation to most fields of human endeavor. Whether we look at warfare, chess, politics, sport, or business, the successful individuals and organizations are seldom the outcome of a purely random process. Nor is superiority in initial endowments of skills and resources typically the determining factor. Strategies that build on the basic four elements almost always play an influential role. Look at the "high achievers" in any competitive area. Whether we review the 42 American presidents, the CEOs of the *Fortune* 500, or our own circles of friends and acquaintances, it is apparent that those who have achieved outstanding success in their careers are seldom those who possessed the greatest innate abilities. Success has gone to those who managed their careers most effectively—typically by combining the four strategic factors. They are goal focused; their career goals have taken primacy over the multitude of life's other goals—friendship, love, leisure, knowledge, spiritual fulfillment—which the majority of us spend most of our lives juggling and reconciling. Indeed, the biographies of leading figures in business, politics, entertainment, and the creative arts often show that remarkable career success is matched by dismal failure in other aspects of living such as friendships and family relations. They know the environments within which they play and tend to be fast learners in terms of understanding the keys to advancement. They know themselves in terms of both strengths and weaknesses. And they pursue their careers with commitment, consistency, and determination.

These same ingredients of successful strategies: clear goals, understanding the competitive environment, resource appraisal, and effective implementation form the key components of our analysis of business strategy. These principles are not new. Over 2,000 years ago Sun Tzu wrote:

> Know the other and know yourself:
> Triumph without peril.
> Know Nature and know the Situation:
> Triumph completely.[1]

A FRAMEWORK FOR ANALYZING BUSINESS STRATEGY

The same four principles that are critical to the design of successful strategies form the analytical foundations on which this book is based. Our framework views strategy as forming a link between the firm and its external environment (see Figure 1.2). The firm embodies three sets of key characteristics:

- ♦ Its goals and values,
- ♦ Its resources and capabilities,
- ♦ Its organizational structure and systems.

The external environment of the firm comprises the whole range of economic, social, political, and technological factors that influence a firm's decisions and its performance. However, for most strategy decisions, the core of the firm's external environment is its *industry*, which is defined by the firm's relationships with customers, competitors, and suppliers.

The task of business strategy, then, is to determine how the firm will deploy its resources within its environment and so satisfy its long-term goals, and how to organize itself to implement that strategy.

Limitations of SWOT Analysis

The distinction between the external environment and the internal environment of the firm is common to most approaches to designing and evaluating business strategies. For example, a common approach is the SWOT framework: Strengths, Weaknesses, Opportunities, and Threats. This framework distinguishes between two features of the internal environment, strengths and weaknesses, and two features of the external environment, opportunities and threats. However, the SWOT framework is handicapped

FIGURE 1.2
The Basic Framework: Strategy as a Link Between the Firm and Its Environment

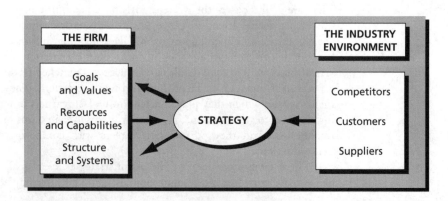

by difficulties in distinguishing strengths from weaknesses and opportunities from threats. For instance:

♦ Is Michael Eisner a strength or a weakness for Walt Disney Company? To the extent that he has masterminded Disney's revival over the past 14 years he is an outstanding strength. Yet, his quadruple heart-bypass surgery and inability to implement a management succession plan suggest that he is also a weakness.

♦ Is the convergence of computing and television broadcasting a threat or an opportunity to Microsoft? To the extent that it offers a basis for new business ventures (such as the MS-NBC news channel/web site), it is an opportunity. To the extent that it leads to an undermining of Microsoft's dominance of computer operating systems and applications software, it is a threat.

The lesson here is that an arbitrary classification of external factors into opportunities and threats, and internal factors into strengths and weaknesses, is less important than a careful identification of these external and internal factors followed by an appraisal of their implications.

Strategic Fit

An important implication of the firm-strategy-industry environment framework is the concept of **strategic fit**. For a strategy to be successful, is must be consistent with the firm's goals and values, with its external environment, with its resources and capabilities, and with its organization and systems. Lack of consistency between the strategy pursued by a firm and its external and internal environments is a common source of failure. For example:

♦ The difficulties of British retailers Laura Ashley and Body Shop may be attributed, in part, to their strategies becoming increasingly decoupled from the core values upon which the companies were founded. Wal–Mart and Marks & Spencer have been more successful in keeping a close fit between strategy and values.

♦ In terms of consistency with the industry environment, the failure of Pan American World Airlines and Eastern Airlines and difficulties at Alitalia and Air France result from a failure to adapt strategies to an increasingly competitive and deregulated airline market. Similarly, Apple Computer's decline during the 1990s reflects a failure to adapt strategy to the evolution of competition and customer requirements in a personal computer market increasingly dominated by the Intel-MS Windows standard.

♦ In terms of the consistency of strategy with internal resources and capabilities, the dismal performance of Tandy Corporation over the past decade may be attributed to its lacking both the technological capabilities to be a successful manufacturer of computers and electronics equipment as well as the retailing capabilities needed to be a successful retailer of computers and consumer electronic equipment. Similarly, the failure of British Satellite Broadcasting in developing satellite TV in the UK can be attributed to pursuing a strategy that required financial resources and marketing agility that the company lacked.[2]

♦ Failure to design organizational structure and management systems to the requirements of a firm's strategy is a common cause of poor performance. The failure of Exxon's Office Systems subsidiary is largely due to the corporation's control systems and management style being unsuited to a strategy of innovation and entrepreneurial responsiveness. More generally, the current reorganizations of large corporations to achieve "delayering," "empowerment," teams, and horizontal coordination are adjustments of structures and systems to meet the requirements of strategies that emphasize flexibility, opportunism, and innovation.

This view of business strategy as the interface between the firm and its business environment implies a different conception of strategy than that inherent in traditional approaches to corporate planning. To better understand the nature of business strategy and its role within the management of the firm, we devote a few pages to tracking its origins and development.

A BRIEF HISTORY OF BUSINESS STRATEGY

Enterprises need business strategies for much the same reasons that armies need military strategies—to give direction and purpose, to deploy resources in the most effective manner, and to coordinate the stream of decisions being made by different members of the organization.

Origins and Military Antecedents

The concepts and theories of business strategy have their antecedents in military strategy. Indeed the term *strategy* derives from the Greek word *strategia* meaning "generalship," itself formed from *stratos,* meaning "army," and *-ag,* "to lead." [3] However, the concept did not originate with the Greeks: Sun Tzu's classic *The Art of War* written about 500 B.C. is regarded as the first treatise on strategy. The military associations with strategy are apparent from dictionary definitions (see Table 1.1).

Military strategy and business strategy share a number of common concepts and principles, the most basic being the distinction between strategy and tactics. **Strategy** is the overall plan for deploying resources to establish a favorable position. A **tactic** is a scheme for a specific action. Whereas tactics are concerned with the maneuvers necessary to win battles, strategy is concerned with winning the war.[4] Strategic decisions, whether in the military or the business sphere, share three common characteristics:

- They are important.
- They involve a significant commitment of resources.
- They are not easily reversible.

Many of the principles of military strategy have been applied to business situations. These include the relative strengths of offensive and defensive strategies; the merits of outflanking over frontal assault; the roles of graduated responses to aggressive initiatives; the benefits of surprise; and the potential for deception, envelopment, escalation, and attrition.[5] At the same time, the differences between business competition and military conflict must be recognized. The objective of war is (usually) to defeat the enemy. The purpose of business rivalry is seldom so aggressive: most business enterprises limit their competitive ambitions, seeking coexistence rather than the destruction of competitors.

The tendency for the principles of military and business strategy to develop as separate bodies of knowledge reflects the absence of a general theory of strategy. The publication of Von Neumann and Morgenstern's *Theory of Games* in 1944 gave rise to the hope that a general theory of competitive behavior would emerge. During the subsequent half century, game theory has revolutionized the study of competition and collaboration both between firms and within firms, and has been applied widely

TABLE 1.1
Some Definitions of
Strategy

- STRATEGY. The art of war, especially the planning of movements of troops and ships etc., into favorable positions; plan of action or policy in business or politics etc.

  —Oxford Pocket Dictionary.

- The determination of the long-run goals and objectives of an enterprise, and the adoption of courses of action and the allocation of resources necessary for carrying out these goals.

  —Alfred Chandler, *Strategy and Structure,*
  (Cambridge, MA: MIT Press, 1962).

- A strategy is the pattern or plan that integrates an organization's major goals, policies and action sequences into a cohesive whole. A well-formulated strategy helps marshal and allocate an organization's resources into a unique and viable posture based upon its relative internal competencies and shortcomings, anticipated changes in the environment, and contingent moves by intelligent opponents.

  —James Brian Quinn, *Strategies for Change: Logical Incrementalism*
  (Homewood, IL: Irwin, 1980).

- Strategy is the pattern of objectives, purposes, or goals and the major policies and plans for achieving these goals, stated in such a way as to define what business the company is in or is to be in and the kind of company it is or is to be.

  —Kenneth Andrews, *The Concept of Corporate Strategy*
  (Homewood, IL: Irwin, 1971).

- What business strategy is all about is, in a word, *competitive advantage* . . . The sole purpose of strategic planning is to enable a company to gain, as efficiently as possible, a sustainable edge over its competitors. Corporate strategy thus implies an attempt to alter a company's strength relative to that of its competitors in the most efficient way.

  —Kenichi Ohmae, *The Mind of the Strategist*
  (Harmondsworth: Penguin Books, 1983).

- Lost Boy: "Injuns! Let's go get 'em!"
  John Darling: "Hold on a minute. First we must have a strategy."
  Lost Boy: "Uhh? What's a *strategy*?"
  John Darling: "It's, er . . . It's a plan of attack."

  —Walt Disney's *Peter Pan.*

in military and political analysis.[6] Nevertheless, as we shall see in Chapters 3 and 4, despite offering striking conceptual insights into competition and bargaining, game theory has yet to fullfill its potential as a widely applicable and practical basis for strategy formulation by firms.[7]

From Corporate Planning to Strategic Management

Indeed, the evolution of business strategy has been driven more by the practical needs of business rather than by the development of theory. The emergence of corporate planning was associated with the problems faced by managers during the 1950s and 1960s in coordinating decisions and maintaining control in increasingly large and complex enterprises. The development of financial budgeting procedures provided a basic mechanism for such coordination and control, but coordinating capital investment decisions required a longer planning horizon than the standard annual budgeting process. The emphasis on longer-term planning during the 1960s reflected concern with achieving coordination and consistency in investment planning during a period of stability and expansion. As companies sought efficiency and risk control—through scale-efficient production, mass marketing, vertical integration, and long-term investments in technology—long-term planning based on economic and market forecasts became a central task of top management. The typical format was a five-year corporate planning document that set goals and objectives, forecast key economic trends (including market demand, the company's market share, revenue, costs, and margins), established priorities for different products and business areas of the firm, and allocated capital expenditures. In 1963, SRI found that the majority of the largest U.S. companies had set up corporate planning departments.[8] Exhibit 1.4 provides an example of such formalized corporate planning.

The diffusion of corporate planning was closely associated with the drive toward diversification as large corporations came to view their management skills as unbounded by industry divisions. Increasingly, corporate planning became focused on the management of growth through diversification. One of the founders of the new field, Igor Ansoff, defined strategy in terms of diversification decisions:

> Strategic decisions are primarily concerned with external rather than internal problems of the firm and specifically with the selection of the product-mix that the firm will produce and the markets to which it will sell.[9]

During the 1970s, portfolio planning matrices (see Chapter 15) came into vogue as frameworks for selecting strategies and allocating resources within the diversified corporation.

EXHIBIT 1.4

Corporate Planning in a Large U.S. Steel Company, 1965

The first step in developing long-range plans was to forecast the product demand for future years. After calculating the tonnage needed in each sales district to provide the "target" fraction of the total forecast demand, the optimal production level for each area was determined. A computer program that incorporated the projected demand, existing production capacity, freight costs etc., was used for this purpose.

When the optimum production rate in each area was found, the additional facilities needed to produce the desired tonnage were specified. Then the capital costs for the necessary equipment, buildings, and layout were estimated by the Chief Engineer of the corporation and vari-

ous district engineers. Alternative plans for achieving company goals were also developed for some areas, and investment proposals were formulated after considering the amount of available capital and the company debt policy. The Vice President who was responsible for long-range planning recommended certain plans to the President, and after the top executives and the Board of Directors reviewed alternative plans, they made the necessary decisions about future activities.

Source: Harold W. Henry, _Long Range Planning Processes in 45 Industrial Companies,_ Prentice-Hall, Englewood Cliffs, 1967, p.65.

Diffusion of corporate planning during the 1960s and early 1970s was part of a wider enthusiasm among both companies and governments for "scientific" techniques of decision making including: cost-benefit analysis, discounted cash flow appraisal, linear programming, econometric forecasting, and macroeconomic demand management. Many economists and social commentators argued that scientific decision making and rational planning by corporations and governments were superior to the haphazard workings of the market economy.

During the 1970s, circumstances changed. Not only did diversification fail to deliver the anticipated synergies, but the oil shocks of 1974 and 1979 ushered in a new era of macroeconomic instability combined with increased international competition from resurgent Japanese, European, and Southeast Asian firms. Increased turbulence forced firms to abandon their corporate plans in favor of more flexible approaches to strategic management where the focus was less on planning for diversification and growth and more on achieving *competitiveness*. This transition from *corporate planning* to what is now termed *strategic management* was associated with increasing focus on competition as the central characteristic of the business environment and competitive advantage as the primary goal of strategy. As Bruce Henderson, founder of the Boston Consulting Group, observed:

> Strategy is a deliberate search for a plan of action that will develop a business's competitive advantage and compound it. For any company, the search is an iterative process that begins with a recognition of where you are now and what you have now. Your most dangerous competitors are those that are most like you. The differences between you and your competitors are the basis of your advantage. If you are in business and are self-supporting, you already have some kind of advantage, no matter how small or subtle . . . The objective is to enlarge the scope of your advantage, which can only happen at someone else's expense.[10]

This refocusing of priorities had important implications for the development of strategy concepts and frameworks. During the late 1970s and into the 1980s, the focus was on firms' market environments with particular emphasis on the analysis of industry structure and competition. Michael Porter of Harvard Business School pioneered the application of industrial organization economics to analyzing the determinants of firm profitability. His work was extended by consulting organizations including the Boston Consulting Group and the Strategic Planning Institute's PIMS (Profit Impact of Market Strategy) project.

During the late 1980s and early 1990s, interest in the role of strategy in building competitive advantage resulted in a shift of interest toward the internal aspects of the firm. Developments in the resource-based view of the firm and organizational competences and capabilities pointed to the firm's resources and capabilities as the primary source of its profitability and the basis for formulating its longer-term strategy.

As the 1990s draw to a close, the field continues its rapid evolution. Key developments include interest in the dynamics of competition and competitive advantage, in the role of knowledge within the firm, in cooperative strategies (particularly strategic alliances and inter-firm networks), and in novel organizational forms. Strategy remains one of the most exciting and fast-developing fields of management. It is fueled by multidisciplinary academic interest and by companies' continual striving to identify and access new sources of profitability and devise new approaches to competing in more established markets.[11]

Table 1.2 summarizes the development of strategic management over time.

TABLE 1.2
The Evolution of Strategic Management

PERIOD	1950S	1960S	1970S	LATE 1970S TO EARLY 1980S	LATE 1980S TO EARLY 1990S	MID TO LATE 1990S
Dominant Theme	Budgetary planning and control	Corporate planning	Corporate strategy	Analysis of industry and competition	The quest for competitive advantage	Strategic innovation
Main Issues	Financial control through operating budgets	Planning growth	Portfolio planning	Choice of industries, markets, and segments, and positioning within them	Sources of competitive advantage within the firm	Strategic and organizational advantage
Principal Concepts and Techniques	Financial budgeting Investment planning Project appraisal	Forecasting Investment planning models	Synergy SBUs Portfolio planning matrices Experience curves Returns to market share	Analysis of industry structure Competitor analysis PIMS analysis	Resource analysis Analysis of core competences	Dynamic sources of competitive advantage Control of standards Knowlege and learning
Organizational Implications	Financial management the key	Rise of corporate planning departments and five-year formal plans	Diversification Multidivisional structures Quest for global market share	Greater industry and market selectivity Industry restructuring Active asset management	Corporate restructuring and business process reengineering Refocusing and outsourcing	The virtual organization The knowledge based firm Alliances and networks The quest for critical mass

THE DISTINCTION BETWEEN CORPORATE AND BUSINESS STRATEGY

As the focus of strategic management has shifted from planning processes to the quest for profit, so the theoretical foundations of the field have been driven by analysis of the sources of profit and the factors that result in differences in profitability between firms. If we accept that the fundamental goal of the firm is to earn a return on its capital that exceeds the cost of its capital, what determines the ability of the firm to earn a such a rate of return? There are two routes. First, the firm may locate in an industry where favorable industry conditions result in the industry earning a rate of return above the competitive level. Second, the firm may attain a position of advantage vis-à-vis its competitors within an industry allowing it to earn a return in excess of the industry average (see Figure 1.3).

These two sources of superior performance define the two basic levels of strategy within an enterprise: corporate strategy and business strategy. **Corporate strategy** defines the scope of the firm in terms of the industries and markets in which it competes. Corporate strategy decisions include investment in diversification, vertical integration, acquisitions, and new ventures; the allocation of resources between the different businesses of the firm; and divestments.

Business strategy is concerned with how the firm competes within a particular industry or market. If the firm is to prosper within an industry, it must establish a competitive advantage over its rivals. Hence, this area of strategy is also referred to as *competitive strategy*. Using slightly different terminology, Jay Bourgeois has referred to corporate strategy as the task of *domain selection* and business strategy as the task of *domain navigation*.[12]

The distinction between corporate and business strategy and their connection to the two basic sources of profitability may be expressed in even simpler terms. The purpose and the content of a firm's strategy is defined by the answer to a single question: How can the firm make money? This question can be elaborated into two further questions: "What business or businesses should we be in?" And, within each business: "How should we compete?" The answer to the first question describes the

FIGURE 1.3
Sources of Superior
Profitability

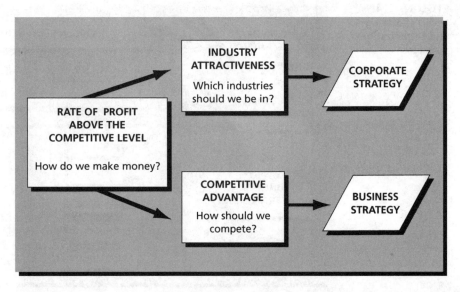

corporate strategy of the company, the answer to the second describes the primary themes of business (or competitive) strategy.

The distinction between corporate strategy and business strategy corresponds to the organization structure of the typical multibusiness corporation. Corporate strategy is the responsibility of the top management team, supported by corporate strategy staff. Business strategy is formulated and implemented primarily by the individual businesses (typically organized as divisions or business units). Figure 1.4 also shows a third level of strategy: functional strategy. **Functional strategies** are the elaboration and implementation of business strategies through individual functions such as production, R&D, marketing, human resources, and finance. They are primarily the responsibility of the functional departments. In single-business firms there is no distinction between corporate and business strategy.

The primary emphasis of this book is business rather than corporate strategy. This is justified by the conviction that the key to the success of an enterprise is establishing competitive advantage. Hence, from an analytical standpoint, issues of business strategy precede those of corporate strategy. Yet these two dimensions of strategy are closely linked: the scope of a firm's business has implications for the sources of competitive advantage, whereas the nature of a firm's competitive advantage is relevant to the range of businesses and markets within which a firm can be successful.

DIFFERENT APPROACHES TO STRATEGY: *DESIGN* VERSUS *PROCESS*

As indicated by its title, the concern of this book is developing an analytical approach to strategic management. The implicit belief is that the senior managers of an organization are able to objectively appraise the enterprise and its environment, to formulate a strategy that maximizes the chances for success in an uncertain future, and to implement that strategy. The emphasis is the formulation of strategy,

FIGURE 1.4
Levels of Strategy
and Organization
Structure

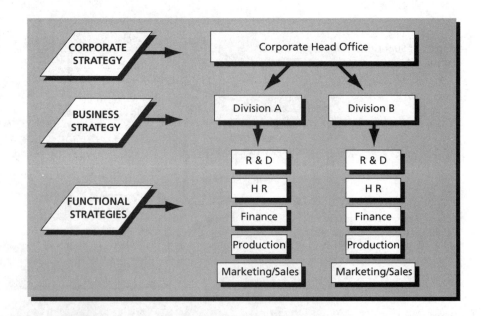

although as we shall see, formulation and implementation cannot be separated: a well-formulated strategy must take account of the process through which it will be implemented, and it is through implementation that strategies are formulated and reformulated.

What has become termed the "design school" of strategy views strategic decision making as a logical process in which strategy is formulated through rational analysis of the firm, its performance, and the external environment. The strategy is then communicated to the organization and implemented down through successive organizational layers.

Such a picture is mostly a fiction: the process is less structured, more diffused, and the dichotomization of formulation and implementation is less apparent. Empirical research by Henry Mintzberg and his colleagues at McGill University into the long-term development of strategy in a number of organizations identified several stages of the strategy process:[13] **Intended strategy** is strategy as conceived of by the top management team. Even here, rationality is limited and the intended strategy is the result of a process of negotiation, bargaining, and compromise, involving many individuals and groups within the organization. However, the **realized strategy** that we observe tends to be only about 10–30 percent of the intended strategy. The primary determinant of a firm's realized strategy is what Mintzberg terms **emergent strategy**—the patterns of decisions that emerge from individual managers adapting to changing external circumstances and the ways in which the intended strategy was interpreted.

The contrast between the rationalist "design school" of strategy and the behaviorist "process school" crystallized in the debate over Honda's strategy in entering the U.S. motorcycle market. According to the Boston Consulting Group, Honda exemplified the analytic approach to strategy formation based on exploiting volume-based economies to attain an unassailable position of cost leadership in the world motorcycle industry.[14] However, Richard Pascale's interviews with the Honda managers actually involved revealed a different story.[15] The initial decision to enter the U.S. market was based on little analysis and included no clear plan of how Honda would build a market position. The outstanding success of the Honda 50cc Supercub was a surprise to the company—Honda had believed that its main opportunities lay with its larger bikes. As Mintzberg observes: "Brilliant as its strategy may have looked after the fact, Honda's managers made almost every conceivable mistake until the market finally hit them over the head with the right formula."[16]

The debate over the Honda story and its implications continues.[17] The key point, however, is not who is right and who is wrong, but recognizing that different approaches are suited to answering different questions. The "process school" of strategy research focuses on the realities of how strategies emerge. The central issues are processes through which strategic decisions are made in practice. The "design school" is more normative in its approach. Its goal is to uncover the factors that determine success to permit managers to develop performance-enhancing strategies.

However, Henry Mintzberg goes further: not only is rational design an inaccurate account of how strategies are actually formulated, it is a poor way of making strategy. "The notion that strategy is something that should happen way up there, far removed from the details of running an organization on a daily basis, is one of the great fallacies of conventional strategic management." The problem is that a divide between formulation and implementation precludes learning. In practice, the two must go hand in hand, with strategy constantly being adjusted and revised in light of experience. Mintzberg uses the images of *crafting* to contrast his conception of strategy formulation from the conventional rational-planning approach:

> Imagine someone planning strategy. What likely springs to mind is an image of orderly thinking: a senior manager, or a group of them, sitting in an office formulating courses of action that everyone else will implement on schedule. The keynote is reason—rational control, the systematic analysis of competitors and markets, or company strengths and weaknesses, the combination of these analyses producing clear, explicit, full-blown strategies.
>
> Now imagine someone *crafting* strategy. A wholly different image likely results, as different from planning as craft is from mechanization. Craft invokes traditional skill, dedication, perfection through the mastery of detail. What springs to mind is not so much thinking and reason as involvement, a feeling of intimacy and harmony with the materials at hand, developed through long experience and commitment. Formulation and implementation merge into a fluid process of learning through which creative strategies emerge.[18]

The approach of this book is to follow a rationalist, analytical approach to strategy formulation in preference to the crafting approach advocated by Mintzberg. This is not because planning is necessarily superior to crafting—we have already noted that strategy is about identity and direction rather than planning. Nor is it because we wish to downplay the role of skill, dedication, involvement, harmony, or creativity. These qualities are essential ingredients of successful strategies and successful enterprises. Strategy development is a multidimensional process that must involve both rational analysis and intuition, experience, and emotion. But, whether strategy formulation is formal or informal, whether strategies are deliberate or emergent, there can be little doubt as to the importance of systematic analysis as a vital input into the strategy process. Without analysis, the process of strategy formulation, particularly at the senior management level, is likely to be chaotic with no basis for comparing and evaluating alternatives. Moreover, critical decisions become susceptible to the whims and preferences of individual managers, to contemporary fads, and to wishful thinking. Concepts, theories, and analytic frameworks are not alternatives or substitutes for experience, commitment, and creativity. But they do provide useful frames for organizing and assessing the vast amount of information available on the firm and its environment and for guiding decisions, and may even act to stimulate rather than repress creativity and innovation.

Central to the rational approach to strategy analysis is the idea that we can systematically analyze the reasons for business success and failure and apply this learning to formulating business strategies. The problem of the rationalist approach, as emphasized in Mintzberg's attacks on strategic planning, is that the analysis is too narrow—it has tended to be overformalized and has emphasized quantitative over qualitative data.[19] The danger of the Mintzberg approach is that by downplaying the role of systematic analysis and emphasizing the role of intuition and vision, we move into a world of new-age mysticism in which there is no clear basis for reasoned choices and in which disorder threatens the progressive accumulation of knowledge.

The goal of this book is to promote analysis that is sound, relevant, and applicable. If strategy analysis does not take account of experiential learning and the practicalities of implementation, it is poor analysis. Similarly the process of strategy formulation must involve intuition, reflection, and the interaction between thought and action. Good analysis should encourage the development of intuition and promote creativity.

Analysis can also greatly facilitate the process of strategy formulation. Analysis provides a conceptual framework for rational discussion of alternative ideas and a vocabulary for communicating the strategy throughout the organization.

THE DIFFERENT ROLES OF STRATEGY WITHIN THE FIRM

What emerges from this discussion of the "process" view of strategy is a recognition that strategic management fulfills multiple roles within the firm. We can view strategy as a vehicle for achieving three key managerial purposes.

Strategy as Decision Support

At the outset of this chapter, we identified strategy as a key element in success. But why is this so? Strategy is a pattern or theme that gives coherence to the decisions of an individual or organization. But why can't individuals or organizations make optimal decisions in the absence of such a unifying theme? Consider Gary Kasparov's defeat in the May 1997 chess tournament by IBM's "Deep Blue." Deep Blue did not need strategy. Because of its phenomenal memory capacity and computing power, it could examine the full set of consequences of each move. In short, it could envisage a huge decision tree covering the entire game—making a strategy unnecessary. For every move by Kasparov, Deep Blue could compute the optimal response. Kasparov was subject to the cognitive limitations that constrain all human beings. Bounded rationality means that the human brain is incapable of assimilating and analyzing all the available information necessary for fully rational choices. In a world of bounded rationality, a strategy is a second-best solution: it establishes a set of guidelines and criteria for how individual decisions will be made. One of Kasparov's handicaps was that because Deep Blue was so thoroughly programmed to respond to Kasparov's chess-playing strategy, he was forced to adopt a chess-playing strategy that was not as well adjusted to his temperament and expertise.

Even in the smallest enterprise, many hundreds of decisions are likely to be made every day. Decisions range from whether to give a discount to a particular customer, to the choice of sending mail by express or regular delivery. It is not possible or desirable to optimize every single decision by considering the full implications of every permutation of decision choices. In these circumstances, strategies such as "We will seek technological leadership in military applications of wireless communication," or "We shall provide the lowest priced gasoline in Ohio," simplify decision making by *constraining* the range of decision alternatives considered, and by acting as a *heuristic*—a rule-of-thumb that reduces the search required to find an acceptable solution to a decision problem.

Strategy as a Vehicle for Coordination and Communication

A strategy helps achieve consistency in decisions over time. Additionally, in complex organizations, a strategy serves as a vehicle for achieving consistent decision making across different departments and individuals. Organizations are composed of many individuals—647,000 in the case of General Motors—all of whom are engaged in making decisions that must be coordinated.

For strategy to provide such coordination requires that the strategy process acts as a communication mechanism within the firm. One of the most important changes in large enterprises over the past two decades has been for the responsibility

EXHIBIT 1.5

Coca-Cola's Project Infinity

Coca-Cola has 43 percent of the U.S. market for carbonated soft drinks. In the United States Coca-Cola products are sold through 2 million stores, 450,000 restaurants, and 1.4 million vending machines. A dominant player with limited growth prospects? Not according to Chairman Roberto Goizueta who calculates Coca-Cola's market share as 3 percent. Why the discrepancy? Goizueta identifies the relevant market as the human race's total consumption of fluids. The purpose of Project Infinity is to galvanize the company into exploiting its infinite opportunities for market growth.

How will this ambitious goal be translated into sales? Rather than looking at Coke's overall share of the U.S. and world market, the company will break down its market share data to identify discrepancies in market share between countries,

localities, and specific outlets. In Bismarck, North Dakota, consumption per person averages 566 eight-ounce servings each year; in nearby Jamestown, consumption is only 314. In Memphis, Tennessee, consumption per head is 50 percent higher than in nearby Hot Springs, Arkansas.

Standing in a shopping center in Atlanta, Jack Stahl, head of Coke's U.S. operations, can see a grocery store, three restaurants, and three vending machines, all of which sell Coke. Saturated market? No, a "microcosm of opportunity" says Stahl. "Nearby apartment buildings and office complexes could support more vending machines. I bet 150 people come into that hair salon each day—why shouldn't it sell Coke?"

Source: "A Coke and a Perm?" Wall Street Journal, May 8, 1997, p. A1.

for strategy formulation to shift from corporate planning departments to line managers. One of the benefits of this transition is that the strategic planning process provides a mechanism for dialogue among corporate, divisional, and business unit managers, and between general managers and functional specialists. For many companies a key vehicle for communicating strategy is the **mission statement:** a summary statement of the essence of the organization's strategy and purpose. We examine mission statements in the next chapter when we discuss the role of goals and values.

Strategy as Target

Strategy links with *mission* and *vision* in defining where the firm wants to be in the future. The purpose of such goal setting is not just to establish a direction to guide the formulation of strategy, but also to set aspirations for the company. Hence, a further role for strategy is as a target for the organization. Hamel and Prahalad argue that a critical ingredient in the strategies of outstandingly successful companies is what they term "strategic intent"—an obsession with achieving leadership within the field of endeavor.[20] Examples of organizational strategic intent include the goal of the Apollo program 'To put a man on the moon by the end of the decade,' McDonald's pronouncement that, "Our vision is to dominate the global food service industry," Komatsu's intent to "Encircle Caterpillar," and Coca-Cola's "Project Infinity" (see Exhibit 1.5).

Hamel and Prahalad extend their argument further. In a dynamic environment, the conventional approach to strategy formulation, which emphasizes the fit between internal resources and external opportunities, may be insufficient to drive long-run competitiveness. Critical to the success of upstart companies such as CNN in television, Apple in computers, Yamaha in pianos, and Southwest Airlines and Virgin Atlantic in air travel was a mismatch between resources and aspirations in which unreasonable ambition became the driving force for innovation, risk taking, and continuous improvement. In place of *strategic fit* and *resource allocation*, Hamel and Prahalad emphasize *stretch* and *resource leverage*.[21]

THE ROLE OF ANALYSIS IN STRATEGY FORMULATION

Recognition of the multiplicity of purposes that a company's strategy fulfills—and, in particular, strategy's role in communicating purpose and setting aspirations—raises further questions about the analytical approach to strategy. Ever since Abernathy and Hayes identified "modern management techniques" as instrumental in the American firms' declining international competitiveness in many sectors,[22] analytical approaches to management have been castigated for being static, conservative, risk averse, inflexible, short term, and detrimental to innovation.

The purpose of this book is not to defend conventional approaches to business strategy analysis but to do better. Management's approach to strategy must be dynamic, flexible, and innovative. It must recognize the powerful role that values and goals play in organizations, and the importance of the strategy process in facilitating communication and coordination. It must recognize the importance of intuition, tacit knowledge, and learning-by-doing in complementing more "scientific" analysis.

It is vital that we recognize the limitations of analysis in guiding strategic management. Unlike mathematics, chemistry, or even economics, strategic management lacks an agreed-upon, internally consistent, empirically validated body of theory. Though it employs theory and theoretical concepts, these are drawn mainly from economics, psychology, ecology and sociology—principally on an ad hoc basis. Even as applied science, strategic management differs substantially from more technically oriented managerial disciplines such as finance and production management. Strategy analysis does not generate solutions the same way that scheduling algorithms or discounted cash flow analysis or the sampling frameworks of market research provide. A major feature of the techniques introduced in this book is that they do not provide solutions. Just as strategic decisions in our personal lives are not amenable to quantitative decision techniques (Should I get married? Have children? Change my career from bond trading to brain surgery? Move to a new location?), the same is true in business. There are simply too many variables to reduce strategy analysis to programmed algorithms.

The purpose of strategy analysis is not to provide answers but to help us understand the issues. Many of the analytic techniques introduced in this book are simply frameworks to identify, classify, and understand the principal factors that influence strategic decisions. Such frameworks are invaluable in understanding the complexities of strategy decisions: the infinite richness of the firm's environment and the tangle of people, resources, structures, and traditions that make up the business enterprise. In some instances, the most useful contribution may be in assisting us to make a start on the problem: by guiding us to the questions we need to answer, and by providing a framework for organizing the information gathered, we are in a superior position to a manager who relies exclusively on experience and intuition. Finally, analytic frameworks and techniques can assist our flexibility as managers.

The analysis in this book is general in its applicability; it is not specific to particular industries, companies, or situations. Hence, it can help increase our confidence and effectiveness in understanding and responding to new situations and new circumstances. By encouraging depth of understanding into fundamental issues concerning competitive advantage, customer needs, organizational capabilities, and the basis of competition—the concepts, frameworks, and techniques in this book will encourage rather than constrain innovation, flexibility, and opportunism.

◆ SUMMARY

This chapter has covered a lot of ground. We have introduced the concept of strategy, explained its role in success, traced its development over time, and examined its purposes and limitations.

The fundamental premise of this chapter is that strategy is an important determinant of success in most areas of human activity. In identifying some common features of successful strategies, we have presented a framework for studying strategic choices that views strategy as a link between an organization and its environment.

In Part II, we examine each of the separate components of this framework: goals, values, and performance; the industry environment; the resources and capabilities of the firm; organization structure; and management systems. These chapters comprise the basic tools of strategy analysis. We then deploy these tools in the analysis of competitive advantage (Part III), in the formulation and implementation of business strategies in different industry contexts (Part IV), and then in the development of corporate strategy (Part V). Figure 1.5 shows the framework for the book.

NOTES

1 Sun Tzu, in *The Art of Strategy: A New Translation of Sun Tzu's Classic "The Art of War,"* trans. R. L. Wing (New York: Doubleday, 1988).

2 "British Satellite Broadcasting and Sky Television," Harvard Business School Case.

3 Roger Evered, "So What Is Strategy?" *Long Range Planning* 16 no. 3 (June 1983): 57–72.

4 For a review of the concepts and principles of military strategy, see B. H. Liddell Hart, *Strategy* (New York: Praeger, 1968).

5 On the links between military and business strategy, see Roger Evered, "So What Is Strategy?" Long Range Planning 16 no. 3 (June 1983) : 57–72. For a survey, see Nigel Campbell, "Lanchester Market Structures: A Japanese Approach to the Analysis of Business Competition," *Strategic Management Journal* 7 (1986): 189–200.

6 On the contribution of game theory to business strategy analysis, see Franklin M. Fisher, "Games Economists Play: A Noncooperative View," *RAND Journal of Economics* 20 (Spring 1989): 113–124; and Colin F. Camerer, "Does Strategy Research Need Game Theory?" *Strategic Management Journal* 12, Special Issue (Winter 1991): 137–152.

7 For a practical and accessible introduction to the application of game theory, see Thomas C. Schelling, *The Strategy of Conflict,* 2nd edition (Cambridge, MA: Harvard University Press, 1980); A. K. Dixit and B. J. Nalebuff, *Thinking Strategically: The Competitive Edge in Business, Politics, and Everyday Life* (New York: W. W. Norton, 1991); and A. Brandenburger and B. J. Nalebuff, *Co–opetition* (New York: Doubleday, 1996).

8 Frank F. Gilmore, *Formulation and Advocacy of Business Policy,* rev. ed. (Ithaca, NY: Cornell University Press, 1970): 16.

9 Igor Ansoff, *Corporate Strategy* (London: Penguin Books, 1985): 18.

FIGURE 1.5
The Structure of
the Book

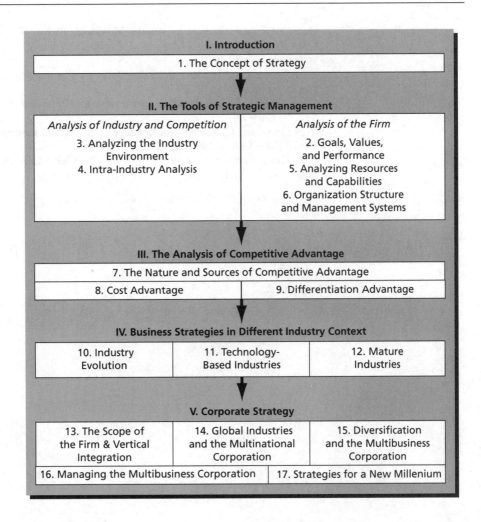

10 Bruce D. Henderson, "The Origin of Strategy," *Harvard Business Review* (November–December 1989): 139–143.

11 For an account of the conceptual and intellectual development of strategic management, see J.–C. Spender, "Business Policy and Strategy: A View of the Field, with Comments on Rumelt, Schendel and Teece (1991)," discussion paper, Graduate School of Management, Rutgers University, 1992.

12 L. J. Bourgeois, "Strategy and the Environment: A Conceptual Integration," *Academy of Management Review* 5 (1980): 25–39.

13 See Henry Mintzberg, "Patterns of Strategy Formulation," *Management Science* 24 (1978): 934–948; "Of Strategies: Deliberate and Emergent," *Strategic Management Journal* 6 (1985): 257–272; and *Mintzberg on Management: Inside Our Strange World of Organizations* (New York: Free Press, 1988).

14 Boston Consulting Group, *Strategy Alternatives for the British Motorcycle Industry* (London: Her Majesty's Stationery Office, 1975).

15 Richard T. Pascale, "Perspective on Strategy: The Real Story Behind Honda's Success," *California Management Review* 26, no. 3 (Spring 1984): 47–72.

16 Henry Mintzberg, "Crafting Strategy," *Harvard Business Review* 65 (July–August 1987): 70.

17 Henry Mintzberg, Richard T. Pascale, M. Goold, Richard P. Rumelt, "The Honda Effect Revisited," *California Management Review* 38 (Summer 1996): 78–117.

18 Mintzberg, op. cit., 66.

19 Henry Mintzberg, "The Rise and Fall of Strategic Planning," *Harvard Business Review* (January–February 1994): 107–114.

20 Gary Hamel and C. K. Prahalad, "Strategic Intent," *Harvard Business Review* (May–June 1989):63–77.

21 Gary Hamel and C. K. Prahalad, "Strategy as Stretch and Leverage," *Harvard Business Review* (March–April 1993): 75–84.

22 W. J. Abernathy and R. H. Hayes, "Managing Our Way to Economic Decline," *Harvard Business Review* (July–August 1980): 67–77.

II.

Tools of Strategic Management

2

Goals, Values, and Performance

The strategic aim of a business is to earn a return on capital, and if in any particular case the return in the long run is not satisfactory, then the deficiency should be corrected or the activity abandoned for a more favorable one.

—Alfred P. Sloan Jr., *My Years with General Motors*
(London: Sidgewick & Jackson, 1963.)

◆ INTRODUCTION AND OBJECTIVES

The first chapter established what strategy is and what it can do. It also provided a framework for developing and appraising business strategies. In this framework, strategy is viewed as linking four sets of factors: the goals and values of the firm, the

31

industry environment, the resources and capabilities of the firm, and its structure and management systems. Hence, strategy may be viewed as the way in which the firm deploys its resources and capabilities within its business environment in order to achieve its goals. In this chapter we explore the first of these topics: the goals and values of the firm and the performance of the firm in attaining them.

Firms possess multiple goals. Their choices of goals and the ways in which they pursue them are influenced and constrained by the values that the firm adheres to. Nevertheless, this chapter assumes that the primary goal of the firm is profit maximization—or, equivalently, maximizing shareholder value. This assumption of profit maximization underlies the analysis of the book as a whole. Most of the frameworks and techniques of strategy you will become familiar with are based on analysis of the sources of profitability and the determinants of differences in profitability between firms. Indeed, for most practical purposes, strategic management can be defined as a quest for profitability.

By the time you have completed this chapter you will be able to:

♦ Evaluate the arguments for shareholder versus stakeholder approaches to the goals of the firm.

♦ Translate goals of profit maximization and value maximization into measurable performance targets defined by accounting returns, cash flows, economic profit, and operating targets.

♦ Apply the principles of valuing companies, business units, and strategies.

♦ Appreciate the role of values in the formulation and implementation of strategy.

STRATEGY AS A QUEST FOR PROFIT

Business is about creating value. Value can be created in two ways: by production and by commerce. **Production** creates value by the physical transformation of products that are less valued by consumers into products that are more valued by consumers, e.g., the transformation of clay into pottery. **Commerce** creates value, not by the physical transformation of materials, but by repositioning them in space and time. **Trade** involves transferring products from individuals and places where they are valued less to individuals and locations where they are valued more. Similarly, **speculation** involves transferring products between a point of time where the product is valued less to a point of time where it is valued more. Thus, the essence of commerce is creating value through **arbitrage** across time and space.

Profitability as the Underlying Goal of the Firm

The value created by firms is distributed among different parties: consumers benefit because they acquire goods and services at prices below the maximum they would have been willing to pay; the suppliers of labor and other inputs receive remuneration in excess of the minimum they would have accepted; the risk takers who take equity stakes in the enterprise receive profits—the surplus of revenues over the costs of the inputs.

If business enterprise creates value for all these participants and their interests diverge from one another, it seems natural to think of the firm as serving multiple constituencies. This **stakeholder view** of the firm sees the business enterprise as a coalition of interest groups including shareholders (whose goal is profit), top management (whose goals include salary, perks, prestige, and power), and employees (who are interested in pay, working conditions, and job security). External stakeholders such as customers, suppliers, and government also have important interests. Even within each stakeholder group, diversity of goals is likely. For instance, managers tend to identify with the interests of their particular division or functional department.[1]

The case for the stakeholder approach to defining the goals of the firm is based on the recognition that the business enterprise is a social institution pursuing the interests of multiple groups. In Japan and continental Europe, Germany in particular, the notion of corporations balancing the interests of multiple interest groups has a long tradition. In German companies, this is institutionalized in the supervisory board that includes representatives of both shareholders and employees. Under the stakeholder view of the firm, a primary role of top management is reconciling the divergent interests of different stakeholders.

Though strategies can be formulated by taking explicit account of multiple goals, the need to establish priorities and tradeoffs results in vastly increased complexity.[2] To avoid this complexity, we make the simple, yet realistic, assumption that business enterprises pursue a single dominant objective—*profit*. The case for the pursuit of profit as the primary goal for firms is supported by four observations.

1. The primary motivation of the owners of companies is profit, since profit determines the income of these individuals. Although shareholders have limited control over the managers of public corporations, in Britain, Canada, the United States, and several other countries, the directors of public corporations are legally obliged to operate in the interests of their shareholders.

2. Increasing pressure of competition—international competition in particular—has caused the interests of different stakeholders to converge. The underlying common interest of all stakeholders is the firm's survival. Survival requires that, over the long term, the firm earn a rate of profit that covers its cost of capital. Despite the upswing in corporate profits during the 1990s, many companies fail to earn a return on capital that covers their cost of capital. In 1994, a year of increasing profitability and rising stock market values in the United States, 533 of the 1,000 largest nonfinancial companies listed on U.S. stock markets earned a net, after-tax operating profit that was less than their cost of capital.[3] Generally speaking, as the heat of international competition increases, fewer and fewer organizations have the luxury of pursuing goals that diverge substantially from profit maximization. If a company is unable—over the long-term—to earn a return on its capital that covers its cost of capital, then ultimately, it will fail due to the inability to attract the capital needed to replace its assets.

3. The external pressure on firms to make profits and operate in the interests of shareholders has also come from financial markets. A feature of the corporate financial environment of the 1980s and 1990s has been a more active "market for corporate control." Increased numbers of corporate acquisitions, many of them hostile, have meant that any company that depresses its share price by failing to maximize profits risks being acquired by owners anxious to operate the company in a more profit-focused manner. Such an acquirer may be a competitor (e.g., BankOne and Nationsbank have both been aggressive acquirers of other U.S. banks), a company that specializes in corporate

restructuring (e.g., a conglomerate such as Tomkins), or a leveraged buyout investment group (e.g., Kohlberg Kravis Roberts, which acquired RJR Nabisco in one of the world's all-time biggest acquisitions). External pressure on top management to operate in the shareholder interest has also come through more active institutional shareholders. The large pension fund, California Public Employees Retirement System, has been especially prominent in pressuring the boards of directors of companies that have failed to generate satisfactory shareholder return.

4. Even beyond a common interest of stakeholders in the survival of the firm, it is likely that there is more community of interests than conflict of interests among different stakeholders. The quest for profits over the long term is likely to require that a company treat its employees well and develop their full potential, act fairly and honorably toward suppliers and customers, and conduct itself responsibly in relation to the environment and society's values. The success of companies such as Levi Strauss, Marks & Spencer, Harley-Davidson, and Sony Corporation suggests that a strong ethical code and promoting the interests of suppliers and employees is quite compatible with superior long-run profitability.

The assumption that the purpose of strategy is to pursue profit over the long term greatly simplifies strategy analysis. At the same time, it does not succeed in eliminating ambiguity. What is the firm to maximize: total profit, margin on sales, return on equity, return on invested capital, or what? Over what time period? With what kind of adjustment for risk? And what is profit anyway: are we concerned with accounting profit, cash flow, or economic surplus?

What Is Profit?

Profit is the surplus of revenues over costs available for distribution to the owners of the firm. If we are to maximize profit, we must be clear about how we measure it. Instructing the managers of a firm to maximize profit only makes sense if there is agreement as to what profit is and how it is measured. The ambiguity of the concept is apparent once we consider the profit performance of companies. Table 2.1 identifies several indicators of profitability. Not only do the different measures result in different rankings of firm performance, but the choice of a particular profit measure is likely to have important implications for strategic choices. Consider the following issues:

Does Profit Maximization Mean Maximizing Total Profit or Rate of Profit?

If the latter, are we concerned with profit as a ratio to sales (*return on sales*), total assets (*return on assets*), or shareholders' equity (*return on equity*)? As an objective, each will lead to perverse results. The instruction to "maximize total profit" is likely to encourage investment in activities that are profitable but where the return falls below the cost of capital. Maximizing the *rate* of profit encourages the firm to divest assets to the point where it is reduced to a rump of a few exceptionally profitable activities.

Over What Time Period Is Profitability Being Maximized?
Whatever measure of profitability is chosen, the specification of time period is critical. The instruction to "maximize next year's profit" will lead to a very different strategy from the instruction to "maximize profit over the next ten years."

How Is Profit to Be Measured? Accounting profit is defined by the accounting principles under which a company's financial statements are drawn up. Thus, a company's profit varies according to the accounting rules of the company's country of domicile. When Daimler-Benz obtained a listing on the New York Stock Exchange in September 1993, the recalculation of its net income using U.S. accounting principles resulted in what was a sizable profit (under German accounting principles) becoming a loss. Not only does a firm's reported profit depend on rules and conventions regarding the treatment of inflation, taxation, investments, R&D, capital gains and losses, exchange rate changes, and extraordinary items, but flexibility in the interpretation of accounting principles means that a firm has discretion over the profits it reports.[4]

From Accounting Profit to Economic Profit

One of the biggest problems with profit as measured by a firm's financial statements is that it combines two types of returns: the *normal return to capital* as a reward to investing and *economic profit* as a pure surplus after all inputs (including capital) have been paid out. In recent years, a number of companies and their financial advisers have encouraged firms to distinguish these two elements and to focus on *economic profit* both as a target and as a measure of performance. To distinguish pure or economic profit from conventional accounting notions of profit, economists and business strategists use the term **rent** or **economic rent** to refer to economic profit.

TABLE 2.1
Performance of Leading U.S. Companies Using Different Profitability Measures

COMPANY	NET INCOME[1] 1995, $m	ROS[2] 1995, %	ROE[3] 1995, %	EVA[4] 1995, $m	MVA[5] 1995, $m	RETURN TO SHARE-HOLDERS[6] 1995, %
General Motors	6,881	4.1	29.5	3,225	-8,172	28.5
General Electric	6,573	9.4	22.2	1,852	80,792	45.3
Exxon	6,470	5.9	16.0	1,113	39,048	38.1
Philip Morris	5,450	10.3	39.0	1,165	51,628	64.8
IBM	4,178	5.8	18.6	2,541	-5,878	25.7
Coca-Cola	2,986	16.6	55.4	2,140	87,820	29.3
Wal-Mart	2,740	2.9	18.6	265	35,974	5.3
Procter & Gamble	2,645	7.9	25.0	624	40,000	36.7
Hewlett-Packard	2,433	7.7	20.6	295	26,037	69.4
Mobil	2,376	3.6	13.2	-926	21,378	37.5

[1.] Net after-tax profits (*Fortune* 500)
[2.] Net income as a percentage of sales revenues (*Fortune* 500)
[3.] Net income as a percentage of shareholders' equity (*Fortune* 500)
[4.] Economic Value Added = Net operating profits after tax *less* cost of capital (*Stern Stewart Performance* 1000, 1997)
[5.] Market Value Added = Total market value (equity + debt), *less* total investment in assets by investors (*Stern Stewart Performance* 1000, 1997)
[6.] Dividend in 1995 + Increase in market price of the shares during 1995/Price of shares at beginning of 1995

The most widely used approach to measuring and utilizing the concept of economic profit is the one devised and popularized by the New York consulting company Stern Stewart & Company.[5] The Stern Stewart analysis centers on Economic Value Added (EVA), which is the Net Operating Profit after Tax (NOPAT) earned by the company *less* its Weighted Average Cost of Capital (WACC). Thus, for Anheuser-Busch, EVA is calculated as follows:

	Operating Profit	$1,756m.
less	Taxes	$617m.
less	Cost of Capital	$904m.*
=	Economic Value Added	$235m.

*Cost of equity 14.3 percent, cost of debt (adjusted for the tax-deductibility of interest payments) 5.2 percent, weighted average cost of capital 11.3 percent, total capital employed $8.0 billion.[6]

The advantages of economic profit over accounting profit are both in setting performance targets for companies and business units and in evaluating performance achieved. As a target, economic profit overcomes the problems associated with instructing managers either to maximize accounting earnings (which encourages firms to overinvest through accepting projects that generate returns at less than the cost of capital) or to maximize rate of return on capital (which encourages underinvestment and the divestment of profitable assets). Thus, maximizing economic profit is consistent with maximizing shareholder value.[7]

In evaluating profit performance, economic profit has the virtue of imposing a tighter financial discipline than does accounting profit by clarifying the fact that businesses earning less than their cost of capital are really making a loss. James Meenan, chief financial officer of AT&T reported that:

> The effect of adopting EVA on AT&T's businesses is staggering. "Good" is no longer a positive operating earnings. It's only when you beat the cost of capital.

The approach has had a particularly dramatic effect on those businesses that suddenly found that, under the new rules, they had been posting negative profitability for years.[8] Many companies have used EVA as the centerpiece of a company-wide system for imposing tight financial discipline and reorienting all aspects of strategy and operations around the goals of maximizing shareholder value. Companies that have reported performance improvements as a result of implementing EVA-based financial control systems include Coca-Cola, Briggs & Stratton, Eli Lilly, and the Burton Group. Exhibit 2.1 comments on the experience of Varity Corporation in implementing EVA.

The Shareholder Value Approach

The merit of EVA is that it corresponds more closely to economic profit than do accounting earnings and, as an objective, is consistent with the pursuit of shareholder interests. At the same time, it does not address the problem of the time period over which profits are to be maximized. Resolution of this problem requires that future profits be capitalized and that the firm maximize their present value. Hence, EVA may be viewed as a halfway move toward a full shareholder value approach.

EXHIBIT 2.1

Deployment of Economic Value Added by Varity Corporation

Varity Corp. was built from the struggling farm-machinery manufacturer, Massey-Ferguson, and is now a profitable supplier of auto components and diesel engines. Chairman and CEO Victor Rice adopted EVA in 1993 in an effort to link Varity's business objectives more closely with investor interests and to create a more financially driven corporate culture. Rice reports that:

EVA permeates every level at Varity from the boardroom to the shop floor. My bonus as well as all senior managers' bonuses are determined solely by whether Varity achieves its EVA target. . . . We believe that this approach enables us to directly align management and shareholder interests. . . . Here are some of the specific ways we've applied EVA:

♦ Varity's EVA was negative $150 million in 1992. We set a five-year target to reach positive EVA in annual increments using a pre-tax cost of capital of 20 percent. By 1995 we were approaching 80 percent of our target.

♦ EVA caused us to take a closer look at our capital structure, recognizing the relatively higher cost of equity versus debt. This was an important factor in our decision to embark on a stock buyback program in which we purchased 10 percent of our outstanding common stock.

♦ EVA identifies operations and projects that earn more than the cost of capital. EVA analysis confirmed our decision to build twenty-first century manufacturing facilities for our Kelsey-Hayes antilock brake business.

♦ We use the EVA model to evaluate potential joint ventures. In 1994, for example, we determined that a joint venture between our UK Perkins diesel-engine business and Ishikawa-jima-Shibaura in Japan would generate returns in excess of cost of capital.

♦ As part of our annual strategic planning process we use EVA analysis to quantify business initiatives such as expansion in new markets and acquisitions.

♦ EVA provides a means of determining whether the sale of businesses or assets is in the best interests of shareholders.

♦ Almost every business process in our 80 plants and offices is influenced by EVA. For example, improvements in cycle times and inventory turns reduce capital needs and, in turn, create value.

♦ Using incentives to create a positive return on capital, EVA encourages managers to behave as if they are shareholders. We link employee bonuses directly to EVA improvement . . . All 4,000 Perkins employees, including union members, are tied to an EVA-based compensation plan.

Source: Victor Rice, "Why EVA Works for Varity," *Chief Executive*, September 1996.

The essence of a shareholder value approach is recognizing that companies operate in the interests of their owners (shareholders), whose interest is maximizing their wealth, i.e., maximizing the value of their shares. What determines the market value of a company's shares? Investment analysts use a variety of methods to estimate and forecast companies' market value. The simplest is to multiply expected earnings by the price earnings (P/E) ratio. Thus, in forecasting the market values of the various parts of the Anglo-American conglomerate, Hanson, prior to its breakup in 1996, some analysts simply estimated the net profits for each of the components (Imperial Tobacco, Millennium Chemicals, Energy

Group, and so on), then multiplied them by the average P/E ratios for each of these industries (tobacco, chemicals, coal and power). The problem with this approach is that it looks only at profits in a single period and it provides no analysis of what determines a company's P/E ratio.

A more satisfactory approach is to view a company as a capital asset whose value is the net present value (NPV) of the cash flows to that asset. Thus, the value of a firm's equity is the NPV of cash flows of the firm available to pay shareholders. Hence, shareholder value maximization uses the same discounted cash flow (DCF) methodology that applied to the analysis of investment projects. In essence, shareholder value maximization views the firm as a collection of investment projects: in the same way that we calculate the NPV of an individual project, we can calculate the NPV of the firm as a whole. Thus, the market value of a company's equity (E) is the sum of net cash flow (C) of the company in each year t, discounted at the company's cost of equity capital (r_e):

$$E_0 = \sum_t \frac{C_t}{(1 + r_e)^t}$$

As with DCF analysis of investment projects, the appropriate measure of profitability is *net cash flow* where:

Net cash flow = (Net income + Depreciation + Other noncash expenses) *less* (Capital expenditures + Increase in working capital)

From a managerial perspective, it may be appropriate to view the value of the firm as not just the value of equity, but the value of all the assets of the firm whether financed by equity or debt. Thus, a slightly different approach to valuing the firm is to view the firm's value (V) as consisting of the value of all its securities, both equity (E) and debt (D), which is the value of cash flows *including interest on debt* ($C\sim$) discounted at the *weighted average cost of capital* (r_{e+d}):

$$V_0 = E_0 + D_0 = \sum_t \frac{C\sim_t}{(1 + r_{e+d})^t}$$

Valuing Companies and Businesses

The DCF approach is widely used as a means of valuing companies and individual business units. The difficulty here is in forecasting cash flows. One approach is to assume that cash flows will grow at a fairly constant rate (g) into infinity. In this case the above equation becomes:

$$V_0 = \frac{C\sim}{(r - g)}$$

For most companies, cash flows can be forecast over the medium term, say five years into the future, at which point a *horizon value* (V_H) can be calculated based either on the book value of the firm at that time or on some more arbitrary forecast of cash flows beyond the medium term:

$$V_0 = C\sim_o + \frac{C\sim_1}{(1 + r)} + \frac{C\sim_2}{(1 + r)^2} + \frac{C\sim_3}{(1 + r)^2} + \frac{C\sim_4}{(1 + r)^4} + \frac{V_H}{(1 + r)^4}$$

Valuing Strategies

The same principles used to value companies and businesses can be applied to evaluating alternative strategies. Thus, for a single business, or for a whole company, the attractiveness of different strategies can be compared by forecasting the cash flows likely to accrue to the business (or company) under each strategy and to select the strategy that results in the highest NPV.

Increasing numbers of companies are introducing shareholder value analysis into their strategic planning processes. At PepsiCo, for example, shareholder value is used as a performance criterion, which acts as a target for each division and business unit, a basis for evaluating strategies and investment proposals, and a guideline for the corporate level's monitoring of business-level performance.[9] The merit of the shareholder value approach is its consistency. The same methodology of DCF analysis and the same objective of shareholder value maximization is used to value individual investment projects, individual business units, alternative business strategies, and the corporation as a whole.

The main steps in applying shareholder value analysis to appraise business strategies are:

♦ Identify strategy alternatives (the simplest approach is to compare the current strategy with the preferred alternative strategy);

♦ Estimate the cash flows associated with each strategy;

♦ Estimate the implications of each strategy for the cost of capital: if a strategy involves increased capital expenditure (requiring borrowing), this may raise the company's cost of debt and also its cost of equity, since the equity will be viewed as more risky;

♦ Select the strategy that generates the highest net present value.

Compared to the appraisal of individual investment projects, special problems arise from DCF analysis of strategies. Whereas individual investment projects have finite lives, the firm (or the business unit) is much longer living, so strategies must also be chosen for the long term. Forecasting cash flows over long periods of time gives rise to particular difficulties. Given the difficulties of forecasting with any precision the cash flows generated by a particular strategy, the dominant approach to the analysis of strategy in this book is *qualitative* rather than *quantitative*. Our ultimate goal is to quantify the impact on firm value of following strategy A rather than strategy B. However, the first step in achieving that goal is to understand the factors that determine a firm's profits in order to select the strategy that offers the best prospect of maximizing profits, even if we are unable to quantify them.

Some of the most useful applications of shareholder value analysis are in relation to corporate strategy decisions involving acquisition, diversification, and divestment. We shall return to these issues in Chapter 15.

Problems of Applying Discounted Cash Flow Approaches to Shareholder Value Maximization

Considerable progress has been made in linking strategic and financial analysis. Yet major problems remain. A key conceptual problem associated with DCF appraisal of strategies is its failure to take account of option values. In applying DCF analysis, there is the problem of short-term bias and difficulties of estimating future cash flows.

Strategies as Options.   Valuation of individual business units within a company is an easier task than the valuation of alternative business strategies. Valuation of business strategy alternatives in terms of net cash flows discounted at an appropriate cost of capital is difficult because most strategies involve a stream of resource-allocation decisions over time where subsequent investment decisions are contingent upon the performance and information generated by previous investments. As we have already noted, in an increasingly turbulent environment, strategy is less a predetermined program of investment plans and more a positioning of the firm to permit it to take advantage of profitable investment opportunities as they arise. Within this view of strategy, investments in early stages of projects are essentially *options* — their value is that they offer the firm the opportunity to make subsequent investments if prospects look favorable at the end of the initial stage. For example, investments in research and development typically do not offer direct returns; their value is in the option to invest in new products and processes that may arise from the R&D. DCF does not accurately value investments where there is a significant option value. At the same time, the option pricing models devised for valuing securities options are not readily applicable to real investments. In order to assess the option value of strategic investments by the firm, it is necessary to specify the successive stages of the investment process, to identify the alternatives available at each stage, and to specify the possible outcomes together with their probabilities.[10]

Merck & Company has been at the forefront of applying option theory to analyze investments in R&D. Merck's CFO, Judy Lewent, observes that: "When you make an initial investment in a research project, you are paying an entry fee for a right, but you are not obligated to continue that research at a later stage." Merck's analysis is based on an adaptation of the Black-Scholes option pricing formula.[11]

Short-Term Bias.   A criticism of the shareholder value approach is that a focus on the market value of a company's shares is likely to divert management's attention away from the critical issues concerned with managing for long-run competitiveness and more toward managing the stock market's perceptions of a company. To the extent that the stock market is myopic, concern with maximizing stock market value may lead to an emphasis on short-term returns to the detriment of long-term profitability.[12] For many years, commentators have argued that the strong shareholder orientation of U.S. and British companies has resulted in a preoccupation with short-term payoffs, underinvestment in capital and R&D, and a willingness to cede markets to Asian competitors willing to take a longer-term view.[13] A study by Michael Porter of U.S. corporate investment found evidence of short-term thinking in the form of low rates of investment, and a bias against investment in intangible assets (such as knowledge and skills) and in long-term projects.[14] However, these findings are countered by a number of studies that find no short-term bias by the stock market.[15]

A key point here is that managing for shareholder value does not mean managing the stock market. It means managing the cash flows of the firm which, it is hoped, will be reflected in the stock market's valuation of a company.

Problems of Estimating Cash Flows.   Establishing profitability as the primary long-run goal for the firm is not controversial. The difficulties arise in specifying the appropriate measure of profit. Whereas accountants favor traditional accounting measures of profitability, finance experts declare that "cash is king." Certainly from a theoretical standpoint, cash flow is the appropriate return to use in valuing the firm.

The problems come in practical application. There is little point in telling managers "Maximize the stock market value of the firm." It is unclear what such an instruction means in terms of decision making. Instructing managers to maximize the present value of future cash flows is more specific, but this runs into two problems. First, we cannot measure future cash flows. All we have available to us are measures of past cash flows and uncertain estimates of the future. Second, there is no separate system of cash flow accounting. All estimates of cash flows are derived from standard accounting measures. Hence, to claim that cash flows are "cleaner" because they are not subject to accountants' shenanigans is only partially true.

The more difficult it is to forecast cash flows far into the future, the more attractive are accounting profits as a performance measure and basis for valuation. For example, if a company is highly profitable, but is investing heavily in expansion, its net cash flows over the medium term are likely to be negative, but its longer-term cash flows will be substantial. The greater the difficulty of forecasting the long term, the more likely it is that DCF valuations undervalue growth companies and growth strategies as compared to an approach that looks at operating profits or economic profits.

PRACTICAL ISSUES IN LINKING VALUE-BASED MANAGEMENT TO STRATEGY

In practice, the gulf between the cash flow and the accounting profit approaches to setting targets and appraising performance is narrower than generally recognized. Different measures of profit tend to be highly correlated. The longer the period of time, the greater the convergence. Which measure of profit is used is less important than recognizing the limitations and biases inherent in that measure. John Kay has shown that, under certain circumstances, accounting measures of profit approximate economic profit.[16] Over the life of the firm, the net present value of net cash flows from operations, economic profit based on historic cost accounting profit, economic profit based on replacement cost measures, and excess returns to shareholders are the same.[17]

Because cash flow estimates are derived from accounting data and because of the difficulties of estimating cash flows far into the future, most practical approaches to implementing shareholder value maximization tend, ultimately, to resort to familiar accounting based measures of profit. Thus:

- ♦ EVA is firmly rooted in the concept of shareholder value maximization, yet it is essentially a single-period measure that adapts standard accounting earnings data.

- ♦ McKinsey and Company's *Value-Based Management* offers a practical guide to managers seeking to maximize the market value of their companies. Despite insisting that "cash is king" when it comes to estimating the value of the company or a single business and evaluating past performance, the McKinsey methodology relies heavily on accounting-based measures. For example, DCF valuation techniques are translated into economic profit formulae (equivalent to the EVA approach), past performance is evaluated in terms of accounting returns (specifically, return on invested capital: defined as net operating income after tax as a percentage of net operating assets), and estimates of future cash flows are based upon assumptions about the return on invested capital and return on sales that the firm will earn in the future.[18]

Some Simple Guidelines

As already noted, the approach of this book is not to use sophisticated models for valuing businesses or strategies, but to concentrate on analyzing the fundamental factors that determine profitability. When it comes to corporate strategy, we focus more explicitly on the valuation of companies and individual businesses, but until then we use a more simplistic approach. Maximization of the value of the firm implies two simple guidelines:

- On *existing* investments, the firm should seek to maximize the its after-tax rate of return.

- On *new* investments, the firm should seek an after-tax rate of return that exceeds its cost of capital.

Analyzing Past Performance and Setting Targets for the Future

For the purposes of evaluating past performance and setting targets for future performance, rate of return on capital continues to be one of the most useful and widely deployed indicators of profitability and value creation. However, in order to diagnose past performance in detail and to set detailed performance targets for the future, it is useful to separate accounting rate of return into its component elements to identify the fundamental "value drivers." Figure 2.1 shows such a disaggregation. The basic components of accounting rate of return are sales margin and capital turnover. Thus:

$$\text{Return on capital employed} = \frac{\text{Profit}}{\text{Capital employed}}$$

$$= \frac{\text{Profit}}{\text{Sales}} \times \frac{\text{Sales}}{\text{Capital employed}}$$

FIGURE 2.1
Disaggregating
Return on Capital
Employed

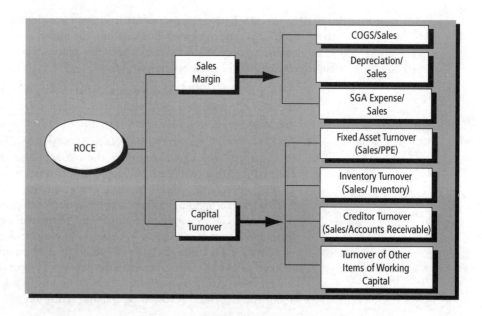

As Figure 2.1 shows, we can further disaggregate sales margin and capital productivity into their constituent items. This approach is useful for two purposes:

1. In diagnosing profit performance, we can relate overall return on capital to specific contributing factors. Thus, in analyzing why General Motors' profitability declined during 1997 and was substantially less than that of Chrysler, we can look at the factors influencing margins such as cost of goods sold (COGS) and sales, general, and administrative (SGA) expenses as well as aspects of capital productivity such as inventory turnover and fixed asset turnover.

2. In setting targets for managers at different levels of the company, the key is to match performance targets to the variables over which different managers exert some control. Thus, for the CEO, it may make sense to set the overall goal of maximizing shareholder value. For the chief operating officer and divisional heads, it makes more sense to set specific goals such as maximizing return on capital employed on the existing asset base and investing in projects where the rate of return exceeds the cost of capital. For functional, departmental, and unit managers, more specific operating targets are preferable. Thus, in a retailing company, store managers might be given targets with regard to sales per square foot and gross margins. Warehouse managers might be required to achieve target levels of inventory turns. Purchasing managers might be required to reduce the cost of goods purchased as a percentage of sales revenue. The chief financial officer might be required to minimize average cost of capital and reduce cash balances. Figure 2.2 relates the drivers of return on capital to the types of targets that might be set at different levels of a company.

Balanced Scorecards

Linking the overall corporate goal of maximizing shareholder value to more specific strategic and operating targets is a central task of a company's control system. An increasingly popular approach to linking corporate level shareholder and strategic goals to more specific business unit, departmental, and individual goals is called "balanced scorecards." The scorecard approach to setting targets and measuring performance was devised by Robert Kaplan (Harvard Business School) and David Norton (Knoll, Norton & Company). Their balanced scorecard includes a set of internally consistent performance measures that combine the answers to four questions.

1. *How do we look to shareholders?* The financial perspective is composed of measures such as cash flow, sales and income growth, and ROE.

2. *How do customers see us?* The customer perspective comprises measures such as goals for new products, on-time delivery, and defect and failure levels.

3. *What must we excel at?* The internal business perspective relates to internal business processes such as productivity, employee skills, cycle time, yield rates, and quality and cost measures.

4. *Can we continue to improve and create value?* The innovation and learning perspective includes measures related to new product development cycle times, technological leadership, and rates of improvement.

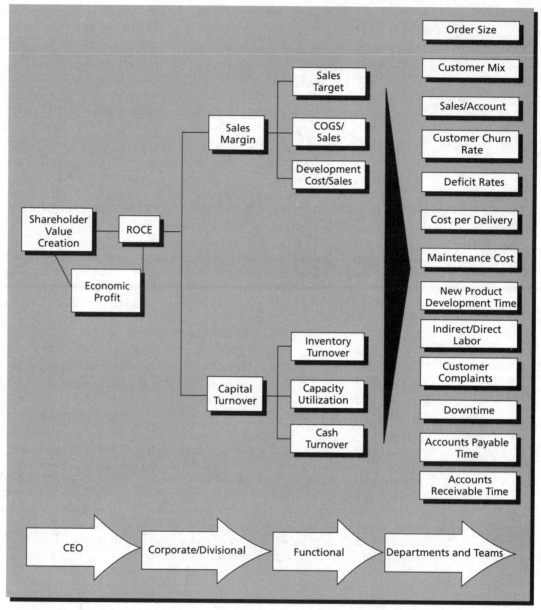

FIGURE 2.2
Linking Value Drivers to Performance Targets

Such a procedure, argue Kaplan and Norton, permits the linking of strategic and financial goals. Thus, at FMC, they report that:

Strategists came up with 5 and 10 year plans, controllers with one year budgets and near-term forecasts. Little interplay occurred between the two groups. But the scorecard now bridges the two. The financial perspective builds on the traditional function performed by controllers. The other three perspectives make the division's long-term strategic objectives measurable.[19]

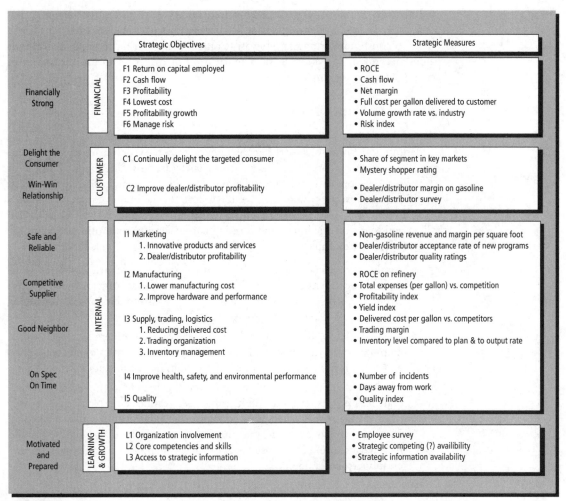

FIGURE 2.3
Balanced Scorecard for Mobil N. American Marketing and Refining

A leading exponent of the balanced scorecard approach is Mobil Corporation's North American Marketing and Refining business (NAM&R). Faced with pressures of unsatisfactory profit performance, the business adopted the scorecards as a means of linking strategy with financial performance goals and translating these into operating objectives tailored to the specific performance requirements of individual business units and functional departments. The scorecard is a mechanism for "cascading down" strategy into specific operating goals. As a result, scorecards provide the measurements by which the performance of each unit and department is appraised and against which performance-related pay bonuses are determined. Figure 2.3 shows NAM&R's scorecard.

VALUES AND MISSION

There is more to business than making money. Profit maximization (shareholder value maximization to be more precise) provides the foundation for strategy analysis, yet it is not the goal that inspired Henry Ford to build a business that profoundly changed twentieth century lifestyles, nor is it the one that causes Bill Gates to continue working at Microsoft rather than retiring to enjoy his billions of dollars; nor does it provide such motivation or direction to the thousands of employees of both companies.

Where Do Values Fit In?

All companies possess broader organizational values that are integral to their sense of identity and purpose, and that constrain, augment, even transcend, the fundamental requirement of profitability. Values such as providing opportunities for employees' development and self-realization, pursuing unmatched product quality, creating a safe working environment, and working for the improvement of the natural environment may constrain the pursuit of profitability, but they also play a vital role in building strategic intent and forming consensus and commitment within the organization. For example:

- ◆ Marks & Spencer's values with regard to employee welfare, customer value, and fair treatment of suppliers form the basis of that company's competitive advantage, which is founded on a network of trusting relationships involving customers, suppliers, and employees.
- ◆ At Body Shop, the enthusiasm and loyalty of customers and the zeal of employees and franchisees are nourished by the principles of environmental and social responsibility espoused by the founder Anita Ruddick.
- ◆ McDonald's ability to sell 60 billion hamburgers in 86 countries and to generate vast profits for itself and its franchisees cannot be explained exclusively by a profit-driven strategy of low costs, standardization, and marketing. McDonald's is sustained by a philosophy that transcends social class and national culture and is enshrined in the principles of "quality, consistency, cleanliness, and value."

What we observe is that the linking of strategy to the broader pursuit of social and moral purpose may facilitate rather than impede profit performance over the long term. The values a firm embraces can assist in building relationships between the firm and others with whom it does business, can help build employee commitment and loyalty, and may offer the basis for differentiation. If human beings are ultimately concerned more with the pursuit of meaning in their lives than with material rewards, then organizations that can help instill within their employees and customers a sense of purpose will have an advantage over those that do not.[20]

The Role of Mission

What emerges is that the goals of the firm extend beyond the basic performance variables that the firm is pursuing: profit, growth, or the balanced interest of stakeholders. Though profit is the overriding performance objective of the firm, the goals of the firm typically embody a sense of overall purpose that directly shapes strategy and unifies the efforts of the many organizational members. This sense of purpose sometimes takes the form of a **vision** that motivated the founding of the company and sustained its development. Examples include Henry Ford's vision of a car for every family; Steve Jobs' vision of one person–one computer; Walt Disney's desire to provide family entertainment that enshrines the values of warmth, brotherhood, joy,

EXHIBIT 2.2

The Chevron Way

Mission

"We are an international company providing energy and chemical products vital to the growth of the world's economies. Our mission is to create superior value for our stockholders, our customers, and our employees.

Vision

Our vision is to be Better than the Best, which means:

- Employees are proud of their success as a team
- Customers, suppliers, and government prefer us
- Competitors respect us
- Communities welcome us
- Investors are eager to invest in us

Our primary objective is to exceed the financial performance of our strongest competitors. Our goal is to be No. 1 among our competitors in total Stockholder Return for the period 1994–1998. We will balance long-term growth and short-term results in the pursuit of this objective.

Our approach to the business is based on

- Committed team values
- Total quality management
- Protecting People and the Environment

We will be guided by the Strategic Intents in our Corporate Strategic Plan and will measure progress with the Vision Metrics.

Vision Metrics

Superior Stockholder Return	*Metric:*	Total Stockholder Return
Superior Financial Performance	*Metrics:*	Return on Capital Employed
		Earnings Growth
Delighted Customers	*Metric:*	Customer Satisfaction
Competitive Operating Advantage	*Metric:*	Operating Expense per Barrel
Public Favorability	*Metric:*	Public Favorability Index
Committed Team	*Metrics:*	Worldwide Employee Survey Results
		Safety Performance

Source: Chevron Corporation 1995 Annual Report, p. 6

and family unity; and at Southwest Airlines, Herb Kelleher's vision of opening air travel to a wider group of leisure travelers while infusing the whole organization with a sense of fun.

As we noted in our discussion of "strategic intent" in Chapter 1, a recognized sense of purpose provides a foundation for a company's strategy. This encouraged an increasing number of companies to formulate a **mission statement** to communicate overall direction and articulate the linkage between a company's vision and values and its strategy. Exhibit 2.2 reproduces Chevron Corporation's statement of mission and vision.

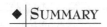

◆ | SUMMARY

In the first chapter we established that strategy is about success and that a successful strategy is one that uses a firm's resources and capabilities within its industry environment in order to achieve its goals. This raises the issue of what the goals of the firm are. The firm operates in the interests of its owners—its shareholders—through maximizing their wealth. This implies profit maximization which, we have seen, raises some complex issues with regard to the meaning and measurement of profit, the relevant time period, and the appropriate rate of discount. Clarifying these issues is vital in setting targets for the firm and evaluating its performance.

A key aspect of the strategic management process within the firm is not simply formulating strategy, but linking strategy to performance through setting performance targets for the firm and its individual businesses and departments, and appraising performance against these targets (typically on an annual basis).

Although we have gone some way to separate broad profitability measures into constituent financial and operational ratios, it is impossible to view the pursuit of profit as the application of mechanistic algorithms to a business. Over the longer term, identifying the determinants of superior profitability requires careful analysis and deep insight into the economics of the industry and characteristics of the firm. This is the task of the remaining chapters in Part II.

Understanding the goals of the firm is not simply proclaiming the supremacy of profit and shareholder value. As we saw in Chapter 1, strategy is not simply identifying and accessing the sources of superior profitability, it is also about communicating, coordinating, and motivating the organization to higher levels of aspiration. It is in these roles that values and vision are important. The values of the firm are not simply a constraint on strategy in terms of limiting the means by which the firm will achieve its performance goals; they directly shape the goals of the firm and may facilitate the attainment of performance goals through building consensus, commitment, and reputation. It is similar with vision. Whereas profit objectives relate to the material goals of a firm's owners, the quest for creativity, power, and recognition may be far more powerful motivating forces. The entrepreneurial spirit behind new business start-ups, and the driving forces behind the continuing development of established corporations tend to be a sense of individual and collective achievement and organizational purpose.

Having recognized that, as motivators, values and a sense of vision supersede material goals, we return to the theme of strategy as a quest for profit. Why do we give the values, vision, and mission such limited attention? Not because they are unimportant. As we have seen, they are likely to be fundamental in providing direction for strategy and building organizational purpose. The point here is that there is little left to say. Goals, values, and vision are not topics for *analysis* but for *discovery*. They need to be recognized, but once their leading role in shaping strategic direction is accepted, the firm still needs to acknowledge that it is unlikely to prosper on values alone. It thus needs to address the issue of rendering unto shareholders the profits they expect. Hence, we proceed by exploring the drivers of firm profitability. Our next port-of-call is the industry environment of the firm.

NOTES

1   R. Cyert and J. March, *A Behavioral Theory of the Firm* (Englewood Cliffs, NJ: Prentice-Hall, 1964).
2   See Kenneth R. MacCrimmon, "An Overview of Multiple Objective Decision Making," in *Multiple Criteria Decision Making*, ed. J. L. Cochrane and M. Zeleny (Columbia, SC: University of South Carolina Press, 1973).
3   *The Stern Stewart Performance 1000: A Ranking of America's Most Value-Adding Companies* (New York: Stern Stewart, 1996).

4   For discussion of the problems of accounting-based measures of profitability, see F. M. Fisher and J. J. McGowan, "On the Misuse of Accounting Rates of Return to Infer Monopoly Profit," *American Economic Review* 73 (1983): 82–87. For a more conciliatory view, see John Kay and Colin Meyer, "On the Application of Accounting Rates of Return," *Economic Journal* 96 (1986): 199–207.

5   Shawn Tully, "The Real Key to Creating Wealth," *Fortune*, September 20, 1993: 38–50.

6   Note that the cost of equity is calculated using the Capital Asset Pricing Model: Firm X's cost of equity = the Risk-free rate of interest + A risk premium. The risk premium is the excess of the stock market rate of return over the risk-free rate multiplied by Firm X's beta coefficient (its measure of systematic risk).

7   Although I focus on Stern Stewart's EVA analysis, there is nothing new or proprietary about the concept of economic profit. A similar approach has been proposed by John Kay in *Foundations of Corporate Success: How Corporate Strategies Add Value* (Oxford: Oxford University Press, 1993). Kay uses the term *added value*, which is defined as ". . . the difference between the (comprehensively accounted) value of a firm's output and the (comprehensively accounted) cost of the firm's inputs. In this specific sense, adding value is both the proper motivation of corporate activity and the measure of its achievement." (p. 19).

8   "EVA: The Real Key to Creating Wealth," *Fortune*, September 20, 1993: 38–50.

9   Alfred Rappaport has been prominent in developing and disseminating the "shareholder value" approach to strategy appraisal. See Rappaport, *Creating Shareholder Value: The New Standard for Business Performance* (New York: Free Press, 1986); also Rappaport "Selecting Strategies That Create Shareholder Value," *Harvard Business Review* (May–June 1981): 139–149; Rappaport, "Linking Competitive Strategy and Shareholder Value Analysis," *Journal of Business Strategy* (Spring 1987): 58–67; Enrique R. Arzac, "Do Your Business Units Create Shareholder Value?" *Harvard Business Review* (January–February 1986): 121–126; and Rappaport, "CFOs and Strategists: Forging a Common Framework," *Harvard Business Review* (May–June 1992): 84–91.

10 Option pricing theory is outlined in R. A. Brealey and S. C. Myers, *Principles of Corporate Finance,* 3rd edition (New York: McGraw Hill, 1988), chapters 20 and 21. For a discussion of option valuation approaches to strategic investments, see Avinash Dixit and Robert Pindyck, "The Options Approach to Capital Investment," *Harvard Business Review* (May–June 1995): 105–115; Stewart C. Myers, "Finance Theory and Financial Strategy," *Interfaces* 14 (January–February 1984): 134–136; and Tom Copeland, Tim Koller, and Jack Murrin, *Valuation: Measuring and Managing the Value of Companies,* 2nd edition (New York: John Wiley, 1995), chapter 15. The application of option theory to strategic management is discussed by Bruce Kogut and Nalin Kulatilaka, "Options Thinking and Platform Investments: Investing in Opportunity," *California Management Review* (Winter 1994): 52–69; and E. H. Bowman and D. Hurry, "Strategy Through the Option Lens: An Integrated View of Resource Investments and the Incremental-Choice Process," *Academy of Management Review* 18, no. 4 (1993): 760–782.

11 Nancy Nichols, "Scientific Management at Merck: An Interview with CFO Judy Lewent," *Harvard Business Review* (January–February 1994): 89–105.

12 Michael T. Jacobs, *Short-Term America* (Boston: Harvard Business School Press, 1991).

13 The MIT Commission on Industrial Productivity, *Made in America* (Cambridge, MA: MIT Press, 1989), chapter 4.

14 Michael E. Porter, "Capital Disadvantage: America's Failing Capital Investment System," *Harvard Business Review* (September–October 1992): 65–82.

15 For example, J. McConnell and C. Muscarella, "Corporate Capital Expenditure Decisions and the Market Value of the Firm," *Journal of Financial Economics* (March 1985): 399–422, found that on average the stock market reacted positively to company announcements of increased capital expenditure. Also, stock prices responded positively to announcements of major corporate write-offs, despite the fact that these depress short term profitability (Copeland, Koller and Murin, op. cit., 90–92).

16 John A. Kay, "Accountants, Too, Could Be Happy in a Golden Age: The Accountant's Rate of Profit and the Internal Rate of Return," *Oxford Economic Papers* 28 (1976): 447–460; and John A. Kay and Colin Meyer, "On the Application of Accounting Rates of Return," *Economic Journal* 96 (1986): 199–207.

17 John A. Kay, *Foundations of Corporate Success: How Business Strategies Create Value* (Oxford: Oxford University Press, 1993): 207.

18 Tom Copeland, Tim Koller, and Jack Murrin, *Valuation: Measuring and Managing the Value of Companies,* 2nd edition (New York: John Wiley, 1995).

19 R. Kaplan and D. Norton, "Putting the Balanced Scorecard to Work," *Harvard Business Review* (September–October 1993): 147.

20 Abraham Maslow, "A Theory of Human Motivation," *Psychological Review* 50 (1943): 370–396, postulated that human beings have a hierarchy of needs, the highest being that of "self-actualization": the realization of one's distinctive psychological potential that goes beyond economic and social fulfillment.

3

Analyzing the Industry Environment

The reinsurance business has the defect of being too attractive-looking to new entrants for its own good and will therefore always tend to be the opposite of, say, the old business of gathering and rendering dead horses that always tended to contain few and prosperous participants.

—Charles T. Munger, Chairman, Wesco Financial Corp.
(extract from the 1986 Annual Report)

OUTLINE

◆ INTRODUCTION AND OBJECTIVES

In this chapter and the next we turn our attention to analyzing the external environment of the firm. In Chapter 1 we observed that profound understanding of the competitive environment is a critical ingredient of a successful strategy. We further noted that for business enterprises, strategy is essentially a quest for profit. Our primary task in this chapter is to identify the sources of profit in the business environment.

The distinction between corporate-level and business-level strategy is relevant here. **Corporate strategy** is concerned with deciding which industries the firm should be engaged in and with the allocation of corporate resources among them. To make such decisions, it is vital that the firm evaluate the attractiveness of different industries in terms of their potential to yield profit in the future. The primary objective of this chapter is to analyze how competition determines industry profitability. Once the determinants of industry profitability are understood, it is possible to forecast the future profit potential of an industry.

Business strategy is concerned with establishing competitive advantage. Identifying the basis of and opportunities for competitive advantage requires an understanding of competition within the industry. It also requires that we understand customers, their needs and motivations, and the means by which these needs are satisfied.

By the time you have completed this chapter you will be able to:

- ◆ Identify the main structural features of an industry that influence competition and profitability.

- ◆ Apply this analysis and explain why some industries are more profitable than others.

- ◆ Use evidence on structural trends within industries to forecast changes in industry profitability in the future.

- ◆ Identify the opportunities available to influence industry structure in order to alleviate the pressures of competition and improve industry profitability.

- ◆ Appreciate the roles of both competitive and cooperative behavior in seeking profit within an industry.

- ◆ Analyze competition and customer requirements in order to identify opportunities for competitive advantage within an industry.

FROM ENVIRONMENTAL ANALYSIS TO INDUSTRY ANALYSIS

The business environment of the firm consists of all the external influences that impact a firm's decisions and performance. The problem here is that, given the vast number and range of external influences, how can managers hope to monitor, let alone analyze, environmental conditions? The starting point is some kind of system or framework for organizing information. For example, environmental influences can be classified by source into economic, technological, demographic, social, and governmental factors; or by proximity: the "micro-environment" or "task environment" can be distinguished from the wider influences that form the "macro-environment."

Though systematic, continuous scanning of the whole range of external influences might seem desirable, such extensive environmental analysis is unlikely to be cost effective and creates information overload. The Royal Dutch/Shell Group, one of the world's largest and most international enterprises, invests more heavily in the systematic monitoring and analysis of its business environment than most other companies. Its scenario analysis (which we look at in detail in Chapter 10) is exceptionally far-sighted and wide-ranging in assessing its business environment. Nevertheless, the group's environmental scanning and analysis focuses on factors that are directly relevant to its strategic planning: in particular, those factors that influence the demand and supply of oil and refined products.[1]

The prerequisite for effective environmental analysis is to distinguish the vital from the merely important. Let's return to first principles. For the firm to make profit it must create value for customers. Hence, the firm must understand its customers. Second, in creating value, the firm acquires goods and services from suppliers. Hence, the firm must understand its suppliers and how to form business relationships with them. Third, the ability to generate profitability from value-creating activity depends on the intensity of competition among the firms that vie for the same value-creating opportunities. Hence, the firm must understand competition. Thus, the core of the firm's business environment is formed by its relationships with customers, suppliers, and competitors. This is the firm's industry environment.

This is not to say that macro-level factors such as general economic trends, changes in demographic structure, or social and political trends are unimportant to strategy analysis. These factors may be critical determinants of the threats and opportunities a company will face in the future. The key issue is how these more general environmental factors impact the firm's industry environment (Figure 3.1). For most firms, global warming is not a crtical issue. For the producers of automobiles, oil, and electricity, it is important since government measures to restrict the production of carbon dioxide and other greenhouse gases will directly affect the demand for their products and their costs of doing business. By focusing on the industry environment, we can determine which of the macro-level influences are important for the firm and which are not.

FIGURE 3.1
The Business Environment

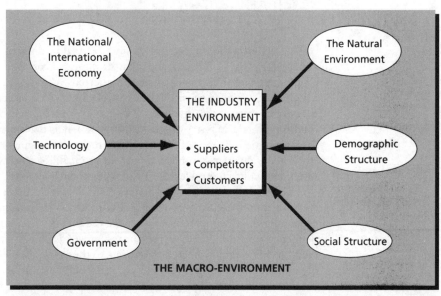

THE DETERMINANTS OF INDUSTRY PROFIT: DEMAND AND COMPETITION

If the purpose of strategy is to help the firm to survive and make money, the starting point for industry analysis is: What determines the level of profit in an industry?

As already noted, business is about the creation of value for the customer. Firms create value by production (transforming inputs into outputs) or arbitrage (transferring products across time and space). Value creation requires that the price the customer is willing to pay the firm exceed the costs incurred by the firm. But value creation does not translate directly into profit. The surplus of value over cost is distributed between customers and producers by the forces of competition. The stronger the competition among producers, the lower the price actually paid by customers compared with the maximum price they would have been willing to pay. In other words, the greater the proportion of the surplus gained by customers (*consumer surplus*), the less is earned by producers (*producer surplus* or *economic rent*). A single supplier of bottled water at an all-night rave can charge a price that fully exploits the dancers' thirst. If there are many suppliers of bottled water, then, in the absence of collusion, competition causes the price of bottled water to fall toward the cost of supplying it.

The surplus earned by producers over and above the minimum costs of production is not entirely captured in profits. Where an industry has powerful suppliers—monopolistic suppliers of components or employees united by a strong labor union—then a substantial part of the surplus may be appropriated by these suppliers (the profits of suppliers or premium wages of union members).

The profits earned by the firms in an industry are thus determined by three factors:

♦ The value of the product or service to customers

♦ The intensity of competition

♦ The relative bargaining power at different levels in the production chain.

Our industry analysis brings all three factors into a single analytic framework.

ANALYZING INDUSTRY ATTRACTIVENESS

Table 3.1 shows the average rate of profit earned in different U.S. industries. Some industries (such as tobacco and pharmaceuticals) consistently earn high rates of profit; others (such as iron and steel, nonferrous metals, airlines, and basic building materials) have failed to cover their cost of capital. The basic premise that underlies industry analysis is that the level of industry profitability is neither random nor the result of entirely industry-specific influences, but is determined, in part at least, by the systematic influence of **industry structure.** As an example of how an attractively structured industry can support a superior profitability, consider the cases of the sausage skin manufacturer, Devro, and tobacco products supplier, UST (see Exhibit 3.1).

The underlying theory of how industry structure drives competitive behavior and determines industry profitability is provided by industrial organization (IO) economics. The two reference points are the theory of monopoly and the theory of perfect competition, which represent the two ends of a spectrum of industry structures. A single firm protected by barriers to the entry of new firms forms a **monopoly** in which it can appropriate in profit the full amount of the value it creates. By contrast, many firms supplying an identical product with no restrictions on entry or

TABLE 3.1
The Profitability Of U.S. Manufacturing Industries

Industry	Return on Equity (1985-95)
Drugs	19.39%
Food and kindred products	13.85%
—of which Tobacco products	18.60%
Instruments and related products	11.24%
Printing and publishing	10.16%
Electrical and electronic equipment	10.00%
Aircraft, guided missiles, and parts	8.36%
Fabricated metal products	8.15%
Rubber and misc. plastics products	9.95%
Paper and allied products	8.47%
Retail trade corporations	8.37%
Petroleum and coal products	7.88%
Textile mill products	7.25%
Wholesale trade corporations	5.72%
Stone, glass and clay products	5.28%
Machinery, exc. electrical	4.29%
Nonferrous metals	4.21%
Motor vehicles and equipment	2.61%
Iron and steel	1.30%
Mining corporations	1.24%
Airlines	(2.84%)

Source: Federal Trade Commission

exit constitutes **perfect competition:** the rate of profit falls to a level that just covers firms' cost of capital. In the real world, industries fall between these two extremes. The U.S. market for smokeless tobacco is close to being a monopoly, the Chicago grain markets are close to being perfectly competitive. Most manufacturing industries and many service industries tend to be **oligopolies:** they are dominated by a small number of major companies. Figure 3.2 identifies some key points on the spectrum. By examining the principal structural features and their interactions for any particular industry, it is possible to predict the type of competitive behavior likely to emerge and the resulting level of profitability.

Porter's Five Forces of Competition Framework

Figure 3.2 identifies four structural variables influencing competition and profitability. In practice, there are many features of an industry that determine the intensity of competition and the level of profitability. A helpful, widely used framework for classifying and analyzing these factors is the one developed by Michael Porter of Harvard Business School.[2] Porter's Five Forces of Competition framework views the profitability of an industry (as indicated by its rate of return on capital relative to its

EXHIBIT 3.1

Sausage Skins and Chewing Tobacco: The Joys of Dominating Niche Markets

Devro International plc is a Scottish company with headquarters in the village of Moodiesburn near Glasgow. With 930 employees and plants in Scotland, Australia, and the United States, Devro holds 56 percent of the world market for collagen sausage skins. The company was listed on the London Stock Exchange in 1993, two years after a management buyout from its parent, Johnson & Johnson. During 1991 and 1992, operating profits averaged 25 percent of sales revenue. Devro holds 94 percent of the UK market, 83 percent of the Australian market, and 40 percent of the U.S. market. Although collagen casings are a substitute for natural gut sausage casings, collagen possesses some clear advantages that have resulted in the steady displacement of natural gut. Scale economies, technology, and Devro's absolute cost advantages pose substantial barriers to would-be entrants. Because casings account for only a small proportion of the sausage manufacturers' total costs, they are relatively insensitive to the price of casing and do not exert substantial bargaining power.

UST Inc. (Formerly U.S. Tobacco) has the distinction of earning the highest return on equity of any company in *Fortune*'s listings (165 percent in 1996, 146 percent in 1995). UST dominates the U.S. market for "smokeless tobacco" (chewing tobacco and snuff) with a market share of 78 percent (in a range of brands including *Skoal*, *Copenhagen*, *Long Cut*, and *Red Seal*). Despite its association with a bygone era of cowboys and rural poverty, chewing tobacco has been a growth market over the past two decades with a surprisingly large number of young consumers. UST's long-established brands, its distribution through tens of thousands of small retail outlets, and the unwillingness of major tobacco companies to enter this market (due to the poor image and social unacceptability of the product), have supported UST's unassailable market position. Federal controls on the advertising of smokeless tobacco products introduced in 1986 have buttressed UST's market position by limiting the opportunities for would-be entrants to market their products.

Source: James Buxton, "A Leaner Business That Has More Bite," *Financial Times*, April 16, 1993, p. 33; *Standard & Poor's Stock Reports*.

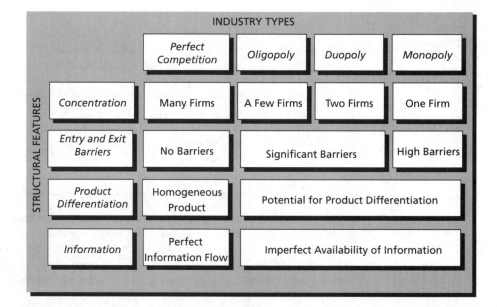

FIGURE 3.2
The Spectrum of Industry Structures

cost of capital) as determined by five sources of competitive pressure. These five forces of competition include three sources of "horizontal" competition: competition from substitutes, competition from entrants, and competition from established rivals; and two sources of "vertical" competition: the bargaining power of suppliers and buyers (see Figure 3.3).

The strength of each of these competitive forces is determined by a number of key structural variables as shown in Figure 3.4.

Competition from Substitutes

The price customers are willing to pay for a product depends, in part, on the availability of substitute products. The absence of close substitutes for a product, as in the case of gasoline or cigarettes, means that consumers are comparatively insensitive to price, i.e., demand is *inelastic* with respect to price. The existence of close substitutes means that customers will switch to substitutes in response to price increases for the product, i.e., demand is *elastic* with respect to price. The introduction of digital personal communication services (PCS) in the United States by Sprint Spectrum and Nextel and in the UK by Hutchinson Orange has increased the substitute competition faced by traditional cellular companies and lowered their margins.

FIGURE 3.3
Porter's Five Forces of Competition Framework

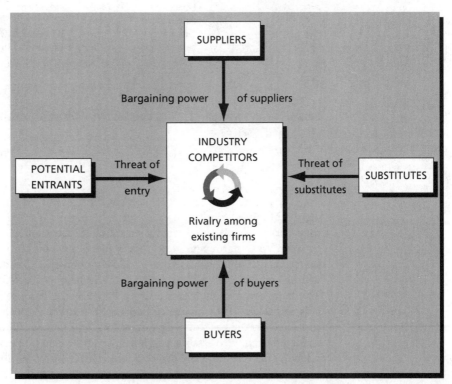

FIGURE 3.4
The Structural Determinants of Competition and Profitability within the Porter Framework

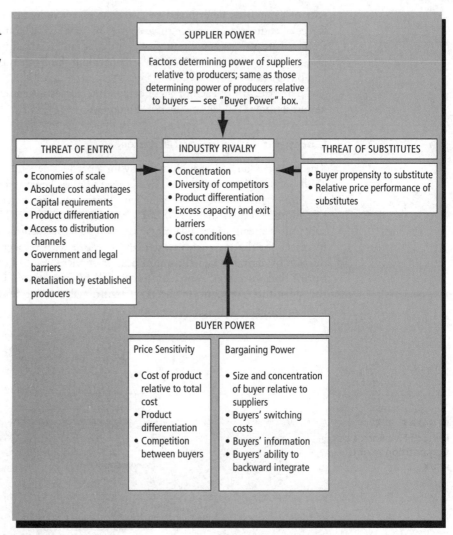

The extent to which substitutes limit prices and profits depends on the propensity of buyers to substitute between alternatives. This, in turn, is dependent on their price-performance characteristics. If city-center to city-center travel between Washington and New York is two hours quicker by air than by train and the average traveler values time at $25 an hour, the implication is that the train will be competitive with air at fares of $50 below those charged by the airlines. The more complex the needs being fulfilled by the product and the more difficult it is to discern performance differences, the lower the extent of substitution by customers on the basis of price differences. The failure of low-priced imitations of leading perfumes to establish significant market share reflects, in part, consumers' difficulty in discerning the performance characteristics of different fragrances.

Threat of Entry

If an industry earns a return on capital in excess of its cost of capital, that industry acts a magnet to firms outside the industry. Unless the entry of new firms is barred, the rate of profit will fall toward its competitive level. The U.S. bagel industry, for example, faced a flood of new entrants in 1996, which caused a sharp diminution of profit prospects. The *threat of entry* rather than actual entry may be sufficient to ensure that established firms constrain their prices to the competitive level. Only American Airlines offers a direct service between Dallas/Fort Worth and Santa Barbara, California. Yet American may be unwilling to exploit its monopoly position if other airlines can easily extend their routes to cover the same two cities. An industry where no barriers to entry or exit exist is **contestable:** prices and profits remain at the fully competitive level, regardless of the number of firms within the industry.[3] Contestability depends on the absence of sunk costs. **Sunk costs** exist where entry requires investment in industry-specific assets whose value cannot be recovered on exit. An absence of sunk costs makes an industry vulnerable to "hit-and-run" entry whenever established firms raise their prices above the competitive level.

In most industries, however, new entrants cannot enter on equal terms with those of established firms. The size of the advantage of established over entrant firm (in terms of unit costs) measures the height of **barriers to entry,** which determines the extent to which the industry can, in the long run, enjoy profit above the competitive level. The principal sources of barriers to entry are: capital requirements, economies of scale, cost advantages, product differentiation, access to channels of distribution, governmental and legal barriers, and retaliation.

Capital Requirements.   The capital costs of getting established in an industry can be so large as to discourage all but the largest companies. The duopoly of Boeing and Airbus in large passenger jets is protected by the prohibitive costs of establishing such a venture. In satellite television broadcasting in Britain, Rupert Murdoch's Sky TV incurred almost $1 billion in capital costs and operating losses and Robert Maxwell's British Satellite Broadcasting spent some $1.8 billion before the two merged in 1991. In other industries, entry costs can be modest. Start-up costs for franchised fast-food restaurants are around $280,000 for a Wendy's and $800,000 for a Burger King.[4]

Economies of Scale.   In industries that are capital or research or advertising intensive, efficiency requires large-scale operation. The problem for new entrants is that they are faced with the choice of either entering on a small scale and accepting high unit costs, or entering on a large scale and running the risk of drastic underutilization of capacity while they build up sales volume. Thus, in large jet engines, economies of scale in R&D and manufacturing have caused consolidation into just three producers (General Electric, Pratt & Whitney, and Rolls-Royce), which are protected by very high barriers to entry. Economies of scale in automobiles have deterred entry into that industry: recent entrants such as Ssangyong of Korea and Proton of Malaysia have incurred huge losses trying to establish themselves.

Absolute Cost Advantages.   Apart from economies of scale, established firms may have a cost advantage over entrants simply because they entered earlier.

Absolute cost advantages tend to be associated with the acquisition of low cost sources of raw materials or economies of learning.

Product Differentiation.   In an industry where products are differentiated, established firms possess the advantages of brand recognition and customer loyalty. The percentage of U.S. consumers loyal to a single brand varies from under 30 percent in batteries, canned vegetables, and garbage bags, up to 61 percent in toothpaste, 65 percent in mayonnaise, and 71 percent in cigarettes.[5] New entrants to such markets must spend disproportionately heavily on advertising and promotion to gain levels of brand awareness and brand goodwill similar to that of established companies. One study found that, compared to early entrants, late entrants into consumer goods markets incurred additional advertising and promotional costs amounting to 2.12 percent of sales revenue.[6] Alternatively, the new entrant can accept a niche position in the market or can seek to compete by cutting price. In producer goods too, reputation and close customer-supplier relationships impose similar problems for new entrants. Despite their huge financial resources, most U.S. commercial banks have chosen to enter investment banking by means of acquiring existing investment banks.

Access to Channels of Distribution.   Whereas lack of brand awareness among consumers acts as a barrier to entry to new suppliers of consumer goods, a more immediate barrier for the new company is likely to be gaining distribution. Limited capacity within distribution channels (e.g., shelf space), risk aversion by retailers, and the fixed costs associated with carrying an additional product result in distributors' reluctance to carry a new manufacturer's product. In the United States and Britain, food and drink processors are increasingly required to make lump-sum payments to the leading supermarket chains in order to gain shelf space for a new product.

Governmental and Legal Barriers.   Some economists claim that the only effective barriers to entry are those created by government. In taxicabs, banking, telecommunications, and broadcasting, entry usually requires the granting of a license by a public authority. In knowledge-intensive industries, patents, copyrights, and trade secrets are major barriers to entry. Xerox Corporation's near monopoly position in the world plain-paper copier business until the mid-1970s was protected by a wall of over 2,000 patents relating to its xerography process. In industries subject to regulation and environmental and safety standards, new entrants may be at a disadvantage to established firms because compliance costs weigh more heavily on newcomers.

Retaliation.   The effectiveness of the barriers to entry also depends on the entrants' expectations as to possible retaliation by established firms. Retaliation against a new entrant may take the form of aggressive price cutting, increased advertising, sales promotion, or litigation. British Airways' retaliation against competition from Virgin Atlantic on its North Atlantic routes included not only promotional price cuts and advertising, but also a variety of "dirty tricks" such as accessing Virgin's computer system, poaching its customers, and attacking Virgin's reputation. Southwest and other low-cost airlines have alleged that selective price cuts by American and other major airlines amounted to predatory pricing designed to drive them out of business. The likelihood of retaliation is influenced by the scale of entry. When Japanese firms first entered the U.S. car and consumer electronics markets, they sought to avoid retaliation by introducing small products in segments that were deemed unprofitable by U.S. producers. A successful retaliatory strategy is one that deters entry by using a threat that is credible enough to intimidate would-be entrants.[7]

The Effectiveness of Barriers to Entry.   Studies by Bain[8] and Mann[9] found profitability was higher in industries with "very high entry barriers" than in those with "substantial" or "moderate to low" barriers. Capital intensity and advertising are key variables that increase entry barriers and raise industry profitability.[10]

Whether barriers to entry are effective in deterring potential entrants depends on the resources of the potential entrants. Barriers that are effective for new companies may be ineffective for firms that are diversifying from other industries. George Yip found no evidence that entry barriers deterred new entry.[11] Entrants were able to successfully overcome entry barriers for one of two reasons. Some possessed resources and capabilities that permitted them to surmount barriers and compete against incumbent firms using similar strategies. American Express, for example, used its brand name to enter a broad range of financial service markets, and Mars used its strong position in confectionery to enter the ice cream market.[12] Others successfully circumvented entry barriers by adopting different strategies from those of incumbent firms. Southwest Airlines used a low-cost, "no-frills" strategy to challenge the major U.S. airlines. Dell Computer used direct-mail distribution and telephone-based customer service to bypass established distribution channels.

Rivalry Between Established Competitors

For most industries, the major determinant of the overall state of competition and the general level of profitability is competition among the firms within the industry. In some industries, firms compete aggressively—sometimes to the extent that prices are pushed below the level of costs and industry-wide losses are incurred. In others, price competition is muted and rivalry focuses on advertising, innovation, and other non-price dimensions. Six factors play an important role in determining the nature and intensity of competition between established firms: concentration, the diversity of competitors, product differentiation, excess capacity, exit barriers, and cost conditions.

Concentration.   Seller concentration refers to the number and size-distribution of firms competing within a market. Seller concentration is most commonly measured by the **concentration ratio:** the combined market share of the leading producers. For example, the four-firm concentration ratio (conventionally denoted "CR4") is the market share of the four largest producers. A market dominated by a single firm, e.g., Xerox in the U.S. plain-paper copier market during the early 1970s, or UST in the U.S. smokeless tobacco market, displays little competition and the dominant firm can exercise considerable discretion over the prices it charges. Where a market is dominated by a small group of leading companies (an oligopoly), price competition may also be restrained, either by outright collusion, or more commonly through "parallelism" of pricing decisions.[13] Thus, in markets dominated by two companies, such as alkaline batteries (Duracell and Eveready), color film (Kodak and Fuji), and soft drinks (Coke and Pepsi), prices tend to be similar and competition focuses on advertising, promotion, and product development. As the number of firms supplying a market increases, coordination of prices becomes more difficult, and the likelihood that one firm will initiate price cutting increases. Despite the strong theoretical arguments, the effect of seller concentration on profitability has been hard to pin down empirically. Richard Schmalensee concludes that: "The relation, if any, between seller concentration and profitability is weak statistically and the estimated effect is usually small."[14]

Diversity of Competitors.   The ability of firms in an industry to avoid price competition also depends on their similarities in terms of origins, objectives, costs, and strategies. The cozy atmosphere of the U.S. steel industry prior to the advent of import competition and the new mini-mills was possible because of the similarities of the companies and the outlooks of their senior managers. By contrast, the inability of OPEC to maintain prices and output quotas is a consequence of differences in objectives, production costs, language, politics and religion among member countries.

Product Differentiation.   The more similar the offerings among rival firms, the more willing customers are to substitute and the greater the incentive for firms to cut prices to increase sales. Where the products of rival firms are virtually indistinguishable, the product is a **commodity** and price is the sole basis for competition. Commodity industries such as agriculture, mining, and basic materials tend to be plagued by price wars and low profits. By contrast, in industries where products are highly differentiated (perfumes, pharmaceuticals, restaurants, management consulting services), price competition tends to be weak, even though there may be many firms competing.

Excess Capacity and Exit Barriers.   Why does industry profitability tend to fall so drastically during periods of recession? The key is the balance between demand and capacity. Unused capacity encourages firms to offer price cuts to attract new business in order to spread fixed costs over a greater sales volume. Excess capacity may not be just cyclical, but part of a structural problem due to over-investment and stagnant or declining demand. In such situations, the issue is whether excess capacity will leave the industry. **Barriers to exit** are costs associated with capacity leaving an industry. Where resources are durable and specialized, and where employees are entitled to job protection, barriers to exit may be substantial.[15] Depressed profits in the European oil refining industry are the result of low demand, over-investment, and barriers to exit in the form of refinery dismantling, environmental cleanup, and employee redundancy. Conversely, growth industries tend to be subject to capacity shortages, which boost profitability, although cash flow in rapidly growing industries can be negative due to high rates of investment (see Table 3.2).

TABLE 3.2
The Relationship Between Real Market Growth and Profitability

	REAL ANNUAL RATE OF MARKET GROWTH				
	Less than –5%	–5% to 0	0 to 5%	5% to 10%	Over 10%
Gross margin on sales	23.5	25.6	26.9	25.7	29.7
Return on sales	7.8	8.3	9.1	8.3	9.4
Return on investment	20.6	23.0	23.2	22.2	26.6
Cash flow/Investment	6.0	4.9	3.5	2.4	-0.1

Source: R. D. Buzzell and B. T. Gale, *The PIMS Principles* (New York: Free Press, 1987) pp. 56–57.

Cost Conditions: Scale Economies and the Ratio of Fixed to Variable Costs.
When excess capacity causes price competition, how low will prices go? The key factor is cost structure. Where fixed costs are high relative to variable costs, firms will take on marginal business at any price that covers variable cost. The consequences for profitability can be disastrous. From 1990 to 1995, the total losses of the U.S. airline industry exceeded total profits during the previous three decades. The willingness of airlines to offer heavily discounted tickets on flights with low bookings reflects the fact that the variable costs associated with filling empty seats on a scheduled flight are close to zero. The devastating impact of excess capacity on profitability in petrochemicals, tires, steel, and memory chips is a result of high fixed costs in these businesses and the willingness of firms to accept additional business at any price that covers variable cost.

Scale economies may also encourage companies to compete aggressively on price in order to gain the cost benefits of greater volume. In consumer electronics, automobiles, and semi-conductors, the cost benefits of market leadership are powerful drivers of inter-firm competition.

Bargaining Power of Buyers

The firms in an industry operate in two types of markets: in the markets for *inputs* they purchase raw materials, components, and financial and labor services from the suppliers of these factors of production; in the markets for *outputs* they sell their goods and services to customers (who may be distributors, consumers, or other manufacturers). In both markets, the relative profitability of the two parties in a transaction depends on relative economic power. Dealing first with the sales to customers, two sets of factors are important in determining the strength of buying power: buyers' price sensitivity and relative bargaining power.

Buyers' Price Sensitivity.   The extent to which buyers are sensitive to the prices charged by the firms in an industry depends upon four major factors.

♦ The greater the importance of an item as a proportion of total cost, the more sensitive buyers will be about the price they pay. Beverage manufacturers are highly sensitive to the costs of metal cans because this is one of their largest single cost items. Conversely, most companies are not sensitive to the fees charged by their auditors, since auditing costs are such a small proportion of overall company expenses.

♦ The less differentiated the products of the supplying industry, the more willing the buyer is to switch suppliers on the basis of price. The manufacturers of T-shirts, light bulbs, and blank videotapes have much more to fear from Wal-Mart's buying power than do the suppliers of perfumes.

♦ The more intense the competition among buyers, the greater their eagerness for price reductions from their sellers. As competition in the world automobile industry has intensified, so component suppliers are subject to greater pressures for lower prices, higher quality, and faster delivery.

♦ The greater the importance of the industry's product to the quality of the buyer's product or service, the less sensitive are buyers to the prices they are charged. The buying power of personal computer manufacturers relative to the manufacturers of microprocessors (Intel, Motorola, Advanced Micro Devices) is limited by the critical importance of these components to the functionality of their product.

Relative Bargaining Power.   Bargaining power rests, ultimately, on refusal to deal with the other party. The balance of power between the two parties to a transaction depends on the credibility and effectiveness with that each makes this threat. The key issue is the relative cost that each party sustains as a result of the transaction not being consummated. A second issue is each party's expertise in leveraging its position through gamesmanship. Several factors influence the bargaining power of buyers relative to that of sellers.

♦ *Size and concentration of buyers relative to suppliers.* The smaller the number of buyers and the bigger their purchases, the greater the cost of losing one. Because of their size, health maintenance organizations (HMOs) can purchase health care from hospitals and doctors at much lower cost than can 6individual patients.

♦ *Buyers' information.* The better informed buyers are about suppliers and their prices and costs, the better they are able to bargain. Doctors and lawyers do not normally display the prices they charge, nor do traders in the bazaars of Tangier and Istanbul. Keeping customers ignorant of relative prices is an effective constraint on their buying power. But knowing prices is of little value if the quality of the product is unknown. In the markets for haircuts, interior design, and management consulting, the ability of buyers to bargain over price is limited by uncertainty over the precise attributes of the product they are buying.

♦ *Ability to integrate vertically.* In refusing to deal with the other party, the alternative to finding another supplier or buyer is to do-it-yourself. Large food processors such as Heinz and Campbell's Soup have reduced their dependence on the oligopolistic suppliers of metal cans by manufacturing their own. The leading retail chains have increasingly displaced their suppliers' brands with their own brand products. Backward integration need not necessarily occur—a credible threat may suffice.

Empirical evidence points to the tendency for buyer concentration to depress prices and profits in supplying industries.[16] PIMS data show that the larger the average size of customers' purchases and the larger the proportion of customers' total purchases the item represents, the lower the profitability of supplying firms.[17]

Bargaining Power of Suppliers

Analysis of the determinants of relative power between the producers in an industry and their suppliers is precisely analogous to the analysis of the relationship between producers and their buyers. Since the factors that determine the effectiveness of supplier power against the buying power of the industry are the same as those that determine the power of the industry against that of its customers, they do not require a separate analysis.

Because raw materials, semi-finished products, and components tend to be commodities supplied by small companies to large manufacturing companies, their suppliers usually lack bargaining power. Hence, commodity suppliers often seek to boost their bargaining power through cartelization—e.g., OPEC, the International Coffee Organization, and farmers' marketing cooperatives. A similar logic explains labor unions.

PIMS studies of the impact of suppliers' bargaining power on firms' profitability is complex. Increasing concentration of a firm's purchases is initially beneficial since it permits certain economies of purchasing. Thereafter, increasing concentration among

TABLE 3.3
The Impact of
Unionization on
Profitability

	PERCENTAGE OF EMPLOYEES UNIONIZED				
	None	1% TO 35%	35% TO 60%	60% TO 75%	Over 75%
ROI(%)	25	24	23	18	19
ROS(%)	10.8	9.0	9.0	7.9	7.9

Source: R.D. Buzzell and B.T. Gale, *The PIMS Principles: Linking Strategy to Performance*
(New York: Free Press, 1987), p.67.

purchasers results in decreased profitability due to increased supplier power. Supplier power is significantly increased by forward integration into its customer's own industry. When a firm faces its suppliers as competitors within its own industry, its ROI is reduced by two percentage points. Unionization is unambiguously associated with decreasing profitability (see Table 3.3).

APPLYING INDUSTRY ANALYSIS

Once we understand how industry structure drives competition which, in turn, determines industry profitability, then we can apply this analysis, first, to forecasting industry profitability in the future and, second, to devising strategies to change industry structure.

Forecasting Industry Profitability

Decisions to commit resources to a particular industry must be based on anticipated returns five to ten years in the future. Over these periods, profitability cannot be accurately forecast by projecting current industry profitability. However, we can predict changes in the underlying structure of an industry with some accuracy. Structural changes are driven by current changes in product and process technology, the current strategies of the leading players, the changes occurring in infrastructure and in related industries, and by government policies. If we understand how industry structure affects competition and profitability, we can use our projections of structural change to forecast the likely changes in industry profitability.

The first stage is to understand how past changes in industry structure have influenced competition and profitability. Exhibit 3.2 explains deteriorating profitability of the world automobile industry in terms of the structural changes that have affected the five forces of competition. The next stage is to identify *current* structural trends and determine how these will impact the five forces of competition and resulting industry profitability. Consider the U.S. casino gambling industry (see Exhibit 3.3). The current strategies of the companies and actions by regulatory authorities have clear implications for structural changes in the industry. These structural trends directly influence competition and profitability.

While it is not possible to predict with any confidence the *quantitative* impact of structural changes, their *qualitative* impact is easier to assess. The main problem is the difficulty of appraising the aggregate effect of multiple structural changes where some are beneficial to profitability, others are detrimental. Thus, a key issue in the casino industry is whether the current merger wave will offset the tendency for increasing excess capacity to depress profitability.

EXHIBIT 3.2

Competition and Profitability in the World Automobile Industry

Despite record profits earned by the U.S. Big Three (GM, Ford, and Chrysler) from 1994 to 1997 and recovery of Japanese and German car makers in 1996–1997, the overall profitability of the world auto industry during the 1990s was dismal. During the six year period from 1990 to 1995, the average return on equity earned by the world's 10 largest car makers was 3.4 percent—substantially below their cost of equity capital. Profitability was far below the levels earned during the 1960s. What factors can explain the deterioration in industry profitability?

Substitute competition remained modest. Despite dire warnings over the imminent demise of private motoring, the automobile increased its position as the dominant mode of personal transportation in the industrialized countries. Despite growing congestion, little shift to public transportation occurred while *telecommuting* remained in its infancy.

New entry was also limited, due mainly to the huge costs of establishing manufacturing and distribution facilities and the large scale economies in the business. New entrants during the 1980s and 1990s included Proton (Malaysia), Ssangyong and Samsung (Korea), and some small companies producing for their domestic markets.

The major force of increased competition was increased rivalry among existing car makers. At the global level, industry concentration increased as many small and medium-sized producers were merged or acquired: in France, Peugeot and Citroen merged; Chrysler acquired AMC; VW acquired Seat and Skoda; BMW acquired Rover; Ford acquired Jaguar. Yet, looking at national markets, the picture was quite different. During the 1960s, national car makers dominated their domestic markets. The process of internationalization resulted in increased import competition and building of foreign plants with the result that every national market featured more companies and lower concentration than three decades earlier. The U.S. market share of the Big Three dropped from 85 to 64 percent, Fiat's share of the Italian market fell from 66 to 40 percent, Rover (formerly British Leyland) saw its UK market share decline from 40 to 11 percent; in Germany, the market share of VW and Mercedes declined from 50 to 28 percent. The leading motor vehicle manufactures in

1994 in terms of number of cars and trucks produced were as follows (figures in thousands):

GM	U.S.	8,619
Ford	U.S.	6,462
Toyota	Japan	4,465
Volkswagen	Germany	3,299
Nissan	Japan	2,839
Chrysler	U.S	2,808
Fiat	Italy	2,143
Peugeot	France	1,890
Renault	France	1,761
Honda	Japan	1,765
Mitsubishi	Japan	1,529
Hyundai	S. Korea	1,255
Mazda	Japan	974
Suzuki	Japan	940
Daimler-Benz	German	930
Kia	S. Korea	691
Daihatsu	Japan	606
BMW	Germany	563
VAZ	Russia	585
Daewoo	S. Korea	523
Isuzu	Japan	456
Volvo	Sweden	448
Fuji	Japan	419

Not only were there more competitors, but their products were becoming increasingly similar. Increasing standardization of designs, technologies, and features resulted in different manufacturers' vehicles in each product category becoming increasingly similar. Competition was further enhanced by excess capacity. Although a strong U.S. economy kept capacity utilization high in North America during 1995 to 1997, elsewhere, the picture was less satisfactory. In Europe, capacity utilization remained low, and union agreements and political pressures presented major barriers to exit. Substantial excess capacity also existed in Japan and Korea. Worldwide, heavy investment in new plants and new process technologies was causing production capacity to grow faster than demand.

The manufacturers were also pressured by increased vertical bargaining power. The power of suppliers had increased greatly. Suppliers of components and sub-assemblies such as Bosch, TRW, Verity, Aisin Seiki, Dana, and Eaton rivaled the auto manufacturers in terms of size and multinationality. Increasingly, technology development was led by the component manufacturers,

---

EXHIBIT 3.2

(Continued)

---

not the auto companies. At the buyer level, there were signs the auto manufacturers might be losing control over their distribution channels. In the United States, the traditional dealer system was being challenged by new "automobile supermarkets" including Automax (owned by Circuit City) and AutoNation (owned by Republic Industries), as well as by Internet sales.

———————

Source: R. M. Grant, "The World Automobile Industry," Georgetown School of Business, 1997.

EXHIBIT 3.3

How Will Structural Change Affect the Profitability of U.S. Casinos?

The 1990s were a period of rapid development for the U.S. casino gambling industry. Increasingly, the industry was viewed, not just by the existing casino operators, but also by municipalities, states, and entertainment companies as offering huge economic potential. The result was expansion on multiple fronts.

In terms of new entry, casino gambling expanded well beyond its traditional locations in Nevada and Atlantic City, NJ. The potential for gambling to offer new revenue sources to governments and opportunities for economic development encouraged the licensing of casinos in Mississippi and the introduction of riverboat casinos. By 1996, 10 states had licensed casinos. The 1988 Indian Gaming Regulatory Act opened the way for some 70 casinos on Indian reservations in 17 states. One of the biggest reservation casinos is Foxwood's, owned by the Mashantucket Pequot tribe in Ledyard, CT.

Additional sources of new capacity have been expansion by existing casino companies in Las Vegas and Atlantic City. In Las Vegas, competition to build the "biggest and best" has resulted in the demolition and rebuilding of a number of leading casinos. Between 1996 and 2000, the number of hotel rooms at Las Vegas casinos will double. New "megacasinos" include the $390 million Luxor, the $450 million Treasure Island, the $1 billion MGM Grand resort, and the $2.5 billion Bellagio (by Mirage Resorts). Rivalry between Donald Trump and Mirage Resorts' Steve Wynn has also expanded capacity in Atlantic City, where excess capacity is already causing several casinos to lose money. Mirage will own 5,500 rooms by 1998. The problems of excess capacity are exacerbated by the high fixed costs of operating casinos.

Increasingly, the Las Vegas casinos are competing through ever more ambitious differentiation. New casinos such as New York, Bellagio, and Monte Carlo are breaking new ground in spectacle, entertainment, theming, and sheer scale. However, the geographical proximity of these casinos means despite differentiation, the casinos will still be battling for the same pool of gamblers.

At the substitute level, Americans' dreams of quick riches were also being met by an expanding number of state lotteries, and an increasing use of games of chance as vehicles for marketing magazines, soft drinks, and credit cards. Traditional forms of gambling such as horse and greyhound racing were attempting to revitalize their appeal through the addition of slot-machine gambling. The expansion of cruise-ship vacations provided new opportunities for offshore gambling.

Whether the pressures of new entry and excess capacity will cause industry margins to collapse depends on the extent to new supply will create its own demand. If new gambling opportunities attract a new breed of gamblers and if the themed megacasinos attract vacationing families, it may be possible for the market to absorb the new capacity. Certainly, gambling in the United States is a growth industry with total revenues rising from $124 billion in 1982 and $304 billion in 1991, to over $500 billion in 1996. But, if the new casinos are simply increasing competition for the narrow group of "high rollers," then the prospects look gloomy.

EXHIBIT 3.3
(Continued)

The final factor to take into account is increasing industry concentration. In recent years, the industry has been consolidating into a small number of hotel/casino companies. Hilton Hotels acquired Bally Entertainment and is seeking to acquire ITT (which owns Caesar's Palace).

Mirage Resorts, Circus Circus, and MGM Grand are also big players seeking to acquire smaller players. A battle for market dominance between a small number of major players may cause a short-medium term shakeout resulting in a more favorable long-term structure.

In other industries, there may be little ambiguity about the impact of structural changes on profitability since the main structural changes are pulling in the same direction. For example:

♦ It seems likely that the profitability of U.S. network broadcasting will decline over the next ten years (1998–2007) in response to an increased number of broadcast networks (the big three—ABC, CBS, and NBC—were joined first by Fox, then by Time Warner); increased competition from substitutes such as direct satellite TV, the Internet, and video games; and increased bargaining power of production studios and local TV stations.

♦ The situation is similar with the issuers of bank credit cards. More competition due to increasing numbers of competitors (including non-bank issuers such as GM, GE, and AT&T), entry from various co-branders (ranging from universities and churches to clubs and airlines), lower demand due to increased consumer indebtedness, and increased substitute competition from ATM cards and electronic transactions through the Internet and other media may affect profitability.

Strategies to Alter Industry Structure

Understanding how the structural characteristics of an industry determine the intensity of competition and the level of profitability provides a basis for identifying opportunities for changing industry structure in order to alleviate competitive preassures. The first issue is to identify the key structural features of an industry that are responsible for depressing profitability. The second is to consider which of these structural features are amenable to change through appropriate strategic initiatives. For example:

♦ In consumer electronics, suppliers of leading brands (such as Sony and Pioneer) have sought to limit the buying power of discount chains by refusing to supply those chains that advertise cut prices or that do not display their products within "an appropriate retailing environment."

♦ In the European and North American oil refining industry, most firms have earned returns well below their cost of capital due to many competitors, excess capacity, and commodity products. Efforts to improve industry profitability include mergers between BP and Mobil in Europe, between Shell and Texaco in the United States (aimed at facilitating capacity reduction), and attempts at product differentiation through performance enhancing additives to gasoline.

♦ Excess capacity has also been a major problem in the European petrochemicals industry. Through a series of bilateral plant exchanges, the number of companies producing each product group has been reduced and capacity rationalization has been facilitated.[18] During 1993, ICI initiated a program of plant swaps with BASF, Bayer, and Dow to reduce excess capacity in European polyurethane production.[19]

♦ Building entry barriers is a vital strategy for preserving high profitability in the long run. A primary goal of the American Medical Association has been to maintain the incomes of its members by controlling the numbers of doctors trained in the United States and imposing barriers to the entry of doctors from overseas.

DEFINING INDUSTRIES: IDENTIFYING THE RELEVANT MARKET

One of the most difficult problems in industry analysis is defining the relevant industry. Suppose Jaguar, a division of Ford Motor Company, is assessing its outlook over the next ten years. In forecasting the profitability of its industry, should Jaguar consider itself part of the "motor vehicles and equipment" industry (SIC 371), the automobile industry (SIC 3712), or the luxury car industry? Should it view its industry as national (UK), regional (Europe), or global?

The first issue is clarifying what we mean by the term "industry"? Economists define an industry as a group of firms that supplies a market.[20] Hence, the key to defining industry boundaries is identifying the relevant market. By focusing on the relevant market, we do not lose sight of the critical relationship among firms within an industry: competition.

A market's boundaries are defined by **substitutability,** both on the demand side and the supply side. Thus, in determining the appropriate range of products to be included in BMW's market, we should look first at substitutability on the demand side. If customers are unwilling to substitute trucks for cars on the basis of price differences, then Jaguar's market should be viewed as automobiles rather than all motor vehicles. Again if customers are willing to substitute among different types of automobiles—luxury cars, sports cars, family sedans, sport utility vehicles and station wagons—on the basis of relative price, then Jaguar's relevant market is the automobile market rather than just the luxury car market.

Even if there is limited substitution by customers between different types of automobile, if manufacturers find it easy to switch their production from luxury cars to family sedans to sports cars and the like, then such supply-side substitutability would suggest that Jaguar is competing within the broader automobile market. The ability of Toyota, Nissan, and Honda to penetrate the luxury car market suggests that supply-side substitutability between mass-market autos and specialty autos is moderately high. Similarly, the automobile industry is frequently defined to include vans and light trucks, since these can be manufactured at the same plants as automobiles (often using the same platforms and engines). So too with "major appliance" manufacturers. They tend to be classified as a single industry, not because consumers are willing to substitute between refrigerators and dishwashers, but because the manufacturers can easily substitute among different appliances.

The same considerations apply to the geographical boundaries of markets. Should Jaguar view itself as competing in a single global market or in a series of separate national or regional markets? The criterion here again is substitutability. If customers are willing and able to substitute cars available on different national markets, and/or if manufacturers are willing and able to divert their output among different countries to take account differences in margins, then a market is global. Whereas the market for jet aircraft is clearly global and the market for dairy products clearly national (or local), automobiles are an especially difficult case. To the extent that most auto manufacturers are multinational corporations, there is considerable supply-side substitutability. However, to the extent that national markets are separated by trade restrictions, regulations, and the manufacturers' tightly controlled distribution channels, the international auto market may be seen as a conglomeration of many national markets with imperfect demand and supply-side substitutability among them.

Ultimately, drawing boundaries around industries and markets is a matter of judgment that must account for the purposes and context of the analysis. Substitutability tends to be higher in the long run than in the short term. Hence, if Jaguar is planning its strategy over a ten year period, its relevant business environment is the global automobile industry. If it is considering its competitive strategy over the next three years, it makes sense to focus on specific national and regional markets—the United States, Japan, the EU, and Mercosur—and on the luxury car market rather than the automobile market as a whole.

Fortunately, the precise delineation of an industry's boundaries is seldom critical to the outcome of industry analysis so long as we remain wary of external influences. Because the five forces framework includes influences from outside the industry— entrants and substitutes—the risks of defining the industry too narrowly are mitigated. For example, if we choose to identify Jaguar's industry as comprising the manufacturers of luxury cars, then we can view substitute competition as sports cars, family sedans, and sport utility vehicles, and view the manufacturers of these vehicles as potential entrants into the luxury car market.

BEYOND THE FIVE FORCES MODEL: DYNAMICS, GAME THEORY, AND COOPERATION

Despite being widely used as a framework for analyzing competition and predicting profitability, Porter's Five Forces of Competition framework is not without its critics. Economists criticize its theoretical foundations. Its basis is the structure-conduct-performance approach to industrial organization economics, which has been largely displaced by game theory approaches. Researchers at McKinsey & Company have identified a number of assumptions in the structure-conduct-performances approach which do not hold in practice. For example, business relationships are not always arms-length. Many relationships are characterized by *privilege* through affection or trust; others are *co-dependent systems* formed by webs of companies, where competition exists between webs and within webs. Thus the "Wintel" web competes with the Apple web, while within the Wintel web, Compaq and Dell compete with one another.[21] Apart from unease over its dubious theoretical foundations, the Five Forces model is also limited by its *static* nature: it views industry structure as stable and externally determined. This determines the intensity of competition, which in turn influences the level of industry profitability. But competition is not some constrained process that determines prices and profits and leaves industry structure unchanged. Competition is a dynamic process through which industry structure itself changes through evolution and transformation. Thus, a model that does not take these features into account fails to recognize that competition changes industry structure both consciously by firms' strategic decisions and as an outcome of the resulting competitive interaction.

The essence of competition, then, is a dynamic process in which equilibrium is never reached and in the course of which industry structures are continually reformed. This is evident in the structural transformation of deregulated industries.

♦ By the mid-1990s, the U.S. airline industry had developed a structure that few of the architects of deregulation had predicted. The economists of the Civil Aeronautics Board had predicted that, in the absence of government regulation of routes and fares, entry would be easy, concentration would fall, and fares would drop to their competitive levels. In practice, the industry has been shaped by the strategies of the leading players: mergers and acquisitions have increased concentration; the hub-and-spoke system has given rise to several local near-monopolies; selective price competition has driven a number of low-cost entrants into bankruptcy; and barriers to entry have been created through control of airport gates and landing slots, computer reservations systems, and frequent flyer programs.

♦ The privatization of British Telecom and the deregulation of the British telecommunications industry heralded a new era of intense competition and rapid and radical structural change. Competition from Mercury was soon followed by cellular phone competitors such as Vodaphone, PCS competitors such as Orange, and cable TV companies offering telephone service.

Schumpeterian Competition

Joseph Schumpeter was the first to recognize and analyze the dynamic interaction between competition and industry structure. Schumpeter focused on innovation as the central component of competition and the driving force behind industry evolution. Innovation represents a "perennial gale of creative destruction" through which favorable industry structures—monopoly in particular—contain the seeds of their own destruction by providing incentives for firms to attack established positions through new approaches to competing. Although identified here with Schumpeter, this view of competition as dynamic process of rivalry is associated more widely with the Austrian school of economics.[22]

The key issue raised by Schumpeter is whether we can use current industry structures as a reliable guide to the nature of competition and industry performance in the future. The relevant consideration is the speed of structural change in industry. If the pace of transformation is rapid, if entry rapidly undermines the market power of dominant firms, if innovation speedily transforms industry structure by changing process technology, by creating new substitutes, and by shifting the basis on which firms compete, then there is little merit in using industry structure as a basis for analyzing competition and profit.

Most empirical studies of changes over time in industry structure and profitability show Schumpeter's process of "creative destruction" to be more of a breeze than a gale. Studies of United States and Canadian industry[23] have found that entry occurs so slowly that profits are undermined only slowly. One survey commented: ". . . the picture of the competitive process . . . is, to say the least, sluggish in the extreme."[24] Overall, the studies show a fairly consistent picture of the rate of change of profitability and structure. Both at the firm and the industry level, profits tend to be highly persistent in the long run.[25] Structural change—notably concentration, entry, and the identity of leading firms—also appears to be, on average, slow.[26]

Some industries, however, conform closely to Schumpeter's model. Jeffrey Williams identifies "Schumpeterian industries" as those subject to rapid product innovation with relatively steep experience curves. In these industries, structure tends to be unstable. In computers, telecommunication services, Internet access, and electronic games, using current trends in industry structure to forecast profitability several years ahead is unreliable for two reasons: the relationship between competition and industry structure is unstable, and changes in industry structure are rapid and difficult to predict. We return to the issues of industry evolution and forecasting industry structure in Chapter 10.

Hypercompetition

Schumpeter's ideas of competition as a process of creative destruction have been developed and extended in Rich D'Aveni's concept of hypercompetition.

> **Hypercompetition** is an environment characterized by intense and rapid competitive moves, in that competitors must move quickly to build advantages and erode the advantages of their rivals. This speeds up the dynamic strategic interactions among competitors.

> Hypercompetitive behavior is the process of continuously generating new competitive advantages and destroying, obsoleting, or neutralizing the opponent's competitive advantage, thereby creating disequilibrium, destroying perfect competition, and disrupting the status quo of the marketplace. This is done by firms moving up their escalation ladders faster than competitors, restarting the cycles, or jumping to new arenas.[27]

The driving force of competition is the quest for profit through establishing competitive advantage. However, rivalry for competitive advantage means that competitive advantage is transitory. Only by continually recreating and renewing competitive advantage can firms sustain market dominance and superior performance over the long haul.

The Contribution of Game Theory

Central to the criticisms of Porter's Five Forces as a static framework is its failure to take full account of competitive interactions among firms. In Chapter 1, we noted that the essence of strategic competition is the interaction among players such that the decisions made by any one player are dependent on the actual and anticipated decisions of the other players. By relegating competition to a mediating variable that links industry structure with profitability, the Five Forces analysis offers little insight into firms' choices of whether to compete or to cooperate; sequential competitive moves; and the role of threats, promises, and commitments. Game theory has two especially valuable contributions to make to strategic management.

1. It permits the framing of strategic decisions. Apart from any theoretical value of the theory of games, the description of the game in terms of:
   - Identifying the players,
   - Specifying each player's options,
   - Establishing the payoffs from every combination of options,
   - Defining sequences of decisions using game trees,

   permits us to understand the structure of the competitive situation and facilitates a systematic, rational approach to decision making.

2. Through the insight it offers into situations of competition and bargaining, game theory can predict the equilibrium outcomes of competitive situations and the consequences of strategic moves by any one player. Game theory provides penetrating insight into central issues of strategy that go well beyond pure intuition. Simple game models (e.g., "prisoner's dilemma") predict cooperative versus competitive outcomes, whereas more complex games permit analysis of the effects of reputation,[28] deterrence,[29] information,[30] and commitment[31]—especially within the context of multiperiod games. Particularly important for practicing managers, game theory can indicate strategies for improving the structure and outcome of the game through manipulating the payoffs to the different players.[32]

Despite the explosion of interest in game theory during the 1980s, practical applications, especially in the area of strategic management, remained limited until the 1990s. Interest in game theory has grown recently as a result of a number of practical guides to the application of the game theory's tools and insights.[33] Game theory has provided illuminating insights into a wide variety of situations, including the Cuban missile crisis of 1962,[34] President Reagan's 1981 tax cut,[35] subsidies for Airbus Industrie, the problems of OPEC in agreeing to production cuts, the competitive impact of Philip Morris's cutting cigarette prices on 'Marlboro Monday' in 1993,[36] and the auctioning of licenses of wavelengths for telecommunications by the U.S. and New Zealand governments.[37]

One of the greatest benefits of game theory is its ability to view business interactions as comprising both competition and cooperation. A key deficiency of the Five Forces framework is in viewing rivalry and bargaining as competitive in nature. The central message of Adam Brandenburger and Barry Nalebuff's book, *Co-opetition*, is recognizing the competitive/cooperative duality of business relationships. Whereas Coca-Cola's relationship with Pepsi-Cola is essentially competitive, that between Intel and Microsoft is primarily complementary. Thus,

- A player is your **complementor** if customers value your product **more** when they have the other player's product than when they have your product alone.
- A player is your **competitor** if customers value your product **less** when they have the other player's product than when they have your product alone.

The **Value Net** recognizes these two types of relationship (see Figure 3.5). It is important to recognize that a player may occupy multiple roles. Microsoft and Netscape compete fiercely to dominate the market for Internet browsers. At the same time, the two companies cooperate in establishing security protocols for protecting privacy and guard-

FIGURE 3.5
The Value Net

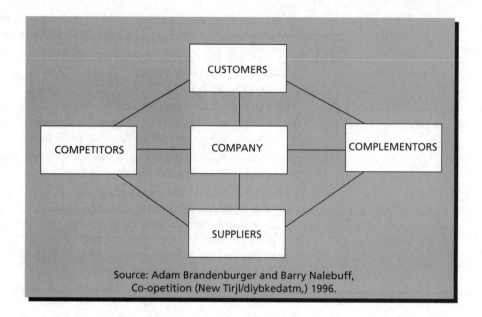

Source: Adam Brandenburger and Barry Nalebuff,
Co-opetition (New Tirjl/diybkedatm,) 1996.

ing against credit card fraud on the Internet. Similarly, with customers and suppliers, though these players are essentially partners in creating value, they are also bargaining over sharing that value. The desire of competitors to cluster together—antique dealers in London's Bermondsey Market and advertising agencies on Madison Avenue—points to the complementary relations among competitors in growing the size of their market and developing its infrastructure.

The most important insights that game theory provides are its ability to identify opportunities for a player to *change the structure of a game in order to improve payoffs*. Consider the following examples:

♦ **The benefits of repeated games.** A classic case of "*prisoners' dilemma*" is purchasing a product where the quality cannot be easily discerned prior to purchase (e.g., a used car). The seller has an incentive to offer low quality, the buyer has an incentive to offer a low price in the likelihood that quality will be poor (see Chapter 9 for a fuller analysis). Both parties would benefit from ensuring that the product was high quality. How can this dilemma be resolved? One answer is to change a *one period game* (single transaction) into a *repeated game* (long-term vendor relationship). Faced with the possibility of a long-term business relationship, the seller has the incentive to offer a quality product, the buyer has the incentive to offer a price that offers the seller a satisfactory return.

♦ **Deterrence.** The payoffs in a game can be changed through increasing the costs to other players of choices that are undesirable to the firm. By establishing the certainty that deserters would be shot, the British army made desertion a less attractive alternative for troops than advancing over no-man's-land to attack German trenches during World War I. Similarly, established airlines have sought to deter Southwest from expanding its route network by the threat of matching Southwest's fares on the new routes.

♦ **Bringing in competitors.** Establishing alliances and agreements with competitors can increase the value of the game by increasing the size of the market and building strength against other competitors. The key is converting win-lose (or even lose-lose) games into win-win games. When Intel developed its 8086 microprocessor, it gave up its monopoly by offering second-sourcing licenses to AMD and IBM. Although Intel was creating competition for itself, it was also encouraging the adoption of the 8086 chip by computer manufacturers (including IBM) who were concerned about overdependence on Intel. Once Intel had established its technology as the industry standard, it developed its family of 286, 386, 486, and Pentium processors and became much more restrictive over licensing. A cooperative solution was also found to Norfolk Southern's competition with CSX for control of Conrail. The 1997 bidding war was terminated when CSX and Norfolk Southern agreed to dismember and share Conrail.

Game theory permits considerable insight into the nature of situations involving interactions among multiple players. It clarifies the structure of relationships and nature of interactions among players, and it identifies the alternative actions available to different players and related these to possible outcomes. Game theory has provided valuable decision support in negotiations and in simulating competitive patterns of action and reaction. War gaming, based on game theory principles, is a popular technique both among military planners and management consultants such as Booz Allen and Coopers & Lybrand. The weaknesses are in the ability to apply game theory to specific business situations and generate unambiguous, meaningful, and accurate predictions. Game theory is excellent in providing insights and understanding; it has been less valuable in predicting outcomes and designing strategies. The cost of game theory's mathematical rigor has been narrowness of application. Game theory provides clear prediction in highly stylized situations involving few external variables and highly restrictive assumptions. The result is a mathematically sophisticated body of theory that suffers from unrealistic assumptions, lack of generality, and an analysis of dynamic situations through a sequence of static equilibria.[38] When applied to more complex (and more realistic) situations, game theory frequently results in either no equilibrium or multiple equilibria, and outcomes that are highly sensitive to small changes in the assumptions. Experience in applying game theory has been mostly disappointing. The game theory-designed FCC auctions for PCS licenses are generally viewed as being a disaster, both for the FCC and for the bidders who used game theory to formulate their bidding strategies. Although game theory is in a phase of rapid development, it is far from providing the theoretical foundations for strategic management. Though we draw on game theory in several places in this book, the emphasis of analysis is less on the analysis of action and response between rivals and other approaches to "playing the game," and more about the transformation of competitive games through building sustainable competitive advantage.[39]

OPPORTUNITIES FOR COMPETITIVE ADVANTAGE: IDENTIFYING KEY SUCCESS FACTORS

Our discussion of hypercompetition and game theory has taken us well beyond the confines of the Five Forces framework. Remember that the primary purpose of that model is to analyze industry attractiveness in order to forecast industry profitability. Hypercompetition explicitly recognizes that competition is a battle for competitive advantage. Game theory also focuses on positioning and maneuvering for advantage.

The purpose of this section is to look explicitly at the analysis of competitive advantage. In subsequent chapters, we develop a more comprehensive analysis of competitive advantage. The purpose here is to identify the potential for competitive advantage within an industry in terms of the factors that determine a firm's ability to survive and prosper—its **Key Success Factors**.[40] In Exhibit 3.4, Kenichi Ohmae of McKinsey and Company in Tokyo discusses Key Success Factors in forestry and their link with strategy.

Like Ohmae, our approach to identifying key success factors is straightforward and commonsense. To survive and prosper in an industry, a firm must meet two criteria: first, it must supply what customers want to buy, second, it must survive competition. Hence, we may start by asking two questions:

♦ What do our customers want?

♦ What does the firm need to do to survive competition?

EXHIBIT 3.4

Probing for Key Success Factors

As a consultant faced with an unfamiliar business or industry, I make a point of first asking the specialists in the business, "What is the secret of success in this industry?" Needless to say, I seldom get an immediate answer, and so I pursue the inquiry by asking other questions from a variety of angles in order to establish as quickly as possible some reasonable hypotheses as to key factors for success. In the course of these interviews it usually becomes quite obvious what analyses will be required in order to prove or disprove these hypotheses. By first identifying the probable key factors for success and then screening them by proof or disproof, it is often possible for the strategist to penetrate very quickly to the core of a problem.

Traveling in the United States last year, I found myself on one occasion sitting in a plane next to a director of one of the biggest lumber companies in the country. Thinking I might learn something useful in the course of the five-hour flight, I asked him, "What are the key factors for success in the lumber industry?" To my surprise, his reply was immediate: "Owning large forests and maximizing the yield from them."

The first of these key factors is a relatively simple matter: purchase of forest land. But his second point required further explanation. Accordingly, my next question was: "What variable or variables do you control in order to maximize the yield from a given tract?"

He replied: "The rate of tree growth is the key variable. As a rule, two factors promote growth: the amount of sunshine and the amount of water. Our company doesn't have many forests with enough of both. In Arizona and Utah, for example, we get more than enough sunshine but too little water, and so tree growth is very low. Now, if we could give the trees in those states enough water, they'd be ready in less than fifteen years instead of the thirty it takes now. The most important project we have in hand at the moment is aimed at finding out how to do this."

Impressed that this director knew how to work out a key factor strategy for his business, I offered my own contribution: "Then under the opposite conditions, where there is plenty of water but too little sunshine—for example, around the lower reaches of the Columbia River—the key factors should be fertilizers to speed up the growth and the choice of tree varieties that don't need so much sunshine."

Having established in a few minutes the general framework of what we were going to talk about, I spent the rest of the long flight very profitably hearing from him in detail how each of these factors was being applied.

Source: Kenichi Ohmae, *The Mind of the Strategist* (Harmondsworth, U.K.: Penguin, 1982): 85.

To answer the first question we need to look more closely at customers of the industry and to view them, not so much as a source of bargaining power and hence as a threat to profitability, but more as the basic rationale for the existence of the industry and as the underlying source of profit. This implies that the firm must identify who its customers are, identify their needs, and establish the basis on which they select the offerings of one supplier in preference to those of another. Once we have identified the basis of customers' preference, this is just the starting point for a chain of analysis. As Table 3.4 shows, if consumers select supermarkets primarily on the basis of price, and if low prices depend on low costs, the interesting questions concern the determinants of low costs.

TABLE 3.4
Identifying Key Success Factors: Some Examples

	WHAT DO CUSTOMERS WANT? (Analysis of demand)	HOW DOES A FIRM SURVIVE COMPETITION? (Analysis of Competition)	KEY SUCCESS FACTORS
Steel	Customers include auto, engineering, and container industries. Customers acutely price sensitive. Customers require product consistency and reliability of supply. Specific technical specifications required for special steels.	Competition primarily on price. Competition intense due to declining demand, high fixed costs, excess capacity, low-cost imports, and exit barriers high. Transport costs high. Scale economies important.	Cost efficiency through scale-efficient plants, low cost location, rapid adjustment of capacity to output, efficient use of labor. Scope for differentiation through quality service and technical factors.
Fashion Clothing	Demand fragmented by garment, style, quality, color. Customers' willingness to pay price premium for fashion, exclusivity, and quality. Mass market highly price sensitive. Retailers seek reliability and speed of supply.	Low barriers to entry and exit. Low seller concentration. Few scale economies. International competition strong. Retail chains exercise strong buying power.	Need to combine effective differentiation with low-cost operation. Key differentiation variables are speed of response to changing high fashions, style, reputation and quality.
Supermarkets	Low prices. Convenient location. Wide range of products. Product range adapted to local customer preferences. Freshness of produce. Cleanliness, service, and pleasant ambience.	Markets localized and concentration normally high. But customer price sensitivity encourages vigorous price competition. Exercise of bargaining power an important influence on input cost. Scale economies in operation and advertising.	Low cost operation requires operational efficiency, scale efficient stores, large aggregate purchases to maximize buying power, low wage costs. Differentiation requires large stores (to allow wide product range), convenient location, easy parking.

The second question requires that the firm examine the basis of competition in the industry. How intense is competition and what are its key dimensions? If competition in an industry is intense, then, even though the product may be highly differentiated and customers may choose on the basis of design and quality rather than price, low cost may be essential for survival. Retailers such as Harrods, Nordstrom, and Tiffany's do not compete on low prices, but in a fiercely competitive retailing sector, their prosperity depends on rigorous cost control.

A basic framework for identifying Key Success Factors is presented in Figure 3.6. Application of the framework to identify Key Success Factors in three industries is outlined in Table 3.4.

Key Success Factors can also be identified through the direct modeling of profitability. In the same way that our Five Forces analysis models the determinants of industry-level profitability, we can also attempt to model firm-level profitability in terms of identifying the key factors that drive a firm's relative profitability within an industry. In Chapter 2, we made some progress on this front. By disaggregating a firm's return on capital employed into individual operating factors and ratios, we can pinpoint the most important determinants of firm success (see Figure 2.2). In many industries, these primary drivers of firm-level profitability are well-known and widely used as performance targets. Exhibit 3.5 gives a well-known profitability formula used in the airline industry then identifies the factors that drive the profitability ratios.

FIGURE 3.6
Identifying Key Success Factors

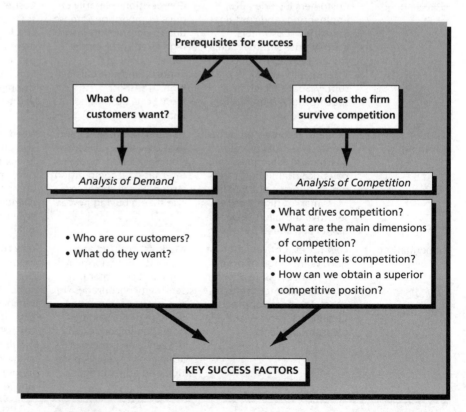

EXHIBIT 3.5

Identifying Key Success Factors Through Modeling Profitability: The Airline Business

Profitability, as measured by operating income per available seat-mile (ASM), is determined by three factors: *Yield*, total operating revenues divided by the number of revenue passenger miles (RPM); *Load factor*, the ratio between RPMs and APMs; and *Cost*, total operating expenses divided by ASMs. Where an ASM is one seat flown one mile with a passenger in it or not, RPM is one seat flown one mile with a passenger in it. Thus:

$$\frac{Income}{ASMs} = \frac{Revenue}{RPMs} \times \frac{RPMs}{ASMs} - \frac{Expenses}{ASMs}$$

Some of the primary determinants of each of these measures are the following:

Revenue/RPMs

- Intensity of competition on routes flown.
- Ability to quickly adjust prices and price structures to changing market conditions through effective yield management.
- Ability to attract business customers.
- Offering superior customer service.

Load Factors

- Competitiveness of prices.
- Efficiency of route planning (e.g., through hub-and-spoke systems)
- Building customer loyalty through quality of service, frequent-flyer programs.

- Matching airplane size to demand for individual flights.

Expenses/ASMs

- Wage rates and benefit levels.
- Fuel efficiency of aircraft.
- Productivity of employees (determined partly by their job flexibility).
- Load factors.
- Level of administrative cost.

In their quest for survival and competitive advantage, the airlines have sought to optimize as many of these factors as possible in order to improve their profitability. In terms of revenue enhancement, several airlines have withdrawn from the most intensely competitive routes, others have sought to achieve a fare premium over the cut-price airlines through punctuality, convenience, comfort, and services (e.g., inflight telephones, personal video monitors with choice of movies). To improve load factors, companies have sought flexibility in allocating plane capacity to routes, and used their computer reservation systems and Internet sales to achieve more flexible pricing. Most notably, companies have sought cost economies through increasing employee productivity, reducing administrative overhead through outsourcing, investing in fuel-efficient aircraft, and reducing wages and benefits.

More generally, the approach introduced in Chapter 2 (see Figure 2.2) to disaggregate return on capital into its component ratios can be extended to identify the specific operational and strategic drivers of superior profitability. Figure 3.7 applies this analysis to identify success factors in retailing.

The value of success factors in formulating strategy has been scorned by some strategy scholars. Pankaj Ghemawat observes that the " . . . whole idea of identifying a success factor and then chasing it seems to have something in common with the ill-considered medieval hunt for the philosopher's stone, a substance that would transmute everything it touched into gold."[41] The objective here in identifying Key Success Factors is less ambitious. There is no universal blueprint for a successful strategy, and even in individual industries, there is no "generic strategy" that can guarantee superior profitability. However, each market is different in terms of what motivates customers and how competition works. Understanding these aspects of the industry environment is a

FIGURE 3.7
Identifying Key Suc-
cess Factors in Retail-
ing Through
Analyzing Drivers of
Return on Capital
Employed

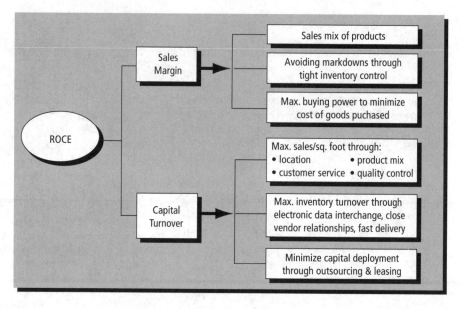

prerequisite for an effective business strategy. This does not imply that firms within an industry adopt common strategies. Since every firm comprises a unique set of resources and capabilities, every firm must pursue unique key success factors.

◆ SUMMARY

In Chapter 1, we observed that understanding one's competitive environment is a key ingredient of a successful strategy. In this chapter, we examined concepts and frameworks to assist us in understanding the business environment of the firm. A key assumption is that to understand competition and the determinants of profitability within an industry, we are not restricted to acquiring experience-based, industry-specific learning over a long period of time. Instead, we can draw on concepts, principles, and theories that can be applied to any industry. Although every industry is unique, the patterns of competitive behavior can be explained and using common analytical frameworks.

The underlying premise of this chapter is that the structural characteristics of an industry play a key role in determining the nature and intensity of the competition within it and the rate of profit it earns. Our framework for linking industry structure to competition and profitability is Porter's Five Forces of Competition model. This provides a simple, yet powerful, organizing framework for classifying the relevant features of an industry's structure and predicting their implications for competitive behavior. The framework is particularly useful for:

- ◆ Predicting industry profitability
- ◆ Indicating how the firm can influence industry structure in order to moderate competition and improve profitability.

The Porter framework suffers from some critical limitations. In particular, it does not take adequate account of the dynamic character of competition. Competition is a powerful force that changes industry structure. In hypercompetitive industries, competing strategies create a process of "creative destruction" that continually transforms industry structure. As for the theoretical weaknesses of the Porter framework, game theory provides a broader theoretical basis for analyzing both competition and cooperation, but, in providing a basis for strategy formulation, its potential has yet to be realized.

Though the Porter framework permits analysis of competition and profitability at the industry level, our industry analysis is also directed toward understanding the opportunities for competitive advantage. Our approach has been to show that by understanding customer demand, the competitive process, and the determinants of firm-level profitability, we can identify Key Success Factors: the prerequisites for survival and success within an industry.

Subsequent chapters draw extensively on the frameworks, concepts, and techniques introduced here. In particular, we develop our industry analysis through considering the evolution of industry structure (Chapter 10) and the characteristics of technology-based industries (Chapter 11), mature industries (Chapter 12), and global industries (Chapter 14). Chapter 4 extends our industry analysis through examining the internal complexity of industries in relation to segmentation, strategic groups, and competitor behavior.

NOTES

1   See, for example, J. P. Leemhuis, "Using Scenarios to Develop Strategies," *Long Range Planning* (April 1985): 30–37; and Pierre Wack, "Scenarios: Shooting the Rapids," *Harvard Business Review* (November–December 1985): 139–150.

2   Michael E. Porter, *Competitive Strategy: Techniques for Analyzing Industries and Competitors* (New York: Free Press, 1980), chapter 1. For a summary, see his article, "How Competitive Forces Shape Strategy," *Harvard Business Review* 57 (March–April 1979): 86–93.

3   W. J. Baumol, John C. Panzar, and Robert D. Willig, *Contestable Markets and the Theory of Industry Structure* (New York: Harcourt Brace Jovanovitch, 1982).

4   "Annual Franchise 500," *Entrepreneur* (January 1996).

5   "Brand Loyalty Is Rarely Blind Loyalty," *Wall Street Journal*, October 19, 1989: B1.

6   Robert D. Buzzell and Paul W. Farris, "Marketing Costs in Consumer Goods Industries," in *Strategy + Structure = Performance*, ed. Hans Thorelli (Bloomington, IN: Indiana University Press, 1977): 128–129.

7   Martin B. Lieberman, "Excess Capacity as a Barrier to Entry," *Journal of Industrial Economics* 35 (June 1987): 607–627, argues that to be credible the threat of retaliation needs to be supported by excess capacity.

8   J. S. Bain, *Barriers to New Competition* (Cambridge, MA: Harvard University Press, 1956).

9   H. Michael Mann, "Seller Concentration, Entry Barriers, and Rates of Return in Thirty Industries," *Review of Economics and Statistics* 48 (1966): 296–307.

10 See, for example, the studies by W. S. Comanor and T. A. Wilson, *Advertising and Market Power* (Cambridge: Harvard University Press, 1974); and L. Weiss, "Quantitative Studies in Industrial Organization," in *Frontiers of Quantitative Economics*, ed. M. Intriligator (Amsterdam: North Holland, 1971).

11 George S. Yip, "Gateways to Entry," *Harvard Business Review* 60 (September–October 1982): 85–93.

12 Guy de Jonquieres, "Europe's New Cold Warriors," *Financial Times*, May 19, 1993: 18.

13 See "U.S. Probes Whether Airlines Colluded on Fare Increases," *Wall Street Journal*, December 14, 1989: B1; and "A Tank Full of Trouble," *Economist*, December 16–22, 1989: 57.

14 Richard Schmalensee, "Inter-Industry Studies of Structure and Performance," in *Handbook of Industrial Organization* 2, ed. Richard Schmalensee and Robert D. Willig (Amsterdam: North Holland, 1988): 976. For evidence on the impact of concentration in banking, airlines, and railroads see D. W. Carlton and J. M. Perloff, *Modern Industrial Organization* (Glenview, IL: Scott, Foresman, 1990): 383–385.

15 The problems caused by excess capacity and exit barriers are discussed in *Strategic Management of Excess Capacity*, ed. Charles Baden Fuller (Oxford: Basil Blackwell, 1990).

16 S. H. Lustgarten, "The Impact of Buyer Concentration in Manufacturing Industries," *Review of Economics and Statistics* 57 (1975): 125–132; and Robert M. Grant "Manufacturer-Retailer Relations: The Shifting Balance of Power," in *Business Strategy and Retailing*, ed. G. Johnson (Chichester: John Wiley & Sons, 1987).

17 Robert D. Buzzell and Bradley T. Gale, *The PIMS Principles: Linking Strategy to Performance* (New York: Free Press, 1987): 64–65.

18 See Joe Bower, *When Markets Quake* (Boston: Harvard Business School Press, 1986).

19 Paul Abrahams, "ICI Seeks Restructure of Polyurethane Industry," *Financial Times*, July 1, 1993: 28.

20 The economist's definition of an industry can differ from normal usage of the term. For example, the U.S. automobile industry tends to be viewed either as comprising U.S.-owned car makers (GM, Ford, Chrysler) or U.S.–located car makers (the Big Three plus the U.S. subsidiaries of foreign-owned auto companies such as Honda, Nissan, and BMW). A market-based definition would focus on all auto companies that supply the U.S. car market wherever their plants are located.

21 Kevin Coyne, "A Comprehensive Model for Strategy Development," paper presented at the Strategic Management Society Conference, Barcelona, October 6, 1997.

22 See Robert Jacobson, "The Austrian School of Strategy," *Academy of Management Review* 17 (1992): 782–807; and Greg Young, Ken Smith, and Curtis Grimm, "Austrian and Industrial Organization Perspectives on Firm-Level Competitive Activity and Performance," *Organization Science* 7 (May–June 1996): 243–254.

23 R. T. Masson and J. Shaanan, "Stochastic Dynamic Limit Pricing: An Empirical Test," *Review of Economics and Statistics* 64 (1982): 413–422; R. T. Masson and J. Shaanan, "Optimal Pricing and Threat of Entry: Canadian Evidence," *International Journal of Industrial Organization* 5 (1987).

24 P. A. Geroski and R. T. Masson, "Dynamic Market Models in Industrial Organization," *International Journal of Industrial Organization* 5 (1987): 1–13.

25 Dennis C. Mueller, *Profits in the Long Run* (Cambridge: Cambridge University Press, 1986).

26 Richard Caves and Michael E. Porter, "The Dynamics of Changing Seller Concentration," *Journal of Industrial Economics* 19 (1980): 1–15; P. Hart and R. Clarke, *Concentration in British Industry* (Cambridge: Cambridge University Press, 1980).

27 Richard D'Aveni, *Hypercompetition: Managing the Dynamics of Strategic Maneuvering* (New York: Free Press, 1994): 217–218.

28 Keith Weigelt and Colin F. Camerer, "Reputation and Corporate Strategy: A Review of Recent Theory and Applications," *Strategic Management Journal* 9 (1988): 137–142.

29 A. K. Dixit, "The Role of Investment in Entry Deterrence," *Economic Journal* 90 (1980): 95–106.

30 P. Milgrom and J. Roberts, "Informational Asymmetries, Strategic Behavior and Industrial Organization," *American Economic Review* 77, no. 2 (May 1987): 184–189; J. Tirole, *The Theory of Industrial Organization* (Cambridge, MA: MIT Press, 1990).

31 Pankaj Ghemawat, *Commitment: The Dynamic of Strategy* (New York: Free Press, 1991).

32 The are two outstanding introductions to the principles of game theory and their practical applications: Thomas C. Schelling, *The Strategy of Conflict*, 2nd edition (Cambridge: Harvard University Press, 1980); and A. K. Dixit and B. J. Nalebuff, *Thinking Strategically: The Competitive Edge in Business, Politics, and Everyday Life* (New York: W. W. Norton, 1991).

33 Avinash K. Dixit and Barry Nalebuff, *Thinking Strategically: The Competitive Edge in Business, Politics, and Everyday Life* (New York: W. W. Norton, 1991); John McMillan, *Games, Strategies, and Managers* (New York: Oxford University Press, 1992); Adam Brandenburger and Barry Nalebuff, *Co–opetition* (New York: Doubleday, 1996).

34 Graham Allison, *Essence of Decision: Explaining the Cuban Missile Crisis* (Boston: Little, Brown, 1971).

35 A. K. Dixit and B. J. Nalebuff, *op cit.*,131–135.

36 "Business War Games Attract Big Warriors," *Wall Street Journal*, December 22, 1994: B1.

37 "Winning the Game of Business," *Business Week*, February 11, 1985: 28.

38 There are numerous critiques of the usefulness of game theory. F. M. Fisher, "The Games Economists Play: A Noncooperative View," *RAND Journal of Economics* 20 (Spring 1989): 113–124, points to ability of game theory to predict almost any equilibrium solution. Colin Camerer describes this as the "Pandora's Box Problem," see C. F. Camerer, "Does Strategy Research Need Game Theory?" *Strategic Management Journal*, special issue, 12 (Winter 1991): 137–152. Steve Postrel illustrates this problem by developing a game theory model to explain the rationality of bank presidents setting fire to their trousers. See S. Postrel, "Burning Your Britches Behind You: Can Policy Scholars Bank on Game Theory," *Strategic Management Journal*, special issue, 12 (Winter 1991): 153–155. Michael E. Porter, "Toward a Dynamic Theory of Strategy," *Strategic Management Journal*, special issue 12 (Winter 1991): 95–117, notes that game theory ". . . stops short of a dynamic theory of strategy . . . these models explore the dynamics of a largely static world."

39 In game theory terminology, we may regard the establishment of competitive advantage through cost or differentiation advantage as a *dominant strategy*. If all players are pursuing such dominant strategies then equilibrium in the game is simple and robust.

40 The term was coined by Chuck Hofer and Dan Schendel, *Strategy Formulation: Analytical Concepts* (St. Paul: West Publishing, 1977): 77, who defined Key Success Factors as ". . . those variables that management can influence through its decisions and that can affect significantly the overall competitive positions of the firms in an industry . . . Within any particular industry they are derived from the interaction of two sets of variables, namely, the economic and technological characteristics of the industry . . . and the competitive weapons on which the various firms in the industry have built their strategies."

41 Pankaj Ghemawat, *Commitment: The Dynamic of Strategy* (New York: Free Press, 1991): 11.

4

Intra-Industry Analysis

Fly a MIG-29 at Mach 2.3. MIGS *etc*, in conjunction with the Russian aerospace industry, has a limited number of high-performance military flight packages available for immediate booking. You need not be a pilot. Flight packages from $7,000. 1-800-MIGS ETC
—extract of advertisement, *Washington Post*, February 6, 1994, p. A22

OUTLINE

- INTRODUCTION AND OBJECTIVES
- SEGMENTATION ANALYSIS
  The Uses of Segmentation
  Stages in Segmentation Analysis
- STRATEGIC GROUPS
- COMPETITOR ANALYSIS
  Competitor Intelligence
  A Framework for Predicting Competitor Behavior
  Applying the Results of Competitor Analysis
- SUMMARY

◆ INTRODUCTION AND OBJECTIVES

If industries are defined by competitive relationships among firms, they are internally heterogeneous and their boundaries ill-defined. A firm's competitive relationships are differentiated by the distance of the relationship and the market context. American Airlines' closest competitors are United Airlines and Delta, whereas more distant competitors are Amtrak and Greyhound bus lines. Between New York and Milan, American's closest competitor is Alitalia, but between New York and Montreal it is Air Canada. None of these airlines competes with MIGS *etc*, which offers air transport services in a unique market segment. Standard industry classifications tend to be based on similarities of customer demand, technology, and raw materials. As a result, conventional industry definitions seldom correspond closely to groups of competing firms. The United States retailing sector includes JC Penney, Safeway Food Stores, Tiffany's, Shell gas stations, and Blockbuster Video. Each of these retailers inhabits a different competitive environment and none competes directly with another.

Such heterogeneity poses problems for industry analysis. In the last chapter, we viewed the industry as a real-world phenomenon with definite structural features that determined competition and profitability. However, if the industry itself is an artificial construct, industry analysis may be misleading. For example, industry analysis tells us that the microcomputer industry is fragmented, with low entry barriers, low brand loyalty, highly price-sensitive customers, and strong supplier power exercised by Intel. This should result in fierce competition and slim margins. Yet, while gross margins on PCs averaged a modest 15 to 25 percent in 1994–1995, PC servers (more powerful microcomputers that distribute programs and data around a network of PCs) averaged a 30 to 40 percent gross margin. For Compaq Computer, servers accounted for only 5 percent of sales, but 25 to 30 percent of profits during 1994.[1] A similar phenomenon occurs in the bread and beer industries. Although both are intensely competitive industries dominated by large companies that benefit from scale economies in production, distribution, and advertising, small companies in the form of mini-bakeries and microbreweries have been successful supplying premium-priced, specialty products to local markets.

For some companies, the central feature of their competitive environment is not the industry, but the behavior of a single competitor. Thus, Pepsi-Cola's competitive environment is dominated by the strategy and marketing tactics of Coca-Cola. For Airbus Industrie, strategic decisions are dominated by its predictions of Boeing's competitive initiatives.

To understand competition more intimately and to identify profit opportunities more precisely, a more detailed look into industries is needed. This chapter explores, at a finer level of analysis, the internal structure of industries.

By the time you have completed this chapter, you will be able to:

♦ Segment an industry into its constituent markets and identify the relative attractiveness of the different segments and the differences in key success factors among them.

♦ Classify the firms within an industry into strategic groups based on similarities in their strategies.

♦ Predict the behavior of individual companies including the competitive moves that they are likely to initiate, and the responses they are likely to evoke from rivals.

SEGMENTATION ANALYSIS[2]

Industries tend to be defined broadly: the automobile industry, the computer software industry, the electric power industry. To analyze competition at a more fine-grained level, we need to define the markets within which firms meet at a more disaggregated level in terms of products and geography.

The Uses of Segmentation

If the nature and intensity of competition varies among the different submarkets that an industry serves, then it is useful to partition an industry into segments and analyze their separate structural characteristics. Such analysis is useful not only for the new entrant in determining the most attractive part of a market to enter, but also for established firms deciding in which segments to maintain a presence and how to allocate resources among them. Although the European refining industry earned dismal rates of profit from 1995 to 1997, attractive margins existed in selected submarkets: notably in diesel fuel and aviation fuel, bitumen in Poland and Hungary, and lubricants in Western Europe.

Differences in customers and competition between segments may also mean differences in key success factors between segments. In the United States beer industry, competing effectively in the market for standard, packaged beer requires cost-efficient operation in the form of large-scale, automated production, regional or national distribution through a vast network of local franchised distributors, and heavy investment in advertising and promotion. However, in the market for specialty beers, success is far more dependent on a carefully crafted, quality, flavorful product; local mystique; and localized distribution that emphasizes freshness and careful handling.

Stages in Segmentation Analysis

Segmentation analysis proceeds in five principal stages; Exhibit 4.1 summarizes these stages and applies them to the European metal container industry.

1. Identify Key Segmentation Variables. The first stage of segmentation analysis is to determine the basis of segmentation. Segment decisions are essentially choices about products and customers, hence segmentation variables relate to the characteristics of the product or characteristics of customers. Figure 4.1 lists a number of segmentation variables. The most appropriate segmentation variables are those that

FIGURE 4.1
The Basis for Segmentation: Customer and Product Characteristics

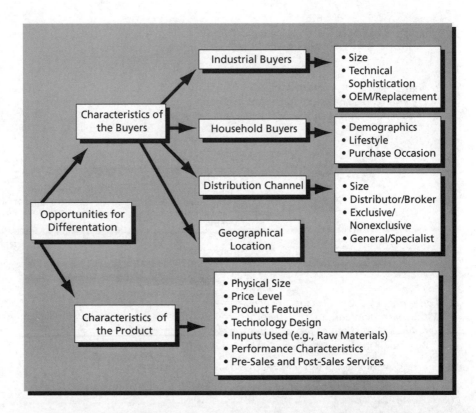

EXHIBIT 4.1

The Main Stages of Segmentation Analysis as Applied to the European Metal Can Industry

1. Identify Key Segmentation Variables and Categories

- Identify segmentation variables.

  (Raw material, can design, can size, customer size, customer's industry, location).

- Reduce the number of segmentation variables by selecting the most significant segmentation variables and by combining closely correlated segmentation variables.

  (Type of can, customer's industry, location).

- Identify discrete categories for each segmentation variable.

  (Type of can: steel 3-piece, steel 2-piece, aluminum 2-piece, general cans, composite cans, aerosols. Type of customer: food processing, fruit juice, pet food, soft drink, beer, oil. Location: France, Germany, Spain/Portugal, Italy, UK, Benelux/Nith).

2. Construct a Segmentation Matrix

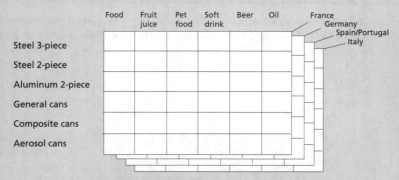

3. Analyze Segment Attractiveness

Apply Five Forces analysis to individual segments.

E.g. Aluminum 2-piece cans to soft drink canners in Italy:

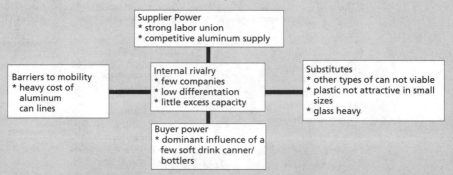

4. Identify Key Success Factors in Each Segment

Within each segment, how do customers choose, and what is needed to survive competition?

5. Analyze Attractions of Broad versus Narrow Segment Scope

- ♦ What is potential to share costs and transfer skills across segments?
- ♦ How similar are Key Success Factors between segments?
- ♦ Are there benefits of segment specialization?

partition the market most distinctly in terms of substitutability among customers (demand-side substitutability) and producers (supply-side substitutability). Market segments are generally associated with price differentials. Indeed, price itself may provide a useful basis for segmenting a market. A classic example of price-based segmentation is that of General Motors during the 1920s. In contrast to Henry Ford's single-model strategy, Alfred Sloan identified six market segments ranging from the lowest price category, $450–$600, to the highest, $2500–$3500. Each of GM's divisions targeted a separate price segment with Chevrolet at the bottom, and Cadillac at the top.[3]

Typically there are many customer and product characteristics that can be used as a basis for segmentation. In order for a segmentation analysis to be manageable, we need to reduce these to two or three. To reduce the number of segmentation variables, do the following:

♦ Identify the most *strategically significant* segmentation variables. In terms of substitutability by customers and by producers, which variables are most important in creating meaningful divisions in a market? In the case of metal containers, geography is critical (cans are expensive to transport long distances), material (influences both demand-side and supply-side substitutability), and customer type.

♦ Combine segmentation variables that are closely correlated. In the case of restaurants, possible segmentation variables such as price level, service (waiter service/self-service), cuisine (fast-food/full meals), and alcohol license (wine served/soft drinks only) could be combined into a single variable, restaurant type, with three categories: full-service restaurants, cafes, and fast-food outlets.

2. Construct a Segmentation Matrix.   Once the segmentation variables have been selected and discrete categories determined for each, the individual segments may be identified using a two- or three-dimensional matrix. Thus, the European metal container industry might be analyzed in a three-dimensional segmentation matrix (see Exhibit 4.1), whereas the world automobile industry might be segmented simply by vehicle type and geographical region (see Exhibit 4.2).

3. Analyze Segment Attractiveness.   Profitability within an industry segment is determined by the same structural forces that determine profitability within an industry as a whole. As a result, Porter's Five Forces of Competition framework is equally effective in relation to a segment as to an entire industry. Exhibit 4.2 applies Five Forces analysis to certain segments of the world automobile industry.

There are, however, a few differences. First, when analyzing the pressure of competition from substitute products, we are concerned not only with substitutes from other industries, but more importantly, substitutes from other segments within the same industry. For example, in deciding whether to introduce a station wagon version of its Mondeo/Contour sedan, Ford's analysis of the station wagon market must consider substitute competition from passenger minivans.

Second, when considering entry into the segment, the major source of entrants is likely to be producers established in other segments within the same industry. Thus, the threat of entry into a segment depends on whether there are barriers that restrict the entry of firms from other segments. These are termed *barriers to mobility* to distinguish them from the barriers to entry that offer protection from outside the industry. Barriers to mobility are key factors in determining the ability of a segment to offer superior returns to those available elsewhere in the industry. Unless there are

EXHIBIT 4.2

Segmenting the World Automobile Market

A global automobile producer such as Ford or Toyota might segment the world auto market by product type and geography. A first-cut segmentation might be along these lines:

REGIONS

	N.America	W. Europe	E. Europe	Asia	Latin America	Australasia	Africa
Luxury cars							
Full-size sedans							
Mid-size sedans							
Small-size sedans							
Station wagons							
Passenger minivans							
Sports cars							
Sport-utility							
Pickup trucks							

(PRODUCTS)

One of the most useful applications of such a segmentation would be an understanding of how profitability in the past had varied between segments and the determinants of such differentials. For example, during the 1990s:

- The North America market for small-sized sedans has always yielded low profits due to the large number of competitors (all the world's major auto producers including a number of low-cost producers such as Hyundai), comparatively low product differentiation (as indicated by the convergence of car designs, automotive technologies, and quality levels), and high level of capacity relative to demand.
- The North America/European markets for passenger minivans have been highly profitable segments due to strong demand relative to capacity and comparatively few participants. Chrysler's survival during the 1980s was primarily due to its strong position within this segment (with its Dodge Caravan and Plymouth Voyager). The influx of companies into minivans was eroding their margins during the late 1990s.
- Worldwide, the market for luxury cars was highly unattractive for most of the 1990s. Despite this traditionally being a high margin segment due to high product differentiation and price insensitivity of buyers, Rolls Royce, Mercedes, Jaguar, and BMW were, as a group, barely profitable. The small size of the segment made it difficult to spread the fixed costs of new model development. Low demand due to recession in Europe and a luxury tax in the United States resulted in an overhang of excess capacity. New entry by Honda (Acura), Toyota (Lexus), and Nissan (Infiniti), together with the acquisition of Jaguar by Ford, had greatly increased competition. Meanwhile, enhancement in the quality and features of mass-produced family sedan made these cars closer substitutes for luxury cars.

Once we understand the factors that determined segment profitability in the past, then we can predict segment profitability in the future.

significant barriers to the mobility of firms from other segments, a segment will be unable to maintain superior profitability to that of the industry.[4] In most industries, the increased flexibility of design and production made possible by computer-aided design and flexible manufacturing systems has had the effect of reducing barriers to mobility. In the automobile industry, high margin segments such as luxury cars, passenger vans, and sport utility vehicles have seen a sharp rise in competition as volume car manufacturers have entered them.

Segmentation analysis can also be useful in identifying unexploited opportunities in an industry. For example, a segmentation matrix of the restaurant industry in a town or locality might reveal a number of empty segments. The interesting question is whether such empty segments represent unexploited opportunities or whether they reflect a lack of customer demand. Consider the market for kitchen appliances. In the early 1960s, microwave ovens and dishwashers were manufactured almost exclusively for the catering trade. A segmentation analysis of the appliance industry might have alerted the firms established in these segments to opportunities for developing these products for the consumer market.

4. Identify the Segment's Key Success Factors. Differences in competitive structure and in customer preferences between segments imply differences in the basis of competitive advantage. Using the same analysis of buyers' purchase criteria and the basis on that firms compete that was outlined in Chapter 3 (see Figure 3.6), we can identify Key Success Factors for individual segments.

For example, the United States bicycle industry can be segmented on the basis of the age-group of the customer (infants, children, youths, adults), price, branding, and distribution channel. Combining and categorizing these segmentation variables results in four major segments each with different Key Success Factors (see Figure 4.2).

FIGURE 4.2
Segmentation and Key Success Factors in the U.S. Bicycle Industry

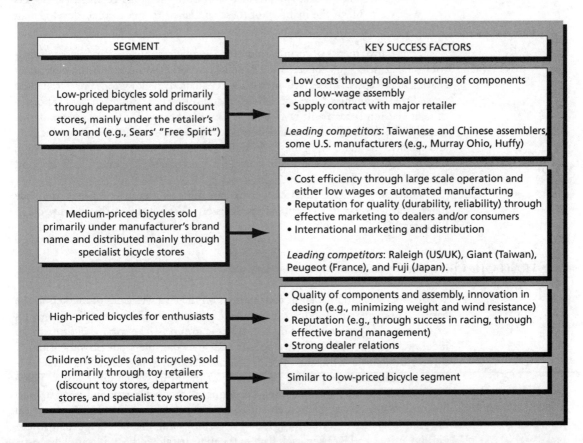

5. Select Segment Scope.   A final issue relating to the choice of which segments to enter concerns the relative advantages of segment specialization versus segment diversity. The advantages of a broad over a narrow segment focus depend on two major factors: similarity of key success factors and the presence of shared costs. In an industry where key success factors are similar across segments, a firm can adopt a similar strategic approach in relation to different segments. If different strategies need to be adopted for different segments, not only does this pose organizational difficulties for the firm, but also the credibility of the firm in one segment may be adversely affected by its strategy in another. Harley-Davidson's introduction of a range of lightweight motorcycles during the early 1970s was a failure, not only because Harley-Davidson could not compete with the Japanese in this segment, but also because of the damage to the firm's reputation in the heavyweight motorcycle segment. Mercedes-Benz seems to be suffering a similar fate with its A-class compact car.

Shared costs mean that broad-segment suppliers can achieve lower costs than their narrow-segment competitors. The vulnerability of narrow-segment specialists to competition from broad-line competitors is constantly being revealed.

♦ In soft drinks, 7 Up's reliance on a single lemon-lime drink made it vulnerable to competition from broad-line competitors such as Coca-Cola and Pepsi. Ultimately, 7 Up, together with Dr. Pepper, was acquired by Cadbury-Schweppes.

♦ The acquisition of specialist auto producers Saab, Lancia, Jaguar, AMC-Jeep, Maserati, Audi, Alfa-Romeo, and Lotus by broad-segment car makers was a result of the inability of these specialists to spread their development costs over a large enough sales volume.

The relative merits of focused and broad-segment strategies vary among industries. The critical issue concerns the benefits of specialization versus the benefits of sharing joint costs. In service industries, William Davidow and Bro Uttal have argued that economies from specialization and differences in key success factors in different customer segments favor a narrow segment focus. By specializing in hernia surgery, Shouldice Hospital near Toronto achieves remarkable levels of productivity and quality.[5] In audio equipment, specialists have continued to dominate the high quality segment against the major consumer electronics companies such as Sony, Matsushita, and Philips.

The issues of specialization versus spreading common costs over multiple markets are similar to diversification decisions. We return to this discussion in Chapter 14.

STRATEGIC GROUPS

Whereas segmentation analysis concentrates on the characteristics of markets as the basis for disaggregating industries, **strategic group analysis** uses the characteristics of firms as the basis for division. A **strategic group** is "the group of firms in an industry following the same or a similar strategy along the strategic dimensions."[6] **Strategic dimensions** include those decision variables that best distinguish the business strategies and competitive positioning of the firms within an industry. These may include product market scope (in terms of product range and geographical breadth), choice of distribution channels, level of product quality, degree of vertical integration, choice of technology, and so on. By selecting the most important strategic dimensions and locating each firm in the industry along them, it is usually possi-

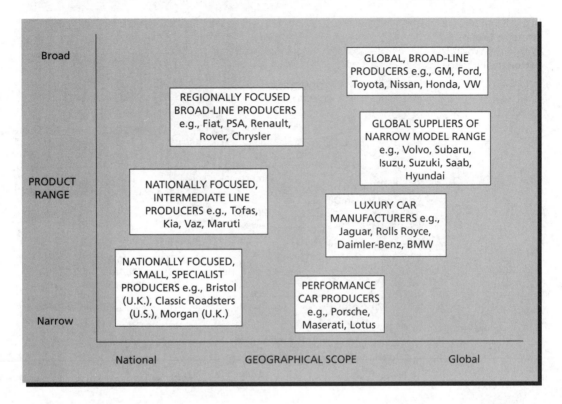

FIGURE 4.3
Strategic Groups in the World Automobile Industry

ble to identify one or more groups of companies that have adopted more or less similar approaches to competing within the industry. Figure 4.3 identifies strategic groups within the world automobile industry, and Figure 4.4 identifies strategic groups within the oil industry.[7]

Strategic groups were developed as a result of empirical analysis of the domestic appliance[8] and brewing industries.[9] Most of the empirical research into strategic groups has been concerned with analyzing differences in profitability among firms.[10] The basic argument is that mobility barriers between strategic groups permit some groups of firms to be persistently more profitable than other groups. In general, the proposition that profitability differences *within* strategic groups are less than differences *between* strategic groups, has not received robust empirical support.[11] The inconsistency of empirical findings may reflect the fact that the members of a strategic group, though pursuing similar strategies, are not necessarily in competition with one another. For example, within the world oil industry, the nationally based integrated oil companies such as Petrobras (Brazil), Indian Oil, Mitsubishi Oil (Japan), and Petronas (Indonesia), are not competing directly with one another, although they are located within the same strategic group. Results from the U.S. airline industry suggest that, though strategic group analysis may not tell us much about profitability differences, it can be useful in helping us understand the types of competitive responses by different firms within an industry.[12]

For our purposes, strategic group analysis is more valuable as a descriptive than a predictive tool. Because strategic group analysis focuses on strategic similarities

FIGURE 4.4
Strategic Groups
Within the World
Petroleum Industry

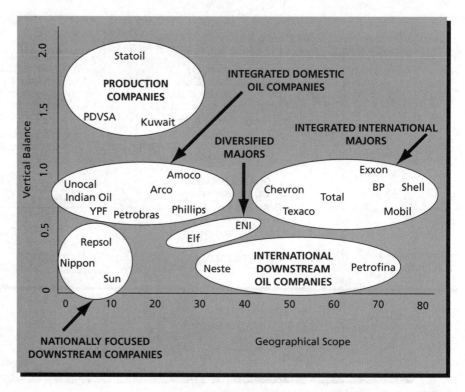

rather than competitive relationships, its potential for explaining inter-firm profitability differences is limited. However, as a means of gaining a broad picture of the types of firms within an industry, the kinds of strategies that have proven viable, and how different firms are positioned in relation to one another, strategic group analysis can contribute substantially to the understanding of industry structure, firm strategy, and industry evolution. This view of strategic groups as a valuable descriptive device is supported by Reger and Huff's evidence that managers within an industry have consistent perceptions of groupings of similar firms.[13]

COMPETITOR ANALYSIS

The purpose of competitor analysis is to predict the behavior of one's closest rivals. The importance of competitor analysis to a company depends on the structure of its industry. In a fragmented industry where firms produce an undifferentiated product, as in the case of most agricultural commodities, market competition is the outcome of the strategies and decisions of so many producers that there is little point in analyzing the behavior of individual firms. In highly concentrated industries, the competitive environment of a company depends critically on the behavior of a few rivals. In household detergents, the industry environment is dominated by the competitive interaction of Procter & Gamble, Colgate-Palmolive, and Lever Brothers (Unilever). The same can be said about large passenger jet aircraft (Boeing and Airbus Industrie), jet engines (GE, Pratt & Whitney, Rolls-Royce), soft drinks (Coke and

Pepsi), news weeklies (*Time*, *Newsweek*, and *U.S. News & World Report*), and the retail market for office supplies (Office Depot, Staples, and Office Max). Similar circumstances exist in more local markets. For the owner of the Shell gas station in the English village of Coalpit Heath, the dominant feature of the local gasoline market is the competitive behavior of the Texaco station across the road.

Even in markets that are not dominated by two or three competitors, the extent of differentiation in the goods and services offered by different firms may mean that a company faces just one or two close competitors whose strategies substantially impact its profitability.

- ♦ In the UK newspaper industry, ten national daily newspapers and a number of regional and local papers compete fiercely. Yet, for *The Independent*, the competitive environment is determined primarily by *The Times* and the *Daily Telegraph*. Among the tabloids *The Sun*, *Daily Mirror*, and *Star* form another intensely competitive group.

- ♦ In the U.S. automobile market, more than 20 manufacturers vie for market share. However, Jaguar's competitive environment is most strongly influenced by the product, pricing, and promotional policies of Mercedes-Benz and BMW.

It is not only through marketing activities that firms' competitive strategies are interdependent. In industries where plant capacity is large relative to the total market, investment decisions are highly interdependent.[14] In petrochemicals, any single firm's calculation of the returns on investment in a new plant must take careful account of other firms' investment plans. Research and development activities show similar interactions. In pharmaceuticals, the returns to research and development depend crucially on being the first company to file for a patent on a new drug. R&D investments require a careful appraisal of whether other firms are pursuing similar avenues of research and, if so, their stage of development.

It is in the analysis of these intensive interactions between small numbers of competitors that applications of game theory described in the previous chapter have proven to be especially useful. The value of game theory is that it provides a structured approach to identifying the choices available to the different players, specifying the payoffs, and showing how the game can be changed to alter the payoffs. The central weakness is that formal game theory models cannot be applied to complex business situations. The approach to competitor analysis followed here is less theoretical but more practical. It focuses on two issues: acquiring information about competitors and predicting their behavior.

Competitor Intelligence

Competitor analysis has three major purposes:

- ♦ To forecast competitors' future strategies and decisions
- ♦ To predict competitors' likely reactions to a firm's strategic initiatives
- ♦ To determine how competitors' behavior can be influenced to make it more favorable

For all three purposes, the key requirement is to understand competitors in order to predict their choices of strategy and tactics and their reactions to environmental changes and our own competitive moves. To understand competitors, it is important to be informed about them. One of the fastest growing areas of corporate activity in recent years has been competitor intelligence. About one-tenth of large U.S. corporations are estimated to have competitor intelligence units, a proportion that has tripled since 1988. **Competitor intelligence** involves the systematic collection and analysis of public information about rivals for informing decision making. *Business Week* notes that Anne Selgas, Eastman Kodak's director of competitive intelligence:

> . . . regularly reads an extensive list of publications that even she considers a tad bizarre. Her favorite is the *Transylvania Times,* a semi-weekly out of tiny Brevard in North Carolina's Transylvania County. A medical film rival—Sterling Diagnostic Imaging Inc.—has a plant there, and Selgas says the paper has lots of hiring and layoff news that helps her understand what's going on.[15]

Historically, European and Asian companies have given greater attention to competitor intelligence than U.S. companies. However, increased competitive pressures and greater need for fast responses have caused many firms to focus greater attention on their competitors. Discount broker Charles Schwab created its competitor intelligence program in 1994, tracking both traditional and new competitors by paying consultants to visit rivals' offices, hiring competing firms' employees, and quizzing customers. The distinction between public and private information is not always clear—the application of trade secrets law to the information carried by an employee moving between firms is especially murky. As a result, competitor intelligence always runs the risk of degenerating into industrial espionage. General Motors' case against Volkswagen over the alleged theft of confidential information by Mr. Lopez and his colleagues is the most publicized recent example. In June 1996, Boehringer Mannheim Corp. sued Johnson & Johnson's Lifescan Inc. for obtaining confidential information relating to its AccuEasy blood-monitoring device through eavesdropping on a sales meeting.

A Framework for Predicting Competitor Behavior

Competitor intelligence is not simply about information. The problem is likely to be too much rather than too little information. The key is a systematic approach that makes clear what information is required and for what purposes it will be used. Our objective is to *understand* our competitor. A characteristic of great generals from Hannibal to Patton has been their ability to go beyond military intelligence and to "get inside the heads" of their opposing commanders. Figure 4.5 shows a basic framework for competitor analysis. There are four main inputs into the analysis.

1. Identifying Current Strategy.   The starting point is identifying the competitor's current strategy. In the absence of any forces for change, a reasonable assumption is that the company will continue to compete in the future in much the same way as it competes at the present. A competitor's strategy may be identified on the basis of what the firm says and what it does. These two are not necessarily the same. As Mintzberg has pointed out, there may be a divergence between intended strategy and realized strategy.[16] Major sources of explicit statements of **strategy intentions** can be found in the annual reports of companies, particularly in the chairman's message to shareholders, and in other statements by senior managers, especially in meetings with investment analysts. With regard to **realized strategy**, emphasis must be given to the competitors' actions and decisions: what capital

FIGURE 4.5
A Framework for
Competitor Analysis

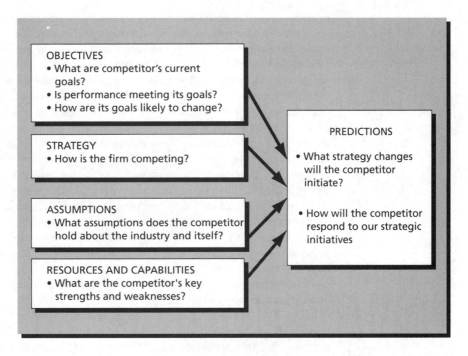

investment projects are being undertaken, what hiring is taking place, what new products are in the pipeline, what acquisitions or strategic alliances have recently been undertaken or rumored, what new advertising and promotional campaigns have been planned? Because of the importance of communicating both to employees who implement the strategy and to the investment community who evaluates the strategy and forecasts its implications for future performance, companies are becoming more explicit about their strategic plans. For example, British Petroleum's web site includes not only the company's annual report to shareholders and 10K report, but also its press releases and reports to analysts. Taken together, these include explicit statements of corporate strategy and strategies for each of BP's businesses (upstream, downstream, chemicals, and alternative energy), together with forecasts of key operating and financial variables. Predictions about future strategies can also be inferred from current decisions: Sears, Roebuck's announcement in 1993 of its intention to sell its Dean Witter financial services subsidiary was seen as a signal that Sears was refocusing on its core retailing businesses and would subsequently devote resources and top management energies into revitalizing its competitive position within U.S. retailing. Similarly, AT&T's desire in 1997 to acquire the regional Bell operator, SBC Communications, was widely viewed as an indicator that AT&T had yet to abandon its old monopolistic ways and embrace aggressive cost and technological competition, and customer-focused marketing in the new, global telecommunications market.

2. Identifying the Competitor's Objectives. To forecast how a competitor might change its strategy, some knowledge of its goals is crucial. Identifying basic financial and market objectives is particularly important. A company driven by short- and medium-term profitability such as Emerson Electric or GEC plc is a very different competitor than a company with long-term market share goals such as Procter & Gamble or Komatsu. A company with a short-term ROI objective is unlikely to react aggressively to the competitive initiative of a rival. Such a reaction would be financially costly in the short term. The demise of the British motorcycle industry and near-disappearance of the U.S. consumer electronics industry have been attributed to the responses of domestic UK and U.S. companies to Japanese competition by withdrawing from competition and retreating to market segments where profits are more secure.[17] Compare the reaction of Procter & Gamble to competition. P&G's obsession with market share means that it is meeting competition willing to finance long-lasting competitive warfare using price cuts, promotions, and advertising. In the case of new products, P&G is willing to accept losses for up to nine years while building a market position.

If the competitor is a subsidiary of a larger corporation, it is important to comprehend the goals of the parent, since these goals impact the strategy of the subsidiary. The means by which the parent controls the subsidiary is also important. How much autonomy does the subsidiary have? A subsidiary's ability to respond to competitive assaults may be restricted by corporate control mechanisms.

The level of current performance in relation to the competitor's objectives is important in determining the likelihood of strategy change. The more a company is satisfied with present performance, the more likely it is to continue with the present strategy. If, on the other hand, the competitor's performance is falling well short of target, then the likelihood of radical strategic change, possibly accompanied by a change in top management, is increased.

Particular problems arise when a competitor is not subject to profitability disciplines. Such competitors can initiate destructive price competition. During the early 1990s, the world aluminum industry was plagued by depressed prices resulting from heavy sales by Russian producers onto world markets. Russian producers were not subject to financial disciplines and were able to acquire energy at below world market prices.

3. Competitors' Assumptions about the Industry.

A competitor's strategic decisions are conditioned by its perceptions (of the outside world and of itself) and by assumptions concerning the industry and about business in general. Both are likely to reflect the theories and beliefs that senior managers hold about their industry and the determinants of success within it. Evidence suggests that, not only do these systems of belief tend to be stable over time, they also tend to converge within an industry. Hence, at any point of time, different firms tend to adhere to very similar beliefs. These industry-wide beliefs about the determinants of success have been described by J-C Spender as "industry-recipes."[18]

Industry-recipes may limit the ability of a firm, and indeed an entire industry, to respond rationally and effectively to external change. The result may be that established firms have a "blindspot" to competitive initiatives of a newcomer. During the 1960s, the Big Three U.S. automobile manufacturers firmly believed that small cars were unprofitable. This belief was based on their own experiences—which were, in part, a consequence of their own cost allocation procedures. As a result, they were willing to yield the fastest growing segment of the U.S. automobile market to Japanese and European imports. Similar beliefs explain the complacency of British and U.S. motorcycle manufacturers in the face of Japanese competition (see Exhibit 4.3).

EXHIBIT 4.3

Motorcycle Myopia

During the 1960s, the motorcycle markets in Britain and the United States were dominated by BSA and Harley-Davidson, respectively. At the beginning of the 1960s, Japanese manufacturers, spearheaded by Honda, began to make inroads into the market for small bikes in both countries. The leading British and U.S. manufacturers discounted the Japanese threat, principally because of their disregard for smaller motorcycles.

Eric Turner, chairman of BSA Ltd (manufacturer of Triumph and BSA motorcycles) commented in 1965:

> The success of Honda, Suzuki, and Yamaha has been jolly good for us. People start out by buying one of the low-priced Japanese jobs. They get to enjoy the fun and exhilaration of the open road and they frequently end up buying one of our more powerful and expensive machines.[26]

Similar complacency was expressed by William Davidson, president of Harley-Davidson:

> Basically, we do not believe in the lightweight market. We believe that motorcycles are sports vehicles, not transportation vehicles. Even if a man says he bought a motorcycle for transportation, it's generally for leisure time use. The lightweight motorcycle is only supplemental. Back around World War I, a number of companies came out with lightweight bikes. We came out with one ourselves. We came out with another in 1947 and it just didn't go anywhere. We have seen what happens to these small sizes.[27]

By the end of the 1970s, BSA and Triumph had ceased production and Harley-Davidson was barely surviving. The world motorcycle industry, including the large bike segments, was dominated by the Japanese.

4. Identifying the Competitor's Capabilities. Predicting a competitor's future strategy is not enough. The key issue for a firm is evaluating the seriousness of a potential challenge. The extent to that a competitor threatens a company's market position depends on the competitor's capabilities. Detailed analysis of resources and capabilities is deferred to the next chapter. At this stage, the key elements are an examination of the firm's principal categories of resources including financial reserves, capital equipment, work force, brand loyalty, and management skills, together with an appraisal of capabilities within each of the major functions: R&D, production, marketing, distribution, and so on.

Circumspection in evaluating a competitor's capabilities is essential before embarking on a strategy that may provoke a competitor. Many brilliant and innovative new companies have failed to withstand the aggressive reactions of established, well-financed incumbents. In the U. S. airline industry, most of the new entrants of the early 1980s had been forced out of business by the end of the decade. Conversely, the trepidation felt by established companies in network software, Internet browser software, on-line news, information, and entertainment over Microsoft's entry in these markets is a result of Microsoft's huge financial resources, its marketing muscle, and its fearsome reputation for market dominance.

Applying the Results of Competitor Analysis

For the purpose of strategy formulation, competitor analysis is useful both in predicting how competitors are likely to behave, and in influencing their behavior.

1. Predicting Competitors' Behavior.   The first question we want to answer is: "What strategy shifts is the competitor likely to make?" This requires that we carefully identify current forces that are likely to provoke a change in strategy. These may be external—a shift in consumer preferences or regulatory change that may have important consequences for the firm—or they may be internal—a failure to achieve current financial or market share targets, or divisive conflict within the company. Whatever the sources, a careful identification of current strategy and goals and the company's assumptions about the industry and its capabilities provide a sound basis on which to forecast the direction of change.

Second, we may wish to forecast a competitor's likely reactions to a proposed strategy change that our own company is initiating. If this strategy change involves an attack on the competitor's market base, then his reactions may be crucial in determining the desirability of the strategy change. The same four elements together provide useful guidance as to the nature, likelihood, and seriousness of a defensive reaction by the competitor. When Honda first attacked BSA/Triumph and Harley-Davidson with the introduction of a large-capacity motorcycle, Honda knew that:

- ◆ Both companies pursued medium-term financial goals rather than market share goals
- ◆ Both firms were benefiting from an upsurge in motorcycle demand; hence, they were not unduly sensitive to losses in market share
- ◆ Both firms believed that, due to their own customer loyalty and brand image, the Japanese producers were not a serious threat in the big bike market
- ◆ Even if BSA/Triumph and Harley-Davidson did react aggressively, the effectiveness of their response would be limited by their weak financial positions and by their lack of innovation and manufacturing capabilities.

2. Influencing Competitors' Behavior: Signaling and Credible Threats.
Understanding one's competitors can assist the firm in influencing its competitors' behavior. Competitor reaction depends not only on what the firm does, but also on what the competitor believes that its rival is doing. The term **signaling** is used to describe the selective communication of information to competitors designed to influence competitors' perceptions and behavior in order to provoke or avoid certain types of reaction.[19] The use of diversionary attacks and misinformation is well-developed in military warfare. In 1944, Allied deception was so good that even during the D-Day landings in Normandy, the Germans believed that the main invasion would occur near Calais.

The principal role of signaling is to provide clear threats to competitors of the company's intention to aggressively react to any rival's competitive move. Such signals need to be credible. It has been argued that some firms deliberately over-invest in order to have available capacity that can be used to flood a competitor's market, if that competitor does not toe the industry line with regard to acceptable competitive behavior. Such strategic excess capacity may be particularly valuable in deterring entrants. The classic example is Alcoa's use of capacity expansion as a warning to potential entrants into the U.S. aluminum industry (United States versus Alcoa,

1945). However, subsequent studies have suggested that this practice is far from prevalent.[20]

The credibility of threats is critically dependent on the reputation of a company.[21] Even though carrying out threats against rivals is costly and depresses short-term profitability, such threats can build a reputation for aggressiveness that deters competitors in the future. The benefits of building a reputation for aggressiveness may be particularly great for diversified companies where reputation can be transferred from one market to another.[22] Hence, Procter & Gamble's protracted market share wars in disposable diapers and household detergents have established a reputation for toughness that protects it from competitive attacks in other markets. *Fortune* magazine identifies Gillette in razors and razor blades, Anheuser-Busch in beer, and Emerson Electric in sink disposal units as examples of companies whose aggressive quest for market share has gained them reputations as "killer competitors," which has encouraged a number of rivals to give up the fight.[23]

Signaling may also be used to maintain a cozy industry environment of cooperation and restrained competition among firms. One means of avoiding price competition in an industry is for firms to follow a pattern of price leadership. In the UK gasoline market, the initiation of a price increase by a firm is normally preceded by a period of consensus building during which the firm tests the water by press releases that announce "the unsatisfactory level of margins in the industry," the "need for a price increase to recoup recent cost increases," and the likelihood that "a price increase will become necessary in the near future."[24]

◆ SUMMARY

The industry analysis in Chapter 3 provided a first stage analysis of a company's industry environment. In this chapter we recognize the internal complexity of industries and go beyond industry-level analysis of competition and success factors to analyze where a firm positions itself within its industry, and how it out-maneuvers rivals.

Segmentation analysis disaggregates industries and markets, permitting a company to:

- Identify segments with the greatest profit potential
- Identify strategies to exploit Key Success Factors within a segment
- Evaluate the merits of a niche strategy, compared with a broader, multisegment strategy

The ability to identify and occupy attractive segments of an industry is critical to success. Hewlett-Packard's superior performance in the office electronics industry during the late 1980s was primarily due to its ability to quickly identify slowing sales and falling margins in the minicomputers segment, and swiftly shift its emphasis toward personal computers (desktops and workstations) and laser printers.[25] Location of attractive industry segments must be supported by clear understanding of Key Success Factors within those segments. The Gap, Gymboree, and Wal-Mart are all successful retailers of children's clothes, but their strategies are quite different, reflecting the different requirements of their respective segments of the children's clothes market.

Analysis of competition may need to extend to an even more micro level. Where a company faces a few close competitors, it is not possible to understand competition without understanding the competitors themselves. Understanding a competitor requires identification of its goals, current strategy, assumptions, and capabilities.

"Getting inside" competitors in order to understand and influence competitive interaction lies at the heart of strategy analysis. An essential characteristic of successful strategists, whether corporate chief executives, military commanders, political leaders, or chess players, is their ability to insightfully analyze their opponents.

NOTES

1 "Computer Companies Rush to Servers to Boost Profits," *Wall Street Journal*, May 6, 1994: B6.
2 This section draws heavily on the approach used by Michael E. Porter, *Competitive Advantage* (New York: Free Press, 1985): chapter 7.
3 Alfred P. Sloan, *My Years with General Motors* (London: Sidgewick & Jackson, 1963): 65, 67.
4 For a formal analysis of mobility barriers, see Richard E. Caves and Michael E. Porter, "From Entry Barriers to Mobility Barriers: Conjectural Decisions and Contrived Deterrence to New Competition," *Quarterly Journal of Economics* 91 (1977): 241–262.
5 William H. Davidson and Bro Uttal, "Service Companies: Focus or Falter," *Harvard Business Review* (July–August 1989): 77–84.
6 Michael E. Porter, *Competitive Strategy* (New York: Free Press, 1980): 129.
7 For further discussion of strategic groups and their role in strategy analysis, see John McGee and Howard Thomas, "Strategic Groups: Theory, Research, and Taxonomy," *Strategic Management Journal* 7 (1986): 141–160.
8 Michael Hunt, *Competition in the Major Home Appliance Industry*, doctoral dissertation, Harvard University, 1973; and Michael E. Porter, "Structure Within Industries and Companies' Performance," *Review of Economics and Statistics* 61 (1979): 214–227.
9 Ken Hatten, Dan Schendel, and Arnold Cooper, "A Strategic Model of the U.S. Brewing Industry," *Academy of Management Journal* 21 (1978): 592–610.
10 Karl Cool and Dan Schendel, "Strategic Group Formation and Performance: The Case of the U.S. Pharmaceutical Industry," *Management Science* 33 (1987): 1102–1124; A. Feigenbaum and H. Thomas, "Strategic Groups and Performance: The U.S. Insurance Industry," *Strategic Management Journal* 11 (1990): 197–215.
11 K. Cool and I. Dierickx, "Rivalry, Strategic Groups, and Firm Profitability," *Strategic Management Journal* 14 (1993): 47–59.
12 Ken Smith, Curtis Grimm, and Stefan Wally, "Strategic Groups and Rivalrous Firm Behavior: Toward a Reconciliation," *Strategic Management Journal* 18 (1997): 149–157.
13 R. K. Reger and A. S. Huff, "Strategic Groups: Cognitive Perspective," *Strategic Management Journal* 14 (1993): 103–124.
14 For an analysis of such interdependence, see Michael E. Porter and A. M. Spence, "The Capacity Expansion Process in a Growing Oligopoly: The Case of Corn Wet Milling," in *The Economics of Information and Uncertainty*, ed. J. McCall (Chicago: University of Chicago Press, 1982).
15 "They Snoop to Conquer," *Business Week*, October 28, 1996: 172–176.
16 Henry Mintzberg, "Opening up the Definition of Strategy," in *The Strategy Process: Concepts, Contexts and Cases*, ed. Quinn, Mintzberg and James (Englewood Cliffs, NJ: Prentice-Hall, 1988).
17 Boston Consulting Group, *Strategy Alternatives for the British Motorcycle Industry* (London: Her Majesty's Stationery Office, 1975); M. Dertouzos, R. Lester, and R. Solow, *Made in America: Regaining the Productive Edge* (Cambridge, MA: MIT Press, 1989).
18 J.-C. Spender, *Industry Recipes: The Nature and Sources of Managerial Judgement* (Oxford: Basil Blackwell, 1989). The propensity for social interaction to result in a convergence of perceptions and beliefs is commonly referred to as "groupthink" and has been discussed by Anne Huff, "Industry Influences on Strategy Reformulation," *Strategic Management Journal* 3 (1982): 119–131.

19 For a review of theory and research on competitive signaling, see O. Heil and T. S. Robertson, "Toward a Theory of Competitive Market Signaling: A Research Agenda," *Strategic Management Journal* 12 (1991): 403–418.

20 Marvin B. Leiberman, "Excess Capacity as a Barrier to Entry: An Empirical Appraisal," *Journal of Industrial Economics* 35 (1987): 607–627.

21 For a survey of the strategic role of reputation, see Keith Weigelt and Colin Camerer, "Reputation and Corporate Strategy: A Review of Recent Theory and Applications," *Strategic Management Journal* 9 (1988): 443–454.

22 P. Milgrom and J. Roberts, "Predation, Reputation, and Entry Deterrence," *Journal of Economic Theory* 27 (1982): 280–312.

23 "Companies That Compete Best," *Fortune*, May 22, 1989: 36–44.

24 Robert M. Grant, "Pricing Behavior in the UK Wholesale Market for Petrol," *Journal of Industrial Economics* 30 (1982): 271–292.

25 "Hewlett-Packard's Screeching Turn Toward Desktops," *Business Week*, September 11, 1989: 106–112.

26 *Advertising Age*, December 27, 1965, quoted by Richard T. Pascale, "Honda A," Harvard Business School, Case 9-384-049, 1983.

27 *Forbes*, September 15, 1966.

5

Analyzing Resources and Capabilities

Analysts have tended to define assets too narrowly, identifying only those that can be measured, such as plant and equipment. Yet the intangible assets, such as a particular technology, accumulated consumer information, brand name, reputation, and corporate culture, are invaluable to the firm's competitive power. In fact, these invisible assets are often the only real source of competitive edge that can be sustained over time.

—Hiroyuki Itami, *Mobilizing Invisible Assets*

◆ INTRODUCTION AND OBJECTIVES

This is an important chapter. We make a major shift in our focus and encounter ideas, concepts, and analytic frameworks that have been responsible for a fundamental rethinking of the sources of profit and the foundations for strategy. The material in this chapter provides the foundation for the analysis of competitive advantage.

By the time you have completed this chapter, you will be able to:

- Explain the role of a company's resources and capabilities as a basis for formulating strategy.
- Identify and appraise the resources and capabilities of a firm.
- Identify the characteristics of resources and capabilities that determine the stream of economic rents they can earn for the firm.
- Recognize that strategy is concerned not only with using the firm's resources and capabilities to maximize returns, but also with building the firm's resource base.
- Develop a framework for resource analysis that integrates the preceding themes into a practical guide for formulating strategies that build competitive advantage.

I begin by explaining why a company's resources and capabilities are so important to its strategy.

THE ROLE OF RESOURCES AND CAPABILITIES IN STRATEGY FORMULATION

Strategy is concerned with matching a firm's resources and capabilities to the opportunities that arise in the external environment. So far, the emphasis of the book has been the interface between strategy and the external environment of the firm. With this chapter, our emphasis shifts to the interface between strategy and the internal environment of the firm, more specifically, with the resources and capabilities of the firm. Figure 5.1 illustrates this shift of emphasis.

The emphasis on the external environment reflects the dominant themes in strategy literature during the 1970s and most of the 1980s. During this period, most developments in strategy analysis concentrated on the industry environment of the firm and its competitive positioning in relation to rivals. During the 1980s, the analysis of industry structure and competitive positioning was closely associated with the work of Michael Porter at Harvard, the analytic approaches of consulting companies (e.g., the Boston Consulting Group's analysis of the role of experience and market share in driving relative costs), and the Strategic Planning Institute's PIMS project, which explored the impact of industry structure and competitive positioning on business unit profitability.

By contrast, strategic analysis of the firm's internal environment remained underdeveloped. Analysis of the internal environment has, for the most part, been concerned with issues of strategy implementation: choices of organizational structure, systems of control, and management style have been viewed primarily as consequences of the strategy adopted.[1] The comparative neglect of internal resources by business strategists contrasts sharply with military strategy, which has been dominated by the analysis of relative resource strength. From the Thirty Years War until World War I, European diplomacy had been based on a resource-based notion of a

FIGURE 5.1
Shifting from an
Industry Focus to a
Resource Focus

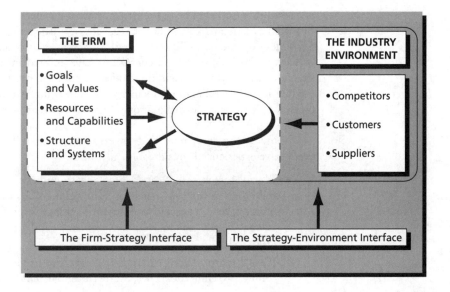

balance of power. The unease among the German High Command over Hitler's military strategy throughout World War II reflected recognition that Germany did not possess the resources to simultaneously wage war on the Eastern, Western, and North African fronts as well as in the sky and sea. The military historian, Liddell Hart, has argued that there is only one underlying principle of military strategy: "concentration of strength against weakness."[2]

During the 1990s, there has been a surge of interest in the role of a firm's resources and capabilities as the principal basis for strategy and the primary determinants of a firm's profitability. These ideas have coalesced into what has become known as the resource-based view of the firm.[3]

Resource-Based Strategy

The starting point for the formulation of strategy must be some statement of the firm's identity and purpose. As we noted in Chapter 2, this generally takes the form of a mission statement that answers the question: "What is our business?" Traditionally, firms have defined their businesses is in terms of the market they serve: "Who are our customers?" and "Which of their needs are we seeking to serve?" In a world where customer preferences are volatile and the identity of customers and the technologies for serving them are changing, a market-focused strategy may not provide the stability and constancy of direction needed as a foundation for long-term strategy. When the external environment is in a state of flux, the firm itself, in terms of its bundle of resources and capabilities, may be a much more stable basis on which to define its identity. Hence, a definition of the firm in terms of what it is capable of doing may offer a more durable basis for strategy than a definition based upon the needs the business seeks to satisfy.[4]

Theodore Levitt's solution to the problem of external change was that companies should define their markets broadly rather than narrowly: railroads should have perceived themselves to be in the transportation business, not the railroad business.[5] But such broadening of the target market is of little value if the company cannot easily develop the capabilities required for serving customer requirements across a wide front. Although railroad companies have entered into airlines, shipping, and trucking, their performance in these markets has been patchy. Perhaps resources and capabilities of the railroad companies were better suited to real estate development, pipelines, or oil and gas exploration—businesses where several of them have prospered.

Many of the companies that have sought to serve broadly defined customer needs have experienced considerable difficulties.

♦ Merrill Lynch, American Express, Sears, and Citicorp's efforts to "serve the full range of financial needs of our customers" by diversifying across stock-broking, retail banking, investment banking, insurance, and real estate brokerage gave rise to serious problems and resulted in disappointing profitability.[6]

♦ Allegis Corporation's attempt to "serve the needs of the traveler" through combining United Airlines, Hertz car rental, and Westin Hotels was a costly failure.

By contrast, several companies whose strategies have been based on developing and exploiting clearly defined internal capabilities have successfully adjusted to and exploited external change.

♦ Honda's strategy since its founding in 1948 has been built around its expertise in the development and manufacture of engines; this capability has successfully carried Honda from motorcycles to a number of gasoline-engined products (see Figure 5.2).

♦ 3M Corporation's expertise in adhesives and thin-film coatings has taken the company from sandpaper, into adhesive tapes, audiotapes and videotapes, road signs, medical products, floppy disks, and over 30,000 other products.

In general, the greater the rate of change in a firm's external environment, the more likely internal resources and capabilities are to provide a secure foundation for long-term strategy. In the fast-moving world of information technology, new companies are built around specific technological capabilities. The products or markets within which the capabilities are applied is a secondary strategic consideration. Motorola, the Texas-based supplier of wireless telecommunications equipment, semiconductors, and direct satellite communications, has undergone many transformations from being a leading supplier of TVs and car radios to its current focus on telecommunication. Yet, underlying these transformations has been a consistent focus on technological leadership in electronic components—semiconductors in particular.

When faced with the imminent obsolescence of one's core products, a critical strategic issue for the firm is whether to orient strategy around external customer needs or internal resources and capabilities. Consider the typewriter manufacturers facing the microcomputer revolution of the 1980s. With the approaching obsolescence of typewriters, there were two strategic alternatives. The companies could pursue their traditional market focus and attempt to acquire the electronic technology necessary to continue to serve the word processing needs of their customers; alternatively, the companies could concentrate on their existing electrical and precision engineering capabilities and seek other markets where these capabilities could be used. Few companies have successfully made the transition from typewriters to personal computers. Olivetti, the Italian typewriter and office equipment manufacturer, built up substantial losses trying to establish itself in PCs.[7] Remington, on the other hand, moved from typewriters into products using similar technical and manufacturing skills: electric shavers and other small electric appliances.

Few companies have successfully maintained their market focus in the face of changing technology. An exception is Eastman Kodak. When Kodak's dominance of the world market for photographic products was threatened by the displacement of chemically based imaging by electronic imaging, Kodak had the choice of either acquiring the electronic imaging capabilities needed to maintaining its position in photographic imaging, or developing its chemical capabilities through its Eastman chemical and Sterling pharmaceutical business. Kodak chose the former. However, by mid-1997, the transition to digital imaging was far from complete. Despite investing over $500 million in digital photography, this business lost over $100 million during the first half of 1997. It remains to be seen whether competitive advantage in digital photography will be achieved by a traditional photographic company such as Kodak, or by an electronics company such as Hewlett-Packard.[8]

Resources as the Source of Corporate Profitability

In Chapter 1, I noted that superior profitability may derive from two sources: location within an attractive industry, and achieving a competitive advantage over rivals. Industry analysis has emphasized market power conferred by favorable industry structures as the primary basis for superior profitability. The implication is that strategic management is concerned with locating within attractive industries and market segments within industries, and adopting strategies that modify industry

FIGURE 5.2
Evolution of Honda: A Strategy Based on Resources and Capabilities

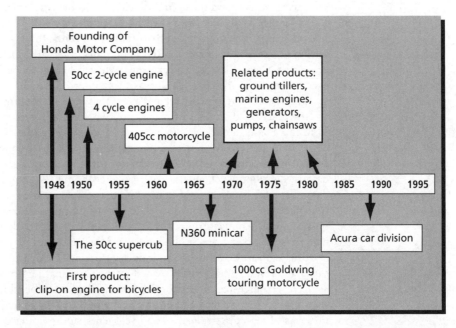

conditions and competitor behavior to moderate competitive pressures. The viability of this approach has been undermined by three factors. First, the increase in competitive pressure across industries due to increased international competition and deregulation has meant that industries that once offered cozy environments for making easy profits are now subject to vigorous price competition. Second, technological and demand changes are causing industry boundaries to become increasingly ill-defined. Third, empirical research has failed to show that industry factors account for a significant proportion of inter-firm profit differentials.[9]

As a result, establishing competitive advantage through the development and deployment of resources and capabilities, rather than seeking shelter from the storm of competition, has become the primary goal for strategy formulation. The resource-based view conceives of the firm as a unique bundle of heterogeneous resources and capabilities. These resources and capabilities are the basis on which a firm's competitive advantage is built and the primary determinant of profitability.

◆ The profitability of Arco's West Coast petroleum business owes nothing to the attractiveness of the U.S. oil business: most of the major players have been selling off their U.S. assets because of poor returns. Arco has earned spectacular returns in this business because of its low-cost Alaskan oil reserves and a tightly integrated transportation, refining, and retailing network within the five Western states.

◆ Though the airline business has been one of the world's least profitable businesses during the 1990s, a few companies have earned rates of return significantly above their cost of capital. British Airways' extensive route network and its marketing and customer service capabilities have provided the basis for a return on equity several times greater than the industry average. Southwest Airlines' operating capabilities, unique corporate culture, and the commitment and flexibility of its employees have resulted in Southwest being the only U.S. airline consistently profitable during the 1990s.

Economists regard the profits associated with industry attractiveness and competitive advantage as distinct types of economic profit (or *rent*). The profits associated with limited competition are referred to as **monopoly rents,** those associated with the possession of superior resources as **Ricardian rents,** after the nineteenth century British economist, David Ricardo, who explained why fertile land was able to earn high returns even when the market for wheat was competitive. Ricardian (or *scarcity*) rent is the return earned by a resources over and above that required to bring it into production.

In practice, distinguishing the profits associated with industry attractiveness from those associated with owning superior resources and capabilities is difficult. A closer look at the Five Forces frameworks suggests that monopoly rents also have their source in firm resources. Barriers to entry, for example, are the result of patents, brands, distribution channels, experience, economies, or some other resource that incumbent firms possess but that entrants can acquire only slowly or at disproportionate expense. A monopoly or oligopoly position in an industry is founded on the possession of manufacturing capacity and sales and distribution facilities that dominate those of other firms in the industry. Some resources may be owned collectively by firms within the industry: an industry standard (which raises costs of entry), or cartel, is a resource collectively owned by the participating firms.

The resource-based view of the firm has had a profound impact on our understanding of strategy formulation. Until the mid-1980s, strategy was seen primarily in terms of selecting industries and segments, and gaining competitive advantage through the pursuit of generic strategies such as cost leadership or differentiation. The resource-based view emphasizes that the key to profitability is not doing the *same* as other firms—locating in the most attractive industries and pursuing the appropriate generic strategy—but exploiting the *differences* among firms. Each firm is a unique collection of highly differentiated resources and capabilities. Establishing competitive advantage is concerned with formulating and implementing a strategy that recognizes and exploits the unique features of each firm. To view Southwest Airlines and Arco as pursing similar strategies of cost leadership is to overlook the essence of their strategies, which is the development and deployment of unique sets of resources and capabilities through strategies and organizational systems that are quite unlike those of any other competitor.

The remainder of this chapter outlines a resource-based approach to strategy formulation. The essence of the approach is that the firm should seek self-knowledge in terms of a thorough and profound understanding of its resources and capabilities. Such a resource-based approach to strategy comprises three key elements:

1. Selecting a strategy that exploits a company's principal resources and capabilities. Companies that have been successful over the long term, such as Matsushita, Procter & Gamble, Coca-Cola, Marks & Spencer, BMW, and Motorola, have achieved a close linkage between their strategies and their resources and capabilities. Companies whose strategies have strayed beyond their resource base (such as Daimler-Benz and Saatchi & Saatchi during the 1980s) suffered loss of direction and deteriorating profitability.

2. Ensuring that the firm's resources are fully employed and their profit potential is exploited to the limit. Walt Disney's remarkable turnaround between 1984 and 1988 involved very little change in basic strategy. The key feature was that Disney's wealth of assets and skills were mobilized to produce greatly increased profit (see Exhibit 5.1).

3. Building the company's resource base. Resource analysis is not just about deploying existing resources. It is crucially concerned with filling resource gaps and building the company's base of resources and capabilities for the future. Honda, Microsoft, Johnson & Johnson, and Motorola are all companies whose long-term success owes much to their commitment to nurturing talent, developing technologies, and building capabilities to permit adaptation to change within their business environments.

Our starting point is to identify and assess the resources and capabilities available to the firm.

THE RESOURCES OF THE FIRM

Resource analysis takes place at two levels of aggregation. The basic units of analysis are the individual resources of the firm: items of capital equipment, the skills of individual employees, patents, brands, and so on. But to examine how the firm can create competitive advantage we must look at how resources work together to create capabilities: this is our second level of analysis. Figure 5.3 shows the relationship among resources, capabilities, and competitive advantage.

Drawing up an inventory of a firm's resources can be surprisingly difficult. No such document exists within the accounting or management information systems of most corporations. The corporate balance sheet provides a partial and distorted

EXHIBIT 5.1

Resource Utilization Revival of Walt Disney

When Michael Eisner arrived at Walt Disney Productions in 1984 to take over as president, the company was heading for its fourth consecutive year of decline in net income and its share price had fallen to a level that was attracting predators. Between 1984 and 1988, Disney's sales revenue increased from $1.66 billion to $3.75 billion, net income from $98 million to $570 million, and the stock market's valuation of the company from $1.8 billion to $10.3 billion. Yet during Eisner's first three years at Disney, initially as president, then as chairman, there was no obvious shift of strategy. All Disney's major strategic initiatives of the 1980s: the Epcot Center, Tokyo Disneyland, Touchstone Films, the Disney Channel, and the acquisition of Arvida Corporation had been launched by the previous management.

So what happened? The essence of the Disney turnaround was the mobilization of Disney's considerable resource base.

Disney's 28,000 acres of land in Florida were put to commercial use. With the help of the Arvida Corporation, a land development company acquired in 1984, Disney began hotel, resort, and residential development of its Florida landholdings. New attractions were added to the Epcot Center, and a new theme park, the Disney-MGM Studio Tour was added. These developments involved DisneyWorld expanding beyond theme parks into resort vacations, the convention business, and residential housing.

In exploiting its huge film library, Disney went far beyond its usual practice of periodic re-releases of the Disney classics. It introduced video-cassette sales of Disney movies and the licensing of packages of movies to TV networks. A single package of films licensed to a European TV network raised $21 million. The huge investments in the Disney theme parks were more effectively exploited through heavier marketing effort and increased admission charges. Encouraged by the success of Tokyo Disneyland, Disney embarked upon further international duplication of its U.S. theme parks with a EuroDisneyland.

The most ambitious feature of the turnaround was Disney's regeneration as a movie studio. As well as maintaining Disney's commitment to high quality family movies (and cartoons in particular), Eisner began a massive expansion of Disney's Touchstone label, which had been established in 1983 with the objectives of putting Disney's film studios to fuller use and establishing Disney in the teenage and adult markets. To achieve fuller utilization, Disney Studios quickly doubled the number of movies in production. Simultaneously, Disney engaged in aggressive recruiting of leading producers, directors, filmmakers, actors, and scriptwriters. In 1988, Disney became America's leading studio in terms of box office receipts. Studio production was further boosted by Disney's increasing TV presence, both though the Disney Channel and programs for network TV.

Above all, the new management team was exploiting Disney's most powerful and enduring asset: the affection of millions of people of different nations and different generations for the Disney name and the Disney characters.

picture of a firm's assets. A useful starting point is a simple classification of the principal types of resources into tangible, intangible, and human resources. Table 5.1 describes the principal categories.

Tangible Resources

Tangible resources are the easiest to identify and evaluate: financial resources and physical assets are identified and valued in the firm's financial statements. Yet balance sheets are renowned for their propensity to obscure strategically relevant information, and to under- or overvalue assets. Historic cost valuation can provide little indication of an asset's market value. A critical issue in the 1994

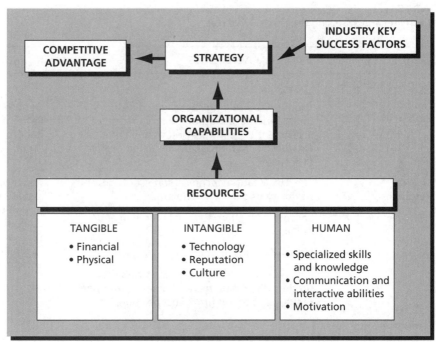

FIGURE 5.3
The Relationships among Resources, Capabilities and Competitive Advantage

battle between Viacom and QVC to acquire Paramount Communications was the value of Paramount's movie library—valued on the balance sheet as capitalized production costs net of depreciation.

Though the balance sheet provides a starting point, it is important to get behind the accounting numbers and look at basic facts pertinent to evaluating the potential of the resources for creating competitive advantage. Information that Bethlehem Steel has fixed assets with a book value of $480 million is of little use in assessing the strategic value of these assets. Where are Bethlehem's plants located, what are their capacities, what is the age and type of the equipment, and how flexible are they with regard to inputs, output variations and product varieties? Ultimately, the value of any durable resource is the net present value of the cash flows that it can generate. This is the greater of the value of the resource in use and the price that can be obtained by selling it to another firm.

A strategic assessment of tangible resources is directed toward answering two key questions:

1. *What opportunities exist for economizing on the use of finance, inventories, and fixed assets?* This may involve using fewer tangible resources to support the same level of business, or using the existing resources to support a larger volume of business. The ability of ConAgra, Nationsbank, and Emerson Electric to create value through acquisition has depended on management's ability to rigorously prune the assets needed to support the turnover of acquired businesses.

2. *What are the possibilities for employing existing assets more profitably?* A company may boost the returns to its tangible resources through utilizing them

TABLE 5.1
Classifying and Assessing the Firm's Resources

RESOURCE	MAIN CHARACTERISTICS	KEY INDICATORS
Tangible Resources		
Financial Resources	The firm's borrowing capacity and its internal funds generation determine its capacity for investment expenditure and its ability to weather fluctuations in demand and profits over time.	Debt to equity ratio Ratio of net cash to capital expenditure Credit rating
Physical Resources	The size, location, technical sophistication, and flexibility of plant and equipment.	Resale values of fixed assets Age of capital equipment
	Location and alternative uses for land and buildings.	Scale of plants Flexibility of plant and equipment
	Reserves of raw materials.	
	Physical resources constrain the firm's set of production possibilities and determine important aspects of the firm's cost position.	
Intangible Resources		
Technological Resources	*Stock of technology* in the form of proprietary technology (patents, copyright, trade secrets) and expertise in the application of technology (know-how).	Number and significance of patents Revenue from patent licenses
	Resources for innovation: research facilities, technical and scientific employees.	R&D staff as a percent of total employment
Reputation	Reputation with customers through the ownership of brands, established relationships with customers, the reputation of the firm's products and services for quality, reliability, etc.	Brand recognition Price premium over competing brands Percent of repeat buying Level and consistency of company performance
	The reputation of the company with suppliers (including the component suppliers, banks and other lenders, employees and potential employees), with government and government agencies, and with the community.	Objective measures of product performance
Human Resources	The *training and expertise* of employees determine the skills available to the firm.	Educational, technical, and professional qualifications of employees
	The *adaptability* of employees determines key aspects of strategic flexibility of the firm.	Compensation relative to industry
	The *commitment and loyalty* of employees determines the capacity of the firm to attain and maintain competitive advantage.	Record of labor disputes Employee turnover rate

more productively. Arco has greatly increased the output and profitability of its Prudhoe Bay oil reserves through the application of enhanced recovery technologies and improved reservoir management techniques. Federal Express has increased the productivity of its huge distribution network by taking over the management of other companies' distribution activities. If an asset is valued more highly by another firm, then returns are maximized by selling it. Since 1990, Chevron has reduced its U.S. oilfield properties from 1,800 to about 300. Maximizing the returns on these small, marginal oil fields has involved selling them to independent operators who can operate them more cost effectively.

Intangible Resources

Over time, tangible resources such as fixed and working capital become less important to the firm in terms of their contribution to value added and as a basis for competitive advantage. Yet, in relation to company financial statements, intangible resources remain largely invisible. For European companies, balance sheets might include intangible items such as "goodwill arising on acquisition," capitalized R&D expenditure, and intellectual property items such as patents, trademarks, and brands. For U.S. companies, however, general accounting principles have resisted the inclusion of intangible resources on company balance sheets. Yet, in 1993, brand valuations were estimated at $39 billion for Marlboro, $33.4 billion for Coca-Cola, and $17.8 billion for Intel.[10] The exclusion or undervaluation of intangible resources from company balance sheets is a major reason for the large and growing divergence between companies' balance sheet valuations ("book values") and stock market valuations (see Table 5.2). Companies with the highest valuation ratios tend to be technology-based companies (e.g., computer and pharmaceutical companies) and companies with very strong brand names (e.g., suppliers of consumer nondurables).

Brand names and other trademarks are a form of **reputational assets**—their value is in the confidence they instill in customers. This value is reflected in the price premium that customers are willing to pay for the branded product over that for an unbranded or unknown brand. Estimates of brand value (or brand equity) measure this price premium, multiply it by the brand's annual sales volume, then calculate a net present value by applying a depreciation factor to the brand's returns in future years. The value of a company's brands can be increased by extending the product/market scope over which the company markets its brands. Philip Morris is expert at internationalizing its brand franchises. Harley-Davidson's brand strength has not only permitted the company to obtain a price premium of about 40 percent above that of comparable motorcycles, but also to license its name to the manufacturers of clothing, coffee mugs, cigarettes, and restaurants .

Reputation may be attached to the company as well as to its brands. For example, Marks & Spencer, the British retailer, has a reputation for quality and customer service that extends beyond its *St. Michael* product brand. Indeed, the reputational assets of Marks & Spencer include its other relationships. Among its employees, M&S has a reputation as a fair employer that offers above average wages, fringe benefits, and opportunities for development and advancement. Among suppliers, M&S is seen as a reliable and supportive long-term partner. In relation to government, M&S has a reputation as a good corporate citizen.

COMPANY	RATIO	INDUSTRY
Northwest Airlines	43.6	Airlines
Glaxo Wellcome (UK)	35.4	Drugs
Avon Products (US)	35.0	Personal care
EMI Group (UK)	33.6	Recorded music
General Mills (US)	32.7	Food processing
TIM (Italy)	27.7	Telecommunications
Coca-Cola (U.S.)	27.6	Beverages
Dampskibsselskabet (Denmark)	26.5	Shipping
Dell Computer (US)	24.2	Computers
SAP (Germany)	22.2	Computer software
Peoplesoft (US)	22.0	Business services
Ciena (US)	21.6	Electrical and electronics products
Microsoft (US)	21.4	Computer software and services
SmithKline Beecham	21.1	Drugs
Gucci Group (Netherlands)	20.9	Consumer goods
Sophus Berendsen (Denmark)	19.7	Diversified
KVBN (Netherlands)	19.1	Food products
UST (US)	18.6	Tobacco
Schering-Plough (US)	16.1	Drugs
Cisco Systems (US)	15.6	Computer software and services

Source: "*Business Week* Global 1000," *Business Week*, July 7, 1997

Apart from reputation, technology forms the most important category of intangible resources. A central issue in valuing technological resources is ownership. Proprietary technology comprises technology in which property rights are established in law: patents, copyrights, and trade secrets. However, once we stray into the broad area of know-how, the distinction between company-owned and employee-owned knowledge is vague. Since technology is only valuable through its application to products and processes, the closer technology is to basic scientific knowledge, the more difficult it is to assess its value. Technological resources are commonly misunderstood and misvalued by top management. Xerox Corporation's squandering of the advances in personal computer technology from its Palo Alto Research facility during the 1980s is legendary. Conversely, some of the most persistently profitable companies are those that have been most astute in exploiting and safeguarding proprietary technologies: Intel, Microsoft, Motorola, and Merck are all examples.

Human Resources

From a resource-based view, human resources are the *productive services* human beings offer the firm in terms of their skills, knowledge, and reasoning and decision-making abilities. Economists refer to these resources as "human capital," which emphasizes the fact that they are durable and created through investment in education and training.

Identifying and appraising the stock of human capital within a firm is complex and difficult. Human resources are appraised at the time of recruitment, where qualifications and experience are used as indicators of performance potential, and in employment, typically through annual performance reviews. The limitations of qualifications, personal recommendation, and traditional performance reviews as indicators of an individual's potential to contribute to the performance of the organization have increasingly been recognized. Assessment methods have difficulty taking into account that most employees work in teams. This means, first, that a critical skill area is the ability to work cooperatively with others, second, that individual performance cannot be directly observed and measured. As a result, firms rely heavily on indirect and perceptual approaches to assessing performance and potential: Does Ms. Jones seem to be enthusiastic; is her demeanor "professional"; does she "fit in"?

Over the past decade, human resource appraisal has become far more systematic and sophisticated. Many companies have established assessment centers specifically for the purpose of providing comprehensive, quantitative assessments of the skills and attributes of individual employees. **Competency modeling** involves identifying the set of skills, content knowledge, attitudes, and values associated with superior performers within a particular job category, then assessing each employee against that profile.[11] The results of such competency assessment can then be used to identify training needs, select for hiring or promotion, and determine compensation. The technique was pioneered by David McClelland of Harvard University and developed subsequently by McBer & Company and the Hay Group.[12] Leading adopters of competency modeling include the U.S. Foreign Service, U.S. Navy, Eastman Kodak,[13] and Westinghouse.[14] A central feature of competency modeling is the emphasis it gives not just to technical and professional abilities, but also to the psychological and social aptitudes so critical in linking technical and professional abilities to overall job performance. For example, Amoco Corporation's evaluation of employee competencies in its upstream activities concentrates on four clusters of competencies:

- **Achieving objectives,** e.g., concern for improvement, risk taking/initiative, ownership/accountability.
- **Problem solving,** e.g., information gathering, evaluation and judgment, systematic problem solving.
- **Interacting with others,** e.g., organizational astuteness, effective communication, confidence.
- **Team work,** e.g., building consensus, coaching and development, focus on development.

The ability of employees to harmonize their efforts and integrate their separate skills may depend not only on the interpersonal skills but also the organizational context. This organizational context as it affects internal collaboration is determined by an intangible resource: the *culture* of the organization. The term **organizational culture** is notoriously loose and ill-defined. It broadly relates to the values, traditions and social norms of an organization. Building on the observations of Peters and Waterman and others that "firms with sustained superior financial performance typically are characterized by a strong set of core managerial values that define the ways they conduct business," Jay Barney identifies organizational culture as a firm resource that is potentially very valuable and of great strategic importance.[15]

ORGANIZATIONAL CAPABILITIES

Resources are not normally productive on their own. A brain surgeon is close to useless without a radiologist, anaesthetist, nurses, surgical instruments, imaging equipment, and a host of other resources. Most productive tasks require that resources collaborate closely together within teams. We use the term **organizational capabilities** to refer to a firm's capacity for undertaking a particular productive activity. Just as an individual may have the capability to play the violin, ice skate, and speak Mandarin, so the organization may have the capability to manufacture widgets, distribute them throughout the Baltic states, and hedge its resulting foreign exchange exposure. The literature uses the terms "capability" and "competence" interchangeably.[16] The key distinctions are the adjectives used to modify the terms. Thus, Selznick used **distinctive competence** to describe those things that an organization does particularly well relative to competitors,[17] and Igor Ansoff used the same term to analyze the basis of firms' growth strategies.[18] Hamel and Prahalad coined the term **core competences** to distinguish those capabilities fundamental to a firm's performance and strategy.[19] Core competences, according to Hamel and Prahalad, are those that:

1. Make a disproportionate contribution to ultimate customer value, or to the efficiency with which that value is delivered, and
2. Provide a basis for entering new markets.[20]

The value of the terms distinctive competence and core competence is that they center attention on the issue of competitive advantage. Our interest is not in capabilities per se, but in capabilities *relative to other firms*. Many companies can produce personal computers; the critical issue is whether they can produce PCs with as low a cost, as high a quality, and with as quick a distribution as Dell Computer. Establishing competitive advantage requires that a firm identify what the firm can do *better* than its competitors.

Prahalad and Hamel castigate U.S. companies for their emphasis on product management as opposed to competence management. They compare the strategic development of Sony and RCA in consumer electronics. Both companies were failures in the home video market. RCA introduced its videodisk system, Sony its Betamax videotape system. For RCA, the failure of its first product marked the end of its venture into home video systems and heralded a progressive retreat from various segments of the consumer electronics industry. RCA was eventually acquired by GE, and the combined consumer electronics division was sold to Thomson of France. Despite the failure of Betamax, Sony continued to develop its capabilities in video technology. It adopted the VHS format and went on to develop a highly successful range of camcorders.

A strategic focus on capabilities rather than products is also observable in Canon's development. Canon's technological capabilities lie in the integration of microelectronics, fine optics, and precision engineering. Figure 5.4 shows how these technologies are common to most of Canon's product introductions during the late 1980s.

Identifying Capabilities: Functions and Activities

Before we can identify which of the firm's capabilities are "distinctive" or "core," we need to identify what capabilities a firm possesses. To examine the firm's capabilities,

FIGURE 5.4
Canon: Products as Outgrowths of Technical Capabilities

	Precision Mechanics	Fine Optics	Microelectronics
Basic camera	✓	✓	
Compact fashion camera	✓	✓	
Electronic camera	✓	✓	
EOS autofocus camera	✓	✓	✓
Video still camera	✓	✓	✓
Laser beam printer	✓	✓	✓
Color video printer	✓		✓
Bubble jet printer	✓		✓
Basic fax	✓		✓
Laser fax	✓		✓
Calculator			✓
Plain-paper copier	✓	✓	✓
Battery PPC	✓	✓	✓
Color copier	✓	✓	✓
Color laser copier	✓	✓	✓
NAVI	✓	✓	✓
Still video system	✓	✓	✓
Laser imager	✓	✓	✓
Cell analyzer	✓	✓	✓
Mask aligners	✓		✓
Stepper aligners	✓		✓
Excimer laser aligners	✓	✓	✓

Source: Prahalad and Hamel, "The Core Competence of the Corporation," *HBR*, May–June 1990.

some classification of the firm's activities is needed. Two main approaches are commonly used:

1. A **functional classification** identifies organizational capabilities in relation to each of the principal functional areas of the firm. Table 5.3 classifies the principal functions of the firm and identifies organizational capabilities pertaining to each function.

2. The **value chain** separates the activities of the firm into a sequential chain. Figure 5.5 shows a typical chain of activities for a manufacturing company based on McKinsey and Company's concept of "the business system."

TABLE 5.3
A Functional Classification of Organizational Capabilities

FUNCTIONAL AREA	CAPABILITY	*EXAMPLE*
CORPORATE HEAD OFFICE	Financial management	Exxon Coca-Cola
	Expertise in strategic control of multibusiness corporation	General Electric ABB
	Effectiveness in motivating and coordinating divisional and business unit management	Royal Dutch/Shell Unilever
	Management of acquisitions	ConAgra, Nationsbank
MANAGEMENT INFORMATION	Comprehensive, integrated MIS network linked to managerial decision making	Wal-Mart Federal Express
RESEARCH AND DEVELOPMENT	Capability in basic research	IBM, Merck
	Fast-cycle development of innovative new products	Sony Hewlett-Packard
	Speed of new product development	Canon
MANUFACTURING	Efficiency in volume manufacturing	Briggs & Stratton Ford Motor Company
	Capacity for continual improvements in production processes	Toyota Komatsu
	Flexibility and speed of response	Benetton Nucor
PRODUCT DESIGN	Design capability	Swatch Apple Computer
MARKETING	Brand management and brand promotion	Procter & Gamble Coca-Cola
	Promoting and exploiting reputation for quality	American Express Ralph Lauren
	Understanding of and responsiveness to market trends	The Limited Campbell Soup
SALES AND DISTRIBUTION	Effectiveness in promoting and executing sales	Rubbermaid Glaxo
	Efficiency and speed of distribution	Federal Express L.L. Bean
	Quality and effectiveness of customer service	Singapore Airlines Marks & Spencer

Michael Porter has proposed a rather more elaborate classification of activities that distinguishes between *primary activities* (those involved with the transformation of inputs and interface with the customer) and *support activities*. Figure 5.6 shows Porter's conceptualization of the value chain. The value chain permits a highly disaggregated approach to appraising a firm's capabilities that is especially useful in outsourcing decisions. If Apple Computer's "core competences" lie in product and software design, should it not seek to outsource other value chain activities such as manufacturing, logistics, and customer service?

FIGURE 5.5
A Simple Value Chain: McKinsey and Company's "Business System"

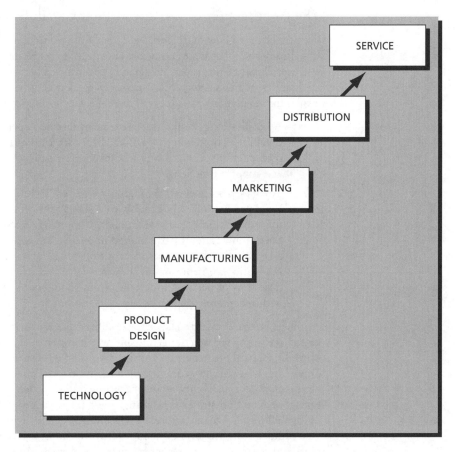

FIGURE 5.6
The Porter Value Chain

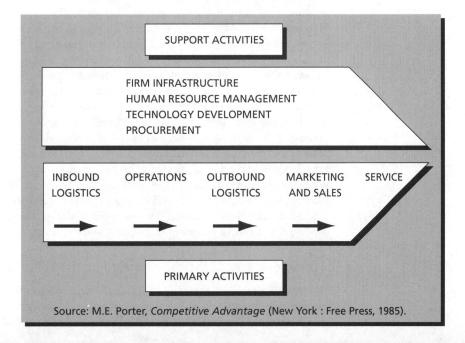

Source: M.E. Porter, *Competitive Advantage* (New York : Free Press, 1985).

The Architecture of Organizational Capabilities

We have observed how capabilities are formed from teams of resources working together. It is also apparent that some capabilities are formed from the integration of more specialized capabilities. Hence, capabilities tend to be organized hierarchically. Some capabilities are highly specific, relating to a narrowly defined task; other, higher-level capabilities involve the integration of a number of more specific capabilities. For example:

♦ A hospital's capability in treating heart disease depends on its integration of capabilities pertaining to patient diagnosis, cardiovascular surgery, pre- and post-operative care, as well as capabilities relating to various administrative and support functions.

♦ Toyota's manufacturing capability—generally referred to as its system of "lean production"—is a highly complex organizational capability requiring the integration of a large number of more specific capabilities relating to the manufacture of particular components and subassemblies, welding and assembly processes, quality control procedures, systems for managing innovation and continuous improvement, and mechanisms for the just-in-time flow of parts and materials from suppliers to the assembly plants and within assembly plants.

Within the firm, specialized capabilities relating to individual tasks are integrated into broader functional capabilities: marketing capabilities, manufacturing capabilities, R&D capabilities, and the like. At the highest level of integration are capabilities that require wide-ranging cross-functional integration. Thus, new product development capability requires the integration of R&D, marketing, manufacturing, finance, and strategic planning.[21] Figure 5.7 shows a hypothetical hierarchy of capabilities for a manufacturer of telecommunication switching equipment.

Although higher-level capabilities involve the integration of lower-level capabilities, it is important to recognize that capabilities cannot be integrated directly. Capabilities can only be integrated through integrating the knowledge of individual persons. This is precisely why higher-level capabilities are so difficult to perform. New product development requires the integration of a wide diversity of specialized knowledge and skill, yet communication constraints mean that the number of individuals who can be directly involved in the process is limited. A common solution has been the creation of cross-functional product development teams. Though setting up such teams would appear to be a straightforward task, research into new product development confirms that a key problem is the team's ability to access and intergrate the vast range of specialized knowledge that is to be imbedded within the product.[22] A major achievement of Japanese industrial corporations has been establishing the structures and complex patterns of coordination needed to integrate knowledge across a broad spectrum, and to greatly reduce the cycle time for new product development. Companies such as Toyota, Sony, Matsushita, and Canon have become models for U.S. and European corporations seeking to accelerate new product development. Chrysler's revival owes much to the restructuring of its new product development processes to imitate those of Honda.

Appraising Capabilities: The Role of Benchmarking

Objective appraisal of capabilities is difficult. In assessing their own competencies, organizations frequently fall victim to past glories, hopes for the future, and their own wishful thinking. Among the failed industrial companies in both America and

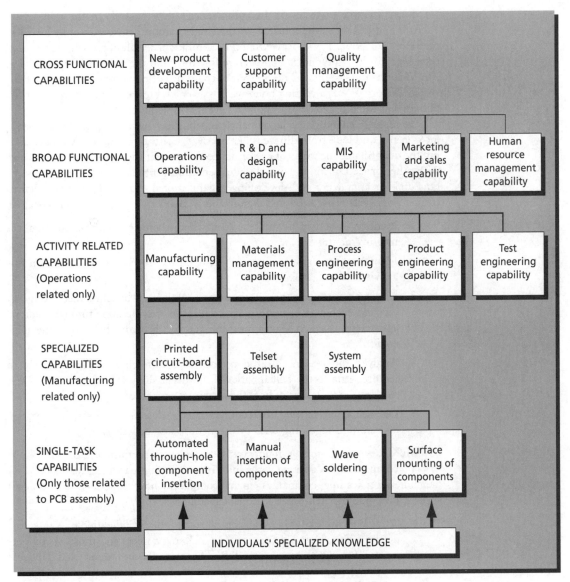

FIGURE 5.7
A Hierarchy of Capabilities: A Telecom Manufacturer

Britain are many that believed themselves world leaders with superior products and customer loyalty:

♦ Sheffield, England once supplied cutlery and silverware to the world. Its stubborn belief in its superior production skills and product quality contributed to its near extinction in the face of foreign competition.[23]

♦ Lack of domestic competition and easy access to sources of coal and iron ore encouraged complacency and chauvinism among U.S. steelmakers concerning their technological prowess and the superior quality of American steel. Neglect of new process technology and customers' preferences resulted in a rapid decline in the face of competition from imports and domestic mini-mills.[24]

Firms may be unaware of the competencies they possess. In the mid-1950s, Richard and Maurice McDonald owned a single hamburger restaurant in San Bernardino, California. It was Ray Kroc, then a milk-shake salesman, who recognized the merits of the McDonalds' approach to fast-food and the potential for replicating the McDonalds' system.[25] The Starbucks chain of coffee houses has a remarkably similar history. It was a visiting housewares salesman, Howard Schultz, who saw the potential of the original Seattle shop and eventually acquired it.

To identify and appraise a company's capabilities, managers must look broadly, look deeply, and look from different perspectives. Critical to objectivity is establishing the quantifiable measures of performance that permit the comparison of the firm with other firms. During the past decade, **benchmarking** has emerged as an important tool for appraising and developing organizational capability through detailed comparisons with other firms and organizations. Benchmarking involves five stages:

1. Identify an activity within the firm where there seems to be potential for improvement.

2. Identify a firm, not necessarily a competitor, that is a world leader in this activity.

3. Undertake performance comparisons with the benchmarked company through exchange of performance data (this may be done through bilateral agreement, through a consulting company or through a benchmarking association).

4. Analyze the reasons for the performance differentials. This is likely to require visits to the benchmarked firm, discussions with the managers and workers, and analysis of how the activity is organized and conducted.

5. Use the new learning to redefine goals, redesign processes, and change expectations regarding one's own functions and activities.

McKinsey and Company found vast differences in performance between best-in-class companies and average companies in performing particular activities.[26] By benchmarking leading companies, many companies have experienced significant success in upgrading their organizational capabilities.

♦ *Xerox.* Benchmarking played a central role in the revitalization of Xerox during the 1980s. Detailed comparisons of Xerox copiers and those of competing manufacturers began in 1979. The comparisons found that Japanese rivals made copiers at half the cost, with product development schedules that were half as long, and involved half as many people. Xerox's defects per thousand in assembly were 10 to 30 times greater than Japanese competitors. The result was the establishment of a continuous program of benchmarking in which every department within Xerox is encouraged to look globally to identify best-in-class companies against which to benchmark. For instance, for inventory control and customer responsiveness, Xerox benchmarked L.L. Bean, the direct-mail clothing manufacturer.

♦ *ICL,* the British computer subsidiary of Fujitsu, benchmarks against a variety of different companies. In manufacturing processes, ICL benchmarks Sun Microsystems. In distribution, ICL benchmarks the retailer Marks & Spencer.[27]

♦ *Bank of America's* vice chairman, Martin Sheen, commented, "We have worked a lot with the Royal Bank of Canada on benchmarking because our sizes and philosophies are comparable and we're not direct competitors. We have had some particularly good exchanges with them on processes. We can also benchmark through the Research Board against an array of competitors reported in a disguised fashion. What these do is to highlight anomalies. You can't get down to a unit cost or systems task level. But if a comparable company has 22 people and we have 60, we can sit down and try to figure out what's going on."

Every organization has some activity where it excels or has the potential to excel. For Federal Express, it is a system that guarantees next-day delivery anywhere within the United States. For Marks & Spencer, it is the ability to ensure a high and consistent level of product quality across a wide range of merchandise through meticulously managed supplier relationships. For McDonald's, it is the ability to supply millions of hamburgers from several thousand outlets throughout the world, with each hamburger almost identical to any other. For General Electric, it is a system of corporate management that reconciles control, coordination, flexibility, and innovation in one of the world's largest and most diversified corporations. All these companies are examples of highly successful enterprises. One reason why they are successful is that they have recognized what they can do well and have based their strategies upon it. Many other companies are not successful. One reason for lack of success is not an absence of distinctive competencies, but a failure to recognize what they are and to design strategy to use them most effectively.

Capability as Resource Integration: Direction and Routine

Organizational capability requires integrating the knowledge and skills of various employees with capital equipment, technology, and various other tangible and intangible resources. But how does this integration occur? The critical management issues concern the integration of human resources. Knowledge and skill are embodied within individual employees in specialized form. Economies of specialization in the acquisition of skills and knowledge mean that it is not feasible for everyone within the company to learn what everyone else knows, hence some mechanism for integrating knowledge and skills is needed. Two primary mechanisms exist: rules and directives, and organizational routines.

Rules and Directives.   Specialized knowledge can be transferred and hence integrated by means of rules and directives. It is not feasible for a McDonald's restaurant manager to learn the full knowledge of the food technologists, chefs, bacteriologists, marketing experts, and milk-shake design engineers whose expertise is embodied within McDonald's organizational capabilities. However, in the voluminous operating manuals that grace every McDonald's manager's office shelf, their knowledge has been distilled into a multitude of highly exacting operating practices.

Organizational Routines.   Virtually all productive activities involve teams of people undertaking closely coordinated activity without significant direction or verbal communication. Richard Nelson and Sidney Winter have used the term **organizational routines** to refer to these regular and predictable patterns of activity made up of a sequence of coordinated actions by individuals.[28] Such routines form the basis of most organizational capabilities. At the manufacturing level, a series of routines govern the passage of raw materials and components through the production process to the factory gate. Sales, ordering, distribution, and customer service activities are similarly organized through a number of standardized, complementary routines. Even top management activity includes routines: monitoring business unit performance, capital budgeting, and strategic planning.

Routines are to the organization what skills are to the individual. Just as the individual's skills are carried out semi-automatically, without conscious coordination, so organizational routines are based on firm-level tacit knowledge that can be observed in the operation of the routine, but cannot be fully articulated by any member of the team—not even the manager. Just as individual skills become rusty when not exercised, so it is difficult for organizations to retain coordinated responses to contingencies that arise only rarely. Hence, there may be a trade-off between efficiency and flexibility. A limited repertoire of routines can be performed highly efficiently with near-perfect coordination—all in the absence of significant intervention by top management. The same organization may find it extremely difficult to respond to novel situations.[29]

Leveraging Resources and Capabilities

Hamel and Prahalad argue that the key to competitive advantage is not initial resource endowments, but a company's ability to leverage its resources and capabilities. They pose the following questions:

♦ If GM outspends Honda four-to-one on R&D, why is GM not the undisputed world leader in powertrain chassis technology?

♦ Why has Sony, with a much smaller research budget than Philips, produced so many more successful innovations?

A firm's resource base has only an indirect link with the capabilities that that firm can generate. The key, according to Hamel and Prahalad, is the firm's ability to *leverage* its resources and capabilities.[30] Resources can be leveraged by:

♦ **Concentrating resources** through the processes of: *converging* resources upon a few clearly defined and consistent goals; *focusing* the efforts of each group, department, and business unit on individual priorities in a sequential fashion; and *targeting* those activities that have the biggest impact on customers' perceived value.

♦ **Accumulating resources** through *mining experience* in order to achieve faster learning, and *borrowing* from other firms—accessing their resources and capabilities through alliances, outsourcing arrangements, and the like.

♦ **Complementing resources** involves increasing their effectiveness through linking them with complementary resources and capabilities. This may involve *blending* product design capabilities with the marketing capabilities needed to communicate these to the market, and *balancing* to ensure that limited resources and capabilities in one area do not hold back the effectiveness of resources and capabilities in another.

♦ **Conserving resources** involves utilizing resources and capabilities to the fullest through *recycling* them through different products, markets, and product generations; and *co-opting* resources through collaborative arrangements with other companies.

♦ **Recovering resources** by increasing the speed with which investments in resources generate cash returns to the firm. A key determinant of resource recovery is new product development cycle time.

Building Capability. The dilemma facing managers is that if capabilities are based on routines that develop through experience with limited management direction, what can the firm do to establish and develop its organizational capabilities? Evidence suggests that management intervention is more effective in destroying capabilities than it is in building them. Company histories tend to support the view that a company's capability profile is highly dependent on the circumstances influencing the establishment and early development of the company. Consider the world's two largest oil and gas companies: Exxon and the Royal Dutch/Shell Group. Although similar in their businesses, their vertical integration, and their multinationality, the two companies have very different capabilities. Exxon is known for its financial management capabilities exercised through rigorous investment controls and performance auditing. Shell is known for its decentralized, international management capabilities, in particular its adaptability to a huge variety of national environments. These differences can be traced back to the companies' nineteenth-century origins. Exxon (as Standard Oil New Jersey) was part of Rockefeller's Standard Oil Trust where it played a key holding company role with responsibilities for the financial management of other parts of the Standard Oil empire. Shell was established to sell Russian oil in China and the Far East, while Royal Dutch was established to exploit Indonesian oil reserves. With head offices thousands of miles away in Europe, it is little wonder that the group developed a decentralized, adaptable management style.

The time it takes to develop and hone complex organizational capabilities also has implications for firms' capacity to adapt to change and the relative advantages of new and established companies in exploiting new opportunities. Dorothy Leonard's study of new product development shows that although core capabilities are essential for new product development, they also represent *core rigidities* in terms of inhibiting companies' ability to access and develop new capabilities.[31]

If established firms' existing capabilities represent barriers to acquiring new capabilities, this implies that in responding to radical change within an industry, or in exploiting entirely new business opportunities, then new firms are at an advantage with respect to established firms. Whereas new firms are faced with the challenge of acquiring entirely new capabilities, established firms are faced with the dual challenges of acquiring new capabilities and dismantling existing obsolete capabilities. It is notable that in personal computers, apart from IBM, Hewlett-Packard, and Toshiba, most of the successful companies were new start-ups: Compaq, Dell, Acer, and Gateway 2000. Many seemingly well-endowed early entrants such as Xerox, GE, DEC, AT&T and Olivetti were unsuccessful.

Replicating Capabilities. Exploiting capabilities to their fullest extent requires that the firm can replicate them internally.[32] Some of the world's most successful corporations are those that have been able to replicate their capabilities in different product and geographical markets. Ray Kroc's genius was in taking the original McDonald's formula and replicating it thousands of times over in a global chain of hamburger restaurants. Other leading service companies—Marriott, BankOne, Club Med, McKinsey and Company—have followed similar patterns of growth through replication. So has Toyota with automobile plants throughout the world.

If routines develop through practice and perfection and if the knowledge is tacit, then replication is far from easy. A critical step is to transfer the tacit knowledge embodied in the routine into explicit knowledge in the form of guidelines and operating procedures.[33] Thus, McDonald's has distilled its system in operating procedures and training manuals, Andersen has transferred the systems integration and management consulting skills of its leading consultants into a set of standard techniques and procedures based on the "Andersen Way."

APPRAISING THE PROFIT-EARNING POTENTIAL OF RESOURCES AND CAPABILITIES

So far, we have established what resources and capabilities are, how they can provide a long-term focus for a company's strategy, and how we can go about identifying them. We also have some basis for appraising strengths and weaknesses of the firm's resource base relative to competitors. However, if the focus of this book is the pursuit of profit, we also need to appraise the potential for resources and capabilities to earn profits for the company.

The profit returns to resources and capabilities ("rents") depend on the extent to which a firm deploys its resources and capabilities to establish and sustain a competitive advantage. We examine this issue in greater detail in the next chapter. In this section, we identify key characteristics of a firm's resources and capabilities that determine their profit earning potential.

The profits that a firm obtains from its resources and capabilities depend on three factors: the ability to **establish** a competitive advantage, to **sustain** that competitive advantage, and to **appropriate the returns** to that competitive advantage. Each of these depends upon a number of resource characteristics. Figure 5.8 shows the principal relationships.

FIGURE 5.8
The Rent-Earning Potential of Resources and Capabilities

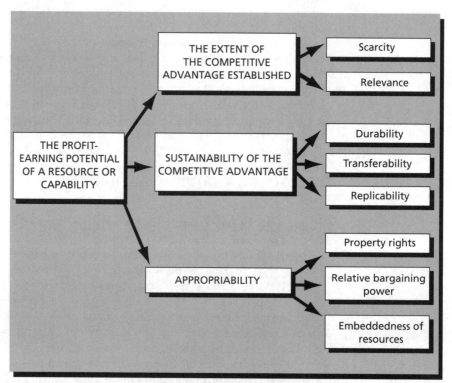

Establishing Competitive Advantage

For a resource or capability to establish a competitive advantage, two conditions must be present. First, a resource or capability must be *scarce*. If it is widely available within the industry, then it may be essential in order to play, but not a sufficient basis for winning. In oil and gas exploration, new technologies such as directional drilling and 3-D seismic analysis are critical to finding new reserves at an economical cost. The problem for firms is that these technologies are widely available in the industry from specialist drilling and computer software companies. The situation is similar for automobiles. Quality remains critical for success, but it is no longer so important a competitive advantage for Toyota and Honda since the diffusion of total quality management has raised quality standards throughout the industry.

Second, the resource or capability must be *relevant*. The British coal mines produced some wonderful brass bands. Unfortunately, these bands did little to assist the mines in meeting competition from cheap South African and American coal and North Sea gas. As retail banking shifts toward automated teller machines and on-line transactions, so the retail branch networks of the banks become less relevant for customer service. Thus, resources and capabilities are valuable only if they can be linked to one or more of the key success factors within an industry: they must assist the firm in creating value for its customers, or in surviving competition.

Sustaining Competitive Advantage

The profits earned from resources and capabilities depend not just on their ability to establish competitive advantage, but also on how long that advantage can be sustained. This depends on the *durability* of the resources and capabilities upon which the competitive advantage is based. It is also affected by rivals' ability to *imitate* the strategy of the company through acquiring the resources and capabilities needed to build the competitive advantage. This requires either that the firm purchase the resources or capabilities required, in which case they must be *transferable*, or that the firm *replicate* them.

Durability.   Some resources are more durable than others and, hence, are a more secure basis for competitive advantage. The increasing pace of technological change is shortening the useful life-span of most capital assets. The result is that industrial companies are increasingly writing down or writing off the book value of fixed assets well before they are fully depreciated. Technological resources such as patents may also be rendered obsolete before their legal life span. Reputation, on the other hand, can show remarkable resilience to the passage of time. Brands such as Heinz sauces, Kelloggs' cereals, Campbell's Soup, Hoover vacuum cleaners, and Singer sewing machines have been market leaders for periods of a century or more. Corporate reputation is similarly long-lived: the reputations of General Electric, Matsushita, and Procter & Gamble as well-managed, responsible, financially sound companies producing reliable products and offering good opportunities to capable employees continue to give these companies credibility and attention in every field of business they enter.

Transferability   The simplest means of acquiring the resources and capabilities necessary for imitating another firm's strategy is to buy them. If rivals can acquire on similar terms the resources required for imitating the strategy of a successful company, then that company's competitive advantage will be short lived. The ability to buy a resource or capability depends on its transferability—the extent to which it is mobile between and among companies. Some resources, such as finance, raw materials, components, machines produced by equipment suppliers, and employees with standardized skills (such as short-order cooks and auditors), are transferable and can be bought and sold with little difficulty. Some resources are not easily transferred. Immobility may arise from several sources.

- *Geographical immobility* of natural resources, large items of capital equipment, and some types of employees may make it difficult for firms to acquire these resources without relocating themselves.

- *Imperfect information* concerning the quality and productivity of resources creates considerable risks for firms seeking to acquire those resources. Such imperfections are especially important in relation to human resources. People are exceptionally heterogeneous and their performance is highly context-specific, particularly within team-based production.[34] The superior information of established firms concerning the characteristics of their resources creates a "lemons" problem for the prospective purchaser.[35] Jay Barney has shown that different valuations of resources by firms can result in their being either underpriced or overpriced, giving rise to differences in profitability between firms.[36]

- *Firm-specific resources* are those whose ownership cannot be easily transferred—or whose value declines upon such transfer.[37] To the extent that brand reputation is associated with the company that created the brand, a change in ownership of the brand name erodes its value. The acquisition of Harrods department store by the Al Fayed brothers raised concerns over the possible detriment of foreign ownership to Harrods' reputation as the quintessential English department store. Employees can also suffer loss of productivity from inter-firm transfer: Gilbert Amelio was less effective as Apple Computer's CEO from 1996 to 1997 than he was as National Semiconductor's CEO. There are also doubts as to whether George Fisher can work the same magic as CEO of Eastman Kodak as he did as CEO of Motorola.

Organizational capabilities, because they are based on teams of resources, are less mobile than individual resources. Even if the whole team can be transferred (e.g., the defection to Volkswagen in March 1993 of Ignacio Lopez, GM's head of worldwide purchasing, and 40 of Opel's purchasing staff[38]), the dependence of the capability on company-specific relationships and culture may mean that capability cannot be easily recreated in the new company.

Replicability.   If a firm cannot buy a resource or capability, then it must build it. In retailing, competitive advantages that derive from store layout, point-of-sale technology, charge cards, and extended opening hours can be copied easily by competitors. In financial services, innovations such as interest rate swaps, stripped bonds, and most other derivatives can similarly be imitated easily by competitors—unlike mechanical or chemical innovations, few new financial innovations can be patented.

Less easily replicable are capabilities based on complex organizational routines. Federal Express's national, next-day delivery service and Nucor's system for steel manufacturing that combines outstanding efficiency with remarkable flexibility are complex capabilities fused into unique corporate cultures. Some capabilities appear simple but prove difficult to replicate. Just-in-time scheduling and continuous improvement through quality circles are relatively simple techniques used to great effect by Japanese companies. Although neither require advanced manufacturing technologies or sophisticated information systems, their dependence on high levels of collaboration through communication and trust has meant that many American and European firms have encountered difficulties in implementing them.

Even where replication is possible, the dynamics of stock-flow relationships may still offer advantages to incumbent firms. Competitive advantage depends on the *stock* of resources and capabilities a firm possesses. These have been built up by investment over time. Dierickx and Cool show that firms that have built up strong positions in particular resources or capabilities possess advantages over imitators due to the dynamics of investing in resources and capabilities.[39] For example, "asset mass efficiencies" mean that a strong initial position in technology, distribution channels, or reputation may mean that subsequent accumulation of these resources can be achieved at a relatively rapid rate. Similarly, "time compression diseconomies" are the additional costs incurred by imitators attempting rapid accumulations of particular resources and capabilities. Thus, "crash programs" of R&D and "blitz" advertising campaigns tend to be less productive than similar expenditures made over a longer period.

Appropriating the Returns to Competitive Advantage

Who gains the returns generated by a resource or capability? We should normally expect that such returns accrue to the owner of that resource or capability. However, ownership is often far from clear cut. Machinery, brand names, or patents are normally owned by the firm that acquired or developed these resources, but even in the case of trademarks and proprietary technology, property rights are ill-defined (as indicated by the extent of litigation in the area of intellectual property). Human beings normally own their own skills and knowledge, yet there is still a vague boundary between the knowledge and skills of the employee and the trade secrets of the employer. Not only is the distinction between the knowledge of the firm and that of the individual unclear, but employment contracts only partially specify what services the firm is buying from the employee.

These issues have become prominent in a number of well-publicized cases. When Mr. Lopez and his colleagues left General Motors for Volkswagen, to what extent were they transferring their individual knowledge and expertise, and to what extent were they taking GM's trade secrets? When a group of employees leave a microelectronics company and set up their own business, to what extent are they plundering the proprietary technology of their former employer? Charles Ferguson has claimed that many high-tech business start-ups in the United States are not simply reflections of the entrepreneurial dynamism of America's IT sector, but the exploitation of corporate knowledge for private gain. This continual leakage of the technological assets of leading United States companies impedes their global leadership.[40]

In professional service firms, ambiguity over company versus individual ownership of knowledge, technology, customer goodwill, and reputation is similarly critical to rent allocation. The prevalence of partnership arrangements among lawyers and accountants reflects the need to avoid this potential conflict. Many of the problems that have arisen in acquisitions of human capital intensive companies are a consequence of such conflicts between the acquiring company and employees of the acquired company over property rights (see Exhibit 5.2).

In the case of team-based organizational capabilities, how are rents distrtributed between the firm and the individual employees who make up the team? The degree of control exercised by a firm and the balance of power between the firm and an individual employee depends crucially on the relationship between individuals' skills and organizational routines. The more deeply embedded are individual skills and knowledge within organizational routines, and the more they are dependent on corporate systems and reputation, then the greater is the firm's ability to appropriate the returns.

Conversely, the closer an organizational capability is identified with the expertise of individual employees, and the more effective are those employees at leveraging their bargaining power, the better able are those employees to appropriate rents. If the individual employee's contribution to productivity is clearly identifiable, if the employee is mobile, and the employee's skills offer similar productivity to other firms—then the employee is in a strong position to appropriate a substantial proportion of his or her contribution to the firm's value added. If the improvements in team

EXHIBIT 5.2

Our Assets Just Walked out on Us!

In the summer of 1987, Martin Sorrell, CEO of WPP Group PLC, bought Lord, Geller, Fredrico, Einstein (LGFE)—one of New York's most respected advertising agencies, best known for its Charlie Chaplin advertisements for IBM. The acquisition followed WPP's purchase of J. Walter Thompson and a string of other agencies that established WPP as one of the world's largest advertising agencies.

Friction between LGFE and its British parent, WPP, over issues of business and creative independence of LGFE reached a climax in March 1988. The chairman, president, and four top executives from LGFE left to establish a new agency, Lord, Einstein, O'Neill & Partners. They were joined on March 22 by over a dozen other key employees. The exit of employees was followed by the defection of clients. One client, the president of the *New Yorker* magazine, explained: "If you're used to working with someone who is generating ideas and helping you, you stay with them. This is a matter of personal loyalties." Meanwhile, the parent company, WPP, was busy taking legal action against the new agency, contending that the former LGFE employees had conspired to take away Lord Geller's business, while at the same time

trying to quash rumors that Lord Geller was about to close.

WPP obtained a temporary injunction against Richard Lord and Arthur Einstein Jr. from soliciting or accepting business from any of LGFE's clients. The new firm also took to the courts, charging Martin Sorrell and WPP with libel and slander.

By the end of 1988, WPP's LGFE subsidiary was in a sorry state. Despite loyalty from a few clients—Schieffelin and Somerset decided to keep its $8 million advertising account for Hennessy cognac with LGFE—many of LGFE's largest clients switched to other agencies. IBM put its $120 million account up for competition and awarded part of it to the new agency Lord, Einstein, O'Neill & Partners. Sears, Roebuck and Pan Am also withdrew their business from LGFE. Following this loss of business, LGFE was forced to lay off one third of its employees. In the meantime the defectors made quick progress: a $30 million advertising account was won from Saab Scania North America, and the court injunction against Lord and Einstein was lifted.

Source: *Wall Street Journal*, March 23, 1988: A1, 21; and subsequent issues.

performance, game attendance, and TV ratings that Patrick Ewing brings to the New York Knicks would work for any basketball team, then it is likely that the $17 million a year that Ewing receives in salary is close to the full value of these benefits. One of the advantages Andersen Consulting possesses over other consulting companies is that its skills are securely firm-based. Its expertise lies in its systems and techniques that are instilled into new recruits and honed through systematic training. Other consulting companies are far more dependent on their individual experts.

DEVELOPING THE RESOURCE BASE OF THE FIRM

So far we have been concerned with the extent to which the firm's existing pool of resources and capabilities can offer sustainable competitive advantage. However, strategy is not just about deploying the firm's resources and capabilities; it is also about *building* its resources base to extend its competitive advantage into the future.

The conventional approach to resource building has focused on **gap analysis.** Having evaluated a company's resources and capabilities with regard to relative strengths and weaknesses, the company formulates a strategy that most effectively uses the company's resource strengths against the key success factors in the company's industry environment. Comparing the chosen strategy against the company's bundle of resources and capabilities, however, may reveal certain resource gaps that need to be closed if the strategy is to be most effective in building competitive advantage.

The turnaround of Walt Disney between 1985 and 1987 (see Exhibit 5.1) involved little in the way of new strategic directions. The principal emphasis was an adjustment of strategy in order to more effectively utilize Disney's existing resources and capabilities. At the same time, these strategy adjustments also pointed to the existence of certain resource gaps. For example, the revitalization of Disney's motion picture business was achieved through heavy investment in creative talent in the form of directors, actors, scriptwriters and cartoonists. The acquisition of the Arvida Corporation provided the real estate development skills necessary to better utilize Disney's huge Florida land holdings. A rebuilt marketing team was instrumental in boosting attendance at Disney's U.S. theme parks.

Acquisitions and strategic alliances may play an important role in filling resource gaps. General Motors' strategy during the 1980s placed heavy emphasis on the need to upgrade manufacturing operations through computer-integrated manufacturing and improved quality. GM's acquisition of Ross Perot's Electronic Data Systems and alliances with Toyota (the NUMMI joint venture), Fanuc (robotics), and a number of technology-based companies were means of accessing the necessary resources and capabilities.

Identifying Resource Gaps

Some companies have made the systematic evaluation and development of organizational capabilities a central part of their strategic planning processes. Amoco, the Chicago-based oil, gas, and chemical company, has given particular prominence to the shaping and development of organizational capabilities, a task that involves close coordination between the strategic planning function and human resource management (see Exhibit 5.3). One of the techniques used by Amoco is a two-dimensional plot of capabilities where one dimension is the importance of the resource or capability to

EXHIBIT 5.3

Developing Organizational Capabilities at Amoco

Among the international oil and gas majors, Amoco is distinguished by its strong commitment to strategy analysis. Amoco's commitment to a strategic approach to managing its business is indicated by Amoco's identification of itself as "a strategically managed company," and its naming its top management team following its 1995 reorganization as the "Strategic Planning Committee." A key feature of Amoco's approach to strategic planning has been the emphasis it has given to building competitive advantage through the development of organizational capability. This has involved integration of strategic planning with human resource management: the strategic planning process identifies the organizational capabilities needed to implement the strategy. HR is responsible for evaluating these capabilities and developing them through recruitment, training, and incentives.

The analysis and development of organizational capabilities is the responsibility of the Organizational Capability Group within Amoco's Human Resources Department. The methods include:

♦ Identifying "capability gaps" by determining the capabilities required by different businesses and functions (Amoco distinguishes those capabilities "needed to win" from those capabilities "needed to play"), and assessing Amoco's performance relative to competitors in terms of superiority or inferiority.

♦ Linking organizational capabilities to individual skills and aptitudes using Competency Modeling—a technique developed by the Macabre Associates (now part of the Hay Group) that identifies the combination of individual competencies required for a particular job type, and a methodology for assessing each individual's competencies against the profile created.

♦ Using the results of these analyses to guide employee appraisal, training, recruitment, and promotion.

The figure below shows the organization capability building process in terms of the link between strategy formulation and human resource management.

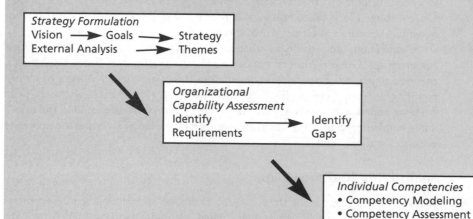

competitive advantage in the business, and the other is the company's strength in that resource or capability relative to competitors. Key gaps exist where a resource or capability is critical to competitive advantage, but where the company's position is one of inferiority to competitors.

Let's look at a hypothetical analysis of the resources and capabilities of Volkswagen A.G. The starting point is to identify the resources and capabilities most important to competitive advantage within the industry. This involves looking not just at the relevance of resources and capabilities to the key success factors of the industry, but also at the other factors that determine rent-earning potential: scarcity, durability, mobility, replicability, and appropriability (see Figure 5.8). Having identified the key resources and capabilities, we can then assess the position of the company relative to industry averages. Table 5.4 lists some of the principal resources and capabilities needed to compete in the world auto industry and assesses VW's competitive position in relation to each. Figure 5.9 plots these on a two-dimensional display. The four quadrants of this display show the main implications of this analysis for strengths and weaknesses and areas for development.

Dynamic Resource Fit

This resource gap approach takes an overly static view of resource analysis. As we examine more fully in the next chapter, competition is a dynamic process in which a firm's competitive advantage is constantly being eroded through imitation and innovation. Michael Porter argues that it is continuous investment in resources and capabilities that is the key to competitive advantage over the long haul.

> Firms create and sustain competitive advantage because of the capacity to continuously improve, innovate, and upgrade their competitive advantages over time. Upgrading is the process of shifting advantages throughout the value chain to more sophisticated types and employing higher levels of skill and technology.[41]

Investment in upgrading resources and capabilities can occur naturally through organizational learning. Hiroyuki Itami has introduced the concept of **dynamic resource fit** to describe the process through which the pursuit of a strategy not only utilizes a firm's resources, but also augments them through the creation of skills and knowledge that are the products of experience.

> Effective strategy in the present builds invisible assets, and the expanded stock enables the firm to plan its future strategy to be carried out. And the future strategy must make effective use of the resources that have been amassed.[42]

Matsushita's multinational expansion has closely followed this principle of parallel and sequential development of strategy and resources. In developing production in a foreign country, Matsushita has typically begun with the production of batteries, then moved on the production of products requiring greater manufacturing and marketing sophistication. Arataroh Takahashi explained the strategy:

> In every country batteries are a necessity, so they sell well. As long as we bring a few advanced automated pieces of equipment for the processes vital to final product quality, even unskilled labor can produce good products. As

TABLE 5.4
Appraising VW's resources and capabilities

RESOURCES	IMPORTANCE[1]	VW'S RELATIVE STRENGTH[2]	COMMENTS
R1. Finance	5	4	VW's financial position weakened by poor cash flows and restructuring costs
R2. Technology	7	5	Despite technical strengths, VW's R&D budgets, patents and recent innovations inferior to GM, Ford, Toyota and Honda
R3. Plant and equipment	8	6	Heavy investment in upgrading manufacturing facilities
R4. Location (proximity to key markets and low cost inputs)	7	3	High-cost German base, weak in United States, strong in Eastern Europe and Latin America
R5. Distribution (dealership network)	8	4	Dealership network less geographically extensive than Ford, GM, or Toyota
CAPABILITIES			
C1. Product development	9	4	Traditional weakness of VW: unable to repeat success of the Beetle or Vanagon
C2. Purchasing	7	5	Traditionally weak—strengthened by Lopez
C3. Engineering	7	9	The core technical strength of VW
C4. Manufacturing	8	5	Problems of high costs, inflexibility, and indifferent quality largely resolved
C5. Financial management	6	3	Has traditionally lacked a strong financial orientation
C6. R&D	6	6	A comparative strength of VW, but becoming less important as technology shifts increasingly to suppliers
C7. Marketing and sales	9	4	Weak in recognizing and meeting customer needs in different national markets
C8. Government relations	4	8	Important in emerging markets

[1] Both scales range from 1 to 10 (1 = very low, 10 = very high).
[2] VW's resources and capabilities are compared against those of GM, Ford, Toyota, Honda, Chrysler, Nissan, Honda, Fiat, and PSA, where 5 represents parity.

they work on this rather simple product, the workers get trained, and this increased skill level then permits us to gradually expand production to items with increasingly higher technology levels, first radios, then televisions.[43]

FIGURE 5.9
Appraising VW'S
Resources and
Capabilities

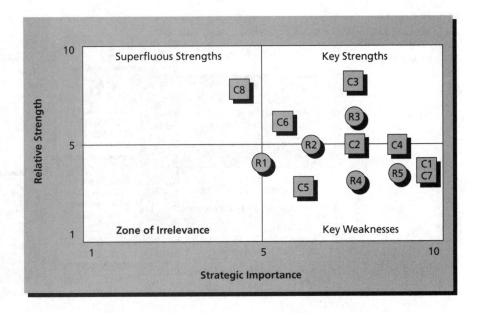

This dynamic resource fit may also provide a strong basis for a firm's diversification. Sequential product addition as expertise and knowledge is acquired is a prominent feature of the strategies of Honda in extending its product range from motorcycles, to cars, to lawn mowers, and boat engines, and of 3M in expanding from abrasives, to adhesives, to computer disks, to video and audiotape, and a broad range of consumer and producer goods.

◆ SUMMARY

We have shifted the focus of our attention from the external to the internal environment of the firm. This internal environment comprises many features of the firm, but for the purposes of strategy analysis, the key issue is what the firm can *do*. This means looking at the resources of the firm and the way resources are brought together to create organizational capabilities. The key chracteristics of resources and capabilities that determine their potential for earning profits for the firm have been identified. At the same time there are other important strategy issues that have remained unresolved. Can firms develop entirely new capabilities, or must top management recognize that distinctive capabilities are the result of building and honing capabilities over long periods of time through processes that are poorly understood? If that is the case, strategy must be concerned with exploiting, preserving, and developing the firm's pool of resources and capabilities, rather than changing them. The resource and capability-based approaches to strategy are still relatively young. There is much to learn. Most of this learning will come from the careful observation of companies as they face the challenges of acquiring, building, and deploying resources and capabilities.

Although much of the discussion has been conceptual and theory-based, the issues are practical. Figure 5.10 emphasizes the applicability of the concepts and

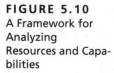

FIGURE 5.10
A Framework for
Analyzing
Resources and Capa-
bilities

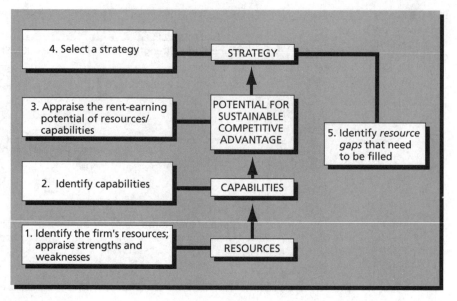

techniques we have covered by summarizing the principal stages in the analysis of resources and capabilities.

Because the resources and capabilities of the firm form the foundation for building competitive advantage, we shall return again and again to the concepts of this chapter. Our first port of call is the structures and systems through which the firm deploys its resources, builds and exercises its capabilities, and implements its strategy.

NOTES

1 Analysis of the internal environment of the firm has also been given prominence by researchers who have investigated the *process* of strategy formulation. Researchers who have approached strategy formulation from a behavioral science perspective view strategy formulation not as rational optimizing decisions made with objective information, but either as an evolving pattern of decisions and actions (see Henry Mintzberg, "Crafting Strategy," *Harvard Business Review* (July–August 1987): 66–75), or as a political process within the firm, (see Andrew M. Pettigrew, "Strategy Formulation as a Political Process," *International Studies of Management and Organization* 7, no. 2 (1977): 78–87.

2 B. H. Liddell Hart, *Strategy* (New York: Praeger, 1954): 365.

3 The "resource-based view" is described in J. B. Barney, "Firm Resources and Sustained Competitive Advantage," *Journal of Management* 17 (1991): 99–120; J. Mahoney and J. R. Pandian, "The Resource-Based View Within the Conversation of Strategic Management," *Strategic Management Journal* 13 (1992): 363–380; M. A. Peterlaf, "The Cornerstones of Competitive Advantage: A Resource-Based View," *Strategic Management Journal* 14 (1993): 179–192; David Collis and Cynthia Montgomery, "Competing on Resources: Strategy in the 1990s," *Harvard Business Review* (July–August 1995): 119–128.

4 J. B. Quinn emphasizes the need for companies to focus their strategies around the activities of their key internal strengths in *Intelligent Enterprise* (New York: Free Press, 1992).

5 Theodore Levitt, "Marketing Myopia," *Harvard Business Review* (July–August 1960): 24–47.

6 Robert M. Grant, "Diversification in Financial Services: Why Are the Benefits So Elusive?" In A. Campbell and K. Luchs (eds.), *Strategic Synergy* (London: Heinemann, 1994).

7 "Olivetti: On the Ropes," *Economist*, May 20, 1995: 60–61.

8 "Blurred Image: Kodak Moment Came Early for CEO Fisher, Who Takes a Stumble," *Wall Street Journal*, July 25, 1997: A1.

9 Richard P. Rumelt, "How Much Does Industry Matter?" *Strategic Management Journal* 12 (1991): 167–185, found that among 2,180 business units, only 4 percent of the variance of return on assets was attributable to the influence of industry.

10 "Coke and Chips," *Financial Times*, September 2, 1993: 7.

11 Edward Lawler, "From Job-Based to Competency-Based Organizations," *Journal of Organizational Behavior* 15 (1994): 3–15.

12 See Lyle Spencer, David McClelland, and S. Spencer, *Competency Assessment Methods: History and State of the Art*, Hay/McBer Research Group (1994); Kathryn Cofsky, "Critical Keys to Competency-Based Pay," *Compensation and Benefits Review* (November–December 1993): 46–52.

13 J. Boroski, D. Blancero, and L. Dyer, "Competency Implications of Changing Human Resource Roles," Center for Advanced Human Resource Studies, Working paper 94–31, Cornell University, 1994.

14 E. G. Vogely and L. J. Schaeffer, "Link Employee Pay to Competencies and Objectives," *HR Magazine* (October 1995): 75–81.

15 Jay Barney, "Organizational Culture: Can It Be a Source of Sustained Competitive Advantage?" *Academy of Management Review* 11 (1986): 656–665.

16 While some attempts have been made to differentiate the two, Gary Hamel and C. K. Prahalad argue in a letter, *Harvard Business Review* (May–June 1992): 164–165, that "the distinction between competencies and capabilities is purely semantic."

17 P. Selznick, *Leadership in Administration: A Sociological Interpretation* (New York: Harper & Row, 1957).

18 Igor Ansoff, *Corporate Strategy* (Harmondsworth: Penguin, 1965).

19 C. K. Prahalad and Gary Hamel, "The Core Competences of the Corporation," *Harvard Business Review* (May–June 1990): 79–91.

20 Gary Hamel and C. K. Prahalad, letter, *Harvard Business Review* (May–June 1992): 164–165.

21 For an illuminating description of the integration of functional and technical capabilities to develop new automobiles, see Clark and Fujimoto (1991).

22 K. B. Clark and T. Fujimoto, *Product Development Performance* (New York: Free Press, 1991); and K. Imai, I. Nonaka, and H. Takeuchi, "Managing the New Product Development Process: How Japanese Companies Learn and Unlearn," in *The Uneasy Alliance*, ed. K. Clark, R. Hayes, and C. Lorenz (Boston: Harvard Business School Press, 1985).

23 Robert M. Grant, "Business Strategy and Strategy Change in a Hostile Environment: Failure and Success Among British Cutlery Producers," in *The Management of Strategic Change*, ed. Andrew Pettigrew (Oxford: Basil Blackwell, 1987).

24 Paul R. Lawrence and Davis Dyer, *Renewing American Industry* (New York: Free Press, 1983): 60–83.

25 McDonald's Web Site (http://www.mcdonalds.com).

26 S. Walleck, D. O'Halloran, and C. Leader, "Benchmarking World-Class Performance," *McKinsey Quarterly* 1 (1991).

27 "First Find Your Bench," *The Economist*, May 11, 1991: 102.

28 R. R. Nelson and S. G. Winter, *An Evolutionary Theory of Economic Change* (Cambridge, MA: Belknap, 1982).

29 This observation is supported by John Freeman and Michael Hannan, "Niche Width and the Dynamics of Organizational Populations," *American Journal of Sociology* 88 (1984): 1116–1145, who observe that in the restaurant industry, specialists survived better than generalists (except where the environment was highly variable, in which case generalists displayed greater adaptability).

30 Gary Hamel and C. K. Prahalad, *Competing for the Future* (Boston: Harvard Business School Press, 1994).

31 Dorothy Leonard-Barton, "Core Capabilities and Core Rigidities," *Strategic Managment Journal*, Special Issue (Summer 1992): 111–126.

32 Sid Winter, "The Four Rs of Profitability: Rents, Resources, Routines, and Replication," in *Resource-Based and Evolutionary Theories of the Firm*, ed. Cynthia Montgomery (Boston: Kluwer, 1995): 147–178.

33 I. Nonaka and H. Takeuchi, *The Knowledge-Creating Company* (New York: Oxford University Press, 1995): chapter 3.

34 A. A. Alchian and H. Demsetz, "Production, Information Costs, and Economic Organization," *American Economic Review* 62 (1972): 777–795.

35 G. Akerlof, "The Market for Lemons: Qualitative Uncertainty and the Market Mechanism," *Quarterly Journal of Economics* 84 (1970): 488–500.

36 Barney, *op. cit.*

37 My definition of resource specificity corresponds to the definition of "specific assets" by Richard Caves, "International Corporations: The Industrial Economics of Foreign Investment," *Economica* 38 (1971): 1–27; it differs from that used by O. E. Williamson, *The Economic Institutions of Capitalism* (New York: Free Press, 1985): 52–56. Williamson refers to assets that are specific to particular *transactions* rather than to particular *firms*.

38 Christopher Parkes, "Tricky Feats at the Top," *Financial Times*, July 17, 1993: 13.

39 Ingemar Dierickx and Karel Cool, "Asset Stock Accumulation and Sustainability of Competitive Advantage," *Management Science* 35 (1989): 1504–1513.

40 Charles Ferguson, *International Competition, Strategic Behavior, and Government Policy in Information Technology Industries*, Ph.D. thesis, MIT, 1987. For a summary and critique see George Gilder, "The Revitalization of Everything: The Law of the Microcosm," *Harvard Business Review* (March–April 1988): 49–61. For a reply see Charles Ferguson, "From the People Who Brought You Voodoo Economics," *Harvard Business Review* (May–June 1988).

41 Michael E. Porter, "Toward a Dynamic Theory of Strategy," *Strategic Management Journal*, Special Issue (Winter 1991): 111.

42 Hiroyuko Itami, *Mobilizing Invisible Assets* (Boston: Harvard University Press, 1987): 125.

43 A. Takahashi, *What I Learned from Konosuke Matsushita* (Tokyo: Jitsugyo no Nihonsha, 1980) (In Japanese). Quoted by Itami, *op. cit.*: 25.

6

Organization Structure and Management Systems

> Ultimately, there may be no long-term sustainable advantage other than the ability to organize and manage.
>
> —Jay Galbraith and Ed Lawler

OUTLINE

◆ INTRODUCTION AND OBJECTIVES

One of the conventions that has misled both scholars and practitioners of strategic management is the idea that there is a distinction between strategy formulation and strategy implementation. This convention holds that the formulation of strategy is based on the identification of the organization's goals and the rational analysis of its external environment and internal resources and capabilities. Once formulated, the strategy is then implemented by selecting the appropriate organization structure and managing its execution through tailoring the management systems of the organization to the requirements of the strategy. This concept of a two-stage strategy process is summed up in the dictum: Strategy follows structure. This supposed division between formulation and implementation is fiction. We have already seen (Chapter 5) that it is impossible to analyze the resources and capabilities of the firm without taking firm structure into account. The capabilities of the firm—the primary repositories of its competitive advantage—are totally dependent on the existence of a structure that coordinates teams of resources to permit productive activities to be performed. More generally, formulating a strategy without taking into account the conditions under which it will be implemented is unlikely to result in a well-designed strategy. The comment "Great strategy, lousy implementation" gives unjustified credit to the strategist. If the design of the strategy does not reflect the organization's capacity for implementation, it is a lousy strategy. The idea that the structure of the organization is integral to its strategy is reflected in Tom Peters' pronouncement that "Strategy *is* structure." Thus, for companies such as Benetton with its closely coordinated network of local suppliers and worldwide network of franchised retailers, General Electric with its 17 business groups coordinated and controlled by corporate headquarters, or Amway with its pyramid of commission-based, independent distributors, the firms' structures are fundamental to defining their strategies.

This chapter introduces key concepts and ideas pertinent to the design of companies' structures and systems. Our approach is concise and selective. Organization design is a broad and rapidly developing field of study that includes organizational theory and its applications to structuring companies and other types of organization. The goal is to introduce some basic principles and to apply these to the aspects of organizational design most pertinent to the formulation and implementation of a firm's strategy. These principles are further developed in later chapters when we consider particular types of strategy or strategies within particular business contexts. For example, Chapter 11, which deals with technology-based industries, considers the structures and systems conducive to innovation and product development. Chapter 14, which explores global strategy, examines the structure and management of the multinational corporation. Chapter 16 develops more fully the management issues facing the multidivisional company.

By the time you have completed this chapter you will be able to:

- Discuss the evolution of the business enterprise, and recognize the key organizational innovations that have shaped the modern corporation.
- Identify the fundamental principles which determine the structural characteristics of complex human organizations.
- Understand the merits and limitations of hierarchy and bureaucratic organizational principles in structuring business enterprises.
- Recognize the alternative approaches to organizing business enterprises and identify the organizational structures appropriate to particular circumstances.

♦ Appreciate the role of information systems, strategic planning, financial control, and human resource management in the coordination and control of corporations.

♦ Understand the forces which are reshaping the organization structures and management systems of companies.

THE EVOLUTION OF THE CORPORATION

Most of the world's production of goods and services is undertaken by corporations. Exceptions include agriculture outside industrialized countries where family-based production predominates, and services such as defense, policing, and education that are usually provided by government organizations. This has not always been so. Until the nineteenth century, the only large corporations were colonial trading companies such as the Dutch East India Company, Hudson's Bay Company, and the United Africa Company. Indeed, much of manufacturing was organized through networks of self-employed, home-based workers. The English woolen industry consisted of home-based spinners who purchased raw wool (on credit) from a merchant to whom they sold the yarn; the merchant resold the yarn to home-based weavers from whom he purchased cloth. This "putting-out" system survived until the onset of the industrial revolution. With the advent of water-powered looms, weavers moved to factories where, initially, they rented looms from the factory owner by the hour. Factory-based manufacture made this system of independent contractors inefficient—it was difficult to schedule machine time, and there was little incentive for the independent workers to look after their rented machines. The emergence of firms where market relationships among workers, machine owners, and merchants were replaced by employment relationships between the owner of capital and the workers was a more efficient means of organizing production. This issue of the *transactions costs* of markets versus the *administrative costs* of firms is revisited in Chapter 13.

Initially, most companies were small. Lack of transportation limited each firm's market to its immediate vicinity, while lack of communication prevented the firm from operating in multiple locations. The railroad and the telegraph changed all that. While new forms of transportation and communication created the opportunity for companies to grow, developments in organization structure and management techniques gave firms the capacity to grow.

In his research into the evolution of large U.S. and European corporations, Alfred Chandler focused on the strategic and administrative roles of top management. When faced with the pressures of managing greater complexity, managers developed new structures and techniques, including specialized staff units, systems of accounting and inventory control, mechanisms of coordination, decision support tools, and systems of communication and information management.[1] Chandler identified two critical transformations in the organization of the modern corporation. The first, during the latter part of the nineteenth century, was the emergence of the modern corporation with multiple operating units and a head office organized by function. The railroad companies (as a result of their rapid geographical expansion) were the first to establish hierarchical organizational structures with management responsibilities specialized by function.

". . . safe, regular reliable movement of goods and passengers, as well as the continuing maintenance and repair of locomotives, rolling stock, and other equipment, required the creation of a sizable administrative organization. It meant the employment of a set of managers to supervise these functional activities over an extensive geographical area; and the appointment of an administrative command of middle and top executives to monitor, evaluate, and coordinate the work of managers responsible for the day-to-day operations. It meant, too, the formulation of brand new types of internal administrative procedures and accounting and statistical controls. Hence, the operational requirements of the railroads demanded the creation of the first administrative hierarchies in American business."[2]

The growing size of firms meant increasing need for finance, while increasing sophistication of management techniques required business leaders with more sophisticated administrative and financial skills. The result was increasing specialization between the roles of owners and managers. Whereas old-time industrialists had been both owners and managers, the evolving structure of the joint-stock company supported by limited liability permitted multiple investors to be separated from salaried, professional managers with boards of directors providing an interface between the two.

The second development was the emergence during the 1920s of the divisionalized corporation, which, over time, replaced both the centralized, functional structures that characterized most industrial corporations and the loosely knit, holding company structure that was a feature of firms that had grown by merger. The pioneers were Du Pont, which adopted a product divisions structure to replace its functional structure in 1920, and General Motors, which arrived at a similar structure but from a quite different starting point.

- ♦ At Du Pont, it was the strain of increasing size and a widening product range that stimulated the adoption of a divisionalized structure. Under its centralized, functional structure, coordination among the various functional departments for each product area became increasingly difficult, and top management became overloaded. As Chandler observed:

  ". . . the operations of the enterprise became too complex and the problems of coordination, appraisal and policy formulation too intricate for a small number of top officers to handle both long-run, entrepreneurial and short-run, operational administrative activities."[3]

  The solution devised by Pierre Du Pont was to decentralize: to create product divisions where the bulk of operational decisions would be made, leaving to the corporate head office the task of coordination and strategic leadership and control.

- ♦ At General Motors, reorganization from a holding company to a more coordinated, divisionalized structure was a response to the acute financial and organizational difficulties including lack of inventory control, absence of a standardized accounting system, lack of information, and a confused product line. The new structure was based on two principles: the chief executive of each division was fully responsible for the operation and performance of that division, while the general office, headed by the president, was responsible for the development and control of the corporation as a whole including
  - ♦ Monitoring divisional return on invested capital
  - ♦ Coordinating the divisions (including establishing terms for inter-divisional transactions)
  - ♦ Establishing a product policy[4]

The primary feature of the divisionalized corporation was the separation of operating responsibilities, which were vested in general managers at the divisional

TABLE 6.1
The Evolution of the
Modern Industrial
Corporation

ENVIRONMENTAL INFLUENCES	STRATEGIC CHANGES	ORGANIZATIONAL CONSEQUENCES
Local markets. Transport and communication slow. Labor-intensive production.	Firms specialized and focused upon local market.	No complex administrative or accounting systems. No middle management.
Railroads, telegraph, and mechanization permit large scale production and distribution.	Geographical expansion: national distribution, large scale production. Broadening of product lines. Forward integration.	Emergence of functional organization structures with top management providing integration. Development of accounting and control systems. Line and staff distinction.
Excess capacity in distribution systems, increased availability of finance. Desire for growth.	Product diversification.	Increased difficulties of cross–functional cordination; top management overload. Functional structure replaced by multidivisional structure: operational management at the division level, strategic management at corporate head office.

level, from strategic responsibilities, which were located at the head office. The divisionalized corporation represented a reconciliation of the efficiencies associated with decentralization with those resulting from centralized coordination. Table 6.1 summarizes some of the key influences on the strategy and structure of corporations.

THE PRINCIPLES OF ORGANIZATIONAL DESIGN

According to Henry Mintzberg:

> Every organized human activity—from making pots to placing a man on the moon—gives rise to two fundamental and opposing requirements: the division of labor into various tasks, and the coordination of these tasks to accomplish the activity. The structure of the organization can be defined simply as the ways in which labor is divided into distinct tasks and coordination is achieved among these tasks.[5]

We begin with these two key dimensions of organization structure.

Specialization and Division of Labor

Firms exist because they are efficient institutions for the organization of economic activities, particularly the production of goods and services. The fundamental source of efficiency in production is *specialization*, especially the *division of labor* into separate tasks. The classic statement on the gains due to specialization is Adam Smith's description of pin manufacture:

> One man draws out the wire, another straightens it, a third cuts it, a fourth points it, a fifth grinds it at the top for receiving the head; to make the head requires two or three distinct operations; to put it on is a peculiar business, to whiten the pins is another; it is even a trade by itself to put them into the papers.[6]

Smith's pin makers produced about 4,800 pins per person each day. "But if they had all wrought separately and independently, and without any of them having been educated to this peculiar business, they certainly could not each have made 20, perhaps not one pin, in a day." Similarly, Henry Ford experienced huge productivity gains by installing moving assembly lines and assigning individuals to highly specific production tasks. Between 1913 and 1914 the time taken to assemble a Model T fell from 10 hours to 90 minutes. More generally, the difference in human productivity between modern industrial society and primitive subsistence society depends on the efficiency gains (including learning, innovation, and capital accumulation) arising from individuals specializing in the production tasks they undertake. The gains from specialization and division of labor are especially important in management, even if the resulting productivity gains are difficult to measure. The nineteenth century owner-manager was strategic planning manager, chief financial officer, chief operating officer, head of human resources, technical director, marketing director, purchasing manager, as well as many other functional roles, all of which are specialized career tracks today.

A critical design issue for all organizations is the optimal degree of job specialization. Although increased specialization results in efficiency gains in individual job performance, there is a tradeoff between specialization gains and the increased coordination needed as division of labor increases. The more an organization needs to adapt its outputs to changes in the external environment, the greater these coordination costs are likely to be. In general, the more stable the environment, the lower coordination costs and the greater the optimal division of labor. This is true both for firms and for entire societies. Civilizations are built on increased division of labor, which is only possible through stability. As Bosnia, Somalia, Afghanistan, and Rwanda have demonstrated so tragically, once chaos reigns, so societies regress toward subsistence mode where each family unit must be self-sufficient.

Coordination

How do individuals undertaking specialized tasks within the firm coordinate their efforts? In the market, coordination is achieved through the **price mechanism**. Price mechanisms also exist within firms. Different departments and divisions may trade on an arm's-length basis where prices are either negotiated or set by corporate headquarters. Though many companies replicate markets internally, the existence of firms reflects the fact that the firm has access to coordination mechanisms that are not available to external markets. The simplest form of coordination involves the mutual adjustment of individuals engaged in related tasks. In soccer or doubles tennis, each player coordinates with fellow team members without any authoritative relationship between or among them. Such mutual adjustment occurs in leaderless teams and work groups. In the case of recurrent activities, efficiency requires that coordination based on mutual adjustment become institutionalized within organizational routines.

Most forms of coordination within organizations involve some form of authority being exercised. This may involve direct supervision through issuing directives: "Iron my *Wall Street Journal*, Smithers," or establishing rules to govern the work of others. Such rules may involve specifications as to how tasks are to be performed: "Place the slice of pickle at the center of the hamburger, spread 0.5 ounces of mustard on the lower side of the top half of the bun . . .," or they may specify required performance standards: "The yield rate from our car-door stamping press is to exceed 95 percent for every shift, except New Year's Day."

Cooperation and Control

The discussion of coordination has dealt only with the technical problem of integrating the actions of different individuals within the organization. Coordination, however, is not simply a technical issue—it is confounded by the problems of different goals among different organizational members. The organizational literature has found it useful to distinguish the technical aspects of achieving effective coordination from the goal-conflict and goal-alignment issues associated with achieving cooperation.[7]

The problem of goal alignment is referred to in the economics literature as the *agency problem*. An **agency relationship** exists when one party (the principal) contracts with another party (the agent) to act on behalf of the principal. The problem of such a relationship is ensuring that the agent acts in the principal's interest. Within the firm, attention has focused on the agency problem that exists between owners (shareholders) and professional managers. The problem of ensuring that managers operate companies to maximize shareholder wealth is at the center of the corporate governance debate. Changes in the way that top managers are remunerated, in particular the increasing emphasis given to stock options and profit-based bonuses, are efforts to improve the alignment of manager and shareholder interests. At the same time, such incentives impose significant costs: stock options and profit-related bonuses are absorbing a growing proportion of companies' operating profits.

Agency problems exist throughout the hierarchy. For individual employees, systems of incentives, monitoring, and appraisal are designed to encourage employees to pursue organizational objectives and overcome employees' tendency either to seek their own self-interest or simply to shirk. The organization structure and its related cultures may itself create problems. Either unintentionally or by design, organizational units create their own subgoals that may not be fully aligned with the overall organizational goals. Such subgoals are typically associated with the individual functional departments of the firm.[8] Bruce Henderson, founder of the Boston Consulting Group, has observed: "Every production man's dream is a factory that always runs at full capacity making a single product that requires no change . . . every salesman would like to give every customer whatever he wants immediately."[9]

Hierarchy

Hierarchy is fundamental to the structure of all organizations. Herbert Simon goes further and identifies hierarchy as present in virtually all complex systems. If a hierarchy is defined as a system composed of interrelated subsystems, examples of hierarchy include:

- The human body, which is composed of a hierarchy of cells, organs, and subsystems such as the respiratory system, nervous system, digestive system, and so on.

- Physical systems are composed at the macro level of planets, stars, and galaxies, and at the micro level of subatomic particles, atoms, and molecules.

- Social systems consist of individuals, families, communities, tribes or socio-economic groups, and nations.

- A book consists of letters, words, sentences, paragraphs, and chapters.

Note that this is a broader concept of hierarchy than that encountered in most discussions of organization design, where hierarchy is identified with *administrative hierarchy* in which organizational members are arranged in superior-subordinate relationships and authority flows downward from the top.

There are two key advantages to hierarchical structures. The first is adaptability. Simon argues that hierarchical forms have the capacity to evolve more rapidly than unitary systems, which are not organized into subsystems. The adaptability of hierarchical systems requires some degree of *decomposability*: the ability of component subsystems to operate with some measure of independence from other subsystems. Thus, in the case of the automobile, its modular structure permits different subassemblies (power units, brakes, air bags, and electronic guidance systems) to be developed without constant communication and coordination with the designers of every other unit. Similarly, defects can be corrected by replacing a single subunit—the engine, the gearbox, or the exhaust system—without having to scrap the entire car. These same advantages exist in modular organizations such as the multidivisional firm: strategic and operational improvements can occur in GE's domestic appliance businesses without requiring the involvement of managers in jet engines and GE Capital. Similarly, GE can acquire a new business or dispose of an existing subsidiary (e.g., Kidder Peabody) without requiring organizational changes throughout the company. The benefits of modular design with *loose coupling* of organizational units is being increasingly recognized in the academic literature.[10]

The second advantage of hierarchy is in economizing on coordination. As we have noted, the gains from specialization come at the cost of coordination. Suppose there are four programmers designing a piece of customized computer software. If they are structured as a "self-organized team," where coordination is by mutual adjustment (see Figure 6.1a), six interpersonal interactions must be managed. Alternatively, suppose the programmer with the biggest feet is selected to be supervisor. In this single hierarchy (Figure 6.1b), there are only three relationships to be managed. However, this says nothing about the quality of the coordination. For instance, the coordination achieved when each team member interacts directly with every other team member may be more effective than when all coordination occurs through a supervisor. The flexibility advantages of modularity and efficiency advantages of hierarchical communication are evident in Nelson Mandela's restructuring of the ANC (see Exhibit 6.1). Let's look more closely at administrative hierarchies associated with *bureaucratic* or *mechanistic* organizational forms.

FIGURE 6.1
Hierarchy Can Econo-
mize on Coordination

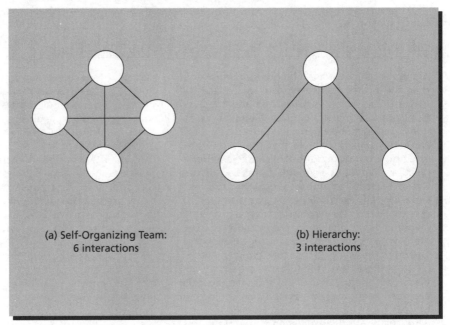

(a) Self-Organizing Team:
6 interactions

(b) Hierarchy:
3 interactions

Bureaucracy

If hierarchy is the basic organizational form for all complex systems, the *administrative hierarchy*, in which power is located at the apex of the hierarchy and delegated downward, has been the basis for structuring most large organizations since early Chinese civilization. Administrative hierarchies operate as *bureaucracies*, the principles of which, according to Max Weber, writing at the end of the nineteenth century, are:

1. *Rational-legal authority* based on "Belief in the legality of enacted rules and the right of those elevated to authority under such rules to issue commands"

2. *Specialization* through a "systematic division of labor" with clear job definitions and individual authority limited to the sphere of work responsibilities

3. *Hierarchical structure* with "each lower office under the control and supervision of a higher one"

4. *Coordination* and *control* through rules and standard operating procedures

5. *Standardized employment rules and norms*

6. *Separation of management and ownership*

7. *Separation of jobs and people*: the organization is defined by positions and their associated responsibilities and authority, not by individuals; there is no ownership of the position by the individual

8. *Formalization* in writing of "administrative acts, decisions, and rules."[11]

The bureaucratic form of organization is highly formalized, eliminating most of the features that characterize human societies and human behavior: cooperation, innovation, personality, variation, and emotion. For this reason, bureaucratic

EXHIBIT 6.1

Hierarchical Structures: The 1952 Mandela Plan for the ANC

Along with many others, I had become convinced that the government intended to declare the ANC (African National Congress) and the SAIC (South African Indian Congress) illegal organizations, just as it had done with the Communist Party. It seemed inevitable that the state would attempt to put us out of business as a legal organization. With this in mind, I approached the National Executive with the idea that we must come up with a contingency plan for such an eventuality. . . . They instructed me to draw up a plan that would enable the organization to operate from underground. This strategy came to be known as the Mandela-Plan, or simply, M-Plan.

The idea was to set up organizational machinery that would allow the ANC to take decisions at the highest level, which could then be swiftly transmitted to the organization as a whole without calling a meeting. In other words, it would allow the organization to continue to function and enable leaders who were banned to continue to lead. The M-Plan was designed to allow the organization to recruit new members, respond to local and national problems and maintain regular contact between the membership and the underground leadership. . . .

I worked on it for a number of months and came up with a system that was broad enough to adapt itself to local conditions and not fetter individual initiative, but detailed enough to facilitate order. The smallest unit was the cell, which in urban townships consisted of roughly ten houses on a street. A cell steward would be in charge of

each of these units. If a street had more than ten houses, a street steward would take charge and the cell stewards would report to him. A group of streets formed a zone directed by a chief steward, who was in turn responsible to the secretariat of the local branch of the ANC. The secretariat was a subcommittee of the branch executive, which reported to the provincial secretary. My notion was that every cell and street steward would know every person and family in his area, so that he would be trusted by his people and know whom to trust. The cell steward arranged meetings, organized political classes, and collected dues. He was the linchpin of the plan.

The plan was accepted and was implemented immediately. Word went out to the branches to begin to prepare for this covert restructuring. Although it was accepted at most branches, some of the more far-flung outposts felt that the plan was an effort by Johannesburg to centralize control over the regions.

As part of the M-Plan, the ANC introduced an elementary course of political lectures for its members throughout the country. These lectures were meant not only to educate but to hold the organization together. They were given in secret by branch leaders. Those members in attendance would in turn give the same lectures to others in their homes and communities.

Source: Nelson Mandela, *Long Walk to Freedom* (London: Little Brown & Co., 1994): 134–135.

---

organizations have been described by Burns and Stalker as *mechanistic*[12] and by Mintzberg as *machine bureaucracies.*[13]

Mechanistic and Organic Forms

Although bureaucratic administrative forms dominated large organizations throughout history—particularly the military and civil service—business enterprises have exhibited a wider range of organizational types. In studying the difficulties experienced by Scottish engineering companies responding to the challenges and opportunities provided by electronic technologies, Burns and Stalker compared mechanistic forms to a less formalized organizational type where coordination was achieved primarily by mutual adjustment, jobs were less narrowly defined, and patterns of interaction were flexible and multidirectional.

They described these companies as *organismic*, subsequently abbreviated to *organic*. Table 6.2 contrasts key characteristics of the two forms.

The merits of bureaucratic as opposed to more organic organizational forms depend on the activities the organization undertakes and the environment in which it operates. Where an organization is producing standardized goods and services (beverage cans, property tax collections, haircuts for army inductees), using well-understood processes, in an environment where change is slow and predictable, then the bureaucratic model with its standard operating procedures and high levels of specialization offers tremendous efficiency advantages. The problems occur when the bureaucratic model has to produce heterogeneous outputs from heterogeneous inputs, using poorly understood technologies, in an environment where change requires constant adjustment. Here the bureaucratic system fails. In some instances, firms may attempt to retain the advantages of bureaucracy by attempting to control variation in the outside environment. The business system perfected by McDonald's is highly mechanistic, including reliance on highly standardized, formalized working practices that are carefully documented in McDonald's operating procedures. This system can only work by McDonald's carefully controlling its inputs to reduce variation: potatoes are carefully selected for size and shape, managers are carefully selected and trained, consumer tastes and expectations are carefully managed through advertising and promotion.

In most organizations, the extent to which a department or unit corresponds to mechanistic or organic type depends on these factors. Thus in most companies, payroll, treasury, taxation, customer support, and purchasing activities tend to be organized along bureaucratic principles; research, new product development, marketing, and business process reengineering tend to be more organic.

TABLE 6.2
Mechanistic vs. Organic Organizational Forms

FEATURE	MECHANISTIC	ORGANIC
Task definition	Rigid and highly specialized	Flexible and less narrowly defined
Coordination and control	Rules and directives vertically imposed	Mutual adjustment, common culture
Communication	Vertical	Vertical and horizontal
Knowledge	Centralized	Dispersed
Commitment and loyalty	To immediate superior	To the organization and its goals
Environmental context	Stable with low technological uncertainty	Unstable with significant technological uncertainty and ambiguity

Source: Adapted from Richard Butler, *Designing Organizations: A Decision-Making Perspective* (London: Routledge, 1991): 76.

The Decline of Bureaucracy

The current unpopularity of bureaucracy in large companies and the movement toward delayering hierarchies can be linked to changes in the nature of the business environment. Global competition, deregulation, and accelerating technological change have made the business environment of most companies less stable and less predictable. These changes have revealed the shortcomings of administrative hierarchy organized along bureaucratic principles.

In the hierarchical model with centralized power and where each manager has a fixed span of control, increases in the size of the firm, in terms of numbers of employees, implies increases in the number of layers of hierarchy. Thus, with a fixed span of control of three, a firm with 4 employees (including the CEO) is organized into two layers, 5 to 13 employees require three layers, from 14 to 41 employees require four layers, and 42 to 122 employees require five layers. (Sketch this for yourself.) Unless the hierarchy can be decomposed into loosely coupled modules, then hierarchical structures suffer from slower and slower decision making and increased loss of control as the size of the organization increases.[14]

The movement to reform and restructure corporate hierarchies does not amount to a rejection of hierarchy as an organizing principle. So long as there are benefits from the division of labor, then hierarchy is inevitable. The critical issues relate to the design and operation of the hierarchy. Two major concerns relate to excessive centralization of decision making and the costs of administration:

Centralization.   Centralized decision making within hierarchies means that information must flow up the hierarchy, and decisions flow down. In fast-moving environments, the key issue is how to preserve the benefits of division of labor while avoiding the inflexibility and slow decision making associated with conventional approaches to coordination. Delayering is an obvious means by which top management can be drawn closer to the organizational front-line without abdicating decision-making power. The key to delayering is to increase managers' spans of control. For Jack Welch at General Electric, widening spans of control has been fundamental to the organization changes he pioneered. Widening spans of control typically involves forcing managers to work harder and changes the basis of control from *supervision* toward *accountability*. Delayering also involves shifting coordination from vertical control processes to more horizontal, voluntaristic collaboration. Finally, speeding response times in large organizations requires decentralization of decision making. Critical to such decentralization is increased modularity with a move toward the loose coupling of modules to one another. The move toward self-directed work groups and interlinked teams is an attempt to create such structures.

Cost.   The trend toward delayering is also linked to increased pressures for cost efficiency. In the administrative hierarchy with a fixed span of control, we observed that increasing the numbers of employees results in increasing the number of hierarchical layers. This also means an increasing ratio of supervisors and managers to operatives. Thus, in the example above, a span of control of three implies that:

♦ With 3 operatives there is 1 administrator (25 percent of employees are administrative)

♦ With 9 operatives there are 4 administrators (31 percent administrative)

- ♦ With 27 operatives there are 13 administrators (32.5 percent administrative)
- ♦ With 81 operatives there are 41 administrators (34 percent administrative)

The Basis for Grouping

If the efficient operation of a complex system requires some form of hierarchy of units and subsystems, how are individuals to be formed into groups and units within the firm? This issue is fundamental to the design of the organization and is complex because it involves comparing the benefits of organizing on one basis to the benefits of organizing along an alternative basis. Multinational, multiproduct companies are continually grappling with the issue of whether they should be structured around product divisions, country subsidiaries, or functional departments, and occasionally undergo the disruption of changing from one to another. Some of the principal bases for grouping employees are common tasks, products, geography, and process.

Common Tasks. The most common basis for organizations to group employees is to departmentalize on the basis of common tasks. Thus, an engineering company might include a machine shop, an assembly line, a maintenance department, a design engineering unit, a quality control department, a finance office, and an administrative support unit.

Products. Where a company produces multiple products, these can provide a basis for structure. Magazine publishing companies tend to be organized with a separate editorial group publishing each title. In a department strore, departments are defined by products: kitchen goods, bedding, lingerie.

Geography. Where a company serves multiple local markets, organizational units can be defined around these localities. Wal-Mart is organized by individual stores, groups of stores within an area, and groups of areas within a region. The Church of England compromises parishes, diocese, and arch-diocese.

Process. A process is a sequence of interlinked activities. An organization may be viewed as a set of processes: the product development process, the manufacturing process, the sales and distribution process, and so on. A process may correspond closely with an individual product, or a process may be dominated by a single task. Functional organizations tend to combine task-based and process-based grouping.

Intensity of Interaction as a Basis for Grouping

The relative merits of different approaches depend on several factors. The fundamental issue is achieving the coordination necessary to integrate the efforts of the various members of the organization. This implies grouping individuals according to the intensity of their coordination needs. Those individuals whose tasks require the most intensive coordination should work within the same organizational unit. Those whose coordination needs are less, or are infrequent, may be separated organizationally.

The principle of organizing according to intensity of coordination combined with the principle of decentralizing through loose coupling is the basis for Oliver Williamson's concept of *hierarchical decomposition*, whereby the organization is sliced vertically—grouping the operating parts into separate entities, the interactions within which are strong, and between which are weak. Slicing the organization horizontally means grouping activities according to frequency of decisions: operating activities involve high-frequency decision making, strategic decisions tend to be low frequency. Hence,

> the hierarchical decomposition principle can be stated as follows: Internal organization should be designated in such a way as to effect quasi-independence between the parts, the high frequency dynamics (operating activities) and low frequency dynamics (strategic planning) should be clearly distinguished, and incentives should be aligned within and between components so as to promote both local and global effectiveness.[15]

To organize according to intensity of interaction requires some understanding of the nature of interdependence between individuals and units within an organization so that intensity of interactions can be recognized. James Thompson defined three types of interdependence. **Pooled interdependence**, the loosest form, exists where the units or individuals operate independently, but are all dependent on one another's performance for the survival of the organization. Thus, in an office equipment service company, each service engineer works individually. **Sequential interdependence** exists where the output of one individual or unit is the input of the other, as in many manufacturing processes, such as an assembly line. **Reciprocal interdependence** is a mutual dependence relationship where the output of each unit is the input of the other, as in the relationship between doctors and nurses within a hospital. Thompson argued that organizations should be structured according to intensity of interdependence: first, putting together tasks involving reciprocal interdependence within the same units; second, creating links between sequentially interdependent units; finally, linking together parts of the organization with pooled interdependence.[16]

Large-scale reorganizations of corporations are typically the result of changes in the relative intensities of interdependence between employees and organizational units resulting from either a change in strategy or a change in the business environment. For example:

♦ Firms operating in a single industry tend to be functionally organized since the primary coordination needs are within each type of activity. However, once firms begin to diversify, close coordination within each business becomes more important than coordination within each function. Hence, most multiproduct corporations adopt the multidivisional structure organized around businesses and product groups.

♦ When country differences were substantial and transportation and communication between countries were slow and expensive, multinational corporations tended to organize around national subsidiaries. Globalization has involved convergence of national market characteristics and easier transportation and communication. The tendency has been for multinationals to move from geographically based structures to organization around worldwide product divisions.

Other Considerations in Grouping Employees and Activities

Coordination requirements are not the only consideration in deciding how to group together employees and activities within the firm. Additional factors include economies of scale, economies of utilization, learning, and standardization of control systems.

Economies of Scale.   There may be advantages in grouping together activities where scale economies are present. Thus, it may be desirable to group together research activities even if there is little coordination among different research projects, simply to exploit scale economies in specialized facilities and technical personnel.

Economies of Utilization.   It may also be possible to exploit efficiencies from grouping together similar activities that result from fuller utilization of employees. Even though there may be little need for individual maintenance engineers to coordinate with one another, establishing a single maintenance department permits maintenance personnel to be utilized more fully than assigning a maintenance engineer to each manufacturing cell.

Learning.   If establishing competitive advantage requires building distinctive capabilities, then firms must be structured to maximize learning. Typically, it was assumed that learning was best achieved by grouping together individuals doing similar jobs—creating a manufacturing engineering department, a quality control department, and a finance function. More recently, it has been observed that the specialized functional and discipline-based knowledge may be less important than *architectural knowledge*—knowing how to link together specialized knowledge from different fields. This implies the creation of multifunctional work groups comprising experts from different knowledge bases.

Standardization of Control Systems.   Tasks may be grouped together in order to achieve economies in standardized control mechanisms. An advantage of the typing pool and the sales department was that employees doing near-identical jobs could be subject to the same system of monitoring, performance measurement, training, and behavioral norms.

ALTERNATIVE STRUCTURAL FORMS

On the basis of these alternative approaches to grouping tasks and activities we can identify three basic organizational forms: the functional structure, the product division structure, and the matrix structure.

The Functional Structure

Single-business firms tend to be organized along functional lines. The benefits of functional structures are that they bring together similar activities within which interdependence tends to be high, and by centralizing these groups of activities offer advantages in scale economies, learning and capability building, and designing and deploying standardized control systems. Since cross-functional integration occurs at the top of the organization, functional structures are conducive to effective control by the CEO and top management team.

Coordination within the functional firm remains a problem, however. Different functions tend to develop their own goals, values, vocabularies, and behavioral norms. Though these may be conducive to integration and effectiveness at the functional level, they can make cross-functional integration difficult. As the size of the firm increases, the pressure on top management to achieve effective integration increases. Because the different functions of the firm tend to be *tightly coupled* rather than *loosely coupled*, to the extent that there is a continuing need for sales, distribution, manufacturing, and purchasing to closely integrate their activities, there is very limited scope for decentralization. In particular, it is very difficult to operate individual functions as semi-autonomous profit centers.

The real problems arise when the firm grows its range of products and businesses. Once the company expands into a new product area, the critical coordination need is between functions within each product area. When IBM entered the personal computer business, it could not build this business through its existing functional structure by asking engineers in R&D, manufacturing managers in operations, product managers in marketing, and sales personnel in sales to collaborate in bringing to market an entirely new product range. IBM established its PC division as a stand-alone operation in a location far from IBM's headquarters.

Although the long-term trend among very large companies has been for product-based, divisionalized companies to replace functionally organized companies, the trend is not entirely one way. As companies mature, the need for strong centralized control and effective functional coordination sometimes takes precedence over tight cross-functional integration at the product level. Apple Computer and General Motors are such examples.

- ♦ When John Scully became CEO of Apple in 1984, Apple was organized by product groups Apple II, Apple III, Lisa, and Macintosh. These product divisions achieved highly effective coordination among hardware engineers, software engineers, production managers, and marketing personnel. The problem was that there was little integration across products: each product was completely incompatible with the others, and the structure failed to exploit scale economies within functions. Scully's response was to reorganize Apple along functional lines in order to gain control, reduce costs, and achieve a more coherent product strategy.

- ♦ General Motors, one of the innovators of the multidivisional structure, has, over the past 20 years been moving toward a more functional structure. As GM's strategic priorities have shifted from differentiation and segmentation toward cost efficiency, it has maintained its brand names (Cadillac, Oldsmobile, Chevrolet, Buick) but merged the separate divisions into a structure that allows exploitation of functional-level scale economies and faster technical transfer (see Figure 6.2).

The Multidivisional Structure

The product-based, multidivisional structure emerged during the twentieth century in response to the coordination problems caused by diversification. The key advantage of divisionalized structures (whether product based or geographically based) is the potential they offer to decentralize decision making. The multidivisional structure is the classic example of a loose-coupled, modular organization where business-level strategies and all operating decisions can be made at the divisional level, and the relationships with the corporate headquarters are limited to corporate planning, budgeting, and the provision of common services. Chapter 16 is devoted to the management of multidivisional companies; here I outline just a few key features.

FIGURE 6.2
General Motors'
Organization Struc-
ture, 1997

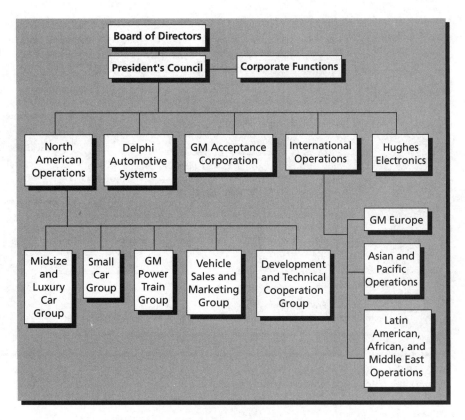

The ability to manage divisions with a common set of management tools permits a wide span of control: at ITT, more than 50 divisional heads and functional and regional managers reported to Harold Geneen. A high level of divisional autonomy is also conducive to the development of divisional heads with well-developed general management capabilities. This facilitates top management succession.

The large, divisionalized corporation is typically organized into three levels: the corporate center, the divisions, and individual business units each representing a distinct business for which financial accounts can be drawn up and strategies formulated. Figure 6.3 shows General Electric's organizational structure at the corporate and divisional levels.

Many divisionalized companies are hybrids—a combination of product-based and geographically based divisions reflecting the varied coordination requirements of different businesses and different countries and regions. Figure 6.4 shows Mobil Corporation's divisional structure. Some of Mobil's "business groups" are defined on a business basis (e.g., Mobil Chemical Company; Supply, Trading and Transportation), some are defined on a geographical area basis (e.g., South America, Asia/Pacific), others combine the two (e.g., North American Exploration and Production). Still other divisions are functionally defined (e.g., Mobil Technology Company). This mixed basis for grouping reflects different coordination priorities. The chemicals business is driven by technology and scale economies since the business is essentially the same from one country to another. The key coordination requirement is *within* the chemicals business; it is more important that Mobil's chemicals business in Germany coordinate with the chemicals business in France than with

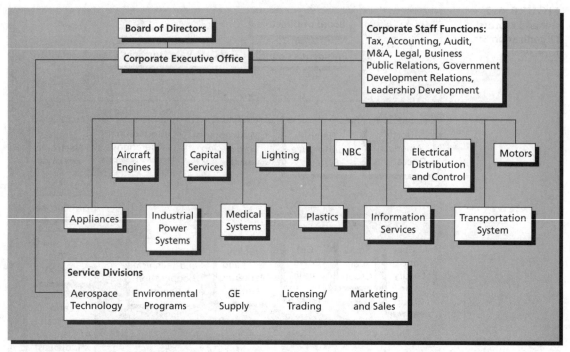

FIGURE 6.3
General Electric's Organization Structure, 1995

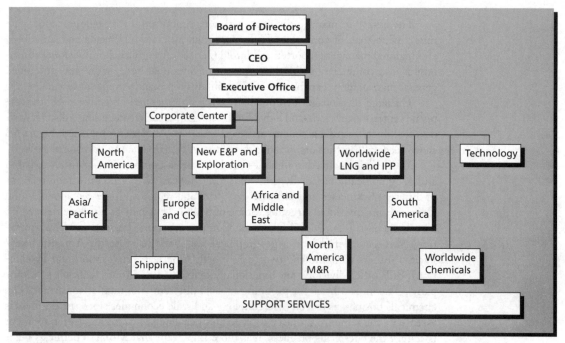

FIGURE 6.4
Mobil Corporation's Organization Structure, 1997

Mobil's other businesses in Germany. In the former Soviet Union (FSU), on the other hand, the dominant factors influencing all Mobil's businesses in the region are the difficult business environment and the need to manage relationships with governments and public sector authorities. Hence, all Mobil's businesses within the FSU are coordinated within a single business group.

Matrix Structures

Whatever the primary basis for grouping, all multiproduct, multinational, and multifunctional companies must ultimately coordinate across all three dimensions: functions, products, and geographical areas. This is formalized within the matrix structure. Essentially, the matrix sacrifices the unity of command that characterizes most hierarchical organizations (especially the military), and was regarded by Henri Fayol as a fundamental principle of effective management, in favor of a dual or even multidimensional authority structure.[17]

Figure 6.5 shows the Shell management matrix (up to Shell's reorganization in 1996). Within this structure, the general manager of Shell's Berre refinery in France reported to his country manager, the managing director of Shell France, but also reported to the business sector head, the coordinator of Shell's refining sector, as well as having a functional relationship with Shell's head of manufacturing.

During the 1960s and 1970s, many companies adopted matrix structures as a means of reconciling the coordination needs of businesses, functions, and geographical areas. However, few companies have attempted to give equal authority to all dimensions of the matrix. In general, most companies have retained some element of the "unity of command" principle by making one dimension of the matrix dominant in terms of budgetary authority, personnel reporting and appraisal, and strategy formulation. Thus, within the Shell matrix the geographically-based structure was dominant: power centered around the country heads and regional coordinators. Under the new structure, it is the business organization that has become preeminent. Where power clearly operates through one organizational dimension, hierarchical coordinations through the other dimensions of the matrix are frequently described as "dotted line" reporting relationships. Thus, in companies organized by business divisions, corporate-level functional heads cannot exercise much authority over their functional counterparts within the divisions, but coordinate through voluntary cooperation over issues such as the transfer of best practices, the negotiation of cross-divisional collaboration, and the organization of training.

The problem of the matrix organization is not that it attempts to coordinate across multiple dimensions—in a complex organization such coordination is essential. The problem is that matrix structures tend to overformalize such relationships with the result that matrix organizations tend to build excessive head office staffs and overcomplex systems. Although Shell prided itself on being one the most decentralized of the oil majors, its decentralized system of almost 200 country subsidiaries was administered by head offices in London and the Hague that employed over 3,000 people. Certainly all organizations need effective control through the standard tools of budgetary, strategic, and human resource planning, but these control mechanisms are best concentrated within one dimension of the organization. The other dimensions can be informal and more voluntaristic. The renouncing of matrix structures by many large multiproduct, multinational corporations has typically meant that multidimensional coordination remains, but the formal structure emphasizes just one dimension.

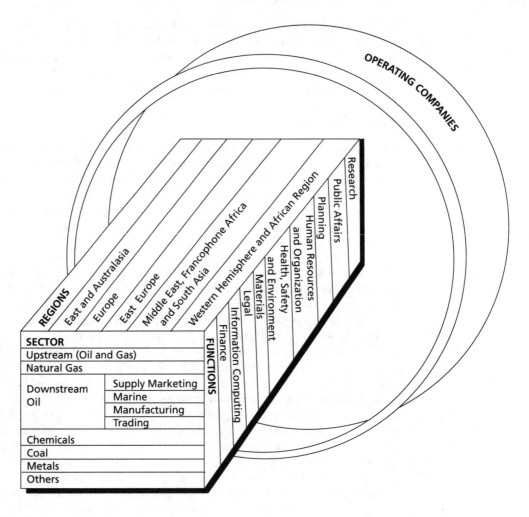

FIGURE 6.5
The Royal Dutch/Shell Group's Matrix Structure (pre-1996)

Nonhierarchical Coordination Structures

Recognition of the rigidities and costs associated with hierarchical, authority-based approaches to coordination have encouraged companies to experiment with alternatives to administrative hierarchies. A variety of organizational forms have appeared, including: team-based organizations, project-based organizations, adhocracies, cluster designs, shamrock organizations, honeycomb organizations, inside-out doughnuts, and networks. Let's look at a few of these more closely.

Project-Based Organizations.   Project-based organizations have long existed in the construction industry, oil exploration, and other industries where the work forms highly differentiated projects of a limited duration. The key feature of these organizations is the coexistence of a continuing organization structure, typically based on functional departments with a temporary organizational structure based on project teams.

Adhocracies. Adhocracies are identified by Mintzberg as innovation-oriented organizations of an extremely organic type with very little formalization of behavior and a maximization of innovation potential through the elimination of standardization.[18] Adhocracies consist of experts who collaborate in nonroutine modes often in multifunctional project teams. Adhocracies tend to exist within new product development groups, research organizations, and consulting firms. Each specialist is valued for his or her expertise and there is little exercise of authority. Adhocracies work well with activities that involve problem solving and nonroutine operations such as new product development, process reengineering, and crisis management.

Shamrock Organizations. The shamrock organization was identified by Charles Handy as another organizational response to the costs and rigidities of coordination within the large enterprise.[19] The downsizing by so many large companies during the 1980s and 1990s has involved concentrating the tightly integrated activities of the firm into a professional core (the first leaf of the shamrock). Outside this core, forming the second leaf of the shamrock, are all those activities that can be contracted out to other companies, which may include not just administrative services such as payroll administration and IT, but also key functions such as manufacturing and distribution. The final leaf is formed by a contingent work force of temporary and part-time workers who support the operation of the core, but do not require a high level of integration with core workers.

Honeycomb Organizations. Honeycomb organizations are self-organizing groups based on the characteristics of biological organisms such as beehives and ants' nests. According to Stuart Kaufman, self-organization is a common feature of complex systems involving a haphazard quest for order in the face of potential chaos. The dynamics of such systems have been analyzed by complexity theory.[20] Among industrial corporations, AES, the Virginia-based power producer, uses the honeycomb principle as its basis for organization. At AES' power plant at Thames, Connecticut, the key elements of the honeycomb philosophy are:

♦ No employee handbooks, manuals, or rules (except safety)
♦ No operating, maintenance, or technical departments
♦ No shift supervisors or maintenance supervisors
♦ No staff, except financial
♦ No "turf"[21]

Common features of all these nonhierarchial structures are:

1. *A focus on coordination rather than control.* The administrative hierarchy combines two organizational tasks: achieving coordination between different specialists and ensuring cooperation through control. A central feature of the newer approaches is their emphasis on coordination, with cooperation being taken care of by financial or professional incentives and greater emphasis on social rather than manegerial control.

2. *Reliance on coordination by mutual adjustment.* Central to all nonhierarchical structures is their dependence on voluntaristic coordination through bilateral and multilateral adjustment. The capacity for coordination through mutual adjustment has been greatly enhanced by information technology. IT eliminates each individual's reliance on the hierarchy for information

flows and permits information and communication to flow horizontally at very low cost.

3. *Individuals in multiple organizational roles.* Reconciling complex patterns of coordination with high levels of flexibility and responsiveness is difficult if job designs and organizational structures are rigidly defined. Adhocracies and team-based organizations feature individuals switching their organizational roles and occupying multiple roles simultaneously. For example, AES has no finance function, no HR function, no safety or environmental affairs functions, and no public relations department. These functions are performed by teams of operating and managerial employees. Thus, at AES' Connecticut plant, a team composed of coal handlers, maintenance engineers, and other plant employees gather each afternoon to manage the plant's finances, including cash management and short-term investments.

MANAGEMENT SYSTEMS FOR COORDINATION AND CONTROL

The relationship between organization structure and management systems may be illustrated by biological and IT analogies. In the human body, the skeleton provides the framework for the structure, while the respiratory system, digestive system, nervous system, and other systems provide the means by which the body operates. In a computer network, the hardware provides the structure and the software provides the systems through which the hardware operates in order to achieve the purposes of the network. Within the corporation, management systems correspond to the role of physiological systems and computer software. Management systems exercise control over the organization. Control relates to both coordination, the need for individuals undertaking specialized tasks and groups undertaking specific activities to coordinate their actions, and cooperation, the need to align the goals and behaviors of individuals and groups with those of the organization. Whereas coordination is mainly about establishing the information and communication systems and procedures that can permit individuals to relate and adjust their separate actions, cooperation involves the establishment of incentives and penalties which encourage individuals to subjugate their goals and desires to those of the organization. Four management systems are of primary importance in achieving control: the information systems, the strategic planning systems, the financial systems, and the human resource management systems.

Information Systems

Information is fundamental to the operation of all management systems. As the work of Chandler and other business historians has shown, the development of the telegraph, telephone, and computer have had a huge impact on the practice of management and the size and structure of the firm. Accounting systems too are means by which information can be collected and organized systematically, then communicated to top management and other parts of the organization.

The administrative hierarchy is founded partly on the centralization of authority that is delegated downward through the hierarchy, and partly on vertical information flows: the ability of the manager to supervise subordinates depends on the upward flow of information to the manager either from direct observation or from written reports and a downward flow of instructions.

Two key aspects of increased information availability are **information feedback** to the individual on job performance, which has made self-monitoring possible and **information networking**, which has allowed individuals to coordinate their activities voluntarily and informally without hierarchical supervision. A central element of total quality management has been recognition that providing regular, even real-time, performance feedback to employees permits employees to take responsibility for quality control, reducing or eliminating the need for supervisors and quality controllers. At Wal-Mart there is continual feedback to the departmental managers for individual product sections within each Wal-Mart store. Feedback includes information on daily sales by product line with comparisons to previous sales and to other stores. This same information system gathers and transmits data from point-of-sale scanners to monitor inventory levels, plan deliveries, and trigger reorders from suppliers. IT facilitates coordination by making information instantaneously available throughout the organization. It can achieve automatic coordination—as when electronic data interchange between Wal-Mart and Procter & Gamble results in sales information from Wal-Mart sales registers causing automatic reordering of Tide detergent.

Strategic Planning Systems

A small, entrepreneurial start-up may operate without any explicit strategy. The firm's strategy is likely to exist only in the head of the founder, and apart from being articulated through verbal communications with employees, suppliers, and other interested parties, may have been made explicit only when a business plan was required by outside investors. Most corporations with an established management structure tend to have some form of strategic planning process, though in small, single business companies the strategy process may be highly informal, with no regular cycle, and may result in little documentation. Most larger companies, especially those with multiple businesses, have more systematic strategic planning processes, the outcome of which is a documented corporate plan that intergrates separate business plans for the individual businesses.

Whether formal or informal, systematic or ad hoc, documented or not, the strategy formulation process is an important vehicle for achieving coordination within a company. As discussed in Chapter 1, the strategy process occupies multiple roles within the firm. It is in part a process for improving decision making by encouraging systematic analysis and bringing together the knowledge from individuals and locations within the company. It is in part a coordination device encouraging consistency between the decisions being made at different levels and in different parts of the organization. It is in part a mechanism for driving performance by establishing consensus around ambitious long-term targets and by inspiring organizational members through creating vision and a sense of mission. In these roles, the strategy process can be important in achieving both coordination and cooperation.

The system through which strategy is formulated varies considerably from company to company. The traditional strategic planning approach is based on an annual strategy cycle that begins with the review of the previous year's performance, reviews and amends goals for the next five years (or whatever the planning period is), then reformulates strategy on the basis of the types of analysis undertaken in this book so far. The emphasis tends to be analysis of developments in the industry environment and assessment of the firm's competitive position with regard to resources and capabilities. The firm's statement of mission and/or vision provides a foundation and guiding light for the strategy-making process. Although many writers have presented "generic frameworks for strategic planning," it is notable that there is little consistency among these different generic frameworks. Moreover, in many companies, the strategy processes are so different that the idea of a "generic framework" has little meaning. Bill Finnie suggests that in a medium-sized, single-business company, a typical strategic planning process might follow the following stages:

1. Corporate objectives meeting in which the CEO reviews last year's strategic plan in relation to the past year's performance and subsequent developments in the industry and in the general business climate. Financial goals and projections might be supplied by the head of finance, and sales projections by the head of marketing.

2. Marketing strategy meeting. A reformulated set of goals are produced and key elements of a market-based strategy are presented (possibly by the head of marketing). A revised financial plan is presented by the head of finance. Adjustments are made and integrated.

3. Long-range planning meeting involving all functional heads. A draft of the strategic plan is presented with identification of gaps between current performance and positioning and future performance and position. A discussion of how to close these gaps culminates in consensus for the strategy over the planning period together with key strategic priorities for the coming year.[22]

Generally speaking, the bigger and more complex the company, the more sophisticated and formalized the strategic planning process. However, the outcome is similar for most firms: a written document agreed to by top management and ratified by the board of directors. The document typically contains:

♦ A **statement of the goals** the company seeks to achieve over the planning period (typically 3–5 years, but longer for some companies). These goals typically include *financial goals* (with regard to revenue, cost reduction, operating profit, return on capital employed, return to shareholders), and *strategic goals* (market share, new products, overseas market positions, new business development, and productivity).

♦ A **set of assumptions** or forecasts about key developments in the external environment to which the company must respond.

♦ A **qualitative statement** of how the shape of the business will be changing in relation to geographical and segment emphasis, and the basis on which the company will be establishing and extending its competitive advantage.

♦ **Specific action steps** with regard to decisions and projects supported by a set of mileposts stating what is to be achieved by specific dates.

♦ A **set of financial projections** including a capital expenditure budget and outline operating budgets.

Although I emphasize documentation, the documents are only records; the important elements of strategic planning are the process of dialogue through which knowledge is communicated, the decision reached, and the commitment to those decisions that is fostered and recognized.

The tendency over time has been for the strategic planning of companies to change in terms of their formality, content, objectives, and the roles of different participants. A study of strategic planning processes in the oil and gas industry found:

♦ Strategic planning was becoming more heavily focused on financial goals, especially profit and shareholder return. This was evident in the growing prominence of performance targets and a greater emphasis on annual financial planning relative to longer-term strategic planning.

♦ Companies were recognizing the impossibility of forecasting the future. Strategies were becoming less dependent on specific forecasts of the future and more on statements of direction and intent, with recognition of the need for flexibility in the face of alternative scenarios.

♦ The strategic planning process has shifted from a *control perspective* in which senior management seeks to use the strategy making as a means of controlling the actions and development of business units and departments, toward more of a *coordination perspective* in which the strategy process is a dialogue permitting the sharing of knowledge and ideas and achieving a convergence of views. As a result, the process has become increasingly informal.

♦ A diminishing role of strategic planning staff as responsibility for strategic decisions and the strategy-making process becomes located among senior managers.[23]

Financial Planning and Control Systems

Financial planning and control systems relate to budgeting activities and financial targets. If profitability is the primary goal of the firm, then it is inevitable that financial systems are the primary mechanism through which top management seeks to control performance. At the center of financial planning is the budgetary process. The **budgetary process** involves setting and monitoring financial estimates with regard to income and expenditure for a fixed period both for the firm as a whole and for divisions and subunits. Budgets play multiple, somewhat ambiguous roles. They are in part an estimate of incomes and expenditures for the future, in part a target of required financial performance in terms of revenues and profits, and in part a set of authorizations for expenditure up to specified budgetary limits. Two types of budget are set: the capital expenditure budget and the operating budget.

Capital Expenditure Budget. The **capital expenditure budget** grows out of the strategic planning system. In setting strategy and performance guidelines, strategic plans also forecast capital expenditure for the strategic planning period (typically between three and ten years). The capital expenditure budget is then set for the upcoming year in terms of actually allocating funds to each division or subsidiary. The annual capital budget is determined primarily by the approvals given for individual capital expenditure projects. Most companies have a standardized approach to evaluating projects and approving them. Project proposals originate in the individual businesses and a request for funding is prepared according to a standardized methodology typically based on a forecast of cash flows discounted according to cost of capital and risk, with indications of the sensitivities of cash flows to key environmental uncertainties. For example, to estimate the net present value of a new copper mine, RTZ would make different estimates for different assumptions about future copper prices; to evaluate investment in a new semiconductor plant in Malaysia, Texas Instruments would examine the sensitivity of the project's NPV to different assumptions about the exchange rate between the U.S. dollar and the Malaysian ringgit. Capital expenditure approvals take place at different levels of a company according to their size. Projects up to $5 million might be approved by a business unit head, projects up to $25 million might be approved by divisional top management, larger projects might need to be approved by the top management committee, while the biggest projects might require approval of the board of directors.

Operating Budget.   The **operating budget** is a pro forma profit and loss statement for the company as a whole and for individual divisions and business units for the upcoming year. It is usually divided into quarters and months to permit continual monitoring and the early identification of variances. The operating budget is part forecast and part target. Performance targets are typically set by the board of directors for the period of the strategic plan. Thus, in 1994, Amoco set its financial objectives as: net income of $3 billion by 1998, an annual rate of earnings growth of 2 to 4 percent over the rate of inflation, return on capital employed of 11 to 13 percent, and return on equity of 13 to 15 percent. Each division typically prepares an operating budget for the following year that is then discussed with the top management committee and, if acceptable, approved. At the end of the financial year, divisional management is called on to review its performance over the past year.

Human Resource Management Systems

Ultimately, achieving coordination and cooperation within an organization is about managing people. Even though strategic planning systems and financial planning systems are about strategies and finances, ultimately they are systems for influencing the ways in which people behave, for example, influencing their priorities and inducing them to make certain decisions rather than others. However, the most direct means by which companies can influence their employees is through human resource management. The central issue for human resource management with regard to strategy implementation is establishing an incentive system that most effectively aligns employee and company goals. The general problem, we have noted, is one of agency: how can a company induce employees to do what it wants? Agency problems are not specific to employment contracts; they arise in all contractual relationships. When my garage presents me with a bill for $3,000 for a new engine, when all I asked for was a $20 oil change, my suspicions are aroused. The problem is greater and more complex in the case of employment contracts, because unlike most market contracts, which are highly specific ("R. Grant agrees to pay D. Hockney $4,500 to prepare all external woodwork on 2208 Cathedral Avenue, and paint with one coat of primer and two coats of top-coat, using quality gloss paint"), employment contracts are imprecise about what is required of the employee. Employment contracts give the right to the employer to terminate the contract for unsatisfactory performance by the employee, but the threat of termination is an inadequate incentive: it imposes costs on the employer and only requires the employee to perform better than a new hire would. Moreover, the employer has imperfect information as to employees' work performance. To ascertain that the employee is using the firm's computer to play games and the firm's telephone to call relatives in New Zealand imposes monitoring costs on the firm. The more employees are engaged in team production activities where their individual output is not separately observable, the greater the potential for shirking.[24]

An employment contract gives the firm the right to assign tasks to an employee within the limits of the job category specified in the employment contract, and the power to dismiss the employee failing to perform these tasks satisfactorily. The firm can ensure the employee's compliance with organizational goals using direct supervision of the type that administrative hierarchies are designed to do. The weaknesses of such administrative supervision are that there is no incentive for performance in excess of the minimum required to avoid dismissal, that supervision imposes costs, and that the system presupposes that the supervisor has the knowledge required to effectively direct the employee.

The key to promoting more effective cooperation is for more sophisticated incentives than threat of dismissal. The principal incentives available to the firm for promoting cooperation are compensation and promotion. The key to designing compensation systems is to link pay either to the inputs required for effective job performance (hours of work, punctuality, effort, numbers of customers visited) or to outputs. The simplest form of output-linked pay is piecework (paying for each unit of output produced) or commission (paying a percentage of the revenue generated).

Relating pay to individual performance is suitable for tasks performed individually. However, firms exist primarily to permit complex coordination among individuals; encouraging such collaboration requires linking pay to team or departmental performance. Where broad-based, enterprise-wide collaboration is required, there may be little alternative to linking pay to company performance through some form of profit sharing.

The process of delaying and dismantling hierarchical control mechanisms has been accompanied by increased reliance on financial incentives as mechanisms for coordination and control. If the remuneration of business unit and departmental heads is linked to their unit and departmental performance, then incentives can replace direct supervision as a control device. In the past, performance-related pay was too small a proportion of total remuneration to exert powerful incentive effects. This is changing. Among the chief executives of U.S. companies with revenues of $2 billion or more, bonuses frequently fall into the range of 50–70 percent of base salary.

Corporate Culture as a Control Mechanism

A final mechanism for coordination and control is corporate culture. **Corporate culture** comprises a set of beliefs, values, and behavioral norms among the members of a company that influence how they think and behave. Corporate culture is manifest in symbols, social practices, rites, vocabulary, and dress. Academic studies have compared car parking practices and the interior design and decor of boardrooms as indicators of different companies' cultures. As with any social group, corporate cultures are complex phonemena. They are embedded within national cultures, and incorporate elements of other outside societies: managers are likely to reflect cultures associated with professional and managerial social classes, hourly workers (other than lawyers and consultants) reflect working class cultures, each ethnic group reflects elements of its own culture. Within the corporation, culture is far from homogeneous: different cultures may be associated with different businesses and functions.

Our interest in culture is as a control mechanism that can substitute for more formal systems of coordination and control. It has been observed that organizations with strong cultures can operate with very wide spans of control (the Roman Catholic Church, Church of Jesus Christ of Latter Day Saints, and Greenpeace are examples). The value of corporate culture is that it facilitates both cooperation and coordination. Cooperation is helped by the shared values among organizational members. Thus, at Apple Computer during the early 1980s, a common culture built around the belief that Apple was leading the microcomputer revolution that would transform and democratize industrial societies permitted intense cooperation with very little formal control. As one cynic noted: "What's the difference between Apple and the Boy Scouts?" "In the Boy Scouts, the kids have adult supervision!" Similar points can be made about other companies whose cultures are dominated by a strong sense of shared values: Ben & Jerry's Ice Cream, Body Shop, Amway, Marks & Spencer, and Wal-Mart.

The role of culture as a control mechanism that is an alternative to bureaucratic control or a market system of control is central to Bill Ouchi's concept of clan control.[25] Ouchi identifies clan control as the primary control mechanism within Japanese corporations, where a powerful culture results in individuals aligning their individual goals and behaviors with those of the organization, with companies reinforcing this identification through lifetime employment and heavy emphasis on socialization during the early years of one's career. Clan control results in savings on monitoring costs as self-control and informal monitoring by coworkers substitutes for managerial supervision and financial incentives.

But the impact of culture is not only in unity of motivation; a corporate culture can also assist coordination. In large, decentralized corporations such as Royal Dutch/Shell, Andersen Consulting, and Matsushita, strong corporate culture creates a sense of identity among employees that facilitates communication and the building of organizational routines, even across national boundaries. This is especially evident in relation to horizontal communication and coordination. The unifying influence of corporate culture is likely to be especially helpful in assisting coordination through mutual adjustment in large cross-functional teams of the type required for new product development. One of the advantages of culture as a coordinating device is that it permits substantial flexibility in the types of interactions it can support.

At the same time, it is important not to generalize about the beneficial impact of culture. The way in which culture affects cooperation and coordination depends not only on the strength of the culture but also on the characteristics of the culture. Salomon Brothers has a strongly individualistic, internally competitive culture—which fosters drive and mutual understanding—but probably does not facilitate cooperation. The British Broadcasting Corporation has a strong culture which reflects internal politicization, professional values, internal suspicion, and a dedication to the public good, but without a strong sense of customer focus.[26]

Integrating Different Control Mechanisms

The past ten years has seen substantial progress in integrating different control systems. As strategy has become more and more focused on creating shareholder value, so financial goals, financial measures, and budgeting have become more closely integrated with strategy formulation. Indeed, preoccupation with profitability and shareholder return has caused a shift in emphasis from strategic to financial planning with a consequent shortening of time horizons. However, for most companies, financial and strategic planning have become closely integrated, the two being seen as complementary to one another. Thus annual performance targets for business units and departments tend to combine financial goals such as return on capital employed, and strategic goals with regard to market share, productivity, new product introduction, and the like.

Linking strategic and financial goals with human resource management has been the final stage of integrating control mechanisms. The essence of such integration is the desegregation of broad, enterprise-wide financial and strategic goals into targets for individual employees. If targets are to be effective motivators, then they must be measurable. The central aspect of the "metrics" movement within management is the ability not just to establish quantitative goals for individual employees and groups, but to create mechanisms for measuring and reporting the attainment of these targets. The balanced scorecard system outlined in Chapter 2 is but one approach to this linking of employee goals to company wide goals.

◆ SUMMARY

The internal structure and systems of the firm are not simply a matter of "strategy implementation," which can be separated from the hard analytics of strategy formulation. Not only is strategy implementation inseparable from strategy formulation, but issues of structure and systems are central to the fundamental issues of competitive advantage and strategy choice—the profile of organizational capabilities in particular.

Despite the importance of these issues, this chapter provides only a brief introduction to some of the key issues in organization design. Although subsequent chapters develop many of themes more fully in relation to particular areas of strategy and particular business contexts, our progress is limited by the weakness of theory in this area. Though our analysis of the industry environment has progressed substantially in recent decades—thanks especially to the contributions from industrial economics and game theory—organization theory is an exceptionally rich field that has yet to see effective integration of the many disciplines on which it is based: sociology, psychology, organizational economics, systems theory, and several others. Many of the concepts, tools, and frameworks are mired in organizational models and practices of a bygone age. While firms are experimenting with radically new organizational forms, we business school academics lag a long way behind in fitting our theories to the facts we observe.

The chapters that follow will have more to say on the organizational structures and management syssstems appropriate to different strategies and to different business contexts.

NOTES

1   Alfred D. Chandler, *Strategy and Structure* (Cambridge: MIT Press, 1962); Alfred D. Chandler, *The Visible Hand: The Managerial Revolution in American Business* (Cambridge: Harvard University Press and Belknap Press, 1977).

2   Alfred D. Chandler, *The Visible Hand: The Managerial Revolution in American Business* (Cambridge: Harvard University Press and Belknap Press, 1977): 87.

3   Chandler, 1962, *op. cit.*: 382–383.

4   Alfred P. Sloan, *My Years at General Motors*, (London: Sidgewick & Jackson, 1963): 42–56.

5   Henry Mintzberg, *Structure in Fives: Designing Effective Organizations* (Englewood Cliffs: Prentice-Hall, 1993): 2

6   Adam Smith, *The Wealth of Nations* (London: Dent, 1910): 5.

7   J. D. Thompson, *Organizations in Action* (New York: McGraw-Hill, 1967).

8   For a formal analysis, see R. Cyert and J. March, *A Behavioral Theory of the Firm* (Englewood Cliffs: Prentice-Hall, 1964).

9   Bruce Henderson, *The Logic of Business Strategy* (New York: Ballinger, 1984): 26–27.

10 R. Sanchez and J. T. Mahoney, "Modularity, Flexibility, and Knowledge Management in Product and Organizational Design," *Strategic Management Journal* 17, Special Issue (Winter 1996): 63–76; J.-C. Spender and P. H. Grinyer, "Organizational Renewal: Top Management's Role in a Loosely Coupled System," *Human Relations* 48 (1995): 909–926.

11   The quotes in this section are from Max Weber, *Economy and Society: An Outline of Interpretive Sociology* (Berkeley: University of California Press, 1968).

12   T. Burns and G. M. Stalker, *The Management of Innovation* (London: Tavistock, 1961).

13   Henry Mintzberg, *op. cit.*, 1993: chapter 9.

14   The control loss phenenon in hierarchies is analyzed in O. E. Williamson, "Hierarchical Control and Optimal Firm Size," *Journal of Political Economy* 75 (1967): 123–138.

15   O. E. Williamson, "The Modern Corporation: Origins, Evolution, Attributes," *Journal of Economic Literature* 19 (1981): 1537–1568.

16   J.D. Thompson, *Organizations in Action* (New York: McGraw Hill, 1967)

17   Henri Fayol, *General and Industrial Management* (London: Pitman, 1949, first published 1916).

18   Henry Mintzberg, *op. cit.*, 1993: chapter 12.

19   Charles Handy, *The Age of Unreason* (Boston: Harvard Business School Press, 1990): chapter 4.

20   For a brief introduction, see "Order Out of Chaos," *Financial Times*, August 22, 1997: 10.

21   "AES Honeycomb (A)" (Harvard Business School: Case 9-395-132, 1995): 9.

22   William C. Finnie, *Hands-On Strategy: The Guide to Crafting Your Company's Strategy* (New York: John Wiley, 1994).

23   Robert M. Grant, "Strategic Planning among the Oil and Gas Majors," paper presented at the Strategic Management Society Conference, Barcelona, 1997.

24   A. Alchian and H. Demsetz, "Production, Information Costs, and Economic Organization," *American Economic Review* 62 (1972): 777–797.

25   William G. Ouchi, *Theory Z* (Reading, MA: Addison-Wesley, 1981).

26   Tom Burns, *The BBC: Public Institution and Private World* (London: MacMillan, 1977).

III.

The Analysis of Competitive Advantage

7

The Nature and Sources of Competitive Advantage

One Saturday afternoon in downtown Chicago, Milton Friedman, the famous free-market economist, was shopping with his wife.

"Look, Milton!" exclaimed Mrs. Friedman, "There's a $20 bill on the sidewalk!"

"Don't be foolish, my dear," replied the Nobel laureate, "If that was a $20 bill, someone would have picked it up by now."

—(Economist's anecdote of doubtful authenticity)

OUTLINE

◆ INTRODUCTION AND OBJECTIVES

This chapter draws together the individual elements of our analysis of competitive advantage that have been covered in prior chapters. Chapter 1 noted that a firm can earn a rate of profit in excess of its cost of capital either by locating in an attractive industry or by establishing a competitive advantage over its rivals. Of these two sources of superior profitability, competitive advantage is the more important. As competition has intensified across almost all industries, very few industry environments can guarantee secure returns; hence, the primary goal of a strategy is to establish a position of competitive advantage for the firm. Kenichi Ohmae has gone as far as to define strategy as the quest for competitive advantage (see Table 1.1). Chapters 3 and 5 provided the two primary components of our analysis of competitive advantage. The last part of Chapter 3 analyzed the *external* sources of competitive advantage: Key Success Factors are the requirements for achieving competitive advantage in an industry in terms of the conditions that must be met to satisfy customers and survive competition. Chapter 5 analyzed the *internal* sources of competitive advantage: the potential offered by the firm's resources and capabilities for establishing and sustaining competitive advantage. Chapter 5 also noted that the firm's ability to establish competitive advantage required that its resources and capabilities be consistent with the key success factors of the industry or market. This chapter develops this analysis further, concentrating on the relationship between competitive advantage and the competitive process. Competition provides the incentive for establishing advantage and is the means by which advantage is eroded. Understanding the characteristics of competition in an industry is fundamental to identifying the nature of opportunities for competitive advantage. The goal is to draw together ideas of competition, success factors, and the returns to resources and capabilities into a wide-ranging and insightful analysis of the nature and sources of competitive advantage. By the time you have completed this chapter, you will be able to:

♦ Identify the circumstances in that a firm can create a competitive advantage over a rival.

♦ Understand how responsiveness and innovation can create competitive advantage.

♦ Predict the potential for competition to erode competitive advantage through imitation.

♦ Recognize the role of resource conditions in creating imperfections in the competitive process and, therefore, opportunities for competitive advantage.

♦ Distinguish the two primary types of competitive advantage—cost advantage and differentiation advantage.

♦ Apply this analysis to formulate business strategies capable of establishing and sustaining competitive advantage in different types of industry.

THE EMERGENCE OF COMPETITIVE ADVANTAGE

To understand how competitive advantage emerges, we must first understand what competitive advantage is. Competitive advantage can be defined as follows:

> When two or more firms compete within the same market, one firm possesses a competitive advantage over its rivals when it earns a persistently higher rate of profit (or has the potential to earn a persistently higher rate of profit).

Competitive advantage, then, is the ability of the firm to outperform rivals on the primary performance goal—profitability. Note that competitive advantage may not be revealed in higher profitability: a firm may trade current profit for investment in market share or technology, or a firm may forgo profits in the interests of customer satisfaction, philanthropy, employee benefits, or executive perks.

External Sources of Change

Differences in profitability between competing firms are a disequilibrium phenomenon—some kind of *change* must take place. The source of the change may be external or internal to the industry: Figure 7.1 illustrates several sources. If external changes are to result in competitive advantage, the changes must have differential effects on companies because each company is different in terms of its resources and capabilities and its strategic positioning. In 1997, the competitive positions of firms within the automobile industry were affected by the fall in the price of crude oil, changing exchange rates (notably the fall of the Japanese yen and German mark against the U.S. dollar), and changing government regulations with regard to emissions and safety. Falling oil prices helped the manufacturers of large cars and sport-utility vehicles, whereas exchange rate movements improved the competitive position of German and Japanese automakers.

How great is the impact of external change on competitive advantage? This depends on the magnitude of external change and the extent of firms' strategic differences. The more turbulent an industry's environment, the greater the number of sources of change, and the greater the differences in firms' resources and capabilities—the greater the dispersion of profitability within the industry. In the world oil industry of the 1960s, the industry environment was relatively stable and the leading firms pursued similar strategies. As a result, competitive advantages, as reflected in inter-firm profit differentials, tended to be small. The toy industry, on the other hand, experiences rapid and unpredictable changes in demand, technology, and fashion, and firms are positioned very differently with regard to capabilities and product lines. Inter-firm profitability tends to be widely dispersed.

FIGURE 7.1
The Emergence of Competitive Advantage

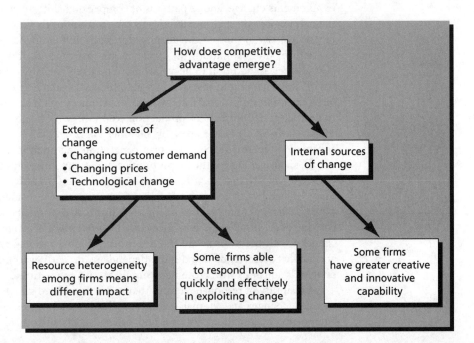

Competitive Advantage from Responsiveness to Change

The role of external change in creating competitive advantage is not simply in *conferring* advantages and disadvantages on otherwise passive firms. The competitive advantage that arises from external change also depends on a firm's ability to *respond* to external change. Any external change creates opportunities for profit. The ability to identify and respond to opportunity lies at the core of the management capability. This capability is called **entrepreneurship**. To the extent that external opportunities are fleeting or subject to first-mover advantage, speed of response is critical to exploiting business opportunity. An unexpected rain shower creates an upsurge in the demand for umbrellas. Those street vendors who position themselves outside a busy railroad station at the onset of rain will benefit most from this business opportunity.

As markets become increasingly turbulent, so responsiveness to external change has become increasingly important as a source of competitive advantage.

- ♦ Wal-Mart's ability to consistently outperform Kmart and other discount retailers is based on a business system that responds quickly and effectively to changes in demand. Wal-Mart's distribution and purchasing is driven by point-of-sale data in a tightly integrated system that results in low inventories, few stockouts, and few forced markdowns.

- ♦ The highly successful textile industry of the Prato region of northern Italy is based on a business model pioneered by Massimo Menichetti in the early 1970s. The Prato model of small, specialized textile and clothing companies competing and cooperating through highly flexible, closely integrated networks is uniquely suited to the fast-paced business environment of fashion clothing.[1]

Responsiveness also involves anticipating changes in the basis of competitive advantage over time. As an industry moves through its life cycle, as customer requirements change, and as patterns of competition shift, so companies must adjust their strategies and their capabilities to take account of the key success factors of the future. Monsanto showed considerable foresight in building its competitive position to outlive the expiration in 1992 of its patents on its artificial sweetener, NutraSweet. In addition to heavy promotion of the NutraSweet brand name and its "swirl" logo, Monsanto invested in scale-efficient production facilities, signed long-term exclusive supply contracts with key customers (such as Coca-Cola), and used trade secrets to protect its production know-how.[2] The joint Mercedes-Swatch *Micro Compact Car* developed by Daimler-Benz and SMH is designed to take advantage of increasing concerns over congestion and pollution.

Responsiveness to the opportunities for competitive advantage provided by environmental change requires one key resource—information—and one key capability—flexibility of response. **Information** is necessary to identify and anticipate external changes. This is dependent on a firm's environmental scanning capability. As the pace of change has accelerated, *environmental scanning* activities have changed with them: firms are less dependent on conventional analysis of economic and market research data and more dependent on "early warning systems" through direct relationships with customers, suppliers, and competitors.

Flexibility of response requires that a firm be able to swiftly redeploy resources to meet changes in external conditions. Traditionally associated with plant and equipment, information systems, and other aspects of "organizational hardware," flexibility is now viewed as primarily dependent on "organizational software"—organization structure, decision-making systems, job design, and culture. Flexibility typically requires fewer levels of hierarchy, greater decentralization of decision making, and informal patterns of cooperation and coordination. Benetton's remarkable responsiveness to emerging market trends and changing customer preferences is achieved through a highly flexible network. The shifting of garment dyeing to the end of the production process is just one means by which Benetton has redesigned its business processes to maximize flexibility.[3] At the retail level, Benetton operates through a system of country and regional agents who coordinate the franchised retail outlets within their territories. At the production level, Benetton's own production facilities are supported by over two thousand subcontractors. A remarkable feature of this vertically integrated network is an absence of formal contracts.

The greater flexibility a company has in responding to changing market circumstances, the less dependent it is on its ability to forecast. Dell Computer is the epitome of the current trend toward speed and agility. A custom order placed at 9 A.M. on Monday can be on a delivery truck by 9 P.M. Tuesday. This permits Dell to customize each computer to the customer's specifications and to operate with less than 14 days of inventory, which not only cuts costs, but permits Dell to adjust rapidly and effortlessly to fluctuations in market demand and upgrade its products quickly to take advantage of technical advances in components. During the first half of 1997, Dell earned a return on equity of over 70 percent—far ahead of any other PC maker.

As fast-response capability becomes an increasingly important key success factor across most industries, interest in time-based management and the role of time as a strategically important resource has grown. George Stalk of the Boston Consulting Group argues that *speed* through time-based manufacturing, time-based sales and distribution, and time-based innovation is the primary competitive advantage of many leading-edge Japanese companies.[4] In automobiles, speed of new product development is a major advantage of Japanese companies (see Table 7.1). During the 1990s, major efforts have been made by U.S. companies to increase their fast-response capabilities by reducing cycle times both in manufacturing and in new product development.

TABLE 7.1
New Product Development Performance by U.S., Japanese, and European Auto Producers

	JAPANESE VOLUME PRODUCER	U.S. VOLUME PRODUCER	EUROPEAN VOLUME PRODUCER	EUROPEAN HIGH-END SPECIALIST
Average Lead Time (months)	42.6	61.9	57.6	71.5
Engineering Hours (in millions)	1.2	3.5	3.4	3.4
Total Product Quality Index	58	41	41	84

Source: Kim B. Clark and Takahiro Fujimoto, *Product Development Performance* (Boston: Harvard Business School Press, 1991): 73.

Competitive Advantage from Innovation: "New Game" Strategies

The source of disturbance that creates the opportunity for competitive advantage may be internal as well as external. Internal change is generated by innovation. **Innovation** not only creates competitive advantage, it provides a basis for overturning the competitive advantage of other firms. Schumpeter's view of the competitive process as "a gale of creative destruction" involved market leadership being eroded not by imitation but by innovation. Innovation is typically thought of in its technical sense: the embodiment of new ideas and knowledge in new products or processes. In a business context, however, innovation also embodies new approaches to doing business. Innovative strategies involve new approaches to competing within an industry. Innovative strategies tend to be the basis of most outstanding success in most industries—far more so than product innovation alone. Many creative business strategies involve little product innovation. Consider the following examples:

- ♦ In the North American steel industry, Nucor, Chaparral Steel, and CoSteel have achieved unrivaled productivity and flexibility by combining new process technologies, flat and flexible organizational structures, and innovative management systems. By 1997, Nucor looked set to overtake USX as America's biggest steel producer.

- ♦ In retailing, competitive advantage is closely associated with novel retailing concepts and new approaches to organizing traditional tasks. In many retail sectors, newcomers have displaced incumbents and dominated their markets by the simple strategy of establishing retail units of unprecedented size. Home Depot in home improvement products, Blockbuster in video rental, Sam's Club in discount warehouses, IKEA in furniture, Virgin in recorded music, and Office Depot in office supplies have all offered a combination of cost savings and greater variety through megastores. Other retailers have achieved success through innovative approaches to differentiation: The Gap, Nordstrom, Pier 1, Gymboree, and Body Shop have all been associated with differentiation through novel retailing concepts.

Charles Baden Fuller and John Stopford provide compelling evidence that, even in mature industries, **strategic innovation** is the primary basis for competitive advantage and the principal driving force of industry change. Central to such innovation is creating customer value through the combination of performance dimensions that were previously viewed as conflicting.

- ♦ Toyota developed its "lean production system," which combined low cost and high quality;

- ♦ Courtaulds, the British acrylic fibers manufacturer, developed large-scale production of its Courtelle fiber and small-lot dyeing to combine low cost and product variety;

- ♦ Richardson, a Sheffield, England, manufacturer of kitchen knives, used its highly flexible management systems and its culture of entrepreneurship and customer focus to achieve low costs with a speed of customer response that was unprecedented within its industry.[5]

Innovation typically requires imagination, intuition, and creativity rather than analysis in the deductive sense. However, a careful examination of how companies compete currently can suggest opportunities for changing the ways in which a company competes. McKinsey and Company has shown that "new game" strategies often differ from "same game" strategies by a reconfiguration of the industry value chain. By reconstructing and rearranging the value chain, a company can change the "rules of the game" so as to capitalize on its distinctive competencies, catch competitors off guard, and erect barriers to protect the advantage created.

McKinsey cites Savin in the North American market for plain-paper copiers as an example of the potency of new game strategies in challenging an established firm with a seemingly impregnable competitive position and an illustration of the application of the value chain in formulating new game strategies (see Exhibit 7.1).

EXHIBIT 7.1

Reconfiguring the Value Chain to Formulate New Game Strategies: Savin and Xerox

For most of the 1970s, Xerox possessed a near monopoly position in the North American market for plain-paper copiers. Xerox's dominance rested, first, upon the wall of patents that the company had built over several decades and, second, on the scale economies and reputation that its market dominance conferred. The first company to compete effectively with Xerox during the late 1970s was Savin. The basis of Savin's challenge was an approach that sought not to imitate Xerox's success but to compete in an entirely different manner.

Savin developed and patented a new low-cost technology. Its product design permitted the use of standardized parts that could be sourced in volume from Japan. Assembly was also undertaken in Japan. The result was a product whose cost was about half that of Xerox's. To avoid the costs of leasing and the need for a costly direct sales force, Savin distributed through existing office equipment dealers.

The principal differences between the approach of Savin and that of Xerox can be seen by comparing the main activities of the companies:

	XEROX	SAVIN
Technology and design	Dry xerography High copy speed Many features	Liquid toner Low copy speed Few features and options
Manufacture	Most manufacturing (including components) in house	Machines sourced from Ricoh in Japan
Product range	Wide range of machines	Narrow range of machines for different volumes and uses
Marketing	Machines leased to customers	Machines sold to customers
Distribution	Direct sales force	Distribution through dealers
Service	Directly operated service organization	Service by dealers and independent service engineers

Source: Roberto Buaron, "New-Game Strategies," McKinsey Staff Paper, March 1980.

The key element in the formulation of new game strategies is to identify a firm's key strengths in terms of resources and capabilities and to devise a strategy that leverages these to the maximum.

♦ Southwest Airlines capitalized on its low-cost, highly motivated employees and flexible organization to build a business system that differs radically from that of the established airlines: it offers point-to-point routes (instead of the usual hub-and-spoke system), provides no in-flight meals, operates a single type of plane, and does not utilize either of the industry's main computerized reservations systems. Southwest's unique approach has given it some of the lowest unit costs in the industry.

♦ Nike built its large and successful businesses on a business system that involved a total reconfiguration of the activities of the traditional shoe manufacturing firm. To begin with, Nike does not manufacture shoes—indeed, it manufactures little of anything. Nike designs, markets, and distributes shoes, but its primary activity is the coordination of a vast and complex global network involving design and market research (primarily in the United States), the production (under contract) of components (primarily in Korea and Taiwan), and the assembly of shoes (in China, the Philippines, India, Thailand, and several other low-wage countries).

♦ Dell Computer's remarkable speed and profitability is similarly based on an innovative reconfiguration of the value chain. Dell sells and offers after-sales service directly to customers by telephone and Internet. Its entire logistics are outsourced. Some components are delivered to customers without passing through Dell's hands, e.g., monitors are shipped directly from supplier to customer to arrive simultaneously with the computer.

The withdrawal by companies from all stages of the value chain that can be undertaken more efficiently by other companies is a central feature of the move toward **virtual corporations**.[6] We discuss this phenomenon in relation to cost analysis (Chapter 8) and vertical integration (Chapter 12).

SUSTAINING COMPETITIVE ADVANTAGE

Once established, competitive advantage is subject to erosion by competition. The speed with which competitive advantage is undermined depends on the ability of competitors to challenge either by imitation or innovation. The essence of the competitive process is the imitation of the strategy of the advantaged firm by rivals. For competitive advantage to be sustained over time requires the existence of barriers to imitation. Rumelt uses the term *isolating mechanisms* to describe "barriers that limit the ex post equilibration of rents among individual firms."[7] The more effective these isolating mechanisms are, the longer competitive advantage can be sustained against the onslaught of rivals. Empirical studies show that the process through which competition destroys the competitive advantage of industry leaders is slow. We have already noted that in most industries, there is considerable variation in the profitability of different firms. Equally interesting is the fact that these differentials are eroded at a slow pace. Even over periods of a decade and more, inter-firm profit differentials tend to persist with little change in the identities of the leaders and the laggards.[8]

To identify the sources of isolating mechanisms, we need to examine the process of competitive imitation. For one firm to successfully imitate the strategy of another, it must meet four conditions:

1. *Identification.* The firm must be able to identify that a rival possesses a competitive advantage.

2. *Incentive.* Having identified that a rival possesses a competitive advantage (as shown by above-average profitability), the firm must believe that by investing in imitation, it too can earn superior returns.

3. *Diagnosis.* The firm must be able to diagnose the features of its rival's strategy that give rise to the competitive advantage.

4. *Resource acquisition.* The firm must be able to acquire through transfer or replication the resources and capabilities necessary for imitating the strategy of the advantaged firm.

Figure 7.2 illustrates these stages and forms of isolating mechanisms that exist at each stage.

Identification: Obscuring Superior Performance

A simple barrier to imitation is to obscure the firm's superior profitability. In the 1951 movie classic *The Treasure of the Sierra Madre*, Humphrey Bogart and his fellow gold prospectors go to great lengths to obscure their find from other prospectors.[9] The most direct means of **obscuring** competitive advantage in order to discourage would-be competitors is simply to forgo short-term profits. The theory of **limit pricing**, in its simplest form, postulates that a firm in a strong market position sets prices at a

FIGURE 7.2
Sustaining Competitive Advantage Against Imitation

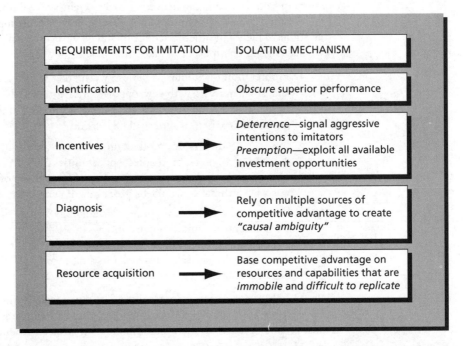

REQUIREMENTS FOR IMITATION	ISOLATING MECHANISM
Identification	*Obscure* superior performance
Incentives	*Deterrence*—signal aggressive intentions to imitators *Preemption*—exploit all available investment opportunities
Diagnosis	Rely on multiple sources of competitive advantage to create *"causal ambiguity"*
Resource acquisition	Base competitive advantage on resources and capabilities that are *immobile* and *difficult* to replicate

level that just fails to attract entrants. A more attractive means of avoiding competition is for the firm to withhold information about its profitability. One advantage of private companies and unincorporated forms of business is that they are not obliged to make their profit performance public. The recent trend to take public companies private has in many cases been motivated by the desire not to disclose performance. Among public companies, diversification and consequent consolidation of accounts can help protect highly profitable subsidiaries from competitive entry.

Incentives to Compete: Deterrence and Preemption

A firm may avoid competition by undermining the incentives for imitation. If a firm can persuade rivals that by imitating its strategy they will not achieve comparable profitability, it may be able to avoid competitive challenges. In Chapter 4 we discussed the role of *signaling:* the manipulation of information by a firm in order to influence the behavior of competitors. **Deterrence** involves making threatening signals toward competitors that encourage the competitor to believe that a strategy of imitation will not prove profitable. The key to deterrence is the promise of retaliation against a competitor that encroaches on the firm's strategic niche. For a threat to be effective in deterring a competitive challenge, it must be credible. Because carrying out a threat is usually costly to both the aggressor and the victim, it needs to be supported by *commitment*.[10] Thus, the threat of aggressive price cuts needs to be backed either by excess capacity or by excess inventories. The credibility of a threat also depends on the reputation of the firm that issues it. Engaging in costly competitive battles may be justified as an investment in reputation. Procter & Gamble, through its hard-fought marketing battles in disposable diapers, household detergents, toothpaste, and elsewhere has built a reputation as a formidable competitor, which deters would-be intruders into its markets. Brandenburger and Nalebuff give examples of how, in the market for NutraSweet, Monsanto deterred Holland Sweetener, and how CSX deterred Norfolk Southern from competing in delivering coal to Gainesville, Florida.[11]

A firm can also deter imitation by **preemption**—occupying existing and potential strategic niches in order to reduce the range of investment opportunities open to the challenger. Preemption can take many forms.

♦ Proliferation of product varieties by a market leader can leave new entrants and smaller rivals with few opportunities for establishing a market niche. Between 1950 and 1972, the six leading suppliers of breakfast cereals introduced 80 new brands into the U.S. market.[12]

♦ Large investments in production capacity ahead of growth of market demand also preempt market opportunities for rivals. Monsanto's heavy investment in plants for producing NutraSweet ahead of its patent expiration was a clear threat to would-be producers of generic aspartame.

♦ Patent proliferation can protect technology-based advantage by limiting competitors' technical opportunities. In 1974, Xerox's dominant market position was protected by a wall of over 2,000 patents, most of which were not used. When IBM introduced its first copier in 1970, Xerox sued it for infringing 22 of these patents.[13]

The ability to sustain competitive advantage through preemption depends on the presence of two imperfections of the competitive process. First, the market must be small relative to the minimum efficient scale of production, such that only a very small number of competitors are viable. Second, there must be first-mover advantage that gives an incumbent preferential access to information and other resources, putting rivals at a disadvantage.

Diagnosing Competitive Advantage: "Causal Ambiguity" and "Uncertain Imitability"

If a firm is to imitate the competitive advantage of another, it must understand the basis of its rival's success. In most industries, there is a serious identification problem in linking superior performance to the resources and capabilities that generate that performance. Consider the remarkable success of Wal-Mart in the discount retailing business. It is easy for Kmart to point to the differences between Wal-Mart and itself. As one Wal-Mart executive commented: "Retailing is an open book. There are no secrets. Our competitors can walk into our stores and see what we sell, how we sell it, and for how much." The difficult task is to identify which differences are critical to the profitability differential between the two retailers. Is it Wal-Mart's store locations (typically in small towns with little direct competition)? Its tightly integrated logistics of purchasing, warehousing, and distribution? Its unique management system? The information system that supports Wal-Mart's logistics and decision-making practices? Or is it the culture that combines rural American values concerning thrift, simplicity, hard work, and customer attentiveness with company traditions that reconcile a sense of family with hard-driving entrepreneurship?

The problem for Kmart and other discount retailers is what Lippman and Rumelt refer to as **causal ambiguity**.[14] The more multidimensional a firm's competitive advantage is and the more each dimension of competitive advantage is based on complex bundles of organizational capabilities rather than individual resources and capabilities, the more difficult it is for a competitor to diagnose the determinants of success. The outcome of causal ambiguity is **uncertain imitability**: where there is ambiguity associated with the causes of a competitor's success, any attempt to imitate that strategy is subject to uncertain success.

Acquiring Resources and Capabilities

Having diagnosed the sources of an incumbent's competitive advantage, the imitator can mount a competitive challenge only by assembling the resources and capabilities necessary for imitation. As we saw in Chapter 5, a firm can acquire resources and capabilities in two ways: it can buy them or it can build them. The period over which a competitive advantage can be sustained depends critically on the time it takes to acquire and mobilize the resources and capabilities needed to mount a competitive challenge.

There is little to add here to the discussion of transferability and replicability in the previous chapter. The ability to buy resources and capabilities from outside factor markets depends on their transferability between firms. Even if resources are mobile, the market for a resource may be subject to **transactions costs**—costs of buying and selling arising from search costs, negotiation costs, contract enforcement costs, and transportation costs. Transactions costs are greater for highly differentiated (or "idiosyncratic") resources.[15]

The alternative to buying a resource or capability is to create it through internal investment. As we noted in the last chapter, where capabilities are based on organizational routines, accumulating the coordination and learning required for their efficient operation can take considerable time. Even in the case of "turn-key" plants, developing the required operating capability can be a problem. Michael Polanyi observed: "I have myself watched in Hungary a new imported machine for blowing electric lamp bulbs, the exact counterpart of which was operating successfully in Germany, failing for a whole year to produce a single flawless bulb."[16] Businesses that require the integration of a number of complex, team-based routines may take years to reach the standards set by industry leaders. GM's attempt to transfer Toyota-style, team-based production from its NUMMI joint venture at Fremont, California, to the GM Van Nuys plant 400 miles to the south involved complex problems of learning and adjustment that remained unsolved two years after the program had begun.[17] Conversely, where a competitive advantage does not require the application of complex, firm-specific resources, imitation is likely to be easy and fast.

- In financial services, many new products such as money market checking accounts, brokerage accounts with checking services, stripped bonds, interest rate swaps, and various financial derivatives typically require resources and capabilities that are widely distributed among banks. Hence, imitation of financial innovations is swift.

- The rapid decline of Filofax, the British manufacturer (and originator) of personal organizers, similarly reflected the ease of replicating the product.[18]

First-Mover Advantage.   A firm's ability to acquire the resources and capabilities needed to challenge an incumbent firm depends on the extent and the sources of first-mover advantage in the market. The idea of **first-mover advantage** is that the initial occupant of a strategic position or niche gains access to resources and capabilities that a follower cannot match. The simplest form of first-mover advantage is a patent or copyright. By establishing a patent or copyright, the first mover possesses a technology, product, or design from which a follower is legally excluded. Early occupancy of a strategic niche can offer other resource advantages. The ability of advantaged firms to acquire superior resources and capabilities confirms the adage that "success breeds success."

- Where the resources required for competing are scarce, e.g., store locations in a new shopping mall or highly specialized employees, first movers can simply preempt these scarce resources.

- Initial competitive advantage offers a profit flow that permits the firm to invest in extending and upgrading its resource base. Pilkington's revolutionary float glass process was a competitive advantage whose life was limited to the term of the patent. However, Pilkington used its profits and income from patent licenses to invest heavily in new plants, expand multinationally by acquiring overseas competitors, and finance R&D into fiber optics and other new uses of glass.

- The first mover in a market establishes reputation with suppliers, distributors, and customers that cannot be initially matched by the follower.

- Where proprietary standards in relation to product design and technology are important to competitive advantage, the first mover may have an advantage in setting the standard.

- Economies of learning suggest that the first mover can build a cost advantage over followers as a result of greater experience.[19]

COMPETITIVE ADVANTAGE IN DIFFERENT MARKET SETTINGS

We have seen that profiting from competitive advantage requires that the firm first *establish* a competitive advantage, and then *sustain* its advantage for long enough to reap its rewards. To identify opportunities for establishing and sustaining competitive advantage in a business requires understanding the characteristics of the competitive process in that specific market. Opportunities for competitive advantage require some form of imperfection of competition. To identify and understand these imperfections in the competitive process, we need to recognize the types of resources and capabilities necessary to compete and the circumstances of their availability.

Our initial discussion of the nature of business in Chapter 1 identified two types of value-creating activity: trading and production. *Trading* involves arbitrage across space (trade) and time (speculation). *Production* involves the physical transformation of inputs into outputs. These different types of business activity correspond to different market types: *trading markets* and *production markets* (see Figure 7.3). We begin with a discussion of a special type of trading market: an efficient market.

Efficient Markets: The Absence of Competitive Advantage

In Chapter 3, we introduced the concept of *perfect competition*. Perfect competition exists where there are many buyers and sellers, no product differentiation, no barriers to entry or exit, and free flow of information. In equilibrium, all firms earn the competitive rate of profit, that equals the cost of capital. The closest real-world examples of perfect competition are financial and commodity markets (for example, the markets for securities, foreign exchange, and grain futures). These markets are sometimes described as *efficient*. An **efficient market** is one in which prices reflect all

FIGURE 7.3
Competitive Advantage in Different Market Settings

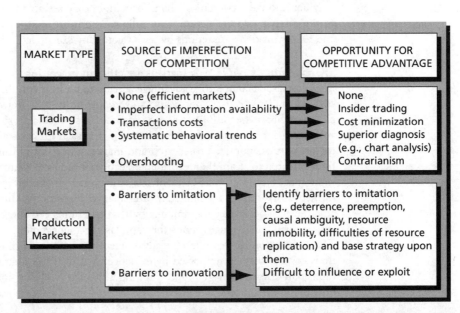

available information. Because prices adjust instantaneously to newly available information, no market trader can expect to earn more than any other. Any differences in ex post returns reflect either different levels of risk selected by different traders or purely random factors (luck). Because all available information is reflected in current prices, no trading rules based on historical price data or any other available information can offer excess returns: it is not possible to "beat the market" on any consistent basis. In other words, competitive advantage is absent.

The absence of competitive advantage in efficient markets is a direct consequence of the types of resources required by participants in these markets. There are only two primary resources required in financial markets: finance and information. If both are equally available to all participants, then there is no basis for one to gain competitive advantage over another.

Competition and Competitive Advantage in Trading Markets

In order for competitive advantage to exist, imperfections (or "inefficiencies") must be introduced into the competitive process. Focusing on the relatively simple case of trading markets, let us introduce different sources of imperfection to the competitive process, showing how these imperfections create opportunities for competitive advantage, and how these imperfections are closely related to the conditions of resource availability.

Imperfect Availability of Information.   Financial markets (and most other trading markets) depart from the conditions for efficiency because of imperfect availability of information. Competitive advantage, therefore, is dependent on superior access to information. The most likely source of superior information is privileged access to private information. Trading on the basis of such information normally falls within the restrictions on "insider trading." Though insider information creates advantage, such competitive advantage tends to be of short duration. Once a market participant begins acting on the basis of insider information, then other operators are alerted to the existence of the information. Even though they may not know the content of the information, they are able to imitate the behavior of the market leader. A commonly followed strategy in stock markets is to detect and follow insider transactions by senior company executives.

Transactions Costs.   If markets are efficient except for the presence of transactions costs, then competitive advantage accrues to traders with the lowest transactions costs. A trader's **transactions costs** as a proportion of turnover depend on the efficiency of his or her information and transactions processing systems and the total volume of transaction. In stock markets, low transactions costs are also attainable by traders who economize on research and market analysis and minimize the transactions required to attain their portfolio objectives. Studies of mutual fund performance show that "Net of all management fees, the average managed investment fund performed worse than a completely unmanaged buy-and-hold strategy on a risk-adjusted basis. Further, the amount by that the funds fell short of the unmanaged strategy was, on average, about the same as the management cost of the funds."[20] The observation that competitive advantage is attained through minimizing transactions costs is further supported by evidence that, over the long term, market index funds outperform managed funds. During 1996, the S&P 500 index beat 75 percent of U.S. fund managers. During the first half of 1997 the figure was 95 percent.[21]

Systematic Behavioral Trends.   If the current prices in a market fully reflect all available information, then price movements are caused by the arrival of new information and follow a random walk.[22] If, however, other factors influence price movements, then there is scope for a strategy that uses an understanding of how prices really do move. Some stock market anomalies are well documented, notably, the "small firm effect," the "January effect" and "weekend effects."[23] More generally, there is evidence that prices in financial markets follow systematic patterns that are the result of "market psychology," the trends and turning points of which can be established from past data. Chart analysis uses hypotheses concerning the relationship between past and future price movements for forecasting. Standard chartist tools include Elliott wave theory, Gann theories, momentum indicators, and patterns such as "support and resistance levels," "head and shoulders," "double tops," "flags," and "candlesticks." There is some evidence that chart analysis outperforms other forecasting techniques.[24] Hence, in markets where systematic behavioral trends occur, competitive advantage is gained by traders with superior skill in diagnosing such behavior.

Overshooting.   Inefficiencies can also arise in trading markets due to the propensity of market participants to overreact to new information with the result that prices **overshoot**.[25] Such overreaction is typically the result of imitative behavior resulting in the creation of *bandwagon effects*. On the assumption that overshooting is temporary and is eventually offset by an opposite movement back to equilibrium, then advantage can be gained through a *contrarian strategy*: acting in the opposite direction to market swings. Warren Buffett, the billionaire chairman of Berkshire Hathaway, is a declared contrarian: "The best time to buy assets may be when it is hardest to raise money," he notes. Prince Alwaleed bin Talal bin Abdulaziz Alsaud also goes against the market tides in acquiring major interests in depressed businesses such as Canary Wharf, EuroDisney, and Apple Computer.[26]

Competition and Competitive Advantage in Production Markets

The transitory nature of competitive advantage in trading markets is a result of the characteristics of the resources required to compete: finance and information. Finance is a relatively homogeneous resource that is widely available. Information, although highly differentiated, is transferable easily and at very low cost; hence, the competitive advantage it offers tends to be fleeting.

Production markets are quite different. Production activities require complex combinations of resources and capabilities, and these resources and capabilities are highly differentiated. The result, as we have noted, is that each producer possesses a unique combination of resources and capabilities. The greater the heterogeneity of firms' endowments of resources and capabilities, the greater the potential for competitive advantage. Thus, as the players in the U.S. steel industry became increasingly diverse during the period from 1970 to 1996, with new companies entering (Nucor, Chaparral, Birmingham Steel, and North Star), and existing companies restructuring, profit differentials widened between innovative mini-mills (such as Nucor and Chaparral) and the lumbering giants (such as USX and Bethlehem).[27]

Differences in resource endowments among firms also have an important impact on the process by which competitive advantage is eroded. Where firms possess very similar bundles of resources and capabilities, imitation of competitive advantages tends to be easy. Where resource bundles are highly differentiated, imitation depends on the speed at which rivals can acquire the needed resources and capabilities for imitation. However, competitive advantages can also be overturned through innovation: the diversity resulting from firms' different resources is conducive to innovation in an industry. For example:

♦ In *car rental services*, the leading players (Avis, Hertz, Budget, General, Alamo) have similar resources and capabilities. One consequence is that competitive advantages are small, and the firms earn similar (low) levels of profitability. The industry is also characterized by a low level of innovation—the business has changed little over the past two decades.

♦ In *medical imaging equipment*, on the other hand, competing firms tend to be of different sizes with different technological resources and different manufacturing, marketing, and service capabilities. Competitive advantages tend to be relatively secure from imitation, but competition through innovation, both product innovation and strategic innovation, tends to be strong.

The potential for creating and sustaining advantage in production markets depends not only on inter-firm differences in resources, but also on the characteristics of the industry. Thus, building on our analysis of the processes through which competitive advantage emerges and is eroded, it is possible to identify various aspects of industry structure that may assist or constrain these forces.

Industry Conditions Conducive to Emergence of Competitive Advantage.

Opportunities for competitive advantage through responding to external change depend on the extent and sources of change in the business environment. Industries subject to a wide range of unpredictable external changes, such as the telecommunications industry, that is subject to rapid regulatory and technological change, are likely to offer a multiplicity of opportunities for creating competitive advantage (even though these opportunities may not support sustainable advantages).

Competitive advantage also emerges through strategic innovation. The more complex an industry in terms of multidimensionality of customer choice criteria and the number of value chain activities, the greater the potential for creating "new game" strategies: the residential homebuilding industry offers greater scope for strategic innovation than the cement industry.

Industry Conditions Conductive to Sustaining Competitive Advantage.

Early on we identified a number of barriers to the erosion of competitive advantage through imitation. Each is likely to depend on characteristics of the industry.

♦ *Imperfection of information.* If the erosion of competitive advantage through imitation first requires potential imitators to *identify* those rivals in possession of competitive advantage and then to *diagnose* the basis of their advantage, then the greater the imperfection of information in an industry, the more difficult such identification and diagnosis. Thus, industries dominated by private companies or partnerships or by specialized units of more diversified companies (such as management consulting and private banking) may be difficult ones in which to identify superior performance. Similarly, industries where competitive advantage is based on complex, multi-layered capabilities, it may be difficult for poorly performing firms to comprehend the success of their better-performing rivals. Thus, in movie production, the long-established leadership of studios such as Paramount, Columbia, Universal, Fox, and Disney may reflect the difficult-to-diagnose secrets of producing "blockbuster" movies, even though the individual (scripts, actors, technicians, and directors) can be hired from the market. Similarly with wireless telephone equipment, the leadership of Motorola and Nokia is based on a complex combination of capabilities in communications technology, semiconductors, product design, manufacturing, and marketing.

♦ *Opportunities for deterrence and preemption.* Competitive advantages can be sustained where the advantaged firm can discourage would-be imitators from mounting competitive challenges. The easier it is for incumbents to preempt viable competitive positions, the easier it is to deter would-be innovators. Thus, industries where valuable first-mover advantages exist because either the market is small (relative to the minimum efficient scale of production), essential resources are scarce or tightly held, industry standards can be set, or economies of learning are important, are likely to be those where competitive advantages are not easily eroded. The rush of Western oil and gas companies into China, Russia, and Azerbaijan has been driven by the desire to tie up exploration licenses and joint ventures before these opportunities disappear.

♦ *Difficulties of resource acquisition.* Finally, industries differ according to their ability to acquire the most strategically important resources. In the bicycle messenger business in London or New York, competitive advantage is easily eroded because the key resources (cyclists, wireless communication, and marketing) are easily acquired. The securities underwriting business (whether for IPOs or corporate bond issues) offers more sustainable advantages because the key resources and capabilities (market expertise, reputation, relationships, retail distribution links, and massive financial reserves) tend to be difficult to assemble. The difficulties of assembling the resources and capabilities needed to challenge the advantages of incumbents increases to the extent that initial resource advantages are cumulative. The ability of successful companies such as Microsoft, Sony, and Procter & Gamble to attract the most talented new graduates is such an advantage.

TYPES OF COMPETITIVE ADVANTAGE

A firm can achieve a higher rate of profit (or potential profit) over a rival in one of two ways: either it can supply an identical product or service at a lower cost or it can supply a product or service that is differentiated in such a way that the customer is willing to pay a price premium that exceeds the additional cost of the differentiation. In the former case, the firm possesses a cost advantage; in the latter, a differentiation advantage. In pursuing **cost advantage**, the goal of the firm is to become the cost leader in its industry or industry segment. Cost leadership is a unique position in the industry that requires that the firm "must find and exploit all sources of cost advantage . . . [and] . . . sell a standard, no-frills product." [28] **Differentiation** by a firm from its competitors is achieved "when it provides something unique that is valuable to buyers beyond simply offering a low price."[29] Figure 7.4 illustrates these two types of advantage.

The two sources of competitive advantage define two fundamentally different approaches to business strategy. A firm that is competing on low cost is distinguishable from a firm that competes through differentiation in terms of market positioning, resource and capabilities, and organizational characteristics. Table 7.2 outlines some of the principal features of cost and differentiation strategies.

FIGURE 7.4
Sources of Competitive Advantage

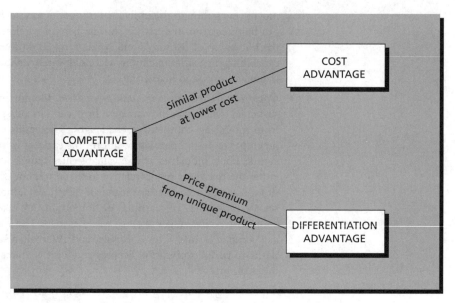

By combining the two types of competitive advantage with the firm's choice of scope—broad market versus narrow segment—Michael Porter has defined three generic strategies: cost leadership, differentiation, and focus (see Figure 7.5).

Porter views cost leadership and differentiation as mutually exclusive strategies. A firm that attempts to pursue both is "stuck in the middle":

> The firm stuck in the middle is almost guaranteed low profitability. It either loses the high volume customers who demand low prices or must bid away its profits to get this business from the low-cost firms. Yet it also loses high-margin business—the cream—to the firms who are focused on high-margin targets or have achieved differentiation overall. The firm that is stuck in the middle also probably suffers from a blurred corporate culture and a conflicting set of organizational arrangements and motivation system.[30]

In practice, few firms are faced with such stark alternatives. Differentiation is not simply an issue of "to differentiate or not to differentiate." All firms must make decisions as to which customer requirements to focus on, and where to position their product or service in the market. A cost leadership strategy typically implies a narrow line, limited-feature, standardized offering. However, such a positioning does not necessarily imply that the product or service is an undifferentiated commodity. In the case of IKEA furniture and McDonald's hamburgers, a low-price, no-frills offering is also associated with a clear market positioning and a unique brand image. The VW Beetle is evidence that a low-cost, utilitarian, mass-market product may achieve a highly differentiated market status. At the same time, firms that pursue differentiation strategies cannot be oblivious to cost.

In most industries, market leadership is held by a firm that maximizes customer appeal by reconciling effective differentiation with low cost. Ford and Toyota are not the lowest cost auto producers. Nor are American Airlines, United, and British Airways the lowest cost airlines. Marks & Spencer and The Gap are not cost leaders in

FIGURE 7.5
Porter's Generic
Strategies

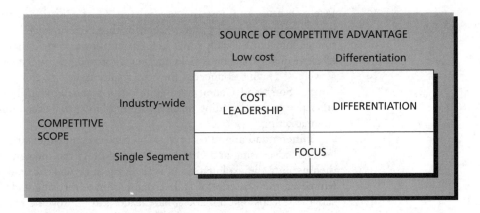

clothing. What all these companies have achieved are market leadership positions based on combining differentiation and low cost in an attractive value-for-money package.

Reconciling differentiation with low cost has been one of the greatest strategic challenges of the 1990s. The success of Japanese companies across a range of consumer goods from autos and consumer electronics to musical instruments was due to their ability to reconcile low costs with unprecedented quality. The principles and methods of *total quality management* that they adopted and developed have exploded the myth that there is a trade-off between high quality and low cost. Numerous studies show that innovations in manufacturing technology and manufacturing management result in simultaneous increases in productivity and quality.[31] Achieving higher quality in terms of fewer defects and greater product reliability frequently involves simpler product design, fewer component suppliers that are more closely monitored, and fewer service calls and product recalls—all of which save cost. Tom

TABLE 7.2
Features of Cost Leadership and Differentiation Strategies

GENERIC STRATEGY	KEY STRATEGY ELEMENTS	RESOURCE AND ORGANIZATIONAL REQUIREMENTS
Cost leadership	Scale-efficient plants Design for manufacture Control of overheads and R & D Avoidance of marginal customer accounts	Access to capital Process engineering skills Frequent reports Tight cost control Specialization of jobs and functions Incentives for quantitative targets
Differentiation	Emphasis on branding advertising, design, service, and quality	Marketing abilities Product engineering skills Creativity Research capability Qualitative performance targets and incentives Strong interfunctional coordination

Peters observes an interesting asymmetry: "Cost reduction campaigns do not often lead to improved quality; and, except for those that involve large reductions in personnel, they don't usually result in long-term lower costs either. On the other hand, effective quality programs yield not only improved quality but lasting cost reductions as well."[32] Having conquered the cost/quality trade-off, companies such as Honda, Toyota, Sony, and Canon have gone on to reconcile worldbeating manufacturing efficiency and outstanding quality, with flexibility, fast-paced innovation, and effective marketing.

Differentiation and cost reduction can be complementary in other ways. High levels of advertising and promotional expenditure can increase market share, which then permits the exploitation of scale economies across a wide range of functions. Moreover, the existence of scale economies in advertising and other differentiation activities means that a market share leader can improve its relative cost position by forcing rivals to compete on product differentiation. The heavy advertising campaign with which Apple launched its Macintosh computer in 1984 was partly motivated by the desire to "up the stakes" for smaller manufacturers of personal computers that did not possess the sales base to justify large-scale advertising. Andersen Consulting's heavy emphasis on media advertising represents a similar strategy in management and IT consulting. In the motorcycle industry, Honda's product strategy of annual model changes increased the pressure on manufacturers who lacked the sales volume to justify such heavy fixed costs of new models.[33]

In the next two chapters, we develop and put into operation these concepts of cost and differentiation advantage by presenting frameworks that can diagnose the sources of cost and differentiation advantage and formulate strategies that exploit these sources of advantage.

♦ | SUMMARY

Making money in business requires establishing and sustaining competitive advantage. Both these conditions for profitability require profound insight into the nature and process of competition within a market. Competitive advantage depends critically on the presence of some imperfection in the competitive process—under "perfect" competition, profits are transitory. Our analysis of imperfections of the competitive process has drawn us back to the resources and capabilities that are required to compete in different markets and to pursue different strategies. Establishing competitive advantage is highly dependent on creativity and luck and is, therefore, difficult to analyze systematically. Sustaining competitive advantage depends on the existence of isolating mechanisms: barriers to rivals' imitation of successful strategies. Though strategic ploys such as deterrence and preemption can act as isolating mechanisms, the major protectors of a firm's competitive positions are likely to be rivals' inability to access the resources and capabilities necessary to compete on equal terms with the advantaged firm. Hence, a major outcome of this analysis is to reinforce the argument made in the previous chapter: the characteristics of a firm's resources and capability are fundamental to strategic decision making and long-term success.

In the next two chapters, we analyze the two primary dimensions of competitive advantage: cost advantage and differentiation advantage. In both of these areas we emphasize the importance of depth of understanding of both the firm and its industry environment. To this end, it is useful to disaggregate the firm into a series of separate but interlinked activities. A useful and versatile framework for this purpose is the value chain, that is an insightful tool for understanding the sources of competitive advantage in an industry, for assessing the competitive position of a particular firm, and for suggesting opportunities to enhance a firm's competitiveness.

NOTES

1 H. Voss, "Virtual Organization," *Strategy and Leadership* 24 (July–August, 1996): 12–24. The Italian model of small firm networks has been documented and analyzed by Gianni Lorenzoni. See G. Lorenzoni and Charles Baden Fuller, "Creating a Strategic Center to Manage a Web of Partners," *California Management Review* 37 no.3 (1995): 146-163; A. and G. Lorenzoni, "Organizational Architecture, Inter-Firm Relationships and Entrepreneural Profile: Findings from a set of SME," *Frontiers of Entrepreneurship Research* (Boston: Babson College: 1993).

2 David J. Teece, "Profiting from Technological Innovation: Implications for Integration, Collaboration, Licensing, and Public Policy," in *The Competitive Challenge: Strategies for Industrial Innovation and Renewal*, ed. David J. Teece (Cambridge, MA: Ballinger, 1987).

3 G. Lorenzoni," Benetton,"in C. Bader Fuller and M. Pitt, *Strategic Innovation* (London, Routledge, 1996): 355–388.

4 George Stalk Jr., "Time—The Next Source of Competitive Advantage," *Harvard Business Review* (July–August 1988): 41-51.

5 Charles Baden Fuller and John M. Stopford, *Rejuvenating the Mature Business* (London and New York: Routledge, 1992).

6 William Davidow and Michael Mallone, *The Virtual Corporation* (New York: Harper Business, 1992).

7 Richard P. Rumelt, "Toward a Strategic Theory of the Firm," in *Competitive Strategic Management*, ed. R. Lamb (Englewood Cliffs, NJ: Prentice-Hall, 1984), 556–570.

8 See John Cubbin and Paul Geroski, "The Convergence of Profits in the Long Run: Interfirm and Interindustry Comparisons," *Journal of Industrial Economics* 35 (1987): 427–442; Robert Jacobsen, "The Persistence of Abnormal Returns," *Strategic Management Journal* 9 (1988): 415–430; and Dennis C. Mueller, "Persistent Profits among Large Corporations," in *The Economics of Strategic Planning*, ed. Lacy Glenn Thomas (Lexington, MA: Lexington Books, 1986): 31–61.

9 The film was based on the book: B. Traven, *The Treasure of the Sierra Madre* (New York: Knopf, 1947).

10 Thomas C. Schelling, *The Strategy of Conflict*, 2nd edition (Cambridge: Harvard University Press, 1980): 35–41.

11 Adam Brandenburger and Barry Nalebuff, *Co-opetition* (New York: Doubleday, 1996): 72–80.

12 Richard Schmalensee, "Entry Deterrence in the Ready-to-Eat Breakfast Cereal Industry," *Bell Journal of Economics* 9 (1978): 305–327.

13 Monopolies and Mergers Commission, *Indirect Electrostatic Reprographic Equipment* (London: Her Majesty's Stationery Office, 1976): 37, 56.

14 S. A. Lippman and Richard P. Rumelt, "Uncertain Imitability: An Analysis of Interfirm Differences in Efficiency under Competition," *Bell Journal of Economics* 13 (1982): 418-438. The analysis of causal ambiguity has been further developed by Richard Reed and Robert DeFillippi, "Causal Ambiguity, Barriers to Imitation, and Sustainable Competitive Advantage," *Academy of Management Review* 15 (1990): 88–102.

15 See O. E. Williamson, "Transaction Cost Economics: The Governance of Contractual Relations," *Journal of Law and Economics* 19 (1979): 153–156.

16 M. Polanyi, *Personal Knowledge: Toward a Post-Critical Philosophy*, 2nd edition (Chicago: University of Chicago Press, 1962): 52.

17 C. Brown and M. Reich, "When Does Union-Management Cooperation Work? A Look at NUMMI and GM-Van Nuys," *California Management Review* 31 (Summer 1989): 26–44.

18 "Faded Fad," *Economist*, September 30, 1989: 68.

19 For an analysis of first-mover advantage, see Marvin Lieberman and David Montgomery, "First-Mover Advantages," *Strategic Management Journal* 9 (1988): 41–58.

20 Frank J. Finn, "Evaluation of the Internal Processes of Managed Investment Funds," *Contemporary Studies in Economic and Financial Analysis*, vol. 44 (Greenwich, CT: JAI Press, 1984): 6.

21 "Index Investing: The Joys of Flying on Autopilot," *Business Week*, June 16, 1997: 128–131.

22 Eugene F. Fama, "Efficient Capital Markets: A Review of Theory and Empirical Work," *Journal of Business* 35 (1970): 383–417.

23 Simon Keane, "The Efficient Market Hypothesis on Trial," *Financial Analysts Journal* (March–April 1986): 58–63.

24 H. Allen and M. Taylor, "Charts, Noise, and Fundamentals in the London Foreign Exchange Market," *Economic Journal*, conference supplement, 100 (1990): 49–59.

25 For empirical evidence, see Werner De Bondt and Richard Thaler, "Does the Stock Market Overreact?" *Journal of Finance* 42 (1985): 793–805.

26 "Arabian Knight," *Business Week*, April 21, 1997: 50–52.

27 "Why Steel Is Looking Sexy," *Business Week*, April 4, 1994: 106–108.

28 Michael E. Porter, *Competitive Advantage* (New York: Free Press, 1985): 13.

29 *Ibid.*, 120.

30 Michael E. Porter, *Competitive Strategy* (New York: Free Press, 1980): 42.

31 See, for example, Jack R. Meredith, "Strategic Advantages of the Factory of the Future," *California Management Review* (Winter 1989): 129–145.

32 Tom Peters, *Thriving on Chaos* (New York: Knopf, 1987): 80.

33 The potential for differentiation to assist the attainment of cost leadership is analyzed by Charles Hill, "Differentiation versus Low Cost of Differentiation and Low Cost: A Contingency Framework," *Academy of Management Review* 13 (1988): 401–412.

8
Cost Advantage

SEARS MOTOR BUGGY: $395

For car complete with rubber tires, Timken roller bearing axles, top, storm front, three oil-burning lamps, horn, and one gallon of lubricating oil. *Nothing to buy but gasoline.*

. . . We found there was a maker of automobile frames that was making 75 percent of all the frames used in automobile construction in the United States. We found on account of the volume of business that this concern could make frames cheaper for automobile manufacturers than the manufacturers could make them themselves. We went to this frame maker and asked him to make frames for the Sears Motor Buggy and then to name us prices for those frames in large quantities. And so on throughout the whole construction of the Sears Motor Buggy. You will find every piece and every part has been given the most careful study; you will find that the Sears Motor Buggy is made of the best possible material; it is constructed to take the place of the top buggy; it is built in our own factory, under the direct supervision of our own expert, a man who has had fifteen years of automobile experience, a man who has for the past three years worked with us to develop exactly the right car for the people at a price within the reach of all.

—*Extract from an advertisement in the Sears Roebuck & Co. catalogue, 1909, p. 1150*

Outline

◆ INTRODUCTION AND OBJECTIVES

Historically, business strategy analysis has emphasized cost advantage as the primary basis for competitive advantage in an industry. This focus on cost advantage reflects the traditional emphasis on price as the principal medium of competition among firms—competing on price depends ultimately on cost efficiency. It also reflects some of the principal strategic preoccupations of large industrial corporations. For much of the twentieth century, the strategies of large corporations have been driven by the quest for economies of scale and scope through investment in mass production and mass distribution. Since the mid-1980s, cost efficiency has remained a priority, but the focus has shifted toward cost cutting through restructuring, downsizing, outsourcing, "lean production," and the quest for dynamic rather than static sources of cost efficiency.

For some industries, cost advantage is the predominant basis for competitive advantage: for commodity goods and services there are few opportunities for competing on dimensions other than cost. But even where competition focuses on product differentiation, intensifying competition has resulted in cost efficiency becoming a prerequisite for profitability. Some of the most dramatic examples of companies and industries being transformed through the pursuit of cost efficiency are in sectors where competition has increased sharply due to deregulation, such as airlines, telecommunications, banking, and electrical power generation.

By the time you have completed this chapter, you will be able to:

♦ Identify the determinants of relative cost within the industry or activity ("cost drivers")

♦ Assess a firm's cost position relative to its competitors and identify the factors responsible for cost differentials

♦ Recommend cost reduction measures

The analysis in this chapter is oriented around these objectives. Further, we examine concepts and techniques for:

♦ Identifying the basic sources of cost advantage in an industry,

♦ Appraising the cost position of a firm within its industry by disaggregating the firm into its separate activities,

♦ Using the analysis of costs and relative cost position as a basis for recommending strategies for enhancing cost competitiveness.

ECONOMIES OF EXPERIENCE

Before we analyze the sources of cost advantage, let's review the concept of the *experience curve*. The experience curve is interesting not only because of its pervasive influence on strategic thinking during the 1970s and early 1980s, but also because it provides a useful introduction into the sources of cost advantage.

The Experience Curve

During the decade that followed the publication of *Perspectives in Experience* by the Boston Consulting Group in 1968, **the experience curve** exercised a powerful influence, not only on the analysis of costs, but on strategy analysis as a whole. It is one of the best known and most influential concepts in the history of strategic management. Its basis is the observed systematic reduction in the time taken to build airplanes and Liberty ships during the Second World War.[1] The concept of **economies of learning** was generalized by BCG to encompass not just direct labor hours, but the behavior of all added costs as cumulative production volume increased. In a series of studies from bottle caps and refrigerators to long distance calls and insurance policies, BCG observed a remarkable regularity in reductions in costs (and prices) that accompanied increases in cumulative production. Doubling of cumulative production typically reduced unit costs (and prices) by 20 to 30 percent. BCG summarized its observations in its Law of Experience:

> The unit cost of value added to a standard product declines by a constant percentage (typically between 20 and 30 percent) each time cumulative output doubles.

"Unit cost of value added" is total cost per unit of production *less* the cost per unit of production of bought-in components and materials. If suppliers of components and materials are subject to similar cost reductions as volume increases, then "unit cost" may be substituted for "unit cost of value added" in the definition.

Figure 8.1 shows a typical experience curve. In logarithmic form, the curve becomes a straight line. The size of the experience effect is measured by the proportion by which costs are reduced with subsequent doublings of aggregate production.

FIGURE 8.1
The Experience Curve

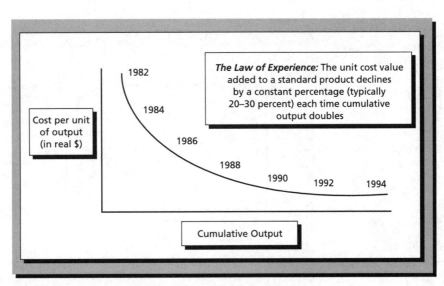

The relationship between unit cost and production volume may be expressed as follows:

$$C_n = C_1 n^{-a}$$

where C_1 is the cost of the first unit of production
          C_n is the cost of the nth unit of production
          n is the cumulative volume of production
          a is the elasticity of cost with regard to output.

Experience curves may be drawn for either an industry or a single firm, and may use either cost or price data. An industry-level experience curve can be constructed by plotting producer price indices against industry output data. Using prices rather than costs assumes that margins are constant. Figure 8.2 shows examples of experience curves estimated by the Boston Consulting Group.

Strategy Implications: The Role of Market Share

The significance of the experience curve lies in its implications for business strategy. If costs decline systematically with increases in cumulative output, then a firm's costs relative to its competitors depend on its cumulative output relative to that of competitors. If a firm can expand its output at a greater rate than its competitors, it is then able to move down the experience curve more rapidly than its rivals and can open up a widening cost differential.

The quest for experience-based cost economies implies that a firm's primary strategic goal should be *market share*. A firm's increase in cumulative output compared to a competitor's depends on each firm's relative market share. If Boeing holds 60 percent of the world market for large commercial jet aircraft and Airbus holds 30 percent, Boeing will reduce its costs at twice the rate of Airbus (other factors being equal).[2]

Hence, the key indicator of competitive advantage, according to the Boston Consulting Group, was *relative market share*. The quest for economies of experience

FIGURE 8.2
Examples of Experience Curves

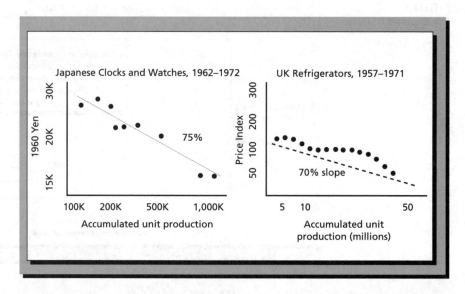

also has important implications for pricing policy.[3] The firm should price its products not on the basis of current costs, but on the basis of anticipated costs.[4] In its study of the British motorcycle industry, BCG observed that British motorcycle manufacturers adopted cost-plus pricing, whereas Honda priced to meet market share objectives. Honda's assumption was that once sufficient sales volume had been achieved, costs would fall to a level that offered a satisfactory profit margin.[5] The quest for experience-based economies also points to the advantages of maximizing volume by offering a broad rather than a narrow product range and expanding internationally rather than restricting sales to the domestic market.

Empirical studies confirm the positive relationship between profitability and market share.[6] As Table 8.1 shows, the positive relationship between profit margin and market share is directly the result of greater productivity: market share leaders tend to have lower rates of investment, receivables, purchases, marketing expenses, and R & D to sales. However, there are difficulties in interpreting the relationship and doubts about the wisdom of pursuing market share as a strategic goal.

- **Causation.** Association is not the same as causation. Does market share confer superior profit, or do profitable firms use their earnings to build market share? The most plausible explanation is that profitability and market share are consequences of some common underlying factor. For example, superior efficiency or innovation results both in high profits and high market share.[7]

- **The unprofitability of investing in market share.** Even if firms with high market shares have cost advantages resulting in superior profitability, this does not necessarily imply that investments aimed at increasing a firm's market share will offer attractive returns. Once the relationship between market share and profitability is well known within an industry, and if all firms have the opportunity of competing for market share through advertising, sales efforts, new capacity, etc.—then the competition for market share will quickly erode any superior profitability available from increased market share.[8]

- **The fallacy of composition.** Pursuing experience economies through pricing for market share may be successful for the individual firm; it can be fatal

TABLE 8.1
The Relationship Between Market Share, Costs, and Profitability

	MARKET SHARE RANK				
	#1	#2	#3	#4	#5 OR BELOW
Investment/Sales	46.3	52.1	52.5	51.4	54.9
Receivables/Sales	14.7	14.7	14.7	14.8	15.3
Inventory/Sales	18.5	19.6	20.5	20.6	22.3
Purchases/Sales	41.8	43.4	45.8	48.8	51.3
Marketing/Sales	8.9	9.5	9.5	9.3	9.2
R&D/Sales	2.1	2.3	1.9	1.8	1.9
Relative Quality (%)	69.0	51.0	47.0	45.0	43.0
Relative Price (%)	105.7	103.8	103.4	103.2	103.0
Pretax Profit/Sales	12.7	9.1	7.1	5.5	4.5

Source: R. D. Buzzell and B. T. Gale, *The PIMS Principles* (New York: Free Press, 1987): 75.

when attempted by several competitors. During the 1970s, U.S. and European producers of steel, petrochemicals, ships, and synthetic fibers followed the lead of their Japanese competitors by investing heavily in large-scale efficient plants while cutting margins in anticipation of lower costs. Overinvestment and aggressive pricing resulted in losses that continued for a decade or more.

THE SOURCES OF COST ADVANTAGE

The key to cost analysis is to go beyond mechanistic and purely empirical approaches such as the experience curve and probe into the factors that determine a firm's cost position. The experience curve combines five sources of cost reduction: economies of scale, economies of learning, improved process technology, improved product design, and process redesign. To these we can add three more factors that further influence the cost position of a firm relative to its competitors: capacity utilization, the cost of inputs, and residual efficiency. These factors, which determine a firm's unit costs (cost per unit of output), are **cost drivers.** Figure 8.3 lists the main drivers of cost advantage.

The relative importance of these different cost drivers vary among different industries as well as among different activities within the firm. By identifying these different cost drivers, we can:

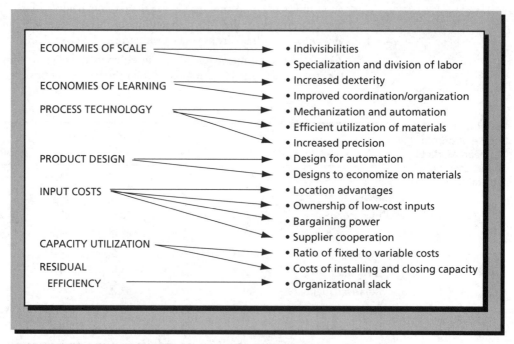

FIGURE 8.3
The Drivers of Cost Advantage

- Diagnose a firm's cost position in terms of understanding why a firm's unit costs diverge from those of its competitors, and
- Make recommendations as to how a firm can improve its cost efficiency.

Let's examine the nature and the role of each of these cost drivers.

Economies of Scale

The predominance of large corporations in most manufacturing and service industries is a consequence of **economies of scale.** Economies of scale exist wherever proportionate increases in the amounts of inputs employed in a production process result in a more than proportionate increase in total output. Hence, as the scale of production increases, unit costs fall. Economies of scale are conventionally associated with manufacturing operations: Figure 8.4 shows a typical relationship between unit cost and plant capacity. The point at which most scale economies are exploited is the Minimum Efficiency Plant Size (MEPS). Scale economies are also important in nonmanufacturing operations such as purchasing, R&D, distribution, and advertising.

Scale economies arise from three principal sources:

1. **Technical input-output relationships.** In many activities, increases in output do not require proportionate increases in input. A 10,000 barrel oil storage tank does not cost five times the cost of a 2,000 barrel tank. Similar volume-related economies exist in ships, trucks, and steel and petrochemical plants.

2. **Indivisibilities.** Many inputs are "lumpy"—they are unavailable in small sizes. Hence, they offer economies of scale as firms are able to spread the costs of these items over larger volumes of output. Most units of capital equipment, such as a body press in an auto plant or a catalytic cracker in an

FIGURE 8.4
A Typical Long-Run
Average Cost Curve
for a Plant

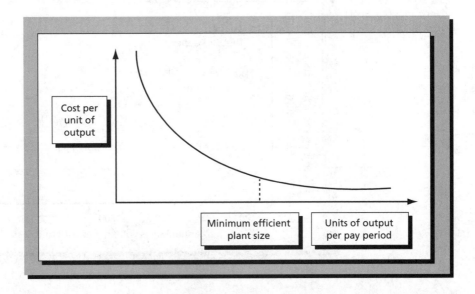

oil refinery, are available only above a certain size. People are also indivisible: a plant probably needs only one gatekeeper and medical officer per shift. For R&D projects and corporate functions such as treasury, tax, and public relations, there is a minimum feasible size to an effective team.

3. **Specialization.** Expanding the number of inputs permits greater task specialization. "Division of labor" is particularly important in this respect. Mass production, pioneered in automobiles by Henry Ford, involves breaking down the production process into a series of separate tasks to be performed by specialized workers using specialized equipment. Specialization of labor increases dexterity, avoids loss of time from workers switching between jobs, and assists mechanization and automation. Similar economies are important in knowledge-intensive industries such as investment banking, management consulting, and design engineering where specialization of labor permits large fims to offer a wide range and depth of expertise.

Scale Economies and Industry Concentration. Scale economies are the single most important determinant of an industry's level of *seller concentration* (the proportion of industry output accounted for by the largest firms). However, the critical scale advantages of large companies are seldom in production. In packaged consumer goods—cigarettes, household detergents, beer, and soft drinks—the tendency for markets to be dominated by a few giant companies results from scale economies in marketing. Advertising is a key indivisibility. The cost of producing and airing a TV commercial nationally is a fixed cost whether the product has a 5 percent or 50 percent market share. The 90-second commercial produced in 1996 for British Airways by M&C Saatchi cost $1.6 million to produce and forms part of a $158 million two-year advertising campaign. Figure 8.5 shows the relationship between sales volume and average advertising costs for different brands of soft drinks.

FIGURE 8.5
Scale Economies in
Advertising: U.S. Soft
Drinks in 1974

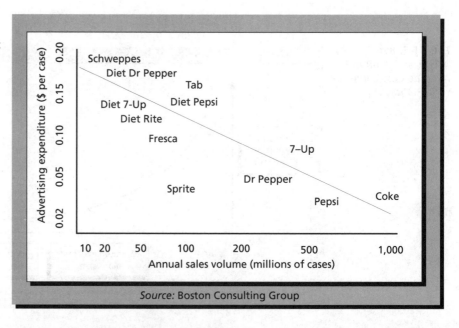

Source: Boston Consulting Group

Consolidation in the world car industry has been driven by the huge costs associated with new model development. The development cost (including plant and tooling) of models introduced during the early 1990s includes:

Ford Escort (new model)	$2 billion
Ford Mondeo/Contour	$6 billion
GM Saturn	$5 billion
Chrysler Neon	$1.3 billion

The small sales volumes of European producers such as Seat (Spain), Saab (Sweden), Skoda (Czech Republic), Rover (UK), Jaguar (UK), and Rolls Royce (UK) have made investment in entirely new models prohibitive and forced mergers with larger competitors. Other small producers have made agreements with larger auto companies to license their designs.[9]

Costs of product development are also the driving force behind the concentration of the large passenger aircraft production into just two companies: Boeing and Airbus. Boeing's cost leadership is based on its ability to amortize development costs over very long runs: almost 1,000 747s were built between 1970 and 1994. Conversely, the supersonic Concorde was a financial disaster for manufacturers, Aerospatiale and British Aerospace (and for their supporting governments), because only 16 were built.

Limits to Scale Economies. The sizes of plants and firms are frequently much smaller than would be implied by the extent of scale economies. Reluctance to fully exploit economies of scale is explained by three reasons.

- **Product differentiation.** Where customer preferences are differentiated, firms may find that the price premium of targeting a single segment with a differentiated product outweighs the higher cost of small volume production. General Motors' rise to market leadership over Ford during the late 1920s is an example of a multimodel differentiation strategy triumphing over a single-model, scale-economy strategy.

- **Flexibility.** Scale-efficient production is likely to involve highly specialized labor and equipment, which tends to be inflexible. In a dynamic environment, very large plants and firms have greater difficulties than smaller units in adjusting to fluctuations in demand and changes in technology, input prices, and customer preferences.[10]

- **Problems of motivation and coordination.** Large units tend to be more complex and more difficult to manage than smaller units. Very large units may never reach maximum efficiency due to problems of strained labor relations, increased supervision costs, and increased waste—and lower levels of employee motivation. One of the world's largest auto assembly plants, VW's Wolfsburg *Halle 54,* provides a classic example of the difficulties of managing very large plants.[11]

Economies of Learning

The principal source of experience-based cost reduction is **learning** by organization members. Repetition reduces costs by decreasing the time required for particular jobs, thus reducing waste and defects, and improving coordination between jobs.[12] For example, in 1943 it took 40,000 labor-hours to build a Convair B-24 bomber. By 1945 it took only 8,000 hours.[13] The more complex a process or product, the greater the potential for learning. Learning effects are important in complex products such as aircraft, process plant construction, and computer software. Learning effects are also important in complex processes. Japanese companies dominate the world market for active-matrix flat screens primarily because of unassailable cost leadership resulting from experience-based learning. The complexity of flat screen manufacture and the fact that a single chip defect may render an entire screen useless, means that yield rate is the key to cost advantage, and learning is the basis of high yields.[14] Learning occurs both at the individual level through improvements in dexterity and problem solving, and at the group level through the development and refinement of *organizational routines* (see Chapter 5 for a further discussion).

Process Technology

For most goods and services, alternative process technologies exist. A particular production method is *technically superior* to another when, for each unit of output, it uses less of one input without using more of any other input. Where a production method uses more of some inputs but less of others, then the relative cost efficiency of the alternative techniques depends on the relative prices of the inputs. Hence, low-cost assembly of consumer electronic products might be achieved in China using labor-intensive techniques, or in Singapore in a fully automated plant.

New process technology may radically reduce costs. Pilkington's float glass process—the manufacture of flat glass by floating molten glass on a bath of molten tin—gave it an unassailable cost advantage in glass production for a sustained period of time. Ford's adoption of moving-assembly line automobile production and interchangeable parts permitted such drastic cost reduction that the automobile was transformed from a rich man's luxury to a form of mass transportation.

When process innovation is embodied in new capital equipment, then diffusion is likely to be rapid. Those firms that are expanding the most rapidly and have the highest rates of net investment will tend to establish cost leadership over their slower growing rivals. However, the full benefits of new process typically require system-wide changes in job design, employee incentives, product design, organizational structure, and management controls.[15] Jaikumar found that the superior performance yielded by flexible manufacturing systems in Japan compared to those in America could be attributed to the failure of American companies to match their management methods to the requirements of the new technology.[16] Between 1979 and 1986, General Motors spent $40 billion on new technology and new plants with a view to becoming the world's most efficient volume manufacturer of automobiles. Yet, in the absence of fundamental changes in organization and management, the productivity gains were meager. Cadillac's state-of-the-art Hamtramck plant in Detroit was a nightmare of inefficiency, line-stoppages, and robots-run-amok. After a tour of the plant, Toyota chairman Eiji Toyoda told a colleague, "It would have been embarrassing to comment on it."[17]

Conversely, process innovations may involve substantial changes in organization and management but comparatively little investment in new hardware. "Lean production" pioneered by Toyota combines JIT, TQM, quality circles, teamworking, job flexibility, and supplier partnerships.[18] Some of the most spectacular turnarounds in production efficiency have been achieved through the application of new approaches to organization and management:

- ♦ The GM-Toyota NUMMI plant at Fremont, California which, using mostly the same employees and capital equipment, went from being one of the lowest productivity auto assembly plants in the United States to one of the highest.[19]
- ♦ Harley-Davidson which, despite limited automation and modest new investment, revolutionized its production processes and performance.[20]

Product Design

Design-for-manufacture—designing products for ease of production rather than simply for functionality and aesthetics—can offer substantial cost savings, especially when linked to the introduction of new process technology. Two key features of the design of new models of automobile have been to permit ease of automated assembly and to increase commonality of components to access scale economies in the manufacture and purchase of components. Thus, car manufacturers have reduced the number of basic "platforms" using standardized engines and major components across different models, while increasing their range of models. Exhibit 8.1 illustrates the potential for design to offer substantial cost economies.

EXHIBIT 8.1

Design for Manufacture: The IBM Proprinter

When IBM introduced its first personal computer in 1983, its least expensive printer cost $5,000. To develop an inexpensive printer for use with its PC, IBM assembled a small technical team of designers, manufacturing engineers, and automation specialists at Charlotte, North Carolina. Working closely together, the team created a design that:

- Reduced the number of parts from 150, found in the typical PC printer, to 60
- Designed the printer in layers so that robots could build it from the bottom up
- Eliminated all screws, springs, and other fasteners that required human insertion and adjustment and replaced them with molded plastic components that clipped together.

Ralph Gomory, former senior vice-president of science and technology at IBM, reported that:

. . . the Proprinter came out essentially as planned. It was made from only 62 parts. It printed faster and had more features than the competition—and the team developed it in half the usual time.

The product was so well-designed for automated manufacture that it turned out to be easy and inexpensive to assemble by hand—so easy in fact that IBM eventually shifted a good deal of Proprinter production from the automated plant in Charlotte to a manual plant in Lexington, Kentucky. An additional benefit was that the Proprinter proved unusually reliable in the field. Fewer parts meant fewer assembly errors, fewer adjustments, and fewer opportunities for things to go wrong later.

With fewer parts and ease of manufacture (the printer could be manually assembled in three and a half minutes), IBM became cost leader in PC printers. Only five months after its launch, the Proprinter was the best-selling printer on the market.

Source: Ralph E. Gomory, "From the Ladder of Science to the Product Development Cycle," *Harvard Business Review*, November–December 1989: 103.

Process Design

Reorganizing production processes can achieve substantial efficiency gains even without new investment in capital or process innovation. What has become popularized as **business process reengineering** (BPR) is the idea that most production processes involve complex interactions among many individuals, and that these processes tend to evolve over time with little conscious or consistent direction. Consultants and "reengineering gurus" Michael Hammer and James Champy have defined BPR as:

> . . . the fundamental rethinking and radical redesign of business processes to achieve dramatic improvements in critical contemporary measures of performance, such as cost, quality, service, and speed.[21]

The idea is to redesign business processes to increase their efficiency in fundamental ways. The essence is to detach from the way in which a process is currently organized and to begin with the question, "If we were starting afresh, how would we design this process?" Although lacking any general theory or design framework, Hammer and Champy point to the existence of a set of "commonalities, recurring themes, or characteristics" that can guide BPR. These include:

♦ Several jobs are combined into one

♦ Workers make decisions

♦ The steps in the process are performed in a natural order

♦ Processes have multiple versions, i.e., processes are designed to take account of different situations

♦ Processes are performed where it makes the most sense, e.g., if the accounting department needs pencils, it is probably cheaper for such a small order to be purchased directly from the office equipment store around the block than to be ordered via the firm's purchasing department

♦ Checks and controls are reduced to the point where they make economic sense

♦ Reconciliation is minimized

♦ A case manager provides a single point of contact at the interface between processes

♦ Hybrid centralized/decentralized operations are prevalent, e.g., through a shared database decentralized decisions can be made while permitting overall coordination simply through information sharing.

BPR has been attributed with achieving major gains in efficiency, quality, and speed (see Exhibit 8.2). On the other hand, there is also considerable evidence of widespread disappointment with the outcomes of reengineering initiatives. One of the major realizations to emerge from BPR exercises is that most production and administrative processes are exceedingly complex. To redesign a process one must first understand it. Process mapping exercises reveal that even seemingly simple business processes, such as the procurement of office supplies, involve complex and sophisticated systems of interactions among a number of organizational members. Reengineering without a complete understanding of the process is hazardous.

Capacity Utilization

Over the short and medium term, plant capacity is more or less fixed, and variations in output are associated with variations in capacity utilization. During periods of low

EXHIBIT 8.2

Process Reengineering at IBM Credit

IBM Credit provides credit to customers of IBM for the purchase of IBM hardware and software. Under the old system, five stages were involved:

1. The IBM salesperson telephoned a request for financing. The request was logged on a piece of paper.
2. The request was sent to the Credit Department where it was logged onto a computer and the customer's creditworthiness was checked. The results of the credit check were written on a form and passed to the Business Practices Department.
3. There the standard loan covenant would be modified to meet the terms of customer loan.
4. The request was passed to the pricer who determined the appropriate interest rate.
5. The clerical group took all the information and prepared a quote letter, which was sent to the salesperson.

Because the process took an average of six days, it resulted in a number of lost sales and held up the sales staff in finalizing deals. After many efforts to improve the process, two managers undertook an experiment. They took a financing request and walked it around through all five steps. The process took 90 minutes!

On this basis, a fundamental redesign of the credit approval process was achieved. The change was replacing the specialists (credit checkers, pricers, and so on) with generalists who undertook all five processes. Only where the request was nonstandard or unusually complex were specialists called in. The basic problem was that the system had been designed for the most complex credit requests that IBM received, whereas in the vast majority of cases no specialist judgment was called for—simply clerical work involving looking up credit ratings, plugging numbers into standard formulae, etc.

The result was that credit requests are processed in four hours compared to six days, total employees were reduced slightly, while the total number of deals increased one hundred times.

Source: Adapted from M. Hammer and J. Champy, *Reengineering the Corporation: A Manifesto for Business Revolution* (New York: Harper Business, 1993): 36–39.

demand, plant capacity is underutilized. This raises unit costs because fixed costs must be spread over fewer units of production. In businesses where virtually all costs are fixed (e.g., airlines, theme parks), profitability is highly sensitive to shortfalls in demand. During periods of peak demand, output may be pushed beyond the normal full-capacity operation. As Boeing discovered in 1997, pushing output beyond capacity operation increases unit costs due to overtime pay, premiums for night and weekend shifts, increased defects, and higher maintenance costs. In declining industries, the ability to speedily adjust capacity to the current level of demand can be a major source of cost advantage. British Steel was Europe's most profitable steel producer for much of the 1980s and 1990s, partly because it adjusted its capacity much faster than its rivals.

Input Costs

When the firms in an industry purchase their inputs in the same competitive input markets, we can expect every firm to pay the same price for identical inputs. In most industries, however, differences in the costs incurred by different firms for similar inputs can be an important source of overall cost advantage. There are several common sources of lower input costs.

Locational Differences in Input Prices.   The prices of inputs may vary between locations, the most important being differences in wage rates from one country to another. In labor-intensive industries such as clothing, footwear, hand tools, and toys, low wage rates give an unassailable cost advantage to producers in developing countries. Similarly, many U.S. companies have relocated labor-intensive administrative tasks—such as insurance claim processing and back-office functions—to Ireland and other English-speaking countries where educational levels are high and employment costs lower than in the United States. Raw material and energy costs also vary between locations. In pulp and paper, Canadian and Scandinavian producers benefit from their access to forests and hydroelectric power. Exchange rate movements exert a major influence on the prices of local inputs. The rise of the yen from 1993 to 1996 severely dented the cost competitiveness of Japanese firms in world markets, while the devaluation of Southeast Asian currencies in 1997 boosted the cost competitiveness of manufacturers exporting from these countries.

Ownership of Low-Cost Sources of Supply.   In   raw   material-intensive industries, ownership or access to low-cost sources may be a key cost advantage. Arco's cost leadership in West Coast gasoline markets—as a result of its Alaskan oil reserves—has made it one of the most profitable of the U.S. oil majors.

Non-Union Labor.   In some labor-intensive industries, cost leaders are often the firms that have avoided unionization. In the U.S. airline industry, unionization is a major source of the cost difference between low-cost carriers and the major airlines (see Table 8.2).

Bargaining Power.   Where bought-in products are a major cost item, differences in buying power among the firms in an industry can be an important source of cost advantage. The dominance of chains such as Wal-Mart, Toys "R" Us, IKEA, and Home Depot in particular areas of retail trade is, to a great extent, a result of superior bargaining power resulting in preferential purchasing terms.[22]

TABLE 8.2
Costs Per Available Seat-Mile in Short-Haul Passenger Transport, 1993

	SOUTHWEST AIRLINES (CENTS)	UNITED AIRLINES (CENTS)
Wages and benefits	2.4	3.5
Fuel and oil	1.1	1.1
Aircraft ownership	0.7	0.8
Aircraft maintenance	0.6	0.3
Commissions on ticket sales	0.5	1.0
Advertising	0.2	0.2
Food and beverage	0.0	0.5
Other	1.7	3.1
Total	7.2	10.5

Source: United Airlines.

Relationships with Suppliers.   Recently companies have developed closer and longer-term relationships with a smaller number of suppliers. Closer coordination permits economies from more effective quality control, just-in-time scheduling, technology transfer, reduced invoicing costs, and accelerated new product development cycles.

Residual Efficiency

In many industries, the basic cost drivers—scale, technology, product and process design, input costs and capacity utilization—fail to provide a complete explanation for why one firm in an industry has lower unit costs than a competitor. Even after taking all these cost drivers into account, unit cost differences between firms remain. These **residual efficiencies** relate to the extent to which the firm approaches its *efficiency frontier* of optimal operation. Residual efficiency depends on the firm's ability to eliminate "organizational slack"[23] or "X-inefficiency":[24] costs in excess of maximum efficiency operation. These costs are typically a consequence of employees' desire—both at managerial and shop-floor levels—to maintain some margin of slack in preference to the rigors of operating at maximum efficiency.

The ability of firms to achieve dramatic cost reductions when faced with bankruptcy is evidence of such slack. Chrysler in 1980, Texaco in 1988, and Continental Airlines in the early 1990s all pulled back from the brink of annihilation through startling cost reductions. In the absence of a threat to the survival of the organization, high levels of residual efficiency are normally the consequence of highly motivated employees—Wal-Mart, Southwest Airlines, and Nucor are examples.

USING THE VALUE CHAIN TO ANALYZE COSTS

Our discussion of costs has used the firm or business as the unit of analysis. In practice, however, the production of a good or service consists of a chain of activities, where each activity has a distinct cost structure determined by different cost drivers.[25] A comprehensive cost analysis requires disaggregating the firm's value chain in order to identify:

♦ The relative importance of each activity with respect to total cost,

♦ The cost drivers for each activity and the comparative efficiency with which the firm performs each activity,

♦ How costs in one activity influence costs in another,

♦ Which activities should be undertaken within the firm and which activities should be outsourced.

A value chain analysis of a firm's cost position consists of the following principal stages:

1. **Disaggregate the firm into separate activities.** Determining the appropriate value chain activities is a matter of judgment. It requires understanding the chain of processes involved in the transformation of inputs into output and its delivery to the customer. Very often, the firm's own divisional and departmental structure is a useful guide. Key considerations are:
   ♦ The separateness of one activity from another,
   ♦ The importance of an activity,
   ♦ The dissimilarity of activities in terms of cost drivers,
   ♦ The extent to which there are differences in the way that competitors perform the particular activity.

2. **Establish the relative importance of different activities in the total cost of the product.** Our analysis needs to focus on the activities that are the major sources of cost. In disaggregating costs, Michael Porter suggests the detailed assignment of operating costs and assets to each value activity. Though the adoption of activity-based costing has made such cost data more available, detailed cost allocation can be a major exercise. Even without such detailed cost data, it is usually possible to identify the critical activities, establish which activities are performed relatively efficiently or inefficiently, identify cost drivers, and offer recommendations.

3. **Compare costs by activity.** To establish which activities the firm performs relatively efficiently and which it does not, benchmark unit costs for each activity against those of competitors.

4. **Identify cost drivers.** For each activity, what factors determine the level of cost relative to other firms? For some activities, cost drivers are evident simply from the nature of the activity and composition of costs. For capital-intensive activities such as the operation of a body press in an auto plant, the principal factors are likely to be capital equipment costs, weekly production volume, and downtime between changes of dies. For labor-intensive assembly activities, critical issues are wage rates, speed of work, and defect rates.

5. **Identify linkages.** The costs of one activity may be determined, in part, by the way in which other activities are performed. Xerox discovered that its high service costs relative to competitors reflected the complexity of design of its copiers, which required 30 different interrelated adjustments.[26] The careful tracing of defects that appear at one stage of a production process to their source in an earlier stage is a key element of total quality management. In recent years, the optimization of activities throughout the value chain has become a major source of cost reduction and speed enhancement has become a key challenge for computer integrated manufacturing. SAP of Germany is a leading supplier of the integration of activities within the firm, whereas Manugistics, 12 Technologies, and several other companies compete for leadership in the market for supply chain management software.

6. **Identify opportunities for reducing costs.** By identifying areas of comparative inefficiency and the cost drivers for each, opportunities for cost reduction become evident. For example:
   - If scale economies are a key cost driver, can volume be increased? One feature of Caterpillar's cost reduction strategy was to broaden Caterpillar's model range and OEM sales of diesel engines to exploit scale economies, R&D, component manufacturing, and dealer support over a larger sales volume.
   - Where wage costs are the issue, can wages be reduced either directly or by relocating production?
   - If a certain activity cannot be performed efficiently within the firm, can the activity be contracted out, or can the component or service be bought in? Outsourcing in the auto industry has extended to the point where at VW's Brazilian plant, external suppliers not only supply components and subassemblies, they are also responsible for installing them on VW's assembly line. Outsourcing of information technology functions has fueled the growth of EDS, Andersen Consulting, and other suppliers of IT services.

Figure 8.6 shows how the application of the value chain to automobile manufacture can yield suggestions for possible cost reductions.

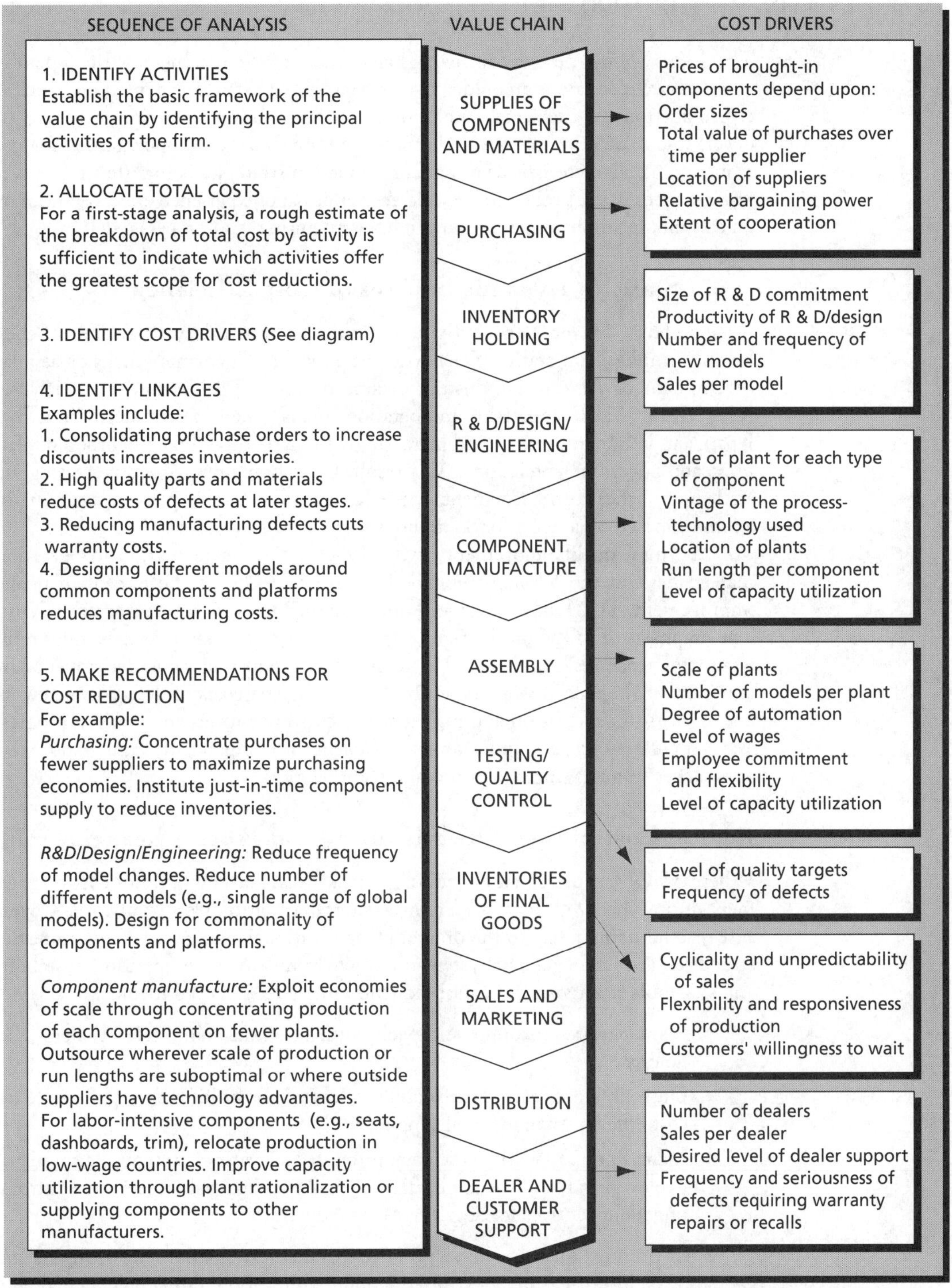

SEQUENCE OF ANALYSIS

1. IDENTIFY ACTIVITIES
Establish the basic framework of the value chain by identifying the principal activities of the firm.

2. ALLOCATE TOTAL COSTS
For a first-stage analysis, a rough estimate of the breakdown of total cost by activity is sufficient to indicate which activities offer the greatest scope for cost reductions.

3. IDENTIFY COST DRIVERS (See diagram)

4. IDENTIFY LINKAGES
Examples include:
1. Consolidating pruchase orders to increase discounts increases inventories.
2. High quality parts and materials reduce costs of defects at later stages.
3. Reducing manufacturing defects cuts warranty costs.
4. Designing different models around common components and platforms reduces manufacturing costs.

5. MAKE RECOMMENDATIONS FOR COST REDUCTION
For example:
Purchasing: Concentrate purchases on fewer suppliers to maximize purchasing economies. Institute just-in-time component supply to reduce inventories.

R&D/Design/Engineering: Reduce frequency of model changes. Reduce number of different models (e.g., single range of global models). Design for commonality of components and platforms.

Component manufacture: Exploit economies of scale through concentrating production of each component on fewer plants. Outsource wherever scale of production or run lengths are suboptimal or where outside suppliers have technology advantages. For labor-intensive components (e.g., seats, dashboards, trim), relocate production in low-wage countries. Improve capacity utilization through plant rationalization or supplying components to other manufacturers.

VALUE CHAIN

SUPPLIES OF COMPONENTS AND MATERIALS

PURCHASING

INVENTORY HOLDING

R & D/DESIGN/ ENGINEERING

COMPONENT MANUFACTURE

ASSEMBLY

TESTING/ QUALITY CONTROL

INVENTORIES OF FINAL GOODS

SALES AND MARKETING

DISTRIBUTION

DEALER AND CUSTOMER SUPPORT

COST DRIVERS

Prices of brought-in components depend upon:
Order sizes
Total value of purchases over time per supplier
Location of suppliers
Relative bargaining power
Extent of cooperation

Size of R & D commitment
Productivity of R & D/design
Number and frequency of new models
Sales per model

Scale of plant for each type of component
Vintage of the process-technology used
Location of plants
Run length per component
Level of capacity utilization

Scale of plants
Number of models per plant
Degree of automation
Level of wages
Employee commitment and flexibility
Level of capacity utilization

Level of quality targets
Frequency of defects

Cyclicality and unpredictability of sales
Flexnbility and responsiveness of production
Customers' willingness to wait

Number of dealers
Sales per dealer
Desired level of dealer support
Frequency and seriousness of defects requiring warranty repairs or recalls

FIGURE 8.6
Using the Value Chain in Cost Analysis: An Automobile Manufacturer

COST CUTTING IN THE 1990S

The 1990s were a new era in managing for cost efficiency. Increased competition and pressure to create shareholder value have resulted in unprecedented pressures for cost reduction. At the same time, a more turbulent business environment and the development of new management tools have opened new opportunities for cost reduction. A characteristic of recent cost reduction strategies is that they rely less on static sources of cost reduction—scale economies and experience effects—and more on continuous improvement, innovation, restructuring, and process redesign.

From Static to Dynamic Sources of Cost Efficiency

Robert Hayes, Steven Wheelwright, and Kim Clark of Harvard Business School identify emphasis on static efficiency at the expense of dynamic efficiency as a key determinant of America's industrial decline during the 1970s and early 1980s.[27] After World War II, leadership in operations management passed from the U.S. to Japan, and U.S. managers turned increasingly to marketing, finance, corporate planning, and government relations. As a result, U.S. companies turned increasingly to static approaches to management, while Japanese companies pioneered a dynamic approach based on a quest for continuous improvement (*kaisan*).

The total quality movement of the 1980s created a revolution in operations management in the West. Although the focus of TQM is the pursuit of quality improvement, TQM also introduced new thinking about the management of costs. The emphasis of TQM on the rigorous analysis of production activities, the simplification of processes, training, and increasing the responsibility and decision-making authority of shop-floor workers results in reducing the costs of defects and rework, lowers costs of supervision and maintenance, cuts inventories and work in progress, and stimulates process innovation.[28] Table 8.3 compares dynamic and static approaches to managing operations and technology.

Radical Cost Surgery: Restructuring and Process Reengineering

Whereas TQM is incremental and long term, the major emphases of cost management during the 1990s have been radical, short-term initiatives to cut costs. **Corporate restructuring** refers to the dramatic organizational changes to adjust strategies, structures, and management systems to an environment of competition, instability, and shareholder activism. The cost reduction measures involved include:

- Plant closures to improve capacity utilization and eliminate obsolete technology;
- Outsourcing of components and services wherever internal suppliers are less cost efficient than external suppliers;
- Increasing managerial efficiency through "delayering" to reduce administrative overhead, and the application of rigorous financial targets and control to provide incentives for aggressive cost reduction.

Such pruning measures have produced dramatic reductions in operating and capital costs. However, further cost reduction requires more fundamental changes in the ways companies do business. BPR represents one approach to achieving efficiency through reorganizing processes. Exhibit 8.3 gives one example of a radical, corporate-wide cost-reduction program.

TABLE 8.3
Characteristics of Dynamic and Static Approaches to Manufacturing

DYNAMIC	STATIC
The Production System	*The Production System*
Artisan mode of production involving:	Production dominated by the imperatives of Scientific Management:
• Problem solving • Creation of knowledge by production workers • Workers' control over the product • Orientation toward the product and the customer	• Quest for the "one best way" • People matched to tasks • Supervise, reward, and punish to ensure conformity of individual efforts and company objectives • Use staff to plan and control
Management of Technology	*Management of Technology*
An emphasis on:	• Science driven, research findings seeking commercial applications • Concentrated in corporate R&D departments • Emphasis on product innovation and on large-scale projects.
• Continual improvement in small steps • Commercial needs establish the R&D agenda (technology pulled in by practical demands) • Product and process innovation intimately related • Teamwork and cross-functional collaboration	

Source: Based on the ideas and concepts in Kim Clark and Robert H. Hayes, "Recapturing America's Manufacturing Heritage," *California Management Review,* Summer 1988: 9–33.

♦ SUMMARY

Cost efficiency may no longer be a guarantee of profitability in today's fast-changing markets, but in almost all industries it is a prerequisite for success. In industries where competition has always been primarily price-based—steel, textiles, and mortgage loans—increased intensity of competition requires relentless cost reduction efforts. In industries where price competition was once muted—airlines, banking, and electrical power—firms have been forced to reconcile the pursuit of innovation, differentiation, and service quality with vigorous cost reduction.

The foundation for a cost reduction strategy must be an understanding of the determinants of a company's costs. The principal message of this chapter is the need to look behind cost accounting data and beyond simplistic approaches to the determinants of cost efficiency, and to analyze the factors that drive relative unit costs in each of the firm's activities in a systematic and comprehensive manner.

Increasingly, approaches to cost efficiency are less about cutting input costs here and accessing additional scale economies there, and more about fundamental rethinking of the activities undertaken by the firm and the ways in which it organizes them. By focusing on those activities in which the firm possesses a cost advantage and outsourcing others, and by extensively reengineering manufacturing and administrative processes, firms have succeeded in achieving dramatic reductions in operating costs.

EXHIBIT 8.3

Cost Cutting at Chevron 1992–93

After a decade during which Chevron's profitability and returns to shareholders lagged those of most other U.S. oil majors, in January 1992, CEO Kenneth Derr announced an "aggressive action plan" involving:

- Capacity reduction and efficiency increases at the Port Arthur refinery, including a cut in employment of 700;
- An acceleration in sales of U.S. oil and gas properties—of Chevron's 1,000 remaining fields at the beginning of 1992, Derr announced the intention to sell 600 of them;
- A program to reduce operating expenses by 50 cents a barrel of sales by mid-1993.

In fact, this cost reduction was achieved before the end of 1992. For 1992 as a whole, operating expenses were reduced by 59 cents for each barrel of product sold, adding $570 million to pre-tax income. Total employment was cut by 6,200 during 1992. For 1993, a further cost reduction target of 25 cents per barrel was established. A key element of the proposed cuts in costs were reductions at the corporate level where a 30 percent cost reduction was targeted. In its report for the third quarter of 1993, Chevron was able to report that it had already exceeded its cost reduction target for 1993: costs had been reduced by over 40 cents a barrel of product sold. After adjusting for special items, Chevron succeeded in cutting operating costs by 7 percent during the first nine months of 1993 compared to the comparable period in 1992. The principal cost reductions occurred in the following areas:

1. *Selling, General and Administrative Expenses.* These were cut from $459 million during the third quarter of 1992 to $359 million during the third quarter of 1993. The biggest cost savings were incurred at corporate headquarters. Between 1992 and 1993, headquarters staff was reduced from 3,600 to 2,600, and headquarters operating costs

from $670 million to $470 million. Of the 1,000 headquarters positions lost, about 550 were by voluntary early retirement. The reductions were primarily in tax, treasury, public affairs, security, law, and human resources. Chairman K. Derr stated, "We regret that these changes will leave some employees without jobs. The cutbacks reflect a business environment that has required us to change our structure and eliminate work that's not absolutely essential to our business."

2. *Chevron Information Technology Company.* A combination of reorganization and outsourcing of IT services resulted in CITC's employment being cut from 2,300 in 1992 to 1,800 in 1993.

3. *Exploration and Production.* During 1992 employee innovations, sales of high-cost oil and gas fields, and a 23 percent reduction in the number of employees cut operating costs by $400 million, or $1.18 per barrel of oil.

4. *U.S. Refining and Marketing.* A key element in Chevron U.S.A. Products' target of reducing operating costs by $300 million was cutting refinery capacity to increase capacity utilization at its Port Arthur (Texas) and Richmond (California) refineries. In retailing, Chevron reduced its number of stations while focusing its marketing efforts on 16 key metropolitan areas in the South and West. From end-1988 to end-1992, Chevron's company-owned and company-leased stations fell from 3,400 to 2,500. At the end of 1993, Chevron was pursuing further capacity reduction. Its Port Arthur and Philadelphia refineries were put up for sale as well as two small refineries in the Northwest and six terminals in the east.

Source: Chevron Annual Reports.

Given multiple drivers of relative cost, cost management implies multiple initiatives at different organizational levels. Careful analysis of existing activities relative to competitors can pinpoint cost reduction opportunities by lowering input costs, accessing scale economies, and better utilizing capacity. At the same time, the firm must seek opportunities for innovation and process redesign in order to exploit new sources of dynamic efficiency.

NOTES

1   Louis E. Yelle, "The Learning Curve: Historical Review and Comprehensive Survey," *Decision Sciences* 10 (1979): 302–328.

2   A rigorous analysis of the profit gains to market share leadership under differently sloped experience curves and different competitive conditions is developed by David Ross, "Learning to Dominate," *Journal of Industrial Economics* 34 (1986): 337–353.

3   For a discussion of the policy implications of the experience curve, see Charles Baden Fuller, "The Implications of the Learning Curve for Firm Strategy and Public Policy," *Applied Economics* 15 (1983): 541–551.

4   This is sometimes referred to as "penetration" pricing, as opposed to "full-cost" pricing, or "skimming."

5   Boston Consulting Group, *Strategy Alternatives for the British Motorcycle Industry* (London: Her Majesty's Stationery Office, 1975).

6   Robert D. Buzzell, Bradley T. Gale, and Ralph Sultan, "Market Share—A Key to Profitability," *Harvard Business Review* (January–February, 1975); Robert D. Buzzell and Fredrick Wiersema, "Successful Share-Building Strategies," *Harvard Business Review* (January–February 1981); Robert Jacobsen and David Aaker, "Is Market Share All That It's Cracked up to Be?" *Journal of Marketing* 49 (Fall 1985): 11–22.

7   Richard Rumelt and Robin Wensley, using PIMS data, found the relationship between market share and profitability to be the result of both being joint outcomes of a risky competitive process. "In Search of the Market Share Effect," paper MGL-63, Graduate School of Management, UCLA, 1981.

8   Robin Wensley, "PIMS and BCG: New Horizons or False Dawn?" *Strategic Management Journal* 3 (1982): 147–158.

9   To be more precise, the economies of amortizing the costs of new product development are *economies of volume* rather than *economies of scale*. The product development cost per unit of production declines not on the *volume of production per unit of time*, but on the *total volume of production over the life of the model.*

10 This argument was first made by David Schwartzman, "Uncertainty and the Size of the Firm," *Economica* (August 1963).

11 Maryann Keller, *Collision* (New York: Doubleday, 1993): 173–177.

12 Leonard Rapping, "Learning and World War II Production Functions," *Review of Economics and Statistics* (February 1965): 81–86.

13 Kim B. Clark and Robert H. Hayes, "Recapturing America's Manufacturing Heritage," *California Management Review* (Summer 1988): 25.

14 "Road Toward Success at Flat Screens Is Full of Bumps," *Wall Street Journal*, April 20, 1994: B4.

15 See, for example: Robert H. Hayes and Ramchandran Jaikumar, "Manufacturing's Crisis: New Technologies, Obsolete Organizations," *Harvard Business Review* (September–October 1988): 85; and Robert M. Grant, A. B. Shani, R. Krishnan, and R. Baer "Appropriate Manufacturing Technology: A Strategic Approach," *Sloan Management Review* 33, no. 1 (Fall 1991): 43–54.

16 Ramchandran Jaikumar, "Postindustrial Manufacturing," *Harvard Business Review* (November–December 1986): 69–76.

17 Maryann Keller, *Collision* (New York: Doubleday, 1993): 169–171.

18 James Womack and Dan T. Jones, *Lean Thinking* (New York: Simon & Schuster, 1996).

19 Clair Brown and Michael Reich, "When Does Union-Management Cooperation Work? A Look at NUMMI and GM-Van Nuys," *California Management Review* (Summer 1989): 28–29.

20 Robert M. Grant, "Roaring Back: Harley-Davidson in 1988," in K.E. Neupert and J.N. Fry (eds.), Cases for Contemporary Strategy Analysis (Oxford: Blackwell, 1996): 167–184

21 Michael Hammer and James Champy, *Reengineering the Corporation: A Manifesto for Business Revolution* (New York: Harper Business, 1993): 32.

22 Robert M. Grant, "Manufacturer-Retailer Relations: The Shifting Balance of Power," in *Retailing and Business Strategy*, ed. G. Johnson (New York: John Wiley, 1987).

23 R. Cyert and J. March, *A Behavioral Theory of the Firm* (Englewood Cliffs, NJ: Prentice-Hall, 1963).

24 H. Leibenstein, "Allocative Efficiency Versus X-Efficiency," *American Economic Review 54* (June 1966).

25 The value chain is introduced and discussed in Chapter 5.

26 "Cutting Costs Without Killing the Business," *Fortune*, October 13, 1986: 72.

27 Robert H. Hayes, Steven C. Wheelwright, and Kim B. Clark, *Dynamic Manufacturing: Creating the Learning Organization* (New York: Free Press, 1988).

28 For a review of the impact of TQM, see David A. Garvin, *Managing Quality: The Strategic and Competitive Edge* (New York: Free Press, 1988).

9
Differentiation Advantage

> If the three keys to selling real estate are location, location, location, then the three keys of selling consumer products are differentiation, differentiation, differentiation.
> — *Robert Goizueta, Chairman, Coca-Cola Co. (died October 18, 1997)*
> If you gave me $100 billion and said, "Take away the soft drink leadership of Coca-Cola in the world," I'd give it back to you and say, "It can't be done."
> — *Warren Buffett, Chairman, Berkshire Hathaway, and Coca-Cola's biggest shareholder*

Outline

◆ INTRODUCTION AND OBJECTIVES

A firm differentiates itself from its competitors "when it provides something unique that is valuable to buyers beyond simply offering a low price."[1] **Differentiation advantage** occurs when a firm is able to obtain from its differentiation a price premium in the market that exceeds the cost of providing the differentiation.

There is almost no limit to a firm's opportunities for differentiating its offering to customers, although the range of differentiation opportunities depends on the characteristics of the product. An automobile or a restaurant offers greater potential for differentiation than standardized products such as cement, wheat, or computer memory chips. These latter products are called "commodities" precisely because they lack physical differentiation. Yet even commodity products can be differentiated in ways that create customer value: "Anything can be turned into a value-added product or service for a well-defined or newly created market," claims Tom Peters.[2] Peters gives the example of Milliken & Company's success in the market for the lowly "shop towel"—towels and cloths for factories, hospitals, and other institutions. Milliken's customers are industrial launderers who rent the towels to the final users. Milliken supplies its customers not just with towels but with a complete service that covers ordering, distribution, inventory control, sales training, promotional materials, audiovisual sales aids, seminars, and market research data. Thus, differentiation extends beyond the characteristics of the product or the service to encompass every possible interaction between the firm and its customers.

The supply-side analysis of differentiation tells us what the firm can do to be different, but the critical issue is whether such differentiation *creates value for customers*. If the purpose of differentiation is to generate profit for the firm, the focus for differentiation analysis must be the potential for differentiation to increase customer satisfaction or lower the customer's costs. Thus, our primary concern in this chapter is the *demand side* of the market. By understanding what customers want, how they chose, and what their motivations are we can identify opportunities for profitable differentiation.

Differentiation strategies are not about pursuing uniqueness for the sake of being different. Differentiation is about understanding the product or service and about understanding the customer. To this extent, the quest for differentiation advantage takes us to the heart of business strategy. The fundamental issues of differentiation are also the fundamental issues of business strategy: Who are our customers? How do we create value for them? And how do we do it more effectively and efficiently than anyone else so that we can earn profit from it?

Because differentiation is about uniqueness, differentiation advantage cannot be achieved simply through the application of standardized frameworks, techniques, checklists, and systems of classification. Differentiation advantage involves identifying new and unique opportunities and developing innovative approaches to exploit them.

This is not to say that differentiation advantage is not amenable to systematic analysis. As we have observed, there are two elements of creating profitable differentiation. On the *supply side*, the firm must be aware of the resources and capabilities through which it can create uniqueness (and do it better than competitors). On the *demand side* the key is insight into customers and their needs and preferences. These two sides form the major components of our analysis of differentiation. This analysis is not intended to constrain or supplant intuition and creativity, but to provide a framework capable of stimulating and guiding novel and creative approaches to generating customer value.

By the time you have completed this chapter you will be able to:

♦ Recognize what differentiation is, recognize its different forms, and appreciate its potential for creating competitive advantage

♦ Analyze the sources of differentiation in terms of customers' preferences and characteristics, and of the firm's capacity for supplying differentiation

♦ Formulate strategies that create differentiation advantage by linking the firm's differentiation capability to customers' demand for differentiation

THE NATURE OF DIFFERENTIATION AND DIFFERENTIATION ADVANTAGE

Differentiation Variables

The potential for differentiating a product or service is partly determined by its physical characteristics. For a product that is technically simple (a pair of socks, a brick), or that satisfies uncomplicated needs (a corkscrew, a nail), or that must meet specific technical standards (a spark plug, a thermometer), differentiation opportunities are constrained by technical or market factors. Products that are complex (an airplane), that satisfy complex needs (an automobile, a vacation), or that do not need to conform to stringent technical standards (wine, toys) offer much greater scope for differentiation.

Beyond these constraints, the potential in any product or service for differentiation is limited only by the boundaries of the human imagination. For simple products such as shampoo, toilet paper, and cigarettes, the proliferation of brands on any supermarket's shelves is testimony both to the ingenuity of firms and the complexity of customer preferences. Differentiation extends beyond the physical characteristics of the product or service to encompass everything about the product or service that influences the value customers derive from it. This means that differentiation includes every aspect of the way in which a company does business and relates to its customers. Thus, McDonald's differentiation advantage within the fast-food business depends not just on the characteristics of the food it serves or the associated services (speed of service, cleanliness), but also the values it projects such as happiness and interest in children. Differentiation is not an activity specific to design and marketing; it infuses all functions and is built into the identity and culture of a company. As a result, companies that supply seemingly basic, no-frills offerings such as Volkswagen during the 1960s and Southwest Airlines during the 1990s may achieve highly differentiated market positions in terms of customers' perceptions.

Differentiation strategy extends beyond *product* differentiation to include all aspects of the *relationship* between a company and its customers. Ultimately differentiation is all about a firm's responsiveness to customer requirements. Tom Peters calls for "total customer responsiveness":

> Every action, no matter how small, and no matter how far from the firing line a department may be, must be processed through the customer's eyes. Will this make it easier for the customer? Faster? Better? Less expensive? . . . Long-term profit equals revenue from continuously happy customer relationships minus cost.[3]

In analyzing differentiation opportunities, a basic distinction is between *tangible* and *intangible* aspects. **Tangible differentiation** is concerned with the observable characteristics of a product or service that are relevant to the preferences and choice processes of customers. These include such characteristics as size, shape, color, weight, design, material, and technology. Tangible differentiation also includes the performance of the product or service in terms of reliability, consistency, taste, speed, durability, safety. The products and services that are complements to the product in question are also important in relation to differentiation potential. These include pre-sales services, after-sales services, accessories, availability and speed of delivery, credit, and the ability to upgrade the product in the future. For consumer products, these differentiation variables directly determine the utility that consumers gain from the product. For producer goods, differentiation variables affect the customer firms' ability to make money in their own businesses—hence these performance variables are valuable sources of differentiation if they lower customer firms' costs or increase their ability to differentiate their own products.

Opportunities for **intangible differentiation** arise because the value that customers perceive in a product or service is not dependent exclusively on the tangible aspects of the offering. There are few products where customer choice is determined solely by observable product features or objective performance criteria. Social, emotional, psychological, and aesthetic considerations are present in choices over all products and services. The desire for status, exclusivity, individuality, and security are extremely powerful motivational forces in choices relating to most consumer goods. Where a product or service is meeting complex customer needs, differentiation choices involve the overall *image* of the firm's offering. Issues of image differentiation are especially important for those products and services whose qualities and performance are difficult to ascertain at the time of purchase ("experience goods"). These include cosmetics, medical services, and education.

Differentiation and Segmentation

Differentiation is different from segmentation. Differentiation is concerned with *how* the firm competes—in what ways the firm can offer uniqueness to its customers. Such uniqueness might relate to *consistency* (McDonald's), *reliability* (Federal Express), *status* (American Express), *quality* (Marks & Spencer), and *innovation* (Sony). Segmentation, in terms of market segment choices, is concerned with *where* the firm competes in terms of customer groups, localities, and product types.

Whereas segmentation is a feature of market structure, differentiation is a strategic choice by a firm. A segmented market is one that can be partitioned according to the characteristics of customers and their demand. Differentiation is concerned with a firm's positioning within a market or a segment in relation to the product, service, and image characteristics that influence customer choice.[4] By locating within a segment, a firm does not necessarily differentiate itself from its competitors within the same segment. A firm may be committed to a differentiation strategy, and yet position itself within the mass market. IBM, General Motors, and Burger King all aim at well-defined positions of differentiation within their markets, while aiming at market share leadership.

However, differentiation decisions may be closely linked to choices over the segments in which a firm competes. By offering uniqueness in its offerings, a firm may inevitably target certain market niches. By selecting performance, engineering, and style as the basis on which BMW competes in the automobile industry, it inevitably appeals to different market segments than does VW.

The Sustainability of Differentiation Advantage

Although strategy analysis has traditionally emphasized cost advantage as the primary basis for establishing a competitive advantage over rivals, in many respects, low cost is a far less secure basis for sustainable competitive advantage than differentiation. The growth of international competition has revealed the fragility of seemingly well-established positions of domestic cost leadership. Across North America and Western Europe, firms whose competitive advantage was based on cost leadership through scale economies and superior process technology have been undermined by competition from countries with lower labor costs. Moreover, in international industries, cost leadership is seldom clearly defined: movements in exchange rates can cause rapid shifts in cost competitiveness. From 1994 to 1996, U.S. carmakers enjoyed global cost leadership as a result of a combination of high productivity and a low dollar. During the first half of 1997, a 20 percent decline of the yen against the dollar revitalized the cost competitiveness of Japanese companies.

Even in relation to domestic competition, cost advantage is increasingly vulnerable:

♦ The increasing pace of technological change means that cost advantages based on scale and experience may be undercut by a competitor's process innovation. During the 1970s, several major European and U.S. steel companies invested heavily in large, integrated iron and steel plants at coastal locations. However, it was the small mini-mill steel firms using a quite different technology that emerged as the cost leaders in the industry.

♦ Where cost advantage is built on technical capabilities, the embodiment of new technology in new equipment and the increased intercompany mobility of personnel speeds the transfer of technology and experience between firms.

The superiority of differentiation advantage over cost advantage in terms of sustainability of competitive advantage is indicated by U.S. companies that have been consistently successful over the long term. Table 9.1 lists companies among the *Fortune* 100 largest U.S. corporations with the highest return to stockholders. The list is dominated by firms whose strategies have been based on differentiation in terms of quality, brand loyalty, and innovation.

ANALYZING DIFFERENTIATION: THE DEMAND SIDE

Successful differentiation involves matching customers' demand for differentiation with the firm's capacity to supply differentiation. Let's begin with the demand side. Analyzing customer demand enables us to determine the potential for differentiation to appeal to customers, their willingness to pay for differentiation, and the most promising positioning in relation to competitors.

Analyzing demand begins with understanding why customers buy a product or service. What are the needs and requirements of a person who is purchasing a personal computer? What is motivating a company when it hires management consultants? Market research systematically explores customer preferences and customer perceptions of existing products. However, the key to successful differentiation is to *understand* customers. In gaining insight into customer requirements and preferences, simple, direct questions about the purpose of a product and its performance attributes can often be far more illuminating than objective market research data obtained from large samples of actual and potential customers. Exhibit 9.1 provides a striking example of the value of simplicity and directness in probing customer requirements.

Product Attributes and Positioning

Virtually all products and services serve multiple customer needs. As a result, understanding customer needs requires the analysis of multiple attributes. Market research has developed numerous techniques for analyzing customer preferences in relation to product attributes in order to guide the positioning of new products and repositioning

TABLE 9.1
Top 30 Companies Among the 100 Largest U.S. Corporations with the Highest Return to Stockholders, 1986–1996

	AVERAGE ANNUAL RETURN %
Intel	43.8
Home Depot	40.2
Compaq Computer	36.9
Johnson & Johnson	31.0
Coca-Cola	29.8
MCI Communications	26.7
Philip Morris	25.0
BankAmerica Corp.	24.2
PepsiCo	23.0
Albertson's	22.7
Motorola	22.5
Merck	22.1
McDonnell Douglas	22.1
Procter & Gamble	21.9
American Stores	21.8
Walt Disney	21.2
UAL	21.0
Kimberly-Clark	20.9
Nationsbank	20.6
Abbot Laboratories	20.6
Enron	20.4
Bell Atlantic	20.3
Chrysler	20.2
Morgan Stanley Group	20.1
Warner-Lambert	20.0
General Electric	19.9
PPG Industries	19.8
Merrill Lynch	19.4
Sara Lee	19.0

Source: "The *Fortune* 500," *Fortune*, April 28, 1997.

of existing products within the market. Techniques include multidimensional scaling, conjoint analysis, and hedonic price analysis.

Multidimensional Scaling. **Multidimensional scaling** permits customers' perceptions of competing products' similarities and dissimilarities to be represented graphically and for the dimensions to be interpreted in terms of key product

EXHIBIT 9.1

Understanding What a Product Is About

Getting back to strategy means getting back to a deep understanding of what a product is about. Some time back, for example, a Japanese home appliance company was trying to develop a coffee percolator. Should it be a General Electric-type percolator, executives wondered? Should it be the same drip-type that Philips makes? Larger? Smaller? I urged them to ask a different kind of question: Why do people drink coffee? What are they looking for when they do? If your objective is to serve the customer better, then shouldn't you understand why that customer drinks coffee in the first place? Then you would know what kind of percolator to make.

The answer came back: good taste. Then I asked the company's engineers what they were doing to help the consumer enjoy good taste in a cup of coffee. They said they were trying to design a good percolator. I asked them what influences the taste in a cup of coffee. No one knew. That became the next question we had to answer. It turns out that lots of things can affect taste—the beans, the temperature, the water. We did our homework and discovered all the things that affect taste . . .

Of all the factors, water quality, we learned, made the greatest difference. The percolator in design at the time, however, didn't take water quality into account at all . . . We discovered next the grain distribution and the time between grinding the beans and pouring in the water

were crucial. As a result we began to think about the product and its necessary features in a new way. It *had* to have a built-in dechlorinating function. It *had* to have a built-in grinder. All the customer should have to do is pour in water and beans . . .

To start you have to ask the right questions and set the right kinds of strategic goals. If your only concern is that General Electric has just brought out a percolator that brews coffee in ten minutes, you will get your engineers to design one that brews it in seven minutes. And if you stick to that logic, market research will tell you that instant coffee is the way to go . . . Conventional marketing approaches won't solve the problem. If you ask people whether they want their coffee in ten minutes or seven, they will say seven, of course. But it's still the wrong question. And you end up back where you started, trying the beat the competition at its own game. If your primary focus is on the competition, you will never step back and ask what the customers' inherent needs are, and what the product really is about.

attributes.[5] For example, a pharmaceutical company's survey of consumer ratings of competing pain relievers resulted in the mapping shown in Figure 9.1.

Conjoint Analysis.   **Conjoint analysis** is a powerful means of analyzing the strength of customer preferences for different product attributes. The techniques require, first, an identification of the underlying attributes of a product and, second, a ranking of hypothetical products that contain alternative bundles of attributes. On the basis of these data, tradeoffs can be analyzed and the simulations can be run to determine the proportion of customers who would prefer a hypothetical new product to competing products already available in the market.[6] A conjoint analysis undertaken by BCG of potential personal computer buyers identified price, manufacturer's reputation, portability, processing capability, memory capacity, word processing capability, and styling as critical attributes. The data gathered on customer preferences and tradeoffs were used to predict the share of customer preferences that the forthcoming Apple Macintosh and IBM PC Junior

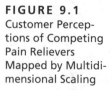

FIGURE 9.1
Customer Percep-
tions of Competing
Pain Relievers
Mapped by Multidi-
mensional Scaling

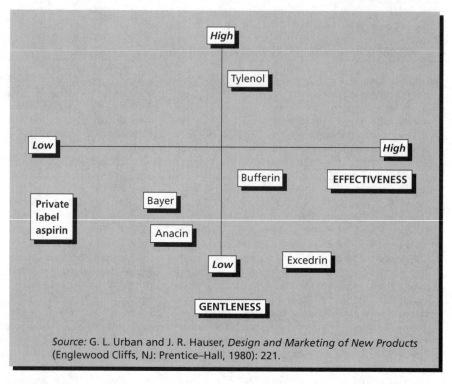

Source: G. L. Urban and J. R. Hauser, *Design and Marketing of New Products* (Englewood Cliffs, NJ: Prentice–Hall, 1980): 221.

would obtain, and to simulate the effects of changing the design features and prices of the new products on customer preferences.[7]

Hedonic Price Analysis.   The demand for a product may be viewed as the demand for the underlying attributes the product provides.[8] The price at which a product can sell in the market is the aggregate of the values derived from each of these individual attributes. **Hedonic price analysis** observes price differences for competing products, relates these differences to the different combinations of attributes offered by each product, and calculates the implicit market price for each attribute. For example, it is possible to relate price differences for automatic washing machines to differences in

- ♦ Capacity
- ♦ Spin speed
- ♦ Energy consumption
- ♦ Features (e.g., number of programs, electronic control)
- ♦ Reliability (as indicated by consumer organizations' data).

By estimating (using multiple regression analysis) the implicit price for each attribute, it is possible to determine the price premium that can be charged for additional units of a particular attribute. In Britain, for example, a machine that spins at 1000 rpm sells at about a $200 price premium to one that spins at 800 rpm.[9] If the cost of adding the faster spin is only $50, it is profitable to differentiate by means of faster spin.

Hedonic price analysis allows us to estimate the price advantage that differentiation will support. In the case of producer goods, it may be possible to calculate even more directly the extent to which differentiation creates value for the customer. For producer goods, creating value for the customer means increasing the customer's profit margin. Where differentiation lowers the buyer's costs, the value of differentiation can be directly calculated. For example, the increase in value to the buyer of a copier that collates and staples is equivalent to the savings in labor costs from undertaking those activities manually.

The Role of Social and Psychological Factors

The problem with analyzing product differentiation in terms of measurable performance attributes is that it does not delve very far into customers' underlying motivations. Very few goods or services are acquired to satisfy basic needs for survival: most buying reflects social goals and values in terms of the desire to find community with others, to establish one's own identity, and to make sense of what is happening in the world. Our discussion of goals in Chapter 2 referred to Maslow's hierarchy of needs: once basic needs for survival are satisfied, there is a progression from security needs, to belonging needs, to esteem needs, to self-actualization needs.[10] Houses, insurance policies, and retirement funds confer security. Other purchases mark social events and bond social relationships—the giving of presents at birthdays and weddings for instance. Many goods and services signal self-image and values. The differentiation strategy by Harley-Davidson extends far beyond the product being supplied. In terms of product alone, Harley-Davidson sells technologically backward, overpriced motorcycles. Why has Harley-Davidson dominated the super-heavyweight segment of the U.S. motorcycle industry? It is not just selling motorcycles, it is offering an image and lifestyle that embodies adventure, defiance, and the American tradition of rugged individualism. Achieving such differentiation has to do with the company, not just its products. Harley-Davidson employees, including top management, play a key role in fostering a sense of identity between the company and its customers through participation in Harley Owners' Group events and other activities. We return to this point when we discuss the role of *integrity* in differentiation.

To understand customer demand and identify potential profitable avenues to differentiation requires that we analyze not only the product and its characteristics, but also customers and their characteristics. If purchase decisions are driven by the need to identify with others, to establish individuality, and to proclaim aspirations, it is vital to look behind the product and investigate the lifestyle, personality, and social grouping of the customer. Such analysis can be both systematic and quantitative in terms of establishing demographic (age, sex, race, location), socioeconomic (income, education), and psychographic (lifestyle, personality type) factors that correlate to patterns of buying behavior.

Yet despite the statistical rigor of formal market research techniques, effective differentiation depends less on analysis than on *understanding* of what customers want and how they behave. The answer, claims Tom Peters, is very simple: business people need to *listen to their customers*. "Good listeners," says Peters, "get out from behind their desks to where the customers are . . . Further, good listeners construct settings so as to maximize "naive" listening, the undistorted sort . . . Finally, good listeners provide quick feedback and act on what they hear."[11] It is important however that "naive listening" is not confused with naive understanding of customer needs. To really understand customer needs and preferences, listening is insufficient.

Companies must observe and analyze customers' use of the product. We will return to this issue when we apply the value chain to differentiation analysis. Ultimately, however, understanding the customer may extend beyond analysis. Johansson and Nonaka show that Japanese companies emphasize intuition and relationships. Satisfying the customer is not about bundling together favored attributes, but is going beyond functionality to provide emotional and aesthetic satisfaction.[12]

Figure 9.2 summarizes this discussion in the form of some basic questions for exploring the potential for differentiation on the demand side of the market.

Broad-Based versus Focused Differentiation

Differentiation, we have observed, may focus on a broad market appeal or on a specific market segment. The choice of market scope has important implications for the orientation of demand analysis. A firm that wishes to establish a broad-based position of differentiation advantage in an industry is primarily concerned with the *general* features of market demand: What general needs are being satisfied by the product? What do customers have in common in terms of their motivations and choice criteria? The firm needs to focus not on the factors that distinguish customer groups and segment their demand, but on the requirements and the aspirations they

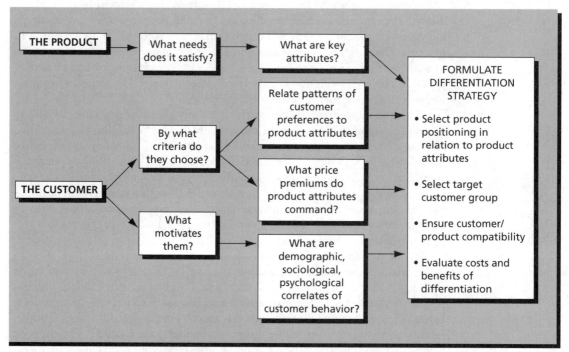

FIGURE 9.2
Identifying Differentiation Potential: The Demand Side

have in common. To establish a position of uniqueness while still appealing to a broad market is no easy task:

♦ McDonald's has extended its appeal across age groups, social groups and national boundaries by emphasizing a few qualities with universal appeal: speed, consistency, value, hygiene, and family lifestyles.

♦ The British retailer Marks & Spencer has been similarly successful in establishing a reputation for product quality and fair dealing that extends across the traditional class divisions that segment British consumer markets.

♦ Honda has positioned itself within the U.S. auto market to achieve a broad-based market appeal in contrast to most American and European brands, which target specific demographic and socioeconomic segments.

Establishing a differentiated niche position in a market necessitates more specific analysis: What are the differences between customers' needs and between the customer groups? What groups of customers are not being adequately served by the existing range of offerings? The emphasis is on the factors that distinguish one group from another and one set of needs from another. In principle, a focused approach to differentiation should displace a broad-based approach. If customers are presented with a wide range of highly targeted product offerings they should prefer a targeted product that matches their particular preferences better than one designed for the broad market. The challenge facing the TV broadcast networks—NBC, ABC, CBS and Fox—is in finding an image and programming format that maintains mass-audience appeal against the cable and satellite channels which nibble away at their viewer ratings by targeting specific groups: children, sports fans, movie watchers, music-video addicts, sci-fi buffs, and the like.

At the same time, segment-focused approaches to differentiation run risks. Apart from the higher unit costs incurred in supplying a narrow rather than broad market, there are dangers that market segments can change over time, or that a firm adopts an inappropriate segmentation in the first place. Segment-focused differentiation based on existing differences between customers is inherently conservative. A problem with General Motors' segmented approach to the U.S. car market was that many consumers within the segments GM had targeted no longer wanted to be identified with the segment that GM had defined for them. GM has worked hard at redefining the brand images of Buick, Oldsmobile, Cadillac, and Chevrolet.

Focused differentiation may be based on an approach to market segmentation that fails to acknowledge customers' needs and preferences. GM's model range targeted each brand to a specific price bracket and particular socioeconomic category. This approach encouraged GM to overlook customers' growing concerns over economy, safety, reliability, and the increasing role of lifestyle rather than income levels in distinguishing customer preferences. If differentiation is really about creating "total customer responsiveness" then analysis should bring us closer to customers' needs and not obscure them.

ANALYZING DIFFERENTIATION: THE SUPPLY SIDE

Though demand analysis identifies customers' demands for differentiation and their willingness to pay for it, creating a differentiation advantage is crucially dependent on a firm's ability to supply differentiation and to do so at a cost that does not exceed the price premium it creates. To identify the firm's potential to supply differentiation, we examine the activities the firm performs and the resources it has access to.

The Drivers of Uniqueness

Differentiation is concerned with the provision of *uniqueness*. A firm's opportunities for creating uniqueness in its offerings to customers are not located within a particular function or activity, but can arise in virtually everything that the firm does. Porter identifies a number of **drivers of uniqueness** over which the firm exercises control. These include:

- Product features and product performance
- Complementary services (e.g., credit, delivery, repair)
- Intensity of marketing activities (e.g., rate of advertising spending)
- Technology embodied in design and manufacture
- The quality of purchased inputs
- Procedures influencing the conduct of each activities (e.g., rigor of quality control, service procedures, frequency of sales visits to a customer)
- The skill and experience of employees
- Location (e.g., with retail stores)
- The degree of vertical integration (which influences a firm's ability to control inputs and intermediate processes).[13]

Most transactions do not involve a single product or a single service, but are a combination of products and services. In analyzing the potential for differentiation, we can distinguish between differentiation of the product ("hardware") and ancillary services ("software"). On this basis, four transaction categories can be identified (see Figure 9.3).[14]

FIGURE 9.3
Differentiation of Hardware and Software

		SOFTWARE	
		Differentiated	Undifferentiated
HARDWARE	Differentiated	SYSTEM	PRODUCT
	Undifferentiated	SERVICE	COMMODITY

Source: Shiv Mathur, "Competitive Industrial Marketing Strategies," *Long Range Planning*, 17, no. 4 (1984).

As markets mature, so "systems" comprising both hardware and software tend to "unbundle," with products becoming increasingly commodities and services being provided by specialized companies. However, the growing sophistication of customer preferences and the quest for differentiation advantage encourage producers to repackage hardware and software into new systems. The personal computer industry is an example. Standardization of the Intel/Windows-based PC has encouraged suppliers to escape the rigors of a commodity business by supplying complete "multimedia, Internet-ready" systems.

Product Integrity

For any firm, the range of differentiation opportunities is wide. The primary issue is likely to be determining which forms of differentiation may be most successful in distinguishing the firm in the market and which are most valued by customers. In establishing a coherent and effective position of differentiation in a market, a firm needs to assemble a complementary package of differentiation measures. If Beck's beer wishes to differentiate itself on the basis of the quality of its ingredients, then it must adopt production methods that are consistent with quality ingredients, and packaging, advertising, and distribution appropriate to a quality, premium-priced product.

Product integrity refers to the consistency of a firm's differentiation; it is the extent to which a product achieves:

> . . . total balance of numerous product characteristics including basic functions, aesthetics, semantics, reliability, and economy . . . Product integrity has both internal and external dimensions. Internal integrity refers to consistency between the function and structure of the product—e.g., the parts fit well, components match and work well together, layout achieves maximum space efficiency. External integrity is a measure of how well a product's function, structure, and semantics fit the customer's objectives, values, production system, lifestyle, use pattern, and self-identity.[15]

In their study of product development in the car industry, Clark and Fujimoto argue that simultaneously achieving internal and external integrity is the most complex organizational challenge facing auto makers since it requires linking close interfunctional collaboration with intimate customer contact. The organizational changes among U.S. and European auto makers, including the growing role of product managers, have attempted to imitate the success of Toyota and Honda in achieving internal-external integration.[16]

Achieving combined internal and external product integrity is critical to all companies that seek differentiation advantage. It is especially important to firms seeking **image differentiation** where the credibility of the image depends critically on the consistency of the image presented. Exhibit 9.2 discusses the differentiation strategy of Body Shop.

Signaling and Reputation

Differentiation is only effective if it is communicated to customers. But customers are not always well informed about the qualities and characteristics of the goods they purchase. The economics literature distinguishes between *search goods*, whose qualities and

EXHIBIT 9.2

Body Shop: The Role of Values in Differentiation

Though Anita Roddick scorns businessmen and management principles, the success of Body Shop reveals an insightful and sophisticated approach to differentiation strategy. In some respects, Body Shop's strategy is consistent with other manufacturers of cosmetics and toiletries—success has always been associated with the establishment of a strong product image that requires consistency among the product, the packaging, the advertising and promotion, the retail environment, and the image of the company.

To this extent, Body Shop is not novel: its products are physically differentiated. This differentiation is carried through to the packaging and to the retail environment in which the products are sold. Indeed, Body Shop goes one step further than most competitors—it only sells its products within its own franchised stores. However, in the nature of its image, Body Shop has contradicted the industry's conventions concerning differentiation advantage. The companies have sought to differentiate their products on the basis of beauty, youth, and sexual attractiveness. Body Shop rejects this "magic"—"My products can only cleanse, moisten, and protect."

Rather, Body Shop appeals to traditional notions of grooming, maintaining, and enhancing faces and bodies through the use of natural ingredients, many of them associated with the traditions of ethnic peoples throughout the world. This differentiation of the product is supported by a strong commitment to research and discovery to identify and examine the use and potential of a whole range of natural products from oatmeal to obscure vegetable oils.

Emphasis on the natural properties of the products is encouraged by packaging that emphasizes simplicity, economy, and information. A similar feeling is communicated by Body Shop's retail outlets, which are open, non-ostentatious and designed to encourage customers to look, read, sample, and interact with sales personnel. Despite the encouragement that the Body Shop gives to employees' individuality and free expression, the retail stores are uniform in their decor and displays and maintain common approaches to customer service.

In contrast to other cosmetic companies, which use advertising and promotion to identify their products with beauty, style, and the fountain of youth, Body Shop communicates its image through its values. In virtually all its words and actions, Body Shop emphasizes commitment to environmental and social responsibility. The primary medium for communication is Body Shop's employees and franchisees. Body Shop exerts special care in selecting its franchisees, rejecting those with prior business experience in favor of those with enthusiasm and commitment to Body Shop ideals. The result is that Body Shop is not simply supplying skin creams and shampoo, it is creating an identity with its customers built around the concepts of naturalness, global environmental responsibility, economic support for indigenous people through trade, and a rejection of traditional business methods (which it sees as exploiting the weak and disregarding the environment).

The problems that Body Shop has encountered in the late 1990s stem from allegations about Body Shop's ethical lapses, in terms of departures from "all natural" ingredients in its products, use of animal-tested ingredients, unfair treatment of franchisees and employees, and weaknesses of its community support and "fair trade" initiatives. Because Body Shop's values are fundamental to its image and relationships with customers, suppliers, franchisees, and employees these criticisms represent a fundamental threat to its competitive position.

_____

Source: Body Shop International, Harvard Business School Case 9-392-032 (1992).

characteristics can be ascertained by inspection, and *experience goods*, whose qualities and characteristics are only recognized after consumption. This latter class of goods includes medical services, baldness treatments, frozen TV dinners, and wine. Even with experience goods, performance attributes may be slow in revealing themselves—only over time can we assess the reliability of a car or the competence of our dentist.

The producer faces a classic *prisoners' dilemma.* The firm can offer a high quality or a low quality product. The customer can pay either a high or a low price. If quality cannot be detected, then equilibrium is established with the customer offering a low price for a low quality product, even though both would be better off with a high quality product sold at a high price (see Figure 9.4).

The resolution of this dilemma is for producers to find some credible means of signaling quality to the customer. The most effective **signals** are those that change the payoffs in the prisoners' dilemma. Thus, an extended warranty is effective because providing such a warranty would be more expensive for a low quality than a high quality producer. Brand names and the advertising that supports them are signals of quality and consistency—because a brand is a valuable asset it acts as a disincentive for providing poor quality. Other signals of quality include packaging, money-back guarantees, the retail environment in which the product is sold, and the supplier's sponsorship of sports and cultural events.

The need for signaling variables to complement performance variables in differentiation depends on the ease with which performance can be assessed by the potential buyer. A perfume can be sampled prior to purchase and its fragrance assessed, but a perfume's ability to augment the identity of the wearer and attract attention remains uncertain. Hence, the key role of branding, packaging, advertising, and lavish promotional events in establishing an identity for the perfume in terms of the implied personality, lifestyle, and aspirations of the user.

Signaling and reputation are especially important for products and services where quality is difficult to ascertain even after purchase. In financial services, the customer cannot easily assess the honesty, financial security, or competence of a broker, fund manager, or insurance company. Hence, the emphasis that financial service companies accord to symbols of security, stability, and competence—large, well-located head offices; conservative and tasteful office decor; smartly dressed, well-groomed employees; historical associations; and perceptions of size.

FIGURE 9.4
The Role of Quality
Signaling

		Producer's strategies	
		High quality	Low quality
Consumer's strategies	High price	7 ⟋ 7	10 ⟋ −5
	Low price	−5 ⟋ 10	3 ⟋ 3

Note: In each cell, the upper right figure is the payoff to the producer, the lower left figure is the payoff to the consumer.

Strategies for reputation building have been subjected to extensive theoretical analysis.[17] Some of the propositions that arise from this research include:

◆ Quality signaling is primarily important for products whose quality can only be ascertained after purchase ("experience goods");

◆ Expenditure on advertising is an effective means of signaling superior quality since suppliers of low quality products will not expect repeat buying, hence it is not profitable for them to spend money on advertising;

◆ A combination of premium pricing and advertising is likely to be superior in signaling quality than either price or advertising alone;

◆ The higher the sunk-costs required for entry into a market and the greater the total investment of the firm, the greater the incentives for the firm not to cheat customers through providing low quality at high cost.

The Costs of Differentiation

Differentiation adds cost. The *direct* costs of differentiation include elements such as the costs of higher quality inputs, the costs of larger inventories in order to guarantee speedy filling of orders, and the costs of heavy advertising to sustain brand strength. The *indirect* costs of differentiation arise through the interaction of differentiation variables with cost variables. To the extent that differentiation narrows the product-market scope of a firm, it also limits the potential for exploiting scale economies. To the extent that differentiation requires product innovation and the introduction of new models, it hampers the exploitation of experience curve economies.

However, not all aspects of differentiation add significant costs. One of the central themes of TQM is that the elimination of product defects results in *cost savings*. The argument that quality incurs costs that are trivial in relation to its market benefits has received widespread empirical support. The PIMS data show that quality adds a significant premium to price while having little or no effect on cost. As a result, quality is strongly associated with superior profitability (see Figure 9.5).

The costs of differentiation can also be offset by expanding the market share of a firm. Hence, they permit exploitation of scale economies. The tendency for many firms to increase their advertising budgets during a recession reflects their desire to spread fixed costs over an expanded sales base.

One means of reconciling differentiation with cost efficiency is to postpone differentiation to later stages of the firm's value chain. Economies of scale and the cost advantages of standardization are frequently greatest in the manufacturing of basic components. Modular design with common components permits scale economies while maintaining considerable product variety. All the major auto makers have reduced the number of platforms and engine types and increased commonality of components across their model ranges, while offering customers an increased variety of colors, trim, and accessory options.[18]

New manufacturing technology has redefined traditional tradeoffs between efficiency and variety. The flexible manufacturing systems and just-in-time scheduling have increased the versatility of many plants, made model changeovers less costly, and made the goal of an "economic order quantity of one" increasingly realistic. At Kawasaki's motorcycle plant in Lincoln, Nebraska, production was switched to mixed-model production on January 1, 1983. Previously, manufacturing had been in lots of at least 200 of each model. Yet by reorganizing the production process,

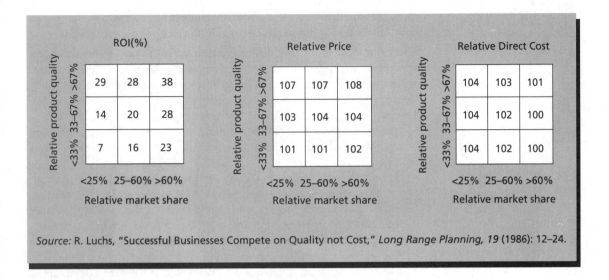

Source: R. Luchs, "Successful Businesses Compete on Quality not Cost," *Long Range Planning, 19* (1986): 12–24.

FIGURE 9.5

adopting just-in-time scheduling, and adapting some machinery, the plant reduced changeover time in frame production from half a day to less than ten minutes.[19]

BRINGING IT ALL TOGETHER: THE VALUE CHAIN IN DIFFERENTIATION ANALYSIS

There is little point in identifying the product attributes customers value most if the firm is incapable of supplying those attributes. Similarly, there is little purpose in identifying a firm's ability to supply certain elements of uniqueness if these attributes are not valued by customers. The key to successful differentiation is in matching the firm's capacity for creating differentiation with customers' potential demand for it. For this purpose, the value chain provides a particularly useful framework. Let's begin with the case of a producer good, i.e., one that is supplied by one firm to another.

Value Chain Analysis of Producer Goods

Using the value chain to identify opportunities for differentiation advantage involves four principal stages.

1. **Construct a value chain for the firm and the customer.** It may be useful to consider not just the immediate customer, but also firms further downstream in the value chain. If the firm supplies different types of customers— for example, a steel company may supply steel strip to automobile manufacturers and white goods producers—draw separate value chains for each of the main categories of customer.

2. **Identify the drivers of uniqueness in each activity.** Assess the firm's potential for differentiating its product by examining each activity in the firm's value chain and identifying the variables and actions through which the firm

can achieve uniqueness in relation to competitors' offerings. Figure 9.6 identifies sources of differentiation within Porter's generic value chain.

3. **Select the most promising differentiation variables for the firm.** Among the numerous drivers of uniqueness that we can identify within the firm, which one should be selected as the primary basis for the firm's differentiation strategy? On the supply side, there are three important considerations:

   ♦ First, we must *establish where the firm has greater potential for differentiating, or can differentiate at lower cost, than rivals.* This requires some analysis of the firm's internal strengths in terms of resources and capabilities.

   ♦ Second, in order to identify the most promising aspects of differentiation, we also need to *identify linkages among activities,* since some differentiation variables may involve interaction among several activities. Thus, product reliability is likely to be the outcome of several linked activities: monitoring purchases of inputs from suppliers, the skill and motivation of production workers, and quality control and product testing.

   ♦ Third, the ease with which different types of uniqueness can be sustained must be considered. The more differentiation is based on resources specific to the firm or skills that involve the complex coordination of a large

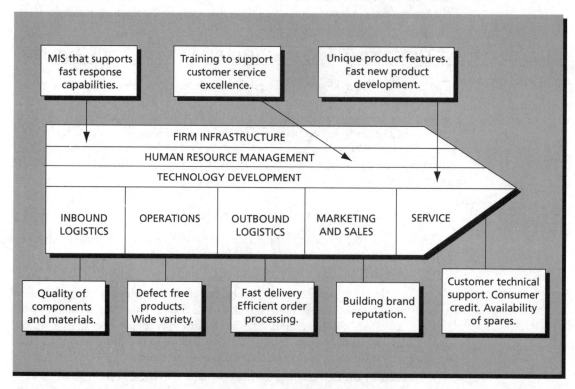

FIGURE 9.6
Using the Value Chain to Identify Differentiation Potential on the Supply Side

number of individuals, the more difficult it will be for a competitor to imitate the particular source of differentiation. Thus, offering business class passengers wider seats and more leg room is an easily imitated source of differentiation. Achieving high levels of punctuality represents a more sustainable source of differentiation.

4. **Locate linkages between value chain of the firm and that of the buyer.** The objective of differentiation is to yield a price premium for the firm. This requires that the firm's differentiation create value for the customer. Creating value for customers requires either that the firm lower the customers' costs, or that the customers be assisted in their own product differentiation. Thus, by completely reorganizing its system of ordering and distribution, Compaq, the world's top PC maker, has radically reduced distribution time and increased delivery reliability. This permits retailers to save inventory costs while offering computers configured to customers' specifications. To identify the means by which a firm can create value for its customers it must locate the linkages between differentiation of its own activities and cost reduction and differentiation within the customer's activities.

Analysis of these linkages can also evaluate the potential profitability of differentiation. The value differentiation creates for the customer represents the maximum price premium the customer will pay. If the provision of just-in-time delivery by a component supplier costs an additional $1,000 a month but saves an automobile company $6,000 a month in reduced inventory, warehousing, and handling costs, then it should be possible for the component manufacturer to obtain a price premium that easily exceeds the costs of the differentiation.

Exhibit 9.3 demonstrates the use of value chain analysis in identifying differentiation opportunities available to a manufacturer of metal containers.

Value Chain Analysis of Consumer Goods

Value chain analysis is most readily applicable to producer goods where the customer is also a company with an easily definable value chain and where linkages between the supplier's and the customer's value chains are readily apparent. However, the same analysis can be applied to consumer goods with very little modification. Few consumer goods are consumed directly; in most cases consumers are involved in a chain of activities before the total consumption of the product.

This is particularly evident for consumer durables. A washing machine is consumed over several years in the process of doing home laundry. The customer's value chain begins with search activity prior to purchase. In the home laundry process, the machine together with water, detergent, and electricity, is used to wash clothes, which are later dried and, possibly, ironed. Continued use of the washing machine requires service and repair. We have a complex value chain for the customer with, potentially, many linkages between the value chains of manufacturer, retailer, and consumer.

Even nondurables involve the consumer in a chain of activities. Consider a frozen TV dinner: it must be purchased, taken home, removed from the package, heated, and served before it is consumed. After eating, the consumer must clean any used dishes, cutlery, or other utensils. A value chain analysis by a frozen foods producer would identify ways in which the product could be formulated, packaged, and distributed to assist the consumer in performing this chain of activities.

EXHIBIT 9.3

A Value Chain Analysis of Differentiation Opportunities for a Manufacturer of Metal Containers

The metal container industry is a highly competitive, low growth, low profit industry. Cans lack much potential for differentiation and buyers (especially beverage and food canning companies) are very powerful. Clearly cost efficiency is essential, but are there also opportunities for differentiation advantage? A value chain analysis can help a metal can manufacturer identify profitable opportunities for differentiation.

- **STAGE 1. Construct value chain for firm and customers.** The principal activities of the can manufacturer and its customers are shown in the diagram.
- **STAGE 2. Identify the drivers of uniqueness.** For each of the can making activities it is possible to suggest several possible differentiation variables. Examples are shown on the diagram.
- **STAGE 3. Select key variables.** To select the most promising differentiation variables, the company's internal strengths must be considered. If the firm has strong technical capabilities, then it might design and manufacture products to meet difficult technical and design specifications, and provide sophisticated technical services to customers. If its

logistics capabilities are strong it might offer fast and reliable delivery, possibly extended to electronic data interchange with customers.

- **STAGE 4. Identify linkages.** To determine differentiation likely to create value for the customer, identify linkages between the can maker's potential for differentiation and the potential for reducing cost or enhancing differentiation within the customer's value chain. The diagram below identifies five such linkages:

1. Designing a distinctive can for customers may assist their own marketing activities.
2. Consistent quality of cans lowers customers' canning costs by avoiding breakdowns and hold-ups on their canning lines.
3. By maintaining high stocks and offering speedy delivery, customers can economize on their own stockholding (they may even be able to move to a just-in-time system of can supply).
4. Efficient order processing can reduce customers' ordering costs.
5. Capable and fast technical support can reduce the costs of breakdowns on canning lines.

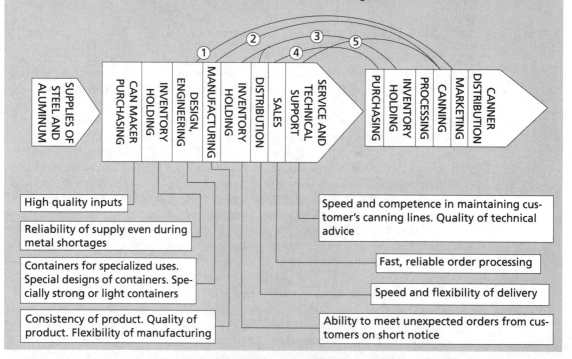

Takahiro Fujimoto has emphasized the need for companies to integrate their design process with the consumption process of the product.[20] For example, as the differentiation advantages of Japanese automobile companies—in terms of reliability and fuel efficiency—are increasingly replicated by U.S. and European producers, so the companies are seeking new sources of differentiation. A full analysis of how customers select, purchase, finance, drive, and service their cars can identify many ways in which auto manufacturers and their dealers can lower the costs of these activities and increase the satisfaction customers receive from them.

◆ SUMMARY

The attraction of differentiation over low cost as a basis for competitive advantage is its potential for sustainability. It is less vulnerable to being overturned by changes in the external environment, and it is more difficult to replicate.

The potential for differentiation in any business is vast. It may involve physical differentiation of the product, it may be through complementary services, it may be intangible. Differentiation extends beyond technology, design, and marketing to include all aspects of a firm's interactions with its customers.

The essence of differentiation advantage is to increase the perceived value of the offering to the customer either more effectively or at lower cost than do competitors. This requires that the firm match the requirements and preferences of customers with its own capacity for creating uniqueness.

The value chain provides a useful framework for analyzing differentiation advantage. By analyzing how value is created for customers and by systematically appraising the scope of each of the firm's activities for achieving differentiation, the value chain permits matching demand-side and supply-side sources of differentiation.

Successful differentiation requires a combination of astute analysis and creative imagination. The two are not antithetical. A systematic framework for the analysis of differentiation can act as a stimulus to creative ideas.

NOTES

1 Michael E. Porter, *Competitive Advantage* (New York: Free Press, 1985): 120.
2 Tom Peters, *Thriving on Chaos* (New York: Knopf, 1987): 56.
3 *Ibid.:* 185.
4 These distinctions are developed in more detail by Peter R. Dickson and James L. Ginter, "Market Segmentation, Product Differentiation and Marketing Strategy," *Journal of Marketing* 51 (April 1987): 1–10.
5 See Susan Schiffman et al., *Introduction to Multidimensional Scaling: Theory, Methods, and Applications,* (Cambridge, MA: Academic Press, 1981).
6 See P. Cattin and D. R. Wittink, "Commercial Use of Conjoint Analysis: A Survey," *Journal of Marketing* (Summer 1982): 44–53.
7 Alan Rowe, Richard Mason, Karl Dickel, and Neil Snyder, *Strategic Management: A Methodological Approach*, 3rd edition (Reading, MA: Addison-Wesley, 1989): 127–128.
8 Kelvin Lancaster, *Consumer Demand: A New Approach* (New York: Columbia University Press, 1971).
9 Phedon Nicolaides and Charles Baden Fuller, *Price Discrimination and Product Differentiation in the European Domestic Appliance Market* (London: Center for Business Strategy, London Business School, 1987).

10 Abraham Maslow, "A Theory of Human Motivation," *Psychological* Review 50 (1943): 370–396.

11 Tom Peters, *Thriving on Chaos* (New York: Knopf, 1987): 149.

12 Johny K. Johansson and Ikujiro Nonaka, *Relentless: The Japanese Way of Marketing* (New York: Harper Business, 1996).

13 Michael E. Porter, *Competitive Advantage* (New York: Free Press, 1985): 124–125.

14 Shiv Mathur, "Competitive Industrial Marketing Strategies," *Long Range Planning* 17, no. 4 (1984): 102–109.

15 Kim Clark and Takahiro Fujimoto, *Product Development Performance* (Boston: Harvard Business School Press, 1991): 29–30.

16 Clark and Fujimoto (1991) *op. cit.:* 247–285.

17 For a survey, see Keith Weigelt and Colin Camerer, "Reputation and Corporate Strategy: A Review of Recent Theory and Applications," *Strategic Management Journal* 9 (1988): 443–454.

18 "Toyota Retooled," *Business Week*, April 4, 1994: 54–57.

19 Richard J. Schonberger, *World Class Manufacturing Casebook: Implementing JIT and TQC* (New York: Free Press, 1987): 120–123.

20 Takahiro Fujimoto, "Managing Effective Development Projects," presentation to Strategic Management Society Conference, San Francisco, October 1989.

IV.

Business Strategies in Different Industry Contexts

10
Industry Evolution

No company ever stops changing . . . Each new generation must meet changes—in the automotive market, in the general administration of the enterprise, and in the involvement of the corporation in a changing world. The work of creating goes on.

—*Alfred P. Sloan Jr., president of General Motors 1923–1937, chairman 1937–1956, in My Years with General Motors*

Outline

◆ INTRODUCTION AND OBJECTIVES

The analysis of competitive advantage in the last three chapters emphasized competition as a *dynamic* process in which firms vie to gain competitive advantage only to see it eroded by imitation and innovation by rivals. The outcome of this process is an industry environment that is continually being reshaped by the forces of competition. This view of competition as a dynamic process contrasts with the *static* approach of the Porter Five Forces of Competition framework (see Chapter 3), which views industry structure as a stable determinant of the intensity of competition in an industry. In practice, industry structures continually evolve, driven both by the forces of competition and by fundamental changes in technology and economic growth. Firms that develop the capabilities and strategies suited to emerging industry circumstances prosper and grow; those that do not are eliminated. The issue we explore in this chapter is whether industry evolution can be anticipated. My central thesis is that, although every industry develops in a unique way, it is possible to detect some typical patterns that are the result of common driving forces. Our task is to identify patterns of industry evolution and the forces that drive them, and explore the implications for competition and competitive advantage.

We will examine the **industry life cycle** as a common pattern of industry development. This permits us to classify industries according to their stage of development. This raises the question, not only of the extent to which the life cycle accurately describes the evolution of different industries, but also whether there is purpose or validity in grouping diverse industries into a single category? The value of classification is in coming to grips with the key elements that determine the strategic character of an industry. The process of choosing a classification scheme and then assigning industries to different categories forces us to consider what is important about an industry. It is useful to highlight the ways in which industries are similar to one another and how they are different. Grouping industries on the basis of strategic similarities can also assist the transfer of management ideas from one industry to another. Although cigarettes, beer, processed foods, and soft drinks are very different products, the fact that they are all mature, branded, disposable consumer goods capable of international distribution provides them with strategic similarities that Philip Morris has been able to exploit.

By the time you have completed this chapter, you will be able to:

♦ Recognize the different stages of the industry life cycle and understand the factors that drive the process of industry evolution

♦ Identify the key success factors associated with industries at different stages of their life cycle

♦ Apply the industry life cycle to issues of strategy implementation in order to identify the organizational structures and management systems appropriate to different stages of the cycle

♦ Use scenarios to explore industry futures

THE LIFE CYCLE MODEL

One of the best-known and most enduring marketing concepts is the **product life cycle.**[1] Products are born, their sales grow, they reach maturity, they go into decline, and they ultimately die. If products have life cycles, so too do the industries that produce them. The industry life cycle is the supply-side equivalent of the product life cycle. Thus, to the extent that an industry produces a range and a sequence of products, the industry life cycle is likely to be of longer duration than that of a single product. Though the 64-bit games produced by Nintendo, Sega, and Sony have a probable life cycle of a few years, the life cycle of the electronic games industry is much longer.

The life cycle is conventionally divided into four phases: introduction, growth, maturity, and decline (see Figure 10.1). Before we examine the features of each of these stages, it is important to understand the forces that are driving industry evolu-

FIGURE 10.1
The Industry Life
Cycle

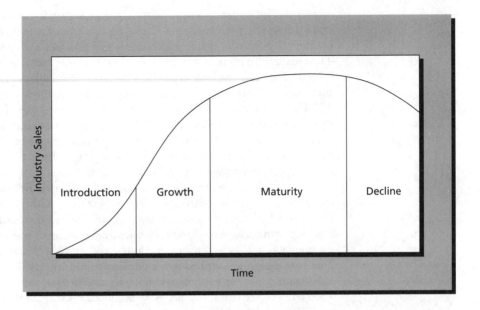

tion. There are two factors that can be identified as fundamental to driving industry evolution: *demand growth* and the *production and diffusion of knowledge.*

Demand Growth

The life cycle and the stages within it are defined by changes in an industry's growth rate over time. The characteristic profile is an S-shaped growth curve.

- In the *introduction stage*, sales are small and the rate of market penetration is low because the industry's products are little known and customers are few. The novelty of the technology, small production scale, and lack of experience means that costs and prices are high, while quality is low. Customers for new products tend to be affluent, innovation-oriented, and risk-accepting.
- The *growth stage* is characterized by accelerating market penetration as product technology becomes more standardized and prices fall. Ownership spreads from higher-income customers to the mass market.
- The onset of the *maturity stage* is caused by increasing market saturation and slowing growth as new demand gives way to replacement demand. Once saturation is reached, demand is wholly for replacement, either direct replacement (customers replacing old products with new products) or indirect replacement (new customers replacing old customers).
- Finally, as the industry becomes challenged by new industries that produce technologically superior substitute products, the industry enters its *decline stage.*

Creation and Diffusion of Knowledge

The second key force driving the industry life cycle is the creation and diffusion of knowledge. New knowledge in the form of product innovation is responsible for an industry coming into being, and the dual processes of knowledge creation and knowledge diffusion continue to drive industry evolution.

In the introduction stage, product technology advances rapidly. There is no dominant product technology, and rival technologies compete for attention. Competition is primarily between alternative technologies and design configurations. The competitive process involves the selection of the more successful from the less successful approaches, and, typically a dominant technology and design configuration emerges. This process of elimination therefore involves *standardization*.[2]

The transition from technological heterogeneity to one of increased standardization typically inaugurates the industry's growth phase. Increased standardization encourages firms to reduce costs through large-scale manufacturing methods. Hence the growth phase is associated with technology shifting from *product innovation* toward *process innovation*. Figure 10.2 shows the typical pattern.

This pattern is evident in the automobile industry. Between 1890 and 1920, cars featured a wide diversity of engine configurations and transmission designs, not to mention body designs and steering and braking systems. Ford's Model T was the first dominant design to emerge with its front-mounted, water-cooled engine, and transmission with a gearbox, wet clutch, and rearwheel drive. In the 1920s, the dominant design was refined to include an all-steel, enclosed body. During the next half century, nonconventional technologies and designs were gradually eliminated. Volkswagen's Beetle was the last mass-produced car with a rear-mounted, air-cooled engine. Renault and Citroën abandoned their distinctive technologies and designs in favor of convention. Even distinctive national differences diminished as American cars became smaller and Japanese and Italian cars became bigger. The fall of the Iron Curtain extinguished the last outposts of nonconformity: by the mid-1990s, East German two-stroke Wartburgs and Trabants were collectors' items. A growing feature of parking lots throughout the world are confused car owners searching along rows of bewilderingly similar vehicles.

Product innovation in automobiles has shifted from being radical to incremental. Most of the innovations in automobiles during the postwar era have involved the

FIGURE 10.2
Product and Process
Innovation Over Time

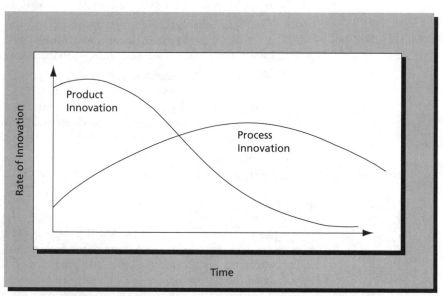

refinement of existing technologies and the application of technologies developed in other sectors (most notably the application of microelectronics and new materials such as plastics and ceramics to cars). Many product innovations have involved the adoption of features and components that were developed many years ago. Table 10.1 identifies some of these.

Once product technology and design stabilize, the challenge is to produce the product at acceptable cost and higher quality. Technological development thus shifts from product to process innovation. The success of the Model T was in Henry Ford's development of moving assembly line production with interchangeable parts. This shifted manufacturing from small-volume, craft-based workshops to huge capital-intensive plants employing large numbers of semi-skilled workers. The second revolutionary process innovation in automobile manufacturing was Toyota's system of "lean production," involving a tightly integrated "pull" system of production embodying just-in-time scheduling, team-based production, continuous improvement, and high levels of flexibility.

Knowledge diffusion is also important on the customer side. Over the course of the life cycle, customers become increasingly informed. As they

TABLE 10.1 From Option to Standard: The Diffusion of Innovations and Features in Automobiles	FEATURE	INTRODUCTION	GENERAL ADOPTION
	Speedometer	1901 by Oldsmobile	Circa 1915
	Automatic transmission	First installed in 1904	Introduced by Packard as an option, 1938. Standard on Cadillacs and other luxury cars, early 1950s
	Electric headlamps	GM introduced in 1908	Became standard by 1916
	All steel body	Adopted by GM, 1912	Became standard, early 1920s
	All steel, enclosed body	Dodge, 1923	Became standard, late 1920s
	Radio	Appears as an option, 1923	Standard equipment, 1946
	Four-wheel drive	Appears 1924	Only limited availability by 1994
	Hydraulic brakes	Introduced 1924	Became standard, 1939
	Shatterproof glass	First used in cars in 1927	Standard feature in Fords, 1938
	Power steering	Introduced 1952	Adopted as standard equipment, 1969
	Antilock brakes	Introduced 1972	Standard on GM cars in 1991
	Air bags	Introduced by GM in 1974	By 1994, most new cars equipped with air bags

Source: Robert M. Grant, "The World Automobile Industry in the 1990s," Georgetown University, mimeograph, 1994.

become more knowledgeable about the performance attributes of rival manufacturers' products, so they are better able to judge value-for-money and become more price sensitive.

How General Is the Life Cycle Pattern?

To what extent do industries conform to this life cycle pattern? The first observation is that the duration of life cycles varies from industry to industry.

+ The life cycle of the railroad industry extended from the 1830s to the 1950s before entering its decline phase.

+ The introduction stage of the U.S. automobile industry lasted about 25 years from the 1890s until growth took off in 1913–1915. The growth phase lasted about 40 years. Maturity, in terms of slackening growth, set in during the mid-1950s.

+ In personal computers, the introduction phase lasted only about four years before growth took off in 1978. Between 1978 and 1983 a flood of new and established firms entered the industry. Toward the end of 1984, the first signs of maturity appeared: growth stalled, excess capacity emerged, and the industry began to consolidate around a few companies. However, continued product innovation caused growth to remain strong through the late 1980s and during the 1990s

+ During the 1980s and 1990s, product life cycles became compressed. Compact discs, introduced in 1984, passed almost immediately from introduction to growth phase. By 1988, compact discs outsold conventional record albums in the United States, and by 1990, only six years since their introduction, the market appeared to be mature.

Industries also differ in their patterns of evolution. Industries supplying basic necessities such as residential construction, food processing, and clothing may never enter a decline phase because obsolescence is unlikely for such needs. Some industries may experience a rejuvenation of their life cycle. In the 1960s, the world motorcycle industry, in decline in the U.S. and Europe, re-entered its growth phase as the influx of new Japanese bikes stimulated the recreational use of motorcycles. The TV set industry has experienced several revivals: the first caused by color TV, the second by the demand for multiple TV sets within a household, and the third spurred by the demand for computer monitors and TV video games. High-definition TV promises a further cycle. These rejuvenations of the product life cycle are not some natural phenomenon—they are typically the result of company strategies fostering breakthrough product innovations or developing new markets for the product.

An industry is likely to be at different stages of its life cycle in different countries. Although the U.S. auto market is in the early stages of its decline phase, markets in China, India, and Russia are in their growth phases. Multinational companies can exploit such differences: developing new products and introducing them into the advanced industrial countries, then shifting attention to other growth markets once maturity sets in. In the automobile and can-making industries, pursuing market growth phases is accompanied by shipping whole plants from North America and Western Europe to Latin America, Eastern Europe, and Asia.[3]

STRUCTURE, COMPETITION, AND SUCCESS FACTORS OVER THE LIFE CYCLE

Changes in demand growth and technology over the cycle have implications for industry structure, competition, and the sources of competitive advantage (Key Success Factors). Table 10.2 summarizes the principal features of each stage of the industry life cycle.

Product Differentiation

Emerging industries are characterized by a wide variety of product types that reflect the diversity of technologies and designs—and lack of consensus over customer requirements. Standardization during growth and maturity phases increases product

TABLE 10.2
The Evolution of Industry Structure and Competition over the Life Cycle

	INTRODUCTION	GROWTH	MATURITY	DECLINE
Demand	High-income buyers.	Readily increasing market penetration.	Mass market, replacement/ repeat buying.	Customers knowledgeable.
Technology	Competing technologies.	Standardization. Rapid process innovation.	Well-diffused technical know-how: quest for technological improvements.	
Products	Poor quality. Wide variety. Frequent design changes.	Design and quality improves. Emergence of dominant design.	Standardization lessens differentiation. Efforts to avoid commoditization by branding.	Commodities the norm.
Manufacturing and Distribution	Short production runs. High-skilled labor content. Specialized distribution channels.	Capacity shortages. Mass production. Competition for distribution.	Emergence of overcapacity. Deskilling of production. Long production runs. Distributors carry fewer lines.	Heavy overcapacity. Reemergence of specialty channels.
Trade	Manufacturing shifts from advanced countries to poorer countries.			
Competition	Few companies.	Entry, mergers, and exits.	Shakeout. Price competition increases.	Price wars, exits.
Key Success Factors	Product innovation. Establishing credible image of firm and product.	Design for manufacture. Access to distribution. Building strong brand. Process innovation.	Cost-efficiency through capital intensity, scale efficiency, and low input costs. High quality. Fast product development.	Reduce overheads, buyer selection. Signal commitment. Rationalize capacity.

uniformity with the result that a product may evolve toward commodity status unless producers are effective in developing new dimensions for differentiation, such as marketing variables, ancillary services (e.g., credit facilities, after-sales service), and product options.[4] A feature of the markets for personal computers, credit cards, securities broking, and Internet access is their increasing commodity status in which buyers select primarily on price.

Industry Structure and Competition

Market growth and technological change are major determinants of the structure of manufacturing and distribution, although it is difficult to generalize about resulting industry structures. In most industries, the introduction phase is associated with a fragmented structure and diversity of products and technologies. Thus, the automobile, aircraft, and personal computer industries all went through their "garage stages" involving numerous small start-ups. The growth stage may also attract further new entry, but soon fragmentation is counteracted by pressures for lower costs through scale efficient production. Rapid consolidation around fewer players is certainly a feature of the transition to maturity when the slowdown of market growth causes excess capacity and a "shakeout" phase for the industry. This shakeout period may mark the onset of aggressive price competition in the industry.

Different industries have different development trends, however. Industries that begin with patent-protected new products are likely to start out as near monopolies, then become increasingly competitive. Plain-paper copiers were initially monopolized by Xerox Corporation (and its affiliates Rank Xerox and Fuji-Xerox), and it was not until the early 1980s that the industry was transformed by the entry of many competitors.

Entry barriers play a key role in the evolution of industry concentration. Where entry barriers rise due to increasing capital requirements (automobiles, commercial aircraft, telecommunications equipment) or product differentiation and access to distribution channels (soft drinks, beer, cosmetics), seller concentration is likely to increase over the life cycle. Where entry barriers fall because technology becomes more accessible or product differentiation declines, concentration may decline over time (credit cards, television broadcasting, steel, frozen foods).

The evolving structure of distribution channels also has an important influence on competition and the overall development of an industry. The typical pattern is for small-scale, specialized distribution channels to give way to larger-scale, more generalized distribution channels. At the retail level, the size of individual retail units increases and independent retailers are displaced by chains (Wal-Mart, Toys "R" Us, Home Depot, and the like). Increasing concentration at one stage of the value chain may encourage increased concentration in other parts as firms seek **countervailing power.**[5]

Location and International Trade

The industry life cycle is associated with changes in the pattern of trade and direct investment that together result in international migration of production.[6] The life cycle theory of trade and direct investment is based on two assumptions. First, that demand for new products emerges first in the advanced industrialized countries of

North America, Western Europe, and Japan and then diffuses internationally. Second, that with maturity, products require fewer inputs of technology and sophisticated skills. The result is the following development pattern:

1. New industries begin in high-income countries (traditionally the United States, but increasingly in Japan and Western Europe) because of the presence of a market and the availability of technical and scientific resources.

2. As demand grows in other markets, they are serviced initially by exports.

3. Continued growth of overseas markets and reduced need for inputs of technology and sophisticated labor skills make production attractive in newly industrialized countries. The advanced industrialized countries begin to import.

With maturity, a reduced need for skilled production workers and an increased perception of the product as a commodity, the production activity shifts increasingly to developing countries in search of low cost labor.

Thus, consumer electronics were initially produced primarily in the United States and Germany. During the early 1960s, production shifted more and more to Japan. The 1980s saw the rise of Korea, Hong Kong, and Taiwan as leading exporters. By the mid-1990s, assembly had moved to lower-wage countries such as China, the Philippines, Thailand, Mexico, and Brazil. We return to these issues of national-level competitiveness in Chapter 14.

The Nature and Intensity of Competition

The consequences of these structural changes over the course of the industry life cycle are for competition: first, to shift from nonprice to price competition and second, to become increasingly intense. During the introduction stage, competitors battle for technological leadership, and competition often features a diversity of technologies and designs. Heavy investments in innovation and limited sales typically make the introduction stage unprofitable, unless one firm gains a major market share through patent protection or by some other first-mover advantage. The growth phase is more conducive to profitability as market demand outstrips industry capacity, though much depends on the effectiveness of barriers to entry. With the onset of maturity, increased product standardization increases the emphasis on price competition. How intense this is depends a great deal on the capacity/demand balance and the extent of international competition. In food retailing, airlines, motor vehicles, and oil refining, maturity is associated with intense price competition and low profits. In household detergents, breakfast cereals, cosmetics, and investment banking, high levels of seller concentration and successful maintenance of product differentiation have resulted in more benign competitive circumstances. Once an industry enters its decline phase, depending on the height of exit barriers and the strength of international competition, price competition may degenerate into destructive price wars.

The pattern of changes in industry structure and competition is summarized in Figure 10.3. The consequences of these changes for profitability over the industry life cycle are shown in Table 10.3.

Maturity in an industry usually corresponds to maturity of the individual firms. Industry membership tends to be stable with long established firms. Lack of radical

TABLE 10.3
Average ROI at Different Stages of the Industry Life Cycle

	REAL RATE OF GROWTH		
	LESS THAN 3%	3% TO 6%	OVER 6%
Growth	22.8%	24.4%	24.3%
Maturity	21.7%	22.0%	24.1%
Decline	16.4%	—22.3%—	

Note: These results are for 6,600 business units on the PIMS database over a four-year period.

Source: Robert D. Buzzell and Bradley T. Gale, *The PIMS Principles (*New York: Free Press, 1987): 58.

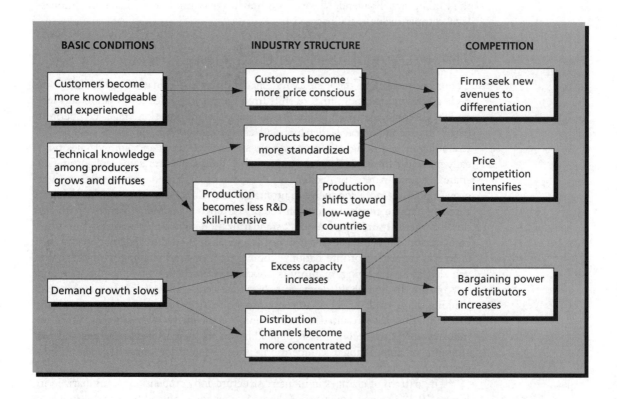

FIGURE 10.3
The Driving Forces of Industry Evolution

innovation and limited opportunities for differentiation also lead to stability of market shares for the leading firms. This stability is partly a product of the heavy investments that leading firms have made in their market positions over long periods of time. The acquisition of experience, reputation, distribution channels, and brand recognition makes it difficult for newcomers to easily dislodge incumbents from their leadership positions. Motor vehicles, oil, chemicals, and branded consumer goods all display such stability. Upheavals in the competitive structures of mature industries are most likely the result of internationalization: new competitors from low-cost countries may undermine the market positions of long-established leaders, as in steel and shipbuilding.

Key Success Factors and Industry Evolution

The changes in competitive structure, customer needs, and resource requirements over the industry life cycle have important implications for key success factors, and hence for business strategies. Several of these strategic implications are shown in Table 10.4.

- ◆ During the **introductory stage** product innovation is the basis for initial entry and for subsequent success. Soon, however, knowledge alone is not enough. As the industry begins its evolution and technological competition intensifies, other requirements for success emerge. In moving from the first generation of products to subsequent generations, investment requirements tend to grow, and financial resources become increasingly important. Capabilities in product development soon need to be matched by capabilities in manufacturing, marketing, and distribution. Hence, in an emerging industry, firms need to support their innovation with a broad array of vertically integrated capabilities.

- ◆ Once the **growth stage** is reached, the key challenge is scaling up. As the market expands, the firm needs to adapt its product design and its manufacturing capability to large-scale production. As Table 10.4 shows, investment in R & D, plant and equipment, and sales tends to be high during the growth phase. To utilize increased manufacturing capability, access to distribution becomes critical. At the same time, the tensions that organizational growth imposes create the need for internal administrative and strategic skills. We consider these issues in Chapter 11.

- ◆ With the **maturity stage,** competitive advantage is increasingly a quest for cost efficiency—or at least, this is the case in those mature industries that tend toward less and less product differentiation. The key success factors thus become the most important cost drivers within that particular industry. Table 10.4 shows that R & D, capital investment, and marketing are lower in maturity than during the growth phase.

- ◆ The transformation to the **decline phase** raises the potential for destructive price competition. Whether a firm has a competitive advantage is secondary to the importance of maintaining a stable industry environment. Hence, company strategies focus on encouraging the orderly exit of industry capacity and building a strong position in relation to residual market demand. We consider the strategic issues presented by mature and declining industries more fully in Chapter 12.

TABLE 10.4
Strategic and Performance Differences Between Businesses at Different Stages of the Industry Life Cycle

	GROWTH	MATURITY	DECLINE
Efficiency Variables			
ROI	.005	.008	−.233*
Capacity Utilization	−.100*	.061*	.107
Employee Productivity	.308*	.127	−.087
Value-Added/Revenue	.155	.063	−.428*
Industry and Product Variables			
Technological Change	.580*	−.159*	−.044
Customization	.185	.151	.035
Relative Product Breadth	−.055	.032*	−.341*
Relative Price	.018	−.049	−.047
Market Share	.030	.062	−.064
R&D Variables			
Sales from New Products/Total Sales	.499*	−.179*	−.383*
Product R&D/Revenue	.537*	.042*	−.365*
Process R&D/Revenue	.484*	−.029*	.003
Production and Investment Variables			
Total Inventory/Revenue	.045	.107	.081
Newness of Plant and Equipment	.323*	−.211*	−.676*
Investment/Revenue	.305*	.028*	−.052*
Backward Vertical Integration	.026	−.043	.001
Forward Vertical Integration	−.030	.029	−.023
Marketing Variables			
Sales Force/Revenue	.278*	−.049*	−.279*
Advertising and Promotion/Revenue	−.250*	−.328*	−.384*

Notes:
1 The table shows the standardized means for each variable for businesses at each stage of the life cycle. Category means that are significantly different from the average for all categories at the 0.05 probability level are indicated by an asterisk.
2 The data were obtained from 1,234 industrial products manufacturing businesses included in the PIMS database during the period 1970–1980.

Source: Carl Anderson and Carl Zeithaml, "Stage of the Product Life Cycle, Business Strategy and Business Performance," *Academy of Management Journal,* 27, 1984: 5–24.

ANTICIPATING AND SHAPING THE FUTURE

Sustaining competitive advantage over time is not just about protecting one's position against imitation, but also ensuring that one's competitive advantage is not rendered obsolete by changes in the industry environment. The threat to IBM in the early 1990s was not about losing its relative strengths in resources and capabilities.

The problem was that changes in the market meant that its enormous investments in internal resources and capabilities (such as its technology base in semiconductors, mainframe computers, and software), its sales and marketing organization, and its customer support capabilities no longer matched industry key success factors as well as they did during the 1970s and 1980s.

The evolution of industries, and with it the changing requirements for success, creates a dilemma for the firm. The firms that are successful at one stage of the life cycle are unlikely to be successful at a subsequent stage because the resources and capabilities that provided the foundation for their success at one stage are not appropriate to the subsequent stage. Woolworth's network of medium-sized, downtown stores that had been the basis of its success during the first six decades of the twentieth century became an increasing liability as demographic and shopping trends left Woolworth stores stranded in unattractive inner-city locations.

Managing with Dual Strategies

The key issue for companies to grasp is that they are competing in two time zones. Strategy is about maximizing performance under today's circumstances; it is also about developing and deploying resources and capabilities for competing in the future. Whereas strategies for the present are primarily concerned with maximizing the effectiveness of current resources and capabilities, competing in the future is concerned with redeploying existing resources and capabilities and developing, extending, and augmenting them. Derek Abell identifies the need for companies to pursue **dual strategies**: managing to optimize performance in the present while simultaneously managing *change* to meet the circumstances of the future.[7] The dilemma facing companies is summed up in the subtitle of Abell's book: *Mastering the Present, Preempting the Future*. Abell cites Nestlé as a company that, during the early 1990s, was concerned with maximizing returns on its present products and brands within the many countries it operates, while simultaneously pursuing its "Nestlé 2000" project aimed at repositioning Nestlé to meet the challenges of a more global, dynamic, and price-competitive marketplace. The issues and decisions involved in managing for the present and for the future are such that companies need **dual planning systems**. Short-term planning, typically with a one-year horizon, needs to focus heavily on strategic fit and performance maximization. Longer-term planning, typically five years or more, needs to develop *vision* and translate that vision into redefining the corporate portfolio, redefining and repositioning individual businesses, developing new capabilities, and redesigning organizational structures and management systems.

Competing for the Future

Gary Hamel and C. K. Prahalad argue that for most companies, emphasis on competing in the present means that too much management energy is devoted to preserving the past and not enough to creating the future.[8] They challenge managers with seven questions:

1. How does senior management's point of view about the future compare with that of your competitors: conventional and reactive, or distinctive and far-sighted?
2. Which business issue absorbs more senior management attention: reengineering core processes or regenerating core strategies?

3. How do your competitors view your company: mostly as a rule follower or mostly as a rule maker?

4. What is your company's strength: operational efficiency or innovation and growth?

5. What is the focus of your company's advantage-building efforts: mostly catching up or mostly getting out in front?

6. What has set your transformation agenda: your competitors or your foresight?

7. Do you spend the bulk of your time as a maintenance engineer preserving the status quo or as an architect designing the future?[9]

Hamel and Prahalad develop what they describe as a "new strategy paradigm" that emphasizes the role of strategy as a systematic and concerted approach to redefining both the company and its industry environment in the future. This compares with the conventional, more static approach which emphasizes the *fit* between the firm's strategy and, on the one hand, the industry environment and, on the other, the firm's resources and capabilities. The key is not to *anticipate* the future, but to *create* the future. We shall return to this point in chapter 12, when we discuss strategic innovation. The main features of their paradigm are summarized in Figure 10. 4.

Concern about the overly short focus of many top management teams at the expense of a longer-term strategic orientation has also been taken up by Michael Porter. Porter points to a growing tendency for companies to confuse measures and

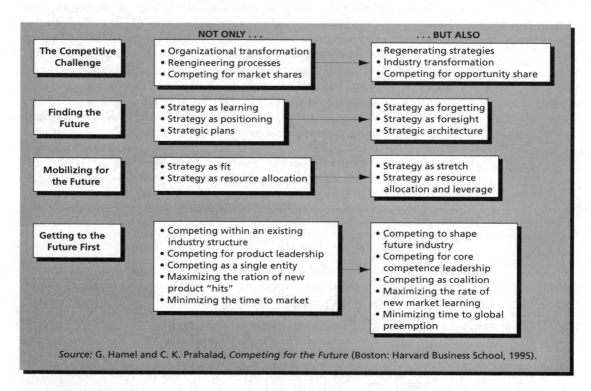

Source: G. Hamel and C. K. Prahalad, *Competing for the Future* (Boston: Harvard Business School, 1995).

FIGURE 10.4
Competing for the Future: Hamel and Prahalad's "New Strategy Paradigm"

programs to promote efficiency and effectiveness with strategic decisions. Strategic decisions involve difficult-to-reverse choices over the allocation of the company's resources. The essence of strategy is choice. The strategic issues facing Apple are whether to continue its focus on developing the distinctive Macintosh computers and operating system, or to adopt the Windows/Intel standard; whether to continue developing both hardware and software, or to specialize in software; whether to maintain its independence or to seek merger. Operational effectiveness issues such as cutting administrative staff, reducing inventories, pressing suppliers for lower component prices, reengineering processes, and implementing TQM may be vitally important, but they are not strategic since they are desirable whichever strategy is adopted.[10]

Preparing for the Future: Scenario Analysis

Whether a company is seeking to adapt to changes in its industry environment or to shape industry evolution, a profound understanding of the forces driving industry change is critical. Increasing inability to forecast the future has resulted in a heavier emphasis on *understanding* the future. Thus, while less and less credence is placed on econometric forecasts, more and more emphasis is being given to scenario analysis. **Scenario analysis** is not a forecasting technique but a process for thinking and communicating about the future. Herman Kahn, who pioneered their use first at the Rand Corporation and subsequently at the Hudson Institute, defined scenarios as "hypothetical sequences of events constructed for the purpose of focusing attention on causal process and decision points."[11] The multiple scenario approach constructs two or more distinct and internally consistent views of how the future may look at 10 to 25 years into the future. Its key value is in combining the interrelated impacts of a wide range of economic, technological, demographic, and political factors into a few distinct alternative stories of how the future might unfold. Scenarios are good exercise for the imagination and are valuable in identifying possible threats and opportunities, generating flexibility of thinking by managers, and developing highly practical approaches to the management of risk. Industry scenarios can be used to develop alternative views of how the market and industry structure may develop and what the implications for competition and competitive advantage might be. Exhibit 10.1 outlines the use of scenarios at Shell.

EXHIBIT 10.1
Multiple Scenario Development at Shell

The Royal Dutch/Shell group of companies has pioneered the use of multiple scenario development as a basis for long-term strategic planning in an industry known for its high risks and very long-term investment projects. In 1967, a "Year 2000" study was inaugurated and scenario development soon became fundamental to Shell's planning process. Mike Pocock, Shell's former chairman, observed: "We believe in basing planning not on single forecasts, but on deep thought that identifies a coherent pattern of economic, political, and social development." Shell views its scenarios as critical to its transition from *planning* toward *strategic management* in which the role of the planning function is not so much to produce a plan, but to manage a *process*, the outcome of which is improved decision making by managers. This involves continually challenging current thinking within the group, encouraging a wider look at external influences on the business, promoting learning, and forging coordination among Shell's 200-odd subsidiaries.   *(continued)*

EXHIBIT 10.1

(Continued)

Shell's global scenarios are prepared about every four years by its corporate-level planning staff. Economic, political, technological, and demographic trends are analyzed and two alternative scenarios are constructed for the development of the world economy over the next 20 years. Thus, Shell's 1984–2005 scenarios were:

- *Next Wave,* which envisaged near-term crisis breaking down structural barriers to change and propelling the global economy into rapid technological progress and strong growth, but accompanied by increasing power of the oil producing nations and stronger competition to oil from gas and electricity.
- *Divided World* in which the barriers to change—protectionism and regulation—stunt growth and technological progress, result in a divide between stagnation in Europe and the developing world and economic development in Asia-Pacific, and are accompanied by weak oil prices.

Once approved by top management, the scenarios are disseminated by reports, presentations, and workshops, where they form the basis for long-term strategy discussion by business sectors and operating companies.

Shell is adamant that its scenarios are not forecasts. They represent carefully thought out stories of how the various forces shaping the global energy environment of the future might play. Their value is in stimulating the social and cognitive processes through which managers think about the future. For example:

- The formulation of scenarios involves bringing out the assumptions and mental models through which managers view their world. All too often these remain hidden and mis-

understood—most importantly by the individuals who hold them. This identification and sharing of implicit assumptions and theories is an important vehicle for mutual learning among different managers.
- The scenario development process permits a deeper and broader understanding of the various forces driving change and how they interact. This can be assisted by sophisticated computer modeling—including simulation.
- The incorporation of scenarios into the strategy formulation process encourages managers to build flexibility into their strategies by envisaging responses to hypothetical situations. Thus, in 1984, Shell had a scenario in which oil was $15 a barrel—which most viewed as inconceivable at a time when oil was $28 a barrel. When the price of oil fell precipitously to $10 in April 1986, Shell was able to adjust more easily than most oil majors because its managers had already considered their responses to dramatically lower prices. Arie De Geus sees scenarios as central to the role of strategic planning as a vehicle for institutional learning.

Sources: J. P. Leemhuis, "Using Scenarios to Develop Strategies," *Long Range Planning,* vol. 18, April 1985: 30–37; Pierre Wack, "Scenarios: Uncharted Waters Ahead," *Harvard Business Review,* September–October 1985: 72 and "Scenarios: Shooting the Rapids," *Harvard Business Review,* November–December 1985: 139; Arie de Geus, "Planning as Learning," *Harvard Business Review,* March–April 1988: 70–74; Paul Schoemacher "Multiple Scenario Development: Its Conceptual and Behavioral Foundation." *Strategic Management Journal,* 14, 1993: 193–214.

◆ SUMMARY

Strategy is about establishing direction into the future. But the future is unknown and, with accelerating changes in the world, is increasingly difficult to predict. However, some regularities are evident in terms of industries' evolutionary paths. The life cycle model provides us with some indications of how industries develop over time.

One use of the life cycle model is allowing us to classifying industries according to their stage of development. This fulfills several purposes:

♦ It acts as a shortcut in strategy analysis. Categorizing industries and applying generalizations about the type of competition likely to emerge and the kinds of strategy likely to be effective provide a quick and useful first-cut analysis for the purposes of strategy formulation.

♦ Classifying an industry requires comparison with other industries. Such comparisons, by highlighting similarities and differences with other industries, can form the basis for a deeper understanding of its structure, competitive character, and sources of advantage.

♦ It directs attention to the forces of evolution within the industry and encourages us to anticipate and manage change.

The dual nature of strategy—maximizing competitive performance in the present while preparing for the future—is a central dilemma for strategic management. If the industry environment is subject to fundamental change, the more successful a company is in achieving fit between its resources and capabilities and the current key success factors, then the greater the difficulties of adapting to the requirements of the future. Despite Gary Hamel urging companies toward strategic revolution, the fact remains that "core capabilities are also core rigidities."[12]

In the next two chapters, we discuss strategy formulation and strategy implementation in industries at different stages of their development: emerging industries and those characterized by technology-based competition and mature industries.

APPENDIX: OTHER APPROACHES TO INDUSTRY CLASSIFICATION

The life cycle is the most common approach to classifying industries by strategic type. However, other approaches to classification have also been proposed. For example, industries can be classified by type of customer (producer goods and consumer goods), by the principal resources used (capital-intensive, technology-intensive, and marketing-intensive professional skill industries), or by the geographic scope of the industry (local, national, global). The critical issue is whether a particular approach to industry classification can offer insight into the similarities and differences among industries for the purposes of formulating business strategies. Here are two useful approaches.

BCG's Strategic Environments Matrix

In the industry life cycle, the stage of maturity of an industry determines the key structural characteristics of an industry, which, in turn, determine the nature of competitive advantage. The Boston Consulting Group's Strategic Environments Matrix reverses this direction: it is the nature of competitive advantage in an industry that determines strategies that are viable, which in turn determine the structure of the industry.

Two variables are used: the number of viable strategy approaches available and the size of the industry leader's potential competitive advantage. The number of strategy approaches depends on the complexity of the industry in terms of the diversity of sources of competitive advantage. Thus, in commodity products where there is no opportunity for differentiation, competitive advantage must be achieved through cost leadership. Furthermore, if all firms face identical input costs and technologies, then scale might be the dominant strategic variable. If an industry's products and customer requirements are complex—as in the case of automobiles, fashion clothing, and restaurants—the sources of competitive advantage are many.

The second variable, the size of the competitive advantage available, depends primarily on the cost and demand characteristics of the industry. Where substantial advantages derive from economies of scale or learning, or brand leadership, or controlling the industry standard, the profit differential associated with competitive advantage may be substantial.

The two variables define four industry types (see Figure A.1):

1. **Volume businesses.** Volume businesses are those with few sources of advantage but with considerable size advantage, typically those where scale advantages are.

2. **Stalemate businesses.** Stalemate businesses are those in which the sources of advantage are few and the size of potential advantage is small. As a result the environment is highly competitive: firms compete with similar strategies, but none is able to obtain significant advantage. This reflects widespread availability of the resources and capabilities needed to compete. These are typically commodity industries where no substantial cost advantages exist. A critical strategic issue is perceiving the emergence of stalemate early on so that a timely exit can be executed. Once a business is embroiled in a stalemate industry, survival and profitability require operational efficiency, low administrative overheads, and a cost-conscious corporate culture.

3. **Fragmented businesses.** Fragmented businesses are those where the sources of competitive advantage are many, but the potential size of the advantage is small. They typically supply differentiated products where brand loyalty is low, technology is well diffused, and scale economies are small. Success factors may include low costs through operational efficiency, focusing on attractive market segment, responding quickly to change, and establishing novel forms of differentiation. Successful companies tend to be entrepreneurial. Franchising is one way of matching the advantages of size

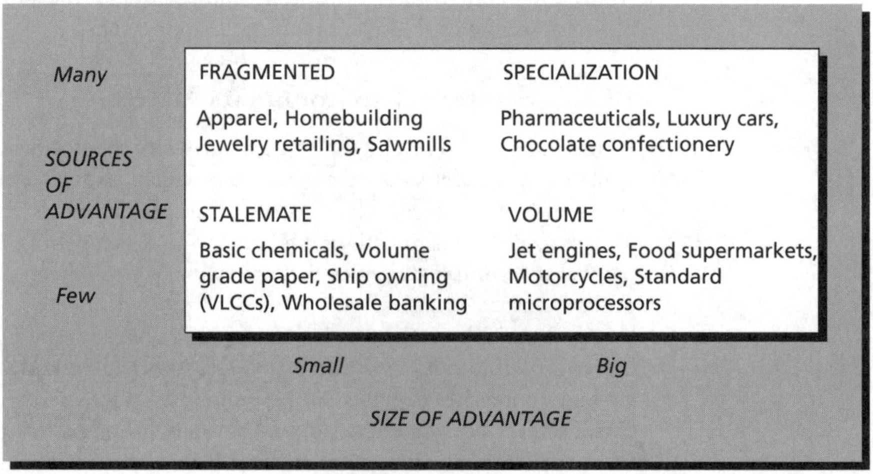

FIGURE A.1
BCG's Strategic Environments Matrix

Many	FRAGMENTED	SPECIALIZATION
	Apparel, Homebuilding Jewelry retailing, Sawmills	Pharmaceuticals, Luxury cars, Chocolate confectionery
SOURCES OF ADVANTAGE	STALEMATE	VOLUME
Few	Basic chemicals, Volume grade paper, Ship owning (VLCCs), Wholesale banking	Jet engines, Food supermarkets, Motorcycles, Standard microprocessors
	Small	*Big*
	SIZE OF ADVANTAGE	

with those of flexibility and decentralization. An alternative strategy is to attempt to transform the business into a specialized or volume business. McDonald's transformed the fast-food industry from a fragmented industry into a specialized/volume industry. Starbucks is achieving a similar feat among gourmet coffee shops.

4. **Specialized businesses.** Specialized businesses are those where the sources of advantage are many and the size of the potential advantage is substantial. Specialization businesses feature varied customer needs, first-mover advantages, brand loyalty, scale economies, and large specific costs associated with serving each market niche with few shared costs (hence, there are no major advantages to firms with a broad market or product scope). Specialization businesses require strategic differentiation: each firm does something different, hence competition is indirect. Competition focuses on product design, innovation, and brand promotion rather than price. BCG's analysis of the strategies appropriate to specialization businesses focuses on two variables: the degree of *environmental stability* and the *ability to systematize* customer and competitor behavior. On the basis of these two variables, Figure A.2 defines four types of businesses and four strategic approaches:

♦ Where the market environment is stable and market behavior is sufficiently regular to permit prediction and systematization, an *analytic* approach to strategy formulation is feasible, involving careful analysis of customer requirements and competitors' behavior.

♦ An environment that is stable but where customers' and competitors' behavior cannot be systematized is conducive to *experimental* approaches to new product introduction and strategy adjustment is appropriate.

♦ Where the environment is variable but where behavior is systematic, *perceptive* skills are the key to competitive advantage—in high-tech environments, the key is to perceive how new technological opportunities can better serve existing customer needs.

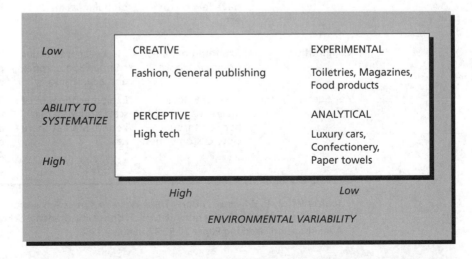

FIGURE A.2
BCG's Analysis of the Strategic Characteristics of Specialization Businesses

♦ Environmental variability combined with inability to systematize requires *creativity* in order to establish competitive advantage. Thus in fashion clothing, not only do markets change quickly but fashion trends and cycles are not amenable to techniques of market analysis.

Classifying Industries According to Competitive Dynamics[13]

Focusing on dynamic aspects of competition, Jeffrey Williams has identified the rate of new product introduction, duration of product life cycles, the rate of decline of unit costs, geographical scope, and the stability of supplier-customer relations as the key strategic features of industries. Williams identifies three industry types, the defining characteristics of which are shown in Table A.1.

1. **Local monopoly markets** sell specialized products to relatively few customers. Firms use highly specialized resources and capabilities to meet highly specific customer requirements. Examples include defense and other government contractors, professional service companies that rely on close client contact (corporate law firms, private bankers), and exclusive consumer product companies (designer clothes, Rolls Royces, and Ferraris). Product differentiation tends to be high: customers are resistant to standardization and elasticity of demand is

TABLE A.1
Williams' Classification of Market Types

	COMPETITIVE ADVANTAGE AND INDUSTRY EVOLUTION		
	Local Monopoly	Traditional Industrial	Schumpeterian
Economies of Experience	Small.	Moderate.	Substantial.
Customer Relations	Stable and long term. Based on close personal contact.	Moderately stable. Emphasis on defending market share.	Unstable with volatile market shares.
Market Scope	Narrow. Firms' markets are local or have few customers.	Markets defined broadly: national or global mass markets.	Typically broad geographically, but often segmented by product/customer type.
Competition	Sheltered markets. Competition weak.	Market share battles; competition on price and advertising.	Intense rivalry on product and process innovation.
Key Success Factors	Dominate local markets and build barriers through close customer ties.	Exploit economies of scale and mass marketing. Market share key.	Fast product innovation. Move quickly down the experience curve. Adopt novel strategies.

Source: Jeffrey R. Williams, "I Don't Think We're in Kansas Any More . . ." A Perspective on Our Expanding Markets, Carnegie-Mellon University, Graduate School of Industrial Administration, Working Paper 20-86-87, January 1988.

low, reflecting customers' preference for specialty products. High-quality, low-volume production with lack of competition encourages craft-based production that is vertically integrated, makes intensive use of highly skilled labor, and places little emphasis on attaining economies of scale or experience.

2. **Traditional industrial markets** are those where market size is large and not heavily segmented and the rate of product innovation is modest. Competition in these markets is dominated by the quest for the benefits of size: economies of scale and brand leadership. Market domination is seldom achieved: products are close substitutes in these markets and market share responds both to price and advertising. The strategy of cost-leadership/brand-awareness/product-variety is exemplified by Unilever, General Motors, and Marks & Spencer. For these strategies to be effective, organizations must emphasize efficiency through control, competence through experience and specialization, and perfection through the elimination of problems and defects. The quest for cost efficiency typically results in continuous cost reduction at a modest annual rate (see Table A.2).

3. **Schumpeterian markets,** driven by a "gale of creative destruction," show the "hypercompetitive" conditions described in Chapter 3. Established products are constantly being displaced by new products that, if successful, show rapid rates of growth. Industries where product innovation is the dominant form of competition include semiconductors, telecommunications, computers, consumer electronics, financial services, recorded music, and certain fashion goods. At the same time, innovations are quickly imitated, and speed in exploiting new products is essential. Hence, success depends not just on product innovation, but also on the manufacturing and marketing capabilities required to move down the experience curve ahead of competitors. Annual reductions in real unit costs in excess of 8 percent are common for these products.

Note that industries may move from one category to another: new process technology, the development of mass markets and deregulation have caused many local

TABLE A.2 Classifying Industries According to Rate of Productivity Growth (as Indicated by Changes in Real Prices)	COMPETITIVE ADVANTAGE AND INDUSTRY REVOLUTION		
	INDUSTRY	PERIOD	AVERAGE ANNUAL REAL CHANGE IN PRODUCER PRICE INDEX (%)
	Local monopoly industries		
	Surgical, orthopedic, and prosthetic appliances	1983–1989	+4.9
	Boot repair	1981–1988	+2.8
	General job printing	1982–1989	+2.6
	Musical instruments	1985–1989	+2.6 *(continued)*

TABLE A.2
Continued

COMPETITIVE ADVANTAGE AND INDUSTRY REVOLUTION		
INDUSTRY	PERIOD	AVERAGE ANNUAL REAL CHANGE IN PRODUCER PRICE INDEX (%)
Map, atlas, and globe cover printing	1982–1989	+2.3
Entertainment	1980–1987	+1.8
Highway construction	1970–1988	+1.7
Burial caskets	1982–1989	+1.7
Residential construction	1970–1988	+1.6
Traditional manufacturing industries		
Passenger cars	1982–1989	+0.3
Wheeled tractors	1982–1989	0.0
Metal cans	1981–1989	−0.1
Electric lamps	1983–1989	−0.7
Gasoline engines (under 11hp)	1982–1989	−0.8
Household refrigerators	1981–1989	−0.9
Dynamic Shumpeterian industries		
Home electronic equipment	1982–1989	−3.6
Microprocessors	1981–1989	−4.6
Microwave cookers	1982–1989	−4.6
Analog integrated circuits	1981–1989	−4.8
Digital PBXs	1985–1989	−4.9
Color TVs (more than 17-inch)	1980–1989	−6.0
Memory integrated circuits	1981–1989	−6.0
Digital computers	1988–1989	−10.3

monopoly industries to become traditional industries. Some industries may be hybrids: thus, in the personal computer industry, components such as keyboards and power supplies are traditional industries, other components such as microprocessors are Schumpeterian industries, while some applications software and customer support are craft-based, sheltered industries. Telecommunications equipment embraces a similar range. These hybrids pose considerable difficulties for strategy and organization.

NOTES

1 The concept of the product life cycle is associated with the work of Everett M. Rogers, *The Diffusion of Innovations* (New York: Free Press, 1962); and Theodore Levitt, "Exploit the Product Life Cycle," *Harvard Business Review* (November–December 1965): 81–94. For a contemporary discussion, see Philip Kotler, *Marketing Management: Analysis, Planning, and Control*, 6th edition (Englewood Cliffs, NJ: Prentice-Hall, 1984), chapter 11.

2 This process may involve intense competition between rival technologies. The video recording industry featured competition between different technologies and formats before the emergence of the VHS format as industry standard. See Richard S. Rosenbloom and Michael A. Cusumano, "Technological Pioneering and Competitive Advantage: The Birth of the VCR Industry," *California Management Review* 29, no. 4 (1987).

3 In the case of metal containers, see "Crown Cork and Seal and the Metal Container Industry" (Boston: Harvard Business School, 1978).

4 In Shiv Mathur's "transaction cycle," differentiation reemerges as products and service are recombined into new systems. See S. Mathur, "Competitive Industrial Marketing Strategies," *Long Range Planning 17, no. 4*, 1984: 102–109.

5 J. K. Galbraith, *American Capitalism: The Concept of Countervailing Power* (Boston: Houghton Mifflin, 1952).

6 R. Vernon, "International Investment and International Trade in the Product Cycle," *Quarterly Journal of Economics* 80 (1966): 190–207.

7 Derek F. Abell, *Managing with Dual Strategies* (New York: Free Press, 1993).

8 Gary Hamel and C. K. Prahalad, *Competing for the Future* (Boston: Harvard Business School, 1995).

9 Gary Hamel and C. K. Prahalad, "Competing for the Future," *Harvard Business Review* (July–August 1994): 122–128.

10 Michael E. Porter, "What Is Strategy?" *Harvard Business Review* (November–December 1996): 61–80.

11 See C. A. R. NcNulty, "Scenario Development for Corporate Planning," *Futures* (April 1977). R. E. Linneman and H. E. Klien, "The Use of Multiple Scenarios by U.S. Industrial Companies: A Comparison Study," *Long Range Planning* (December 1983): 94–101, found that over half of *Fortune* 500 companies were using multiple scenario analysis by the beginning of the 1980s. P. Malaska, "Multiple Scenario Approach and Strategic Behavior in European Companies," *Strategic Management Journal* 6 (1985): 339–355, found scenario analysis used most widely in petroleum, transportation equipment, and electricity industries.

12 Dorothy Leonard Barton, "Core Capabilities and Core Rigidities: A Paradox in Managing New Product Development," *Strategic Management Journal* 13 (Summer 1992): 111–126.

13 This section draws on the work of Jeffrey R. Williams, which is contained in the following papers: "The Productivity Base of Industries," working paper 1983–84, Graduate School of Industrial Administration, Carnegie-Mellon University, May 1984; "I Don't Think We're in Kansas Any More. . . : How Market Settings Influence CIM Strategies," *Long Range Planning* 23 (February 1990); "How Sustainable Is Your Competitive Advantage," *California Management Review* (Spring 1992).

11

Technology-Based Industries and the Management of Innovation

Whereas a calculator on the ENIAC is equipped with 18,000 vacuum tubes and weighs 30 tons, computers in the future may have only 1,000 vacuum tubes and perhaps weigh only 1.5 tons.

—*Popular Mechanics, March 1949*

Outline

- INTRODUCTION AND OBJECTIVES
- COMPETITIVE ADVANTAGE IN TECHNOLOGY-INTENSIVE INDUSTRIES
    The Innovation Process
    The Profitability of Innovation
    Property Rights in Innovation
    Complementary Resources
    The Characteristics of the Technology
    Lead Time
    The Effectiveness of Different Mechanisms for Protecting Innovation
- STRATEGIC ISSUES IN MANAGING TECHNOLOGY AND INNOVATION
    Alternative Strategies to Exploit Innovation
    Alternative Development Models: Corporatism versus Silicon Valley
    Timing Innovation: To Lead or to Follow?
    Controlling Industry Standards
    Managing Risks
- IMPLEMENTING TECHNOLOGY STRATEGIES: CREATING THE CONDITIONS
    FOR INNOVATION
    From Strategy Formulation to Promoting Innovation
    The Conditions for Creativity
    From Invention to Innovation: The Challenge of Cross-Functional Integration
- SUMMARY

◆ INTRODUCTION AND OBJECTIVES

Industries where competition centers on innovation and the application of technology provide some of the most fascinating and complex competitive environments in which to apply the concepts of strategy analysis. Consider the following:

- ◆ In 1985, the personal computer industry was dominated by Apple and IBM; their combined stock market value was six times that of Intel and Microsoft. By June 1997, Intel and Microsoft were worth $318 billion, compared to $86 billion for IBM and Apple. How did Intel and Microsoft become the dominant players in the worldwide personal computer industry?

- ◆ Why did the brilliant British inventor, Clive Sinclair, inventor of the digital watch and pocket TV, developer of the world's cheapest personal computer, and pioneer of electrically powered personal transportation fail to establish a successful industrial enterprise to rival Sony or Hewlett-Packard?

- ◆ Why are some technology-intensive industries such as medical electronics, aerospace, and chemicals dominated by long-established, giant corporations, and others, such as software, computers, and biotechnology led by start-ups?

In this chapter we explore the characteristics of technology-intensive industries and the determinants of competitive advantage within them that give rise to such phenomena.

By technology-intensive industries, we mean both *emerging industries* (those in the introductory and growth phases of their life cycle) as well as the more mature industries (such as pharmaceuticals, chemicals, telecommunications, and electronics) where technology continues to be the major driving force of competition. The issues we examine, however, are also relevant to a much broader range of industries. Although industries such as food processing, fashion goods, automobiles, and domestic appliances are hardly technology-based, innovation and technology utilization are important sources of competitive advantage. Hence, the management of technology is an important component of strategy analysis not just for companies such as Microsoft and Glaxo, but also for Benetton, Michelin, and American Airlines.

In this chapter, we explore market environments in which technology is the driving force of competition and derive insights and principles for the strategic management of technology. Our focus is on innovation. Innovation involves the development of new technology that creates new industries (biotechnology, fiber-optics, digital wireless communication), the application of existing technology to create new products (personal computers, diagnostic imaging), the enhancement of existing products (automobiles, cameras), and the application of technology to business processes (electronic data interchange, computer integrated manufacturing).

By the time you have completed this chapter, you will be able to:

- ◆ Analyze how technology influences industry structure and competition.

- ◆ Identify the factors that determine the returns to innovation, and evaluate the potential for an innovation to establish competitive advantage.

- ◆ Formulate strategies for exploiting innovation and managing technology.

- ◆ Design the organizational conditions needed to successfully implement such strategies.

This chapter is organized as follows. First, we examine the links among technology, industry structure, and competition in technology-intensive industries. Second, we explore the potential for innovation to establish sustainable competitive advantage. Third, we deal with key issues in the design of strategies for technology-intensive industries, including the timing of entry, the optimal means of exploiting an innovation, and the control of industry standards. Finally, we examine the organizational conditions for the successful implementation of technology-based strategies.

COMPETITIVE ADVANTAGE IN TECHNOLOGY-INTENSIVE INDUSTRIES

Our center of attention in the analysis of competitive advantage in technology-based industries is innovation. Innovation is responsible for industries coming into being, and innovation creates competitive advantage. The role of innovation in creating competitive advantage was discussed in Chapter 8. Let's look more closely at the linkage between innovation and profitability.

The Innovation Process

Invention is the creation of new products and processes through the development of new knowledge or, more typically, from new combinations of existing knowledge. **Innovation** is the initial commercialization of invention by producing and marketing a new good or service or by using a new method of production. Once the innovation has occurred, if successful, it becomes diffused: on the demand side, through customers purchasing the good or service; on the supply side, through imitation by competitors. Not all invention progresses into innovation: among the patent portfolios of most technology-intensive firms are numerous inventions that have never been commercialized. Typically, this is because the patent is unlikely to result in a commercially viable product or process. An innovation may be the result of a single invention or multiple inventions. Product innovation in chemicals and pharmaceuticals may involve invention of a single new chemical compound. The first automobile, on the other hand, embodied a multitude of inventions from the wheel, invented some 5,000 years previously, to the internal combustion engine. Some innovations may arise from little or no new technology: the Swatch/Mercedes Benz "Smart Car" is certainly innovative, although it does not necessarily embody new inventions.

The basis of invention is the creation or reconfiguration of *knowledge*. Samuel Morse's telegraph, patented in 1840, was based on several decades of research into electromagnetism from Ben Franklin to Orsted, Ampere, and Sturgion. The compact disc embodies knowledge about lasers.

The pattern of development from knowledge creation to invention and innovation is shown in Figure 11.1. At each of these stages, substantial lags may occur:

♦ Xerography was invented by Chester F. Carlson in 1938 by combining established basic knowledge about electrostatics and printing. The first patents were awarded in 1940. Patent rights were purchased by Xerox Corporation, which launched its first office copiers in 1958. By 1974, the first competitive machines were introduced by IBM, Kodak, Ricoh, and others.

♦ The jet engine, employing Newtonian principles of forces, was patented by Frank Wittle in 1930. The first commercial jet airliner, the Comet, flew in 1957. Two years later, the Boeing 707 was introduced.

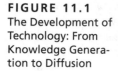

FIGURE 11.1
The Development of
Technology: From
Knowledge Genera-
tion to Diffusion

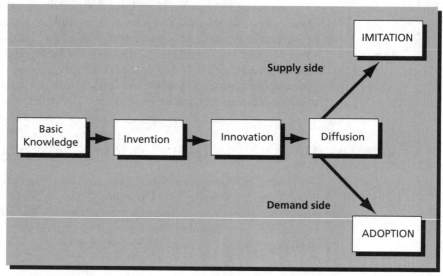

The trend over time is for the lags between knowledge generation, invention, innovation, and diffusion to become shorter. The mathematics of *fuzzy logic* were developed by Lofti Zadeh at Berkeley during the 1960s. By the early 1980s, Dr. Takeshi Yamakawa of the Kyushu Institute of Technology had registered patents for integrated circuits embodying fuzzy logic, and in 1987, a series of fuzzy logic controllers for industrial machines was launched by Omron of Kyoto. By 1991, the world market for fuzzy logic controllers was estimated at $2 billion.[1]

Chapter 10 outlined typical patterns of technology development and their implications for products, industry structure, and the shifting basis of competitive advantage. Emerging industries are characterized by intense product innovation typically involving competition among different technologies and different design configurations. The emergence of a technical standard and dominant product designs are critical points in industry evolution because they mark the transition from radical to incremental product innovation and from product to process innovation.[2] This evolutionary process has important implications for competitive advantage. In the next section, we examine the issues of technological leadership in the early stages of industry development, sustaining innovation advantages, and the determinants of success in battles over standards.

The Profitability of Innovation

As discussed in Chapter 8, innovation is fundamental to the creation of competitive advantage. As Emerson remarked: "If a man . . . make a better mousetrap than his neighbor, though he build his house in the woods, the world will make a beaten path to his door." In terms of our industry analysis, emerging and technology-based industries tend to be attractive in terms of their profit potential: they are growing, product differentiation tends to be high, and proprietary requirements may result in high entry barriers and limits to competition. At the same time, these industries tend to have high and continuing investment requirements and high risks.

The empirical evidence on technological intensity, innovation, and profitability is mixed. PIMS data show R&D intensity and the rate of new product introductions to be negatively related to profitability, although lags between expenditure on innovation and returns may obscure the relationship.[3] Over the longer term, high market share companies in research-intensive industries earned above-average returns, although firms in these industries with above-average patents-to-sales ratios did not earn significantly higher returns."

What emerges is that the returns on innovation depend on the particular circumstances of the firm and its industry. The central issue is the relationship between innovation and competitive advantage. Analyzing the returns on innovation draws on the same criteria that we established in Chapter 5 for evaluating the returns on resources and capabilities:

♦ To what extent does the innovation create competitive advantage from innovation through its *relevance to the key success factors* in the market and its *scarcity* (is it truly unique?)?

♦ To what extent can the competitive advantage from innovation be *sustained?* In terms of its *durability,* will the innovation become quickly obsolete—like the "electronic pets" popular among children during 1997? In terms of *imitation,* can the innovation be acquired or replicated by rivals?

♦ Can the innovator establish the property rights and/or bargaining power needed to *appropriate* the returns to the innovation?

In the case of innovation, the issues of sustainability and appropriability are inseparable and the term **regime of appropriability** is used to describe the conditions that influence the distribution of returns to innovation. The point here is that most innovations benefit multiple parties: the innovator, users (customers), imitators, and suppliers. The critical issue is how the total value created by an innovation is distributed among these different parties (see Figure 11.2). In a *strong* regime of appropriability, the innovator is able to capture a substantial share of the value created: Searle's NutraSweet artificial

FIGURE 11.2
Appropriability: The Distribution of the Benefits from Innovation

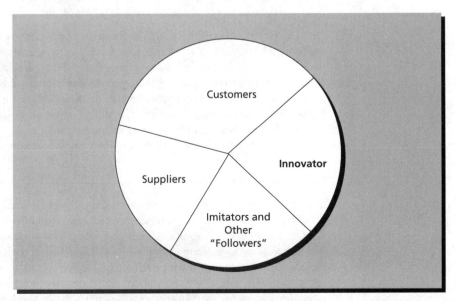

sweetener (later acquired by Monsanto), Glaxo's Zantac, and Pilkington's float glass process generated huge profits for the innovators. In a *weak* regime of appropriability, other parties derive most of the value: in personal computers, the benefits generated were huge, but the primary beneficiaries were not the innovators (MITS, Apple Computer, Xerox), but imitators such as (IBM, Compaq, Dell), suppliers (Intel, Microsoft) and, above all, users.

Four factors are critically important in determining the extent to which innovators are able to appropriate the value of their innovation: property rights, complementary resources, the characteristics of the technology with regard to complexity and transferability, and lead time.

Property Rights in Innovation

Appropriating the returns to innovation depend, to a great extent, on the ability to establish property rights in the innovation. Recognition of this fact prompted the English Parliament to pass the 1623 Statute of Monopolies, which established the basis of patent law. The current law defines what has come to be termed *intellectual property* (related to patents, copyright, trademarks, and trade secrets) as follows:

♦ **Patents** are exclusive rights to a new and useful product, process, substance, or design. Obtaining a patent requires that the invention is novel, useful, and not excessively obvious. Patent law varies from country to country. In the United States, a patent is valid for 17 years (14 for a design).

♦ **Copyrights** give exclusive production, publication, or sales rights to the creators of artistic, literary, dramatic, or musical works. Examples include articles, books, drawings, maps, photographs, and musical compositions.

♦ **Trademarks** are words, symbols, or other marks used to distinguish the goods or services supplied by a firm. In the United States, they are registered with the Patent Office. Trademarks provide the basis for brand identification.

♦ **Trade secrets** offer less well-defined legal protection. Trade secret protection chiefly relates to chemical formulas, recipes, and industrial processes.

The effectiveness of these legal instruments of protection depends on the type of innovation being protected. While patents and copyright establish property rights, their disadvantage is that they make information public. For some new chemical products and basic mechanical inventions, patents can provide effective protections. For products that involve new configurations of existing components or new manufacturing processes, patents may be less effective due to opportunities to innovate around the patent. Where patenting divulges information that may assist competitors, firms may prefer secrecy to patenting as a means of protecting innovation.

Complementary Resources

Innovation involves bringing new products and processes to market. This requires more than invention, it requires the diverse resources and capabilities needed to finance, produce, and market the innovation. These are referred to as **complementary resources** (see Figure 11.3). Complementary resources may include complementary technologies: the commercialization of the jet engine required the technical development of wings, fuselages, fuel systems, instrumentation, and control systems; Microsoft software and Intel microprocessors are similarly complementary to one another.

FIGURE 11.3
Complementary
Resources

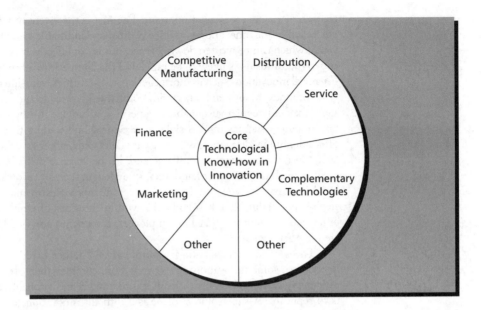

The characteristics and availability of the complementary resources required to commercialize an innovation are critical to the appropriability of the returns to an innovation. If the required complementary resources are owned by other firms or individuals, then the returns to innovation are shared between the innovator and these owners. The issue here is one of bargaining power which, in turn, hinges on dependence. The value of the Wankel rotary engine was limited by the wide range of specialized complementary resources it required: these included investment in the redesign of automobiles and the provision of specialized service and repair facilities. These requirements for specialized complementary resources not only limited the returns to the inventor, but also discouraged the adoption of the innovation both by auto makers and consumers. Where complementary resources are generic, the owners of complementary resources have less bargaining which encourages the adoption of the innovation and enhances its returns. Thus, the huge returns earned by NutraSweet reflect the ability of food and drink companies to substitute NutraSweet for sugar without special investments in new equipment, plants, product redesign, or changes in packaging or distribution.

The role of complementary resources also affects the ease of imitation. If imitation requires access not only to the innovation but also to a range of specialized complementary resources, this creates a more substantial barrier to imitation. For example, Polaroid's leadership in instant photography is protected by a package of specialized complementary resources relating to the technology embodied in the camera, the film, the brand name, the manufacturing facilities and know-how, and Polaroid's strong position in distribution channels.

The Characteristics of the Technology

The extent to which an innovation can be copied depends not just on legal protection through patents and copyrights but also on the characteristics of the technology. Two characteristics are especially important. The first is the extent to which the knowledge embodied in the innovation is tacit or codifiable. **Codifiable knowledge,** by definition, is that which can be written down. Hence, if it is not effectively protected by patents or copyright, diffusion is likely to be rapid and the competitive advantage not sustainable. Financial innovations such as mortgage-backed securities, zero-interest bonds, and new types of index options embody readily codifiable knowledge and are not patentable. As such, they only confer sustainable competitive advantage if supported by complementary resources such as human skills in designing and trading them and the ability to offer liquidity by developing secondary markets with sufficient volumes of trade. Similarly, Coca-Cola's recipe is codifiable and, in the absence of trade secret protection, is easily copied. On the other hand, **tacit knowledge,** such as Toyota's systems for assembling its cars and Nucor's advanced process technologies in mini-mill production of steel, is not codifiable but is embodied within the skills of employees and within the organizational routines that link employees. Experience shows that these innovations are not easily imitated.

The second characteristic is **complexity.** Whether based on tacit or codifiable knowledge, some innovations are simply more complex than others. The more complex an innovation, the more difficult it is to unravel and, probably, the more difficult it is to replicate. A supersonic airplane is a difficult innovation to copy because of the number and complexity of the technologies involved. A Rubik's Cube (a popular toy in the early 1980s) was a simple innovation to copy. The simpler an innovation, the more important patents and copyrights are likely to be for its protection. For complex innovations, secrecy is likely to be the more effective means of protection. However, even complex innovations can be copied through reverse engineering. During the Second World War, British and German armaments producers became especially adept at reverse-engineering captured military hardware. During the 1970s, the rapid closing of the technological gap between Japanese and U.S. industry was achieved in part through Japanese reverse-engineering of state-of-the-art U.S. products.

Lead Time

Tacitness and complexity do not provide lasting barriers to imitation. The protection they provide is that of time. Hence, the competitive advantage that innovation confers should be regarded as temporary: it is a window of opportunity in which the innovator may build on the initial advantage. The essence of this advantage is **lead time:** the innovator has the opportunities to invest in further technical development, production facilities, and market position that will be available to rivals only in the future. The critical issue is to exploit it effectively and not allow the opportunity to pass. British high-tech companies have been notorious for their failure to exploit lead time advantages. DeHaviland with the Comet (the world's first jet airliner), EMI with its CT scanner, Clive Sinclair and the home computer, are all examples of companies that failed to capitalize on their lead time through investing in continued producer development, scale efficient production, and market presence. Microsoft, Intel, and Motorola, on the other hand, are brilliant at exploiting lead time advantage. All three companies solidify initial lead time advantages with large scale investments in production and marketing, and all press to extend their lead time through continual investment in new products that render their earlier product generations obsolete.

The innovator's lead-time advantage can be reinforced by learning efficiencies. Even though AMD and Cyrix has been successful at cloning Intel's Pentium range of microprocessors with a surprisingly short time lag, Intel has used its time advantage and its 90 percent world market share in this category of microprocessor to move quickly down its experience curve, cut prices, and so pressure the profit margins of AMD and Cyrix. Lead time is likely to be important for all innovative products where the experience curve is steep. The ballpoint pen, invented by Ladislao Biro, is a classic example: at Christmas 1945, Biro pens sold at Gimbel's New York store for $12.50; by 1950, ballpoint pens were being sold for 15 cents.[4]

The Effectiveness of Different Mechanisms for Protecting Innovation

How effective are these different mechanisms in protecting technological advantage and permitting innovators to appropriate the returns on their innovations? Empirical evidence shows tremendous variability across industries, but the principal conclusion is that patent protection is of limited effectivess in most industries. One survey found that across 12 industries, patents were judged essential to the development of commercially important inventions in:

- ♦ 65 percent of pharmaceutical inventions
- ♦ 30 percent of chemical inventions
- ♦ 10–20 percent of petroleum, machinery, and metal products inventions
- ♦ Less than 10 percent of electrical equipment, instruments, primary metals, office equipment, motor vehicles, rubber, and textiles inventions.[5]

A landmark study of the appropriability of the returns to R&D by researchers at Yale and Columbia found that patents were less effective at protecting both process and product innovations than were lead-time advantages, learning curve advantages, and sales and service networks (see Table 11.1). The study also found that lead times before competitors could duplicate new products and processes also tended to be short—with patents offering little lead time advantage. (see Table 11.2).

TABLE 11.1
Protecting Innovation: The Effectiveness of Different Barriers to Imitation

METHOD OF APPROPRIATION	OVERALL SAMPLE MEANS	
	PROCESSES	PRODUCTS
Patents to prevent duplication	3.52	4.33
Patents to secure royalty income	3.31	3.75
Secrecy	4.31	3.57
Lead time	5.11	5.41
Moving quickly down the learning curve	5.02	5.09
Sales or service efforts	4.55	5.59

Note: The means show responses from 650 individuals across 130 lines of business. The range was from 1 (= not at all effective) to 7 (= very effective).

Source: R. C. Levin, A. K. Klevorick, R. R. Nelson, and S. G. Winter, "Appropriating the Returns from Industrial Research and Development," *Brookings Papers on Economic Activity 3* (1987): 794.

TABLE 11.2
The Time Required to Duplicate an Innovation

	LESS THAN 6 MONTHS	6–12 MONTHS	1–3 YEARS	3–5 YEARS	MORE THAN 5 YEARS	TIMELY DUPLICATION NOT POSSIBLE
Major patented new product	2	6	64	40	8	9
Major unpatented new product	3	22	89	12	1	2
Major patented new process	0	4	72	37	9	7
Major unpatented new process	2	20	84	17	2	4

Source: R. C. Levin, A. K. Klevorick, R. R. Nelson, and S. G. Winter, "Appropriating the Returns from Industrial Research and Development," *Brookings Papers on Economic Activity 3* (1987).

STRATEGIC ISSUES IN MANAGING TECHNOLOGY AND INNOVATION

Now that we understand some of the factors that determine the potential for innovation to establish and sustain competitive advantage, what are the implications for how we manage technology and innovation?

Alternative Strategies to Exploit Innovation

How should an innovator maximize the returns to his or her innovation? A range of alternatives face any individual or firm. Figure 11.4 ranks these from the lowest level of involvement by the innovator in commercialization—licensing—to the highest level of involvement, internal commercialization—which may involve the creation of a new enterprise or establishing a new unit within an existing enterprise. In between, there are various opportunities for collaboration with other companies. This may take the form of an informal alliance, subcontracting certain activites to outside companies (e.g., outsourcing manufacturing or appointing an agent to handle all marketing and sales within a designated geographical area), or a joint venture, a new company created and owned by two or more partners. Figure 11.4 summarizes some of the key distinctions among these strategic alternatives in terms of risk and resource requirements.

The choice of strategic mode depends on two main sets of factors: the characteristics of the innovation, and the resources and capabilities of the firm.

Characteristics of the Innovation.   The key issue here is the extent to which the firm can establish property rights through patents. The licensing option is only viable where an innovation has clearly defined patent rights. Thus, in pharmaceuticals, licensing is widespread. Because patents are clear and defensible, specialist R&D companies can appropriate a major part of the potential value of their inven-

	Licensing	Outsourcing Certain Functions	Strategic Alliance	Joint Venture	Internal Commercialization
Risk and Return	Low investment risk, but returns also limited (unless patent position very strong). Some legal risks	Lowers capital investment, but may create dependence on suppliers/partners	Benefits of flexibility, risks of informal structure	Shares investment and risk. Potential for partner disagreement and culture clash	High investment requirement and corresponding risks. Benefits of control
Competing Resources	Few	Allows access to outside resources and capabilities	Permits pooling of the resources and capabilities of more than one firm		Requires internal provision of the full range of resources and capabilities needed for commercialization
Examples	Konica licensing its digital camera to Hewlett Packard. Dolby sound reduction system	Pixar's computer animated movies (e.g., "Toy Story") marketed and distributed by Disney Co.	Apple and Sharp build the "Newton" PDA	Microsoft and NBC formed MSNBC	TI's development of its Digital Signal Processing chips. W. T. Gore and Associates' "Gore-Tex"

FIGURE 11.4
Alternative Strategies for Exploiting Innovation

tion through license agreements. Similarly, Dolby's sound reduction business is built entirely on licensing the Dolby technology. On the other hand, Steve Jobs and Steve Wozniak, developers of the Apple I and Apple II computers, had little option other than to go into business themselves—the absence of proprietary technology ruled out licensing as an option.

The Resources and Capabilities of the Firm. As Figure 11.4 shows, the different strategic options require very different capabilities. Developing the innovation requires research, development, and creativity. Thus, a high proportion of major inventions are associated either with individuals or small organizations. Of the major innovations of the first seven decades of the twentieth century, most were contributed by individual inventors—frequently working in their garage or garden shed.[6] Among 27 key inventions of the postwar period, only seven emerged from the R&D departments of established corporations.[7] Hence, the organizations that are best at innovation are frequently those that do not possess the range of resources required for commercialization. These small start-ups have to resort to licensing, outsourcing, or strategic alliances in order to access the complementary resources needed to take their innovation to market. Alternatively, they may seek to be bought out by a larger concern. In biotechnology and electronics, a two-stage model for innovation is common: the technology is initially developed by a small, technology-intensive start-up, which then licenses to a larger concern. Conversely, large, established corporations are more capable of internal commercialization, drawing on their wealth of resources and capabilities. Thus, companies such as Sony, GE, and IBM tend to rely on internal development of innovations. Companies such as these have tended to form more joint ventures, strategic alliances, and outsourcing arrangements as they recognize the need to access capabilities outside their corporate boundaries.

As firms recognize the economic value of their intellectual property, so they are becoming more strategic about protecting and exploiting their knowledge assets. During the 1950s and 1960s, the leading companies in electronics R&D, IBM and AT&T, virtually gave away access to their vast patent portfolios. During the 1980s and 1990s, companies have pursued far more strategic licensing practices. During 1990–95, Texas Instruments' royalty income exceeded its overall net income.

As Grindley and Teece show, licensing is used not only to generate income, but to gain access to other companies' technologies. In semiconductors and electronics, cross-licensing arrangements, whereby one company gives access to its patents across a field-of-use in exchange for access to another company's patents, plays a key role in permitting "freedom-to-design": the ability to design products which draws upon technologies owned by different companies.[8]

Alternative Development Models: Corporatism versus Silicon Valley

Different approaches to the exploitation of innovation are one aspect of a broader question: What type of industry structure is most conducive to the successful innovation? Two rival models can be identified:

♦ The *Corporate model* typical of technology-based industries in Japan and Germany and of the chemical and aerospace sectors in the United States, in which the innovation process from R&D to production and marketing is nurtured and controlled within large, technologically diverse, mature corporations.

♦ The *Silicon Valley model* named after the semiconductor-computer hardware-computer software cluster based in the San Jose area of California. This model is also apparent in the biotechnology industries of the United States and Britain and in the cluster of communications and Internet companies in the Greater Washington area. This model features loose corporate control. Innovation is associated with small, start-up companies, many of them spun off from earlier start-ups. These innovations are exploited through various collaborative relationships ranging from loose networks of strategic alliances to more formalized joint ventures, and involving financing first through venture capitalists, and subsequently through initial public offerings of stock.[9]

George Gilder has praised the dynamism and inventiveness of the Silicon Valley model for its ability to harness creativity and entrepreneurial drive, for its flexibility, and for its ability to permit different types of companies to undertake different stages and different aspects of the innovation so as to exploit their distinctive capabilities.[10] Charles Ferguson, on the other hand, sees these free-wheeling entrepreneurial start-ups as permitting the individual exploitation of the technologies developed within large corporations, which ultimately stunts the development of broad-based innovative capabilities among leading technology-based firms.[11] The key arguments here are: first, that to effectively develop and exploit innovation, technology and the full range of complementary resources needed to exploit the innovation need to be brought together within the same company; second, technological development is not about single innovations but a *technological trajectory* comprising a stream of related innovations. Motorola's development from car radios, to TVs, to semiconductors, to wireless communication equipment, to direct satellite communication services is such a trajectory. Its success requires a process of continual technology building. Success should not be viewed in terms of particular products or innovations but as the development of technological and manufacturing capability within electronics and communication. Thus, "technology leakage" as a result of Motorola's engineers' leaving to start their own companies represents a weakening of these core capabilities.

Different development models may be appropriate to different industries and different national cultures. There is no doubt that the entrepreneurial approach of California's Silicon Valley based on start-ups, spin-offs, and interfirm networks has been outstandingly successful in fostering creativity. It has also encouraged the transfer of knowledge among universities (notably Stanford and Berkeley), corporate research labs (such as Bell Labs and Xerox PARC), and companies (Fairchild Semiconductor, Hewlett-Packard, and IBM have all played leading roles in seeding new technology-based enterprises).

It is also apparent that the corporate model has worked outstandingly well in the Japanese consumer electronics industry (notably for companies such as Matsushita, Toshiba, and Sony) and in the world's chemical industry. As the U.S. semiconductor-computer-software sector increasingly consolidates around a handful of key players (Intel, Microsoft, Hewlett-Packard, IBM, and Sun, to name a few) the issue arises as to whether the entrepreneurial model of Silicon Valley is developing into the hybrid form observed in the pharmaceutical industry: a dominant group of key players with close links with a fringe of creative start-ups that pioneer R&D in biotechnology and other areas at the edge of technology.

Timing Innovation: To Lead or to Follow?

To gain competitive advantage in emerging and technologically intensive industries is it best to be a leader or a follower in innovation? As Table 11.3 shows, the evidence is mixed: in some products the leader has been the first to grab the prize, in others the leader has succumbed to the risks and costs of pioneering. Optimal timing of entry into an emerging industry and the introduction of new technology is a complex issue. The extent of first-mover advantages (or disadvantages) associated with pioneering depends on the following factors:

The Extent to Which Innovation Can Be Protected by Property Rights or Lead Time Advantages.   If an innovation is appropriable through patent or copyright protection or through lead time advantage such as learning, there is likely to be advantage in being an early mover. This is especially the case where patent protection is important, as in pharmaceuticals. Here competition can take the form of a patent race where the rewards are winner-take-all.

The Importance of Complementary Resources.   The more important the complementary resources in exploiting an innovation, the greater the costs and risks of pioneering. Several firms have already failed in their attempts to develop and market an electric automobile. The problem of the pioneer, as General Motors is discovering, is that the development costs are huge, partly because of the need to orchestrate the development of a number of technologies (batteries and other power-storage devices, electric motors, and weight-reducing new materials), and partly because of the need to establish facilities for service and

TABLE 11.3
Leaders, Followers, and Success in Emerging Industries

PRODUCT	INNOVATOR	FOLLOWER	THE WINNER
Jet airliner	De Haviland (Comet)	Boeing (707)	Follower
Float glass	Pilkington	Corning	Leader
X-ray scanner	EMI	General Electric	Follower
Office PC	Xerox	IBM	Follower
VCRs	Ampex/Sony	Matsushita	Follower
Diet cola	R.C. Cola	Coca-Cola	Follower
Instant camera	Polaroid	Kodak	Leader
Pocket calculator	Bowmar	Texas Instruments	Follower
Microwave oven	Raytheon	Samsung	Follower
Plain-paper copier	Xerox	Canon	Not clear
Fiber optic cable	Corning	Many companies	Leader
Video games player	Atari	Nintendo/Sega	Followers
Disposable diaper	Procter & Gamble	Kimberley-Clark	Leader
Internet browser	Netscape	Microsoft	Unclear

Source: Based in part on David Teece, *The Competitive Challenge: Strategies for Industrial Innovation and Renewal* (Cambridge, Ballinger, 1987): 186–188.

recharging. Meanwhile it is not clear what will be the dominant electrical vehicle technology, or even if there will be a mass market for such vehicles. The resource requirements change as an industry evolves: as industry infrastructure develops so firms can access complementary resources from specialist firms. In the British frozen foods industry, Birds Eye, the pioneer, was forced to make huge investments in a frozen foods distribution network, including the leasing of frozen food cabinets to retailers. However, by the mid-1970s, the growth of public cold stores and refrigerated trucking companies meant companies introducing new frozen food products could enter with much smaller investments.

The Presence of Technical Standards.   Product markets vary as to whether they tend toward the establishment of technical standards or not. We discuss the circumstances that promote the emergence of standards later. In the meantime, note that the more important are product standards, the greater the advantages of being an early mover in order to influence those standards. Once a standard has been set, displacing it becomes exceptionally difficult. IBM had little success with its PS2 operating system against the entrenched position of Microsoft Windows. However, in establishing a technical standard, there may also be some risk of entering too early before the direction of technological development is clear. Although IBM's 1981 entry into personal computers was comparatively late, a dominant technology or design had not emerged despite the strength of Apple and Commodore in the market. Hence, IBM was able to establish a dominant de facto standard for the industry.

The choice of timing is not only dependent on the characteristics of the technology and the industry, but also on the resources and capabilities and goals of the individual firm. A small, technology-based firm may have no choice but to pioneer the introduction of an innovation. Given its lack of complementary resources, its only chance of building sustainable competitive advantage is to grab first-mover advantage and to use this to develop the necessary complementary resources before more powerful rivals appear. For the large, established firm with financial resources and strong production, marketing, and distribution capabilities, a follower strategy may be more attractive. The costs of failure are greater for the established firm with a reputation and brands to protect, and the effective utilization of its complementary resources requires the existence of a significant market and stabilization of product ethnology and design. Consider the following examples:

♦ In personal computers, Apple was a pioneer, IBM a follower. The timing of entry was probably optimal for each. Apple's resources were its imagination and its technology. Its strategic window occurred at the very beginning of the industry when these strengths could make the biggest impact. IBM had enormous strengths in manufacturing, distribution, and reputation. It could use these resources to establish competitive advantage even without a clear technological advantage. The important thing for IBM was to delay its entry to the point when market and technological risks had been reduced and the industry had reached a stage of development where strengths in large-scale manufacturing, marketing, and distribution could be brought to bear.

♦ Competition between Netscape and Microsoft is a classic case of the innovative start-up. Netscape, fighting to maintain its lead against the late-coming Microsoft juggernaut, loaded with complementary resources, the most important of which being access to most of the world's PC users through its huge Windows market.

♦ Although General Electric entered the market for CT scanners some four years after EMI, GE was able to overtake EMI within the space of three years because of its ability to apply vast technological, manufacturing, sales, and customer service capabilities within the field of medical electronics.

♦ As a start-up company, PictureTel had little choice but to pioneer the development of videoconferencing. However, by 1996, PictureTel was facing some powerful competitors in this fast-growing market. All of these competitors were able to use their strengths in complementary resources to their advantage in the market for videoconferencing services. Thus, MCI and British Telecom were able to use their telephone systems, communications expertise, and established relations with corporate clients, while Intel was competing with its Proshare system that converts a desktop PC into a videoconferencing system.[12]

Controlling Industry Standards

Table 11.4 lists a number of companies whose success is closely associated with their control of standards within a particular product category.

Why do standards emerge in some product markets and not in others? As we noted in Chapter 10, most products tend to develop a dominant design: a convergence of different companies' product offerings around a common configuration that sets the standard for further product development. The Ford Model T in automobiles, the Boeing 707 in passenger jet aircraft, the IBM PC in microcomputers are all examples of dominant designs. Some product markets, however, go beyond dominant design to the establishment of uniform product standards. In some cases, this is done by official bodies, such as the U.S. National Institute of Standards and the International Organization for Standardization (ISO); in others, de facto standards emerge. It is the latter we are interested in since the ability of firms to own and control these are sources of rent. Morris and Ferguson refer to the technical standards that are critical components of a dominant design paradigm as **architectural standards**.[13] An **architectural controller** is a company that controls one or more of

TABLE 11.4 Examples of Companies That Control Industry Standards	COMPANY	PRODUCT CATEGORY	STANDARD
	Microsoft	Personal computer operating systems	Windows
	Intel	PC microprocessors	*86 series
	Matsushita	Videocassette recorders	VHS system
	Iomega	High capacity PC disk drives	Zip and Jaz drives
	Intuit	Software for on-line financial transactions	Quicken software
	AMR	Computerized airline reservation system	Sabre

the architectural standards by which the entire information package is assembled. Even in an "open systems" environment, these architectural standards play an important role. Thus, in a typical in-company computer network:

- Intel owns the microprocessor design
- Microsoft or Sun owns the operating system
- Novell or Microsoft owns the network software
- Adobe or Hewlett-Packard owns the printer page description system
- McAfee owns the anti-virus software.

Though dominant designs emerge through a competitive process of survival of the fittest, the emergence of technical standards is the result of an additional force for uniformity: **network externalities.** Network externalities exist where there are complements between individuals' utility functions such that the value of a product or service to a user depends on the number of others who are using that product or service. The classic example of network externality is the telephone. Since there is little satisfaction to be gained from talking to oneself on the telephone, the value of a telephone to each user depends on the number of other users connected to the same telephone system. Network externalities do not require everyone to use the same product, but that the different products be *compatible* with one another through some form of common interface. Network externalities arise from many sources:

1. Products where user satisfaction depends on the number of other users—the telephone and other network products are examples. The same phenomenon may arise with best-selling novels, blockbuster movies, and hit TV shows: one consumes in order to feel a part of popular culture and to participate in social conversation.

2. Availability of after-sales service. The advantage of driving a popular Ford model over a Morgan sports car is that spare parts and repair are available for the Ford in many locations.

3. Economizing on training. Familiarity with Microsoft Office is an advantage when seeking employment. Since the majority of companies in the English-speaking world use this suite of applications software, the chance of needing to reinvest in software training is smaller.

4. Availability of complementary products. Many products are used with a range of complementary products: VCRs, PCs, and stereo systems all require software (videocassettes, applications software, recorded music). The value of the product depends on the range of software available, which in turn depends on the number of users. The accelerating decline of the Apple Macintosh is primarily a result of a decreasing availability of leading-edge software as software developers increasingly concentrate on Windows-based applications. Few of you will be interested in buying Grant's Incredible Pneumatic Stereo system if the only recorded music available is Rob Grant singing "My Way."

More and more, firms are recognizing that the ownership of proprietary standards is one of the most valuable resources in technologically based industries. The classic case of missed opportunity is that of IBM in personal computers. IBM was remarkably successful in setting the key technical standards for the industry; its problem was that it did not own these standards. It was Intel and Microsoft that owned the critical parts of the IBM standard and that profited from it.

Profiting from standards requires two elements: first, setting the standard, second, retaining some proprietary interest in the standard in order to appropriate part of its value. There is a tradeoff between the two. Consider the following cases:

♦ In personal computers, IBM was highly successful in setting the standard, partly because it did not restrict access to its technology. Its product specifications were openly available to "clone makers," and its suppliers (including Microsoft and Intel) were free to supply them. IBM was unsuccessful in appropriating the returns to the standard; indeed, the standard became referred to less as the "IBM standard" and more as the "Wintel standard" (Windows/Intel). For Apple, the situation was the reverse. It kept tight control over its Macintosh operating system and product architecture, but in the process forfeited the opportunity of setting the industry standard.

♦ In VCRs, Matsushita's VHS format won against Sony's Betamax format not because of the technical superiority of VHS, but because Matsushita did not insist on such tight ownership of its technology and was more effective in gaining acceptability in the market. The key here was Matsushita's encouragement of adoption through licensing of the VHS system to Sharp, Philips, GE, RCA, and other competitors.

The tradeoff between market penetration and appropriability is shown in Figure 11.5. The innovator who enforces no ownership rights and gives away the innovation to anyone who wants it will probably maximize market penetration. On the other hand, the innovator who is most restrictive in enforcing ownership rights will probably have difficulty building a bandwagon big enough to establish market leadership. In recent battles over technical standards, the desire to gain market leadership has encouraged firms to be less and less restrictive over ownership in the interests of building their market bandwagon. Thus, in the battle for dominance of Internet browser software, both Microsoft (with its *Explorer*) and Netscape (with its *Navigator*) are close to giving away their products in the interests of wresting market leadership. In a quest to set the industry standard for digital audio recordings, Sony (with its minidisk system) is competing against Philips (with its Digital Compact Cassette). Both companies have sought to build alliances with other companies and both companies have supported their technologies by investing heavily in their music subsidiaries (Sony's Columbia records and Philips' Polygram). Though neither system looks to be close to establishing a standard, Philips seems to be losing the contest.[14]

Once established, technical and design standards tend to be highly resilient. Standards are difficult to displace due to learning effects and network effects. Learning effects cause the dominant technology and design to be continually improved and refined. A new technology, even though it may have the potential to overtake the existing standard, will initially be inferior. Such was the fate of the Wankel rotary engine. Continued refinement over one hundred years has given the standard four-cycle engine a remarkable combination of efficiency, economy, and reliability. Although the Wankel rotary engine is believed by many to be potentially superior, the fact that it was only adapted by a single manufacturer (Mazda) has meant that there has never been the continuous development needed to overcome its initial technical problems.

FIGURE 11.5
Profiting from Technical Standards: The Tradeoff between Acceptability and Appropriability

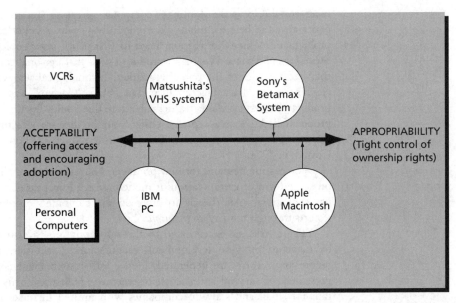

Even where the existing standard is inherently inferior, replacing it may be exceedingly difficult due to network effects. The case of the typewriter keyboard is classic. The standard QWERTY arrangement was invented in 1873. It was designed to *slow* the speed of typing to prevent the typing bards on mechanical typewriters from locking together. In 1932, the Dvorak Simplified Keyboard (DSK) was patented and was shown to offer considerable gains in typing speed. The QWERTY keyboard has persisted because its enormous network effects were reinforced by the investments of millions of people in touch typing and manufacturers in keyboard layouts.[15]

The absence of a clear technical standard may delay market acceptance of a new product if potential customers have a fear of becoming stranded with an obsolete design. The slow movement of cellular telephone systems in the U.S. from analog to digital technology may be attributed in part to uncertainty created by continuing competition between TDMA and CDMA systems. Such uncertainty over which technology will dominate may even cause the death of the product. The failure of quadraphonic sound to displace stereophonic sound during the 1970s resulted from incompatible technical standards among manufacturers of audio equipment. The absence of a dominant standard discouraged recorded music companies from investing in quadraphonic records and tapes, and consumers from investing in quadraphonic systems.[16] Similar uncertainty has arisen over high-definition television (HDTV).[17]

Managing Risks

Emerging industries are characterized by both technological and market uncertainty. Technological uncertainty is exacerbated not only by the unpredictability of technological innovation, but also by inefficiencies of competition in selecting the best technologies: the adoption of the QWERTY keyboard layout and the emergence of

Microsoft DOS as the dominant computer operating system in the 1980s are evidence that the best technology does not always win. Market uncertainty is equally problematic. When Xerox introduced its first plain-paper copier in 1959 and when Steve Jobs and Steve Wozniak introduced their first personal computer in 1977, neither had any idea of the potential market. Technological achievement is not a sufficient basis for market acceptance: Du Pont's "Corfam" was a technically superb product: the first synthetic leather substitute that could "breathe" like leather. But the product failed to gain acceptance either from the shoe manufacturers or their customers, and after running up losses of almost $100 million, Du Pont ceased production of Corfam in 1971.[18]

Forecasting demand for new products is hazardous since all forecasting is based on some form of extrapolation or modeling based on past data. One appoach is to use analogies.[19] Another is to draw on the combined insight and experience of experts through the *Delphi technique*.[20]

These risks are exacerbated by the substantial up-front investments that must be made in product development, manufacturing facilities, and marketing well before any returns are generated. Hence, effective management of risk is a vital ingredient of survival and success in emerging industries. This is especially important for small and start-up companies with limited financial resources. There are several approaches to coping with and reducing vulnerability to risk.

Cooperating with Lead Users.   During the early phases of industry development, careful monitoring of and response to market trends and customer requirements is essential to avoid major errors in technology, design, and performance. Von Hippel argues that lead users provide a vital source of market data for developing new products.[21] Hence, identifying users whose present strong needs will become general market trends in the future and developing close ties with such customers can be vital to maintaining technological progressiveness. Cooperation with lead users yields three major benefits:

1. An "early warning system" for emerging needs and technological trends.
2. Assistance in the conception and development of new products and processes. In electronic instruments, customers' ideas initiated most of the successful new products introduced by manufacturers.[22] Similarly, in aluminum refining, fabricators have been the source of the majority of innovations.
3. By targeting early adopters, the firm can achieve an early cash flow to contribute to further development expenditures.

In industrial products, the most innovative and technologically conscious customers are easy to identify, and their decisions may have an important influence on the technological choices of other firms, too. In consumer products, early adopters are frequently young, educated, affluent consumers in urban areas, although this is not always the case—Nike has test-marketed new product ideas with inner-city street gangs. In electronics and aerospace, governments (the military in particular) play a crucial role as early adopters providing technical input, finance, and field-testing. (However, dependence on government contracts to support R&D may encourage overengineering and inattentiveness to design-for-manufacturability.)

Limiting Risk Exposure.   The high level of risk in emerging industries requires that firms adopt financial and investment practices that minimize their exposure to adversity. Uncertainties over development costs and the timing and amount of future cash flows require a strong balance sheet with limited debt financing.

♦ Apple's ability to survive the many mishaps in its history is owed much to its financial conservatism, including a commitment to a strong cash position and low debt.

♦ Hewlett-Packard's commitment to financing all expansion out of retained earnings has been an important source of strength for the company in navigating a course through technological and market turbulence.

Limiting risk exposure also requires economizing on capital expenditure commitments and other sources of fixed cost. The collapse of EMI's CT scanner business in 1980 may be attributed, in part, to EMI's vulnerability to competition from GE and a downturn in market demand that was exacerbated by its "go-it-alone" strategy. In attempting, single-handedly, to establish itself as a major player in the world medical electronics business, EMI was playing with high stakes.

Innovating companies can reduce their exposure to risk by limiting their capital commitments. Smaller players in high-tech, high-risk industries from biotech to toys are increasingly focusing on core capabilities and outsourcing most traditional business functions. Even large, established companies are resorting increasingly to strategic alliances and joint ventures in developing new, technology-based businesses.

Flexibility. The high level of uncertainty in emerging industries makes flexibility critical to long-term survival and success. Because technological and market changes are difficult to forecast, it is essential that top management closely monitor the environment and respond quickly to demand fluctuations, changing customer preferences, changing patterns of distribution, and the emergence of new customer segments. According to Tom Peters, a vital element in flexibility is recognizing and responding to failures. Peters quotes the late Sichiro Honda, the founder of Honda Motor Company: "Many people dream of success. To me success can only be achieved through repeated failure and introspection. In fact, success represents the 1 percent of your work that only comes from the 99 percent that is called failure."[23] Honda's flexibility and responsiveness to failure was apparent in Mr. Kawashima's account of Honda's initial entry into the U.S. motorcycle market:

By the first week of April 1960, reports were coming in that our machines were leaking oil and encountering clutch failure. This was our lowest moment. Honda's fragile reputation was being destroyed before it could be established. As it turned out, motorcycles in the United States are driven much farther and much faster than in Japan. We dug deeply into our precious cash reserves to air freight our motorcycles to the Honda testing lab in Japan . . . Our lab worked 24-hour days benchtesting the bikes to replicate the failure. Within a month, a redesigned head gasket and clutch spring solved the problem. But in the meantime, events had taken a surprising turn. Throughout our first eight months we had not attempted to move the 50cc Supercubs. While they were a smash success in Japan, they seemed wholly unsuitable for the U.S. market where everything was bigger and more luxurious . . . We used the Honda 50s ourselves to ride around

Los Angeles on errands. They attracted a lot of attention. One day we had a call from a Sears buyer. While persisting in our refusal to sell through an intermediary, we took note of Sears' interest . . . When the larger bikes started breaking, we had no choice. We let the 50cc bikes move. And surprisingly, the retailers who wanted to sell them weren't motorcycle dealers, they were sporting goods stores. The excitement created by the Honda Supercub began to gain momentum.[24]

Fast response to market reactions was similarly critical to the early success of Apple Macintosh. The original Macintosh launched in 1984 was a technologically brilliant product in search of a market. The problem was that the Mac was a fun computer that was unsuitable for business use. During 1985 and 1986, Apple initiated a host of strategic initiatives including cooperation with Microsoft on business applications software, opening the Mac to third-party developers, upgrading speed and memory, and targeting the desktop publishing market. The result was a transformation in Macintosh's market positioning and appeal.[25]

Managing the risks associated with innovation also requires that investment criteria be adjusted so that investments are not biased against R&D projects. One of the problems of discounted cash flow analysis of investment projects is that such appraisal fails to take account of the *option value* of R&D. Research into a promising technology is unlikely to generate financial returns directly. Its value is that it gives a company a position within an emerging technology that offers the potential for further investment in new products that may generate high profits. In drug research, oil exploration, and other high-risk activities, companies are increasingly using option-pricing models to evaluate investments in research companies.[26]

IMPLEMENTING TECHNOLOGY STRATEGIES: CREATING THE CONDITIONS FOR INNOVATION

As I have noted previously, strategy formulation cannot be separated from its implementation. Nowhere is this more evident than in technology-intensive buinesses.

From Strategy Formulation to Promoting Innovation

Our analysis so far has taught us about the potential for generating competitive advantage from innovation and about the design of technology-based strategies, but it has said little about the conditions under which innovation is achieved. The danger is that strategic analysis can tell us a lot about making money out of innovation, but this isn't much use if we cannot generate innovation in the first place. If the essence of innovation is creativity and one of the key features of creativity is its resistance to planning, it is evident that strategy formulation must pay careful attention to the organizational processes through which innovations emerge and are commercialized. Because the features of new products and processes are unknown at the time when resources are committed to R&D and there is no predetermined relationship between investment in R&D and the output of innovations, the productivity of R&D depends heavily on the organizational conditions that foster innovation. Hence, the most crucial challenge facing firms in emerging and technology-based industries is: How does the firm create conditions that are conducive to innovation?

To answer this question we must return to the critical distinction between invention and innovation. Invention is dependent on creativity. Creativity is not simply a matter of individual brilliance; it depends on the organizational conditions that foster ideas and imagination at the individual and group levels. Similarly, innovation is not just a matter of acquiring the resources necessary for commercialization; innovation is a cooperative activity that requires interaction and collaboration between technology development, manufacturing, marketing, and various other functional departments within the firm.

The Conditions for Creativity

Invention has two primary ingredients: knowledge and creativity. Only by understanding the determinants of creativity, then fostering it through the appropriate organizational environment, can the firm hope to innovate successfully. Creativity is an individual act that establishes a meaningful relationship between concepts or objects that had not previously been related such that a new insight or invention is produced. Such reconceptualizing is triggered by accidents: an apple falling on Isaac Newton's head or James Watt observing a kettle boiling. Creativity also requires personal qualities. Research shows that creative people share certain personality traits: they are curious, imaginative, adventurous, assertive, playful, self-confident, risk-taking, reflective, and uninhibited.

Motivating creativity presents a further challenge. Creatively oriented people are typically responsive to different incentives than those who are effective in motivating other members of the organization: "They desire to work in an egalitarian culture with enough space and resources to provide the opportunity to be spontaneous, experience freedom, and have fun in the performance of a task that, they feel, makes a difference to the strategic performance of the firm. Praise, recognition, and opportunities for education and professional growth are also more important than assuming managerial responsibilities."[27]

Creativity is likely to be stimulated by human interaction. Michael Tushman's research into communication in R&D laboratories concludes that developing communication networks is one of the most important aspects of the management of R&D.[28] An important catalyst to interaction is *play*, which creates an environment of inquiry, liberates thought from conventional constraints, and provides the opportunity to establish new relationships by rearranging ideas and structures at a safe distance from reality. Apple Computer placed considerable emphasis on creating an atmosphere of playfulness.

> Almost every building had its own theme, so meeting and conference rooms . . . are named by employees who decide upon the theme of their building. In our "Land of Oz" building, the conference rooms are named "Dorothy" and "Toto." Our Management Information Systems Group has meeting rooms named "Greed," "Envy," "Sloth," "Lust," and the remaining deadly sins. It's not an accident that many of these are the symbols of childhood (popcorn included). William Blake believed that in growing up, people move from states of innocence to experience, and then, if they're fortunate, to "higher innocence"—the most creative state of all.[29]

These conditions for creativity have far-reaching organizational implications. Anita Roddick of Body Shop cultivated a culture of "benevolent anarchy—encouraging questioning of established ways and going in the opposite direction to everyone else."[30] In particular, creativity requires an organizational structure and management system that are quite different from those appropriate to the pursuit of cost efficiency. Table 11.5 contrasts some characteristics of the two types of organization.

Although innovation requires creativity, creativity needs to be stimulated by and directed toward *need*. Few important inventions have been the result of spontaneous creative activity by technologists; almost all have resulted from grappling with practical problems. James Watt's redesign of the steam engine was conceived while repairing an early Newcomen steam engine owned by Glasgow University. The basic inventions behind the Xerox copying process were the work of Chester Carlson, a patent attorney who became frustrated by the problems of accurately copying technical drawings. These observations reaffirm the notion that "necessity is the mother of invention," which explains why customers are such fertile sources of innovation—they are most acutely involved with matching existing products and services to their needs.[31] The relocation of R&D from corporate research departments to operating businesses is motivated by the desire to link technology development more closely with the needs of the business. It also permits the businesses to be better posi-

TABLE 11.5
The Characteristics of "Operating" and "Innovating" Organizations

	OPERATING ORGANIZATION	INNOVATING ORGANIZATION
Structure	Bureaucratic. Specialization and division of labor. Hierarchical control.	Flat organization without hierarchical control. Task-oriented project teams.
Processes	Operating units controlled and coordinated by top management which undertakes strategic planning, capital allocation and operational planning.	Processes directed toward generation, selection, funding and development of ideas. Strategic planning flexible, financial and operating controls loose.
Reward Systems	Financial compensation, promotion up the hierarchy, power and status symbols.	Autonomy, recognition, equity participation in new ventures.
People	Recruitment and selection based upon the needs of the organization structure for specific skills: functional and staff specialists, general managers, and operatives.	Key need is for idea generators which combine required technical knowledge with creative personality traits. Managers must act as sponsors and orchestrators.

Source: Based on Jay R. Galbraith and Robert K. Kazanjian, *Strategy Implementation: Structure, Systems and Processes*, 2nd edition (St. Paul, MN: West, 1986).

tioned to utilize the output of R&D units—so avoiding the fate of Xerox Corporation's PARC facility during the 1980s.[32]

From Invention to Innovation: The Challenge of Cross-Functional Integration

The commercialization of new technology imposes more complex organizational requirements: in addition to creativity and technological expertise, innovation requires production facilities and processes that permit efficient manufacture, marketing capability to manage product introduction, and distribution and customer support. Engineer-inventor John Endacott offers the following advice, "Having the idea is the easy bit. My advice to anyone coming up with a new invention is: Think about it, enjoy thinking about it, and then throw the idea in the bin."[33] There are substantial differences in an organization that conceives and designs an innovative product and one that makes it and takes it to market. Operating functions such as production and sales must be organized differently from technology and product development functions, giving rise to the need for differentiation and integration among departments.[34]

Tension between the operating and the innovating parts of organizations is inevitable. Innovation upsets established routines and threatens the status quo. The more stable the operating and administrative side of the organization, the greater the resistance to innovation. Elting Morrison provides a fascinating analysis of the opposition by the U.S. naval establishment to continuous-aim firing, a process that offered huge improvements in gunnery accuracy. [35]

Two organizational innovations have proven valuable in achieving the needed integration of technology development and other key functions of the business that is so important for the effective commercialization of innovation, new product development in particular.

Cross-Functional Product Development Teams.   Cross-functional product development teams have proven to be highly effective mechanisms for integrating the different functional capabilities required to develop a new product, and for developing communication and cooperation across functional divisions. Japanese companies in automobiles, electronics, and construction equipment have been the most prominent pioneers of product development teams. Imai, Nonaka, and Takeuchi show how the structure of the product development teams facilitates knowledge integration, learning, and swift development of innovative and defect-free new products.[36] The U.S. auto producers have adopted many of these features in the redesigns of their own new model development processes. The Ford Taurus was one of Detroit's first team-based product development efforts (see Exhibit 11.1). Clark and Fujimoto's study of new automobile development in Japan, the United States, and Europe provides fascinating insight into the organization of product development efforts and the advantages derived from "overlapping" the different stages of product development rather than simply sequencing them, and from providing strong leadership through "heavyweight" product managers.[37]

Product Champions.   There is a host of evidence pointing to the key role of individuals in the innovation process. In the same way that the key individual is

EXHIBIT 11.1
Product Development at Ford: From a Sequential to a Team Approach

The sequential approach: pre-Taurus

"Designers designed a car on paper, then gave it to the engineers, who figured out how to make it. Their plans were passed on to the manufacturing and purchasing people . . . The next step in the process was the production plant. Then came marketing, the legal and service departments, and finally the customers. If a glitch developed, the car was bumped back to the design stage for changes. The farther along in the sequence, however, the more difficult it was to make changes."

The team approach: the Taurus

"With Taurus . . . we brought all disciplines together, and did the whole process simultaneously as well as sequentially. The manufacturing peo-ple worked with the design people, engineering people, sales and purchasing, legal, service and marketing. In sales and marketing we had dealers come in and tell us what they wanted in a car to make it more user-friendly . . . We had insurance companies—Allstate, State Farm, American Road—tell us how to design a car so when accidents occur it would minimize the customer's expense in fixing it . . . We went to all stamping plants, assembly plants and put layouts on the walls. We asked them how to make it easier to build . . . It's amazing the dedication and commitment you can get from people."

Source: Taurus project leader, Veraldi. Quoted by Mary Walton, *The Deming Management Method* (New York: Mead & Co., 1986):130–131.

typically the creative force in invention, the individual is likely to be the driving force behind successful commercialization efforts. A common characteristic of companies that are consistently successful in innovation is their ability to capture and direct individuals' drive for achievement and success by creating roles of "product champions" within the organization. Given resistance to change within organizations and the need to forge cross-functional integration, leadership by committed individuals can help overcome vested interests in stability and functional separation. Schon's study of 15 major innovations concluded that: "the new idea either finds a champion or dies."[38] A British study of 43 matched pairs of successful and unsuccessful innovations similarly concluded that that a key factor distinguishing successful innovation was the presence of a "business innovator" to exert entrepreneurial leadership.[39] 3M Corporation is exemplary in the use of product champions to develop new product ideas and grow them into new business units (see Exhibit 11.2). The organizational challenge of reconciling the entrepreneurial vigor required for new product innovation with the efficiency and control required for operating established businesses has been resolved in some corporations by creating new venture divisions. These seek to create the flexibility and entrepreneurial climate associated with start-up companies but within the confines of the mature corporation.

EXHIBIT 11.2

Innovation at 3M: The Role of the Product Champion

Start little and build

"We don't look to the president, or the vice-president for R&D to say, all right, now Monday morning 3M is going to get into such-and-such a business. Rather, we prefer to see someone in one of our laboratories, or marketing or manufacturing, or new products bring forward a new idea that he's been thinking about. Then, when he can convince people around him, including his supervisor, that he's got something interesting, we'll make him what we call a 'project manager' with a small budget of money and talent, and let him run with it. "

In short, we'd rather have the idea for a new business come from the bottom up than from the top down. Throughout all our 60 years of history here, that has been the mark of success. Did you develop a new business? The incentive? Money, of course. But that's not the key. The key . . . is becoming the general manager of a new business . . . having such a hot project that management just has to become involved whether it wants to or not."

—*Bob Adams, vice president for R&D, 3M Corporation*

Scotchlite

"Someone asked the question, 'Why didn't 3M make glass beads, because glass beads were going to find increasing use on the highways?' . . . I had done a little working in the mineral department on trying to color glass beads we'd imported from Czechoslovakia and had learned a little about their reflecting properties. And, as a little extra-curricular activity, I'd been trying to make luminous house numbers—and maybe luminous signs as well—by developing luminous pigments.

"Well, this question and my free-time lab project combined to stimulate me to search out where glass beads were being used on the high-way. We found a place where beads had been sprinkled on the highway and we saw that they did provide a more visible line at night . . . From there, it was only natural for us to conclude that, since we were a coating company, and probably knew more than anyone else about putting particles onto a web than anybody, we ought to be able to coat glass beads very accurately on a piece of paper.

"So, that's what we did. The first reflective tape we made was simply a double-coated tape—glass beads sprinkled on one side and an adhesive on the other. We took some out here in St. Paul and, with the cooperation of the highway department, put some down. After the first frost came, and then a thaw, we found we didn't know as much about adhesives under all weather conditions as we thought . . .

"We looked around inside the company for skills in related areas. We tapped knowledge that existed in our sandpaper business on how to make waterproof sandpaper. We drew on the expertise of our roofing people who knew something about exposure. We reached into our adhesive and tape division to see how we could make the tape stick to the highway better."

The resulting product became known as "Scotchlite," its principal application was in reflective signs, only later did 3M develop the market for highway marking. The originator of the product, Harry Heltzer, interested the head of the New Products Division in the product, and he encouraged Heltzer to go out and sell it. Scotchlite was a success and Heltzer became the general manager of the division set up to produce and market it. Heltzer later went on to become 3M's president.

Source: "The Technical Strategy of 3M: Start More Little Businesses and More Little Businesses," *Innovation*, no. 5, 1969.

◆ SUMMARY

In emerging industries and other industries where technology is the primary medium of competition, the nurturing and developing of innovation is the fundamental source of competitive advantage and the focus of strategy formulation. Does this mean that the principles of strategic management are fundamentally different in technology-based industries from other types of business environments? In many respects, the strategic issues we have discussed in this chapter are the same as those we covered in the previous chapters of the book. For example, the analysis of the determinants of the returns to innovation covered almost the same factors as our analysis of the returns to resources and capabilities: relevance to customer needs, barriers to imitation, and appropriability through well-established property rights.

At the same time, some aspects of strategic management in technology-based industries are distinctive. An issue with technology-based industries is the rapid rate of change and the difficulty of forecasting change. Conditions of Schumpeterian "creative destruction" (or in Rich D'Aveni's terminology, *hypercompetition*), mean that traditional approaches to strategy formulation based on forecasting must be abandoned in favor of strategic management approaches that combine a clear sense of direction based on vision and mission, with the flexibility to respond to and take advantage of the unexpected.

Despite this turbulence and uncertainty, the principles of strategic analysis are critically important in guiding the quest for competitive advantage in technology-intensive industries. Our analysis has been able to guide us on key issues such as:

- Whether an innovation has the potential to confer sustainable competitive advantage
- The relative merits of licensing, alliances, joint ventures, and internal development as alternative strategies for exploiting an innovation
- The factors that determine the comparative advantages of being a leader or a follower in innovation.

This chapter also pointed to the central importance of strategy implementation in determining success. The key to successful innovation is not resource allocation decisions, but creating the structure, integration mechanisms, and organizational climate conducive to innovation. No other type of industry environment reveals so clearly the inseparability of strategy formulation and strategy implementation. Strategies aimed toward the exploitation of innovation, choices of whether to be a leader or a follower, and the management of risk must take careful account of organizational characteristics.

Technology-based industries also reveal some of the dilemmas that are a critical feature of strategic management in complex organizations and complex business environments. For example, technology-based industries are unpredictable, yet investments in technology must be made with a time horizon of a decade or more. Successful strategies must be responsive to changing market conditions, but successful strategies also require long-term commitment. The fundamental dilemma is that innovation is an unpredictable process that requires creating a set of conducive organizational conditions, whereas strategy is about resource-allocation decisions: how can a company create the conditions for nurturing innovation while planning the course of the company's development? As John Scully of Apple has observed, "Management and creativity might even be considered antithetical states. While management demands consensus, control, certainty, and the status quo, creativity thrives on the opposite: instinct, uncertainty, freedom, and iconoclasm."[40]

Fortunately, the experiences of companies such as Apple, 3M, Sony, Merck, and Honda point to solutions to these dilemmas. The need for innovation to reconcile individual creativity with coordination points toward the advantages of cross-functional team-based approaches over the isolation of R&D in a separate "creative" environment. Moreover, the need to reconcile innovation with efficiency points toward the advantage of parallel organizational structures where, in addition to the "formal" structure geared to the needs of existing businesses and products, an informal structure exists, which is the source of new products and businesses. The role of top management in balancing creativity with order and innovation with efficiency becomes critical. The success of companies in both Japan and Silicon Valley in managing technology (especially compared with the poor innovation performance of many large, diversified U.S. and British corporations) points to the importance of technological knowledge among senior managers.

The increasing pace of technological change and intensifying international competition suggests that the advanced, industrialized countries will be forced to rely increasingly on their technological capabilities as the basis for international competitiveness. Strategies for promoting innovation and managing technology will become more important in the future.

NOTES

1 "The Logic That Dares Not Speak Its Name," *Economist*, April 16, 1994: 89–91.

2 William J. Abernathy and James M. Utterback, "Patterns of Technological Innovation," *Technology Review* 80 (June–July 1978): 40–47; and Utterback and Abernathy, "a Dynamic Model of Product and Process Innovations," *Omega* 3 (December 1975): 639–656.

3 R.D. Buzzell and B.T. Gale, *The PIMS Principles* (New York: Free Press, 1987): 274.

4 "Bic and the Heirs of Ball-Point Builder Are No Pen Pals," *Wall Street Journal*, May 27, 1988: 1, 27.

5 David J. Teece, "Profiting from Technological Innovation: Implications for Intergration, Collaboration, Licensing and Public Policy," in *The Competitive Challenge: Strategies for Industrial Innovation and Renewal*, ed. D.J. Teece (Cambridge, MA: Ballinger, 1987): 190.

6 J. Jewkes et al., *The Sources of Invention*, 2nd edition (London: Macmillan, 1969).

7 D. Hamberg, *Essays in the Economics of Research and Development* (New York: John Wiley, 1966).

8 Peter Grindley and David Teece, "Managing Intellectual Capital: Licensing and Cross-Licensing in Semiconductors and Electronics," *California Management Review* 39 (Winter 1997).

9 A. Saxenian, "Regional Networks and the Resurgence of Silicon Valley," *California Management Review* 33 (Fall 1990): 89–112.

10 George Gilder, "The Revitalization of Everything: The Law of the Microcosm," *Harvard Business Review* (March–April 1988): 49–66.

11 Charles H. Ferguson, "From the People Who Brought You Voodoo Economics," *Harvard Business Review* (May–June 1988).

12 "PictureTel Fights to Stay in the Picture," *Business Week*, October 28, 1996, 168–169.

13 Charles R. Morris and Charles H. Ferguson, "How Architecture Wins Technology Wars," *Harvard Business Review* (March–April 1993): 86–96.

14 Charles Hill, "Establishing a Standard: Competitive Strategy and Technological Standards in Winner-Take-All Industries," *Academy of Management Executive* XI, no. 2 (May 1997): 7–25.

15 P. David, "Clio and the Economics of QWERTY," *American Economic Review* 75 (May 1985): 332–337; and Stephen Jay Gould, "The Panda's Thumb of Technology," *Natural History* 96, no. 1 (1986).

16 Steve Postrel, "Competing Networks and Proprietary Standards: The Case of Quadraphonic Sound," *Journal of Industrial Economics* 24 (December 1990): 169–186.

17 "Bandwagons and Barriers," *Economist,* February 27, 1993: 69.

18 Robert F. Hartley, *Management Mistakes,* 2nd edition (New York: John Wiley & Sons, 1986): 56–66.

19 For example, data on rates of market penetration and price decline for household appliances such as electric toothbrushes and compact disc players were used to forecast the market demand for high-definition TVs in the United States (B.L. Bayus, "High-Definition Television: Assessing Demand Forecasts for the Next Generation Consumer Durable," *Management Science* 39 (1993): 1319–1333.)

20 See B.C. Twiss, *Managing Technological Innovation,* Second edition (New York: Longman, 1980).

21 Eric von Hippel, "Lead Users: A Source of Novel Product Concepts," *Management Science 32* (July 1986).

22 Eric Von Hippel, "Users As Innovators," *Technology Review,* no. 5 (1976): 212–239.

23 Tom Peters, *Thriving on Chaos* (New York: Knopf, 1987): 259–266.

24 Richard T. Pascale, "Honda (B)" (Boston: Harvard Business School, Case No. 384-050): 5–6.

25 John Scully, *Odyssey* (Toronto: Fitzhenry and Whiteside, 1987): 323–359.

26 Nancy Nicholls, "Scientific Management at Merck: An Interview with CFO Judy Lewent," *Harvard Business Review* (January–February 1994): 89–105.

27 Louis W. Fry and Borje O. Saxberg, "Homo Ludens: Playing Man and Creativity in Innovating Organizations," discussion paper, Department of Management and Organization, University of Washington, 1987.

28 Michael L. Tushman, "Managing Communication Networks in R&D Laboratories," *Sloan Management Review* (Winter 1979): 37–49.

29 John Scully, *Odyssey:* 187–188.

30 L. Grundy, J. Kickel, C. Prather, "Building the Creative Organization," *Organizational Dynamics* (Spring 1994): 22–37.

31 Eric Von Hippel, *The Sources of Innovation* (New York: Oxford University Press, 1988), provides strong evidence of the dominant role of users in the innovation process.

32 "The Lab That Ran Away from Xerox," *Fortune,* September 5, 1988; "Barefoot into PARC," *Economist,* July 10, 1993: 68.

33 "Making Bright Ideas Shine," *Financial Times,* March 25, 1993: 12.

34 P. Lawrence and S. Lorsch, *Organization and Environment: Managing Differentiation and Integration* (Cambridge: Harvard Univeristy Press, 1967).

35 Elting Morrison, "Gunfire at Sea: A Case Study of Innovation," in *Readings in the Management of Innovation,* ed. Michael Tushman and William L. Moore (Cambridge, MA: Ballinger, 1988): 165–178.

36 K. Imai, I. Nonaka, and H. Takeuchi, "Managing the New Product Development Process: How Japanese Companies Learn and Unlearn," in *The Uneasy Alliance,* ed. K. Clark, R. Hayes, C. Lorenz (Boston: Harvard Business School Press, 1985).

37 Kim Clark and Takahiro Fujimoto, *Product Development Performance: Strategy, Organization, and Management in the World Auto Industry* (Boston: Harvard Business School Press, 1991).

38 D. A. Schon, "Champions for Radical New Inventions," *Harvard Business Review* (March–April 1963): 84.

39 R. Rothwell et al., "SAPPHO Updated—Project SAPPHO Phase II," *Research Policy* 3 (1974): 258–291.

40 John Scully, *Odyssey:* 184.

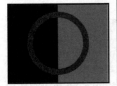

12

Competitive Advantage in Mature Industries

We are a true "penny profit" business. That means that it takes hard work and attention to detail to be financially successful—it is far from being a sure thing. Our store managers must do two things well: control costs and increase sales. Cost control cannot be done by compromising product quality, customer service, or restaurant cleanliness, but rather by consistent monitoring of the "vital signs" of the business through observation, reports, and analysis. Portion control is a critical part of our business. For example, each Filet-O-Fish sandwich receives 1 fluid ounce of tartar sauce and 0.5 ounces of cheese. Our raw materials are fabricated to exacting tolerances, and our managers check them on an ongoing basis. Our written specification for lettuce is over two typewritten pages long. Our french fries must meet standards for potato type, solid and moisture content, and distribution of strand lengths.

—*Edward H. Rensi, President and Chief Operating Officer,*
McDonald's U.S.A.[1]

Outline

◆ Introduction and Objectives

Although technology-based enterprises provide some of the most exciting examples of real-world strategy—the battle between Netscape and Microsoft in Internet browsers, the management problems of Apple Computer, the jockeying for position in telecommunications services—if importance is measured by share of GDP rather than share of press commentary, mature industries continue to be the economic backbone of the industrialized nations.

Despite their heterogeneity—mature industries range from insurance to steel—from a strategic perspective they present several similarities. The purpose of this chapter is to explore the characteristics of mature industries, the strategies through which competitive advantage can be established within them, and the implications of these strategies for organizational structure, management systems, and leadership style. As we shall see, maturity does not imply lack of opportunity. Companies such as Home Depot (hardware retailing), Nike (footwear, apparel), Virgin Group (music, airlines, financial services), Nucor (steel), and MBNA (banking) have established strong positions in their industries through innovative strategies. Coca-Cola and Gillette have achieved combinations of profitability and growth that make any high-tech company envious.

By the time you have completed this chapter, you will be able to:

◆ Recognize the principal strategic characteristics of mature industries

◆ Identify key success factors within mature industries and formulate strategies directed toward their exploitation

◆ Locate and analyze opportunities for strategic innovation in mature industries to establish competitive advantage

◆ Design organizational structures and management systems that can effectively implement such strategies

Key Success Factors in Mature Environments

Maturity has two principal implications for competitive advantage: first, it tends to reduce the number of opportunities for establishing competitive advantage; second, it shifts these opportunities from differentiation-based factors to cost-based factors.

Diminishing opportunities for competitive advantage in mature industries stem from:

1. Less scope for differentiation advantage resulting from increased buyer knowledge, product standardization, and less product innovation;

2. Diffusion of technology means that cost advantages through superior process technology or more advanced capital equipment methods are difficult to obtain and sustain;

3. A highly developed industry infrastructure together with the presence of powerful distributors makes it easier for new or established firms to attack firms that have highly differentiated market positions or strong positions in particular segments;

4. The vulnerability of cost advantage to exchange rate movements and the emergence of low-cost overseas competitors.

However, as Warren Buffett ("The Sage of Omaha") notes, not all mature industries tend toward cost-based competition: a critical distinction is between "franchises" and "businesses."

> The economic strength of the once-mighty media enterprises continues to erode as retailing patterns change and entertainment choices proliferate. In the business world, unfortunately, the rearview mirror is always clearer than the windshield: no one linked to the media business saw the economic deterioration that was in store for the industry.
>
> The fact is that the newspaper, television, and magazine properties have begun to resemble businesses rather than franchises in their economic behavior. Let's take a quick look at the characteristics separating these two classes of enterprise.
>
> An economic franchise arises from a product or service that (1) is needed or desired; (2) is thought by customers to have no close substitute; and (3) is not subject to price regulation. The existence of all three conditions is demonstrated by a company's ability to price its product or service aggressively and thereby earn high rates of return on capital. Moreover, the franchises can tolerate mismanagement. Inept managers may diminish a franchise's profitability, but they cannot inflict mortal damage.
>
> In contrast, "a business" earns exceptional profits only if it is a low-cost operator or if supply of its product or service is tight. Tightness in supply usually does not last long. With superior management, a company may maintain its position as a low-cost operator for a much longer time, but even then unceasingly faces the possibility of competitive attack. And a business, unlike a franchise, can be killed by poor management.
>
> Until recently, media properties possessed the three characteristics of a franchise, and consequently could price aggressively and be managed loosely. Now, however, consumers looking for information and entertainment elsewhere enjoy greatly broadened choices as to where to find them. Unfortunately demand can't expand in response to the new supply: 500 million American eyeballs and a 24-hour day are all that's available. The result is that competition has intensified, markets have fragmented, and the media industry has lost some—though far from all—of its franchise strength.[2]

Cost Advantage

If cost is the overwhelmingly important key success factor in most mature industries, what are the primary sources of low cost? Three cost drivers tend to be especially important.

Economies of Scale. In capital intensive industries, or where advertising, distribution, or new product development are important elements of total cost, economies of scale are important sources of interfirm cost differences. The increased standardization that accompanies maturity greatly assists the exploitation of such scale economies. The significance of scale economies in mature industries is indicated by the fact that the association between ROI and market share is stronger in mature industries than in emerging industries.[3]

Low-Cost Inputs.   Where small competitors are successful in undercutting the prices of market leaders in mature industries, it is frequently through their access to low-cost inputs. Established firms can become locked into high-cost positions through unionization of their workforces or through inertia. The decline in the market share of the U.S. steel majors over the past three decades is partly the result of union agreements over wages, benefits, and working practices that guaranteed high-cost production. During the 1970s and 1980s they steadily lost ground to overseas suppliers and domestic mini-mills, both of which benefited from lower labor costs. New entrants into mature industries may gain cost advantages by acquiring plant and equipment at bargain-basement levels. The emergence of Tosco as one of the largest and most profitable oil refiners in the United States has been based on its acquisition of refineries sold off by the majors as unprofitable assets. Similarly, the acquisition of financially troubled savings and loan institutions by major U.S. banks from 1988 to 1992 represented a remarkably low-cost method of expanding geographical coverage.

Low Overheads.   During the early 1990s, the most profitable companies in mature industries tended to be those that had achieved the most substantial reductions in overhead costs. From 1992 to 1994, Chrysler was the most profitable of the world's largest auto producers, primarily because it had gone furthest in slashing its costs during the 1980s. The resurgence of British Steel as the most profitable of the world's integrated steel companies during the 1990s demonstrates the benefits of pruning administrative overheads, rationalizing capacity, and abandoning restrictive working practices. Inefficiency in mature firms can be pervasive and institutionalized. Its elimination frequently requires shock treatment in the form of a threat to the existence of the firm. In the oil industry, it was not until the oil price collapse of 1986, that the oil companies began to address the fundamental issues of cost reduction and restructuring.[4] During the late 1980s and early 1990s, the most profitable oil companies were those that pursued the most aggressive cost cutting, notably Exxon and Arco. By 1997, these had been joined at the top of the earnings league by British Petroleum, which had spent the period 1982 to 1996 reducing employment from 143,000 to 53,150, redeploying assets, and reorganizing to promote efficiency.

The effectiveness of cost efficiency in improving profit performance in mature industries is supported by research into performance turnarounds among mature businesses. Hambrick and Schecter's study of U.S. businesses that had experienced sharp improvements in ROI over a four-year period identified three successful turnaround strategies.

1. **Asset and cost surgery**—aggressive cost reduction through reduction of excess capacity; halting of new investment in plant and equipment; and cutbacks in R&D, marketing expenditures, receivables and inventories;

2. **Selective product and market pruning**—refocusing on segments that were most profitable or where the firm possessed distinctive strength;

3. **Piecemeal productivity moves**—adjustments to current market position rather than comprehensive refocusing or reorganizing, including reductions in marketing and R&D expenditures, higher capacity utilization, and increased employee productivity.[5]

The importance of cost reduction is confirmed by Grinyer, Mayes, and McKiernan's study of substantial and sustained performance improvements by a sample of British companies (most of which were long-established companies in mature industries). Apart from changes in management, the factor that most frequently distinguished the "sharpbenders" from the control group of companies was the intensive effort by the former to reduce production costs.[6]

Segment and Customer Selection

In general, the profitability of mature industries is constrained by sluggish demand growth, lack of product differentiation, and customers' bargaining power. However, sharp differences in profit rates can arise between industry segments. Not only do growth rates of demand vary between segments, but the structure of segments with regard to concentration, buyer power, and potential for differentiation varies considerably. As a result, choice of segments is likely to be a key strategy issue in mature industries. Across a range of mature industries, the most profitable companies are often those that have made the most astute segment choices. Among discount stores, Wal-Mart's success was based on its locations in small and medium-sized towns where competition was comparatively weak. In chemicals, Du Pont, Ciba-Geigy, BASF, and Akzo Nobel have focused on specialty chemicals in a quest for higher margins and to escape the commodity chemical rollercoaster.

Widespread and far-reaching segment refocusing was undertaken by the major oil companies between 1986 and 1996. Upstream, all the leading oil companies divested and traded oil assets as they sought to focus on those oilfields where they possessed a competitive advantage (either through technical capabilities or the presence of existing production infrastructure). All the majors radically pruned their North American oil and gas holdings. Refocusing was guided, in part, by each company's distinctive capabilities: Shell shifted its exploration and production toward deep-sea oil fields, reflecting its expertise in undersea drilling and platform building; Texaco concentrated on mature oil fields where it could exploit its expertise in enhanced oil recovery techniques; Total, Elf and ENI utilized their expertise in managing government relations to position themselves in some of the most politically difficult locations in Asia and the former Soviet Union. Similar refocusing occurred downstream. By 1994, not one of the oil majors was marketing nationally within the United States, while in Europe each company concentrated on those countries where its market shares were greatest.

The Quest for Differentiation

Cost leadership, we have noted, is difficult to sustain, particularly in internationally competitive industries. Maintaining a low-cost position requires constant attention to operational efficiency and an unrelenting search for small cost reductions across the whole range of the firm's activities. Hence, attaining some insulation from the constant threat of price competition through some degree of differentiation is particularly attractive in mature industries. The problem is that the trend toward standardization narrows the scope for differentiation and reduces customer willingness to pay a substantial premium for differentiation. Hence, the creation of meaningful differentiation in mature industries represents one of the greatest challenges to managers in mature industries.

Standardization of the physical attributes of a product and convergence of consumer preferences constrains but does not eliminate the potential for differentiation. Product standardization is frequently accompanied by increased differentiation of complementary services and image. In the auto industry, increased similarity among the competing models of different manufacturers has encouraged firms to compete on financing terms, leasing arrangements, warranties, after-sales services, and the like. In consumer goods, maturity is often associated with the focus of differentiation shifting from physical product characteristics to image. Deeply entrenched consumer preferences for Coke or Pepsi and Marlboro or Camel cigarettes are a tribute to the capacity of brand promotion over long periods of time to differentiate near-identical products.

Across a broad range of mature industries, we can observe firms attempting to escape from the treadmill of price competition among standardized offerings through a multitude of differentiation variables. The intensely competitive retail sector produces particularly interesting examples. The dismal profitability earned by many of the variety chains, department stores, drug stores, and supermarkets (notably Woolworth's, Kmart, Montgomery Ward, Federated Department Stores, Revco, and Thrifty-Payless) contrasts sharply with the sales growth and profitability of stores that have established clear differentiation through variety, style, and ambiance (The Gap, Circuit City, Pier 1, Barnes & Noble, Timberland). Table 12.1 lists large U.S. retailers with the highest and lowest returns to investors. A similar pattern is evident for British retailers where retailers establishing novel forms of differentiation (Body Shop, Next, Tie Rack) have outperformed more staid retailers (Great Universal Stores, Littlewoods, W. H. Smith, J. Sainsbury). However, the process of creative destruction means that competitive advantage is difficult to sustain: fallen stars include British retailers such Laura Ashley, Conran Stores, Sock Shop, Asda; and U.S. retailers such as Barney's, Macy's, Saks, and Montgomery Ward.

Innovation

We have characterized mature industries as industries where the pace of technical change is low. We have also noted that the quest for differentiation in mature industries requires innovation—finding new approaches to uniqueness in terms of image, retail ambiance, novel approaches to segmentation, or new forms of product delivery. The potential for innovation to create competitive advantage in mature industries extends beyond the differentiation of products and services. Steel, textiles, food processing, insurance, and hotel services are industries where the pace of product and process innovation is modest. In none of these industries does R&D expenditure as a percentage of sales revenue exceed 0.8 percent.[7] But it is precisely because of strong competition in these mature industries and the limited potential for technology-based advantage that creates impetus for innovation in marketing, product design, customer service, and organization. This quest for new ways of doing business is what we referred to in Chapter 6 as "strategic innovation." In relation to the innovation cycles identified by Abernathy and Utterback, it seems likely that there is a third phase of innovation, **strategic innovation,** which becomes most prominent once product and process innovation have begun to slacken (see Figure 12.1).

Because every strategic innovation is unique, it is difficult to adopt a systematic approach to analyzing opportunities for new strategic approaches. In Chapter 6, we suggested value chain analysis as a means of identifying the potential for "new game strategies." Understanding the sequence of activities currently being undertaken by the firm (and by competitors) may facilitate the search for a reconfiguration of the sequence of activities in new strategic format. Benetton and Dell Computer may both be viewed as companies whose success has involved reconfiguring the conventional value chain in terms of establishing novel systems for the production of products and their distribution to the customer.

TABLE 12.1
The Highest and Lowest Performing U.S. Retailers, Measured by Return to Investors

	AVERAGE ANNUAL TOTAL RETURN TO INVESTORS, 1986–1996 %	SALES 1996 $ BILLIONS
Top Performers		
Home Depot (Georgia)	40	19.5
Dollar General	28	2.1
Vons (Calif.)	24	5.4
The Gap (Calif.)	23	5.2
American Stores	22	18.7
Albertson's (Idaho)	22	13.8
Lowe's (N.C.)	20	8.6
Walgreen (Illinois)	19	11.8
Circuit City Stores (Virginia)	15	7.0
Wal-Mart Stores (Ark.)	15	106.1
Kroger (Ohio)	15	25.1
May Department Stores (Missouri)	15	12.6
Laggards		
Hechinger (Maryland)	−18	2.2
Penn Traffic (NY)	−16	3.4
Costco (Washington)	−2	19.6
Kmart (Mich.)	1	31.4
Tandy (Texas)	2	6.3
Safeway (Calif.)	3	17.3
Limited (Ohio)	3	8.7
Woolworth (NY)	4	8.1
Mercantile Stores (Ohio)	5	3.0
Long's Drug Stores (Calif.)	8	2.8

Source: Fortune, May 30, 1993: 214.

Derek Abell points to the redefinition of markets and market segments as offering important opportunities for new strategies.[8] Market boundaries may be redefined by means of:

♦ Inclusion of *new customer groups:* thus fashion houses such as Giorgio Armani, Gucci, and Christian Dior have progressively expanded their customer bases.

♦ The *addition of products or services* that perform new but related functions: thus Arco has redefined its retailing business from the retailing of gasoline and lubricants to the provision of a wide range of goods and services to motorists through its "AM-PM" outlets.

Baden Fuller and Stopford's analysis of strategic innovation in mature industries focuses on the reconciliation of multiple (often opposing) performance goals in

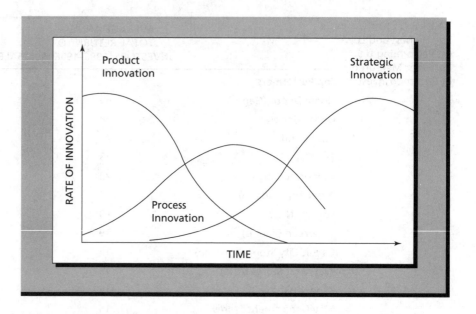

order to create new options. Based on in-depth analysis of company success stories in mature industries, they conclude that:

1. *Maturity* is a state of mind, not a state of the business; every enterprise has the potential for rejuvenation.

2. It is the firm that matters, not the industry. The industry sets a *context* not a *prison* for the firm. Not only can the creative firm achieve success within a hostile industry environment, the firm can transform its industry environment. Look what Honda did to the motorcycle markets of North America and Europe during the 1960s.

3. Strategic innovation is the basis for competitive advantage in industries where the potential for competitive advantage seems limited. The essence of strategic innovation is reconciling alternatives: quality at low cost (Toyota), variety at low cost (Courtaulds), speed at low cost (Benetton), and so on.

4. Businesses should be selective in choosing their strategic territory. An island kingdom is more defensible than the Hapsburg Empire. The firm's market scope needs to be limited by its resources and capabilities.

5. The pursuit of strategic innovation requires an entrepreneurial organization with freedom to experiment and the capacity to learn.

6. Rejuvenation requires a sequence of strategic and organizational development. The key stages are to *galvanize* top management commitment, to *simplify* by eliminating outdated and unnecessary activities and control systems, to *build* the strategic infrastructure and capabilities needed to implement the new vision, and to *leverage* advantages and maintain the momentum.[9]

These are formidable challenges of the mature enterprise. In Chapter 11 we noted the hostility of the status quo to innovation. It is hardly surprising that across many mature industries, the strategic innovators are newcomers or established firms headed by an outsider to the industry.

- In U.S. network broadcasting, newcomer Fox Broadcasting Company, owned by Australian newspaper entrepreneur, Rupert Murdoch, was the major innovative force of the past decade.[10]

- In the archaic Sheffield cutlery industry, the only firm to pursue radical innovation was Richardson Sheffield. The firm was distinguished by its ownership, initially by an American entrepreneur, and subsequently by an Australian company.[11]

- In the U.S. steel industry the outstanding strategic innovator was Nucor, created by Ken Iverson out of Nuclear Corporation of America, a technology-based industrial materials producer. Although Iverson was an engineer with experience in metallurgy, but not in steel making. Iverson searched the world for new steel making and casting technology. Using innovative processes, computer integration and flexible working practices, in the U.S. steel industry Nucor pushed mini-mill technology into new product areas. Nucor was the world's first mini-mill to manufacture flat rolled steel.[12]

- AES, the world's largest and most innovative independent power producer- was founded in 1981 by Dennis Bakke and Roger Sant. Neither had business experience in the industry. The two met while working for the Federal Energy Administration during the 1970's.[13]

This propensity for strategic innovation in mature industries to be led by outsiders may reflect the tendency for long-established firms and their executives to be trapped within conventional thinking about key success factors and business practices within their own industries. Chapter 4 noted how the ability of established firms to respond effectively to competitive threats may be limited by systems of belief that converge within the industry. J-C Spender refers to these common cognitive patterns among managers within an industry as "industry recipes."[14] Studies of **cognitive maps,** the mental frameworks through which managers perceive and think about their environments and their companies, yield fascinating insights into why some firms are able to adapt better than others to a changing business environment. A study of organizational renewal among railroad companies found that the ability of managers to learn in the form of changing their mental models of the business was critical to their capacity to renew themselves.[15]

The propensity for well-entrenched industry recipes to hamper strategic innovation and so cause deteriorating international competitiveness was apparent in the U.S. steel and automobile industries during the 1970s and early 1980s. Maturity in these industries during the period 1930–1960 was associated with emphasis on scale efficiency, increasing organizational rigidity, and a growing inability to respond to opportunities for product and process innovation. Only when challenged by new competitiors—the minimills in steel, and the Japanese in autos—did these industries embarked upon strategic challenge.[16] Gary Hamel believes that most companies are reaching the limits of incremental improvement (cost cutting, quality enhancement, reengineering, and the like), only through strategic innovation can they achieve dramatic improvements in performance:

> Who has been creating new wealth in the American grocery business? Though companies like Procter & Gamble, Kroger and other traditional leaders have created a lot of value in the past decade, industry revolutionaries

like Boston Market, Starbuck's Coffee, Trader Joe's, Petco, ConAgra, and Wal Mart have created even more . . . Who is going to create new wealth in the auto industry? Unless they develop new strategies, it probably won't be GM, Ford Nissan, Chrysler, or their traditional dealers but instead the new megadealers such as CarMax, Auto-By-Tel, AutoNation USA, and Driver's Mart—companies that are reinventing the retailing and distribution of the auto industry from the customer backward.[17]

How do companies break away from their traditional mindsets and achieve strategic innovation? According to Hamel, the role of strategy should be to foster revolution through reorganizing the strategy-making process. This means breaking top management's monopoly over strategy formulation and bringing in younger people from further down the organization and gaining involvement from those on the peripheries of the organization. It means fostering, creating, and making people comfortable with change.[18] Strategic innovation goes well beyond rethinking strategies, it also requires delivering new strategies through new approaches to structuring the mature business.

STRATEGY IMPLEMENTATION IN MATURE INDUSTRIES: STRUCTURE, SYSTEMS AND STYLE

If the key to success in mature industries is achieving operational efficiency and reconciling this with innovation and customer responsiveness, this implies that competitive advantage in mature businesses is critically dependent on structure, systems, and management style.

Efficiency Through Bureaucracy

To the extent that maturity implies environmental stability, lack of technological change, and an emphasis on cost efficiency particular organizational and managerial characteristics are called for. As we observed in Chapter 6, at the beginning of the 1960s, Burns and Stalker argued that, whereas dynamic environments require "organismic" organizational forms characterized by decentralization, loosely defined roles, and a high level of lateral communication; stable environments required a "mechanistic" organization characterized by centralization, well-defined roles, and predominantly vertical communication.[19] Henry Mintzberg describes this highly formalized type of organization dedicated to the pursuit of efficiency as the **machine bureaucracy**.[20] The principal requirement for efficiency is the specialized operation of routine tasks through division of labor closely controlled by management. Such forms of organization are typically found in industries devoted to large-scale production where the basis for efficiency is the application of Frederick Taylor's principles of scientific management. Division of labor extends to management as well as operatives. The machine bureaucracy displays a high level of vertical and horizontal specialization. Vertical specialization is reflected in the concentration of strategy formulation at the apex of the hierarchy, while middle and junior management supervise and administer through the application of standardized rules and regulations. Horizontal specialization in the company is organized around functional departments rather than product divisions.

The machine bureaucracy as described by Mintzberg is a caricature of actual organizations—probably the closest approximations are found in government departments performing highly routine administrative duties. However, in most mature industries, the features of bureaucracy are familiar. Even in dynamic, fast-moving companies such as McDonald's, operating procedures are formulated into a set of precise, written rules that govern virtually every part of the business (see the quotation that introduces this chapter). The organizational characteristics of bureaucracy are clearly apparent among some of the huge industrial enterprises found in automobiles, steel, and the oil industry. The key features of these mature organizations are summarized in Table 12.2.

The Bureaucratic Model in Decline

As was noted in Chapter 6, the 1990s have seen growing unpopularity of bureaucratic approaches to management. This trend is especially evident in mature industries. Five factors have caused the reversal.

TABLE 12.2 Strategy Implementation in Mature Industries: Traditional Features of Organization and Management		
STRATEGY	Primary goal is cost advantage through economies of scale, capital-intensive production of standardized product/service. Dichotomization of strategy formulation (the preserve of top management) and strategy implementation (carried down the hierarchy).
STRUCTURE	Functional departments (e.g., production, marketing, customer service, distribution). Distinction between line and staff. Clearly defined job roles with strong vertical reporting/delegation relationships.
CONTROLS	Performance targets are primarily quantitative and short term and are elaborated for all members of the organization. Performance is closely monitored by well-established, centralized management information systems and formalized reporting requirements. Financial controls through budgets and profit targets particularly important.
INCENTIVES	Incentives based on achievement of individual targets and are in the form of financial rewards and promotion up the hierarchy. Penalties exist for failure to attain quantitative targets, for failure to adhere to the rules, and lack of conformity to company norms.
COMMUNICATION	Primarily vertical for the purposes of delegation and reporting. Lateral communication limited often achieved through inter-departmental committees.
MANAGEMENT	Primary functions of top management: control and strategic decision making. Typical top management styles: *the politician*—the organizational head who can effectively wield power through understanding and manipulating organizational processes and building consensus (e.g., Alfred Sloan Jr. of General Motors); and *the autocrat*—the CEO who is able to lead and control through aggressive use of power and sheer force of personality (Lee Iacocca of Chrysler and Al Dunlap of Sunbeam).

Increased Environmental Turbulence.   Bureaucracy is conducive to efficiency in stable environments. However, the centralized, structured organization cannot readily adapt to change. Achieving flexibility to respond to external change requires greater decentralization, less specialization, and looser controls.

Increased Emphasis on Innovation.   The organizational structure, control systems, management style, and interpersonal relationships conducive to efficiency are likely to hinder innovation. As mature industries recognize the potential for innovation in the form of technological transfer from other industries (e.g., electronics, biotechnology) and new approaches to differentiation and competition, so the disadvantages of formalized, efficiency-oriented organizations have become increasingly apparent.

New Process Technology.   The efficiency advantages of bureaucratized organizations arise from the technical virtues of highly specialized, systematized production methods. The electronics revolution has changed the conditions for efficiency. Computer-integrated manufacturing processes permit cost efficiency with greater product variety, shorter runs, and greater flexibility. As automation displaces labor-intensive, assembly-line manufacturing techniques, there is less need for elaborate division of labor and greater need for job flexibility. Simultaneously, the electronic revolution in the office is displacing the administrative bureaucracy that control and information systems once required.

Alienation and Conflict.   The dependence of bureaucracy on departmentalization, layering, and the control of some employees by others is conducive to alienation and conflict.

The Japanese Example.   Across a range of mature industries from motorcycles and steel to cosmetics and retailing, Japanese firms have demonstrated remarkable success with organizations that feature many of the hierarchical characteristics of Western mature corporations, but fewer of the rigidities. The ability of leading Japanese firms to reconcile efficiency with innovation, and control with opportunism has been an important factor in the rethinking that is taking place in North America and Europe.

In response, firms in mature industries have undergone substantial adjustment over the past decade. Among large mature corporations—first in the United States, subsequently in Europe, and increasingly in Japan—management hierarchies have been pruned, decision making decentralized and accelerated, and more open communication and flexible collaboration fostered. These changes are evident in:

♦ Strategic decision processes that increase the role of the business-level managers, and reduce the role of corporate management; an emphasis on the strategy formulation *process* as more important than *strategic plans* per se.

♦ This shifting of decision-making power to the business level has been accompanied by shrinking corporate staffs.

♦ Less emphasis on economies of large-scale production and increased responsiveness to customer requirements together with greater flexibility in responding to changes in the market place.

♦ Increased emphasis on teamwork as a basis for organizing separate activities to improve interfunctional cooperation and responsiveness to external requirements.

♦ Wider use of profit incentives to motivate employees and less emphasis on controls and supervision.

These trends amount to a closer convergence between the organizational and managerial characteristics of firms in mature industries and those located in the newer, more technologically oriented industries. At the same time, the primary emphasis on cost efficiency remains. It is not that the goal of cost efficiency has been superseded, rather that the conditions for cost efficiency have changed. The most powerful force for organizational change in mature industries has been the inability of highly structured, centralized organizations to maintain their cost efficiency in an increasingly turbulent business environment. As we observed in Chapter 9, the requirements for *dynamic efficiency* are different from the requirements for *static efficiency*. Dynamic efficiency requires flexibility, which necessitates higher levels of autonomy and nonhierarchical coordination.

Achieving dynamic efficiency through increased flexibility and autonomy does not mean less control, but a change in control mechanisms. By relying more on cost controls and profit targets, firms can permit greater autonomy to unit managers while maintaining rigorous demands for cost efficiency. The corporate restructuring initiated by Rawl at Exxon, Iacocca at Chrysler, and Walters, Horton, and Simon at British Petroleum involved a dismantling of a major part of corporate bureaucracy combined with the imposition of demanding financial targets on business units with draconian sanctions for failure to meet targets. A key element of these sanctions is a greater willingness by the corporate headquarters of mature corporations to divest underperforming divisions and to fire senior executives associated with poor financial performance.

STRATEGIES FOR DECLINING INDUSTRIES

The transition from maturity to decline can be a result of technological substitution (typewriters, railroads), changes in consumer preferences (men's suits), or demographic shifts (babyware in Italy). Shrinking market demand gives rise to strategic issues that are distinct from those encountered in other mature industries. Among the key features of declining industries are:

- Excess capacity
- Lack of technical change (reflected in a lack of new product introduction and stability of process technology)
- A declining number of competitors, but some entry as new firms acquire the assets of exiting firms cheaply
- High average age of both physical and human resources
- Aggressive price competition.

Despite the inhospitable environment declining industries normally offer, research by Kathryn Harrigan has uncovered several examples of declining industries where at least some participants earned surprisingly attractive rates of profit. These included electronic vacuum tubes, premium cigars, and leather tanning. However, in such industries as prepared baby foods, rayon, and economy cigars, decline was accompanied by aggressive price competition, company failures, and instability.[21]

The consequences of decline for competition and profitability depend on two key factors: the balance between capacity and output during decline, and the nature of demand for the product or service.

Adjusting Capacity to Declining Demand

The smooth adjustment of industry capacity to declining demand is the key to stability and profitability during the decline phase. In industries where capacity exits from the industry in an orderly fashion, decline can occur without trauma. Where substantial excess capacity persists, as has occurred in the steel industries of America and Europe and in ocean-going oil tankers from 1974 to 1984, the potential for an industry bloodbath exists. The ease with which capacity adjusts to declining demand is dependent on the predictability of decline, barriers to exit, and the strategies of the surviving firms.

The Predictability of Decline.   If decline can be forecast, the more likely it is that firms can plan for it. The problems of the steel industry, oil refining, and oil transport during the late 1970s were exacerbated by the unpredictability of the oil price shock of 1974. The more cyclical and volatile the demand, then the more difficult it is for firms to perceive the trend of demand even after the onset of decline.

Barriers to Exit.   Barriers to exit impede the exit of capacity from an industry. The three most important sources of barriers to exit are:

1. **Durable and specialized assets.** Just as capital requirements impose a barrier to entry into an industry, those same investments also discourage exit. The longer they last and the fewer the opportunities for using those assets in another industry, the more companies are tied to that particular industry. The intensity of price competition in steel, acetylene, and rayon during the 1970s was partly a consequence of the durability and lack of alternative uses for the capital equipment employed.

2. **Costs incurred in plant closure.** Apart from the accounting costs of writing off assets, substantial cash costs may be incurred from redundancy payments to employees, compensation for broken contacts with customers and suppliers, and costs incurred in dismantling and demolishing the plant.

3. **Managerial commitment.** In addition to financial considerations, firms may be reluctant to close plants for a variety of emotional and moral reasons. Resistance to plant closure and divestment arises from pride in company traditions and reputation, managers' unwillingness to accept failure, loyalties to employees and the local community, and the desire not to offend government.

The Strategies of the Surviving Firms.   Smooth exit of capacity ultimately depends on the decisions of the industry players. The sooner companies recognize and address the problem, the more likely it is that independent and collective action can achieve capacity reduction. In the European petrochemical industry, for example, the problem of excess capacity was partially solved by a series of bilateral exchanges of plants and divisions—ICI swapped its polyethylene plants for BP's PVC plants.[22] Stronger firms in the industry can facilitate the exit of weaker firms by offering to acquire their plants and take over their after-sales service commitments.

The Nature of Demand

Where a market is segmented, the general pattern of decline can obscure the existence of pockets of demand that are not only comparatively resilient, but also price inelastic. For example, despite the obsolescence of vacuum tubes after the adoption of transistors, Harrigan observed that GTE Sylvania and General Electric earned excellent profits supplying vacuum tubes to the replacement and military markets.[23] As late as 1994, it was noted that the U.S. system of air traffic control depended on vacuum tubes supplied by a few specialist companies.[24] In fountain pens, survivors in the quality pen segment such as Cross and Mont Blanc have achieved steady sales and high margins through appealing to high income professionals and executives. Decline may be punctuated by periodic upswings of demand: during 1996–1997 the quality cigar market was revived by a sudden return to fashion.

Strategy Options in Declining Industries

Conventional strategy recommendations for declining industries are either to divest or to harvest, i.e., to generate the maximum cash flow from existing investments without reinvesting. However, these strategies assume that declining industries are inherently unprofitable. If profit potential exists, then other strategies may be attractive. Harrigan and Porter[25] identify four strategies that can be profitably pursued either individually or sequentially in declining industries.

Leadership. By gaining leadership, a firm is well placed to outstay competitors and play a dominant role in the final stages of the industry's life cycle. Once leadership is attained, the firm is in a good position to switch to a harvest strategy and enjoy a strong profit stream from its market position. Possible maneuvers in establishing leadership are:

♦ Build market share and compete aggressively to encourage rivals to exit.

♦ Buy market share by acquiring competitors.

♦ Purchase competitors' plants.

♦ Reduce competitors' exit costs by producing spare parts and private label goods for them.

♦ Demonstrate commitment to the industry.

♦ Disclose forecasts of declining future demand, which helps dispel any overly optimistic hopes that some competitors may cling to.

♦ Raise the stakes. Take initiatives such as product or process improvements that pressure competitors to follow, making it costly for them to stay in the business.

Niche. Identify a segment that is likely to maintain a stable demand and other firms are unlikely to invade, then pursue a leadership strategy to establish dominance within the segment. The most attractive niches are those that offer the greatest prospects for stability and where demand is most inelastic.

Harvest. A harvesting strategy is one that maximizes the firm's cash flow from its existing assets, while avoiding further investment as much as possible. Harvesting strategies seek to maximize cash flow by raising prices wherever possible, and cutting costs by rationalizing the number of models, number of channels, and number of customers. Note, however, that a harvest strategy can be difficult to implement effectively. If competition is strong, harvesting may result in an unintended acceleration of

FIGURE 12.2
electing a Strategy
in a Declining
Industry

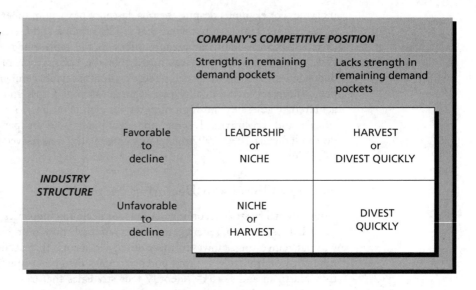

decline, particularly if employee morale is adversely affected by a strategy that offers no development or long-term future for the business.

Divest.   If the future looks bleak, the best strategy may be to divest the business in the early stages of decline before a consensus has developed as to the inevitability of decline. Once industry decline is well established, finding buyers may be extremely difficult.

Choosing the most appropriate strategy requires a careful assessment both of the profit potential of the industry and the competitive position of the firm. Harrigan and Porter pose four key questions:

1. Can the structure of the industry support a hospitable, potentially profitable decline phase?

2. What are the exit barriers that each significant competitor faces?

3. Do your company strengths fit the remaining pockets of demand?

4. What are your competitors' strengths in these pockets? How can their exit barriers be overcome?

Selecting an appropriate strategy requires matching the opportunities remaining in the industries to the company's competitive position. Figure 12.2 shows a simple framework for strategy choice.

◆ SUMMARY

Mature industries present challenging environments for the formulation and implementation of business strategies. Competition—price competition in particular—is usually strong and competitive advantage is often difficult to build and sustain: cost advantages are vulnerable to imitation, differentiation opportunities are limited by the trend to standardization. Stable positions of competitive advantage in mature industries are traditionally associated with cost advantage from economies of scale or experience, and differentiation advantage through brand loyalty. Such strategies are typically implemented through hierarchical organizations, with high levels of specialization and formalization, and centralized decision making directed toward maximizing static efficiency.

Increased dynamism of mature industries resulting from international competition, economic turbulence, and greater pressure for innovation has had two consequences. First, the conditions for cost efficiency have changed. In a dynamic environment, cost efficiency is less dependent on scale, specialization, and rigid control, and more on rapid adjustment to change. Second, as competition has become more intense, companies (especially those in the advanced industrialized countries) have been forced seek new sources of competitive advantage through innovation and differentiation. Reconciling the pursuit of scale economies with the need for responsiveness and flexibility, and the requirements of cost efficiency with the growing need for innovation and differentiation poses complex strategic and organizational challenges. Some of the most successful companies in mature industries—Wal-Mart in retailing, BP in oil and gas, Nike in shoes and sportswear, and Coca-Cola in beverages—are companies that have achieved flexibility through dismantling bureaucratic structures and procedures, have exploited new technology to combine variety and flexibility with efficiency, have encouraged high levels of employee commitment, and have relentlessly pursued financial targets. We return to some of these challenges and firms' responses to them in Chapter 17.

NOTES

1   Edward H. Rensi, "Computers at McDonalds," in *Strategies . . . Successes . . . Senior Executives Speak Out,* ed. J. F. McLimore and L. Larwood (New York: Harper & Row, 1988): 159–160.

2   Letter to shareholders, *The 1991 Annual Report of Berkshire Hathaway Inc.*

3   Robert D. Buzzell and Bradley T. Gale, *The PIMS Principles* (New York: Free Press, 1987): 279.

4   R. Cibin and Robert M. Grant, "Restructuring among the World's Leading Oil Companies," *British Journal of Management* 7 (December 1996): 283–308.

5   Donald C. Hambrick and Steven M. Schecter, "Turnaround Strategies for Mature Industrial-Product Business Units," *Academy of Management Journal* 26, no. 2 (1983): 231–248.

6   Peter H. Grinyer, D. G. Mayes, and P. McKiernan, *Sharpbenders* (Oxford: Basil Blackwell, 1988).

7   "R&D Scoreboard," *Business Week,* June 20, 1988: 139–160.

8   Derek Abell, *Managing with Dual Strategies* (New York: Free Press, 1993): 75–78.

9   Charles Baden Fuller and J. Stopford, *Rejuvenating the Mature Business* (London: Routledge, 1992), especially chapters 3 and 4.

10 *Fox Broadcasting Company,* Harvard Business School, Case Series, 1989.

11 Robert M. Grant and Charles Baden Fuller, "The Richardson Sheffield Story," in *Strategic Innovation,* ed. Charles Baden Fuller and M. Pitt (London: Routledge, 1996).

12 Frank C. Barnes, "Nucor," in *Strategic Management,* ed. G. G. Dess and A. Miller (New York: McGraw-Hill, 1993): 804–832.

13 "Team Approach: A Power Producer Is Intent on Giving Power to its People," *Wall Street Journal,* July 3, 1995: A1.

14 J-C Spender, *Industry Recipes: The Nature and Sources of Managerial Judgment* (Oxford: Basil Blackwell, 1989). On a similar theme, see also Anne S. Huff, "Industry Influences

on Strategy Reformulation," *Strategic Management Journal* 3 (1982): 119–131; and Gerry Johnson, "Strategic Frames and Formulae," *Strategic Management Journal* 8 (1987).

15 P. S. Barr, J. L. Stimpert, and Anne S. Huff, "Cognitive Change, Strategic Action, and Organizational Renewal," *Strategic Management Journal* 13, Special Issue (Summer 1992): 15–36.

16 Paul R. Lawrence and Davis Dyer, *Renewing American Industry* (New York: Free Press, 1983), chapter 2, "Autos: On the Thin Edge,"and chapter 3, "Steel: The Slumping Giant."

17 G. Hamel, "Killer Strategies That Make Shareholders Rich," *Fortune,* June 23, 1997.

18 G. Hamel, "Strategy as Revolution," *Harvard Business Review* 96 (July–August 1996): 69–82

19 T. Burns and G. M. Stalker, *The Management of Innovation* (London: Tavistock Institute, 1961).

20 Henry Mintzberg, *Structure in Fives: Designing Effective Organizations* (Englewood Cliffs, NJ: Prentice-Hall, 1983), chapter 9.

21 Kathryn R. Harrigan, *Strategies for Declining Businesses* (Lexington, MA: D. C. Heath, 1980).

22 Joe Bower, *When Markets Quake* (Boston: Harvard Business School Press, 1986).

23 Kathryn R. Harrigan, "Strategic Planning for Endgame," *Long Range Planning* 15 (1982): 45–48.

24 "U.S. to Shake Up Air Traffic Bureaucracy," *The Washington Post*, May 2, 1994: A1, A11.

25 Kathryn R. Harrigan and Michael E. Porter, "End-Game Strategies for Declining Industries," *Harvard Business Review* (July–August 1983): 111–120.

V.

Corporate Strategy

13

Vertical Integration and the Scope of the Firm

The idea of vertical integration is an anathema to an increasing number of companies. Most of yesterday's highly integrated giants are working overtime at splitting into more manageable, more energetic units—i.e., de-integrating. Then they are turning around and re-integrating—not by acquisitions but via alliances with all sorts of partners of all shapes and sizes.

—*Tom Peters, Liberation Management*

Outline

◆ INTRODUCTION AND OBJECTIVES

Chapter 2 introduced the distinction between *corporate* strategy and *business* strategy. Corporate strategy is concerned primarily with the decisions over the *scope* of the firm's activities, including:

♦ *Product scope.* How specialized should the firm be in terms of the range of products it supplies? Cummins Engine is a specialized company. It is involved almost exclusively in manufacturing diesel engines. British American Tobacco is highly diversified with interests in cigarettes, retailing, insurance, cosmetics, and engineering.

♦ *Geographical scope.* What is the optimal geographical spread of activities for the firm? In the restaurant business, most companies serve small local markets. McDonald's operates in close to one hundred countries throughout the world.

♦ *Vertical scope.* What range of vertically linked activities should the firm encompass? In the computer industry, IBM has traditionally been highly vertically integrated, producing many components and much of its software internally and managing its own direct sales and service organization. Gateway 2000, on the other hand, has a much shorter value chain: it relies heavily on third-party suppliers and distributors.

Business strategy (also known as *competitive strategy)* is concerned with how a firm competes within a particular market. The distinction may be summarized as follows: corporate strategy is concerned with *where* a firm competes; business strategy is concerned with *how* a firm competes.[1] The major part of this book has been concerned with issues of business strategy. For the next four chapters, the emphasis is on corporate strategy: decisions that involve the *scope of the firm.*

I begin with vertical integration because it takes us to the heart of many of the issues relevant to determining the optimal scope of the firm and, in particular, the role of transactions costs in drawing the boundaries of the firm and the types of relationships between firms. Also, issues of vertical integration are among some of the most prominent strategic questions that companies face during the 1990s. For example, vertical de-integration through outsourcing has been an important trend across most industries and a key aspect of corporate restructuring. The past decade has also seen the emergence of new forms of vertical relationships as companies have combined the benefits of close vertical cooperation with the flexibility of market transactions. By the time you have completed this chapter, you will be able to:

♦ Identify the relative efficiencies of firms and markets in organizing economic activity and apply the principles of **transaction cost economics** to determining the boundaries of firms

♦ Assess the relative merits of vertical integration and market transactions in organizing vertically related activities and understand the circumstances that influence their comparative advantages

♦ Identify a range of possible relationships among vertically related firms, including spot market transactions, long-term contracts, franchise agreements, and alliances

♦ Explain why some types of vertically related activities are integrated within a single company, whereas others are performed by separate companies

♦ Identify the critical considerations pertinent to make-or-buy decisions and the extent to which a firm should vertically integrate

♦ Design the most advantageous form of relationship between a firm and its suppliers and customers.

TRANSACTIONS COSTS AND THE SCOPE OF THE FIRM

In Chapter 6, we noted that firms came into existence because they were more efficient in organizing production than market contracts between independent workers. Let us explore this issue in more detail and apply our analysis to the determinants of firm boundaries.

Firms, Markets, and Transactions Costs

Since the industrial revolution of the eighteenth and nineteenth centuries, the general pattern of development of large firms has been for them to expand their scope. Alfred Chandler's research has documented over a century of growth in the vertical, geographical, and product scope of firms in response to technological change, the development of transportation and communications systems, and managerial and organizational innovation.[2] Expansion in the size and scope of firms represents a shift in the relative roles of markets and firms in the organization of economic activity.

Although the capitalist economy is frequently referred to as a "market economy," in fact, it comprises two forms of economic organization. One is the *market mechanism* where individuals and firms make independent decisions that are guided and coordinated by market prices. The other is the *administrative mechanism* of firms where decisions over production, supply, and the purchases of inputs are made by managers and imposed through hierarchies. The market mechanism was characterized by Adam Smith, the eighteenth century Scottish economist, as the "invisible hand" because its coordinating role does not require conscious planning. Alfred Chandler has referred to the administrative mechanism of company management as the "visible hand" because it is dependent on coordination through planning.

Why do institutions called "firms" exist in the first place? The firm is an organization that consists of a number of individuals bound by employment contracts with a central contracting authority. But firms are not essential for conducting complex economic activity. When I recently remodeled my basement, I contracted with a self-employed builder to undertake the work. He in turn subcontracted parts of the work to a plumber, an electrician, a joiner, a drywall installer, and a painter. Although the job involved the coordinated activity of several individuals, these self-employed specialists were not linked by employment relations but by market contracts ("$4,000 to install wiring, lights, and sockets"). What determines which activities are undertaken within a firm, or between individuals or firms coordinated by market contracts? Ronald Coase's answer was relative cost.[3] If the *transactions costs* associated with organizing across markets are greater than the *administrative costs* of organizing within firms, we can expect the coordination of productive activity to be internalized within firms. This situation is illustrated in Figure 13.1. With regard to vertical scope, which is more efficient: three independent companies, one producing iron ore, the next producing steel, and the third producing ships, or having all three stages of production within a single company? In the case of geographical scope, which is more efficient: three independent companies each operating a beverage can plant in three separate countries, or a single company operating the three plants? In the case of product scope, should cigarettes, beer, and food products be produced by three separate companies, or are there efficiencies to be gained by merging all three into a single company called, say, Philip Morris, where the allocation of employees and managers between each company is done by corporate management?

Trends in Aggregate Concentration

Figure 13.2 shows the growing importance of large corporations in the U.S. economy during most of this century. Similar patterns exist for other industrialized countries. As indicated by Chandler, this growth is the result of the widening scope of large corporations: companies have integrated backward and forward, they have

FIGURE 13.1
Transactions Costs
and the Scope of
the Firm

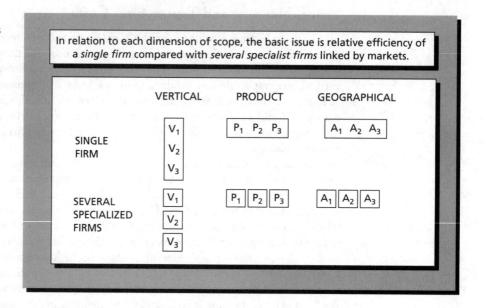

expanded from serving local to national to international markets, they have grown
from being specialized enterprises to supplying a wide range of goods and services.
This, presumably, is the result of the costs of administering transactions internally
within the firm falling as compared with organizing those transactions across markets. Two factors have been especially important in increasing the efficiency of firms
as organizing devices. One is communications and information technologies. The
telegraph, telephone, and computer have played an important role in facilitating
communications within firms and expanding the decision-making capacity of man-

FIGURE 13.2
Aggregate Concen-
tration over Time:
100 Largest Compa-
nies' Share of U.S.
Industrial Output,
1928–1990

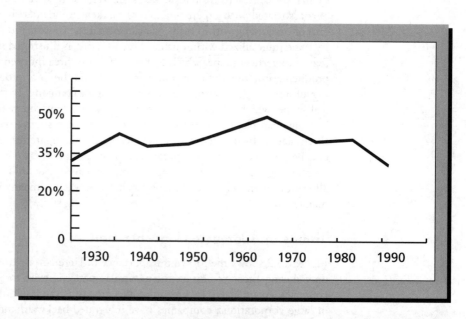

agers. The second is the principles and techniques of management. Beginning with the dissemination of double-entry bookkeeping and emerging principles of bureaucracy in the nineteenth century, and the fundamentals of management and organizational design in the early twentieth century, management knowledge has advanced at an accelerating pace.[4] Key developments have included the multidivisional organizational form, matrix organizations, discounted cash flow investment appraisal, the principles of statistical control, scheduling analysis, market research techniques, and a whole host of other management tools. By the mid-1960s, this displacement of the coordinating role of markets by the internal management systems of vertically integrated, diversified, multinational corporations had amounted to the replacement of the *market* economy by the *corporate* economy. In 1969, J. K. Galbraith predicted that the inherent advantages of firms over markets in allocating resources and permitting long-term planning would result in increasing dominance of capitalist economies by a small number of giant corporations.[5]

During the 1980s and the 1990s, these predictions were refuted by a sharp reversal of the trend toward increased aggregate concentration. Although the majority of large companies have continued to expand internationally, the dominant trends of the last 15 years have been "downsizing" and "refocusing" as large industrial companies have reduced both their product scope through focusing on their core businesses, and their vertical scope through outsourcing activities. These changes seem to be associated with the more turbulent business environment that followed the first oil shock of 1973–1974, floating exchange rates in 1972, the invention of the integrated circuit, and the upsurge of international competition. The implication seems to be that during periods of instability, the costs of administration within firms tend to rise as the need for flexibility and speed of response overwhelms traditional management systems.

Oliver Williamson's contribution to economics has been his analysis of the nature and sources of the transactions costs, which form the basis for a theory of economic organization.[6] His analysis offers penetrating insights into corporate strategy decisions concerning the scope of the firm and the design of relationships among firms. We proceed by applying his analysis to vertical integration and, in doing so, introduce concepts and ideas that are also relevant to decisions concerning multinational growth and product diversification.

THE COSTS AND BENEFITS OF VERTICAL INTEGRATION

Changing ideas about the efficiency of large corporations as organizers of economic activity have exerted a strong influence on firms' vertical integration strategies. Twenty years ago the dominant belief was that vertical integration offered superior coordination as well as protection from the vagaries of the market. The prevailing wisdom today is that vertical specialization is conducive to flexibility and the development of core competencies, and that most of the benefits of vertical coordination can be achieved through inter-firm collaboration. Let's explore some of these issues.

Defining Vertical Integration

Vertical integration refers to a firm's ownership of vertically related activities. The greater the firm's ownership and control over successive stages of the value chain for its product, the greater its degree of vertical integration. The extent of vertical integration is indicated by the ratio of a firm's value added to its sales revenue. Highly integrated companies—such as the major oil companies that own and control their value chain from exploring for oil down to the retailing of gasoline, tend to have low expenditures on bought-in goods and services relative to their sales.

Vertical integration can occur in two directions:

♦ *Backward integration*—where the firm takes ownership and control of producing its own inputs (e.g., Henry Ford's upstream expansion from automobile assembly to the production of his own components, back to the production of basic materials including steel and rubber).

♦ *Forward integration*—where the firm takes ownership and control of its own customers (e.g., PepsiCo acquiring its local bottlers).

Vertical integration may also be *full integration* or *partial integration*:

♦ *Full integration* exists between two stages of production A and B when all stage A's production is sold internally and all stage B's requirements are obtained internally. Thus, at most integrated steel plants, all pig iron production goes into steel making, and none is purchased from outside.

♦ *Partial integration* exists when stages A and B are not internally self-sufficient. Thus, car manufacturers have traditionally been partially backward-integrated into components. For example, most of General Motors's spark plugs, instruments, and ignition equipment are supplied externally, although for many of these items a portion is produced by its Delco division. Partial integration is also typical among integrated oil companies. "Crude rich" companies (such as Statoil) produce more oil than they refine and are net sellers of crude oil; "crude poor" companies (such as Exxon) have to supplement their own production with purchases of crude to keep their refineries supplied.

Technical Economies from the Physical Integration of Processes

Analysis of the benefits of vertical integration has traditionally emphasized economies arising from the physical integration of processes. Thus, most steel production is undertaken by integrated steel producers in plants that first produce pig iron from iron ore and then convert iron to steel. Linking the two stages of production at a single location reduces transportation and energy costs. Similar economies arise in pulp and paper production.

However, although these considerations explain the need for the co-location of plants, they do not explain why vertical integration in terms of *common ownership* is necessary. Why can't iron and steel production or pulp and paper production be undertaken by separate firms owning facilities that are physically integrated with one another?

Thus, we must look beyond technical economies to justify vertical integration. The key is to understand the implications of technical economies of linked processes for transactions costs.

The Sources of Transactions Costs

Consider the value chain for steel cans, which extends from mining iron ore to delivering cans to the canning company. Between the production of iron and steel, most production is vertically integrated. Between the production of steel and steel cans, there is very little vertical integration: the can producers such as Crown, Cork and Seal, and Metal Box are specialist packaging companies that purchase steel strip from steel companies.

The absence of significant benefits from vertical integration between steel companies and can companies reflects low transactions costs in the market for steel strip: competitive supply, conditions, and information are readily available, and the switching costs for buyers and suppliers are low. The same is true for many other commodity products: few jewelry companies own gold mines; few flour milling companies own wheat farms.

But pig iron is also a commodity product with potentially competitive supply conditions. However, once physical integration occurs in order to exploit technical economies, if the iron and steel stages of production are owned by separate firms, then the market now becomes a series of **bilateral monopolies.** Several problems of market contracts arise.

1. The *small numbers problem.* With a monopoly supplier and a monopoly buyer, there is no equilibrium price—it depends on bargaining. The result is likely to be unproductive investments whose aim is only to improve the bargaining power of one party relative to the other.

2. Disincentives for *transaction-specific investments.* At an integrated iron and steel complex, the two companies make investments that are specific to the particular transaction. This is a source of risk. The iron producer may be discouraged from upgrading or expanding facilities for fear that the steel producer may not make complementary investments.

3. *Opportunism and strategic misrepresentation.* Transaction-specific investments give rise to the small numbers problem (typically, bilateral monopoly), which can cause opportunistic behavior. Thus, in the knowledge that the steel producer is a captive customer, the iron producer may be tempted to bargain for a better price by misrepresenting costs or product quality.

4. *Taxes and regulations on market transactions.* Transactions costs may take the form of government taxes or regulations imposed by government. While a graduate student in Britain, high taxes on alcoholic beverages encouraged me to backward integrate into producing my own wine and beer. OPEC's crude oil quotas on its members have encouraged the national oil companies to forward-integrate into refining and petrochemicals as a means of cheating on their quotas.

These conditions increase the transactions costs of market contracts. Under conditions of small numbers, transaction-specific investments, imperfect information, and taxes or regulations imposed on market transactions, vertical integration can reduce costs. That is not to say that market contracts cannot be adjusted to take account of these circumstances. For example, long-term contracts can avoid opportunism, inspection and quality-control procedures can avoid some forms of misrepresentation and opportunism, and provisions for arbitrating disputes can be built into contracts. But all these solutions impose costs. Thus, long-term contracts must take account of changing circumstances. In writing a long-term contract, provision needs to be made for inflation, the changing quantities demanded and supplied by each party need to be reconciled, quality and technical specifications must be established, and the circumstances of *force majeure* must be specified. Not only does this increase the initial costs of the contract, it may also give rise to continuing costs for contract enforcement and interpretation as well as opportunism on the part of one or other of the parties. McDonald's franchise contracts are long-term in order to encourage transaction-specific investment by both franchiser and franchisee, yet changing circumstances frequently give rise to costs through contract disputes. For example, McDonald's opening new outlets in colleges and gas stations is often viewed by franchisees as infringing on their territorial exclusivity.

Administrative Costs of Internalization

The presence of transactions costs in intermediate markets is not enough to justify vertical integration. Vertical integration avoids the costs of using the market, but internalizing the transactions means that there are now costs of administration. The efficiency of the internal administration of vertical relations depends on several factors.

Differences in the Optimal Scale of Operation Between Different Stages of Production.   Federal Express is a major purchaser of trucks and vans, but it has never considered setting up its own truck manufacturing company or acquiring an existing producer. To begin with, the transactions costs associated with buying trucks is low—Federal Express can purchase trucks very efficiently using either spot or long-term contracts. A second factor is the difference in the optimal scale of operation. Although Federal Express purchases over 25,000 trucks each year, these purchases are far below the output needed for efficiency as a manufacturer. Ford produced 2 million commercial vehicles in 1995. The risk, therefore, is that vertical integration may therefore result in high costs in those activities where minimum efficient size is very high. This explains why specialist vehicle producers are much less backward-integrated than volume producers. In auto assembly, the minimum efficient scale is around 200,000 units a year. In engine manufacture, the minimum efficient scale is in excess of one million units a year. Hence, small automobile manufacturers tend to buy rather than make engines.

Managing Strategically Different Businesses.   One of the major sources of administrative costs of vertically related businesses arises from coordinating businesses that, in strategic terms, are very different. A major disadvantage to FedEx of owning a truck manufacturing company is that the management systems and organizational capabilities required for truck manufacturing are very different from those required for express delivery. These considerations may explain why vertical integration between manufacturing and retailing companies is rare. Manufacturing and retailing are quite different types of businesses: manufacturing requires technological, process, and product development capabilities; retailing requires rapid response capability, astute buying, and constant attentiveness to managing the customer interface. Many of the problems of the computer and consumer electronics company, Tandy, may be attributed to these problems of encompassing manufacturing and retailing within a single company. Strategic dissimilarities between businesses have encouraged a number of companies to vertically de-integrate. Marriott's decision to split into two separate companies, Marriott International and Host Marriott, was influenced by the belief that *owning* hotels is a strategically different business from *operating* hotels. Similarly, several British breweries have split into a manufacturing company that produces beer and a catering/entertainment company that operates pubs.

Developing Distinctive Capabilities.   Where vertical integration combines activities with different organizational capabilities, the result may be that the lack of specialization inhibits the development of individual capabilities. Conversely, by specializing in a narrow range of activities, this may induce learning and innovation. The trend for manufacturing and service companies to outsource information services to specialist IT companies is an example of this. It is increasingly difficult for industrialized corporations to maintain IT capabilities that match those of specialists such as EDS, IBM, and Andersen Consulting. However, this assumes that organizational capabilities in different vertical activities are independent of one another. Where one capability builds on capabilities in vertically adjacent activities, vertical integration may help develop distinctive capabilities. Thus, Motorola's success in wireless communication equipment rests to a significant extent on its technical capabilities in semiconductors. In the semiconductor industry itself, a key debate is over the merits of integrating design and fabrication as compared to "fab-less" semiconductor companies. Where complementarities exist between design capability and manufacturing capability, vertical integration is desirable. In the case of digital logic integrated circuits, design and manufacturing capabilities are largely independent, and such activities are commonly undertaken by separate design and fabrication companies.[7]

Competitive Effects of Vertical Integration.   Monopolistic companies have used vertical integration as a means of extending their monopoly positions from one stage of the industry to another. The classic cases are Standard Oil, which used its power in transportation and refining to foreclose markets to independent producers; and Alcoa, which used its monopoly position in aluminum production to squeeze independent fabricators of aluminum products in order to advantage its own fabrication subsidiaries. Such cases are rare. As economists have shown, once a company monopolizes one vertical chain of an industry, there is no further monopoly profit to be extracted by extending that monopoly position to adjacent vertical stages of the industry. A greater concern is that vertical integration may make independent suppliers and customers less willing to do business with the vertically integrated company because it is now perceived as a competitor rather than as a supplier or customer. Such implications followed Disney's acquisition of ABC. Other studios (e.g., Dreamworks) became less interested in collaborating with ABC in developing new programming as well as in advertising their new movie releases on ABC.

Flexibility.   Both vertical integration and market transactions can claim advantage with regard to different types of flexibility. Where the required flexibility is rapid responsiveness to uncertain demand, there may be advantages in market transactions. The lack of vertical integration in the construction industry reflects, in part, the need for flexibility in adjusting both to cyclical patterns of demand and to the different requirements of each project. Vertical integration may also be disadvantageous in responding quickly to new product development opportunities that require new combinations of technical capabilities. Ever since IBM outsourced most of the components for its PC in 1981, fast-cycle product development in electronics has involved extensive outsourcing and technical collaboration. During the 1990s, some of the most rapidly growing companies in the electronics sector have been contract electronics manufacturers.[8] However, where system-wide flexibility is required, a vertically integrated set of activities may offer a more effective means of achieving simultaneous adjustment at every level. For example, the integrated oil majors with their company-owned filling stations have led independent filling stations supplied by independent refiners and gas companies in introducing unleaded gasoline and natural gas for motor vehicles.

Compounding Risk.   To the extent that vertical integration ties a company to its internal suppliers, vertical integration represents a compounding of risk insofar as problems at any one stage of production threaten production and profitability at all other stages. The problem with a strike at a General Motors brake plant in 1997 was that it halted production of GM's auto assembly plants.

What we observe is that the overall balance of costs and benefits associated with vertical integration depends on the costs associated with the internalization of vertical transactions as compared with the costs of undertaking them in separate companies linked by market transactions. Whether there are net benefits to vertical integration depends on many factors relating both to the industry and the individual firm. Table 13.1 summarizes some of these.

TABLE 13.1
Vertigal Integration (VI) versus Market Transactions: Some Relevant Considerations

CHARACTERISTICS OF THE VERTICAL RELATIONSHIP	IMPLICATIONS FOR VERTICAL INTEGRATION
How many firms are there in the vertically related activity?	The fewer the companies, the greater the attraction of VI.
Do transaction-specific investments need to be made by either party?	The greater the requirements for specific investment, the more attractive is VI.
Does limited availability of information provide opportunities to the contracting firm to behave opportunistically (i.e., cheat)?	The greater the difficulty of specifying and monitoring contracts, the greater the advantages of VI.
Are market transactions subject to taxes and regulations?	VI is attractive if it can circumvent taxes and regulations.
How much uncertainty exists with regard to the circumstances prevailing over the period of the contract?	Uncertainty raises the costs of writing and monitoring contracts, and provides opportunities for cheating, therefore increasing the attractiveness of VI.
Are two stages similar in terms of the optimal scale of operations?	The greater the dissimilarity in scale, the more difficult is VI.
How strategically similar are the different stages in terms of key success factors and the resources and capabilities required for success?	The greater the strategic dissimilarity, the more difficult is VI.
How uncertain is market demand?	The greater the unpredictability of demand, the more costly is VI.
Does VI increase risk through requiring heavy investment in multiple stages and compounding otherwise independent risk factors?	The heavier the investment requirements and the greater the independent risks at each stage, the more risky is VI.

Source: Fortune, May 30, 1993: 214.

DESIGNING VERTICAL RELATIONSHIPS

Our discussion so far has compared vertical integration with arms-length relationships between buyers and sellers. In practice, there is a variety of relationships through which buyers and sellers can interact and coordinate their interests.

Long-Term Contracts and "Quasi-Vertical Integration"

In discussing market transactions, our focus has been on spot contracts. A **spot contract** is a single, current transaction such as a shopper buying a loaf of bread from a bakery, a broker selling 100 IBM shares on the NYSE, or Mobil Oil purchasing a cargo load of crude from Kuwait Oil Corporation. However, spot contracts are not the only—nor even the most common—type of market transaction between companies. Supplying components and raw materials to manufacturing firms usually involves a long-term relationship between the supplier and the manufacturer. Similarly, most supply relationships between manufacturers, distributors, and retailers are long term. In some cases, long-term relationships are formulated into written contracts that specify the terms of the agreement and the responsibilities of each party; in other cases, the relationship may be based on trust and implicit understandings. Figure 13.3 shows a range of different vertical relationships.

As already indicated, spot transactions work well where there are many buyers and sellers, a standard product, and little need for transaction-specific investment by either party. When there are few buyers and sellers, where a customized product or

FIGURE 13.3
Different Types of Vertical Relationships

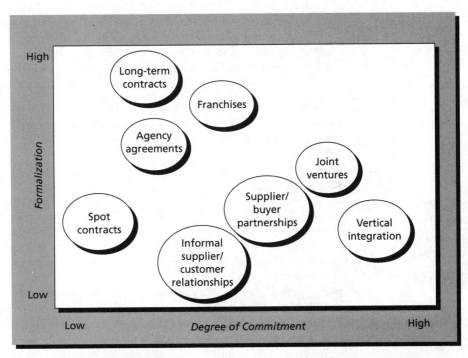

service is being supplied, or where transaction-specific investments are needed, long-term vertical contracts can be a viable alternative to full vertical integration. Where the vertical relationships are especially close and long term, they are referred to as **quasi-vertical integration** or as **value-adding partnerships.**[9]

In selecting among different types of relationships and designing the contractual form, two considerations are critical to efficiency.

1. **Allocation of risk.** Any arrangement beyond a spot contract must cope with uncertainties over the course of the contract. A key feature of any contract is that its terms involve, often implicitly, an allocation of risks between the parties. How risk is shared is dependent partly on bargaining power and partly on efficiency considerations. In the case of contracts between automobile manufacturers and component suppliers, prices are often fixed for six or twelve months, resulting in the component supplier accepting the risk that costs will vary over the contract period. In the case of supply agreements for natural gas, large customers, such as electrical power producers, can purchase on fixed-price contracts; small customers, such as residential users, have much less bargaining power and accept contracts that allow the gas supplier to vary prices.

2. **Incentive structures.** For a contract to minimize transactions costs it must provide an appropriate set of incentives to the parties. Thus, unless a contract for the supply of ready-mixed concrete to construction projects specifies the proportions of cement, sand, and gravel, there is an incentive to supply substandard concrete. However, achieving completeness in the specification of contracts also bears a cost. The $400 toilet seats supplied to the U.S. Navy may reflect the costs of meeting specifications that filled many sheets of paper. Very often, the most effective incentive is the promise of future business. Hence, some of the most successful long-term vertical relationships are supplier agreements where there is no formal agreement but an understanding that satisfaction and responsiveness will lead to a long-term business relationship. But for such "relational contracts" there must be some disincentives to opportunism. Transaction-specific investments made by each party represent an "exchange of hostages" that may act as a disincentive to opportunism.

Exhibits 13.1 and 13.2 describe two examples of long-term vertical contracts that succeed in combining the close cooperation associated with vertical integration, while avoiding some of the administrative costs and rigidities that vertical integration can impose.

Some Recent Trends

The ability for long-term "relational contracts" to offer the flexibility of market transactions while avoiding many of the transactions costs of spot contracts has resulted in a strong trend away from vertical integration throughout many industries in Western Europe and North America. This has been stimulated in part by observation of the close collaborative relationships that many Japanese companies have with their suppliers. During the late 1980s, Toyota and Nissan directly produced about 20 to 23 percent of the value of their cars, whereas Ford accounted for 50 percent of its production value and GM for about 70 percent. Yet, as Jeff Dyer has shown, the Japanese automakers have been remarkably successful in achieving close collaboration in technology, quality control, design and scheduling of production and deliveries.[10]

EXHIBIT 13.1

McDonald's Restaurants Franchise System

A franchise agreement is a contract between the franchisor who owns a brand name and other associated trademarks and has developed a system for supplying a product or service, and the franchisee who purchases the right to use the trademarks and the business system at a specified location. The purpose of the franchise is to offer the coordination advantages of vertical integration while maintaining the flexibility advantages associated with independent contracting companies. Many of the transactions costs associated with market exchanges are avoided by a contract that is long term, comprehensive, and supported by a close relationship between franchisor and franchisee. The reputation that McDonald's has established through many thousands of franchise agreements over a long period gives the new franchisee trust in the relationship and also provides a disincentive for McDonald's to engage in opportunistic behavior. Cooperation is also fostered through the comprehensive training program for franchisees in which McDonald's instills its philosophy and values within the new franchisee. At the same time, because the relationship is between separate firms, the franchise relationship avoids several of the problems of vertical integration. The franchisee brings his own capital, hence reducing financial requirements and risk for the franchisor. McDonald's Restaurants Inc. and the individual franchised restaurant are very different businesses. In terms of scale, one is global and the other local. In terms of capabilities, McDonald's is involved in managing a complex system requiring advanced management information systems, new product development, and sophisticated marketing, whereas the individual restaurant is involved in food and drink preparation, customer service, and maintaining the premises. The franchise system in which the franchisee works for profit provides direct incentives for increasing revenue and reducing costs.

It is interesting to note that McDonald's, along with other fast-food suppliers, has moved from franchising its restaurants toward increased direct ownership and management. This development reflects two factors. First, in the United States at least, McDonald's is less dependent on the financial and managerial resources and the local knowledge of its franchisees. It is in new markets that McDonald's prefers franchises or joint ventures in order to tap local expertise and market knowledge. Second, developments in McDonald's management information systems, communication network, staff training methods, and operating techniques have lowered the costs of internal administration as compared to the costs of managing and monitoring franchise agreements.

The response of Western companies has been twofold:

1. Companies have redefined their relationships with their suppliers. Rather than rely on competitive tendering and written agreements, manufacturers are increasingly seeking the improved flexibility and closer coordination that can occur through long-term cooperation. In the automobile manufacturing and electronics industries, large companies have drastically reduced their number of vendors and have introduced supplier certification programs under which suppliers show that they can meet the standards required by the manufacturer, after which relationships are based more on trust and mutual interest in continued business than on legally enforceable contracts.

2. Companies have focused on a smaller number of vertical activities and increasingly outsourced components and business services. Driven by the quest for cost savings, companies are scutinizing every activity within their

EXHIBIT 13.2

Managing Supplier Relations at Marks & Spencer PLC

Marks & Spencer PLC is undoubtedly the most successful retailer in Britain in the twentieth century. Established in the 1890s, M&S has achieved near continuous growth in revenue and profit over the last half century. The company is primarily a supplier of clothing but in the 1970s expanded into gourmet and convenience foods. Central elements of M&S strategy are its commitment to high quality and value for money and its policy that all its merchandise is sold under its own "St. Michael" brand name and is exclusive to M&S. The foundation of M&S's achievement of unique products of high quality and moderate prices is its system of supplier relations.

The interesting feature of these relationships is that they are long term (often extending over decades), and they are based upon a common understanding, but there is no written contract. The absence of a formal contract permits a high degree of flexibility, and the potential for highly sophisticated patterns of cooperation between M&S and its suppliers. For example, M&S involves itself in numerous aspects of the supplier's business including product design, quality control, purchasing of inputs, manufac-turing methods, human resource policies, and delivery schedules. The supplier is encouraged to make substantial investments in equipment and know-how that are specific to the needs of M&S. Why is it that suppliers are willing to become dependent upon M&S and invest in adapting their business system to meet the specific needs of this single customer? Surely this is very risky for the supplier. The critical factor is the incentive structure. M&S procurement policies have been developed over a century. They are well known, and M&S has developed an unparalleled reputation for fair dealing. Any new supplier has the knowledge that previous suppliers have been treated well, and the long-term relationship that M&S is willing to build has made many of its suppliers highly profitable. Because M&S's reputation is its greatest asset, it is unlikely to engage in behavior that might put that reputation at risk.

Source: K. K. Tse, *Marks & Spencer: Anatomy of Britain's Most Efficiently Managed Company* (New York: Pergamon, 1985).

value chains and asking whether it can be undertaken more efficiently and effectively by outside suppliers. Outsourcing by European and North American companies has been accompanied by global sourcing of components and services.

The evidence from widely different companies and industries points to the success of these new vertical relationships in enhancing company performance. IBM and Chrysler are among the once-integrated companies that have outsourced components and services and restructured supplier relationships. The result has been lower costs, increased flexibility and accelerated new product development.[11] Hewlett-Packard, Cisco Systems, and Sun Microsystems are companies whose collaborative supplier networks are central to their strategies.

The extent of outsourcing and vertical de-integration has given rise to a new organizational form: the **virtual corporation,** where the primary function of the company is coordinating the activities of a network of suppliers.[12] Although the virtual corporation has advantages of flexibility and the ability to select from a wide range of external capabilities, there is a danger that overreliance on external suppliers of manufacturing and technology causes degeneration into the **hollow corporation.** The risk is that, though incremental moves to outsource can be justified on the basis of cost efficiency, in the long run, companies lose the ability to innovate and develop.[13] This argument is closely linked to the concept of *core competences* discussed in Chapter 5. The most valuable and difficult to replicate capabilities of a company are those that involve integration across different technologies and knowledge bases: as more and more activities are outsourced, the company's know-how becomes narrower. Hamel and Prahalad argue that core competences are embodied in "core products" that, in many cases, are components (e.g., the engine of a car, the microprocessor of a personal computer). If industrial companies increasingly outsource and are reduced to the role of being assemblers and marketers, their long-term competitiveness becomes jeopardized.[14]

◆ SUMMARY

Decisions over the vertical range of activities encompassed within the firm raise critical issues concerning the basis of a firm's competitive advantage both now and in the future as well as about the linkages between different vertical activities. In determining whether a firm should undertake a particular activity or rely on an outside supplier, the most common question is whether the firm possesses a competitive advantage in that activity. However, a key aspect of any vertical chain is the nature of the linkages between activities cannot be appraised individually. In determining whether to undertake any activity, the firm must compare the transactions costs of buying from or supplying to another firm, as compared with the administrative costs of managing the internal relationship. Vertical linkages are not just about the costs of managing the transaction; there are also implications for competitive advantage. To what extent is the firm's competitive advantage at each stage enhanced by its involvement in adjacent stages? This is especially relevant with regard to the ability to extend and upgrade competitive advantage in the future and respond to external changes. The danger is that decisions made with respect to today's market and technological circumstances may be suboptimal with regard to tomorrow's competitive circumstances. Hewlett-Packard sources a substantial portion of its specialized integrated circuits (ICs) from its internal IC unit. In determining whether to maintain a presence in IC development and production, the issues for HP are not simply relative costs and the transactions costs of outsourcing highly specialized ICs. The critical strategic issue is the contribution of in-house IC technology to HP's remarkable ability to adapt its product market strategy to changing market circumstances by redeploying its considerable product development capabilities.

Thus, vertical integration decisions involve two sets of questions. First, which activities to be conducted internally and which to be outsourced. Second, the choice of vertical arrangements with external suppliers and buyers—whether spot contracts, long-term contracts, or some form of strategic alliance. Both types of decision are critically dependent on the firm's competitive strategy and its perception of its core competences: that is, those capabilities that are fundamental to its competitive advantage over the long term. As a result, we are likely to see very different vertical arrangements among firms within the same industry. In microwave ovens, Samsung is highly vertically integrated, whereas Emerson Electric is heavily dependent on external suppliers. Within the same company, different vertical relationships are likely between different activities. HP's highly successful range of laser printers use some internally sourced ICs; other components are purchased on both spot and long-term contracts. At the same time, the core printing mechanism is the result of a long-established alliance with Canon.

NOTES

1   In practice, determining where business strategy ends and corporate strategy begins is far from clear. Issues of scope are important in determining how a firm competes within a particular market, and issues of competitive advantage are critical in determining whether a firm should backward-integrate, diversify, or expand overseas. For example, we have considered segmentation decisions (PepsiCo's introduction of Diet Pepsi) to be business strategy, and diversification decisions (PepsiCo's acquisition of Kentucky Fried Chicken) to be corporate strategy. Outsourcing decisions (PepsiCo's outsourcing of certain transportation services) we consider within business strategy. Vertical integration (PepsiCo's acquisition of many of its bottlers) we view as corporate strategy. In all these examples, the critical issue is where we draw industry boundaries.

2   Alfred Chandler Jr., *Strategy and Structure* (Cambridge: MIT Press, 1962); *The Visible Hand: The Managerial Revolution in American Business* (Cambridge: MIT Press, 1977); and *Scale and Scope: Dynamics of Industrial Capitalism* (Cambridge: Harvard University Press, 1990).

3   R. H. Coase, "The Nature of the Firm," *Economica* 4 (1937): 386–405.

4   Although double-entry bookkeeping was invented in the fifteenth century, its use as a tool of management control did not become widespread until the nineteenth century (K. Hoskin and L. Zan, "A first *Discorso del Maneggio:* Accounting and the Production of Management Discourse at the Venice Arsenal," EIASM Working Paper 97-01, 1997.

5   J. K. Galbraith, *The New Industrial State* (Harmondsworth, U.K.: Penguin, 1969).

6   Oliver E. Williamson, *Markets and Hierarchies: Analysis and Antitrust Implications* (New York: Free Press, 1975); and Oliver E. Williamson, *The Economic Institutions of Capitalism: Firms, Markets and Relational Contracting* (New York: Free Press, 1985).

7   K. Monteverde, "Technical Dialogue as an Incentive for Vertical Integration in the Semiconductor Industry," *Management Science* 41 (1995): 1624–1638.

8   "Financial Times Survey: Contract Electronics Manufacture," *Financial Times,* March 16, 1993.

9   R. Johnston and P. R. Lawrence, "Beyond Vertical Integration—The Rise of the Value-Adding Partnership," *Harvard Business Review* (July–August 1988): 94–101.

10 J. H. Dyer, "Effective Interfirm Collaboration: How Firms Minimize Transaction Costs and Maximize Transaction Value," *Strategic Management Journal* 18 (1997): 535–556; J. H. Dyer, "Specialized Supplier Networks as a Source of Competitive Advantage: Evidence from the Auto Industry," *Strategic Management Journal* 17 (1996): 271–292.

11 J. H. Dyer, "How Chrysler Created an American Keiretsu," *Harvard Business Review* (July–August, 1996): 42–56.

12 See: "The Virtual Corporation," *Business Week,* February 8, 1993, 98–104; Arnoud De Meyer, *Creating the Virtual Factory* (Fontainebleau: INSEAD, 1993); and W. H. Davidow and M. S. Malone, *The Virtual Corporation* (New York: HarperCollins, 1992).

13 David Teece, "When Is Virtual Virtuous?" Presentation to Strategic Management Society, Paris, October 1994. In the semiconductor industry, there is evidence that the trend toward separation between chip design and chip fabrication is reversing. This is driven by, first, a shortage in worldwide foundry capacity and, second, the need for close coordination between the design and fabrication of advanced chips. See "Real Men Have Fabs," *Business Week,* April 11, 1994, 108–112.

14 C. K. Prahalad and Gary Hamel, "The Core Competences of the Corporation," *Harvard Business Review* (May–June 1990): 79–91.

14

Global Strategies and the Multinational Corporation

ABB is a company with no geographic center, no national ax to grind. We are a federation of national companies with a global coordination center. Are we a Swiss company? Our headquarters is in Zurich, but only 100 professionals work at headquarters and we will not increase that number. Are we a Swedish company? I'm the CEO, and I was born and educated in Sweden. But our headquarters is not in Sweden and only two of the eight members of our board of directors are Swedes. Perhaps we are an American company. We report our financial results in U.S. dollars and English is ABB's official language. We conduct all high-level meetings in English. My point is that ABB is none of those things—and all of these things. We are not homeless. We are a company with many homes.

—*Percy Barnevik, CEO, Asea Brown Boveri*

Outline
- INTRODUCTION AND OBJECTIVES
- IMPLICATIONS OF INTERNATIONAL COMPETITION FOR INDUSTRY
  ANALYSIS
  Competition from Potential Entrants
  Rivalry Among Existing Firms
  The Bargaining Power of Buyers
  Defining Market Boundaries: National or Global?
- ANALYZING COMPETITIVE ADVANTAGE IN AN INTERNATIONAL CONTEXT
  National Influences on Competitiveness: Comparative Advantage
  Porter's *Competitive Advantage of Nations*
  Consistency Between Strategy and National Conditions
- APPLYING THE FRAMEWORK: INTERNATIONAL LOCATION OF PRODUCTION
  Determinants of Geographic Location
  Location and the Value Chain
- APPLYING THE FRAMEWORK: FOREIGN ENTRY STRATEGIES
  Strategy Alternatives for Overseas Production
  International Alliances and Joint Ventures
- MULTINATIONAL STRATEGIES: GLOBALIZATION VERSUS NATIONAL
  DIFFERENTIATION
  The Benefits of a Global Strategy
  Strategic Strength from Global Positioning

◆ INTRODUCTION AND OBJECTIVES

The most important and pervasive force changing and challenging the business environment over the past four decades has been internationalization. Falling barriers to trade and international capital flows have opened new business opportunities while transforming the competitive structure of most industries. Internationalization has occurred through two mechanisms. The first is the growth of international trade. The growth of world trade has consistently outstripped the growth of world output, increasing export/sales and import/penetration ratios for all countries and all industries. For the United States, the share of imports in sales of manufactured goods rose from less than 4 percent in 1960 to 22 percent in 1996. Trade in commercial services (transportation, communications, information, financial services, and the like) grew even faster than merchandise trade. From 1994 to 1996, world exports of services grew at an annual rate of about 13 percent, compared to 7 percent for merchandise exports. The second aspect of internationalization has been overseas direct investment by corporations. Foreign direct investment by companies in the industrialized countries amounted to $259 billion in 1995.

As a result, domestic industries that were dominated by local companies such as building materials, metal fasteners, banking, telecommunication services, hotels, and power generation are increasingly open to trade and/or multinational corporations. Some industries have been transformed by internationalization. The U.S. television market still features many of the leading brands of half a century ago (RCA, GE, Magnavox, and Zenith), yet manufacturing has moved almost entirely to Asia and Latin America. All the leading U.S. television manufacturers are foreign owned: General Electric/RCA consumer electronics division by the French company Thomson, Magnavox by Philips of the Netherlands, Motorola's TV business by Matsushita, Warwick by Sanyo, and Zenith by LG of South Korea. The internationalization has had a profound impact on the economic performance of countries as well as companies. By 1996, Hong Kong and Singapore, once bases for low-wage manufacturing, had per capita GDP above $24,000 (at purchasing power parity rates of exchange). This exceeds all the European Union members except Luxembourg and Denmark. Despite recent financial difficulties, the prosperity of Hong Kong, Singapore, and the other Asian "tigers" continues to be based on international trade: Singapore's total trade was 140 percent of its GDP in 1996.

The driving force for internationalization, both trade and direct investment, is twofold: first, to exploit market opportunities in other countries, and, second, to exploit production opportunities by establishing production activities wherever they can be conducted most efficiently. The resulting "globalization of business" has meant the creation of networks of international transactions comprising merchandise trade, flows of services (including technology), flows of people (especially those with highly developed skills), flows of factor payments (especially interest, profits, and licensing and royalty income), and flows of capital.

This chapter examines the implications of the internationalization of the business environment for the formulation and implementation of company strategy. Most important, the chapter introduces the national environment as a primary influence on firm strategy: it forms a critical dimension of the firm's competitive environment and has a profound impact on its opportunities for competitive advantage. By the time you have completed this chapter, you will be able to:

♦ Apply the tools of industry analysis to global industries, including identifying the impact of trade and direct investment on industry structure and competition and appraising the critical differences between national markets within the same industry

♦ Analyze how the national environment of the firm influences its competitive advantage, in particular, how the national context affects the resources and capabilities of the firm and the choice of strategies through which the firm can best exploit these national conditions

♦ Formulate strategies for exploiting overseas business opportunities including overseas entry strategies and overseas production strategies, and determine the appropriate degree of globalization or national differentiation

♦ Design organizational structures and management systems appropriate to the pursuit of international strategies.

Our first task is to extend the framework of strategy analysis to take account of international competition. Let me begin by outlining the implications of international competition for the analysis of industry and competition. We then examine the implications of international competition for competitive advantage.

IMPLICATIONS OF INTERNATIONAL COMPETITION FOR INDUSTRY ANALYSIS

Internationalization, we have noted, affects industry structures and competition through trade and international investment. According to the extent and mechanism for internationalization, it is possible to identify four types of industry (see Figure 14.1). The trend over time has been for industries to move from the category of **sheltered industries** outward. By the late 1990s, industries that had once been sheltered (banking, insurance, retailing, telecommunications, cement) were subject to increasing international trade and direct investment. Industries left in this category were fragmented service industries (dry cleaning, hairdressing, auto repair), some small-scale manufacturing (handicrafts, homebuilding), and industries producing nontradable products (fresh milk, ice cream, furniture). If a product is tradable, is not nationally differentiated, and is subject to substantial scale economies, then internationalization tends to develop through trade. Thus, commercial aircraft, shipbuilding, and mainframe computers tend to be **trading industries**. Where trade is restricted by transportation costs or trade barriers, where products are nationally differentiated, or where scale economies in production are unimportant, then internationalization tends to proceed through direct investment. Thus, Kellogg's breakfast cereals, Unilever, Burger King, and Andersen Consulting all operate in these **multinational industries**. In **global industries,** both trade and direct investment are important.

To illustrate the impact of internationalization on industry, consider the U.S. and British markets for automobiles in 1970 and 1992. Two changes stand out. First, competition has increased. In the United States, CR3 (the combined market share of the

FIGURE 14.1
The Internationaliza-
tion of Industries

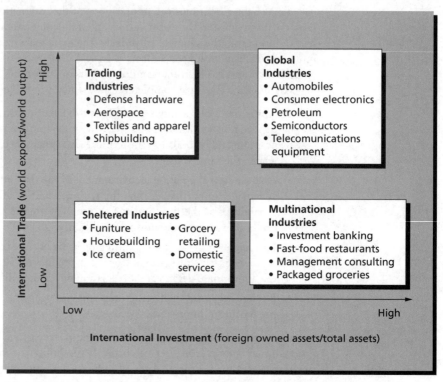

three largest suppliers) was 0.78 in 1970 and 0.65 in 1996. For the United Kingdom, the corresponding figures were 0.66 and 0.52. Second, the principal players in the different national markets have increasingly become the same. Nationally focused companies (such as Seat, Rover, and American Motors) have been absorbed by global players.

The trends we observe in autos are replicated in other industries—in some cases, much more dramatically. In automobiles, internationalization began early this century. During the 1900s, cars manufactured in Britain, France, and the United States were exported all over the world. During the 1920s, Ford and GM established subsidiaries in Europe, Asia, and Australia. In banking, insurance, telecommunications, and power generation, internalization has been much more recent and precipitous.

The consequences of the internationalization of competition for industry attractiveness are mostly adverse. Although internationalization offers increased investment and marketing opportunities to companies, it also means increased intensity of competition. For some industries (such as motor vehicles and steel), the adverse impact of internationalization on profitability is clear, however, for most industries the impact of increased international competition has been swamped by the upsurge in profitability that has resulted from the cost cutting and increased shareholder value orientation over the past decade.

The impact of internationalization on competition and industry profitability can be analyzed within the context of Porter's Five Forces of Competition framework. If we define markets as nationally bounded and industries as the set of suppliers to a national market, then internationalization has important influences on entry, internal rivalry, and buyer power.

Competition from Potential Entrants

The growth of international trade indicates a substantial lowering of barriers to entry into national markets. Multilateral tariff reduction during successive GATT rounds, falling real costs of transportation, the removal of exchange controls, internationalization of standards, and convergence between customer preferences have made it much easier for producers in one country to supply customers in another. Many of the entry barriers that were effective against potential domestic entrants may be ineffective against potential entrants that are established producers in overseas countries.

Rivalry Among Existing Firms

Internationalization increases internal rivalry within industries because it lowers seller concentration and increases the diversity of competing firms.

Seller Concentration.   International trade typically means that more suppliers are competing for each national market. Consider the U.S. auto market. In 1970, GM, Ford, and Chrysler together held 84 percent of total sales, and there were just five manufacturers with market shares greater than 2 percent. By 1996, the combined share of the Big Three had fallen to 65 percent, and there were eight manufacturers with market shares greater than 2 percent. In European countries, the fall in market share of the national leaders (Fiat in Italy, Renault and Peugeot-Citroën in France, British Leyland in the United Kingdom, Seat in Spain) was even more dramatic. What we are observing is that internationalization is decreasing concentration in national markets, while increasing concentration at the global level as competition forces companies to either exit or merge.

Diversity of Competitors.   Lower entry barriers and concentration ratios only partly explain the increasing intensity of competition between established firms. Equally important is the increasing diversity of competitors, which causes them to compete more vigorously while making cooperation more difficult. The **conscious parallelism** observed in the pricing behavior among oligopolistic industries of the 1960s reflected the similarities among domestic companies in their costs, strategies, goals, and perceptions. The entry of overseas competitors into domestic markets upsets such patterns of coordination partly because of the lack of common interest among companies with different costs, goals, and strategies. This is not to say that coordination, even collusion, is impossible on a global scale, but most instances of international collusion involve very small numbers of firms.[1]

The Bargaining Power of Buyers

A further implication of the internationalization of business is that large customers can exercise their buying power far more effectively. Automobile manufacturers increasingly look worldwide in sourcing components. Large retailers can use the threat of shifting their purchases to overseas manufacturers in order to negotiate favorable terms from domestic suppliers.

Defining Market Boundaries: National or Global?

The increase in international trade and direct investment raises the issue of whether it makes sense to define industries on the basis of national markets or whether industry boundaries need to be defined on a broader regional or global basis. In Chapter 3, we established *substitutability* both on the demand side and the supply side as the critical determinant of market boundaries. For many industries, it is clear that national markets are simply segments within a broader global market. In commercial aircraft, turbines, and crude oil production, the markets are clearly global: customers are willing to purchase from supplies wherever they are located, producers are willing to shift supplies to whichever countries offer the best market prospects. In commercial aircraft, Boeing's principal competitor is Airbus; in copiers, Xerox's leading competitor is Canon; in color film, Kodak's leading competitor is Fuji. Other markets are clearly national (or even local): the markets for newspapers, dairy products, cement, and legal services. Other industries are less easy to classify as global or national. Ford, Toyota, General Motors, and Volkswagen compete with one another in most of the countries of the world, yet competition tends to occur through clearly defined national markets. Because customers are supplied by local dealers, and because dealers are tied to individual auto manufacturers, there is limited scope for customers to substitute internationally. National regulations (with regard to safety and pollution) and dealership and warranty restrictions discourage the flow of cars between distributors in different countries ("gray imports"). Moreover, many players are nationally focused: Maruti in India, Tofas in Turkey, even Chrysler has 80 percent of its sales in North America. As we noted in Chapter 3, industries need to be defined differently for different companies and different purposes. Ford needs to analyze the global market in decisions over expanding engine capacity, but must examine national markets in considering pricing policy, marketing, and dealer support.

ANALYZING COMPETITIVE ADVANTAGE IN AN INTERNATIONAL CONTEXT

The growth of international competition has been associated with some stunning reversals in the competitive positions of different companies. Consider again the world auto industry. In 1966, British Leyland produced 800,000 cars, ahead of Ford of Europe with 732,000, Toyota with 316,000, and BMW with 98,000. By 1992, British Leyland, then the Rover Cars subsidiary of British Aerospace, produced 405,000 cars, compared with 4.2 million by Toyota, 1.6 million by Ford of Europe, and 598,000 by BMW (which acquired Rover in 1994).

To understand how competitive advantage has shifted within global industries, we need to extend our framework for analyzing competitive advantage to include the influence of each firm's national environment. Establishing competitive advantage requires that the firm match its internal strengths in resources and capabilities to the key success factors of the industry. When firms are located in different countries, the resources and capabilities available to them depend not only on their internal stocks of resources and capabilities, but also on the conditions of resource availability within their countries. Figure 14.2 shows this extended framework for the analysis of competitive advantage.

National Influences on Competitiveness: Comparative Advantage

The role of national resource availability on international competitiveness is the subject of the **theory of comparative advantage.** The theory states that a country has a comparative advantage in those products that make intensive use of those resources

FIGURE 14.2
Analyzing Competitive Advantage within an International Context

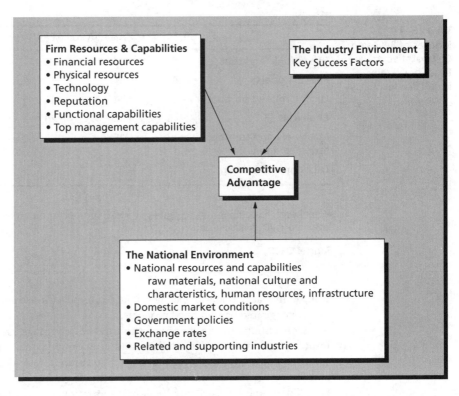

available in abundance within that country. Thus, the Philippines has an abundant supply of unskilled labor. The United States has an abundant supply of technological resources—trained scientists and engineers, research facilities, and universities. The Philippines has a comparative advantage in the production of products that make intensive use of unskilled labor, such as clothing, handicrafts, toys, shoes, and assembly of consumer electronic products. The United States has a comparative advantage in technology-intensive products, such as microprocessors, computer software, pharmaceuticals, medical diagnostic equipment, and management consulting services.

The term comparative advantage refers to the relative efficiencies of producing different products. However, so long as exchange rates are well behaved (they do not deviate far from their purchasing power parity levels), then comparative advantage should be translated into competitive advantage.

The role of resource availability in determining comparative advantage among countries is evident in the pattern of international trade. The advanced industrialized nations tend to be net importers of labor-intensive products and products requiring low levels of technical and scientific skills (typically products in the mature phases of their life cycles). The principal exports of the advanced countries are products whose production is capital and technology-intensive and services that require sophisticated human skills (consulting, information, medical, and financial services). Table 14.1 shows revealed comparative advantage, as revealed by trade performance, for several product groups and several countries. Positive values show comparative advantage, negative values show comparative disadvantage. Thus, Japan has a strong

TABLE 14.1
Indexes of Revealed Comparative Advantage for Certain Broad Product Categories

	USA	CANADA	GERMANY	ITALY	JAPAN
Food, drink, and tobacco	.31	.28	−.36	−.29	−.85
Raw materials	.43	.51	−.55	−.30	−.88
Oil and refined products	−.64	.34	−.72	−.74	−.99
Chemicals	.42	−.16	.20	−.06	−.58
Machinery and transportation equipment	.12	−.19	.34	.22	.80
Other manufacturing	−.68	−.07	.01	.29	.40

Note: Revealed comparative advantage for each product group is measured as: (Exports less Imports)/Domestic Production.

Source: OECD.

comparative advantage in machinery and transportation equipment, and a strong disadvantage in oil and refined products.

Conventionally, the theory of comparative advantage has focused on natural resource endowments, population, and the capital stock. However, empirical research points to the critical role played by cultural, religious, and social factors, and "home grown" resources such as technology, human capital, management capabilities, and infrastructure (e.g., transportation and communications facilities, and the legal system).[2] The remarkable advances in competitiveness and real incomes of South Korea, Taiwan, Hong Kong, Malaysia, and Singapore are especially interesting. Despite enormous differences in political conditions and industrial structure, these countries have limited natural resources, heavy investments in education, and a strong Confucian influence in common. Conversely, a central issue in the current debate over U.S. educational policy is whether the level and the quality of public investment in education is consistent with the maintenance of America's international position as a high-wage, high-skill economy at the forefront of innovation.[3]

Government influences comparative advantage through its policies and provision of infrastructure. Contrast the economic and comercial success of colonial Hong Kong with its laissez-faire government, rule of law, and efficient communication and transportation infrastructure with the impact of public policies on industrial and commercial development in the Soviet Union and much of Africa.

The size of a country's domestic market influences comparative advantage in industries where the minimum efficient size of operation is large or where demand is so segmented that a large total market is required for niches to be of a viable size.[4] Size of home market has been a traditional advantage for U.S. firms and has been a key motivation for the creation of free trade areas such as the European Union, Mercosur, and NAFTA.

Porter's *Competitive Advantage of Nations*

In a major study of the pattern and determinants of comparative advantage among 13 industrialized nations, Michael Porter offers an important extension of our understanding of the impact of national conditions on firms' competitive advantage.[5] Porter's analysis is built on three principles:

1. The competitive performance of a country depends on the performance of the firms within it. However, the national environment exerts a powerful influence on the performance of the firm: it provides the home base within which firms develop their identity, resources and capabilities, and critical managerial behaviors.[6]

2. For a country to sustain a competitive advantage in a sector over time requires *dynamic* advantage: its firms must broaden and extend the basis of their competitive advantage by innovation and upgrading their resources and capabilities. Thus, Japanese success in automobiles reflects their companies' ability to continuously advance the basis of their competitive advantage. By contrast, Britain's failure across many manufacturing sectors displays a tendency for firms to attain positions of competitive advantage but to allow that advantage to atrophy through a lack of continuous innovation and upgrading.

3. The impact of the national environment on firms' competitive performance is less about national resource availability and more about the *dynamic conditions* that influence innovation and the upgrading.

Porter's analysis of how national conditions influence firms' competitive advantage in internationally competing industries is summarized in his national diamond framework (see Figure 14.3).[7]

Factor Conditions.   Whereas the conventional advantage of comparative analysis focuses on endowments of broad categories of resource, Porter's analysis emphasizes, first, "home grown" resources and, second, the role of highly specialized resources. For

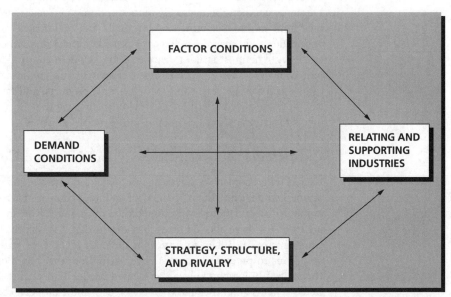

FIGURE 14.3
Porter's National Diamond Framework

example, in analyzing Hollywood's preeminence in film production, Porter points to the local concentration of skilled labor, including the roles of UCLA and USC schools of film. Also, resource constraints may encourage the development of substitute capabilities: in Japan, lack of raw materials has spurred miniaturization and low-defect manufacturing; in Italy, restrictive labor laws have stimulated automation.

Related and Supporting Industries.   For many industries, a critical resource is the presence of related and supporting industries. One of the most striking of Porter's empirical findings is that national competitive strengths tend to be associated with "clusters" of industries. One such cluster is U.S. strength in semiconductors, computers, and computer software. For each of these industries, critical resources are the other related industries. In Germany, a mutually supporting cluster exists around chemicals, synthetic dyes, textiles, and textile machinery.

Demand Conditions.   Demand conditions in the domestic market provide the primary driver of innovation and quality improvement. For example:

♦ The preeminence of Swiss and Belgian chocolate makers may be attributed to their highly discerning domestic customers.

♦ The dominance of the world market for cameras by Japanese companies owes much to Japanese enthusiasm for amateur photography and their eager adoption of innovation in cameras.

♦ The success in high-performance cars of German companies (Mercedes, BMW, Porsche), compared to their much weaker position in mass-produced autos, may be linked to Germans' love of quality engineering and their irrepressible urge to drive on autobahns at terrifying speeds.

Strategy, Structure, and Rivalry.   National competitive performance in particular sectors is inevitably related to the strategies and structures of firms in those industries. Porter puts particular emphasis on the role of competition between domestic companies in driving innovation and the upgrading of competitive advantage. Domestic competition is usually more direct and personal than that between companies from different countries. As a result, the maintenance of strong competition within domestic markets is likely to provide a powerful stimulus to innovation and efficiency. The most striking feature of the Japanese auto industry is the presence of nine companies, all of which compete fiercely within the domestic market. The same can be said for cameras, consumer electronic products, and facsimile machines. This lack of domestic competition may help explain why the efforts of European governments to create "national champions" in so many industries has been so unsuccessful.[8]

Consistency Between Strategy and National Conditions

Establishing competitive advantage in global industries requires congruence between business strategy and the pattern of the country's comparative advantage. For example, in the British cutlery industry, competition from South Korean manufacturers benefiting from low wage and low steel costs means that it was virtually impossible for companies such as J. Billam to survive in the mass market for stainless steel cutlery. The only firms to prosper, or even survive, were those that relied on technology (such as Richardson in kitchen knives), or focused on the high-quality silverware segment. In stereo systems and other audio products, U.S. and European companies (such as Bose and Bang & Olufsen) have survived by focusing on skill-intensive and design-intensive products; Sony, Matsushita, and other Japanese producers compete on the basis of product innovation and highly automated assembly; the low end of the market (e.g., retailers' own brands) is supplied by companies in Thailand, Malaysia, and Korea.

The linkage between the firm's competitive advantage and its national environment is not a simple one of consistency between the strategy pursued and resources and capabilities available within the national economy. It also relates to the development of the firm's organizational capabilities. The firm's development of its internal capabilities is closely linked to the characteristics of the culture and social structure of the country in which these capabilities are being developed. The capabilities of Japanese companies in integrating diverse technologies into innovative new products (electronic musical instruments, color copying machines) and in quality enhancement through continuous improvement, owes much to Japanese traditions of assimilating outside ideas and cooperative behavior. Similarly, the excellence of U.S. firms in financial management and pioneering new industries through entrepreneurship may link with U.S. traditions of individualism and materialism. Thus, the design of long-term strategies that simultaneously develop market positions and organizational capabilities need to recognize the potential for harnessing national characteristics. It could be argued that a common characteristic of outstandingly successful companies in different countries: Exxon, Coca-Cola, and GE in the United States, News Corporation in Australia, Ericsson in Sweden, Armani and ENI in Italy, has been these companies' ability to link their capabilities with key national characteristics.

APPLYING THE FRAMEWORK: INTERNATIONAL LOCATION OF PRODUCTION

To examine the role of firm resources and country resources in international strategy decisions, we look at two types of decisions that face internationalizing companies: first, the decision of where to locate their production activities and, second, the decision of how to enter a foreign market.

So far, our discussion of the linkage between the competitive advantage of the firm and its national environment has assumed, implicitly, that each firm is based within its home country. In fact, a primary motivation of multinational strategies is to access the resources and capabilities available in other countries. Whether a firm markets its product in many countries or only in its domestic market, it must decide where it is to produce it. Some firms market globally but concentrate production in their home country (Honda, Toyota, and Matsushita were like this for most of the 1970s; Boeing and Rolls Royce are like it today). Other multinationals, especially in service industries, establish stand-alone country subsidiaries, where each country unit produces for its own national market. Such companies have been called "multidomestic" corporations (examples include the tobacco company BAT and French water and utilities company Generale des Eaux). Other companies have geographically dispersed locations where each location plays a specialized role within a global network.

Determinants of Geographical Location

The decision of where to manufacture requires consideration of three sets of factors:

1. **National resource conditions.** Where national resource conditions exert a dominant influence on a firm's competitive advantage, it must locate where national resource conditions are favorable. For Nike and Reebok, low labor

costs are of prime importance in shoe assembly, hence, these companies locate where labor costs are low: China, Thailand, India, and the Philippines. Similarly, most of the world's leading producers of computers and telecommunications equipment have established R&D facilities in the United States (commonly in California's Silicon Valley) in order to exploit U.S. microelectronics expertise. In the German automobile industry, high labor costs have encouraged the relocation of assembly elsewhere. BMW and Mercedes-Benz have built plants in the United States; VW has moved production to Central and Eastern Europe (see Table 14.2).

2. **Firm-specific competitive advantages.** For firms whose competitive advantage is based on internal resources and capabilities, location depends on where those resources and capabilities can best be deployed. The competitive advantages of Toyota, Nissan, and Honda rest primarily on their own technical, manufacturing, and product development capabilities. Traditionally, these companies concentrated production within Japan where they could exploit scale economies. During the 1980s, they demonstrated the ability to transfer these competitive advantages to overseas locations.

3. **Tradability issues.** The ability to locate production away from markets depends on transportability. High transportation costs may necessitate local production, and differences in national customer preferences may encourage local production. Production close to the market may also result from governments' import restrictions as a means of forcing global corporations to establish manufacturing operations in local markets.

Location and the Value Chain

Location decisions must take account of the fact that the production of any good or service is composed of a vertical chain of activities and the input requirements of

TABLE 14.2
Hourly Compensation (in U.S. Dollars) for Motor Vehicle Workers (Including Benefits)

	1975	1981	1984	1986	1988	1990	1991	1993
United States	9.55	17.03	19.02	20.09	20.80	22.48	24.21	26.40
Mexico	2.94	5.27	2.55	2.03	1.96	2.79	3.33	4.35
Brazil	1.29	2.53	1.79	—	—	—	—	—
Japan	3.56	7.61	7.90	11.80	16.36	15.77	18.15	23.92
Korea	0.45	1.33	1.74	1.84	3.20	5.78	6.42	7.55
Taiwan	0.64	1.86	2.09	2.23	3.50	4.76	5.72	6.64
France	5.10	9.11	8.20	11.06	13.54	15.94	15.89	16.77
Germany	7.89	3.34	11.92	16.96	23.05	27.58	28.65	33.41
Italy	5.16	8.21	8.00	11.03	14.51	17.97	19.10	16.66
Spain	—	7.03	5.35	7.74	10.85	15.00	15.93	15.83
UK	4.12	8.10	7.44	9.22	11.95	13.87	13.84	14.70

Source: U.S. Department of Labor.

each varying considerably. The result is that different countries are likely to offer differential advantage at each stage of the value chain. International trade patterns show a clear trend toward specialization, not only in specific products but in specific stages of production. Table 14.3 offers two examples.

In electronic products such as televisions and computers, the production of components is capital and research intensive and subject to substantial scale economies. Component production is thus concentrated in the more advanced industrialized countries, traditionally in the United States and Japan, increasingly in Taiwan, Korea, and Malaysia. Assembly is more labor-intensive and is concentrated in the industrializing economies of Asia and Latin America.

A similar pattern exists in textiles and apparel. Fiber production is concentrated in the countries with comparative advantage in agricultural production (for cotton and

TABLE 14.3
Comparative Advantage in Textiles and Consumer Electronics by Stage of Processing

INDUSTRY	COUNTRY	STAGE OF PROCESSING	INDEX OF REVEALED COMPARATIVE ADVANTAGE
Textiles and Apparel	Hong Kong	1	−0.96
		2	−0.81
		3	−0.41
		4	+0.75
	Italy	1	−0.54
		2	+0.18
		3	+0.14
		4	+0.72
	Japan	1	−0.36
		2	+0.48
		3	+0.78
		4	−0.48
	U.S.A.	1	+0.96
		2	+0.64
		3	+0.22
		4	−0.73
Consumer Electronic Products	Brazil	1	−0.62
		2	+0.55
	Hong Kong	1	−0.41
		2	+0.28
	Japan	1	+0.53
		2	+0.97
	S. Korea	1	−0.01
		2	+0.73
	U.S.A.	1	+0.02
		2	−0.65

Notes: Revealed comparative advantage is measured as: (Exports − Imports)/(Exports + Imports). For Textiles and Apparel, the stages of processing are: 1. fiber (natural and manmade) 2. spun yarn 3. textiles 4. apparel. For consumer electronics, the stages of processing are: 1. components 2. finished products.

Source: United Nations.

wool) and chemical production (for synthetic fibers). Spinning yarn and weaving cloth tend to be capital-intensive and occur both in the newly industrialized and mature countries. Clothing is labor-intensive—here the developing countries have a clear comparative advantage. Hence, a key aspect of globalization is for companies to examine their value chains to determine the optimal location for individual activities.

Identifying the Optimal Location for Each Individual Activity.   To determine the best location for each activity, the firm needs to identify the principal inputs into each stage and then match these to the costs and availability of these inputs in different countries. Nike is a classic example of a company exploiting national comparative advantages at each stage of its value chain: its R&D and design are located within the U.S.; the production of fabric, rubber, and plastic shoe components in Korea, Taiwan, and China; assembly in India, China, the Philippines, Thailand, and other low-wage locations; marketing and distribution in the United States, Europe, and other affluent countries.[9] The costs of different locations may be strongly influenced by government subsidies and tax breaks. Also, location decisions must also take account of a firm's existing geographical spread of production facilities: although Germany is a high-cost manufacturing base for VW, this is where it has its major investments in plant and human capital, and where it has benefited from economies of learning.

Linkages Between Activities.   The benefits derived from breaking the value chain and locating individual activities in different countries must be traded off against the costs of weaker linkages between stages in the chain. Transportation costs are one consideration. Another is increased inventory costs. Where learning curves are steep, the time costs of shipping components can be great: semiconductors can lose 5 percent of their value while being shipped from Asia to the United States. Just-in-time scheduling has increased the attraction of geographically concentrated component manufacture and assembly. As Table 14.4 shows, the labor cost advantages of producing cars for the U.S. market in Mexico are offset by the costs of importing components, shipping finished cars, and increased inventory. Dispersed activities also means increased problems of coordination and control. The importance of close linkages through geographical proximity depends on the strategy of the company. Dell Computer, with its emphasis on fast delivery and customizing to meet customer specifications, must manufacture close to its markets. Packard Bell, competing on low prices, offers a narrow product range, assembled in Southeast Asia.

Figure 14.4 summarizes the relevant criteria in location decisions.

TABLE 14.4
The Cost of Producing a Compact Automobile, U.S. and Mexico, 1992

	U.S. ($)	MEXICO ($)
Parts and components	7,750	8,000
Labor	700	140
Shipping costs	300	1,000
Inventory	20	40
Total	8,770	9,180

Source: U.S. Office of Technology Assessment, October 1992.

FIGURE 14.4
International Location of Industrial Activities within the Value Chain

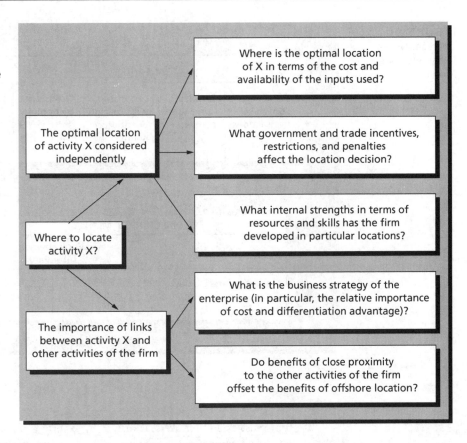

APPLYING THE FRAMEWORK: FOREIGN ENTRY STRATEGIES

Many of the considerations relevant to locating production activities also apply to choosing the mode of foreign market entry. A firm enters an overseas market because it believes that it will be profitable. This assumes not only that the overseas market is attractive—that its structure is conducive to profitability—but also that the firm can establish a competitive advantage vis-à-vis local producers and other multinational corporations (MNCs). We discussed the analysis of industry and market profitability in Chapters 3 and 4. Our focus here is on how the firm can best establish competitive advantage in a foreign market.

In exploiting an overseas market opportunity, a firm has a range of options with regard to mode of entry. These correspond closely to the firm's strategic alternatives with regard to exploiting innovation (see Chapter 11). The basic distinction is between market entry by means of *transactions* and market entry by means of *direct investment.* Figure 14.5 shows a spectrum of market exploitation options arranged according to the degree of commitment by the firm. Thus, at one extreme there is exporting through individual spot-market transactions; at the other, there is the establishment of a fully owned subsidiary that undertakes a full range of functions.

How does a firm weigh the merits of different market entry modes? Among the critical considerations are the following:

1. **Is the firm's competitive advantage based on firm-specific or country-specific resources?** If the firm's competitive advantage is country-based, then the

FIGURE 14.5
Overseas Market
Entry: Alternative
Modes

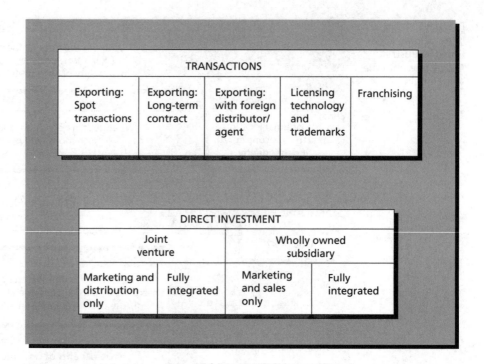

firm must exploit an overseas market by exporting. Thus, to the extent that Hyundai's competitive advantage in the U.S. car market is its low Korean wage rates, it must produce in Korea and export to the United States. If Toyota's competitive advantage is company-specific, then assuming that advantage is transferable within the company, Toyota can exploit the U.S. market either by exports or by direct investment in U.S. production facilities.[10]

2. **Is the product tradable and what are the barriers to trade?** If the product is not tradable because of transportation costs or import restrictions, then accessing that market requires entry either by investing in overseas production facilities or by licensing the use of key resources to local companies within the overseas market.

3. **Does the firm possess the full range of resources and capabilities for establishing a competitive advantage in the overseas market?** Competing in an overseas market is likely to require that the firm acquire additional resources and capabilities, particularly those related to marketing and distributing in an unfamiliar market. Accessing such country-specific resources is most easily achieved by establishing a relationship with firms in the overseas market. The form of relationship depends, in part, on the resources and capabilities required. If a firm needs marketing and distribution, then it might appoint a distributor or agent with exclusive territorial rights. If a wide range of manufacturing and marketing capabilities is needed, the firm might license its product and/or its technology to a local manufacturer. In technology-based industries, firms frequently exploit their innovations internationally by licensing their technology to local companies. In marketing-intensive industries, firms may offer their brands to local companies

through trademark licensing. Alternatively, a joint venture might be sought with a local manufacturing company. The difficulties that U.S. companies faced when entering the Japanese market encouraged many to form joint ventures with local companies (e.g., Fuji-Xerox, Caterpillar-Mitsubishi). Typically, such joint ventures combined the technology and brand names of the overseas partner with the local market knowledge and manufacturing and distribution facilities of the local partner.

4. **Are the firm's resources appropriable?** Whether a firm licenses the use of its proprietary resources or chooses to exploit them directly (either through exporting or direct investment) depends partly on appropriability considerations. In chemicals and pharmaceuticals, the patents protecting product innovations tend to offer strong legal protection, in which case patent licenses to local producers can be an effective means of appropriating their returns. In computer software and computer equipment, the protection offered by patents and copyrights is looser, which encourages exporting rather than licensing as a means of exploiting overseas markets. With all licensing arrangements, key considerations are the capabilities and reliability of the local licensee. This is particularly important in licensing brand names where the licenser must carefully protect the brand's reputation. Thus, Cadbury-Schweppes licenses to Hershey the trademarks and product recipes for its Cadbury's range of chocolate bars for sale in the United States. This arrangement reflects the fact that Hershey has production and distribution facilities in the U.S. that Cadbury cannot match, and that Cadbury views Hershey as a reliable business partner. The need to exert close control over the use of one's trademarks, technologies, and trade secrets is reflected in the design of **franchising** systems. These involve licensing of trademarks and technology in a fully packaged business system. In service industries, notably fast-food restaurants, franchising is the most common internationalization strategy.

5. **What transactions costs are involved?** A key issue that arises in the licensing of a firm's trademarks or technology concerns the **transactions costs** of negotiating, monitoring, and enforcing the terms of such agreements as compared with internationalization through a fully owned subsidiary. It is notable that McDonald's first outlets in the United Kingdom were directly managed rather than franchised. The primary reason was that given British traditions of poor service and indifferent cuisine, direct management avoided the difficulties of monitoring and guiding British franchisees. Issues of transactions costs are fundamental to the choices between alternative market entry modes. Barriers to exporting in the form of transport fees and tariffs are forms of transactions costs; other costs include exchange rate risk and information costs. Transactions cost analysis has been central to theories of the existence of multinational corporations. In the absence of transactions costs in the markets either for goods or for resources, companies exploit overseas markets either by exporting their goods and services or by selling the use of their resources to local firms in the overseas markets.[11] Thus, multinationals tend to predominate in industries where:

- ♦ Firm-specific intangible resources such as brands and technology are important (transactions costs in licensing the use of these resources favor direct investment)

♦ Exporting is subject to transactions costs in product markets
♦ Customer preferences are reasonably similar between countries.

Strategy Alternatives for Overseas Production

This analysis has examined alternative strategies for exploring overseas *market* opportunities. The same type of analysis can be performed by analyzing overseas *production* opportunities. A firm can access the resources and capabilities available for producing in an overseas country either by *transactions* (e.g., importing) or by *direct investment*. Thus, Exxon accesses the crude oil production of the North Sea both by importing oil purchased on long-term contracts with Statoil, BP, and other producers, and on spot-contracts through the London and Rotterdam oil markets. At the same time, Exxon also has production facilities in the North Sea—some of which are wholly owned, and some of which are joint ventures with Shell and other companies. Nike's production of shoes in Asia is entirely through long-term contacts with local production companies. Multinational companies have traditionally been interested in overseas production for two main reasons: to access raw materials and cheap labor and to provide local production to overseas markets. Increasingly, however, direct investment by multinational firms is driven not only by the quest for overseas markets, raw materials, and lower-cost labor, but also by the desire to access technology. Kenichi Ohmae's view that multinational firms need to be based in all three of the world's leading industrial centers—North America, Japan, and Europe—in order to be "where the action is" is supported by evidence from Paul Almeida that, within the semiconductor industry at least, a key role of the foreign subsidiaries of multinational corporations is gaining access to locally available technological knowledge.[12]

International Alliances and Joint Ventures

During the last decade and a half, one of the most striking features of the development of international business has been the upsurge in the numbers of joint ventures and other forms of strategic alliance across national borders. Consider for example the U.S. and Japanese automobile companies: despite the intense competition between them—which extends from the marketplace into government policies and international relations—there has been a remarkable growth in collaborative arrangements between them (see Figure 14.6).

Interfirm, cross-border collaboration is scarcely a new phenomenon. The Royal Dutch/Shell Group, a joint venture between Royal Dutch Petroleum and Shell Transport and Trading, dates from the turn of the century. Recent years have seen international collaboration extend to many industries, with automobiles, information technology, communications, pharmaceuticals, and aerospace in the forefront. In many developing and emerging market countries, joint ventures are a consequence of government policy: host governments require foreign multinationals to take a local partner. The more usual rationale is the desire of companies in different countries to access a complementary set of resources and capabilities. The key is not simply the firm's inability to develop the needed resources and capabilities internally, but the time it takes to do so. America Online could have expanded into Europe on its own, but its alliance with Bertelsmann permitted more rapid market penetration. Similarly, alliances and joint ventures between Xerox and Fuji, Chrysler and Mitsubishi, and Walt Disney and the Oriental Land Company facilitated the U.S. companies' entry into the Japanese market. The success of international joint ventures and other forms of strategic alliance has been mixed. There are plenty of examples of international joint ventures that have been spec-

FIGURE 14.6
Allliances and
Joint Ventures:
U.S. & Japanese
Auto Producers

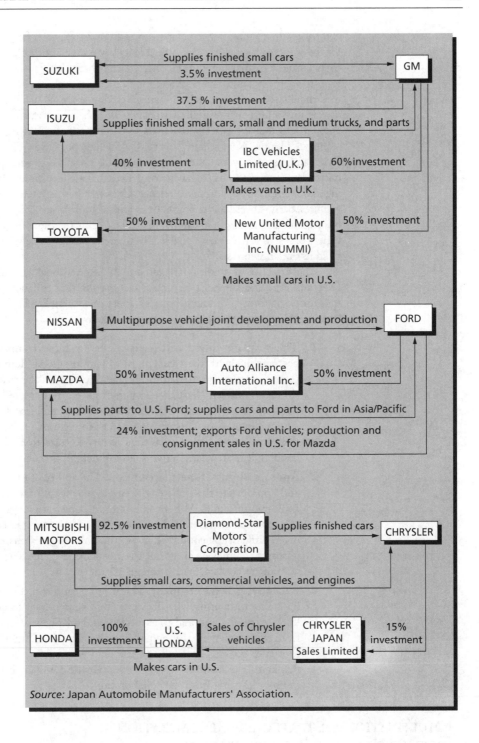

Source: Japan Automobile Manufacturers' Association.

tacular failures. Joint ventures that share management responsibility are far more likely to fail than those with a dominant parent or with independent management.[13] The greatest problems arise between firms that are also competitors—reconciling cooperation with competition requires a tolerance for ambiguity that is unusual among North American companies. In alliances between Japanese and Western firms, a frequent pattern has been for the Western partner to make available its key resources of technology or distribution to its Japanese partner in return for short-term benefits, only to see its Japanese collaborator reemerge as a resurgent competitor.[14] Such experiences point to Japanese companies' more systematic approach to managing complex relationships, which involve both competitive and cooperative dimensions. In the U.S. auto parts industry, 126 companies entered into joint ventures with Japanese parts suppliers in order to supply the U.S. plants of Honda, Nissan, and Toyota. Conflicting objectives, divergent management styles, and disputes over quality and labor practices resulted in widespread failure.[15] The critical issues appear to be (1) having objectives that are realistic and explicit and (2) having a willingness to learn from experience. Corning Glass, a veteran of international joint ventures, derives over half its profits from joint ventures. Sun Microsystems has built its business on alliances with a variety of partners. Texas Instruments' joint ventures with a variety of Asian partners have enabled TI to invest heavily in new fabrication plants and build its presence in Asia.[16]

The effective strategic management of international alliances, argue Hamel, Doz, and Prahalad, depends on a clear recognition that collaboration is competition in a different form.[17] Though both partners must benefit if the alliance is to continue, sharing benefits depends on three key factors:

1. **The strategic intent of the partners.** Japanese companies have entered partnerships with the clear intent of gaining global dominance, and in this respect strategic partnerships are just one step on the road to global expansion. By contrast, Western companies have often entered partnerships with the goal of giving up manufacturing to more efficient Japanese producers. The willingness of Western companies to yield major items of value-added to former competitors limits their ability to learn from their partners and is likely to lead to a cumulative abandonment of activities and capabilities.

2. **Appropriability of the contribution.** The ability of each partner to capture and appropriate the skills of the other depends on the nature of each firm's skills and resources. Where skills and resources are tangible or explicit, they can easily be acquired. Where they are tacit and people-embodied, they are more difficult to acquire. To avoid the unintended transfer of know-how to partners, Hamel et al. argue the need for a "gatekeeper" to monitor and administer contacts with strategic partners.

3. **Receptivity of the company.** The more receptive a company is in terms of its ability to identify what it wants from the partner, to obtain the required knowledge or skills, and to assimilate and adapt them, the more it will gain from the partnership. In management terms, this requires the setting of performance goals of what the partnership is to achieve for the company and managing the relationship to ensure that the company is deriving the maximum of learning from the collaboration.

MULTINATIONAL STRATEGIES: GLOBALIZATION VERSUS NATIONAL DIFFERENTIATION

So far, we have viewed international expansion, whether by export or by direct investment, as a means by which a company can exploit its competitive advantages not just in its home market but in foreign markets too. However, there is more to internationalization than simply extending the geographical boundaries of a company's market. International scope may also be a source of competitive advantage over nationally based competitors. In this section, we explore whether, and under what conditions, firms that operate on an international basis, either by exporting or by direct investment, are able to gain a competitive advantage over nationally focused firms. If such "global strategies" have potential for creating competitive advantage, in what types of industry are they likely to be most effective? And how should they be designed and deployed in order to maximize their potential?

The Benefits of a Global Strategy

A global strategy is one that views the world as a single, if segmented, market. Theodore Levitt of Harvard Business School has argued that companies that compete on a national basis are highly vulnerable to companies that compete on a global basis.[18] The superiority of global strategies rests on two assumptions:

- *Globalization of customer preferences*. National and regional preferences are disappearing in the face of the homogenizing forces of technology, communication, and travel. "Everywhere everything gets more and more like everything else as the world's preference structure is relentlessly homogenized," observes Levitt. Nor is this trend restricted to technology-based products such as pharmaceuticals, aircraft, and computers; it is just as prevalent in branded consumer goods such as Coca-Cola, Ralph Lauren menswear, and McDonald's hamburgers.

- *Scale economies*. Firms that produce standardized products for the global market can access scale economies in product development, manufacturing, and marketing that offer efficiency advantages that nationally based competitors cannot match. In automobiles, consumer electronics, investment banking, and many other industries, domestic firms have increasingly lost ground to global competitors.

Pursuing a global strategy does not necessarily imply that a company becomes multinational: indeed, maximizing the benefits of scale economies favors geographically concentrated production and serving world markets through exporting. This was the traditional strategy of Japanese companies in motorcycles, consumer electronics, and office equipment during the 1960s and early 1970s. Conversely, many European and American multinational corporations (MNCs) used **multidomestic** rather than global strategies: each country was served by a fairly autonomous national subsidiary that managed a full range of functional activities. For example, until the late 1970s, General Motors' overseas subsidiaries (Opel in Germany, Vauxhall in Britain, and Holden in Australia) produced their own range of models under their own brand names for their own domestic markets. The advantage of this strategy is that it permitted flexibility in relation to local conditions, particularly in allowing differentiation on the basis of local preferences, while avoiding the administrative complexities associated with centralized control from a remote corporate head office.

Levitt's thesis is not that customers are the same the world over—national and regional differences in customer preferences do exist. However, underlying national differences is a commonality of people's goals. When presented with a choice between a lower-priced, globally standardized product and a higher-priced, nationally differentiated alternative, most customers favor the former.

Levitt's globalization thesis is a subject of continuing controversy. Critics have attacked his assumptions concerning the homogenization of national preferences and the extent of scale economies. National differences in customer preferences continue to exert a powerful influence on the markets for packaged groceries, recorded music, drinks, clothing, and furniture. Also, costs of national differentiation can be surprisingly low if common basic designs and common major components are used. Flexible manufacturing systems have reduced the costs of customizing products to meet the preferences of particular customer groups.

Domestic appliances provide an especially interesting test of the globalization hypothesis. Levitt used the European market for washing machines to illustrate his argument concerning the benefits of global over national strategies. Hoover, which designed its washing machines to meet the requirements of each national market, lost market share to the Italian manufacturers that produced large volumes of standardized washing machines for the European market as a whole. Subsequent analysis has shown that national preferences have remained remarkably durable: French washing machines are primarily top-loading, elsewhere in Europe machines are mainly front-loading, the Germans prefer higher spin speeds than the Italians, U.S. machines feature agitators rather than revolving drums, and Japanese machines are small. As a result, some nationally focused players such as Hotpoint in the UK have been more profitable than the pioneers of globalization, Electrolux and Whirlpool.[19] National market differences are especially important for products and services supplied to governments and public agencies. As Volker Jung, a director of Siemens, noted, "All politics are local politics. Politicians will always find a way not to buy non-local products."[20]

Most products and services combine global commonalities with national distinctiveness. Even the exemplars of globalization engage in national differentiation: McDonald's offers teriyaki chicken burgers in Japan, pizzas in some parts of the United States, and beer in Germany; Coca-Cola's Hi-C soy milk is popular in Southeast Asia and its Georgia coffee drink is consumed mainly in Japan. The key to successful globalization lies in ensuring uniformity in components and activities where important scale economies are present, while catering to cultural and language differences that do not impede scale efficiency. Thus, the 1998 Honda Accord is global car, but one whose dimensions, accessories, trim, and paintwork are adapted to meet different national preferences.

Strategic Strength from Global Positioning

The competitive advantage from a global approach to manufacturing, marketing, and distribution extends beyond the cost advantages from scale economies. Even in the absence of cost advantages from global scales of operation, there are clear strategic advantages from an international scope. Because the global competitor faces different competitive conditions in different countries, it can use its strength in some national markets to leverage its position in others. Such leveraging requires cross-subsidization: using the cash flow from countries where market position is strong to finance competition against nationally focused competitors in other markets. While the classic form of cross-subsidization—predatory pricing—is likely to contravene both GATT antidumping rules and national antitrust laws, cross-subsidization also occurs through heavy advertising, sales promotion, and dealer support.[21]

Faced with aggressive competition from the local subsidiary of a foreign MNC, the domestic competitor is in a weak position: it has no overseas revenues to finance aggressive competition in its home market. Such was the position U.S. television manufacturers faced against strong Japanese competition in the 1970s. The most effective response to competition in one's home market may be to retaliate in the foreign MNC's own home market. Thus, when Kodak was attacked by Fuji in the U.S. market—an attack that was symbolized by Fuji's sponsorship of the 1984 Olympic Games in Los Angeles—Kodak responded by attacking Fuji in Japan.[22] To effectively exploit such opportunities for national leveraging, some overall global coordination of competitive strategies in individual national markets is required. This has implications for the strategic role of corporate headquarters in coordinating national strategies.

MNCs are increasingly recognizing the advantages of strong market positions in the world's largest economies. During the 1980s, European and Japanese companies scrambled to establish positions within the United States. Companies such as British Petroleum, Siemens, Thomson, Sony, ICI, and Unilever all made large U.S. acquisitions, while Japanese banks and auto companies tended to build U.S. subsidiaries from scratch. Similarly, a number of newly globalizing U.S. companies (including banks and computer companies) have established strong footings in Europe and East Asia. The head of McKinsey and Company's Tokyo office, Kenichi Ohmae, argues the case for *Triad Power*. His thesis is that pressures of technological change, convergence of customer preferences, scale economies, and protectionism require successful world players to become true insiders within the *three* major markets of the world: the United States, Europe, and Japan.[23]

Strategy and Organization within the Multinational Corporation

The Evolution of Multinational Strategies and Structures

Balancing the benefits of globalization against those of adaptation to national market conditions is a central issue not only for the strategy of multinational firms but also for their organizational structures. As we have already observed, strategy and structure are not easily changed in the short or medium term and the strategy-structure configurations adopted by today's MNCs tend to reflect the choices made by the companies at the time of their international expansion. Because of their size and international spread, MNCs are likely to find fundamental changes in their organizational structure especially difficult: once an international distribution of functions, operations, and decision-making authority has been determined, reorganization can be difficult and costly, particularly when host governments become involved. The result is that early choices with regard to strategy and structure have a lasting impact on the development of organizational capability. Bartlett and Ghoshal identify three phases in the development of MNCs, each associated with a different choice with regard to globalization/centralization versus national differentiation/decentralization. The allocation of decision making between the parent company and overseas subsidiaries associated with each phase is shown in Figure 14.7.

Pre–Second World War: The Era of the European Multinationals.   During the early decades of the twentieth century, European multinationals—companies such as Unilever, Royal Dutch/Shell, ICI, Philips, and Courtaulds—were

FIGURE 14.7
The Development of
the Multinational
Corporation

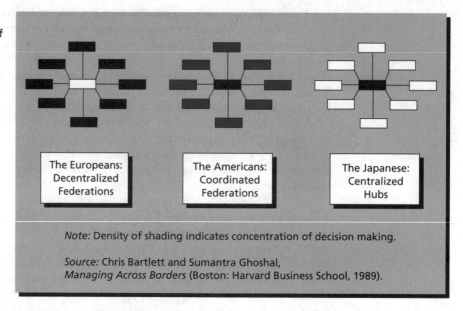

The Europeans:
Decentralized
Federations

The Americans:
Coordinated
Federations

The Japanese:
Centralized
Hubs

Note: Density of shading indicates concentration of decision making.

Source: Chris Bartlett and Sumantra Ghoshal,
Managing Across Borders (Boston: Harvard Business School, 1989).

pioneers of international development. These companies have been described by
Bartlett and Ghoshal as "multinational federations": each national subsidiary was
permitted a high degree of operational independence from the parent company,
undertaking its own product development, manufacturing, and marketing.[24] The
"hands-off" approach of the corporate head office to its overseas subsidiaries was a
response to conditions at the time of internationalization: international transportation and communication were slow, costly, and unreliable, and national markets were
highly differentiated. Parent company control of the subsidiary involved the
appointment of senior managers to subsidiaries, the authorization of major capital
expenditures, and the flow of dividends from subsidiary to parent.

Post–Second World War: The Era of the American Multinationals.   The
emergence of the United States as the world's dominant industrial nation at the end
of the Second World War was followed by two decades during which companies
such as GM, Ford, IBM, Coca-Cola, Caterpillar, Gillette, and Procter & Gamble
became clear international leaders in their respective industries. Although the subsidiaries of these U.S. multinationals typically operated with a high degree of autonomy in terms of product introduction, manufacturing, and marketing, the U.S.
parent companies occupied a dominant position within the groups. Because the
United States was the largest and most affluent market in the world, the U.S. base
acted as the source of new products and process technology for the company. The
primary competitive advantage of overseas national subsidiaries was their ability to
utilize new products, process technology, and marketing and manufacturing know-
how developed in the United States.

The 1970s and 1980s: The Japanese Challenge.   During the 1970s, Japanese companies emerged as leading global players across a number of manufactur-

ing industries from steel and shipbuilding to electronics and automobiles. A distinguishing feature of the Japanese multinationals was their pursuit of global strategies from centralized domestic bases. Companies like Honda, Toyota, Matsushita, and NEC concentrated R&D and manufacturing in Japan, while overseas subsidiaries were initially for sales, distribution, and customer support. By building plants of unprecedented scale to service growing world demand, Japanese companies were able to exploit substantial scale and experience advantages.

Matching Global Strategies and Structures to Industry Conditions

Although global preeminence in manufacturing industries passed from the European to American to Japanese companies between 1920 and 1980, it is not possible to point to any particular strategy/structure combination as uniquely successful for MNCs. The strength of European multinationals is their adaptation to the conditions and requirements of individual national markets. The strength of the U.S. multinationals is their ability to transfer technology and proven new products from their domestic strongholds to their national subsidiaries. That of the Japanese global corporations is the efficiency advantages derived from global integration.

The relative merits of each configuration depend on market and competitive conditions—and hence the key success factors—in different industries. In semiconductors, electronics, and motorcycles, the importance of scale economies and the lack of national differences in customer requirements underscore the benefits of global strategies and structures. Where scale economies are more modest relative to the size of national markets and where national market differences are important—such as processed foods, recorded music, beer, children's clothing, and furniture—responsiveness to national customer preferences takes precedence. In a number of industries, there are considerable benefits from global integration, and also the need to respond to differentiated national requirements. Capital and technology intensive products (such as telecommunications equipment, military hardware, and power generating equipment) supplied to public authorities in different countries are typical examples. Exhibit 14.1 shows how different strategy/structure configurations have had different success in three different industry environments.

Emergence of the "Transnational Corporation"

During the 1990s, multinational firms have tried to reconcile the scale economies of global integration with the differentiation benefits of national adaptation. Increased competitive pressure has pushed companies accross all industries toward achieving cost-efficiency through the global integration of manufacturing and technology development. At the same time, the resilience of national market differences and the need for swift response to local circumstances has required greater decentralization. Accelerating technological change further exacerbates these contradictory forces: despite the cost and "critical mass" benefits of centralizing research and new product development, innovation occurs at multiple locations within the MNC and requires nurturing of creativity and initiative throughout the organization. A key tradeoff is the decentralization conducive to *generating innovation*, and the global centralization conducive to efficiency and effectiveness in *exploiting innovation*. Thus, Philips, with its decentralized, nationally responsive organization structure, has been extremely successful in encouraging companywide innovation. In its TV business, its Canadian subsidiary developed its first color TV, its Australian subsidiary developed its first stereo sound TV, and its British

EXHIBIT 14.1

Matching Multinational Strategy to Industry Characteristics

Consumer Electronics

During the 1980s Matsushita was highly globally integrated, Philips was the most multinational in terms of international spread and responsiveness of national subsidiaries to local requirements, whereas GE was primarily U.S.-based and oriented toward the requirements of the North American market. During the 1980s, customer preferences for consumer electronic products were highly uniform across countries, and competitive advantage was strongly determined by the ability of companies to access global economies in product development and manufacturing, and coordinate the global marketing of new products and new models. By the end of the 1980s, Matsushita was the clear winner, Philips was still hanging on (despite dismal profitability), and GE had exited from the industry.

Branded, Packaged Consumer Goods

In branded, packaged consumer goods, national differences remained strong during the 1980s. Unilever, with its locally responsive multinational spread, and Procter & Gamble, despite its strong U.S. and European bases, increased their global leadership. Meanwhile, Kao, the leading Japanese soaps and personal hygiene products supplier, largely failed in its attempts to penetrate international markets.

Telecommunications Equipment

In contrast to electronics and branded, packaged consumer goods, telecommunications equipment is subject to substantial global scale economies in R&D and manufacturing, *and* requires responsiveness to the specific requirements of national telecommunication companies. ITT, the most international of the major players, was increasingly unable to achieve the integration necessary to leverage its global position. NEC, despite its technological capabilities and dominant position in Japan, has so far failed to develop a strong position in Europe or North America. One of the most successful companies has been Ericsson, which, despite its small domestic market, has effectively combined global integration with national responsiveness.

Source: Chris Bartlett and Sumantra Ghoshal, *Managing Across Borders* (Boston: Harvard Business School, 1989).

subsidiary developed teletext TVs. However, lack of global integration has constrained its ability to successfully exploit its innovation on a global scale. Ever since its V2000 VCR system lost out to Matsushita's VHS system, Philips has been on the losing side of a number of battles over technical standards (including its digital audio tape).

Developing the organizational capability to pursue both responsiveness to national markets and global coordination simultaneously requires, according to Christopher Bartlett, "a very different kind of internal management process than existed in the relatively simple multinational or global organizations. This is the "transnational organization."[25] The distinguishing characteristic of the **transnational** is that it becomes an integrated network of distributed and interdependent resources and capabilities (see Figure 14.8). Features of the transnational corporation include:

♦ Each national unit is a source of ideas, skills, and capabilities that can be harnessed for the benefit of the total organization.

♦ National units achieve global scale economies by designating them the company's world source for a particular product, component, or activity.

♦ The center must establish a new, highly complex managing role that coordinates relationships among units but does so in a highly flexible way. The key is to focus less on managing activities directly and more on creating an organizational context that is conducive to the coordination and the resolution of differences. Creating the right organizational context involves "establishing clear corporate objectives, developing managers with broadly based perspectives and relationships, and fostering supportive organizational norms and values."[26]

The transnational form is more of a direction of development than a clear organizational form. It represents a convergence of the different strategy configurations of MNCs. Thus, traditional "decentralized federations" such as Philips and Royal Dutch/Shell have reorganized to achieve greater integration within their far-flung empires of national subsidiaries, whereas Japanese global corporations such as Toyota and Matsushita are drastically reducing the role of their Japanese headquarters and increasing the roles of their national subsidiaries. Meanwhile, American multinationals such as Ford and GM are moving in two directions: while they reduce the role of their U.S. bases they are simultaneously increasing integration among their different national subsidiaries. Exhibit 14.2 discusses the move toward the integrated, global network form at Ford and Unilever.

FIGURE 14.8
The Transnational Corporation: Reconciling Global Integration with Local Responsiveness

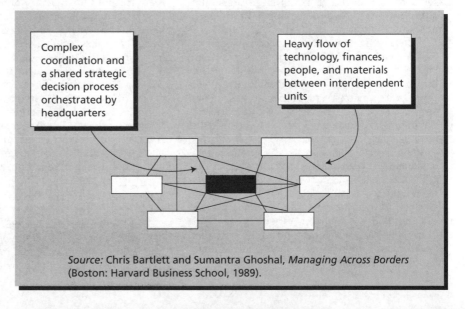

Complex coordination and a shared strategic decision process orchestrated by headquarters

Heavy flow of technology, finances, people, and materials between interdependent units

Source: Chris Bartlett and Sumantra Ghoshal, *Managing Across Borders* (Boston: Harvard Business School, 1989).

EXHIBIT 14.2

Building the Transnational Corporation: Unilever and Ford

Unilever

Unilever was formed in 1930 from the merger of the Dutch company, Margerine Unie, and the British soap company, Lever Brothers. Over the following seven decades, the company evolved through a process of trial-and-error into a global food, cleaning products, and toiletries group. A key aspect of this evolution has been the changing relationship between the parent company and the national subsidiaries. During the 1940s and 1950s, each national subsidiary became locally managed with a high degree of autonomy. This decentralization was balanced by heavy investment in management education and development designed not only to train managers, but also to create a common culture. In 1955, the Four Acres management training center near London was opened. Unilever seeks the best and brightest university graduates who are trained in groups of 25 to 30 for similar managerial positions. This shared experience creates an informal network of equals who continue to meet and exchange information and ideas across different companies and countries. Coherence and coordination is further enhanced by an extensive system of attachments whereby a manager is placed for a short or long period of time at the head office or in another subsidiary. These cross-postings help build managers' worldwide informal networks, and establish unity and a common sense of purpose across national cultures. Managers' personal networks are an important mechanism for the transfer of ideas.

Unilever is organized primarily on a geographical basis with subsidiaries in each country responsible for a particular business. Thus, in Britain, Lever Brothers Ltd. supplies soaps and household detergents, Walls Ice Cream Ltd. supplies ice cream, and Birds Eye Foods Ltd. produces and distributes frozen foods. In addition there are worldwide product groups. Thus, food products are divided into five strategic groups: edible fats, ice cream, beverages, meals and meal components, and professional markets. The balance between centralized requirements and local adaptability varies by function and product. Thus, in the food category there are *global fast-foods* (hamburgers, fried chicken, soft drinks), *international foods* (Indian, Chinese, and Italian foods sold in many national markets), and *national foods* (steak and kidney pies in Britain).

According to CEO Floris Maljers, flexibility in a matrix organization is essential for it to operate as a transnational: "I like to use an analogy with a dance called the quadrille. This is an old-fashioned dance in which four people change places regularly. This is also how a good matrix should work, with sometimes the regional partner, sometimes the product partner, sometimes the functional partner, and sometimes the labor-relations partner taking the lead. Flexibility rather than hierarchy should always be a transnational's motto—today and in the future."

Ford

In 1970, Ford was an archetypal U.S. multinational with a dominant North American core and more-or-less stand-alone subsidiaries in Britain, Germany, Australia and elsewhere, each of which designed, manufactured, and marketed its own line of autos. For example, in Britain, Ford's most popular car was the British-made *Cortina*, in Germany it was the German-built *Taunus*.

The quest for scale economies in engineering and design and component manufacture encouraged increasing international integration. This began with the formation of Ford of Europe, and continued with the consolidation and integration of new product development and manufacturing. Small car design was located primarily in Ford of Europe and in Mazda in Japan; large car design was centered in Dearborn. Ford's smallest car, the *Festiva/Fiesta* is manufactured in South Korea and Spain; its *Escort* is manufactured in Michigan, Mexico, Britain, and Germany; the Mercury *Capri* is made in Australia. Similar global specialization occurred in engines and other major subassemblies.

Under Chairman Alex Trotman, the *Ford 2000* initiative aimed at greatly increasing the extent of international integration. The *Mondeo/Contour* was Ford's first serious attempt at developing a world car. The primary challenge of *Ford 2000* was to develop global models of automobile faster and at a much lower cost than the $6 billion that the *Mondeo/Contour* had cost.

Sources: Floris A. Maljers, "Inside Unilever: The Evolving Transnational Company," *Harvard Business Review* (September–October 1992): 46–51. Maryann Keller, *Collision: GM, Toyota, Volkswagen and the Race to Own the 21st Century* (New York: Doubleday, 1993); Ford Motor Company Annual Reports.

◆ SUMMARY

Internationalization of the business environment creates opportunities and threats for business enterprises. The most serious implications are for companies used to the predictable and muted competition in domestic markets sheltered from the full blast of international rivalry. The competitive pressures being felt by European airlines such as Air France and Alitalia, medium-sized European automakers such as Renault and Peugeot-Citroën, British investment banks, and Japanese rice producers are just a few examples.

One of the difficulties that managers face in coming to grips with the threats and opportunities of the global business environment is the quantum leap in complexity caused by the transition from a national to an international environment. The contribution of this chapter is applying the fundamental concepts of strategy and extending the basic frameworks of strategy analysis to enable us to deal with the complexity of international business. We have shown how the internationalization of business affects a firm's prospects for profitability both through influencing industry structure and by changing the conditions for competitive advantage. With regard to competitive advantage, a critical issue is the influence of national conditions on a firm's potential for competitive advantage. The analysis of competitive advantage is critically important to success in internationally competing industries. Because internationalization increases the intensity and diversity of competition, achieving competitive advantage is critical to success. And because internationalization greatly widens firms' opportunity sets, the potential for competitive advantage becomes the primary guideline for focusing a firm's strategy.

Internationalization imposes increased demands on firms' resources and capabilities while also giving firms access to a wider range of resources and capabilities. As a result, companies often pursue different strategies overseas than in their home markets. International expansion has involved companies in exporting, direct investment, licensing, joint ventures, and collaborative alliances in order to take advantage of international opportunities. The strategy chosen depends on the resources and capabilities that underlie a firm's competitive advantage in relation to those required to exploit the particular opportunity.

In the same way that competitive advantage is more complex in an international context, so too are the means of implementing international strategies. Reconciling the efficiency advantages of international operations with the need to adapt to different market conditions in different countries is a particularly difficult challenge. Traditional matrix structures involving geographical, functional and product-based organization are giving way to new and more sophisticated organizational structures and management systems. Such changes also have important implications for the skills and expertise of managers. An increasingly common feature of large U.S. corporations is the tendency for top management positions to be occupied by executives with substantial experience in overseas subsidiaries.

NOTES

1 During the 1930s, Standard Oil of New Jersey (now Exxon) and the Royal Dutch/Shell Group effectively regulated competition in the international oil industry. The world cigarette industry for much of the twentieth century was neatly divided between American Tobacco and the Imperial Tobacco Group of Britain. American Tobacco agreed not to compete within the British Empire, Imperial agreed to keep outside the Americas, while

exports to other countries were handled by a jointly owned subsidiary British-American Tobacco (BAT). See M. Corina, *Trust in Tobacco* (London: Michael Joseph, 1975).

2 A key finding was that *human capital* (knowledge and skills) was more important than *physical capital* in explaining the pattern of U.S. trade—the so-called *Leontief Paradox*. See W. W. Leontief, "Domestic Production and Foreign Trade," in *Readings in International Economics,* ed. Richard Caves and H. Johnson (Homewood, IL: Irwin, 1968).

3 M. Dertouzos, Richard Lester, Robert Solow, and the MIT Commission on Industrial Productivity, *Made in America: Regaining the Productive Edge* (Cambridge: MIT Press, 1989).

4 Paul Krugman, "Increasing Returns, Monopolistic Competition, and International Trade," *Journal of International Economics* 9 (November 1979): 469–479.

5 Michael E. Porter, *The Competitive Advantage of Nations* (New York: Free Press, 1990).

6 Porter's view differs sharply from those observers who point to the emergence of the "stateless corporation" (ABB's Percy Barnevik among them). Although the national market is comparatively unimportant to a number of MNCs (ABB, Nestlé, Royal Dutch/ Shell Group, Philips, and Hoffman-La Roche), that is not to say that their capabilities, strategy, and management style are not influenced by their national home base. See "The Stateless Corporation," *Business Week,* May 14, 1990: 98–106.

7 For a review of the Porter analysis, see Robert M. Grant, "Porter's *Competitive Advantage of Nations:* An Assessment," *Strategic Management Journal* 12 (1991): 535–548.

8 This analysis also suggests that measures to support local industries through subsidies, currency devaluation, or import protection, to the extent that they reduce competitive pressure, may discourage efficiency, innovation and quality upgrading.

9 *Nike: International Context,* HBS Case Services, Harvard Business School, Boston, 1985, Case 9-385-328; and *Nike in China,* HBS Case Services, Harvard Business School, Boston, 1985, Case 9-386-037.

10 The role of firm-specific assets in explaining the multinational expansion is analyzed in Richard Caves, "International Corporations: The Industrial Economics of Foreign Investment," *Economica* 38 (1971): 1–27.

11 The role of transactions cost is explained in D. J. Teece, "Transactions Cost Economics and Multinational Enterprise," *Journal of Economic Behavior and Organization* 7 (1986): 21–45. See also "Creatures of Imperfection," in "Multinationals: A Survey," *Economist,* March 27, 1993: 8–10.

12 Kenichi Ohmae, *Triad Power: The Coming Shape of Global Competition* (New York: Free Press, 1985); Paul Almeida, "Knowledge Sourcing by Foreign Multinationals: Patent Citation Analysis in the U.S. Semiconductor Industry," *Strategic Management Journal* 17, Special Issue (Winter 1996): 155–165.

13 J. Peter Killing, "How to Make a Global Joint Venture Work," *Harvard Business Review* (May–June 1982): 120–127.

14 See Robert Reich and Eric Mankin, "Joint Ventures with Japan Give Away Our Future," *Harvard Business Review* (March–April, 1986).

15 "When U.S. Joint Ventures with Japan Go Sour," *Business Week,* July 24, 1989.

16 Texas Instruments, *Annual Report, 1996.*

17 Gary Hamel, Yves Doz, C. K. Prahalad, "Collaborate with Your Competitors—and Win," *Harvard Business Review* (January–February 1989): 133–139.

18 Theodore Levitt, "The Globalization of Markets," *Harvard Business Review* (May–June, 1983): 92–102.

19 Charles Baden Fuller and John Stopford, "Globalization Frustrated," *Strategic Management Journal* 12 (1991): 493–507.

20 "Footloose Across Europe's Frontiers," *Financial Times,* March 9, 1993: 15.

21 Gary Hamel and C. K. Prahalad, "Do You Really Have a Global Strategy?" *Harvard Business Review* (July–August 1985): 139–148.

22 R. C. Christopher, *Second to None: American Companies in Japan* (New York: Crown, 1986).

23 Kenichi Ohmae, *Triad Power: The Coming Shape of Global Competition* (New York: Free Press, 1985).

24 Christopher Bartlett and Sumantra Ghoshal, *Managing Across Borders: The Transnational Solution* (Boston: Harvard Business School Press, 1989).

25 Christopher Bartlett, "Building and Managing the Transnational: The New Organizational Challenge," in *Competition in Global Industries,* ed. Michael E. Porter (Boston: Harvard Business School Press, 1986): 377.

26 *Ibid.:* 388.

15
Diversification Strategy

We will have our usual array of Berkshire products at the meeting and this year will add a sales representative from GEICO [Berkshire Hathaway's insurance subsidiary]. At the 1995 meeting, we sold 747 pounds of candy, 759 pairs of shoes, and over $17,500 of Word Books. In a move that might have been dangerous had our stock been weak, we added knives last year from our Quikut subsidiary and sold 400 sets of these. (We draw the line at soft fruit however.) All these goods will again be available this year.

—*Warren Buffett, Invitation to Berkshire Hathaway's 1996 Shareholders' Meeting.*

Outline

◆ INTRODUCTION AND OBJECTIVES

Decisions over which businesses the firm is to operate in are some of the most fundamental strategy decisions. They are guided by the firm's mission statement.

Xerox's definition of itself as "The Document Company," Eastman Kodak's identity as a "picture company," and AT&T's as "the world's networking leader," provide a context and boundaries that guide choices over which businesses the companies will participate in. Ideas about a company's identity may change radically over time. Exxon has gone from being a petroleum and chemical company in the 1960s, to a "broad-based energy and technology company" in the early 1980s, only to refocus on oil, gas, and chemicals in the 1990s. Microsoft began as a supplier of microcomputer operating software, expanded into application and networking software, and is now emerging as broad-based supplier of software, information services, and entertainment. Other companies have moved in the opposite direction. ITT, a leading conglomerate of the 1970s, split into separate hotel, insurance, and automotive companies in 1994. AT&T spun off its NCR and Lucent Technologies businesses in 1995–96.

At first glance, diversification decisions appear impossibly complex. How does Richard Branson decide whether his Virgin Group should supply passenger train services and life insurance? How can Westinghouse Electrical weigh the merits of transforming itself from a manufacturer of turbines and power equipment into a TV and radio broadcaster?

In practice, we make these types of decisions every day in our personal lives. If my car doesn't start in the morning, should I try to fix it myself or have it towed directly to the garage? There are two considerations. First, is repairing a car an attractive activity to undertake? If the garage charges $50 an hour, but I can earn over $200 an hour consulting, then car repair is not attractive to me. Second, am I any good at car repair? If I am likely to take twice as long as a skilled mechanic, then I possess no competitive advantage in car repair.

Diversification decisions by firms involve the same two issues:

♦ How attractive is the industry to be entered?
♦ Can the firm establish a competitive advantage within the new industry?

These are the very same factors we identified in Chapter 1 (see Figure 1.3) as determining a firm's profit potential. Hence, no new analytic framework is needed for appraising diversification decisions: diversification may be justified either by the superior profit potential of the industry to be entered, or by the ability of the firm to create competitive advantage in the new industry. The first issue draws on the industry analysis developed in Chapter 3; the second draws on the analysis of competitive advantage developed in Chapters 5 through 8.

Our primary focus is on the latter question: under what conditions does operating multiple businesses assist a firm in gaining a competitive advantage in each? This leads into exploring linkages between different businesses within the diversified firm—what has often been referred to as "synergy."

By the time you have completed this chapter, you will be able to:

♦ Discuss the factors that have caused past and current trends in diversification and "refocusing"
♦ Identify the conditions under which diversification creates value for shareholders
♦ Evaluate the potential for synergy among businesses by sharing and transferring resources and capabilities within the diversified firm

♦ Appraise the conditions that determine whether diversification or inter-firm collaboration is more effective in exploiting synergies across different businesses

♦ Recognize the organizational and managerial issues that diversification gives rise to and why diversification so often fails to realize its anticipated benefits.

TRENDS IN DIVERSIFICATION OVER TIME

As a background to our analysis of diversification decisions, let's begin by examining the factors which have influenced diversification strategies in the past.

Postwar Diversification

Since the early nineteenth century, large companies have expanded their scope across geographical areas, across the value chain, and across products. During the twentieth century, especially during the first three decades after World War II, diversification—the expansion of companies across different product markets—was the most prominent source of corporate growth. The diversification patterns of large U.S. corporations have been carefully documented by Alfred Chandler.[1] Systematic evidence of diversification by the *Fortune* 500 during the postwar period has been provided by Wrigley[2] and Rumelt.[3] Over time, the number of single business companies among the ranks of the *Fortune* 500 fell steadily, whereas the most diversified companies—both related business and unrelated business—increased in number (see Table 15.1). Similar trends are apparent among large companies in other industrialized nations (see Tables 15.2 and 15.3). The 1960s and 1970s saw the height of the diversification boom with the emergence of conglomerates such as ITT and Allied-Signal in the United States and Slater-Walker and BTR in the UK, and a rush by mature industrial corporations to diversify by acquisition.

Factors Driving Diversification

The diversification trend that lasted into the mid-1970s was a consequence of several factors. Chapter 13 pointed to the developments in management techniques and organizational forms that reduced the costs of internal administration compared to the transactions costs of markets. Foremost among these developments was the multidivisional structure, which allowed companies to add divisions without overloading corporate management. During the 1950s and 1960s, multidivisional structures spread rapidly across North America and Europe, assisted by the efforts of McKinsey and Company and other management consultants in reorganizing large corporations. The rapid advancement of the "science of management" propagated the view that the essence of management was not the deployment of industry-specific, experiential knowledge, but the application of the tools and principles of general management. The universality of the principles of management implied that professional managers could run widely diversified corporations through the application of a common set of financial controls, capital appraisal systems, human resource management policies, and decision rules. The development of the concepts and techniques of corporate strategy during the late 1960s and early 1970s added further weight to the view that professional managers were not constrained by

	1949 %	1954 %	1959 %	1964 %	1969 %	1974 %
Single Business Companies	42.0	34.1	22.8	21.5	14.8	14.4
Vertically Integrated Companies	12.8	12.2	12.5	14.0	12.3	12.4
Dominant Business Companies	15.4	17.4	18.4	18.4	12.8	10.2
Related-Business Companies	25.7	31.6	38.6	37.3	44.4	42.3
Unrelated-Business Companies	4.1	4.7	7.3	8.7	18.7	20.7
	100.0	100.0	100.0	100.0	100.0	100.0

Note: Single business companies have more than 95% of their sales within their main business. Vertically integrated companies have more than 70% of their sales in vertically related businesses. Dominant-business companies have between 70% and 95% of their sales within their main business. Related-business companies have more than 70% of their sales in businesses which are related to one another. Unrelated-business companies have less than 70% of their sales in related businesses.

Source: Richard Rumelt, "Diversification strategy and profitability," *Strategic Management Journal*, 3 (1982): 359–370.

industry boundaries. The simple logic that had driven opportunistic growth of conglomerates was refined into a more sophisticated analysis of corporate strategy decisions concerning industry choice and competitive positioning. Portfolio planning techniques provided top management with a general framework to view their different businesses, providing what Goold and Luchs call a "helicopter view" of the company.[4] (We discuss these portfolio techniques in Chapter 16.) The result was a standardized basis on which to make diversification and divestment decisions, allocate resources, and establish strategies for individual businesses.

Motivational factors were also important. From the 1950s into the early 1980s, large corporations in North America, Europe, and Japan were driven more by a quest for growth than by the desire to maximize profitability. In the benign economic environment of the 1950s and 1960s, earning returns in excess of cost of capital was easy and shareholders were quiescent. Under these circumstances, many corporate CEOs became rampant empire-builders, using diversification and acquisition as their favored strategic weapons.

Refocusing During the 1980s and 1990s

The past two decades have seen a sharp reversal in the trend toward diversification. In Britain, companies that had diversified most extensively during previous years became less diversified during the late 1970s and early 1980s.[5] Between 1980 and 1990, the average index of diversification for the *Fortune* 500 declined from 1.00 to 0.67.[6] Among U.S. companies, unprofitable diversified businesses were increasingly being divested during the later 1980s, and a number of diversified companies fell prey to leveraged buyouts.[7] Despite the fact that acquisition activity was extremely heavy during the 1980s—some $1.3 trillion in assets were

TABLE 15.2
Changes in the Diversity of the 305 Largest British Manufacturing Companies, 1960–1980

	1960 %	1970 %	1975 %	1980 %
Single Business Companies	34.2	14.5	12.5	9.5
Vertically Integrated Companies	2.0	3.3	3.4	3.0
Dominant Business Companies	23.5	26.0	21.6	24.7
Related-Business Companies	32.0	44.4	49.0	49.7
Unrelated-Business Companies	7.4	11.8	13.5	13.2
	100.0	100.0	100.0	100.0

Source: Azar P. Jammine, *Product Diversification, International Expansion and Performance: A Study of Strategic Risk Management in U.K. Manufacturing*, Ph.D. dissertation, London Business School (1984): 215.

acquired, including 113 members of the *Fortune* 500—only 4.5 percent of acquisitions during the 1980s represented unrelated diversification.[8] Moreover acquisitions by the *Fortune* 500 were outnumbered by dispositions. One study of acquisitions and divestitures by large, diversified, U.S. corporations found that the dominant trend was the divestiture of unrelated businesses and a restructuring around fewer, more closely related businesses.[9]

Factors That Cause Refocusing

Increased industrial specialization by companies is the result of three principal factors: management's emphasis on shareholder value rather than growth, increased turbulence in the business environment, and new ideas about corporate strategy and the nature of the firm.

Emphasis on Shareholder Value. The forces driving companies' refocusing on core businesses were reviewed in Chapter 13. The overwhelmingly important

TABLE 15.3
Diversification Among 118 Large Japanese Industrial Corporations, 1958–1973

	1958 %	1963 %	1968 %	1973 %
Single Business Companies	26.3	24.6	19.5	16.9
Vertically Integrated Companies	13.2	15.3	18.6	18.6
Dominant Business Companies	21.0	16.9	18.7	17.8
Related-Business Companies	30.7	35.6	36.4	39.8
Unrelated-Business Companies	8.8	7.6	6.8	6.8
	100.0	100.0	100.0	100.0

Source: H. Itami, T. Kagono, H. Yoshihara, and A. Sakuma, "Diversification Strategies and Economic Performance," *Japanese Economic Studies*, 11, no. 1 (1982): 78–110.

factor driving the retreat from diversification was the reordering of corporate goals from growth to profitability. The new emphasis on profitability was the result of several factors. The economic downturns and interest-rate spikes of the mid-1970s, the early 1980s, and 1989–1990, revealed the inadequate profitability of many large, diversified corporations. A second factor was increased pressure on incumbent management from shareholders and financial markets. Shareholder activism has been led by institutional shareholders, especially by pension funds such as California's Public Employees Retirement System. The result of such pressure has been to increase the influence of independent members of boards of directors and to unseat incumbent management. The increasing insecurity of top management positions is indicated by the ousting of a number of CEOs during the early 1990s. These included Robert Stempel at General Motors, James Robinson at American Express, Ken Olsen at Digital Equipment, and John Akers at IBM.[10]

The surge in leveraged buyouts during the 1980s was a key ingredient in a more active market for corporate control. Where an incumbent management team had destroyed shareholder value, corporate raiders saw the opportunity to use debt financing to mount a takeover bid, and then to oust existing management in favor of a team that would embark on aggressive restructuring. Kohlberg Kravis Roberts' $25 billion takeover of the tobacco and food giant RJR Nabisco in 1989 is the most famous of these leveraged buyouts.[11] The RJR Nabisco buyout demonstrated that even the largest U.S. corporations were not safe from acquisition. Other large tobacco companies faced similar threats: Philip Morris and BAT Industries have both been pressured to separate their core tobacco businesses from their diversified businesses. Corporate management teams have been judged increasingly by the extent to which they have increased stock market valuation. In the case of diversification, the results are salutary. Not only do companies tend to earn lower rates of return in their diversified businesses than in their core businesses, but diversifying acquisitions have destroyed value—principally because the acquisition premiums paid have exceeded any increase in the profitability of the acquired companies.

Turbulence and Transactions Costs.   The increased turbulence of the business environment may also have caused large, diversified corporations to be less efficient as mechanisms for allocating resources than specialized companies coordinated by financial and labor markets. Dynamic market conditions expose the sluggishness of the complex corporate planning and capital budgeting systems of diversified corporations, and overload the decision-making capacity of corporate top management. As a result, the performance of diversified corporations appears to have deteriorated compared to more specialized companies. The shifting balance between the relative efficiencies of large diversified corporations and specialized companies accessing resources through factor markets may also have been influenced by the increasing efficiencies of the markets for finance and labor. The spin-offs of Zeneca pharmaceuticals by ICI; NCR and Lucent Technologies by AT&T; Millenium Chemicals, Imperial Tobacco, and Energy Corporation by Hanson; and ITT Industries and Hartford Insurance by ITT Corporation were influenced, in part, by the belief that these companies could better exploit their growth opportunities by drawing directly on external markets for finance, human resources, and technology.

The "back to basics" trend is certainly strong in North America and Western Europe, but is less evident elsewhere in the world. In East Asia, there is no apparent divestment trend among large diversified corporations. A handful of *chaebols*—Samsung, Daewoo, Hyundai, and Goldstar—continue to dominate the South Korean business sector, while in Southeast Asia sprawling conglomerates such as Charoen Pokphand of Thailand, Lippo of Indonesia, and Keppel Group of Singapore have increased their prominence.[12] These geographical differences may be partly explained by transactions costs: outside the United States and Western Europe, markets for financial, information, and labor are less efficient, offering internalization advantages to diversified companies.

Trends in Management Thinking.   New ideas about corporate strategy have also influenced patterns of corporate evolution. There is less confidence over the applicability of a common set of management principles and techniques to many different business, and greater emphasis has been given to the role of resources and capabilities as the basis of the competitive advantage. This encourages firms to focus on their major strengths in resources and capabilities and avoid the risks of spreading themselves too thinly. If deploying core resources and capabilities requires diversification into new product markets, this is more likely to occur through collaborative arrangements with other companies rather than through internal diversification or outright acquisition.

This is not to imply that ideas concerning synergies from operating in multiple product markets are dead. Indeed, the 1990s have seen continuing interest in economies of scope and the transferability of resources and capabilities across industry boundaries. The major change is that strategic analysis has become much more precise about the circumstances in which diversification can create value from multibusiness activity. Mere linkages between businesses are not enough: the key to creating value is the ability of the diversified firm to share resources and transfer capabilities more efficiently than alternative institutional arrangements, where the additional costs of management do not outweigh the value created. Figure 15.1 summarizes some of the key developments in diversification strategy over the past 40 years.

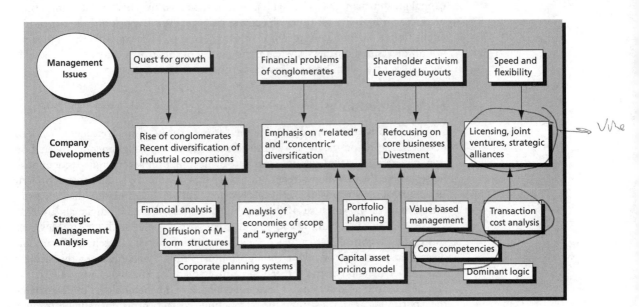

FIGURE 15.1
The Evolution of Management Thinking on Corporate Strategy and Diversification

MOTIVES FOR DIVERSIFICATION

Diversification strategies tend to be driven by three major goals: growth, risk reduction, and profitability. As we shall see, although growth and risk reduction have been prominent motives for diversification, they tend to be inconsistent with the creation of shareholder value.

Growth

We noted that an important factor in the reversal of the postwar diversification trend was a reordering of corporate objectives. To the extent that managers pursue their own individual interests and are motivated by financial gain, status, security, and power, there are good reasons to expect that they will pursue *growth* at the expense of profitability. Evidence shows that top management's salaries and prestige are correlated with corporate size rather than corporate profitability. Robin Marris' theory of managerial capitalism assumes that managers' growth preferences encourage the firm to invest at a greater rate than is consistent with profit maximization, causing valuation ratios to decline to just short of the point where the firm becomes vulnerable to acquisition.[13]

For firms in declining industries, managers' aversion to contraction provides particularly pressing motives for diversification. Thus, the diversification by tobacco companies and oil companies during the 1970s and 1980s was driven by declining sales in domestic markets, although most of the diversification went into less profitable industries and had the effect of destroying shareholder value.[14] The propensity for managers to pursue their own goals rather than those of company owners is one aspect of the **agency problem:** the problem faced by a *principal* (in this case, the owners of a firm) ensuring that his *agent* (in this case, the top management team) operates in his interests.

Top management's ability to pursue objectives other than profitability is constrained by at least two factors. First, over the long term a firm must earn a return on capital greater than its cost of capital or it does not survive. Second, if management sacrifices profitability for other objectives, managers run the risk of losing their jobs either from a shareholders' revolt or from acquisition. This explains why companies sell off diversified businesses when their control of the firm is threatened by a takeover bid or by a fall in profitability that attracts potential predators.[15]

Risk Reduction

A second motive for diversification is the desire to spread risks. To isolate the effects of diversification on risk it is useful to consider "pure" or "conglomerate" diversification: diversification that extends corporate ownership over several independent businesses where the cash flow stream of each separate businesses is unchanged. So long as the cash flow streams of the businesses are imperfectly correlated, then diversification reduces the variance of the combined cash flow. Since individuals are risk-averse, such risk reduction would be consistent with shareholder interests. However, this ignores a critical factor: to achieve diversification of risk, shareholders can hold diversified portfolios or invest through mutual funds. Not only does this achieve wider diversification than even the most diversified corporations can attain, it can also be achieved at lower cost. The transactions costs to shareholders of diversifying their portfolios are far less than the transactions costs to firms diversifying through acquisition. Not only do acquiring firms incur the heavy costs of using investment banks and legal advisers, they must also pay an acquisition premium in order to gain control of an independent company.

The **capital asset pricing model** (CAPM) formalizes this argument. The theory postulates that the risk that is relevant to determining the price of a security is not the overall risk (variance) of the security's return, but **systematic risk**: that part of the variance of the return that is correlated with overall market risk. Systematic risk is measured by the security's **beta coefficient**. Corporate diversification does not reduce systematic risk: if three separate companies are brought under common ownership, in the absence of any other changes, the beta coefficient of the combined company is simply the weighted average of the beta coefficients of the constituent companies. Hence, the simple act of bringing different businesses under common ownership does not create shareholder value through risk reduction.[16]

Empirical studies are generally supportive of the absence of shareholder benefit from diversification that simply combines independent businesses. Studies of conglomerates in the United States have shown that their risk-adjusted returns to shareholders are typically no better than those offered by mutual funds or by matched portfolios of specialized companies.[17] Another study found that unrelated diversification failed to lower either systematic or unsystematic risk, though moderate, closely related diversification did reduce both.[18]

If risk reduction from diversification is to create shareholder value, there must be imperfections in the securities markets that make corporate diversification more efficient or feasible than "homemade" portfolio diversification by investors. For example, if individuals are unable to purchase the securities of companies in Russia or China, multinational diversification by Western companies may offer benefits of global risk-spreading that investors cannot access individually.

All this has been from the viewpoint of the owners of the firms. Let us consider the benefits of risk-spreading available to other stakeholders in the firm. If cyclicality in the firm's profits is accompanied by cyclicality in employment, then so long as employees are transferable between the separate businesses of the firm, there may be benefits to employees from diversification's ability to smooth output fluctuations. Managers appear to be especially enthusiastic about the risk-spreading benefits of diversification. Managers' risk aversity is motivated by their desire to protect their independence and their jobs. Downturns in profit, even if only temporary, can stimulate concern among shareholders and stock analysts. Downturns may make the company temporarily dependent on financial markets for borrowing and may encourage takeover bids.

Special issues arise once we consider the risk of bankruptcy. For a marginally profitable firm, diversification can help avoid cyclical fluctuations of profits that can push it into insolvency. It has been shown, however, that diversification that reduces the risk of bankruptcy is beneficial to the holders of corporate debt rather than to equity holders. The reduction in risk that bondholders derive from a diversifying merger is the **coinsurance effect**.[19] Managers and other employees are also likely to have strong interests in any strategy that reduces the risk of bankruptcy.

Are there circumstances where reductions in unsystematic risk can create shareholder value? If there are economies to the firm from financing investments internally rather than resorting to external capital markets, then the stability in the firm's cash flow which results from diversification may reinforce independence from external capital markets. Among the major oil companies (Exxon, Shell, Mobil, BP), one of the benefits of extending across upstream (explorations and production), downstream (refining and marketing), and chemicals is that the negative correlation of the returns from these businesses increases the overall stability of the companies' cash flows. This in turn increases their capacity to undertake huge risky investments such as offshore oil production, transcontinental pipelines, and natural gas liquefaction plants.

Profitability

If we return to the assumption that corporate strategy should be directed toward the interests of shareholders, what are the implications for diversification strategy? We have already revisited our two sources of superior profitability: industry attractiveness and competitive advantage. For firms contemplating diversification, Michael Porter proposes three "essential tests" to be applied in deciding whether diversification will truly create shareholder value:

1. *The attractiveness test.* The industries chosen for diversification must be structurally attractive or capable of being made attractive.

2. *The cost-of-entry test.* The cost of entry must not capitalize all the future profits.

3. *The better-off test.* Either the new unit must gain competitive advantage from its link with the corporation, or vice versa.[20]

The Attractiveness and Cost-of-Entry Tests. A critical realization in Porter's "essential tests" is that industry **attractiveness** is insufficient on its own. Although diversification is a means by which the firm can access more attractive investment opportunities than are available in its own industry, it faces the problem of entering the new industry. The second test, **cost of entry,** explicitly recognizes that the attractiveness of an industry to a firm already established in an industry may be different from its attractiveness to a firm seeking to enter the industry. Indeed, many industries offer above-average profitability precisely because they are protected by barriers to entry. Firms entering attractive industries such as pharmaceuticals, management consulting, or investment banking face a difficult dilemma. On the one hand they may enter by acquiring an established player, in which case not only does market price of the target firm reflect the superior profit prospects of the industry, but the diversifying firm must also offer an acquisition premium of between 20 and 40 percent over the market price to gain control. The history of diversification is littered with companies that overpaid in order to gain a position in a seemingly attractive industry.[21] If, on the other hand, diversifying firms enter by creating new corporate ventures, then they must directly confront the barriers of that industry. This involves high risk and low returns over a long period: a study of 68 diversifying ventures by established companies found that, on average, break-even was not attained until the seventh and eighth years of operation.[22]

The "Better-Off" Test. Porter's third criterion for successful diversification—the **better-off** test—addresses the basic issue of competitive advantage: if two businesses producing different products are brought together under the ownership and control of a single enterprise, is there any reason why they should become any more profitable? Diversification has the potential to enhance the competitive advantage of the diversified business, the original core business, or both businesses.

In the case of Sony's acquisition of Universal Studios/Columbia Pictures, Morgan Stanley's acquisition of Dean Witter Discover, or Gillette's purchase of Duracell, the gains to both acquirer and acquiree were anticipated as a result of the potential for enhancing competitive advantage. However, though the opportunities for value creation from exploiting synergies between different businesses are many, the practical difficulties of exploiting such opportunities have made diversification a corporate minefield. Let us examine the issues systematically.

COMPETITIVE ADVANTAGE FROM DIVERSIFICATION

If the primary source of value creation from diversification is exploiting linkages between different businesses, what are the linkages and how are they exploited? Here we explore market power, economies of scope, and transactions costs as sources of value from diversification, and look at the role of the diversified firm in exploiting them.

Market Power

One of the issues that has occupied antitrust authorities in the United States and Europe is whether diversification can enhance profitability, not by increasing efficiency, but by creating market power. It has been claimed that large diversified companies could exercise market power through three mechanisms:

1. **Predatory pricing.** Just as global corporations derive strength from their ability to finance competitive battles in individual markets through cross-subsidization, so conglomerates can similarly use size and diversity to discipline or even drive out specialized competitors in particular product markets. The key competitive weapon is predatory pricing—the ability to cut prices below the level of rivals' costs and sustain losses over the period needed to cause the competitor to exit or sell out.

2. **Reciprocal buying.** A diversified company can leverage its market share across its businesses by reciprocal buying arrangements with customers. This means giving preference in purchasing to firms that become loyal customers for another of the conglomerate's businesses. For instance, General Dynamics' acquisition of Liquid Carbonic Corporation in 1957 was based on the belief that General Dynamics' subcontractors could be encouraged to shift their purchases of industrial gases to Liquid Carbonic.[23]

3. **Mutual forbearance.** Corwin Edwards has argued that:

   When one large conglomerate enterprise competes with another, the two are likely to encounter each other in a considerable number of markets. The multiplicity of their contacts may blunt the edge of their competition. A prospect of advantage in one market from vigorous competition may be weighed against the danger of retaliatory forays by the competitor in other markets. Each conglomerate may adopt a live-and-let-live policy designed to stabilize the whole structure of the competitive relationship.[24]

Despite the plausibility of these arguments, evidence on anticompetitive practices of these types is sparse. Although common patterns of diversification among competing firms in the same industry point to firms' awareness of the need to build countervailing strategic positions, examples of firms exercising anticompetitive practices based on diversified market positions are few judging by scarcity of antitrust actions of this type.

Increased used of game theory has resulted in renewed interest in "multimarket competition" among diversified firms. Where the products produced by different divisions of a diversified company are substitutes, coordinated pricing increases margins—a result referred to as the **efficiency effect.**[25] In repeated games involving players that meet in multiple markets, companies are likely to refrain from aggressive action in any one market for fear of triggering more generalized warfare.[26]

Economies of Scope

The most general argument concerning the benefits of diversification focuses on the presence of economies of scope in common resources. If a certain input is used in the production of two products and this input is available only in units of a certain minimum size, then a single firm producing both products is able to spread the cost of the input over a larger volume of output and so reduce the unit costs of both products.[27] Thus economies of scope exist for similar reasons as economies of scale. The principal difference is that the cost reduction we gain from economies of scope arises from the increase in production volume achieved by producing multiple products. Economies of scope are exploited in different ways according to the characteristics of the resources and capabilities in question.

Tangible Resources.   Tangible resources such as distribution networks, information technology systems, sales forces, and research laboratories offer economies of scope by eliminating the duplication of facilities between businesses and creating a single shared facility. The greater the fixed costs of these items, the greater the associated economies of scope are likely to be. Entry by cable TV companies into telephone services, and telephone companies into cable TV are motivated by the desire to spread the costs of networks and billing systems over as great a volume of business as possible. A variety of companies including gas and electricity utilities envisage becoming single-point suppliers of a full range of electricity, gas, telephone, and TV services to households.

Economies of scope are available due to centralized administrative and support services at corporate headquarters. Among diversified companies, accounting, legal services, government relations, and information technology tend to be centralized. Increasingly, companies are forming **shared service organizations** in which these services are supplied to operating divisions on an arms-length basis. Similar benefits arise from centralizing research activities in a corporate R & D lab. Companies such as Philips, IBM, Matsushita, Du Pont, and Xerox can support large-scale corporate research labs that support basic research applicable to multiple businesses. In aerospace, the ability of leading U.S. suppliers to spread research expenditures over both defense and civilian products has given these companies an advantage over overseas competitors without access to large military contracts.[28]

Intangible Resources.   Intangible resources such as brands, corporate reputation, and technology offer economies of scope primarily due to the ability to transfer them from one business area to another at low marginal cost.[29] Thus, when American Express diversified its range of financial services by acquiring Shearson Lehman Brothers, IDS Financial Services, and Trade Development Bank, the new subsidiaries all clearly identified their new affiliations by prominent display of the American

Express blue and white corporate logo and the addition of the suffix "An American Express Company" to their company names. The strategy was outlined as follows:

> . . . we are creating a new kind of enterprise—one with multiple distribution channels that target select market segments with strong brand-name products and services. One expression of our multiple marketing strategy is the new logos and names for the American Express family. Our marketing strategy for the decade ahead is to sharpen our focus on the individual brand names as well as on the multiple distribution channels and carefully targeted market segments these brand names represent. At the same time, each business will continue to draw on the marketing power and identification of the American Express name.[30]

Organizational Capabilities. Organizational capabilities can also be transferred within the diversified company. For example:

- ♦ Philip Morris leveraged Miller Brewing Company from 7th to 2nd in terms of U.S. market share by applying the same brand management, advertising, and market segmentation skills that had proved so successful with Marlboro cigarettes. In both cases, Philip Morris repositioned the brand toward the mass market, increased advertising and promotional expenditure, segmented the market through sub-branding, improved packaging, and invested in production capacity.

- ♦ Motorola's remarkable long-term success in semiconductors and wireless telecommunication products has been built on the development of a set of core technological capabilities that are transferred and integrated across a number of different business areas. These technological capabilities relate to the development of microelectronic and communications technology, the embodiment of new technology into innovative, well-designed new products, and quality-based manufacturing.[31]

Some of the most important capabilities in influencing the performance of diversified corporations are general management capabilities located at the corporate level. Consider the case of General Electric. In an era when conglomerates are being dismantled, GE has achieved remarkable shareholder returns. Although GE does a remarkable job of transferring capabilities between its different businesses ("best practices"), its core capabilities lie at the corporate level in terms of the ways in which it motivates and develops its managers, its ability to reconcile decentralized decision making with centralized control, and its ability to coordinate geographical expansion. Similar observations could be made about 3M. While 3M's capabilities in technical know-how, new product development, and international marketing reside within the individual businesses, it is the corporate management capabilities and the systems through which they are exercised that maintain, nourish, coordinate, and upgrade these competitive advantages.

Economies from Internalizing Transactions[32]

Although economies of scope provide cost savings from sharing and transferring resources and capabilities, does a firm have to diversify across these different businesses in order to exploit those economies? The answer is no. Economies of scope in resources and capabilities can be exploited simply by selling or licensing the use of the resource or capability to another company. In Chapter 11, we observed that a firm can exploit proprietary technology by licensing it to other firms. In Chapter 14, we noted how technology and trademarks are licensed across national frontiers as an alternative to direct investment. The same can be done to exploit resources across different industries. Harley-Davidson exploits its brand name across many products. However, it sticks to manufacturing motorcycles and licenses its brand name to the manufacturers of T-shirts, clothing, key rings, cigarettes, and studded leather underwear. Walt Disney exploits the enormous value of its trademarks, copyrights, and characters partly through diversification into theme parks, live theater, ice shows, and hotels; and partly through licensing the use of these assets to publishers of music and comics, clothing and toy manufactures, food and drink processors, and the franchisees of Disney retail stores. Disney earns over $700 million a year from such licensing.

Even tangible resources can be shared across different businesses through market transactions. Airport and railroad station owners exploit economies of scope in their facilities not by diversifying into catering and retailing, but by leasing out space to specialist retailers and restaurants. Caterpillar exploits economies of scope in its parts distribution network, not by diversifying into the supply of a wider range of parts, but by distributing parts for Chrysler, Hyundai, Hewlett-Packard, and Siemens.[33]

What determines whether economies of scope are better exploited internally within the firm through diversification, or externally through market contracts with independent companies? The key issue is relative efficiency: what are the transactions costs of market contracts, as compared with the costs of managing economies of scope within the diversified enterprise? Transactions costs include the costs involved in drafting, negotiating, monitoring, and enforcing a contract. The costs of internalization consist of the management costs of establishing and coordinating the diversified business.[34]

Consider the case of Walt Disney Company. Why does Disney choose to license Donald Duck trademarks to a manufacturer of orange juice rather than set up its own orange juice company? Why does it own and operate its own Disneyland and DisneyWorld theme parks rather than license its trademarks to independent theme park companies? And why, in the case of Tokyo Disneyland, did it choose a licensing arrangement with the Oriental Land Company, which owns and operates Tokyo Disneyland?

These issues are complex. Much depends on the characteristics of the resource or capabilities. Though the returns to patents and brand names can often be appropriated efficiently though licensing, complex general management capabilities may be near impossible to exploit through market contracts. There is little scope for Sony to deploy its new product development capabilities other than within its own business. A similar situation occurs with Berkshire Hathaway and its skills in identifying attractive acquisition candidates then nurturing the management of these companies. The more deeply embedded a firm's capabilities within the management systems and the culture of the organization, then the greater the likelihood that these capabilities can only be deployed internally within the firm. Even with simpler resources, market contracts may not be effective in protecting the value of the resources in question. Texaco has chosen to exploit its coal gasification technology internally by developing its own power generation plants rather than license the technology, for fear that licensing would not adequately safeguard its proprietary interests.

The Diversified Firm as an Internal Market System

What we observe is that economies of scope alone do not provide an adequate rationale for diversification—economies of scope must be supported by the presence of transactions costs. However, the presence of transactions costs in any nonspecialized resource can offer efficiencies from diversification, even where no economies of scope are present. Consider the case of financial capital. Where significant costs are incurred in using external capital markets (the margin between borrowing and lending rates, and the underwriting costs of issuing securities), diversified companies can benefit from lower costs of capital by building a balanced portfolio of cash generating and cash absorbing businesses. A central role of the corporate head office in diversified corporations is to allocate capital among the different businesses according to the profit prospects of the different investment opportunities. In this respect, the diversified corporation represents an internal capital market in which the different businesses compete for investment funds.

Some companies operate highly sophisticated internal financial markets. Since 1985, British Petroleum Finance International has managed the financing of BP's 50+ operating companies, undertaken standard accounting functions, traded in foreign exchange, managed leasing, and offered 24-hour trading in short-term instruments through offices in London, New York, and Melbourne.[35] A key advantage of internal corporate banks is that they are not subject to the myriad regulations that raise the costs of using external financial institutions.[36]

Efficiencies also arise from the ability of diversified companies to transfer employees—especially managers and technical specialists—between their divisions, and to rely less on hiring and firing. As companies develop and encounter new circumstances, so different management skills are required. The costs associated with hiring include advertising, the time spent in interviewing and selection, and the costs of "head hunting" agencies. The costs of dismissing employees can be very high where severance payments must be offered. A diversified corporation has a pool of employees and can respond to the specific needs of any one business through transfer from elsewhere within the corporation. Not only are such internal transfers less costly than external transfers, they are also much less risky because of the superior information the firm possesses on internal job candidates. The broader set of opportunities available in the diversified corporation as a result of internal transfer may also result in attracting a higher caliber of employee. Graduating students compete intensely for entry-level positions with diversified corporations such as Matsushita, General Electric, Unilever, and Nestlé.

Information Advantages of the Diversified Corporation

An important benefit of internal capital and labor markets within the diversified corporation is that the corporate head office of the diversified corporation has better access to information than is available to external capital and labor markets. As a result, the diversified corporation may be more efficient in reallocating labor and capital among its divisions than are external capital and labor markets in allotting labor and capital among independent businesses. In the case of capital, these information advantages may be especially great for new ventures. Despite a well-developed market for venture capital in the United States and Europe, the risks associated with such ventures are compounded by limited information available to potential lenders and investors. A diversified company such as

3M or Hewlett-Packard has full access to the information on performance and prospects for each of its business units.

These information advantages may be even greater in the case of labor. A key problem of hiring from the external labor market is not just cost but limited information. A résumé, references, and a day of interviews are an uncertain indicator of how an otherwise unknown person will perform in a specific job. The diversified firm that is engaged in transferring employees between business units and divisions has access to much more detailed information on the abilities, characteristics, and past performance of each of its employees. This informational advantage exists not only for individual employees but also for groups of individuals working together as teams. As a result, in diversifying into a new activity, the established firm is at an advantage over the new firm, which must assemble a team from scratch with poor information on individual capabilities and almost no information on how effective the group will be at working together. As a result, in an economy where new industries are constantly arising, there are reasons to expect that diversification by established firms offers some advantages over exploiting new opportunities than entirely new ventures.[37]

DIVERSIFICATION AND PERFORMANCE

Our theory concerning the circumstances under which diversification can create value for shareholders is well developed and clear in its predictions. How do these predictions work in practice?

The Findings of Empirical Research

The implications of the analysis so far for the relationships between diversification and firm performance are as follows. First, to the extent that diversified companies can allocate resources and monitor managers more effectively than the market system, diversified firms should achieve higher profitability and higher growth than specialized firms. Second, because of the importance of economies of scope in shared resources, diversification into *related* industries should be more profitable than diversification into *unrelated* industries.

Initially, empirical research into the impact of diversification on firm performance produced clear and consistent findings on the second hypothesis. A study by Richard Rumelt found that, though diversification per se showed no clear relationship with profitability, sharp differences emerged between different diversification strategies. In particular, firms that diversified into businesses closely related to their core activities were significantly more profitable than those that pursued unrelated diversification. Subsequent research confirmed Rumelt's findings both for the United States and for other countries (notably Canada, West Germany, and Japan). At the same time, the problems associated with wide-ranging unrelated diversification were highlighted by the poor performance of conglomerates such as LTV, ITT, and Allegheny International. The apparent consistency of the evidence was such that in 1982, Tom Peters and Robert Waterman were able to conclude:

> . . . virtually every academic study has concluded that unchannelled diversification is a losing proposition.[38]

These findings together with their own observations of excellent companies provided the basis for one of Peters and Waterman's "golden rules" of excellence—*Stick to the Knitting:*

> Our principal finding is clear and simple. Organizations that do branch out but stick very close to their knitting outperform the others. The most successful are those diversified around a single skill, the coating and bonding technology at 3M for example. The second group in descending order, comprise those companies that branch out into related fields, the leap from electric power generation turbines to jet engines from GE for example. Least successful, as a general rule, are those companies that diversify into a wide variety of fields. Acquisitions especially among this group tend to wither on the vine.[39]

More recent studies have less consistent results. The apparent superior performance of related diversifiers can be attributed as much to industry factors as to the type of diversification strategy.[40] Other studies have found unrelated diversification to be more profitable than related.[41]

It seems likely that there are limits to the degree of diversity that can be profitably managed. Thus, very high levels of diversification give rise to problems of excessive complexity. Among British companies, diversification was associated with increased profitability up to a point, after which further diversification was associated with declining profitability (see Figure 15.2). However, in all the studies of diversification and profitability, *association* does not imply *causation*. It seems likely that the positive association between diversification and profitability that several studies found may be due to profitable companies channeling their cash flows into diversifying investment, rather than diversification causing higher profitability.

The most powerful evidence concerning the relationship between diversification and performance is that which has accumulated over the past decade from the refocusing initiatives by a large number of North American and European companies. The evidence, ranging from conglomerates such as ITT and Hanson, to the oil majors, tobacco companies, and engineering companies such as Daimler-Benz, is that narrowing business scope leads to increased profitability and increased stock market valuation. Undoubtedly the relationship between diversification and profitability has shifted over time—the declining relative performance of highly diversified companies points to the impact of environmental turbulence on the costs of managing large complex corporations. The stock market's verdict on diversification is unambiguous. The high price-earnings ratios attached to conglomerates during the 1960s have been replaced by a "conglomerate discount." The result is that diversified companies have come under attack from leveraged-buyout specialists seeking to add value through dismembering these companies. Costas Markides has found refocusing announcements by diversified companies have been accompanied by abnormal stock market returns.[42] Conversely, the tendency for acquisition announcements to generate abnormal stock market returns to the acquiring companies during the 1960s and 70s, was reversed by the 1980s.[43]

The inability of research to clearly identify related diversification as more profitable than unrelated is troubling given the arguments concerning economies of scope. Two factors may be important. First, related diversification may offer greater potential benefits, but may also pose more difficult management problems

The Relationship
Between Diversity
and profitability
among 304 British
Manufacturing
Coompanies,1972–84.

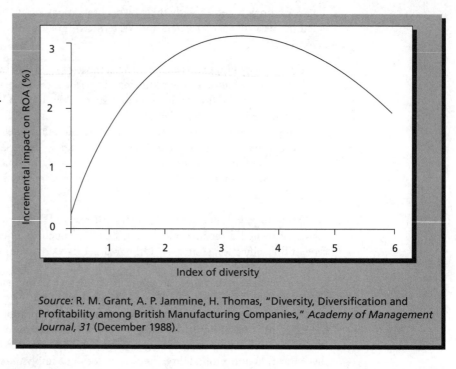

Source: R. M. Grant, A. P. Jammine, H. Thomas, "Diversity, Diversification and Profitability among British Manufacturing Companies," *Academy of Management Journal, 31* (December 1988).

for companies. Second, it is not entirely clear what "related" and "unrelated" diversification really are. The issues concerning the management of the diversified corporation are addressed in Chapter 16. Suffice it to say at this point, that economies of scope from sharing and transferring resources and capabilities among different businesses within the diversified corporation need to managed and such management is not costless.

The Meaning of Relatedness in Diversification

The issue of what we mean by relatedness is critically important in determining the product scope of the company. Our discussion of economies of scope has defined relatedness in terms of the sharing and transfer of resources and capabilities between businesses. Distinguishing the potential for exploiting economies of scope between businesses is no easy matter and researchers have used simple criteria to determine whether businesses are related. Typical criteria are similarities between industries in terms of technologies and markets. Using the first criterion, oil exploration, medical diagnostic imaging, and electronic arcade games would be related through their common dependence on 3D computer imaging. Under the second criterion, gasoline, automobile repair, and fast-food are related because they are sold to the same customers through the same retail outlets (service stations).

These types of links tell us little about the potential for economies of scope in resources and capabilities. Moreover, similarities in technology and markets refer primarily to relatedness at the *operational* level—in manufacturing, marketing, and distribution activities. These operating-level commonalities may not offer substantial economies in resource sharing—the management costs of common systems of purchasing and distribution tend to be high relative to the savings. Conversely, some of the most important sources of value creation within the diversified firm are the ability to apply common general management capabilities, strategic management systems, and resource allocation processes to different businesses. Such economies depend on the existence of *strategic* rather than *operational* commonalities among the different businesses within the diversified corporation.[44]

- ◆ Berkshire Hathaway is involved in insurance, candy stores, furniture, kitchen knives, jewelry, and footwear. Despite this diversity, all these businesses have been selected on the basis of their ability to benefit from the unique style of corporate management established by Chairman Warren Buffett and CEO Charles Munger.

- ◆ ABB comprises a wide range of businesses. Yet they share certain strategic similarities: they tend to be international, capital intensive, and engineering based. All fit with ABB's decentralized, yet closely integrated, system of corporate management.

The essence of such strategic-level linkages is the ability to apply similar strategies, resource allocation procedures, and control systems across the different businesses within the corporate portfolio. Table 15.4 lists some of the strategic factors that determine similarities among businesses in relation to corporate management activities.[45]

Unlike operational relatedness where the benefits of exploiting economies of scope in joint inputs are comparatively easy to forecast and even to quantify, relatedness at the strategic level may be much more difficult to appraise. There are numerous examples of companies that identified potential synergies between businesses

TABLE 15.4 The Determinants of Strategic Relatedness Between Businesses	CORPORATE MANAGEMENT TASKS	DETERMINANTS OF STRATEGIC SIMILARITY
	Resource Allocation	Similar sizes of capital investment projects. Similar time spans of investment projects. Similar sources of risk. Similar general management skills required for business unit managers.
	Strategy Formulation	Similar Key Success Factors. Similar stages of the industry life cycle. Similar competitive positions occupied by each business within its industry.
	Targeting, Monitoring, and Control of Business Unit	Goals defined in terms of similar performance variables. Similar time horizons for performance targets.

Source: R. M. Grant, "On Dominant Logic, Relatedness, and the Link Between Diversity and Performance," *Strategic Management Journal*, 9 (1988): 641.

that in practice prove either elusive or nonexistent. A classic example is the creation and rapid demise of the Allegis Corporation (see Exhibit 15.1).

Actual relatedness between businesses is not the same as perceived relatedness. There has been a good deal of recent interest in business relatedness as a cognitive concept. Prahalad and Bettis refer to this as **dominant logic.**[46] Certainly a dominant logic in the form of a common view within the company as to its identity and rationale is a critical precondition for effective integration (this issue is discussed further in Chapter 16). There is a danger, however, that dominant logic may not be underpinned by any true economic synergies. In the same way that Allegis Corporation attempted to diversify around serving the needs of the traveler, so General Mills diversified into toys, fashion clothing, specialty retailing, and restaurants on the basis of "understanding the needs and wants of the homemaker."

EXHIBIT 15.1

The Rise and Fall of Allegis

On May 1, 1987, Richard J. Ferris, Chief Executive of UAL Inc., inaugurated a new era in the company's history under the new name of Allegis Corporation. The name change symbolized the metamorphosis of UAL from an airline into a diversified travel company. Ferris explained the company's mission as follows:

> . . . Allegis is United, the airline industry leader. It is Hertz, the top car-rental company. It is Westin, a luxury hotel group. Allegis is Covia whose Apollo product is a multinational computer reservations network. It is MPI, a full-service direct marketing agency. It is United Vacations, a wholesale travel tour operator. And Allegis will soon be Hilton International, when we complete our purchase of that leading company with 88 luxury hotels in 42 countries.

Allegis Corporation . . . caring for travelers worldwide . . . a distinctive partnership of companies . . . where people are pledged to service and quality.

Allegis will be the world's premier travel-related corporation—recognized by customers, employees, and investors as the source of superior quality and value.

Allegis customers will prefer the services of its worldwide operating partnership because they represent the best in dependability, comfort, and convenience . . . and because they are delivered by people whose attention to detail enhances every aspect of the travel experience . . .

Allegis will also be unwavering in its dedication to bring quality and care back into the total travel experience. So we pledge to you, our customers, value, convenience, dependability, security, comfort—in sum, ease of travel that no other single corporation can match.

On June 9, only six weeks after formally adopting the Allegis name, Dick Ferris was ousted by the board. The car rental and hotel subsidiaries were sold, and the company reverted to its name of United Airlines Inc.

EXHIBIT 15.1
(Continued)

What had gone wrong? Allegis broke two out of three of Porter's "essential tests" of a diversification strategy. First, its cost of entry, in terms of the prices it paid for companies during its two-year, $2.3 billion acquisition binge, was too high. Second, in terms of the "better-off" test, it appeared that Ferris had greatly overestimated the synergies to be exploited in bringing together airlines, hotels, and car rental under a common ownership. Indeed, it was not apparent that the chief benefit, providing one-stop shopping for the business traveler through an integrated reservations system, could not be achieved equally well by collaboration among independent companies.

While market-relatedness provided the principal benefits, the stumbling blocks for the company were the strategic dissimilarities between the different businesses. While Allegis' up-market hotel chains competed on the basis of service and reputation, the principal requirement for success in the deregulated airline industry was rigorous cost cutting and the maintenance of high load factors through quick-footed operational management. Allegis' focus on servicing the needs of the business traveler deflected its attention from its critical need: reducing costs and increasing efficiency at United Airlines.

Sources: Richard J. Ferris, "From Now On," *Vis-à-Vis* (March 1987): 13; "Allegis: Is a Name Change Enough for UAL?" *Business Week*, March 2, 1987: 54–58; "The Unraveling of an Idea," *Business Week*, June 22, 1987: 42–43.

◆ SUMMARY

Diversification is like sex. Its attractions are obvious, often irresistible. Yet the experience is often disappointing. For top management it is a minefield. The diversification experiences of large corporations are littered with expensive mistakes: Exxon with Exxon Office Systems, GE with Utah International and Kidder Peabody, Ford and General Motors' forays into car rental, American Express with Shearson Lehman, Daimler-Benz in aerospace, Coca-Cola in wine, AT&T with NCR. Yet despite so many costly failures, the urge to diversify continues to captivate senior managers. Part of the problem is the divergence between managerial and shareholder goals. While diversification has offered meager rewards to shareholders, it is the fastest route to building vast corporate empires. A further problem is hubris. A company's success in one line of business tends to result in the top management team becoming overconfident of its ability to achieve similar success in other businesses.

Yet, if companies are to survive and prosper over long periods of time they must change, and this change inevitably involves redefining the businesses in which the company operates. Hewlett-Packard and Motorola are among the longest-established companies in the fast-paced U.S. electronics industry. The success and longevity of both have been based on their ability to adapt their product lines to changing market opportunities. While Motorola has moved from car radios to TVs to semiconductors to wireless communication equipment to communication services, HP has shifted from measuring instruments to computers and printers, to cameras and other imaging products. Although many firms appear to have rejected diversification in favor of "refocusing" and "downsizing," in reality companies have no choice other than to continually move into new products and new areas of business. As new technologies and deregulation continue to reshape the telecommunications industry, firms such as AT&T and British Telecom must develop wireless networks, digital technologies, data transfer, Internet support, information services, and the like.

The critical issue for managers is to avoid the errors of the past through better strategic analysis of diversification decisions. The objectives of diversification need to be clear and explicit. Shareholder value creation has provided a demanding and illuminating criterion with which to appraise investment in new business opportunities. Rigorous analysis may also counter the tendency for diversification to be a diversion—a form of escapism resulting from the unwillingness of top management to come to terms with difficult competitive circumstances in the firm's core businesses.

The analytical tools at our disposal for evaluating diversification decisions have developed greatly in recent years. Twenty years ago, diversification decisions were based on vague concepts of synergy that involved the identification of linkages between different industries. More specific analysis of the nature and extent of economies of scope in resources and capabilities has given greater precision to our analysis of synergy. At the same time, we recognize that economies of scope are insufficient to ensure that diversification creates value. The critical issue is the optimum organizational form for exploiting these economies. The transactions costs of market must be compared against the management costs of the diversified corporation. These management costs depend heavily on the top management capabilities and management systems of the particular company. This type of analysis has caused many companies to realize that economies of scope can often be exploited more efficiently and with less risk through collaborative relationships with other companies rather than through diversification.

NOTES

1 Alfred Chandler Jr., *Strategy and Structure: Chapters in the History of the Industrial Enterprise* (Cambridge, MA: MIT Press, 1962); and *The Visible Hand: The Managerial Revolution in American Business* (Cambridge, MA: Harvard University Press, 1977).

2 Leonard Wrigley, *Divisional Autonomy and Diversification*, doctoral dissertation, Harvard Business School, 1970.

3 Richard P. Rumelt, *Strategy, Structure and Economic Performance* (Cambridge, MA: Harvard University Press, 1974); Richard P. Rumelt, "Diversification Strategy and Profitability," *Strategic Management Journal* 3 (1972): 359–370.

4 Michael Goold and Kathleen Luchs, "Why Diversify? Four Decades of Management Thinking, "*Academy of Management Executive* 7, no. 3 (August 1993): 7–25.

5 Azar P. Jammine, *Product Diversification, International Expansion and Performance: A Study of Strategic Risk Management in U.K. Manufacturing*, doctoral dissertation, London Business School, 1984.

6 G. F. Davis, K. A. Diekman, and C. F. Tinsley, "The Decline and Fall of the Conglomerate Firm in the 1980s: A Study in the De-Institutionalization of an Organizational Form," Northwestern University, September 1993.

7 For a discussion of restructuring of diversified companies, see R. E. Hoskisson and M. A. Hitt, *Downscoping: How to Tame the Diversified Firm* (New York: Oxford University Press, 1994).

8   A. Shleifer and R. W. Vishny, "The Takeover Wave of the 1980s," *Science* 248 (July–September, 1990): 747–749.

9   J. R. Williams, B. L. Paez, L. Sanders, "Conglomerates Revisited," *Strategic Management Journal* 9 (1988): 403–414.

10 "The King Is Dead," *Fortune*, January 11, 1993: 34–46.

11 B. Burrough, *Barbarians at the Gate: The Fall of RJR Nabisco* (New York: Harper & Row, 1990).

12 "South-East Asia's Octopuses," *Economist*, July 17, 1993: 61.

13 Robin Marris, *The Economic Theory of Managerial Capitalism* (London: Macmillan, 1964).

14 Robert M. Grant and R. Cibin, "Strategy, Structure and Market Turbulence: The International Oil Majors, 1970–1991," *Scandinavian Journal of Management* 12, no. 2 (1996): 165–188.

15 David A. Ravenscraft and F. M. Scherer, "Divisional Selloff: A Hazard Analysis," in *Mergers, Selloffs and Economic Efficiency* (Washington, DC: Brookings Institute, 1987); and Michael E. Porter, "From Competitive Advantage to Corporate Strategy," *Harvard Business Review* (May–June 1987): 43–59.

16 See, for example, Stephen A. Ross and Randolph W. Westerfield, *Corporate Finance* (Homewood, IL: Irwin, 1988).

17 See, for example, H. Levy and M. Sarnat, "Diversification, Portfolio Analysis and the Uneasy Case for Conglomerate Mergers," *Journal of Finance* 25 (1970): 795-802; R. H. Mason and M. B. Goudzwaard, "Performance of Conglomerate Firms: A Portfolio Approach," *Journal of Finance* 31 (1976): 39–48; F. W. Melicher and D. F. Rush, "The Performance of Conglomerate Firms: Recent Risk and Return Experience," *Journal of Finance* 28 (1973): 381–388; J. F. Weston, K. V. Smith, and R. E. Shrieves, "Conglomerate Performance Using the Capital Asset Pricing Model," *Review of Economics and Statistics* 54 (1972): 357–363.

18 M. Lubatkin and S. Chetterjee, "Extending Modern Portfolio Theory into the Domain of Corporate Strategy: Does It Apply?" *Academy of Management Journal* 37 (1994): 109–136.

19 Stephen A. Ross and Randolph W. Westerfield, *Corporate Finance* (St. Louis: Times Mirror/Mosby College, 1988): 681.

20 Michael E. Porter, "From Competitive Advantage to Corporate Strategy," *Harvard Business Review* (May–June 1987): 46.

21 In the rush to enter movie production, Sony, Matsushita, and Viacom are widely regarded as having overpaid for Columbia Pictures, MCA, and Paramount, respectively. Commercial banks and other financial service companies also appear to have overpaid for their acquisitions of investment banks.

22 Ralph Biggadike, "The Risky Business of Diversification," *Harvard Business Review* (May–June 1979).

23 Erwin Blackstone, "Monopsony Power, Reciprocal Buying and Government Contracts: The General Dynamics Case," *Antitrust Bulletin* 17 (Summer 1972): 445-462.

24 U.S. Senate, Subcommittee on Antitrust and Monopoly Hearings, *Economic Concentration*, Part 1, Congress, 1st session, 1965: 45.

25 D. Besanko, D. Dranove, and Mark Shanley, *Economics of Strategy* (New York: Wiley, 1996): 428–429.

26 B. D. Bernheim and M. D. Whinston, "Multimarket Contact and Collusive Behavior," *Rand Journal of Economics* 2 (1990): 1–26.

27 The formal definition of economies of scope is in terms of "sub-additivity." Economies of scope exist in the production of goods $x_1, x_2, \ldots x_n$, if:

$$C(X) < C(x_i)$$

Where $X = \Sigma_i x_i$, $C(X)$ is the cost of producing all n goods within a single firm, and $\Sigma_i C(x_i)$ is the cost of producing the goods in n specialized firms. See W. J. Baumol, John

C. Panzar, Robert D. Willig, *Contestable Markets and the Theory of Industry Structure* (New York: Harcourt Brace Jovanovich, 1982): 71–72.

28 More generally, research intensity is strongly associated with diversification. For the U.S. see C. H. Berry, *Corporate Growth and Diversification*, (Princeton: Princeton University Press, 1975); for the U.K. see Robert M. Grant, "Determinants of the Interindustry Pattern of Diversification by U.K. Manufacturing Companies," *Bulletin of Economic Research*, 29 (1977): 84–95.

29 Among service companies, the ability to transfer corporate reputation across different service markets was found to be an important influence on the profitability of diversification. See P. R. Nayyar, "Performance Effects of Information Asymmetry and Economies of Scope in Diversified Service Firms," *Academy of Management Journal* 36 (1993): 28–57.

30 *American Express Company 1984 Annual Report*: 3.

31 "Keeping Motorola on a Roll," *Fortune*, April 18, 1994: 67–78.

32 This section draws heavily on Robert M. Grant, "Diversification and Firm Performance in a Changing Economic Environment," in *Firm-Environment Interaction in a Changing Productive System*, ed. H. Ergas et al. (Milan: Franco Angeli, 1988).

33 "A Moving Story of Spare Parts," *Financial Times*, August 29, 1997: 7.

34 This issue is examined more fully in David Teece, "Towards an Economic Theory of the Multiproduct Firm," *Journal of Economic Behavior and Organization* 3 (1982): 39–63.

35 "Inside the New In-House Banks," *Euromoney*, February 1986: 24–34.

36 Robert K. Ankrom, "The Corporate Bank," *Sloan Management Review* (Winter 1994): 63–72.

37 Armen A. Alchian and Harold Demsetz, "Production, Information Costs, and Economic Organization," *American Economic Review* 62 (1972): 777–795, argue that the collection and processing of information is the basic role of management and provides the primary rationale for the existence of the firm.

38 Tom Peters and Robert Waterman, *In Search of Excellence* (New York: Harper & Row, 1982): 294.

39 *Ibid.*: 294.

40 H. K. Christensen and C. A. Montgomery, "Corporate Economic Performance: Diversification Strategy versus Market Structure," *Strategic Management Journal* 2 (1981): 327–343; R. A. Bettis, "Performance Differences in Related and Unrelated Diversified Firms," *Strategic Management Journal* 2 (1981): 379–383.

41 See, for example, A. Michel and I. Shaked, "Does Business Diversification Affect Performance?" *Financial Management* 13, no.4 (1984): 18–24; and G. A. Luffman and R. Reed, *The Strategy and Performance of British Industry, 1970–80* (London: Macmillan, 1984).

42 C. Markides, "Consequences of Corporate Refocussing: Ex Ante Evidence," *Academy of Management Journal* 35 (1992): 398–412.

43 G. A. Jarrell, J. A. Brickly, and J. M. Netter, "The Market for Corporate Control: Empirical Evidence Since 1980," *Journal of Economic Perspectives* 2, no. 1 (Winter 1988): 49–68.

44 For a discussion of relatedness in diversification, see J. Robins and M. F. Wiersema, "A Resource-Based Approach to the Multibusiness Firms: Empirical Analysis of Portfolio Interrelationships and Corporate Financial Performance," *Strategic Management Journal* 16 (1995): 277–300; and J. Robins and M.F. Wiersema, "Measurement of Related Diversification: Are the Measures Valid for the Concepts?" Discussion paper, Graduate School of Management, University of California, Irvine, November 1997.

45 For a discussion of the role of strategic linkages between businesses in affecting the success of diversification, see Robert M. Grant, "On Dominant Logic, Relatedness, and the Link Between Diversity and Performance," *Strategic Management Journal* 9 (1988): 639–642.

46 C. K. Prahalad and R. A. Bettis, "The Dominant Logic: A New Linkage Between Diversity and Performance," *Strategic Management Journal* 7 (1986): 485–502.

16

Managing the
Multibusiness Corporation

Some have argued that single-product businesses have a focus that gives them an advantage over multibusiness companies like our own—and perhaps they would have, but only if we neglect our own overriding advantage: the ability to share the ideas that are the result of wide and rich input from a multitude of global sources.

GE businesses share technology, design, compensation and personnel evaluation systems, manufacturing practices, and customer and country knowledge. Gas Turbines shares manufacturing technology with Aircraft Engines; Motors and Transportation Systems work together on new propulsion systems; Lighting and Medical Systems collaborate to improve x-ray tube processes; and GE Capital provides innovative financing packages that help all our businesses around the globe. Supporting all this is a management system that fosters and rewards this sharing and teamwork, and, increasingly, a culture that makes it reflexive and natural at every level and corner of our Company.

—*Jack Welch (Letter to Share Owners, General Electric Company 1993 Annual Report)*

Outline

◆ INTRODUCTION AND OBJECTIVES

In the last chapter, I argued that the case for diversification depended ultimately on the ability of the diversified corporation to exploit the sources of value from operating across multiple businesses more effectively than specialized firms linked by market contracts or by other forms of collaboration. Chapters 13 and 14 arrived at the same conclusion in relation to vertical integration and multinational operations. Hence, the critical issues for companies whose scope extends over multiple stages of the value chain, over multiple countries, or over multiple industries are first, whether value can be derived by operating across these activities, countries, and industries; and, second, how the company is to be structured and managed to ensure that these sources of value are exploited more effectively than any other set of organizational arrangements. These issues explain the inability of empirical research to establish the impact of vertical integration, multinational expansion, and diversification on profitability. Not only does it depend on the particular case (there is more scope for adding value by diversifying from jet engines into industrial turbines, than from jet engines into ice cream), but it also depends on the ability of the individual firm to manage multimarket activity.

In this chapter we examine the management of multimarket activity using multibusiness corporations. By "multibusiness corporation" I mean not just firms that operate across different industries, but any firm that manages multiple activities and multiple markets. The common characteristic of such firms is that they are multidivisional: they consist of a number of divisions, subsidiaries, and/or business units, coordinated and controlled by a corporate headquarters. Our emphasis is less on the *content* of strategy than on the organizational structures, management systems, and leadership styles through which strategy is *formulated* and *implemented* within these multibusiness companies. As we will see, corporate strategy is not simply a matter of answering the question, "What businesses should we be in?" Some of the most difficult issues of corporate strategy are the roles and activities of the corporate head office and the relationships between the businesses and the corporate center. We are concerned with five main areas of corporate-level strategic management:

1. The composition of the company's portfolio of businesses (decisions over diversification, acquisition, and divestment);

2. Resource allocation among the company's different businesses;

3. The role of head office in the formulation of business unit strategies;

4. Controlling business unit performance;

5. Coordinating business units and creating overall cohesiveness and direction for the company.

By the time you have completed this chapter, you will be able to:

♦ Discuss the central issues of formulating and implementing corporate strategy

♦ Deploy the concepts and techniques necessary for making judgments about these issues

♦ Evaluate the relationships between the resources and capabilities of the firm, its corporate strategy, and the implementation of the strategy through an appropriate organization structure, management systems, and leadership style.

THE STRUCTURE OF THE MULTIBUSINESS COMPANY

Chapter 1 introduced the distinction between business strategy and corporate strategy and observed that, within the multibusiness company, corporate management takes primary responsibility for corporate strategy, and divisional management takes primary responsibility for business strategy. This corporate/divisional distinction is the most characteristic feature of the multibusiness corporation. Whether we are referring to a diversified corporation (such as Berkshire Hathaway), a multinational corporation (such as Coca-Cola) or a vertically integrated corporation (such as Alcoa), virtually all multibusiness corporations are organized as multidivisional structures where business-level decisions are concentrated among the divisions, subsidiaries, and/or business units and the corporate center exercises overall coordination and control.

As we saw in Chapter 6, the multidivisional structure is the dominant organizational form for all businesses that spread their activities over different products, countries, or vertical businesses. The emergence of this organizational form and the systems of strategic planning and financial control with which it is associated is one of the leading management innovations of the twentieth century. From its early development at Du Pont and General Motors, the multidivisional structure has been adopted throughout North America, Europe, Japan, and elsewhere.

The multidivisional form sets the basic structure for the formation and implementation of corporate strategy. The initial rationale for the multidivisional firm was the separation of strategic and operational decision making. Increasingly, the distinction between the corporate headquarters and the divisions is the separation of corporate-level from business-level decision making.

The Theory of the M-Form Corporation[1]

Chandler's historical analysis of divisionalized structures has been provided with theoretical underpinnings by Oliver Williamson. The efficiency advantages of the divisionalized firm (or **M-form** in Williamson's terminology) rest on four propositions:

1. **Bounded rationality.** Managers are limited in their cognitive, information processing, and decision-making capabilities. Hence, the top management team cannot be responsible for all coordination and decision-making within a complex organization—management responsibilities must be decentralized.

2. **Decision-making responsibilities should be separated according to the frequency with which different types of decisions are made.** Thus, decisions that are made with high frequency (e.g., operating decisions) need to be separated from decisions that are made infrequently (e.g., strategic decisions).

3. **Minimizing the need for communication and coordination.** In the functional organization, decisions concerning a particular product or business area must pass up to the top of the company before all the relevant information and expertise can be brought to bear. In the divisionalized firm, so long as close coordination between different business areas is not necessary, most decisions concerning a particular business can be made at the divisional level. This eases the information and decision-making burden on top management.

4. **Global rather than local optimization.** Functional organizations are likely to give rise to managers, even at a senior level, who emphasize functional interests over the objectives of the organization as a whole. In the multidivisional firm, locating strategic decision making in a general head office means that companywide interests are given primacy. Also, at the divisional level, the interests of the business and of products are emphasized over functional interests.

The multidivisional structure, with its separation of the corporate head office and the operating divisions, may also confer advantages in relation to allocating resources and avoiding agency problems.

Allocation of Resources.   Resource allocation within any type of administrative structure is a political process in which power, status, and influence triumph over commercial considerations. As was argued in Chapter 15, one advantage of the multidivisional company is its ability to create an internal market system in which capital is allocated according to financial and strategic considerations. The multidivisional company can achieve this through operating a competitive internal capital market where budgets are linked to past and projected divisional profitability, and individual projects are subject to a standardized appraisal and approval process. The efficiency of this process is enhanced by the extent and quality of information that is available within the divisionalized company.

Resolution of the Agency Problem.   A second shortcoming of the managerially controlled corporation is the tendency for salaried top management to pursue goals that conflict with the wealth-maximizing goals of owners. To the extent that the multibusiness, multidivisional company places a layer of corporate management between the shareholders and operating management, this organizational form might be expected to exacerbate the agency problem. However, Williamson argues to the contrary, that given the limited power of shareholders to discipline and replace managers, and the tendency for top management to dominate the board of directors, the multidivisional form may act as a partial remedy to the agency problem. The rationale is as follows: The corporate management of the multidivisional company acts as an interface between the stockholders and the divisional managers and can ensure adherence to profit goals. Because divisions and business units are typically profit centers, financial performance can readily be monitored by head office, and divisional managers held responsible for performance failures. The multidivisional corporation thus creates the disciplines of the capital market *within* the diversified corporation. So long as corporate management is focused on shareholder goals, the informational and control advantages of the multidivisional company can provide a particularly powerful system for enforcing profit maximization at the divisional level: the key tools being corporate management's ability to allocate funds, threaten divestiture, and reward or fire divisional presidents. General Electric under Jack Welch, ITT under Harold Geneen, Hanson under Lord Hanson, and Emerson Electric under Charles Knight are all companies where the multidivisional structure proved to be highly effective in imposing a strong profit motivation among divisional managers. Oliver Williamson explains this merit of the multidivisional corporation as follows:

> . . . the M-form conglomerate can be thought of as substituting an administrative interface between an operating division and the stockholders where a market interface had existed previously. Subject to the condition that the conglomerate does not diversify to excess, in the sense that it cannot competently evaluate and allocate funds among the diverse activities in which it is engaged, the substitution of internal organization can have beneficial effects in goal pursuit, monitoring, staffing, and resource allocation respects. The goal-pursuit advantage is that which accrues to M-form organizations in general: since the general management of an M-form conglomerate is disengaged from operating matters, a presumption that the general office favors profits over functional goals is warranted. Relatedly, the general office can be regarded as an agent of the stockholders whose purpose is to monitor the operations of the constituent parts. Monitoring benefits are realized in the degree to which internal monitors enjoy advantages over external monitors in access to information—which they arguably do. The differential ease with which the general office can change managers and reassign duties where performance failures or distortions are detected is responsible for the staffing advantage. Resource allocation benefits are realized because cash flows no longer return automatically to their origins but instead revert to the center, thereafter to be allocated among competing uses in accordance with prospective yields.[2]

The assumption that the corporate management of diversified, multidivisional companies is more likely to create shareholder value and less likely to run companies as personal fiefdoms does not appear to be borne out by history: Armand Hammer at Occidental Petroleum, Russ Johnson at RJR Nabisco, Howard Hughes at Hughes Corporation, the Saatchi brothers at Saatchi & Saatchi all pursued empire-building at the expense of shareholder return. Corporate executives of diversified companies may be less emotionally committed to particular businesses, but this does not necessarily mean that they are more predisposed to shareholder return than to Bokassa-type personal grandeur.

The proposition that the multidivisional structure is more efficient for the management of diversified firms has been tested in a number of studies. Most studies have found that among diversified firms, those with multidivisional structures have outperformed both looser holding companies and more centralized unitary forms.[3]

The Divisionalized Firm in Practice

Despite the theoretical arguments in favor of the divisionalized corporation and empirical evidence of its efficacy, close observation reveals that its reconciliation of the benefits of decentralization with those of coordination is far from perfect. Henry Mintzberg points to two important rigidities imposed by divisional structures.[4]

Constraints on Decentralization.   Although operational authority in the M-form firm is dispersed to the divisional level, the individual divisions often feature highly centralized power that is partly a reflection of the divisional president's personal accountability to the head office. In addition, the operational freedom of the divisional management exists only so long as the corporate head office is satisfied with divisional performance. Monthly financial reviews typically mean that variances in divisional performance precipitate speedy corporate intervention.

Standardization of Divisional Management.   In principle, the divisional form permits divisional management to be differentiated by the business needs of each. In practice, there are powerful forces for standardization across divisions through common control systems, common management development processes, corporate's tendency to promote similar types of managers to top divisional positions, and a common corporate culture. The problems of common management systems and a common corporate culture in managing diversity was apparent in Exxon's management of Exxon Office Systems, its office electronics subsidiary during the early 1980s.

THE ROLE OF CORPORATE MANAGEMENT

We have looked at the structure of the multibusiness corporation and observed how the multidivisional structure is conducive to the efficient management of multimarket activity. However, we have yet to consider the bigger question of what corporate management must do in order to create value within the multibusiness corporation. The fundamental issue is this: the multibusiness corporation brings together a number of separate businesses that are placed under the control of a corporate headquarters. If this arrangement is to add value, then the additional profits generated within the different businesses must more than offset the costs of the corporate headquarters. To explore the potential for corporate management to add value, we must consider the role and functions of corporate managers. In Chapter 1, corporate strategy was defined by the answer to the question, "What business are we in?" This encompasses issues of diversification, acquisition, divestment, and the allocation of resources. It should be apparent from the last three chapters that the functions and responsibilities of corporate management extend much further. Corporate strategy is certainly concerned with shaping the business portfolio. Equally important, however, are the administrative and the leadership roles of corporate management in terms of implementing corporate strategy, participating in divisional strategy formulation, coordinating the different divisions, and fostering cohesion, identity, and a sense of direction within the company. These functions extend beyond what is normally thought of as "corporate strategy." For this reason, Goold, Campbell and Alexander refer to the role of the corporate headquarters in the multibusiness company as "corporate parenting."[5]

The role of corporate management in the diversified company can be examined in relation to the means by which the corporate center can add value to the businesses it manages. These can be grouped into three areas:

♦ Managing the corporate portfolio, including the diversification, divestment, and resource allocation;

♦ Exercising guidance and control over the individual businesses within the corporate portfolio, including the formulation of business strategy and the imposition of financial incentives and controls;

♦ Managing linkages among businesses by sharing and transferring resources and capabilities.

I now outline each of these corporate management activities and indicate the conditions under which they can create value.

MANAGING THE CORPORATE PORTFOLIO

Fundamental to corporate strategy are decisions concerning the composition and balance of the corporate portfolio. These include extensions of the portfolio through diversification, deletions from the portfolio through divestment, and changes in the balance of the corporate portfolio through the allocation of investment funds and other resources between the different businesses. Whereas additions to and deletions from the corporate portfolio represent major but infrequent corporate strategy decisions, the allocation of resources among businesses is a vital, ongoing strategic responsibility of corporate management. Although the resource allocation process focuses on capital budgeting, the assignment and transfer of senior divisional managers is also a vital corporate management activity. Strategic management within multibusiness companies has been closely associated with the development and application of portfolio planning models, and more recently with the application of shareholder value models to restructuring strategies.

GE and the Development of Strategic Planning Techniques

From the development of portfolio planning in the 1970s to the restructuring of the 1980s, General Electric more than any other company has been a source of corporate strategy concepts and innovations and a pioneer of corporate management techniques. GE has been a leading member of *Fortune* magazine's "America's Most Admired Corporations" since its listings began. The key feature of GE's success is its highly effective and constantly evolving system of corporate management. As one executive remarked, "When Japanese managers come to visit us, they don't ask to see our research centers or manufacturing facilities. All they want to know is about our management system."[6]

In response to the challenges of managing a widely diversified corporation organized into 46 divisions and over 190 businesses, GE developed a number of techniques for corporate-level strategic planning in the 1970s that were widely adopted by other companies. In 1969, GE launched a series of initiatives aimed at developing a more effective system of corporate planning backed by better analytical techniques. Working with the Boston Consulting Group, McKinsey and Company,

Arthur D. Little, and the Harvard Business School, GE spawned three innovations that were to transform the formulation and implementation of corporate strategy.

- *Portfolio Planning Models.* All three consulting companies developed simple, matrix-based frameworks to evaluate business unit performance, formulate business unit strategies, and assess the overall balance of the corporate portfolio.

- *The Strategic Business Unit.* The SBU is a business for which it is meaningful to formulate a separate strategy. Typically an SBU is a business consisting of a number of closely related products and for which most costs are not shared with other businesses. McKinsey recommended the reorganization of GE into SBUs for formulating and monitoring business strategies.

- *The PIMS Database.* The PIMS database (first encountered in Chapter 3) began as an internal database that comprised strategic, market, and performance data on each of GE's businesses for assisting strategy formulation by providing analysis of the impact of market structure and strategy variables on profitability.

Portfolio Planning Models: The GE/McKinsey Matrix

The best-known products of GE's corporate planning initiatives of 1969–1972 are the portfolio planning models developed by McKinsey, BCG, and A. D. Little. The basic idea is to represent the businesses of the diversified company within a simple graphic framework that can be used to assist strategy analysis in four areas.

1. **Allocating resources**. Portfolio analysis examines the position of a business unit in relation to the two primary sources of profitability: industry attractiveness and competitive position. This indicates the attractiveness of the business for the purposes of investment.

2. **Formulating business unit strategy**. The positioning of the business in relation to industry attractiveness and competitive position indicates the strategic approach that should be taken with regard to capital investment and can point to opportunities for repositioning the business.

3. **Analyzing portfolio balance**. The primary usefulness of a single diagrammatic representation of the company's different businesses is the ability of corporate management to take an overall view of the company. This permits planning the overall balance of:
   - *Cash flows*—by balancing cash-generating businesses against cash-absorbing businesses, the diversified company can achieve independence from external capital markets
   - *Growth*—by balancing a mix of businesses in different stages of their life cycles, the diversified company can stabilize its growth rate and achieve continuity over time.

4. **Setting performance targets**. To the extent that positioning with regard to industry attractiveness and competitive position determine profit potential, portfolio planning matrices can assist setting performance targets for individual businesses.

The two axes of the GE/McKinsey matrix (see Figure 16.1) are the familiar sources of superior profitability for a firm: industry attractiveness and competitive advantage. Industry attractiveness is computed on the basis of the following factors:

- Market size
- Market growth (real growth rate over 10 years)
- Industry profitability (3-year average return on sales of the business and its competitors)
- Cyclicality (average annual percent trend deviation of sales)
- Inflation recovery (ability to cover cost increases by higher productivity and increased prices)
- Importance of overseas markets (ratio of international to U.S. market)

Business unit competitive position is computed on the basis of the following variables:

- Market position (as indicated by share of the U.S. market, share of the world market, and market share relative to that of leading competitors)
- Competitive position (superior, equal, or inferior to competitors) with regard to quality, technology, manufacturing, distribution, marketing, and cost
- Return on sales relative to that of leading competitors.

Strategy recommendations are shown by three regions of Figure 16.1:

- Business units that rank high both on both dimensions have excellent profit potential and should be *grown*
- Those that rank low on both dimensions have poor prospects and should be *harvested* (managed to maximize cash flow with little or no new investment)
- In-between businesses are candidates for a *hold* strategy.

FIGURE 16.1
Portfolio Planning
Models: The GE/
McKinsey Matrix

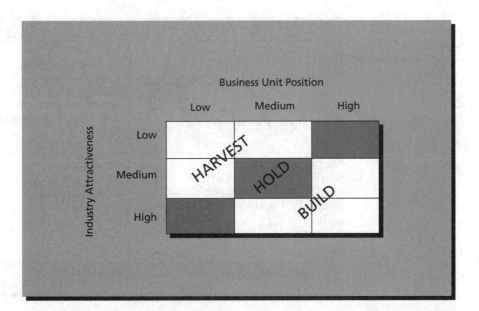

The value of this technique is its simplicity: even for a complex and diverse company such as General Electric, which in 1980 consisted of 43 SBUs, all the firm's SBUs can be shown on a single diagram. Thus, though the matrix may be simplistic, its power lies in its ability to display the relative strategic positions of all the company's businesses and to compress a large amount of data into two dimensions.

Portfolio Planning Models: BCG's Growth-Share Matrix

The Boston Consulting Group's matrix is similar: it also uses industry attractiveness and competitive position to compare the strategic positions of different businesses and draw strategy inferences. However, unlike the McKinsey matrix it uses single variables for each axis: industry attractiveness is measured by *market growth rate*, competitive position by *relative market share* (the business unit's market share relative to that of its largest competitor).

The four quadrants of the BCG matrix predict patterns of profits and cash flow and offer strategy recommendations as to appropriate strategies. These are summarized in Figure 16.2.

The BCG's growth-share matrix is even more elementary than the McKinsey matrix and at best it can provide only a rough, first-cut analysis. Nevertheless, the BCG matrix has been widely used by companies who have found value in its very simplicity, in particular:

♦ Because information on only two variables is required, the analysis can be prepared easily and quickly;

♦ It assists senior managers in cutting through vast quantities of detailed information to reveal key differences in the positioning of individual business units;

FIGURE 16.2
Portfolio Planning Models: The BCG Growth-Share Matrix

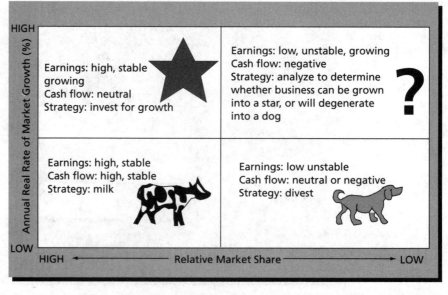

- ◆ The analysis is versatile—it can be applied not only to business units, but also to analyzing the positioning and performance potential of different products, brands, distribution channels, and customers;
- ◆ It provides a useful point of departure for more detailed analysis and discussion of the competitive positions and strategies of individual business units.

The ability to combine several elements of strategically useful information in a single graphical display is indicated by the application of the matrix to a diversified food processing company. Not only can the display show the positioning of the business units with regard to market growth and relative market share, it can also indicate the relative sales revenues of the units, their patterns of distribution, and movements in strategic position over time (see Figure 16.3).

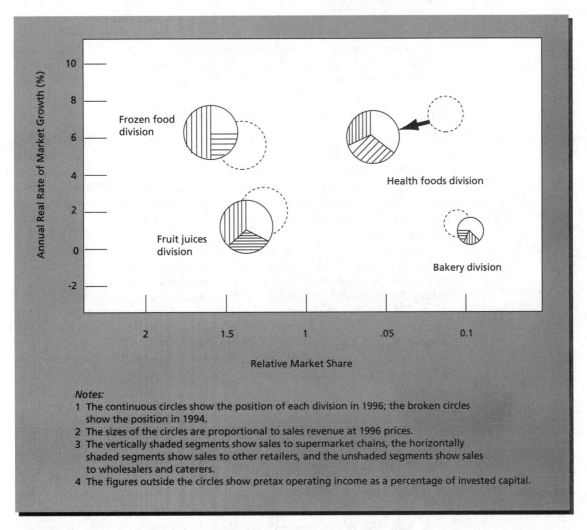

Notes:
1 The continuous circles show the position of each division in 1996; the broken circles show the position in 1994.
2 The sizes of the circles are proportional to sales revenue at 1996 prices.
3 The vertically shaded segments show sales to supermarket chains, the horizontally shaded segments show sales to other retailers, and the unshaded segments show sales to wholesalers and caterers.
4 The figures outside the circles show pretax operating income as a percentage of invested capital.

FIGURE 16.3
Application of the BCG Matrix to the BM Foods Inc.

The declining use of the portfolio planning matrices such as the BCG growth-share matrix and the McKinsey matrix reflects their weaknesses as analytical tools.

- Both are gross oversimplifications of the factors that determine industry attractiveness and competitive advantage. This is especially true of the BCG matrix, which uses just two variables: market share is not a good indicator of competitive advantage; market growth is a poor proxy for market profit potential .

- The positioning of businesses within the matrix is highly susceptible to measurement choices. For example, relative market share in the BCG matrix depends critically on how markets are defined: Is BMW's North American auto business a "dog" because it holds about 1 percent of the total auto market, or a cash cow because BMW is market leader in the luxury car segment?

- The approach assumes that every business is completely independent. Where linkages exist between businesses units, regarding each as a stand-alone business inevitably leads to suboptimal strategy choices: Mobil's downstream businesses in Canada may appear to be "dogs," yet to the extent that they permit high capacity utilization in U.S. refineries, they support the competitive positions of Mobil's U.S. businesses.

Value-Based Approaches to Corporate Restructuring

If portfolio analysis was a key framework for strategy analysis during the diversification era of the 1970s, the refocusing of the 1980s and 1990s has been closely associated with the application of shareholder value analysis to corporate strategy decisions. In appraising the business portfolio of a company, the fundamental criterion to be applied to each business is whether the market value of the company is greater *with* that business, or *without* it (i.e., selling it to another owner or spinning it off as a separate entity).

The application of value-based management tools has been salutary for the top management teams of many multibusiness corporations. As noted in the previous chapter, the majority of diversifying acquisitions have destroyed shareholder wealth—the acquisition premiums paid have greatly exceeded the value of any increased performance resulting from the acquisitions. Conversely, stock market valuations have responded positively to divestments, or even to the anticipation of divestment.

Applying the techniques of shareholder value analysis outlined in Chapter 2, McKinsey and Company has proposed a systematic framework for increasing the market value of multibusiness companies through corporate restructuring. McKinsey's "pentagon framework" consists of a five-stage process illustrated in Figure 16.4. The five stages of the analysis are:

1. **The current market value of the company.** The starting point of the analysis is the current market value of the company, which comprises the value of equity plus the value of debt (as we know from Chapter 2, this equals the market's expectations of the net cash flow of the company discounted at the company's weighted average cost of capital).

2. **The value of the company as is.** Since the current market value represents the market's valuation of the company, there may be potential to enhance market value simply by managing external perceptions of the company

FIGURE 16.4
Corporate Restructuring to Create Value: The McKinsey Pentagon

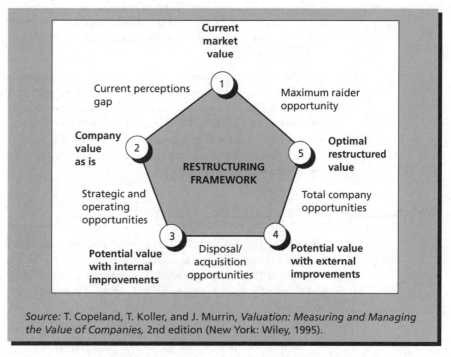

Source: T. Copeland, T. Koller, and J. Murrin, *Valuation: Measuring and Managing the Value of Companies,* 2nd edition (New York: Wiley, 1995).

without any changes to strategy or operations. Over the past ten years, companies have devoted increasing attention to managing investor expectations by increasing the flow of information to shareholders and investment analysts and investing in investor relations departments.

3. **The potential value of the company with internal improvements.** As we shall see in the next section, the corporate head office of a company has opportunities for increasing the overall value of the company by making strategic and operational improvements to individual businesses that increase their cash flows. Strategic opportunities include exploring growth opportunities such as investing in global expansion, repositioning a business in relation to customers and competitors, or strategic outsourcing. Operating improvements would include cost-cutting opportunities and taking advantage of the potential to raise prices.

4. **The potential value of the company with external improvements.** Once top management has determined the value of its constituent businesses and of the company as a whole, it is then in a position to determine whether changes in the business portfolio will increase overall company value. The key issue is whether an individual business, even after strategic and operating improvements have been made, could be sold for a price that is greater than its potential value to the company.

5. **The optimum restructured value of the company.** This is the maximum value of a company once all the potential gains from changing investor perceptions, making internal improvements, and taking advantage of external

opportunities have been exploited. The difference between the maximum restructured value and the current market value represents the profit potential available to a corporate raider from taking advantage of the restructuring opportunities.

This type of analysis has been traditionally associated with leveraged-buyout specialists and other corporate raiders. However, faced with the increasing threat of acquisitions, such analysis is increasingly being undertaken by corporate management teams of established companies. The restructuring transformations of the oil majors have followed this process: increasing the value of existing companies through cost cutting, while taking advantage of external opportunities through trading assets and selling businesses.[7]

MANAGING INDIVIDUAL BUSINESSES

Despite the emphasis given to economies of scope and other types of linkage among the businesses within the multibusiness firm, some of the most important opportunities for corporate headquarters to create value arise from what Goold, Campbell and Alexander call "stand-alone influence." This relates to the corporate parent's ability to:

> . . . appoint the general manager of each business and influence management development and succession planning within the businesses. It can approve or reject budgets, strategic plans, and capital expenditure proposals and it can influence the shape and implementation of these plans and proposals. It can provide advice and policy guidance to the businesses. The parent also influences the businesses by the hints and pressures passed on through both formal and informal line management meetings and contacts, and, more indirectly, through the corporate culture.[8]

The various means by which the corporate headquarters exercises influence over the different businesses can be classified into input control and output control mechanisms. **Input control** or **behavior control** relates to control exercised by corporate-level management over the decisions of business-level managers. This occurs through influence over and approval of business-level strategies and business-level investment proposals. **Output control** or **outcome control** relates to corporate-level control over performance by setting performance targets and incentives and penalties associated with meeting or falling short of these targets. Although most companies use a combination of input and output controls, there is an unavoidable trade-off between the two: more of one implies less of the other. If a company exerts tight control over business-level decisions, then it must accept the performance outcomes that arise from those decisions. If the company exerts rigorous controls relating to performance in terms of annual profit targets, then the company must give business-level managers the freedom to make the decisions necessary to achieve these targets. Here we concentrate on two aspects of corporate influence: influence over business strategy formulation, and financial control.

Business Strategy Formulation

Whereas corporate strategy is formulated and implemented by top management, business strategies are formulated jointly by corporate and divisional managers. In most diversified, divisionalized companies, initiation of strategy proposals is the responsibility of divisional managers and the role of corporate managers is to probe, appraise, amend, and approve divisional strategy proposals. Most companies operate some form of annual planning cycle in which the strategies for individual businesses are determined and these business-level strategies are aggregated to form the corporate strategy. Exhibit 16.1 describes key elements of the planning process at Exxon Corporation.

Performance Control and the Budgeting Process

Most multidivisional companies operate a dual planning process: strategic planning concentrates on the medium and long term, financial planning controls short-term performance. Typically, the first year of the strategic plan includes the performance plan for the upcoming year in terms of an operating budget, a capital expenditure budget, and strategy targets relating to market share, new product introductions, and output and employment levels. Annual performance plans are agreed on between business-level management and corporate-level management, are monitored on a monthly or quarterly basis, and are reviewed more extensively in meetings between business and corporate management after the end of each financial year.

The corporate head office is responsible for setting, monitoring, and enforcing performance targets for the individual divisions. Performance targets may be financial (return on invested capital, gross margin, growth of sales revenue), strategic (market share, rate of new product introduction, market penetration, quality), or both. Performance targets may be short term (monthly, quarterly), medium term (annual), or long term (five years). The primary function of the management information system in a diversified corporation is to enable the head office to monitor divisional performance and identify deviations from targets.

Incentives for achieving target performance include financial returns (salary, bonuses, stock options), promotion, and intangible rewards that enhance organizational status and self-image (e.g., praise, recognition). Sanctions include blame and loss of reputation, demotion, and ultimately, dismissal. Some diversified companies have proved to be highly effective in using performance monitoring and a combination of incentives and sanctions to create an intensely motivating environment for divisional managers. At ITT, Geneen's obsession with highly detailed performance monitoring, ruthless interrogation of divisional executives, and generous rewards for success developed a highly motivated, strongly capable group of young, senior executives who were willing to work unremittingly long hours, and who demanded as high a standard of performance from their subordinates as Geneen did of them.[9] The existence of precise, quantitative performance targets that can be monitored on a short-term (monthly or quarterly) basis can provide an intensely competitive internal environment that is highly effective in motivating a business unit and divisional managers. Hanson's "high-wire" profit targets provide a relentless pressure for cost cutting within its diverse businesses, while PepsiCo's obsession with monthly market share results nourishes an intense and aggressive, marketing-oriented culture. As one PepsiCo executive explained, "The place is full of guys with sparks coming out of their asses."[10]

For companies in rapidly developing and technology-based industries, formulating and implementing appropriate controls is a difficult task. Despite the clarity

EXHIBIT 16.1

Strategic Planning at Exxon

In terms of profitability and shareholder return, Exxon has been one of the most successful of the oil and gas majors as well as being one of the world's largest and most international companies. Exxon's management system has been especially successful at reconciling longer term strategic planning needs with rigorous, shorter term financial control. Key features of Exxon's planning system are :

1. *Responsibility for strategy lies with corporate, divisional, and business managers.* Exxon's reorganization during 1986–1988 focused decision-making responsibility and accountability on individual managers, disbanding the committees, dual reporting mechanisms, and formal systems that had diffused responsibility and obscured accountability. Corporate strategy is formulated by the Management Committee, composed of Exxon's executive directors. Divisional strategies are the responsibility of the Divisional Presidents and their management teams. Linkage between corporate and divisional strategies is provided by the "contact directors." Each executive director is the "contact director" for one or more divisions.

2. *Strategic planning is process oriented and combines formal and informal aspects.* Strategic planning is not about developing plans in some formal sense, it is about ensuring the appropriate direction for the corporation as a whole. The key is effective communication between the Board and the operating divisions to share ideas and information, to improve strategic thinking through dialogue and challenge, and to achieve overall coordination. The contact directors play a key role in this.

3. *Stewardship* is a doctrine of managerial responsibility and accountability that makes each executive responsible in a personal way to the corporation and its shareholders.

4. *Simultaneously top-down and bottom-up strategic decision making.* Strategy is a result both of top-down priorities and guidelines, and bottom-up decision making from those closest to the individual businesses.

Exxon has a regular annual planning cycle as follows:

	The Regular Planning Calendar		**Anytime**
Spring	**Economic Outlook**	Planning Department	**Strategy**
	Energy Outlook	Planning Department	**Studies**
Sept.	**Business Plans**	Divisions	
Oct.	**Corporate Plan**	Planning Department and Management Committee	undertaken
Nov.	**Financial Forecast**	Controller	as and when
	Budget: —Operating	Divisions, Controller, Management Committee	needed
	—Capital		
	Stewardship Basis	Divisions, Planning Department, Management Committee	
Feb.	**Stewardship Reviews**	Divisions, Planning Department, Management Committee	
Aug./Sept.	**Investment Reappraisals**	Divisions, Controller, Management Committee	

EXHIBIT 16.1

(Continued)

The principal stages of the planning cycle are as follows:

1. *The Economic Outlook and Energy Outlook* are prepared by the Economics Division and the Energy Division of the Corporate Planning Department. Each look out 10–15 years at the key macroeconomic and market variables to provide an informed and consistent basis for strategic plans.

2. *Business Plans* are developed during the Spring and Summer by individual businesses and are aggregated and refined at the Divisional level. They outline long-term goals, the means by which these goals will be attained, and the specific projects and types of project that will be undertaken. Their time horizon is 10 years for upstream, 5 years for downstream and chemicals. The business plans are submitted to the Corporate Planning Department during early to mid-October. It is then the task of Corporate Planning to aggregate these plans into a single Corporate Plan.

3. *The Financial Forecast* is the financial plan for a two-year period. The financial forecast is a compilation of the plans for individual businesses and divisions comprising forecasts of revenues, operating costs, capital expenditures, interest and other expenses, income, and cash flow.

4. *The Budget* includes operating and capital budgets are set for the next year.

5. *The Stewardship Basis* is a statement of annual targets against which the next year's performance by each division will be judged. This is determined by the Division and draws on the financial forecast and the business plans. The objectives include:
   - Financial objectives
   - Operating targets (e.g., wells drilled, contracts signed, capacity utilization, throughput)
   - Safety and environmental objectives
   - Strategy mileposts

   A key aspect of the stewardship process is to identify performance measures that reflect *controllable* aspects of the business. Thus, profit performance targets are set such that they can be adjusted for unforecasted price and exchange rate movements.

6. *Stewardship Reviews.* In February of each year, each Division's performance for the previous year is evaluated against its stewardship objectives. These reviews involve presentations by the Divisional top management to the Management Committee.

7. *Investment Reappraisals* occur in August and September and involve the Divisions reporting back on the outcomes of specific investment projects.

8. *Strategic Studies* are ad hoc projects by the Corporate Planning Department that address specific issues such as: What should Exxon's strategy for Thailand be? How should Exxon grow its position in the European market for natural gas? What are the implications for Exxon's minerals business of the 1996–97 fall in the price of copper?

Exxon's Strategic Planning Process

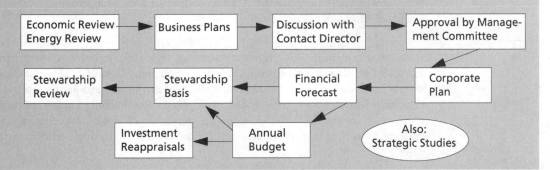

and measurability of financial and sales targets, they may stunt innovation. One approach to reconciling the unpredictability and long time horizons in technology-based industries with effective corporate control is to establish a series of **milestones** that set dates for achieving specific stages in the development of products, projects, or the business as a whole. Milestones might include the signing of particular contacts, the production of a product prototype, the market launch of a new product, achieving a particular level of market penetration, or reducing costs by a specific level. The merit of this approach is that it can reconcile specific short-term targets with longer strategic goals.

The attainment of performance targets is enforced through various incentives and penalties. The trend over time has been for business-level managers to have their remuneration tied closely to business performance. Unsatisfactory performance may lead to the replacement of divisional top managers and ultimately, to the divestment of the division or business unit. The nature and extent of corporate control is likely to depend on the ability of the business to achieve its performance targets. Unsatisfactory performance is likely to lead to loss of autonomy with outcome control being replaced by much closer corporate intervention in business-level decision making. General Electric's hands-off management of its investment banking subsidiary Kidder Peabody was replaced by meticulous corporate scrutiny following a collapse of profitability and scandals involving insider-trading and phantom trading in mortgage-backed securities.[11]

Strategic Management Styles

In their study of corporate strategy among large, British, multibusiness companies, Goold and Campbell found that these forms of control corresponded to the two basic types of strategic management style. Focusing on two corporate management functions—involvement in business strategy formulation and performance control—Goold and Campbell identified three corporate management styles: financial control, strategic control, and strategic planning (plus two additional categories, centralized control and holding company, which they believed to be largely defunct among diversified companies).[12] Figure 16.5 shows these categories.

The principal contrast is between companies where the corporate head office plays an important role in formulating and coordinating business unit and divisional strategies (the **strategic planning style**) and those where the corporate head office concentrates on financial management (the **financial control style**). A third style, **strategic control**, identified with ICI, Courtaulds, Plessey, and Vickers, is a hybrid of the other two. It aims to balance a high degree of divisional autonomy with the benefits of head office coordination.

Strategic Planning.   A strategic planning style of corporate management was found in British Petroleum, Cadbury-Schweppes, Lex, and STC. In these companies, there was substantial involvement by corporate headquarters in business unit planning. Strategies tended to emphasize establishing long-term competitive advantage that was reflected in performance goals that emphasized strategic objectives (market share, innovation, quality leadership) over financial

FIGURE 16.5
The Role of Corporate HQ:
Goold & Campbell's Corporate
Management
Styles

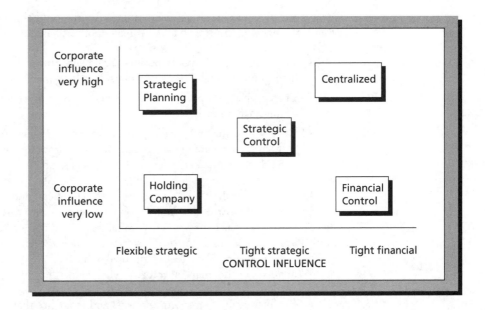

objectives, and the long term over the short term. Weaknesses of the strategic planning style include:

♦ The lack of autonomy for top divisional management, which may result in lack of initiative and "ownership"

♦ The tendency for strategy making to be slow and cumbersome and, hence, unresponsive to new circumstances and opportunities

♦ The lack of diversity that may result from the unitary view imposed by corporate

A strategic planning style is appropriate for companies whose businesses are small in number, do not span to wide a range of products and industries, and where links are strong between them (particularly through shared skills and resources). The style is more appropriate to companies that compete in international and technology-intensive markets where longer-term, strategic goals are more important than short-term profit targets.

Financial Control. The financial control style is associated with conglomerates such as BTR, General Electric Company, and the former Hanson (now dismantled into a number of constituent companies). Corporate headquarters has limited involvement in business strategy formulation; this is the responsibility of divisional and business unit managers. The primary influence of headquarters is through short-term budgetary control. The objective is for the divisions and business units to accept and pursue ambitious profit targets. Because targets were short term, quantitative, and easily measured, they provided strong motivation to managers to increase efficiency and expand business into profitable areas. Careful monitoring of performance by headquarters—with rigorous questioning of managers responsible for deviations from target—maintains constant pressure on divisional management and creates a challenging working environment. Apart from being conducive to profitability, the financial control style has three important benefits:

♦ The autonomy it gives to business units encourages the development of top management capabilities among business-level managers.

♦ The emphasis on profit encourages managers to break away from ineffective strategies at an early stage.

♦ Because the major operating and strategic decisions are taken at business unit level, corporate managers can focus on corporate issues and do not need to have an intimate knowledge of the business units.

Despite the emphasis on "managing by the numbers" and monetary incentives among financial control companies, John Roberts points to the key role of the "psychological contract" between divisional heads and corporate management: the motivation and commitment of divisional managers results from their decision-making autonomy and their feeling of "ownership."[13]

Weaknesses of the financial control style include:

♦ The bias against long-term projects and strategies that results from a short-term focus (Chapter 4 notes the vulnerability of financially managed businesses to those that pursue long-term strategic goals)

♦ Its difficulty of achieving coordination and cooperation between businesses when every business is competing internally for funds and recognition.

The financial control style is suited to companies characterized by broad business diversity, with investment projects that are mainly short and medium term in fruition, and in low-tech industries with limited international competition.

Table 16.1 summarizes key features of the two styles.

Using PIMS in Strategy Formulation and Performance Appraisal

The PIMS program grew out of General Electric's internal database on the strategic, market, and performance characteristics of its business units. It was subsequently extended and developed by the Strategic Planning Institute, which conducts research and provides advisory services to the member companies. The PIMS database now includes information on some 5,000 business units used to estimate the impact of strategy and market structure on business-level profitability. Table 16.2 shows an estimated PIMS equation. PIMS is used by multibusiness companies in the following ways:

♦ *Setting performance targets for business units.* A key problem in setting performance targets and appraising the adequacy of business unit performance is determining the appropriate level of profitability for different types of business. PIMS analysis shows how a business's profitability is determined by some 30 strategy and industry variables. Hence, by plugging in the actual levels of a business's strategy and industry variables into the PIMS regression estimates, it is possible to calculate that business's "Par ROI": the normal level of ROI for a business given its profile of strategic and industry characteristics.

TABLE 16.1
Characteristics of
Different Strategic
Management Styles

	STRATEGIC PLANNING	FINANCIAL CONTROL
Business Strategy Formulation	Business units and corporate center jointly fomulate strategy. Center responsible for coordination of strategies among business units.	Strategy formulated at business unit level. Corporate HQ largely reactive offering little coordination.
Controlling Performance	Primarily strategic goals with medium- to long-term horizon.	Financial budgets set out annual (and shorter term) targets for ROI and other financial variables.
Advantages	Can exploit linkages among businesses. Can give appropriate weight to innovation and longer term competitive positioning.	Business units given autonomy and initiative. Business units can respond quickly to change. Encourages development of business unit managers. Highly motivating.
Disadvantages	Loss of divisional autonomy and initiative. Conducive to unitary view. Resistance to abandoning failed strategy.	Short-term focus discourages innovation, building longer term competitive position, and sharing resources and skills among businesses. Businesses may be willing to give ground to determined competitors.
Style suited to:		
Portfolio Structure	Small number of businesses across narrow range of sectors with close interrelations.	Many businesses across wide range of industries. Linkages ideally few.
Type of Investments	Large projects with long-term paybacks.	Small capital investments with short payback periods.
Environmental Features	Industries with strong technological and global competition.	Mature industries (technical change modest or slow). Stable industry environment without strong international competition.
UK Examples	BP, BOC, Cadbury-Schweppes, Lex Group, STC, United Biscuits	Hanson , BTR, General Electric Company, Ferranti, Tarmac

TABLE 16.2
The PIMS Multiple Regression Equations: The Impact of Industry and Strategy Variables on Profitability

PROFIT INFLUENCES	IMPACT ON:	
	ROI	ROS
Real market growth rate	0.18	0.04
Rate of price inflation	0.22	0.08
Purchase concentration	0.02	N.S.
Unionization (%)	-0.07	-0.03
Low purchase amount:		
low importance	6.06	1.63
high importance	5.42	2.10
High purchase amount:		
low importance	-6.96	-2.58
high importance	-3.84	-1.11
Exports-Imports (%)	0.06	0.05
Customized products	-2.44	-1.77
Market share	0.34	0.14
Relative quality	0.11	0.05
New products (%)	-0.12	-0.15
Marketing, percentage of sales	-0.52	-0.32
R & D, percentage of sales	-0.36	-0.22
Inventory, percentage of sales	-0.49	-0.09
Fixed capital intensity	-0.55	-0.10
Plant newness	0.07	0.05
Capital utilization	0.31	0.10
Employee productivity	0.13	0.06
Vertical integration	0.26	0.18
FIFO inventory valuation	1.30	0.62
R^2	0.39	0.31
F	58.3	45.1
Number of cases	2,314	2,314

Note: For example, if Real Market Growth Rate of a business was to increase by one percentage point, the equation predicts that its ROI would rise by 0.18 percent.

Source: Robert D. Buzzell and Bradley T. Gale, *The PIMS Principles: Linking Strategy to Performance* (New York: Free Press, 1987): 274.

"Par ROI" represents a benchmark that can be used as the basis for profitability targets or can be used as a basis for evaluating actual profitability.

♦ *Formulating business unit strategy.* Because the PIMS regression equations estimate the impact of different strategy variables on ROI, these estimates can indicate how a business can adjust its strategy in order to increase its profit performance.

♦ *Allocating investment funds between businesses.* Past profitability of business units is a poor indicator of the return on new investment. PIMS "Strategic Attractiveness Scan" indicates investment attractiveness based on (a) estimated future real growth rate of the market and (b) the "Par ROI" of the business. The analysis offers predictions as to the "strategic attractiveness" of investment in the business, and the cash flow that can be expected from the business.

MANAGING INTERNAL LINKAGES

The main opportunities for creating value in the multidivisional company arise from the opportunities to exploit economies from sharing resources and transferring capabilities through the linkages that exist among different businesses within the company. These opportunities exist at several levels.

Common Corporate Services

The most basic form of resource sharing in the multidivisional company is the centralized provision of common services and functions. These include basic corporate management functions such as strategic planning, financial control, cash and risk management and other accounting functions, internal audit, taxation, government relations, and shareholder relations. They also include those services used by the businesses that are more efficiently provided on a centralized basis. These include research, engineering, human resources management, legal services, management development, purchasing, and any other services common to several businesses and where there are advantages either of economies of scale or learning benefits from centralized provision.

In practice, the benefits of centralized provision of common services tend to be smaller than many corporate managers anticipate. Although there is little doubt that centralized provision can result in avoiding the costs of duplication, the key problem tends to be a lack of incentive among corporate headquarters staff and specialized corporate units to exploit cost efficiencies or to meet the needs of their business-level customers. During the 1960s and 1970s many companies found that their corporate staffs tended to grow under their own momentum with few obvious economies from central provision and no obvious benefits to the businesses in terms of superior services. Indeed, in HRM and technical services it was common to observe a duplication of services between corporate and business levels.

As a result, many companies separated their corporate headquarters into two groups: a corporate management unit responsible for supporting the corporate management team in core support activities such as strategic planning, finance and legal, and a shared services organization responsible for supplying common services such as research, engineering, training, and information technology to the businesses. The tendency has been to create market incentives for these shared service organizations by requiring them to supply services on an arms-length basis to internal operating units, frequently in competition with independent suppliers of the same services (see Exhibit 16.2).

EXHIBIT 16.2

Amoco's Shared Services Organization

In 1995, Amoco embarked on a radical reorganization of its internal structure. Formerly organized around a large corporate headquarters and three major operating divisions (upstream, downstream, chemicals), Amoco moved to a much more decentralized structure. The three big divisions were broken up into 17 business groups. The corporate headquarters (plus staff units from the former divisions) were formed into two groups: a small Corporate Roles group supporting the top management team now organized as the Strategic Management Committee, and a larger Shared Services Organization.

Corporate Roles comprises the Controller, Treasurer, Financial Operations, Corporate Planning, Corporate Secretary, and "Amoco Progress."

Shared Services includes: Human Resources, IT, Government Relations, Public and Government Affairs, Purchasing, Facilities and Services, Business Processing, Analytical Services, Environment-Health-Safety, Supply, Engineering and Construction, Tax, Auditing, and Legal Services. These 14 service groups supply common services to the business groups. The service groups initially have a "monopoly" on supplying services internally, but after three years, the businesses will be free to obtain services from inside or outside the Amoco group, and the Shared Services Organization will compete with outside providers.

The new structure of Amoco is intended to foster more decentralized decision making, greater accountability, increased focus on profitability and shareholder returns, and increased responsiveness to customer needs and market opportunities.

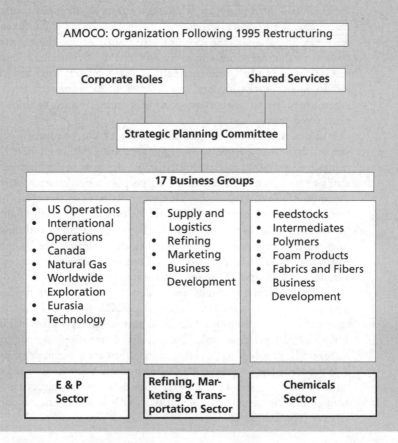

Business Linkages and Porter's Corporate Strategy Types

Corporate management can add value by managing many different types of linkage among business units. These may include:

♦ *Internal trading relationships* (these are likely to be especially important among geographically related and vertically related businesses)

♦ *Coordinating external relationships* (for example, pooling purchases, and providing an integrated approach to government, labor unions, and external interest groups)

♦ *Sharing common resources* (such as research facilities and distribution networks)

♦ *Transferring know-how, intangible resources, and functional capabilities.*

Michael Porter has argued that managing such linkages is the most important source of shareholder value arising from corporate strategy. He identifies four corporate strategy types.

Portfolio Management. Portfolio management is where the parent company simply acquires a portfolio of attractive, soundly managed companies, allows them to operate autonomously, and links them through an efficient internal capital market. This corresponds to the traditional *holding company,* a contemporary example of which is Berkshire Hathaway. Value is created by acquiring companies at favorable prices, closely monitoring their financial performance, and operating a highly effective internal capital market.

Restructuring. British conglomerates BTR and the former Hanson, and U.S. leveraged buyout operators such as KKR have created value by restructuring: acquiring poorly managed companies then intervening to dispose of underperforming businesses and assets, restructure liabilities, and change management and reduce costs in ongoing businesses.

Transferring Skills. Transferring capabilities among business units can create or enhance competitive advantage: Philip Morris' transfers of marketing and distribution capabilities among its tobacco, beer, and Kraft-General Foods businesses. On the other hand, AT&T's acquisition of NCR failed to achieve its intended transfer of computing and communication capabilities. Creating value by sharing skills requires not only that commonalities exist between the businesses in terms of similar skills being applicable and important, but also that mechanisms are established to transfer these skills through the personnel exchange and best practice transfer.

Sharing Activities. Porter argues that the most important source of value arises from exploiting economies of scope in common resources and activities. For these economies to be realized, corporate management must play a key coordinating role, including involvement in formulating business unit strategies and intervention in operational matters to ensure that opportunities for sharing R&D, advertising, distribution systems, and service networks are fully exploited. Such sharing is facilitated by:

♦ A strong sense of corporate identity

♦ A corporate mission statement that emphasizes the integration of business-level strategies

 ♦ An incentive for cooperation among businesses
 ♦ Inter-business task forces and other vehicles for cooperation.

The Corporate Role in Managing Linkages

The closer the linkages among businesses, the greater the opportunities for creating value from sharing resources and transferring capabilities, and the greater the need for corporate headquarters to manage coordination of divisional strategies and activities. In the conglomerate, the independence of each business limits the opportunities for managing linkages. The coordinating role of the head office is restricted to managing the budgetary process and establishing "framework conditions" for divisional planning in the form of economic forecasts, scenarios, and a common format for strategic plans.

In more closely related companies such as the highly vertically integrated oil companies, or companies with close market or technological links (such as IBM, Procter & Gamble, American Express, and Alcoa), corporate management is likely to play a much greater coordinating role. This is likely to involve not only coordination of strategies but also operational coordination in order to exploit the economies of scope and transferable skills discussed in Chapter 15. One indicator of the impact of divisional interrelationships on the coordinating role of corporate management is the size of the corporate headquarters in different types of companies. Berkshire Hathaway, which has almost no linkages among its businesses, has a corporate staff of about 50. Hewlett-Packard with about the same sales, but with much closer linkages between its divisions, has close to 3,000 employees at its Palo Alto head office.

The need to marry decentralized decision making with multiple dimensions of coordination gives rise to complex issues of organizational design within the multibusiness company. Virtually all multibusiness companies are organized around some form of matrix; even companies that are based on product divisions tend to have a geographical organization through country managers who coordinate government relations, taxation, and legal affairs within each country; and functional heads responsible for coordination and best practice transfer in manufacturing, marketing, and other functions across the corporation.

Opportunities for sharing and transferring resources and capabilities may also be accessed through various types of ad hoc organizational arrangements such as **cross-divisional task forces.** Such task forces might be formed for the introduction and dissemination of total quality management, to reengineer financial management practices, to promote fast-cycle new product development, to coordinate business development in Vietnam, and so on.

Corporate management may also encourage divisional managers to exploit interbusiness linkages through exhortations to divisional managers. A key aspect of the top-down aspect of corporate planning is for the CEO to identify companywide issues for divisional managers to take account of in their strategies and operating decisions. The annual planning cycle typically begins with the CEO issuing corporate priorities and performance targets that might include cross-divisional issues such as expansion into China, increasing inventory turnover, integrating IT networks, and the like.

Exploiting linkages between businesses requires careful management, and this imposes costs. Though Porter may be right that the *potential* for value creation increases as a company moves from a loose, "portfolio-management" strategy toward the more integrated "shared-activity" strategy, it is not apparent that this potential is always realized. A study by Lorsch and Allen compared corporate management practices and corporate-divisional relationships in three conglomerates (which engaged in "portfolio management" and "restructuring"), with those of three vertically integrated paper companies (which pursued "transfer of skills" and "sharing of activities").[14] The coordinated requirements of the paper companies resulted in greater involvement of head office staff in divisional operations, larger head office staffs, more complex planning and control devices, and lower responsiveness to change in the external environment. By contrast, the conglomerates made little attempt to exploit linkages even if they were present:

> . . . the conglomerate firms we had studied seemed to be achieving appreciable degrees of financial and managerial synergy but little or no operating synergy. Some of the firms saw little immediate payoff in this operating synergy; others met with little success in attempting to achieve it.[15]

Corporate headquarters' capacity to successfully manage linkages between businesses is likely to depend on corporate management's understanding of its different businesses. This understanding of the different businesses and their relationships is not simply dependent on the existence of shared resources and transferable capabilities, but also on corporate management's ability to comprehend these similarities. As we noted in the last chapter, the mind-set and underlying rationale that gives cohesiveness to the diversified company has been defined by C. K. Prahalad and Richard Bettis as the dominant logic of the enterprise.[16] They define **dominant logic** as "the way in which managers conceptualize the business and make critical resource allocation decisions."[17] For a diversified business to be successful, argue Prahalad and Bettis, there must be sufficient strategic similarity among the different businesses so that top management can administer the corporation with a single dominant logic. For example:

- ♦ Emerson Electric comprises a number of different businesses (electric motors, air conditioning, electrical appliances, control instruments), but the common goal of being a low-cost producer in each of its businesses provides a unifying thread. [18]

- ♦ Unilever's dominant logic is that it is an international manufacturer and marketer of branded, packaged consumer goods. Pursuing this logic has encouraged Unilever to exit animal feeds, transportation, packaging, and most recently, chemicals.

- ♦ Jack Welch's restructuring of GE's business portfolio was preceded by his conceptualizing of GE as three intersecting circles each containing 15 businesses. One circle was GE's core businesses (such as lighting, appliances, and turbines), the second was high technology businesses (such as aerospace, medical equipment, and electronics), the third was service businesses (such as financial and information services).[19]

Such strategic similarities can promote learning within the company as strategies that prove successful in one business can be applied in others. At the same time, the tendency for headquarters to encourage uniformity in the strategies applied in different businesses can cause a failure to fit strategy to the circumstances of the individual business. Although Philip Morris successfully transferred its marketing capabilities from its cigarette business to Miller Brewing, the deployment of these same capabilities and approaches at its 7-Up soft drink subsidiary was a costly failure. [20]

RECENT TRENDS IN THE MANAGEMENT OF MULTIBUSINESS CORPORATIONS

Defining corporate management styles in terms of "parenting roles" as compared to "systems of corporate control" represents a shift in emphasis symbolic of a wider transition in thinking about the role of corporate in the multibusiness corporation. Key features of this transition are:

- A view of corporate headquarters less as the apex of a hierarchy and more as a support service for the businesses.
- Less emphasis on formal systems and techniques, and more on relationships and informal interaction.
- Decentralization of both operational and strategic decisions from corporate to divisional levels.
- Emphasis on the role of headquarters, and the CEO in particular, as a catalyst and driver of organizational change.

Reinventing General Electric

In the same way that General Electric was the pioneer in the development of formalized approaches to corporate strategy and control, it has also been a prime mover in the dismantling of these formal controls in favor of a more flexible, informal, and dynamic approach to corporate strategy. The "reinventing" of GE has been closely associated with the role of CEO Jack Welch, who took over in 1981. Welch's tenure began with an intensive period, which transformed the composition of GE's business portfolio through acquisitions and disposals. This portfolio restructuring was accompanied by radical internal restructuring through aggressive cost cutting and heavy emphasis on international expansion.

Toward the mid-1980s, Welch's attention shifted from the business portfolio to the structure, systems, and style of GE. Several major changes were initiated by Welch.

Delayering.   Welch's fundamental criticism of GE's management was that it was slow and unresponsive. A precondition for a more nimble enterprise was fewer levels of management. Welch eliminated GE's *sector* level of organization (which combined a number of businesses and within each business pressed for the flattening of management pyramids through reducing the layers of hierarchy from nine or ten to four or five):

> We used to have things like department managers, subsection managers, unit managers, supervisors. We're driving those titles out . . . We used to go from the CEO to sectors, to groups, to businesses. We now go from the CEO to businesses. Nothing else.[21]

Changing the Strategic Planning System.   During the 1970s, GE had developed a systematic and formalized approach to strategy formulation and appraisal. Welch believed the system was not only slow and inefficient, but it also stifled innovation and opportunism. A Harvard case study outlines the changes:

> Nowhere was the change more striking than in the area of strategic planning and operational reviews. Although the basic processes were retained, the old staff-led, document-driven process of the 1970s was largely replaced by a

more personal, less formal, but very-intensive face-to-face discussions and small meetings. To cut through the bureaucracy Welch asked each of his 13 business heads to reduce the complex, multivolume planning documents to a slim "playbook" that summarized key strategic issues and actions. On each page, they provided concise answers to questions about their global, market dynamics, key competitive activity, major competitive risks, and proposed GE business responses. These documents became the basis for a half-day shirtsleeve review in mid-summer. Business heads and their key people (usually from three to ten in total) met with the Office of the CEO members and their key staff in an open dialogue on core plans and strategies.[22]

Redefining the Role of Headquarters.   The changes in the strategic planning system is indicative of a broader set of changes in the role of the corporate headquarters. Welch viewed headquarters as interfering too much in the businesses, generating too much unnecessary paper, and failing to add value. His objective was to "turn their role 180 degrees from checker, inquisitor, and authority figure to facilitator, helper, and supporter of the 13 businesses. Ideas, initiatives, and decisions could now move quickly." Welch explained his view of corporate HQ as follows:

> What we do here at headquarters . . . is to multiply the resources we have, the human resources, the financial resources, and the best practices . . . Our job is to help, it's to assist, it's to make these businesses stronger, to help them grow and be more powerful.[23]

The Coordinating Role of Corporate.   Placing increased emphasis on informal aspects of corporate-business relations increased the role of corporate in facilitating coordination across GE's businesses. The Corporate Executive Council was reconstituted to include the leaders of GE's 13 businesses and several key corporate executives. It met two days each quarter to discuss common problems and issues. The Council became an important vehicle for identifying and exploiting synergies.

By 1990, Welch had formulated his notions of coordination and integration within his view of the "boundaryless company." A key element of this concept was a blurring of internal divisions so that people could work together across functional and business boundaries. Welch aimed at "integrated diversity"—the ability to transfer the best ideas, most developed knowledge, and most valuable people freely and easily between businesses.

> Boundaryless behavior is the soul of today's GE . . . Simply put, people seem compelled to build layers and walls between themselves and others, and that human tendency tends to be magnified in large, old institutions like ours. These walls cramp people, inhibit creativity, waste time, restrict vision, smother dreams and, above all, slow things down . . . Boundaryless behavior shows up in the actions of a woman from our Appliances business in Hong Kong helping NBC with contacts needed to develop satellite television service in Asia . . . And finally, boundaryless behavior means exploiting one of the unmatchable advantages a multibusiness GE has over almost any other company in the world. Boundaryless behavior combines 12 huge global businesses—each number one or number two in its markets—into a vast laboratory whose principal product is new ideas, coupled with a common commitment to spread them throughout the Company.[24]

Corporate Managers as Drivers of Organizational Change

Devolution of decision making authority from corporate to business level did not imply a passive role for the corporate HQ. In many respects, corporate became more interventionist in attempting to influence business operations. A critical role for corporate was in attempting to drive large-scale organizational change. An example of this was GE's "Work-Out" initiative that encourages the businesses to establish forums where employees could speak their minds about management and to propose changes in business and operating practices. Work-Out was a vehicle for cultural change in which the relationship between boss and subordinate was redefined and the creativity of employees was unleashed. Large-scale organizational change in other mature organizations is typically associated with chief executives who have adopted the role of change-maker. In the oil sector, Lawrence Rawl at Exxon, Lucio Noto at Mobil, James Kinnear at Texaco, David Simon (preceded by Robert Horton and Peter Walters) at BP, Serge Tchuruk at Total, and Franco Bernabe at ENI have all adopted the role of pioneering organizational change.[25]

Redefining the Corporate Role at Other Companies

Although General Electric is one of the best-known among the companies that have radically altered their corporate strategies and the structures, systems, and styles through which those strategies are implemented, the changes at GE reflect factors that have affected most multibusiness corporations. These include the overriding need to establish competitive advantage within each of the business areas in which the firm competes, the need for responsiveness to external change, the need to foster innovation, and the need for cost efficiency. The problem for large diversified corporations is that these challenges require conflicting adjustments. For example:

- ♦ Rigorous financial controls are conducive to cost efficiency and autonomy; flexible controls are conducive to responsiveness and innovation.
- ♦ Multibusiness companies have typically been based on the advantages of exploiting existing resources and capabilities across different markets, yet competitive advantage in the future is dependent on the creation of new resources and capabilities.
- ♦ Active portfolio management based on the maximization of shareholder value is best achieved with independent businesses; the creation of competitive advantage increasingly requires the management of business interdependencies.

The central dilemma is one that has preoccupied GE: how to exploit the resource advantages of the large company, while achieving the responsiveness and creativity associated with small companies.

The implication is that the management systems of multibusiness companies must also become more sophisticated and flexible. In Chapter 14, we noted how conflicting pressures for globalization and local adaptability were resolved by multinationals moving toward a "transnational" structure. Similar tendencies are observable in managing the tensions within diversified corporations. At IBM, it is interesting to observe that CEO Lou Gerstner resisted stock market pressures for a breakup of the company in favor of limited and selective divestment. The internal changes occurring at IBM under the leadership of Gerstner parallel many of the changes introduced by GE:

- Aggressive cost cutting and employee reduction

- Encouraging responsiveness and flexibility through greater autonomy, while more effectively exploiting internal resources and capabilities through internal coordination

- A breaking down of corporate boundaries and an increased willingness to learn from other companies and to collaborate with other companies in strategic alliances.

Coordination is less about managing the sharing and transfer of resources and capabilities and more about promoting the overall cohesiveness of the diversified company. The corporate strategy of a diversified company is not completely described by the portfolio of businesses the company holds. Just as the single-business company needs clarity of purpose to provide its strategy with direction and its employees with commitment, so the diversified firm typically needs an identity and a rationale that gives meaning to its strategy beyond the composition of its portfolio. Hence, key roles of corporate management in coordinating the diversified company are providing *leadership*, defining *mission*, and establishing a set of values and beliefs that create a unifying **corporate culture.**

Unity within the diversified company may be achieved partly through strategic similarities (or dominant logic) between the different businesses. But companies also need a stronger integrating force if it is to develop the loyalty and commitment necessary to mobilize the efforts and talents of its employees. Because of its very diversity, the multibusiness corporation may find it difficult to establish a common culture that bonds the various businesses and the scattered employees to one another. LVMH, the French producer of Moet champagne, Hennessy cognac, Dior and Givenchy perfumes, and Louis Vuitton luggage is a company that has made great efforts to establish a unifying set of values and traditions: "the common cultural trunk is based on the permanent search for quality of the products and the management, human relations based on responsibility and initiative, and rewarding competences and services."[26] A major theme in American Express's "one enterprise" program aimed at integrating its various financial service companies has been the development of a common set of values oriented around quality, outstanding customer service, and marketing excellence.

Corporate Management in ABB

Asea Brown Boveri (ABB) was created in 1987 from the merger of Asea and Brown Boveri. It combines a very high level of international spread with a very high level of diversification. Because of its success in reconciling decentralization with integration within a large and highly complex enterprise, ABB has been identified by several management scholars (including Christopher Bartlett and Sumantra Ghoshal) as an exemplar of the emerging model of the multibusiness corporation.[27] Bartlett and Ghoshal identify the key features of ABB that exemplify emerging management trends.

1. **Matrix organization**. The M-form model is one of a number of product divisions reporting to a corporate HQ. Most large industrial organizations are matrices where a business unit/subsidiary general manager reports both to a sector manager and a country or regional manager.

2. **Radical decentralization**. The fundamental units of organization in ABB are not product divisions as assumed in the traditional M-form model, but individual businesses within each country of which ABB possesses 1,300. These are free-standing legal entities with average employment of 200. These businesses are where strategic and operating decisions are made. Between them and the corporate headquarters is a single management layer formed by worldwide business area managers and country managers. However, the intermediate layer is exceptionally lean, and corporate HQ employs less than 100 people.

3. **Bottom-up management**. The M-form presupposes that decision-making power has been devolved from corporate down to the divisions. In ABB authority lies with the individual businesses. Each has its own balance sheet and is able to retain one-third of its net income. Front-line managers are entrepreneurs—not implementors of corporate and divisional decisions.

4. **Informal collaboration and integration**. The traditional view of economies of scope in the diversified corporation views corporate HQ as exploiting economies in joint resources (corporate research labs, corporate provision of MIS and administrative services). In ABB it is horizontal linkages between the front-line business units facilitated by country and business area managers through which capabilities are transferred and common resources are shared.

Bartlett and Ghoshal identify three central management processes occurring in the multibusiness corporation: the **entrepreneurial process** (decisions about the opportunities to exploit and the allocation of resources), the **integration process** (how organizational capabilities are built and deployed), and the **renewal process** (the shaping of organizational purpose and the initiation of change).[28] In traditional approaches to the multibusiness corporation, all three processes have been centered within the corporate HQ, the key feature of ABB, and the Bartlett-Ghoshal "managerial theory of the firm" is the distribution of these functions between three levels of the firm: corporate ("top management"), the business and geographical sector coordinators ("middle management"), and the business units ("front-line management"). The critical feature of the relationships between these management levels and between the individual organizational members form a social structure based on cooperation and learning. Figure 16.6 illustrates their framework.

◆ SUMMARY

The formulation and implementation of corporate strategy presents top management with a tangle of issues of almost impenetrable complexity. The tendency for multibusiness corporations to also expand multinationally represents a further quantum leap in complexity. The difficulty of establishing ground rules for corporate strategy reflects several factors. First, the variety of objectives and rationales for diversification. Second, the size and administrative complexity of multibusiness corporations involved. Third, the long period of development of many multibusiness corporations that results in inertia and an institutionalized culture. Fourth, the inability of empirical research to offer clear guidance as to the correlates of superior performance in multibusiness corporations:

- Diversified companies may be more or less successful than specialized companies
- Closely linked diversified businesses may be more or less successful than conglomerates

FIGURE 16.6
Corporate Management Processes in the New Multi-business Company

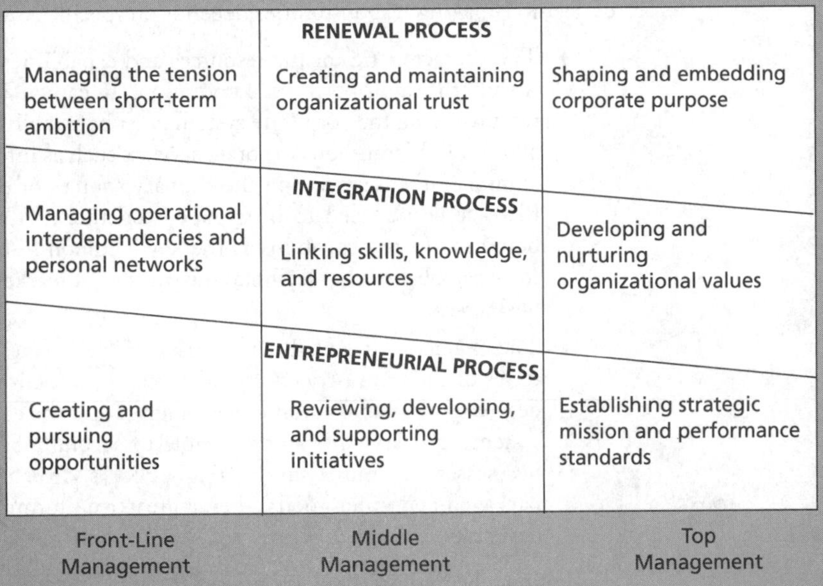

	RENEWAL PROCESS	
Managing the tension between short-term ambition	Creating and maintaining organizational trust	Shaping and embedding corporate purpose
Managing operational interdependencies and personal networks	**INTEGRATION PROCESS** Linking skills, knowledge, and resources	Developing and nurturing organizational values
Creating and pursuing opportunities	**ENTREPRENEURIAL PROCESS** Reviewing, developing, and supporting initiatives	Establishing strategic mission and performance standards
Front-Line Management	Middle Management	Top Management

Source: C. A. Bartlett and S. Ghoshal, "Beyond the M-Form: Toward a Managerial Theory of the Firm," *Strategic Management Journal,* special issue, 14 (Winter 1993): 23–46.

♦ Exploiting shared resources and skills can lead to cost efficiencies and the transfer of competitive advantages, but it can also lead to high administrative cost, management inertia, and inflexibility.

♦ For some diversified companies, rigorous financial controls are conducive to high performance; in others longer-term strategic goals are more effective.

Designing the appropriate organizational structure, management systems, and leadership style of a multibusiness corporation depends critically on *fit* with the corporate strategy of the company. Fundamental to this fit is the *rationale* for the firm. Diversification may create value in different ways. Each source of gain from diversification is likely to imply a quite different approach to managing the firm. For a conglomerate firm, value can be created through the strategic judgment of the CEO with regard to business prospects and company valuation, and the ability to operate a highly efficient internal capital market. Hence, organization and management systems should be oriented toward a clear separation of business levels on corporate decisions and a highly effective system for budgetary control and project evaluation. For a technology-based diversified corporation, value is created through the transfer and integration of knowledge, ideas, and expertise. The company must be organized in order to facilitate the transfer and application of knowledge. Corporate HQ is likely to play a critical role in technological guidance and in divisional integration.

At a more detailed level, the design of structure and systems, and the allocation of decision-making responsibilities depends on specific issues such as:

♦ The characteristics of the resources and capabilities that are being exploited within the multibusiness corporation. If capital is the primary common resource, then the corporate system must be established to ensure its efficient allocation. If common corporate services such as information technology and administrative services are the primary sources of economies of scope, then these activities need to be grouped together at the corporate level. If the brand marketing capability is the key common resource, then systems need to be established that facilitate the transfer of marketing capabilities between businesses.

♦ The characteristics of the businesses. If the businesses are highly diverse in terms of their industry characteristics and competitive positions, then a high degree of divisional autonomy is required and the establishment of corporate systems that are sufficiently flexible to accommodate that flexibility. If the businesses are more similar (e.g., P&G's diversification across branded, packaged consumer goods) then a greater uniformity of systems and style is desirable.

Ultimately, finding the appropriate structure, systems, and style with which to manage a multibusiness corporation is dependent on establishing an identity for the company. The failure of most of the conglomerates of the 1960s and early 1970s was either that they failed to establish a clear identity, or that their identity was so closely linked with a single person (e.g., Geneen at ITT) that the companies found difficulty surviving the demise of that person. In other cases, the rationale on which the identity was based was found to be flawed (e.g., Allegis Corp.). Conversely, the success of diversifed corporations such as General Electric, Matsushita, Canon, Emerson Electric, and ABB reflects a cohesiveness between the businesses of the company, the strategies being pursued, the structure of the organization, and its management style. This permits a sense of identify and clarity of vision with regard to the fundamental strategic question, *"What kind of company are we seeking to become?"*

NOTES

1   This section draws heavily on Oliver E. Williamson, *Markets and Hierarchies: Analysis and Antitrust Implications* (New York: Free Press, 1975); and Oliver E. Williamson, "The Modern Corporation: Origins, Evolution, Attributes," *Journal of Economic Literature* 19 (1981): 1537–1568.

2   Oliver E. Williamson, "The Modern Corporation: Origins, Evolution, Attributes," *Journal of Economic Literature* 19 (1981): 1558–1589.

3   See, for example, Peter Steer and John Cable, "Internal Organization and Profit: An Empirical Analysis of Large UK Companies," *Journal of Industrial Economics* 21 (September 1978): 13–30; Henry Armour and David Teece, "Organizational Structure and Economic Performance: A Test of the Multidivisional Hypothesis," *Bell Journal of Economics* 9 (1978): 106–122; and David Teece, "Internal Organization and Economic Performance," *Journal of Industrial Economics* 30 (1981): 173–199.

4   Henry Mintzberg, *Structure in Fives: Designing Effective Organizations* (Englewood Cliffs, NJ: Prentice-Hall, 1983): chapter 11.

5 M. Goold, A. Campbell, and M. Alexander, *Corporate-Level Strategy: Creating Value in the Multibusiness Company* (New York: Wiley, 1994)

6 "General Electric: Strategic Position—1981," Harvard Business School Case 381-174, 1981: 1.

7 R. Cibin and R. M. Grant "Restructuring Among the World's Largest Oil Companies," *British Journal of Management* 7 (December 1996): 411–428.

8 Michael Goold, Andrew Campbell, and Marcus Alexander, *Corporate Level Strategy: Creating Value in the Multibusiness Company* (New York: Wiley, 1994): 90.

9 Geneen's style of management is discussed in chapter 3 of Richard T. Pascale and Anthony G. Athos, *The Art of Japanese Management*, (New York: Warner Books, 1982).

10 "Those Highflying PepsiCo Managers," *Fortune*, April 10, 1989: 79.

11 "GE's Costly Lesson on Wall Street," *Fortune*, May 9, 1988: 79; "General Electric's Wall Street Shock," *Economist*, May 28, 1994: 71–72.

12 M. Goold and A. Campbell, *Strategies and Styles* (Oxford: Blackwell, 1987).

13 J. Roberts, "Strategy and Accounting in a U.K. conglomerate," *Accounting, Organizations and Society* 15 (1990): 107–126.

14 Jay W. Lorsch and Stephen A. Allen III, *Managing Diversity and Interdependence: An Organizational Study of Multidivisional Firms* (Boston: Harvard Business School Press, 1973).

15 *Ibid.*: 168.

16 C. K. Prahalad and R. Bettis, "The Dominant Logic: A New Linkage Between Diversity and Performance," *Strategic Management Journal* 7 (1986): 485–502.

17 *Ibid.*: 490.

18 "Shades of Geneen at Emerson Electric," *Fortune*, May 22, 1989: 39.

19 "General Electric—Going with the Winners," *Fortune*, March 26, 1984: 106.

20 *The Seven-Up Division of Philip Morris Inc.*, Harvard Business School, 1989.

21 "GE Chief Hopes to Shape Agile Giant," *Los Angeles Times*, June 1, 1988: D1.

22 "General Electric: Jack Welch's Second Wave (A)," Harvard Business School Case 9-391-248, 1991.

23 Jack Welch, "GE Growth Engine," speech to employees, 1988.

24 "Letter to Share Owners," *General Electric Company 1993 Annual Report* (Fairfield, CT, 1994): 2.

25 R. M. Grant, "The Chief Executive as Change Agent," *Planning Review* 24, no. 1 (December 1995): 9–11.

26 Roland Calori, "How Successful Companies Manage Diverse Businesses," *Long Range Planning* 21 (June 1988): 85; "LVMH Tries to Adjust After a Life of Luxury," *Financial Times*, June 11, 1993: 26.

27 C. A. Bartlett and S. Ghoshal, "Beyond the M-Form: Toward a Managerial Theory of the Firm," *Strategic Management Journal* 14, Special Issue (Winter 1993): 23–46.

28 C.A. Barlett and S. Ghoshal, "Beyond Structure to Process," *Harvard Business Review* (January-February 1995); and "Beyond the M-Form: Toward a Managerial Theory of the Firm," *Strategic Management Journal* 14, Special Issue (Winter 1993): 23–46.

17

Strategies for a New Millennium

Standing on the threshold:
"Before man reaches the moon your mail will be delivered within hours from New York to California, to England, to India or to Australia by guided missiles . . . We stand on the threshold of rocket mail."
—*Arthur E. Summerfield, U.S. Postmaster General, 1959*[1]

Outline

◆ INTRODUCTION

What a decade it has been!

In terms of the corporate sector, the 1990s have been one of unparalleled opportunity. In North America and some parts of Europe, companies have enjoyed a level of profitability and shareholder return unmatched since the 1960s.

423

In terms of strategic management, the 1990s have been a period of rapid development. Advances in strategic thinking and analysis have been the result of increased integration of the concepts and theories drawn from disciplines such as economics, sociology, psychology, biology, and systems theory. Synthesis across disiciplines and between theory and practice has promoted accelerating theoretical and empirical progress. One indicator of this progress is that strategic management is less obviously a net importer of ideas and findings from its contributing disciplines. In areas such as the analysis of competition, determinants of long-run profitability, organizational structure and the design of interfirm relationships, and the management of technology, it is the strategic management scholars who are breaking new ground and influencing thinking in the related disciplines.

At the same time, formidable challenges lie ahead. The late 1980s and early 1990s appear to be a watershed in the development of firms. The trajectory of development of the post-war period has been reversed, and many of the features of "managerial capitalism" including diversification, vertical integration, large corporate staffs, and meticulous corporate planning have been undone. The driving force for change has been the application of the rigorous yardstick of shareholder value against all aspects of strategy, structure, and managerial decisions. However, the limits of downsizing, refocusing, restructuring, and reengineering are fast being approached. What lies beyond is unclear. It is certain that the future gains in performance will not come so easily. The challenge is to identify and exploit new sources of competitive advantage. These are likely to result from innovation and the development of capabilities based on superior and unique approaches to complex integration within and across firms. Unlike the other chapters of this book, the objective of this chapter is not to equip you with tools and frameworks that you can deploy directly in your own companies or in case analysis. My approach is exploratory: to introduce you to the trends and ideas that are reshaping our thinking about business strategy as a preliminary stage to developing new tools and frameworks. Let us begin by examining current trends and identifying some of the ideas influencing contemporary thinking about strategy and competitive advantage.

THE NEW ENVIRONMENT OF BUSINESS

In terms of the business sector in general, the 1990s have been a period of unprecedented opportunity. These are opportunities for trade, investment, and entrepreneurship that have sprung from revolutionary changes: the collapse of communism in the Soviet Union and Eastern Europe, worldwide privatization and deregulation, increased freedom of trade following the Uruguay Round and creation of the World Trade Organization, and the formation of regional free-trade areas (NAFTA, Mercosur, and the enlarged European Union). If internationalization has been one key driver, technology has been the other. The 1980s saw the rise of the personal computer industry and the explosive growth of microelectronics, but it has been in the 1990s that the full impact of the digital revolution has been felt by the world of business. It is a testament to the pervasive impact of information and communications technology that government statisticians have been unable to measure its impact on productivity!

The telecommunications sector reflects the combined impact of these forces more clearly than almost any other industry. Beginning with the breakup of AT&T, privatization of British Telecom, and growth of wireless communication at the beginning of decade, the industry has been propelled into a hypercompetitive ferment. The explosive growth of the Internet, the introduction of PCS and direct satellite communications, the convergence of communication with computing and entertainment, privatization of state-owned telephone companies, and the removal of restrictions on market entry and pricing have caused continual reconfiguration of the competitive environment. Strategic moves have included the emergence of new companies, the battle over digital standards, the formation of alliances to exploit new markets, the creation of new services, and a variety of different approaches to vertical integration and outsourcing and bundling and unbundling.

Looking ahead to 2000 and beyond, it seems likely that these two same forces—internationalization and digital technologies—will continue to reshape the business environment and provide the primary sources of business opportunity. The trend to increased international openness and interaction appear difficult to derail. Among the former isolationist nations of the world, only North Korea is resisting integration with the global economy. All the others that had pursued policies of protectionism or "separate development," including China, Russia and the Comecon countries of Eastern Europe, Iran, India, Syria, South Africa, Tanzania, Albania, and many others, have abandoned isolation and are actively seeking foreign investment and increased participation in world markets. Even Cuba is seeking access to international flows of capital, trade, and technology despite the restrictions of its own ideology and the U.S. embargo.

Expanding trade and financial flows and more intense international competition increase the pressures for convergence among national policies. When countries are competing for inward flows of foreign investment and technology and domestic firms are battling for world market share, taxes and regulations that might appear desirable in a closed economy can become prohibitively expensive in an open economy in terms of lost investment and lost jobs. The increasing inability of the Soviet Union to compete in a world economy driven by technology, customer focus, and entrepreneurial responsiveness was fundamental to its collapse. The partial dismantling of the "welfare state" in Britain and Sweden, the continuing difficulties of France's *dirigiste* state-dominated economy, and the unsustainability of the Japanese and South Korean models of government-orchestrated capitalism reflect the same forces.

Information and communications technology is reinforcing the internationalization process. The remarkable ability of the Internet to bypass existing marketing systems and distribution channels, especially in business-to-business transactions, has exploded the market potential for small companies. At its web site "Salami.com," Eastern Meat Farms has expanded the market for its Italian-style deli products from Franklin Square, NY, to Japan and beyond.[2] More generally, the ability of buyers and suppliers of any size to use "electronic markets" to find one another anywhere in the world without human intermediaries has the potential to generate the greatest expansion in the market system since the invention of money.

Information technology is creating new industries and redrawing the boundaries of exiting industries. The convergence of communication and entertainment through web-TV and the joint delivery of telecommunications and cable TV, is now set within a larger debate over the potential for bundling these services with other utility-type services such as power, gas, and water.

As industries and customer requirements change, so the competitive positions of established enterprises are undermined—while opportunities appear for both new and existing firms. The future shape of the financial services sector is especially difficult to predict. As retail branch-banking increasingly gives way to on-line banking, the biggest asset of the retail banks—their branch networks—becomes a liability in meeting new customer needs. As a variety of companies jockey for position within the emerging value chain of on-line banking—software companies such as Microsoft and Intuit, on-line service providers such as AOL and AT&T, banks such as Citibank and Nations-bank—the battle for competitive advantage is between rivals with very different bundles of resources and capabilities. In investment banking too, as firms rush to create vertically integrated powerhouses (e.g., the mergers between Morgan Stanley and Dean Witter Discover and between Travelers Group and Salomon Brothers), there is the risk that these giant players will be undone by technology-driven restructuring of distribution channels. The Internet has permitted corporations to access the capital market without relying on investment banks. Logos Research Systems was one of the first initial public offering (IPOs) undertaken by direct placement of stock with individual investors through the Internet.[3] Across the economy as a whole, "middlemen," whether investment banks, commercial banks, wholesalers, real estate brokers, employment agencies, or car dealers, are threatened by the same trends: IT permits "disintermediation." In other words, buyers and sellers can be brought directly into contact without the need for intermediaries.

DIRECTIONS IN STRATEGIC MANAGEMENT PRACTICE

To understand where we are going, we must know where we are coming from. Let me outline the key trends of the current decade, then identify the major influences of the present.

Trends of the 1990s

At the practical level, firms' strategies have been driven by two dominant forces. The first is pressure for shareholder return, the second, adjusting to turbulence.

The shareholder value movement of the past decade has had a huge impact on companies' strategies, their management, and their performance. Pressure on management from shareholders (especially pension funds) and from the financial markets (especially through the threat of takeover), has created strong pressure on top management to maximize returns to shareholders. This has been most evident in the "Anglo-Saxon business systems" of North America, the UK, and Australia, but is increasingly evident in Continental Europe and Japan.

At the level of corporate strategy, the major impact has been the move to refocusing. With the exception of some service industries and some technology-based sectors, large corporations have divested diversified operations and concentrated on "core businesses." In terms of vertical scope, outsourcing has resulted in greater selectivity over which stages of the value chain firms wish to engage in. At the business strategy level, the key driver has been cost reduction. The widespread downsizing among industrial corporations is partly the result of refocusing, but also a consequence of radical cost cutting. Pressure to increase profitability has meant pressure to reduce costs. The elimination of large numbers of managers and administrative staff, cuts in inventories, increased utilization of capital equipment, divestment of assets whose returns fall short of cost of capital, and reengineering of processes are all outcomes of preoccupation with the bottom line.

These cost-cutting, profit-enhancing initiatives have been undertaken, to a great extent, not by the familiar command-and-control mechanisms of the corporate bureaucracy, but by a management system that sets targets for managers, but then gives them substantial discretion as to how these targets are achieved. As noted in Chapter 16, the emphasis of control has shifted from input or behavior control, to **outcome control.** This dissemination of authority within the corporation, widely described as "empowerment" has involved linking decision-making responsibilities with clear accountability. Achieving accountability requires careful monitoring of actual performance against performance targets and leads to far more elaborate quantification of performance goals than existed before. The movement toward **metrics,** which have been closely identified both with total quality management and the empowerment trend of the past decade, represent the increasing sophistication and fine-tuning of this outcome-based control system—the **balanced scorecard** approach (see Chapter 2) is one example of this.

The drive to decentralization of decision making is also a response to external turbulence. As we noted in Chapter 6, administrative hierarchies with centralized decision making tend to break down under the pressure of environmental turbulence. This is partly because of increased volume of decisions, partly because of the need for faster organizational responses, and partly because of the inability of rules and routines to deal with new circumstances. The need for increased flexibility and responsiveness has resulted in a number of changes to companies' strategies and structures, including:

- *Emphasis on dynamic sources of efficiency.* These include rapid capacity adjustment, rescheduling of production, minimizing downtime from production line changeovers, and flexible manufacturing systems, rather than static sources of efficiency, such as economies of scale, economies from dedicated production facilities, and vertical integration.

- *Emphasis on time reduction.* A key priority in process reengineering, whether manufacturing processes, order fulfillment processes, or new product development processes, has been the reduction of cycle time. Achieving time reduction has required tighter integration of activities and processes, cross-functional linkages, integrated information networks, and a shift from production-driven "push" processes to customer-driven "pull" processes.

Key Influences on Strategy

Many of the changes in companies' strategies during the 1990s were strongly influenced by strategy concepts developed and popularized by business school academics, consultants, and, in some cases, leading-edge corporations. Four concepts have exerted particular influence.

Resource-Based Theory, Organizational Capabilities, and Core Competences.

Recognition of the role of resources and capabilities (competences) as a basis for competitive advantage and the foundation of corporate profitability has had a pervasive influence of companies' strategies. Resource and competency-based thinking has provided the conceptual underpinnings for refocusing and outsourcing and recent thinking on *dynamic capabilities* has influenced strategies toward flexibility and responsiveness.[4]

Dynamic Approaches to the Analysis of Industry and Competition.

An increasingly apparent feature of the business environment of the 1990s has been the instability of industry boundaries. This has been most apparent in the *hypercompetitive* industries such as computing, entertainment, communication and information services, but also in seemingly less turbulent environments such as electricity, financial services, natural gas, retail distribution, and commercial real estate. The result has been to renew interest in Schumpeterian analysis of competition and the Austrian school of economics more generally,[5] and to reinvigorate the quest for realism and relevance in applications of game theory.[6] Although the theory of games has been with us for half a century, its usefulness as a tool of strategy analysis is only recently becoming evident.

Emphasis on Network Effects, the Role of Standards, and Bandwagon Effects in Establishing and Sustaining Competitive Advantage.   A central feature of competition in new technology-based industries and new product generation have been pitched battles for the control of technical standards. The lesson of the VHS/Betamax battle in video and Macintosh/Windows rivalry in microcomputer operating systems has been the critical role of strategic management in influencing standards. Game theory, the principles of strategic commitment, and analyses of bandwagon effects have provided substantial insight into the dynamics of these situations.[7]

Modern Financial Analysis.   In understanding the sources of shareholder value, financial theory has had a major impact on clarifying the implications of shareholder value maximization for strategy, and dispelling delusions concerning the risk-spreading benefits of diversification. By carefully distinguishing accounting from economic profit, identifying the risk relevant to shareholders (systematic risk), showing that shareholders can diversify risk more cheaply than can companies, showing that debt is typically cheaper than equity capital, and providing rigorous analysis of the agency issues associated with the separation of ownership from control, financial theory has not only linked strategic and financial analysis much more closely, but encouraged strategy to become much more focused around a quest for the sources of profitability. In linking shareholder value analysis to the problems of uncertainty and the need for flexibility, **option theory** is providing a whole new set of tools for the appraisal of strategic investments.[8]

NEW DIRECTIONS IN STRATEGIC THINKING

Beyond Downsizing

At the sharp end of business practice, the key challenge to company executives is maintaining the momentum that has been built up over the past decade. The most daunting aspect of the new millennium (particularly for U.S. companies) is the prospect that because the economic environment of the 1990s has been so favorable, and because the strategies of downsizing, refocusing, and delayering have been so successful, the expectations built into current stock market valuations are almost bound to lead to disappointment. The past decade has seen a sharp reversal in the post-war trend toward lower real return on capital among companies, and a significant redistribution of income from labor (wages, salaries, and benefits) to capital (profits). Figures 17.1 and 17.2 show these trends.

These trends reflect a combination of factors. In the United States, a benign macroeconomic environment in terms of low interest rates, subdued inflation, buoyant consumer demand, and a low U.S. dollar have boosted corporate profitability. Looking more internationally, the key influences have been the impact of technological change on productivity and profit-focused company strategies.

The problem for senior management is that the principal sources of increased profitability in the past (cost-cutting, divesting underperforming assets, and reengineering processes) are no longer available. The "low-hanging fruit" has been picked and future bounty requires new approaches to harvesting.

For many companies, the simple answer is to shift from cost-cutting mode to revenue-growing mode. Yet, in view of the emerging business environment of the next decade, it is not apparent that the returns on new investment will earn anything like the returns on existing investments. Despite the current problems of East and Southeast Asia, demand continues to grow in North America, parts of Europe, and Latin America; so too does industrial capacity. In automobiles, semiconductors, microcomputers, oil and gas production, and petrochemicals, current rates of new capital investment threaten to swamp increases in world demand over the next five years. Even if companies are successful in continuing to cut costs and boost productivity, in the current competitive environment, it seems likely that these cost reductions will accrue to customers through lower prices rather than to stockholders through higher profits.

Under these circumstances, the challenge to top management is to identify and access new sources of profitability. The current rekindling of interest in strategic management reflects the importance and the complexity of this task. Yet the focus of strategic management continues to shift. If the focus of strategy formulation during

FIGURE 17.1
Return on Equity (in percent) of U.S. Manufacturing Corporations, 1985–1996

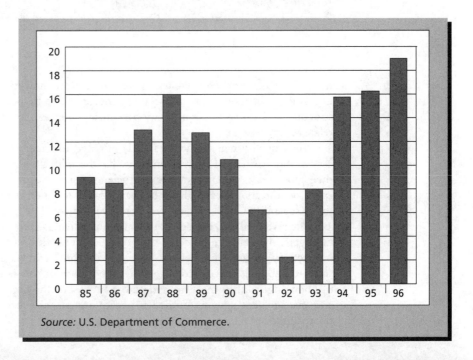

Source: U.S. Department of Commerce.

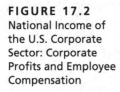

FIGURE 17.2
National Income of
the U.S. Corporate
Sector: Corporate
Profits and Employee
Compensation

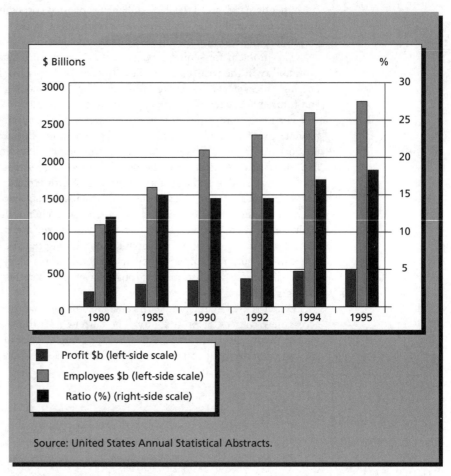

Source: United States Annual Statistical Abstracts.

the 1980s was *positioning*—which markets to be in and how to position within them in relation to market share and segment choice, where to locate in relation to cost structure and differentiation positions—during the late 1990s the critical issues relate to *organization*.

Total quality management (TQM) initiated this reorientation; business process reengineering (BPR) reinforced it. By the mid-1990s, companies looked to their processes as primary sources of efficiency, speed, quality, and flexibility. Interest in organizational capabilities has carried this focus on organization much further. Capabilities such as new product development, fast-cycle order fulfillment, and effective deal making are not located in individual processes or in individual managers, they are the outcome of a complex network of activities involving the interactions of large numbers of people. Work on "architectural capabilities" and "meta-capabilities" have recognized the importance of this large-scale integration of knowledge within the firm and across firms, but the organizational structures and management systems needed to create and sustain such capabilities remain poorly understood.[9]

The MIT Initiative on Inventing the Organizations of the 21st Century has identified eight questions that represent urgent challenges for today's business leaders.

1. **Learning to adapt.** How can an organization effectively deal with constant and multidimensional change? How can it boost its capacity to adapt?

2. **Structure.** How should a company be organized for maximum responsiveness to continuous and often unpredictable changes in the marketplace?

3. **Skills.** What leadership qualities are needed to guide tomorrow's organizations? What skills will be crucial at all levels of an organization operating in such a dynamic environment?

4. **Management styles.** What happens when "command and control" styles of management collide with ongoing efforts to empower workers? When more employees have access to more information, how should decisions be made?

5. **Impact of information technology.** What will happen to industry structures when electronic markets and information highways transform traditional patterns of marketing and commerce?

6. **New ways of working.** With increased capacity for communication and coordination, how will individuals work together? Will there be less need for co-location in offices and factories and more "telecommuting"?

7. **Innovation.** If the winners are those companies that are first to recognize and implement innovations, how can companies create internal environments that spur continuous innovation?

8. **Measures of success.** As intellectual capital and other intangibles play a larger role in a firm's success, how are accounting measures to be adapted to more accurately portray the true assets, liabilities, and long-term prospects of a company?[10]

New Concepts of the Firm

The spectacular success of the corporate sector in generating shareholder value over the period 1988–1997 and the resurgence of U.S. business over this same period owes much to a model of the firm built on shareholder sovereignty, resolution of agency problems through financial incentives and individual insecurity, and performance-based management built around an integrated system of metrics. If the success of this system has focused on undoing the inefficiencies, lethargy, and self-indulgence of the corporatism that flourished in the 1960s and 1970s, it is not apparent that this management model will foster competitiveness under a post-downsizing era.

The critical requirements of the future are likely to be accessing more complex sources of advantage and achieving more effective reconciliation of the contradictions between short-run vs. long-run optimization, individual initiative vs. coordinated response, cost efficiency vs. innovation, and global integration vs. local responsiveness. Attaining these performance goals is likely to require a model of the firm that embodies a richer set of human relationships. The ascendancy of the shareholder-oriented, economically rational model of the firm has left alternative approaches to management—notably the human relations, sociotechnical systems, and stakeholder approaches—in the shadows. There is current evidence that management concepts based on a socially richer conception of the firm may be reappearing.

Senge's concept of the **learning organization** goes beyond a concept of the firm as a social institution and views the firm as a social organism that is also a knowledge system.[11] Arie de Geus extends this concept of the firm as organism to draw more heavily on biological analogies. The key to survival and prosperity in the long run, notes de Geus, is adaptivity. Based on a study of the world's longest-living companies (including Stora, a Swedish paper company founded in the thirteenth century, Japan's 400-year old Sumitomo, 195-year old Du Pont, and Pilkington, the British glass maker founded in the 1820s), de Geus identifies longevity with: *financial conservatism*; *sensitivity* to the external environment reinforced by organizational mechanisms that promote adaptation (such as "flocking"); *cohesion* in terms of strong sense of identity infused through a strong corporate culture, yet with significant *tolerance* for individuality.[12]

Biological analogies have exerted strong influences on organizational design and the role of management among Japanese companies. Kao Corporation bases its philosophy and management systems on the concept of the company as a living organism. For example, when facing localized problems, employees are expected to act as an immune system—focusing their attention on the threat to the system and mobilizing to contain and eliminate the "infection." Kyocera, the multinational manufacturer of ceramic semiconductor components, bases its structure around some 400 "amoebas"—cells comprising a single self-organizing team of 3–50 members, that can divide as their work expands or as they develop internal specialities.

The idea of the firm as an organism rather than a machine is central to Margaret Wheatley and Myron Kellner-Rogers' concept of self-organization.[13] As with other living organisms, organizations have the capacity to self-organize, to sustain themselves, to adapt to change, to develop leadership as and when needed, to create new structures and systems. Examples of self-organization include communities reorganizing after a disaster, the World Wide Web, crowds of 100,000+ or more attending impromptu rock festivals, or the densely packed humanity navigating the sidewalks of Hong Kong. Synchronized behavior is common to social insects, flocks of birds, and schools of fish. Computer simulations of such coordinated behavior require only two or three rules for individuals to follow. In the case of organizations, there are three essential requirements for self-organization:

♦ *Identity.* Organizations need to be founded on an intent which drives the sense-making process within the organization.

♦ *Information.* Information provides the medium through which an organization relates to its environment and through which the individuals within the organization know how to react to external changes.

♦ *Relationships.* Relationships are the pathways through which information is transformed into intelligent, coordinated action. The more access individuals have to one another, the greater the possibilities for organized activity. Responsiveness to a wide range of external circumstances necessitates every individual having a wide range of connections to other individuals with the potential for unplanned connections.[14]

The issue of adaptability is also the basis for the attack on rationality both in strategy making (where Henry Mintzberg has been a leading critic[15]) and more generally as a basis for managerial action. David Hurst argues that the American approach to management based on rational objectivity is seriously flawed intellectually and socially, the result being a limited capacity for adaptation. On an intellectual basis, rationality-based management is based on a misplaced faith in objectivity:

> . . . business realities do not exist independently of their observers. Economies, markets, organizations, and strategies are constructed rather than natural objects. Thus, objectivity is never absolute—it is always relative to some frame of reference developed from the past. Because real change means that the frames themselves have to be altered, a rigid objectivity freezes this process.[16]

The social problem of objectivity is that it inevitably creates distance between the senior managers who perpetrate change programs and those being managed. This distancing is lethal: acceptance of change requires a mutual acceptance that everyone in the organization shares a common fate.

THE KNOWLEDGE-BASED VIEW OF THE FIRM

A starting point in the quest for new sources of profitability would be to ask, "Where are there opportunities for exploiting existing resources more effectively?" The quest for shareholder value has focused primarily on squeezing maximum productivity from physical and financial assets. Yet a number of recent books have suggested that the most important resource of the firm is the knowledge embedded within the firm's people and its systems.[17] The resulting surge of interest in knowledge as the critical resource of the firm and the fundamental management challenge, has resulted in an emerging conceptualization of the firm and the nature of management identified as the **knowledge-based view of the firm.** This approach identifies knowledge as the central resource of the firm, not only because of its quantitative importance to value added, but also because of its strategic importance. It embodies many characteristics relevant to establishing sustainable competitive advantage: knowledge is *scarce*, it is costly to *replicate*, it is often difficult to *transfer*, and it gives rise to complex *appropriability* issues. Two critical issues arise in relation to knowledge management: the first is *knowledge utilization*, the second is *knowledge creation*.

Knowledge Utilization

A first requirement for effective utilization is to identify the knowledge available within the organization. **Knowledge audits** establish an inventory of proprietary technology and know-how in the same way that accounting systems identify and value a firm's tangible assets. Formal systems for deploying knowledge have focused on *information technology* and the role of *networks* and *groupware* in linking organizational members. Recognition that the major source of knowledge is the expertise and know-how of employees has directed attention to human resource planning and appraisal. For example, **competency modeling** identifies the knowledge requirements of different occupations and can guide appraisal and training. Companies such as Dow Chemical, Andersen Consulting, IBM, Polaroid, and Skandia are developing corporate-wide systems to track, access, exploit, and create organizational knowledge, typically under the leadership of a director or vice president of "knowledge" or "intellectual capital."

Managing knowledge is made complex by its heterogeneity. In particular, different types of knowledge vary in their transferability. The critical distinction is between **explicit knowledge,** which is capable of articulation (and hence transferable at low cost), and **tacit knowledge,** which is manifest only in its application and is not amenable to transfer. The ease with which knowledge can be transferred (especially through IT systems) also depends on whether different units of knowledge can be aggregated.[18]

A critical challenge of knowledge management is that, though knowledge must be created and stored in specialist form, producing goods and services requires the application of many types of knowledge. Hence, the critical organizational task of the firm is integrating multiple types of knowledge while maintaining the efficiencies of specialization in creating and maintaining knowledge.

Most knowledge is subject to economies of scale and scope. This is especially the case with explicit knowledge that, once created, can be deployed in additional applications at low marginal cost. Effective exploitation of knowledge therefore requires that it be internally replicated; yet sustaining competitive advantage also requires that other firms be unable to replicate that same knowledge. The power and beauty of McDonald's strategy is a business system that integrates many, many types of knowledge and that can be replicated thousands of times over in each McDonald's hamburger restaurant, yet is so embedded in McDonald's systems and culture, that others cannot easily copy it.

Some of the most interesting and far-reaching implications of the knowledge-based view concern organizational design and distribution of decision-making authority. In terms of structuring organizations, the knowledge-based view can help us understand the deficiencies of hierarchy as an organizing device and reformulate some of the principles of organization design. If a major part of knowledge is tacit and its transfer sticky, hierarchy is ineffective as a mechanism for knowledge integration since no manager can efficiently integrate the knowledge of his or her subordinates.

Many current trends in organizational design can be interpreted as attempts to access and integrate the tacit knowledge of organizational members while recognizing the barriers to the transfer of such knowledge. The recent vogue for team-based structures, where team membership is fluid depending on the knowledge requirements of the task at hand, is one response to the deficiencies of hierarchy. The essence of a team-based organization is recognition that integration is best achieved through the direct involvement of individual specialists and that official coordinators ("managers") cannot effectively coordinate if they cannot access the range of specialist knowledge the task requires. The ubiquity of team-organized processes in production activities is implicit recognition that know-how is located among individual operatives and only they can integrate it. The displacement of scientific management by various forms of participative, employee-empowering management approaches partly reflects the motivational benefits of these systems, but it is also a result of the greater efficiency of these systems in accessing and integrating the relevant knowledge. Total quality management is a nonhierarchical, team-based organizing technology that permits an organization to access and utilize individuals' knowledge located at low levels of the organization. In "higher level" integration, new product development for example, difficulties of transferring tacit knowledge from specialists to department heads, imply that cross-functional teams comprising specialists is a far better approach to knowledge integration than a committee of heads of functional departments.

The principles of knowledge management are central to the concept of modularity in organizational design discussed in Chapter 6. Modular structures involve separating the total system into a number of subsystems and standardizing the interfaces between them. The principles of knowledge management can play an important role in optimizing the design of such modular systems. A key distinction here is between the component knowledge required by the subsystems and the **architectural knowledge** required for the linking of the various subsystems.

Implications for the allocation of decision-making authority in the firm follow. The discussion of organizational design links closely with the distribution of decision-making authority within the organization. The conventional basis for the analysis of decision making is **delegation.** Decision-making rights reside in the owners of the firm. As representatives of owners, the board of directors confers decision-making powers on senior management, which in turn delegates authority down the hierarchy. The knowledge-based view points to the importance of co-locating decision making and knowledge. Whether this involves decentralization or centralization of decision making depends very much on the characteristics of the knowledge required. Decisions that require idiosyncratic and tacit knowledge (which in not readily transferable), must be made where this knowledge is located. Thus, most operating decisions that require detailed knowledge of the workers involved, the specifics of the machinery and equipment, and other local circumstances are best decentralized. Decisions that require explicit, easily aggregated knowledge can be centralized. Thus, most accounting decisions, which require knowledge of the firm's cash balances and foreign exchange and interest rate exposures, are most effectively undertaken at a single decision point. The situation is similar with many purchasing and corporate financing decisions.

Knowledge Creation

The major emphasis of writers on knowledge and the firm has been the challenge of knowledge creation. This reflects a shift in the focus of firm strategy from competitive advantage based on superior resource positions and superior resource exploitation toward competitive advantage based on innovation. Central to innovation is the acquisition and reconfiguration of knowledge. The stream of management thinking on organizational learning points to the management challenge of knowledge *acquisition* being very different from that of knowledge *utilization* with regard to organizational structure, management systems, values, and leadership style.

Some of the most influential thinking on knowledge creation has been provided by Ikujiro Nonaka, professor of knowledge at University of California, Berkeley. He points to **knowledge conversion** as the central organizational process through which knowledge is created. This knowledge creation involves a **knowledge spiral** through which knowledge is converted between the tacit and explicit domains (the "epistemological dimension") and among individuals, groups, and the whole organization (the "ontological dimension") (see Figure 17.3). There are four key modes of knowledge conversion (see Figure 17.4).

1. **Socialization.** The sharing of experiences such that tacit knowledge is passed between individuals (e.g., the apprenticeship system), from individuals to the

FIGURE 17.3
Spiral of Organizational Knowledge Creation

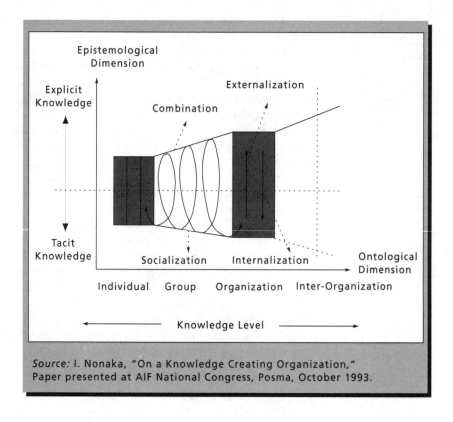

Source: I. Nonaka, "On a Knowledge Creating Organization," Paper presented at AIF National Congress, Posma, October 1993.

FIGURE 17.4
Modes of the Knowledge Conversion

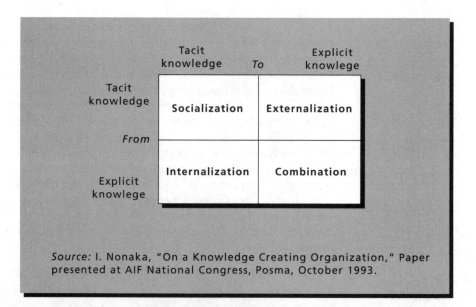

Source: I. Nonaka, "On a Knowledge Creating Organization," Paper presented at AIF National Congress, Posma, October 1993.

organization through the development of culture and shared mental models, and from the organization to individuals.

2. **Externalization.** The conversion of tacit into explicit knowledge through its articulation and systematization within the organization. Nonaka places considerable emphasis on the role of analogy and metaphor in this process (e.g., Canon's use of the beer can to develop its concept of a drum cylinder for its mini-copier).

3. **Combination.** Combination involves the conversion of explicit knowledge held by individuals and units into explicit knowledge at the organizational level, then subsequent conversion of organizational knowledge back to the individual in different form. This is the key role of the information systems of the firm.

4. **Internalization.** Internalization is conversion of explicit knowledge, whether at the individual or organizational level into tacit knowledge in the form of individual know-how and organizational routines.

NEW ORGANIZATIONAL FORMS

The performance requirements are clear. Firms need to move beyond cost efficiency and active asset management to boost innovation, seek new avenues to create customer satisfaction, exploit information technology, and combine a long-term focus on identity and mission with rapid response to external change. At the same time, they must not lose sight of the value of market power and the role of critical mass in exploiting economies and scale and scope and influencing standards. The difficulty is that our theoretical tool box doesn't offer much guidance about the kinds of structures and systems most effective in attaining these disparate goals. The most we can do is to note some of the ideas and examples that are influencing thinking in the business community.

Process-Based Organizations

A key development of the 1990s was the recognition of the role of processes in organization design. If business process reengineering directed attention at processes at the micro level, attention to organizational capabilities has encouraged a more integrated view of processes: identifying how individual processes fit together in sequences and networks of complementary activities. Such processes include product development processes, order fulfillment processes (spanning the whole chain of activities from supplying information to potential customers, to customer selection and ordering, to manufacturing, through to distribution), and customer relations processes involving the entirety of a company's interactions with its customers through marketing and after-sales services. In many cases, these macro processes extend beyond the company. Thus, supply-chain management involves linking internal logistics with those of suppliers and suppliers' suppliers. Effecting coordination and change within these processes for companies organized around functions and business units requires painful adjustment. Volvo's reorganization of its order fulfillment process in order to achieve a 14-day cycle between customer order and customer receipt of a customized automobile involved a Herculean effort to reorganize and reintegrate all the component processes: the order process, the production planning process, the distribution process, and the delivery-to-dealers process.[19] Bartlett and

Ghoshal view the move from the traditional "structure/systems" approach to a processes-based approach as a phenomenon associated with a number of companies, all of which have reached the limits of complexity in their formal structures. In Chapter 16, we noted how Bartlett and Ghoshal identify three critical processes on a corporate level. These processes were emphasized in a number of the companies they studied, including ABB, 3M, Kao, Canon, and Intel. Together these corporate processes amount to a view of the corporation as a dynamic rather than a static entity.

♦ *The entrepreneurial process* is a bottom-up process through which individuals initiate ideas and pursue them to create new products and whole new businesses; it is central to the continued development of 3M, Canon and Intel.

♦ *The competence-building process,* through which top management's role is viewed not as "defining, controlling, or allocating competence, but as creating an environment that allows it to develop and diffuse deep within the organization" is the way in which Kao Corporation develops competences as solutions to the problems that challenge it.

♦ *The renewal process* is the way in which the status quo, in terms of strategies and the assumptions that underlie them, is challenged. As Kao's chairman Yoshio Maruta proclaims, "Past wisdom must not be a constraint but something to be challenged. Yesterday's success formula is often today's obsolete dogma." Such a role has characterized a number of leaders of corporate transformation, notably Jack Welch at GE: "An institution ought to stretch itself to the point where it almost becomes unglued."

Project-Based Organizations

Traditional corporate structures were based on the management of continuous or repetitive processes: manufacturing pins or automobiles, supplying hamburgers or insurance policies. Another set of organizations developed on a project basis: construction companies and management consultancies. Increasingly, these project-based organizations, which feature temporary cross-functional teams have become viewed as models for organizing the dynamic, innovative, ambidextrous organization. Management consulting companies are some of the largest and most advanced form of project-based company. Though organized for operational purposes into project teams, management consultants are also assigned to geographically located offices, each of which has responsibilities for developing and responding to local market needs. Knowledge management is typically organized around "practice centers," which specialize by industry (health care, financial services, manufacturing) or by type of expertise (strategic planning, change management, process reengineering). One of the most extreme and interesting examples of project-based organization is Oticon Holding A/S, the Danish manufacturer of hearing aids. On New Year's Day, 1990, CEO Lars Kolind abolished Oticon's formal organization and announced the formation of a project-based company in which individuals typically work on several of the company's 100+ projects. The ten-person top management team acts as project owners, but provides only advice and does not make decisions. Communication is primarily verbal with very little paper and no individually allocated offices.[20]

Parallel Structures

In the same way that strategies serve dual goals—deploying existing resources and capabilities most effectively for the present, while positioning the enterprise to meet the challenges of the future[21]—a similar duality is required from organization structure: the enterprise must be organized for efficient operation of present activities, and at the same time be engaged in innovation and adaptation to prepare itself for the future. It is difficult to design a single structure to achieve these different goals. Operational efficiency typically requires high levels of specialization and coordination through rules and routines. Innovation and adaptation require low levels of specialization and coordination through planning and mutual adjustment, both of which are likely to be communication intensive. Reconciling different performance objectives and different time frames may require multiple structures to exist simultaneously within the organization. Bushe and Shani identify the role of **parallel learning structures**—organizational arrangements that exist outside the formal structure of the enterprise in order to facilitate organizational learning.[22] Their concept may be broadened: parallel structures may exist for a number of dynamic goals in addition to learning, and within the same organization, multiple parallel structures may exist. Examples of parallel structures include the following:

- At 3M, the formal structure exists in terms of business units, and divisions within which individuals have clearly defined job tasks. In addition, there is an informal structure for the purpose of new product development whereby individuals are permitted, indeed encouraged, to "bootleg" time, materials, and use of facilities to work on new product ideas. If new products that emerge from the informal structure are deemed promising, they are taken within the formal structure to be launched, and ultimately may form the basis for a business unit within the formal structure.

- Total Quality Management is a tool for changing work practices in order to eliminate defects and improve performance. Implementing TQM is typically through the creation of a parallel structure of quality circles, often coordinated by quality management committees and task forces. Thus, Texaco's "Star Quality" program created a hierarchy of quality management groups extending up to the corporate level quality team chaired by the CEO.

- GE's "Work-Out" program is a classic example of a parallel structure effecting change within the formal structure. The essence of Work-Out is a distancing of the parallel structure formed around "town-hall" type Work-Out sessions from the formal structure. To achieve this, Work-Out sessions were held at venues outside the company, all norms regarding hierarchical positions and authorities were suspended, and free interchange of ideas was encouraged. The outcome was a powerful device for initiating change within the formal structure in unusually short periods of time.

- Business Process Reengineering and other radical change initiatives are typically initiated and implemented by task forces operating outside the formal structure. Thus, Chevron's "breakthrough teams" were formed from multiple functions and multiple vertical levels in the company and were challenged to devise ways of finding substantial reductions in costs. The result was a series of far-reaching proposals for reorganizing and outsourcing information technology, restructuring the corporate head office, and reducing operating costs.

Networks and Virtual Organizations

A key feature of the changes in strategy, structure, and management systems has been less distinction between what happens within the firm and what happens outside it. Organization theory emphasizes the distinction between the organization and its environment, while economics distinguishes between markets and hierarchies as alternate organizational mechanisms. The growth of interfirm collaboration and the development of "contingent workforce"—people who work for companies but who are not covered by long-term employment contracts—has blurred this distinction, and theory has recognized a continuum of organizational forms and a multiplicity of contractual forms that make it clear that spot markets and unitary firms are just two specific organizational forms. As "command and control" modes of management give way to less formal patterns of coordination, so internal relationships within the firm are less differentiated from external relationships. The immediate implication is that the boundaries of the firm are less distinct and more permeable. Jack Welch's concept of the **boundaryless firm** is one where neither the internal divisions within the firm, nor the external boundaries are barriers to cooperation and communication. If cooperation across individuals and small enterprises can achieve the close coordination conventionally associated with corporations, the large, integrated company may disappear as the dominant organizational form in many industries. We have already noted how in the Italian clothing industry networks of small firms simultaneously achieve integration, flexibility, and innovation. Such networks are seen in many industries and countries from the shoemaking in India[23] to residential construction in the United States. In evolving toward a pure network form, a single corporation often acts as a hub (e.g., Sun Microsystems in computer workstations, Airbus Industrie in the European passenger aircraft industry).[24] Increasingly however, the network of firms may increasingly exhibit the characteristics and behavior of single corporation—hence the term **virtual corporation.**[25] The potential for networks of small firms to emulate the advantages of large corporations is evident in the Italian motorcycle industry. Newcomers such as Aprilia and established survivors such as Ducati prosper depite production volumes that the Boston Consulting Group proclaimed to be hopelessly uneconomic in its famous report.[26] The success of these small players is based on their extensive networks of suppliers and partners.[27]

New Modes of Leadership

New organizational structures and strategic priorities point to new models of leadership. The era of restructuring and shareholder focus has been associated with "change-masters"[28]—highly visible, individualistic, often hard-driving management styles of CEOs such as Al Dunlap at Sunbeam, Jack Welch at GE, Lucio Noto at Mobil, John Harvey-Jones at ICI, and Franco Bernabe at ENI. These leaders have typically combined centralization and decentralization: they have exerted a dominant influence on key strategic issues (such as downsizing, major acquisitions, and divestments), on organizational structure, and the corporate structure, but have typically encouraged a diffusion of both strategic and operational decision making.

If the post-downsizing era is to emphasize innovation, large-scale integration of capabilities in complex and flexible patterns, and extensive cooperation across multiple companies, then the types of leadership skills required by companies are likely to differ.

As the need for innovation and flexibility cause companies to evolve from mechanistic to organic structures, so their leaders are unable to operate as dominant decision makers. Mark Youngblood, an organizational change consultant, argues that for organic-type companies such as Microsoft, Cisco Systems, Intel, Starbucks and Harley-Davidson, the key responsibilities of leaders are:

♦ Clarifying shared vision

♦ Enriching the culture

♦ Developing alignment between the different parts of the organization and among shared vision, strategy, organizational design, and human resources

♦ Promoting understanding in interpreting information and events within the context of the shared vision

Among the attributes required by leaders are the need to create what Collins and Porras refer to as "Big Hairy Audacious Goals."[29]

In a study of 19 companies, including SmithKline Beecham, Royal Dutch/ Shell, and Levi Strauss, Arthur Andersen's Next Generation Research Group found a high degree of consistency between companies in the leadership competences that the companies identified as critical to their future development and success (see Table 17.1). They found a notable emphasis on "soft" skills:

The balance has clearly shifted from attributes traditionally thought of as masculine (strong decision-making, leading the troops, driving strategy, waging competitive battle) to more feminine qualities (listening, relationship-building, and nurturing). The model today is not so much "take it on your shoulders" as it is to "create the environment that will enable others to carry part of the burden." The focus is on unlocking the organization's human asset potential.[30]

TABLE 17.1
Leadership Competencies

THE LEADERSHIP NEEDS OF ORGANIZATIONS. THE ABILITY TO:	
• build confidence	• form networks
• build enthusiasm	• influence others
• cooperate	• use information
• deliver results	

REQUIRED COMPETENCES OF BUSINESS LEADERS:	
• Business literacy	• Proactivity
• Creativity	• Problem-solving
• Cross-cultural effectiveness	• Relation-building
• Empathy	• Teamwork
• Flexibility	• Vision

Source: Ruth L. Williams and Joseph P. Cothrel, "Building Tomorrow's Leaders Today," *Strategy and Leadership* 26 (September–October, 1997): 17–23.

◆ SUMMARY

Although the future is always unknowable, its origins lie in the present. From what we observe today, we can identify many of the key developments of the next few years. The trends that we discern in technology, economic development, government policies, social structure, demographics, and lifestyles will play a major role in shaping the business environment of at least the first few years of the new millennium. We have also been able to review some of the predictions for the kinds of strategic priorities for achieving competitive advantage in this emerging environment and the kinds of capabilities needed to implement these strategies. It is highly likely that innovation, flexibility, and responsiveness will be key success factors in most sectors over the next decade.

The most difficult issues concern the internal structures, systems, and styles needed to build and exercise these capabilities. Though there is a broad consensus that the structures and systems that were so successful during the first seven decades of the twentieth century will not serve enterprises so well in the twenty-first century, there is little agreement on the characteristics of the emerging organizational forms.

Again, however, it would appear that the future is already here. Experiments in new approaches to organizing and managing are occurring everywhere. From AES's "honeycomb" structure, and Sun Microsystems' networks of alliances, to Kao Corporation's learning organization based on "biological self-control," different companies are devising new approaches to reconcile a host of seemingly incompatible performance objectives. Despite the developments that are taking place in strategy, organizational theory, and a number of other management disciplines, our intellectual tools for dealing with these issues remain woefully inadequate. The challenge for us all is to apply what we know, recognize what we don't know, and engage in reflective observation in order to extend our domain of understanding.

NOTES

1 I am grateful to K. J. White, *Shazam: User's Reference Manual* (Version 6.0, University of British Columbia, 1987) for this quotation.

2 "Italian Sausage That Sizzles in Cyberspace," *Business Week,* September 23, 1996: 118.

3 "Logos Research Systems: For This Virtual IPO, Reality Bytes," *Business Week,* September 23, 1996: 142–143.

4 Henk Volberda, "Toward the Flexible Form: How to Remain Vital in Hypercompetitive Environments," *Organization Science* 7, no. 4 (1996): 359–374; David J. Teece, G. Pisano, and A. Shuen, "Dynamic Capabilities and Strategic Management," *Strategic Management Journal* 19 (1997): 509–534.

5 See, for example Robert Jacobson, "The Austrian School of Strategy," *Academy of Management Review* 17 (1990): 782–807; Mary Tripsas, "Unraveling the Process of Creative Destruction: Complementary Assets and Incumbent Survival in the Typesetter Industry," *Strategic Management Journal* 18, Special Issue (Summer 1997): 119–142; and Rich D'Aveni, *Hypercompetition* (New York: Free Press, 1994).

6 For example: Adam Brandenburger and Barry Nalebuff, *Coopetition* (New York: Doubleday, 1996).

7 M. Katz and C. Shapiro, "Technology Adoption in the Presence of Network Externalities" *Journal of Political Economy* 94 (1986): 822–884; *Standardization as a Tool of Competitive Strategy,* ed. Landis Gabel (New York: North Holland, 1987).

8 Bardia Kamrad, "Valuing Real Options," *Georgetown Business* (June 1997); A. K. Dixit and R. S. Pindyck, "The Options Approach to Capital Investment," *Harvard Business Review* (May–June 1995): 105–115.

9   See Rebecca Henderson, "The Evolution of Integrative Capability: Innovation in Cardiovascular Drugs," *Industrial and Corporate Change* 3 (1994): 607–630.

10 T. W. Malone, M. S. Scott Morton, and R. R. Halperin, "Organizing for the 21st Century," *Strategy and Leadership* 24 (July–August 1996): 6–11.

11 Peter Senge, *The Fifth Discipline* (London: Century, 1990).

12 A. de Geus, *The Living Company* (Boston: Harvard Business School Press, 1997). See also "How to Live Long and Prosper," *Economist*, May 10, 1997: 59.

13 M. J. Wheatley and M. Kellner Rogers, *A Simpler Way* (Berrett-Koehler, 1996); M. J. Wheatley, *Leadership and the New Science*.

14 M. J. Wheatley and M. Kellner Rogers, "Self-Organization: The Irresistible Future of Organizing," *Strategy and Leadership* 24 (July–August 1996): 18–25.

15 Henry Mintzberg, *The Rise and Fall of Strategic Planning* (New York: Free Press, 1994).

16 D. K. Hurst, "When It Comes to Real Change, Too Much Objectivity May Be Fatal to the Process," *Strategy and Leadership* 25 (March–April 1997): 8.

17 I. Nonaka and H. Takeuchi, *The Knowledge Creating Company* (New York: Oxford University Press, 1995); J. B. Quinn, *Intelligent Enterprise* (New York: Free Press, 1992); Dorothy Leonard-Barton, *The Wellsprings of Knowledge* (Boston: Harvard Business School Press, 1996); Peter Senge, *The Fifth Discipline* (London: Century, 1990); J. Roos, G. Roos, and L. Edvinson, *Intellectual Capital* (London: Macmillan, 1997).

18 J.-C. Spender's approach to the analysis of knowledge within the firm distinguishes *types of knowledge* and *levels of knowledge*. He identifies four major categories of knowledge:

	Individual	Social
Explicit	CONSCIOUS	OBJECTIFIED
Implicit	AUTOMATIC	COLLECTIVE

See J.-C. Spender, "Organizational Knowledge, Collective Practice, and Penrose Rents," *International Business Review* 3 (1994): 353–367; J.-C. Spender, "Making Knowledge the Basis of a Dynamic Theory of the Firm," *Strategic Management Journal* 17, Special Issue (Winter 1996): 45–63.

19 Suzanne Hertz and Johny Johansson, "Process Management in Networks: The New Volvo Story," discussion paper, Stockholm School of Economics/Georgetown University, 1997.

20 "This Organization Is Disorganization," *Fast Company*, April 1997: 77–83.

21 Derek F. Abell, *Managing With Dual Strategies* (New York: Free Press, 1993).

22 G. A. Bushe and A. B. Shani, *Parallel Learning Structures* (Reading, MA: Addison-Wesley, 1991).

23 Peter Knorringa, *Economics of Collaboration: Indian Shoemakers Between Market and Hierarchy* (New Delhi: Sage, 1996).

24 G. Lorenzoni and Charles Baden Fuller, "Creating a Strategic Center to Manage a Web of Partners," *California Management Review* (1995).

25 William Davidow and Michael Malone, *The Virtual Corporation* (New York: Harper Business: 1992); Henry Cheesebrough and David J. Teece, "When Is Virtual Virtuous? Organizing for Innovation," *Harvard Business Review* (May–June 1996): 65–73.

26 Boston Consulting Group, *Strategy Alternatives for the British Motorcycle Industry* (London: Her Majesty's Stationery Office, 1975).

27 Gianni Lorenzoni and Andrea Lipporini, "Relational Strategies and Learning by Interacting Mechanisms in the Italian Motorcycle Industry." Paper presented at Strategic Management Society Conference, Barcelona, October 7, 1997.

28 Rosabeth Moss Kanter, *The Change Masters* (New York: Simon & Schuster, 1983).

29 Collins and Porras, *Built to Last* (New York: Harper Business, 1996).

30 Ruth L. Williams and Joseph P. Cothrel, "Building Tomorrow's Leaders Today," *Strategy and Leadership*, 26 (September–October, 1997): 17–23.

Index

Classic Readings to Complement Your Strategy Text...

THE STRATEGY READER

Edited by SUSAN SEGAL-HORN, *Open University Business School*

THE STRATEGY READER includes contributions by Porter, Mintzberg, Senge, Hamel and Prahalad, among others, presenting landmark statements on notable positions and approaches. The less familiar essays have been carefully selected for the variety of insight and contrasting perspective they offer on diverse topics. The reader provides your students with a comprehensive overview of the continuing debates in the field of strategic management.

The analytical aspect of strategy is well represented in the vast range of articles included, however, it also shows that analysis is not a sufficient condition for strategic thinking, which ultimately depends on the exercise of sound judgement. THE STRATEGY READER has been designed to complement any major textbook in strategic management and business policy. It will appeal to students seeking to broaden their understanding of the contribution strategic management can make to the successful development of organizations.

FEBRUARY - 6 ¾ x 9 ¾ - 480 PAGES
0-631-20901-8 - PAPERBACK
0-631-20900-X - HARDCOVER

SPECIAL FEATURES

▶ Includes over 20 classic readings by established leaders in the discipline

▶ Provides an ideal supplement to any major strategy textbook

▶ Guides students through the text with extensive editorial commentary

ABOUT THE EDITOR

SUSAN SEGAL-HORN is Reader in Strategic Management and is the Strategy Module Course Leader at the Open University Business School.

Call Toll Free in North America
(800) 216-2522

Outside of North America call
+44 (0)1235 465500

VISIT BLACKWELL ON THE WEB!

http://www.blackwellpublishers.co.uk

http://www.blackwellpub.com

CONTENTS